American Literary Scholarship

1972

American Literary Scholarship

An Annual / 1972

Edited by J. Albert Robbins

Essays by Ralph H. Orth, Nina Baym, Hershel Parker, Bernice Slote, Hamlin Hill, William T. Stafford, Michael Millgate, Jackson R. Bryer, J. A. Leo Lemay, M. Thomas Inge, G. R. Thompson, Warren G. French, James H. Justus, Alvin H. Rosenfeld, Linda W. Wagner, Walter J. Meserve, John T. Flanagan, George Monteiro.

Duke University Press, Durham, North Carolina, 1974

© 1974, Duke University Press. Library of Congress Catalogue Card Number 65-19450. I.S.B.N. 0-8223-0324-8. Printed in the United States of America by Heritage Printers.

Foreword

This volume completes the first decade of *American Literary Scholarship*. With *ALS 1973* James Woodress will resume editorship of the series, which he commenced and edited for the first five years. Scholars who have published during 1973 are urged to send copies of books and reprints of articles to him (Department of English, University of California, Davis, Calif. 95616) or to the author of the appropriate *ALS* chapter. (Fifteen authors will remain unchanged from *ALS 1972*. Four will be new: Chap. 1, Walter Harding, New York State University College, Geneseo, N.Y. 14454; Chap. 7, James B. Meriwether, University of South Carolina, Columbia, S.C. 29208; Chap. 14, Richard Crowder, Purdue University, Lafayette, Ind. 47907; and Chap. 18, Michael Hoffman, University of California, Davis, Calif., 95616).

I thank all contributors who have given their expertise, judgment, and time to make this and the preceding four volumes possible. The reading of a mass of scholarship, the formulation of informative and judicious evaluations, and the composition of all this into readable essays do not add up, as I know, to a task easily done with a few hours in the library and a couple of nights at the typewriter.

As in the past, we are indebted to Jackson Bryer (section head of the American literature portion of the *MLA International Bibliography*) for providing our people with advance listing of items for the year. We could not meet our publication schedule without this special help. We are indebted also to Harrison Messerole, MLA Bibliographer, for assisting in many ways, including advance listings of festschriften.

Because the Center for Editions of American Authors has recently examined and certified the one hundredth volume, it seems appropriate to recognize the event by a description of that enterprise, which involves so many American literary scholars. I thank Professor Don L. Cook, general editor of the Howells edition, for his comments on the project. They appear as an Afterword in this volume. A recent list of titles so far published or sealed and ready for publication can be found in the September 1973 (directory) issue of *PMLA* on pages 976–77.

Finally, I turn to a topic of some sensitivity, with reluctance but with the belief that the point needs to be made. In the foreword for last year's *ALS* I noted the quantitative proliferation of scholarship. Some of this is genuine increment but, alas, some of it is detritus. In reading the eighteen chapter manuscripts for this year's volume, I was struck as never before by a reiterated refrain: this article adds nothing new, that one should never have been published. Assuming, as I do, that *ALS* contributors are conscientious judges and careful referees, I cite some of their complaints in evidence.

— One "gracelessly written" article "does not advance the state of knowledge of her important subject; indeed, by its innocent citation of well-refuted arguments it might actively retard knowledge."

— One author "makes some comparisons which seem more obvious now than when [an older scholar] made them three decades before."

— One author "seems to have stopped reading scholarship about the time Eisenhower was reelected."

— One author's article is "of marginal value." He "seems unaware that considerable earlier work renders his own contribution gratuitous."

— One author's article "is worth looking at only as a curious throwback to the criticism of an earlier day—its argument dependent upon serious misreadings of this and several other novels."

— One article "is loosely argued and shows little familiarity with the accumulated criticism and scholarship."

— One article "should not have been published."

— One author "trivializes one of the greatest scenes" in the novel in question.

— One author "discovers" a source previously recorded by another scholar in 1970.

On the year's work in general:

— "There is still the lamentable tendency toward repetitiveness (a result primarily of slack scholarship) and a flailing about for critical approaches to replace the much-abused New Critical ones."

These reiterated plaints attest to substantive naïveté, carelessness, unoriginality—and ignorance of published scholarship. Many *ALS* contributors treat ill-informed and shallow articles by not mentioning them at all. If there are so many which draw notices of questionable quality there must be many more passed over in silence.

This is not the place to go into the vexed matter of the pressures for publication. Those pressures of requirements for promotion and tenure which encourage the proliferation of published mediocrity are unhappily a fact of academic life in some institutions. But with the torrent of matter seeking print, it is the editors of journals, it seems to me, who are culpable. All journals, old and new, which profess to address the scholarly community, have an incumbent responsibility to insure that all material accepted meets a standard worthy of the respect of the most demanding scholars. To compromise high standards is a disservice to scholarship in a time when we cannot afford the expense to libraries of subscriptions to marginal journals and cannot afford the erosion of a scholar's time to weed out the mediocre from the worthy.

J. Albert Robbins

Indiana University

Table of Contents

Key to Abbreviations

ABC / American Book Collector
ABR / American Benedictine Review
AH / American Heritage
AI / American Imago
AIM / Annals of Internal Medicine
AION-SR / Annali dell'Istituto Universitario Orientale
AL / American Literature
ALR / American Literary Realism, 1870–1910
ALS / American Literary Scholarship: An Annual
Americana Norvegica / Harald S. Naess and Sigmund Skard, eds., Americana Norvegica, Vol. 3, Studies in Scandinavian-American Interrelations (Oslo, Universitetsforlaget, 1971)
Américas (Pan American Union)
Amerikanische Literatur / Alfred Weber and Dietmar Haack, eds., Amerikanische Literatur im 20. Jahrhundert (Göttingen, Vanderhoeck and Ruprecht, 1971)
AmerS / American Studies
AN&Q / American Notes and Queries
Antaeus (New York)
AntigR / Antigonish Review
APR / American Poetry Review (Philadelphia)
AQ / American Quarterly
Arbor (Madrid)
Archiv / Archiv für das Studium der Neueren Sprachen und Literaturen
ArQ / Arizona Quarterly
AS / American Speech
ASch / American Scholar
ASoc / Arts in Society
ASR / American-Scandinavian Review
AtM / Atlantic Monthly

ATQ / American Transcendental Quarterly
AW / American West
BA / Books Abroad
BB / Bulletin of Bibliography
BlackW / Black World
BNYPL / Bulletin of the New York Public Library
Boundary 2 (State Univ. of New York, Binghamton)
BRMMLA / Bulletin of the Rocky Mountain Modern Language Assn.
BSUF / Ball State University Forum
BuR / Bucknell Review
BYUS / Brigham Young University Studies
BzJA / Beihefte zum Jahrbuch für Amerikastudien (Heidelberg, Carl Winter)
Cabellian / The Cabellian: A Journal of the Second American Renaissance
Calamus: Walt Whitman Quarterly (Tokyo)
Caliban (Toulouse)
CanL / Canadian Literature
CCTET / Conference of College Teachers of English of Texas, Proceedings
CE / College English
CEA / CEA Critic (College English Assn.)
CEAA / Center for Editions of American Authors
Celebration of Life / William R. Mueller, Celebration of Life: Studies in Modern Fiction (New York, Sheed and Ward)
CentR / The Centennial Review (Mich. State Univ.)
CHA / Cuadernos Hispanoamericanos (Madrid)

ChiR / Chicago Review
CHSB / Connecticut Historical Society Bulletin
CimR / Cimarron Review (Okla. State Univ.)
CL / Comparative Literature
CLAJ / CLA Journal (Coll. Language Assn.)
CLQ / Colby Library Quarterly
CLS / Comparative Literature Studies
ColQ / Colorado Quarterly
Commentary
Commonweal
CompD / Comparative Drama
ConL / Contemporary Literature
ConnR / Connecticut Review
ConS / Concord Saunterer (Concord, Mass.)
Contemporary American Novelists / Charles B. Harris, Contemporary American Novelists of the Absurd (New Haven, Conn., College and Univ. Press, 1971)
Costerus: Essays in English and American Language and Literature (Amsterdam)
Courier (Syracuse Univ. Library Associates)
CP / Concerning Poetry (Western Wash. State Coll.)
CR / Critical Review (Melbourne)
Crazy Horse (Southwest Minn. State College, Marshall)
CRevAS / Canadian Review of American Studies
Crit / Critique: Studies in Modern Fiction
Criticism (Wayne State Univ.)
CWH / Civil War History
DAI / Dissertation Abstracts International
Democratic Humanism / Harold Kaplan, Democratic Humanism and American Literature (Univ. of Chicago Press)
Diamond Bessie / Wilson M. Hudson, ed. Diamond Bessie and the Shepherds (Austin, Texas, Encino Press)
DR / Dalhousie Review
DWB / Dietsche Warande en Belfort
EA / Etudes anglaises

EAL / Early American Literature
ECS / Eighteenth-Century Studies
EDB / Emily Dickinson Bulletin
Edda (Oslo)
EE / Exercise Exchange (Univ. of Vermont)
EIHC / Essex Institute Historical Collections
EJ / English Journal
ELH / ELH, Journal of English Literary History
ELN / English Language Notes
ELT / English Literature in Transition (1800–1920)
Encounter (London)
ES / English Studies
ESQ / ESQ: A Journal of the American Renaissance (Washington State Univ.; formerly Emerson Society Quarterly)
ESRS / Emporia State Research Studies
ETJ / Educational Theatre Journal
Expl / Explicator
Fabula: Zeitschrift für Erzählforschung (Berlin)
FCHQ / Filson Club Historical Quarterly (Louisville)
FHA / Fitzgerald-Hemingway Annual
FI / Forum Italicum
FMLS / Forum for Modern Language Studies (Univ. of St. Andrews, Scotland)
Folklore (London)
Folklore and Folklife / Richard M. Dorson, ed., Folklore and Folklife: An Introduction (Univ. of Chicago Press)
FourQ / Four Quarters (LaSalle College, Philadelphia)
Foxfire
From Irving to Steinbeck / Motley Deakin and Peter Lisca, eds., From Irving to Steinbeck: Studies of American Literature in Honor of Harry R. Warfel (Gainesville, Univ. of Fla. Press)
GaR / Georgia Review
Genre
GHQ / Georgia Historical Quarterly
Greyfriar: Siena Studies in Literature

(Siena College, Loudonville, N.Y.)
HAB / Humanities Association Bulle-
tin (Univ. of New Brunswick,
Canada)
Harper's / Harper's Magazine
HEQ / History of Education Quarterly
Historian: A Journal of History (Allen-
town, Pa.)
HL / Humanistica Lovaniensis
HLB / Harvard Library Bulletin
HLQ / Huntington Library Quarterly
HNH / Historical New Hampshire
Hollins Critic
HSELL / Hiroshima Studies in English
Language and Literature
HSL / Hartford Studies in Literature
HTR / Harvard Theological Review
HudR / Hudson Review
IF / Indiana Folklore
IJAS / Indian Journal of American
Studies (Hyderabad)
IllQ / Illinois Quarterly
Images of Women / Susan K. Cornil-
lon, ed., Images of Women in
Fiction: Feminist Perspectives
(Bowling Green, Ohio, Bowling
Green Univ. Popular Press)
Imagination and the Spirit / Charles
A. Huttar, ed., Imagination and the
Spirit: Essays in Literature and
the Christian Faith Presented to
Clyde S. Kilby (Grand Rapids,
Mich., Eerdmans, 1971)
IMH / Indiana Magazine of History
IN / Indiana Names
In Honor of Austin Wright / In Honor
of Austin Wright, Carnegie Series
in English, No. 12 (Pittsburgh,
Carnegie-Mellon Univ.)
IowaR / Iowa Review
JA / Jahrbuch für Amerikastudien
JAF / Journal of American Folklore
JAH / Journal of American History
JAmS / Journal of American Studies
JHI / Journal of the History of Ideas
JHS / Journal of Historical Studies
JLN / Jack London Newsletter
JML / Journal of Modern Literature
JNH / Journal of Negro History
JNT / Journal of Narrative Technique
(Ypsilanti, Eastern Mich. Univ.
Press)

JPC / Journal of Popular Culture
JQ / Journalism Quarterly
JRUL / Journal of the Rutgers
University Library
KanQ / Kansas Quarterly
KFQ / Keystone Folklore Quarterly
KFR / Kentucky Folklore Record
KN / Kwartalnik Neofilologiczny
(Warsaw)
KRQ / Kentucky Romance Quarterly
L&I / Language and Ideology
(Montreal)
L&P / Literature and Psychology
(Univ. of Hartford)
LaS / Louisiana Studies
LC / Library Chronicle (Univ. of Pa.)
LCrit / Literary Criterion (Univ. of
Mysore, India)
LHY / Literary Half-Yearly
LibN / Library Notes (Duke Univ.)
Lillabulero
Literatur und Sprache / Hans
Helmcke, et al., eds., Literatur
und Sprache der Vereinigten
Staaten: Aufsätze zu Ehren von
Hans Galinsky (Heidelberg, Carl
Winter, 1969)
LitR / Literary Review (Fairleigh
Dickinson Univ.)
Lore of Faith / Thomas E. Cheney,
ed., Lore of Faith and Folly (Salt
Lake City, Univ. of Utah Press,
1971)
LWU / Literatur in Wissenshaft und
Unterricht (Kiel)
M&N / Man and Nature (Lincoln,
Mass.)
Major Writers / Everett H. Emerson,
ed., Major Writers of Early
American Literature (Madison,
Univ. of Wis. Press)
MarkhamR / Markham Review
MD / Modern Drama
Meanjin / Meanjin Quarterly (Univ.
of Melbourne)
MFR / Mississippi Folklore Register
MFS / Modern Fiction Studies
MHM / Maryland Historical Magazine
MichA / Michigan Academician
MinnR / Minnesota Review
MissQ / Mississippi Quarterly
MLQ / Modern Language Quarterly

MLR / Modern Language Review
ModA / Modern Age (Chicago)
Modern American Fiction / Wolody-
myr T. Zyla and Wendell M.
Aycock, eds., Modern American
Fiction: Insights and Foreign
Lights (Proceedings of the
Comparative Literature Sympo-
sium, Vol. 5; Lubbock, Texas
Tech Univ.
Montana: The Magazine of Western
History
MPS / Modern Poetry Studies
MQ / Midwest Quarterly
MQR / Michigan Quarterly Review
MR / Massachusetts Review
Ms.
MSE / Massachusetts Studies in
English
MSS / Manuscripts
MTJ / Mark Twain Journal
Myths and Realities / Berkley Kalin
and Clayton Robinson, eds., Myths
and Realities: Conflicting Values
in America (Mississippi Valley
Collection Bulletin, No. 5;
Memphis, Tenn., Memphis State
Univ.)
NALF / Negro American Literature
Forum
Names: Journal of the American
Name Society
NAR / New American Review (New
York, Simon and Schuster)
NCarF / North Carolina Folklore
NCCL / Newsletter on the Conference
on Christianity and Literature
(Adrian College, Adrian, Mich.)
NCF / Nineteenth-Century Fiction
NCHR / North Carolina Historical
Review
NEQ / New England Quarterly
NewL / New Letters
New Yorker
NH / Nebraska History
NHJ / Nathaniel Hawthorne Journal
NLauR / New Laurel Review
NLH / New Literary History
NMW / Notes on Mississippi Writers
NOQ / Northwest Ohio Quarterly
Novel: A Forum on Fiction

NR / Nassau Review (Nassau
Community College, Garden City,
N.Y.)
NRs / Neue Rundschau
NS / Die neueren Sprachen
NYFQ / New York Folklore
Quarterly
NYQ / New York Quarterly
NYRB / New York Review of Books
NYTBR / New York Times Book
Review
Observations and Reflections /
Francis E. Abernethy, ed.,
Observations and Reflections on
Texas Folklore (Austin, Encino
Press)
OH / Ohio History
OhR / Ohio Review (formerly Ohio
University Review)
On the Novel / B. S. Benedikz, ed.,
On the Novel: A Present for Walter
Allen on His 60th Birthday from
His Friends and Colleagues
(London, Dent, 1971)
Open Letter (Toronto)
PAAS / Proceedings of the American
Antiquarian Society
Paideuma / Paideuma: A Journal
Devoted to Ezra Pound Scholarship
(Orono, Maine)
Papers on Poe / Richard P. Veler, ed.,
Papers on Poe: Essays in Honor
of John Ward Ostrom (Springfield,
Ohio, Chantry Music Press)
PAPS / Proceedings of the American
Philosophical Society
ParisR / Paris Review
Parnassus / Parnassus: Poetry in
Review (New York)
PBSA / Papers of the Bibliographic
Society of America
PF / Pennsylvania Folklife
PH / Pennsylvania History
Phylon
Players
PLL / Papers on Language and
Literature
PMHB / Pennsylvania Magazine of
History and Biography
PMHS / Proceedings of the Massa-
chusetts Historical Society

PMLA / PMLA, Publications of the
Modern Language Association
PoeS / Poe Studies
Poetry
PP / Philologica Pragensia
PR / Partisan Review
Proceedings / Proceedings: Pacific
Northwest Conference on Foreign
Languages
Proof / Proof: The Yearbook of
American Bibliographical and
Textual Studies (Univ. of S.C.)
Prose (New York)
PrS / Prairie Schooner
QH / Quaker History: Bulletin of the
Friends Historical Association
QJLC / Quarterly Journal of the
Library of Congress
QJS / Quarterly Journal of Speech
QQ / Queen's Quarterly
RALS / Resources for American
Literary Study
RBPH / Revue Belge de Philologie
et d'Histoire
Renascence
Rendezvous: Journal of Arts and
Letters
RES / Review of English Studies
RIH / Rhode Island History
RLM / Revue des Lettres Modernes
RLT / Russian Literature Triquarterly
(Ann Arbor, Mich.)
RomN / Romance Notes
RoR / Romanian Review
RQ / Riverside Quarterly (Univ. of
Saskatchewan)
RS / Research Studies (Wash. State
Univ.)
SA / Studi Americani
SAB / South Atlantic Bulletin
Salmagundi
SAmL / Studies in American
Literature (Hiroshima Univ.)
SAQ / South Atlantic Quarterly
S&S / Science and Society
SatR / Saturday Review
SB / Studies in Bibliography: Papers
of the Bibliographic Society of
the University of Virginia
SBHT / Studies in Burke and His
Time
SBL / Studies in Black Literature

SCB / South Central Bulletin
SCHM / South Carolina Historical
Magazine
SCMLA / South Central Modern
Language Association
SDR / South Dakota Review
SELit / Studies in English Literature
(English Literary Society of
Japan, Univ. of Tokyo)
Serif / The Serif (Kent State Univ.,
Ohio)
SF&R / Scholars' Facsimiles and
Reprints
SFQ / Southern Folklore Quarterly
SHR / Southern Humanities Review
ShS / Shakespeare Survey
SIR / Studies in Romanticism
SLJ / Southern Literary Journal
SM / Speech Monographs
Smithsonian (Washington, D.C.)
SMS / Steinbeck Monograph Series
(Muncie, Ind., John Steinbeck
Society of America)
SNL / Satire Newsletter
SNNTS / Studies in the Novel
SoQ / Southern Quarterly (Univ. of
So. Miss.)
SoR / Southern Review
SoRA / Southern Review: An Aus-
tralian Journal of Literary Studies
(Univ. of Adelaide)
Spectrum (Atlanta, Ga. State Univ.)
SR / Sewanee Review
SS / Scandinavian Studies
SSCJ / Southern Speech Communi-
cation Journal
SSF / Studies in Short Fiction
Stages of the Clown / Richard Pearce,
Stages of the Clown: Perspectives
on Modern Fiction from Dostoyev-
sky to Beckett (Carbondale, So.
Ill. Univ. Press, 1970)
StAR / St. Andrews Review (St.
Andrews Presbyterian Coll.)
StH / Studies in the Humanities
(Indiana Univ. of Pa.)
StQ / Steinbeck Quarterly
Studies in Theatre and Drama /
Oscar G. Brockett, ed., Studies
in Theatre and Drama: Essays in
Honor of Hubert C. Heffner
(The Hague, Mouton)

Style
Sumac (Fremont, Mich.)
SWR / *Southwest Review*
TCL / *Twentieth Century Literature*
TDR / *The Drama Review*
TFSB / *Tennessee Folklore Society
   Bulletin*
The Cry of Home / Herald Ernest
   Lewald, ed., *The Cry of Home:
   Cultural Nationalism and the
   Modern Writer* (Knoxville, Univ.
   of Tenn. Press)
The Politics / George A. Panichas,
   ed., *The Politics of Twentieth-
   Century Novelists* (New York,
   Hawthorn Books, 1971)
Thoth (Syracuse Univ.)
Thought
ThQ / *Theatre Quarterly* (London)
THQ / *Tennessee Historical Quarterly*
TJQ / *Thoreau Journal Quarterly*
TLS / *Times Literary Supplement*
   (London)
Toward a New Earth / John R. May,
   *Toward a New Earth: Apocalypse
   in the American Novel* (Notre
   Dame, Ind., Univ. of Notre Dame
   Press)
TPJ / *Tennessee Poetry Journal*
TQ / *Texas Quarterly*
TR / *Tamkang Review* (Taipei)
TS / *Theatre Survey*
TSB / *Thoreau Society Bulletin*
TSE / *Tulane Studies in English*
TSL / *Tennessee Studies in Literature*
TSLL / *Texas Studies in Literature
   and Language*
TUSAS / Twayne United States Au-
   thors series (New York, Twayne
   Publishers)
Typology / Sacvan Bercovitch, ed.,
   *Typology and Early American
   Literature* (Amherst, Univ. of
   Mass. Press)
UHQ / *Utah Historical Quarterly*

UMPAW / University of Minnesota
   Pamphlets on American Writers
UMSE / *University of Mississippi
   Studies in English*
UR / *University Review* (Kansas
   City, Mo.)
USMALB / U.S. Military Academy
   Library Bulletin (West Point,
   N. Y.)
UTQ / *University of Toronto Quarterly*
UWR / *University of Windsor Review*
   (Windsor, Ontario)
*Ventures: Magazine of the Yale
   Graduate School*
VH / *Vermont History*
VLit / *Voprosy Literatury*
VMHB / *Virginia Magazine of His-
   tory and Biography*
VQR / *Virginia Quarterly Review*
WAL / *Western American Literature*
War and Society / J. L. Granatstein
   and R. D. Cuff, eds., *War and
   Society in North America* (To-
   ronto, Nelson, 1971)
WascanaR / *Wascana Review* (Re-
   gina, Sask.)
WCR / *West Coast Review*
WF / *Western Folklore*
WHR / *Western Humanities Review*
WMQ / *William and Mary Quarterly*
World (New York; formerly *Saturday
   Review*)
WVUPP / *West Virginia University
   Philological Papers*
WWR / *Walt Whitman Review*
WWS / Western Writers Series
   (Boise, Idaho, Boise State College)
XUS / *Xavier University Studies*
Yankee (Dublin, N. H.)
YCGL / *Yearbook of Comparative
   and General Literature*
YR / *Yale Review*
YULG / *Yale University Library
   Gazette*
ZAA / *Zeitschrift für Anglistik und
   Amerikanistik* (East Berlin)

Part I

1. Emerson, Thoreau, and Transcendentalism

Ralph H. Orth

The year's work on the Transcendentalists was marked by the publication of two significant volumes presenting primary texts by Emerson and Thoreau, by half a dozen books of moderate significance, and by a flood of articles and notes of the most varied quality. In addition, twenty-two dissertations were concerned directly or partially with the Transcendentalists.

The great disparity in the quality of this material is a matter of some concern. With five publications currently printing material specifically on Emerson and Thoreau, there are few articles so feeble or third-hand that they cannot reach print somewhere. An informal count shows that there were twenty-nine articles or notes on Emerson and seventy-seven on Thoreau published in 1972, plus twenty-one pieces of reprinted material (most of it in *ATQ*, and most of it unnecessary) and the twenty-two dissertations—about one hundred and fifty items in all. While some of these articles are first-rate, traversing this plain of Nauset to find them is enough to weary the hardiest traveler and points up the necessity for this yearly summary.

Approximately two-thirds of this mass of material is specifically noted below, and all of it (with the exception of a few fugitive items) has been examined. Hopefully there will be some increase in quality in 1973.

i. Texts, Editions, Bibliographies

One major series was concluded with the publication of the third and final volume of *The Early Lectures of Ralph Waldo Emerson* (Cambridge, Harvard Univ. Press, Belknap), edited by Robert E. Spiller and Wallace E. Williams. Surviving manuscripts of three lecture series are published: that on Human Life, given in 1838–1839; that on The Present Age, given 1839–1840; and that on The Times, given 1841–1842. Also published is Emerson's Address to the People of East Lexington, January 15, 1840. The progressive incompleteness of the lecture manuscripts presented a formidable editorial problem. Of the first series, which consisted of ten lectures, eight survive complete and two are incomplete; of the second—also ten lectures—three survive complete, six are incomplete, and one is missing; and of the third, consisting of eight lectures, one survives complete, one is incomplete, and the other six are missing. (Three of the missing lectures were printed in the *Dial*, so that some sort of text survives.) The editors speculate that so many of the later manuscripts are non-existent because Emerson by 1841 had developed a lecture style that could easily be carried over directly into print as essays, making extensive rewriting for publication unnecessary. As in the previous volumes, the surviving lectures are presented in clear text, with over one hundred pages of textual notes in the back. An analytical index for the three volumes is also provided. Despite the varying state of the manuscripts, the editors promise a further series of the later lectures based on the same editorial principles. It should be noted that this important series was brought to its conclusion without the help of the MLA's Center for Editions of American Authors.

The year was also marked by the appearance of the second volume of *The Writings of Henry D. Thoreau* (Princeton, Princeton Univ. Press), a CEAA-supported project: *The Maine Woods*, edited by Joseph J. Moldenhauer. Like the first volume, *Walden*, issued in 1971, it is a model of everything a definitive edition should be: not only a work of distinguished scholarship but a handsome book as well. These are compact, well-printed works, easy to hold and read, and as unpretentious as their author himself. *The Maine Woods* is textually complex, since the book was published after Thoreau's death and the printed texts that contributed to it are of varying reliability. The editor has consequently chosen four different copy-texts: for "Ktaadn," the 1848 *Union Magazine* printing with Thoreau's corrections; for "Chesuncook," the printer's manuscript for the 1858 *Atlantic Monthly* printing, supplemented by the periodical text where the fair copy has disappeared; for "The Allegash and East Branch," the extant fragments of Thoreau's last draft plus the first edition of 1864; and for the "Appendix," the first edition exclusively. The result is an eclectic text, closer to Thoreau's intention than any yet printed. The textual apparatus is divided into four sections corresponding to the four parts of the work, and subdivided into the categories required by textual analysis. The textual notes especially are well written, informed, and judicious. There is a lengthy textual introduction describing all of the extant manuscripts and printed texts, but the editors have chosen not to include a historical introduction, such as accompanied *Walden*. In all, intelligence and taste are evident everywhere in this volume, including the woodland green, brown, and black of the covers and the selection of the illustrations. (A droll defense of textual editing is made by Moldenhauer in "On the Editing of *The Maine Woods*," *TJQ* 4,iv:15–20, where he links the textual editor and Thoreau in their common belief in the value of "strenuous seeing.")

Wendell Glick in "Thoreau Rejects an Emerson Text" (*SB* 25:213–16) prints two translations of Tacitus's eulogy of Agricola: that delivered by Thoreau at the Concord services for John Brown in December 1859 and that which occurs in the printed text of Thoreau's remarks and was made by Thoreau himself. Because the first version, preserved in the Morgan Library, is in Emerson's handwriting, Glick conjectures that it is Emerson's own, but it actually comes from the London 1831 edition of Tacitus's *Works* edited by Arthur Murphy, which Emerson owned.

Thoreau's note requesting that he not be considered a member of the First Parish of Concord, mentioned in "Civil Disobedience," has been discovered in the records of the Town of Concord and is reproduced in *TSB* 120:7. Its date: January 6, 1841.

A substantial contribution to our knowledge of Thoreau's literary intentions in the years after *Walden* is William L. Howarth's "Successor to *Walden*? Thoreau's 'Moonlight—An Intended Course of Lectures'" (*Proof* 2:89–115). Howarth analyzes the surviving leaves of the lecture, "Moonlight," delivered in October 1854, and a related group of manuscripts dealing with moonlight walks transcribing passages from the journals of 1850–1854. He conjectures that the material may have been intended for a course of lectures (as Thoreau indicated on one of the manuscripts) or even as a book-length successor to *Walden*. He also shows that the essay, "Night and Moonlight," published in *Excursions* (1863), is a truncated, badly arranged version of the lecture prepared by Sophia Thoreau to fill out the volume.

A manuscript page from Thoreau's Indian notebooks, and a transcription, are presented by Richard F. Fleck in *ConS* 7,ii:1–6. A notebook kept by Richard Fuller, Margaret's brother, during his walk with Thoreau to Wachusett Mountain in 1842 is reprinted in *TSB* 121:1–4; unfortunately it says little about Thoreau, consisting largely of rapturous philosophizing, and breaks off in the middle. A letter from Sophia Thoreau to Daniel Ricketson about her late brother written in May 1866 is transcribed, with notes, by Thomas Blanding in *ConS* 7,iii:1–6. A letter not included in Richard L. Herrnstadt's *Letters of A. Bronson Alcott* is printed by Arthur W. Biddle in *ATQ* 13:36–37.

Newspaper accounts of two lectures by Emerson and one by Thoreau are reprinted by Kenneth W. Cameron in "Emerson and Thoreau Lecture at Lynn" (*ATQ* 14:158–64). An early review of *Walden*, from the *Christian Register*, August 26, 1854, is printed in *TSB* 118:7–8. Edmund Schofield, *TSB* 119:4, points out a number of errors in Robert Stowell's *Thoreau Gazetteer*.

Thoreau: The Major Essays, edited by Jeffrey L. Duncan (New York, Dutton), is a good paperback collection that includes all the essays likely to interest a general reader. Editorial comment is at a minimum.

Checklists of current commentary about Emerson and Thoreau are provided in *ESQ* (18:294–97) and in *TSB* (all issues).

ii. Biography, Literary History, Sources and Influence

The current interest in Women's Liberation is undoubtedly the cause of the surge of interest in Margaret Fuller in the popular magazines, though it has not yet resulted in any substantial reevaluation of her in the learned journals. Two primarily biographical articles, Joseph J. Deiss, "Men, Women and Margaret Fuller" (*AH* 23:43–47,94–97), and Fred C. Shapiro, "The Transcending Margaret Fuller" (*Ms.* Nov.: 36–39), enhance her image at the expense of Emerson's until the latter begins to assume the proportions of Mephistopheles.

The critical reputations of both Emerson and Thoreau are considered in Jay B. Hubbell's *Who Are the Major American Writers?* (Durham, N.C., Duke Univ. Press). This work, which reviews attempts by critics, creative writers, and literary journals of both the nineteenth and twentieth centuries to establish a canon of "great" American authors, is both engrossing and depressing. Estimates vary

so widely from generation to generation that the whole effort begins
to seem like a waste of time. The book does, however, document the
fluctuations in Emerson's fame and the gradual rise in Thoreau's.
    *The Recognition of Ralph Waldo Emerson: Selected Criticism
Since 1837* (Ann Arbor, Univ. of Mich. Press), edited by Milton R.
Konvitz, is similar in format to previously published collections in
this series. Many of the selections are familiar and important: the
attack by Andrews Norton on the Divinity School Address, the
lengthy estimate by Theodore Parker, Matthew Arnold's balanced
view, John Jay Chapman's defense, the idiosyncratic estimate by
D. H. Lawrence, the attack by James Truslow Adams on Emerson's
"shallow optimism." As in any such collection, the question of those
omitted looms as large as that of those included. Arguments might be
made for the inclusion of equally important and representative criticism by people like Alcott, V. L. Parrington, F. O. Matthiessen, Yvor
Winters, and Stephen Whicher. More serious is the lack of editorial
substance. Konvitz makes no attempt in his introduction to explain
why the excerpts are grouped as they are, or what phases can be
marked in the progress of Emerson's reputation. The headnotes to the
excerpts run usually to less than a dozen lines and are non-interpretive.
There is no bibliography of other significant criticism that the reader
is encouraged to consult. Of course the title promises only "selected
criticism," but it is possible to hope for somewhat more direction
than that.
    A minor and not very satisfactory volume is *Henry David Tho-
reau: Studies and Commentaries*, edited by Walter Harding, George
Brenner, and Paul A. Doyle (Rutherford, N.J., Fairleigh Dickinson
Univ. Press). It is a collection of papers given at a Thoreau Festival
held at Nassau Community College in Garden City, Long Island, in
1967. The fact that such gatherings rarely cohere, as John C. Broderick noted in last year's *ALS*, is amply demonstrated by this volume,
whose contents range from the perceptive to the sophomoric. The
most significant of the papers, by Alfred Kazin, was published in
slightly revised form in the *Atlantic Monthly* for May 1969 and subsequently reviewed in *ALS 1969*, p. 12. Others of note are discussed in
the appropriate sections below.
    Joel Myerson in "A Calendar of Transcendental Club Meetings"
(*AL* 44:197–207) lists all of the known meetings of the Transcendental Club, based upon references in the journals or letters of, among

others, Emerson, Alcott, Frederick Henry Hedge, Theodore Parker, and Convers Francis. Identified when possible are "the places at which the meetings were held, the topics of discussion, and the persons in attendance." Thirty meetings in all are documented, from September 8, 1836, to *circa* September 20, 1840.

Jeanne M. Zimmer in "A History of Thoreau's Hut and Hut Site" (*ESQ* 18:134–40) traces the further uses of Thoreau's structure through several owners, including Emerson and Hugh Whelan, until eventually parts of it were used to repair a barn, which still stands. She also describes the various attempts to determine and commemorate the site of the hut, culminating in Rowland Robbins's unearthing of the foundation in 1945 and the designation of Walden Pond as a national landmark in 1965.

Joel Myerson, in " 'In the Transcendental Emporium': Bronson Alcott's 'Orphic Sayings' in the *Dial*" (*ELN* 10:31–38), describes the disastrous public reception of Alcott's Sayings, which became the focal point of criticism of the new-fledged *Dial*. The numerous lampoons of Alcott's oracularism are not without their humor even today.

Two articles concern themselves with Emerson's sources. Arlen J. Hansen (*ESQ* 18:184–85) cites Emerson's familiarity with Porphyry's *Life of Plotinus* as an indication that Plotinus should be considered an early source of Emerson's knowledge of Neoplatonism. J. Edward Schamberger (*ESQ* 18:179–83) traces Emerson's awareness of the concepts of the Reason and the Understanding to his reading of Dugald Stewart and Richard Price at Harvard.

Seven articles link Transcendentalist figures with their contemporaries. The most significant of them, Randolph J. Bufano's "Emerson's Apprenticeship to Carlyle, 1827–1848" (*ATQ* 13:17–25), recounts in some detail, but without any new illumination, the course of friendship between Emerson and Carlyle up until Emerson's second visit to England in 1847–1848, when it effectively ended with Carlyle's statement that there was a "line of separation" between the two men "as deep as the pit." He emphasizes the temperamental and philosophical differences between the two men which a transatlantic correspondence ameliorated but did not conceal. Throughout, especially for Emerson, the friendship was one of "hope deferred and expectation unfulfilled," but it could not survive a direct confrontation over such subjects as the nature of the hero and slavery.

The other six articles point out links with Hawthorne, Longfel-

low, Melville, and Emily Dickinson. Emerson's "The Snow-Storm"
and Emily Dickinson's "Publication—is the Auction" are compared by
Mario L. D'Avanzo in " 'Unto the White Creator': The Snow of Dickinson and Emerson" (*NEQ* 45:278–80). The purity of artistic creation
is seen as central to both poems. D'Avanzo (*ATQ* 14:11–13) discusses
the Emersonian context of Dickinson's "The Reticent Volcano." Some
superficial comments on Emerson as the prototype of Plotinus Plinlimmon in Melville's *Pierre* are made by Mildred K. Travis in *ATQ*
14:47–48. Edward C. Peple, Jr., in "Hawthorne on Thoreau: 1853–
1857" (*TSB* 119:1–3) cites a number of occasions during Hawthorne's
term as American consul at Liverpool when he recommended Thoreau to various English acquaintances, to the extent of writing to
America for copies of *Walden* and *A Week* to be sent to them. (Raymona Hull in *TSB* 121:7–8 quotes several additional comments by
Hawthorne.) Edward Stephenson in "Longfellow Revised" (*TSB*
118:4–5) shows how Thoreau, in *Cape Cod*, subtly changed a line in
Longfellow's poem "Seaweed" to make it more accurately reflect his
own theory of artistic creation. Finally, Margaret Fuller figures in
Darrell Abel's "Hawthorne on the Strong Division-Line of Nature"
(*ATQ* 14:23–31). Abel sees Hawthorne's primarily satiric attitude
toward "the transcendental heifer" as balanced by an awareness of
the justice of Fuller's view that "wholly masculine" men and "purely
feminine" women are both incomplete.

Two articles attempt to define the significance of Emerson for our
day. Earl Rovit in "Emerson: A Contemporary Reconsideration"
(*ASch* 41:429–38) sees Emerson's central achievement as the creation
of a personality which is forever in a state of tension, seeing and
glorying in the irreconcilability of opposites, avoiding any movement
toward finality of vision. In a prose which crackles with electric metaphors, Rovit calls such concepts as the Over-Soul and compensation
"energy-grounds" for Emerson's art, and speaks of the essays as "wired
together like an electrical relay system . . . suddenly vitalized under
high voltage in the consciousness of the reader." Despite a few too
many such passages, the essay is an excellent analysis of Emerson's
continuing importance as a believer in the individual in an age given
over to group action and collectivism. Ann Douglas Wood in "Recon-
siderations—Ralph Waldo Emerson" (*New Republic*, 1&8 Jan.: 27–
29) sees *Representative Men* as Emerson's attempt to provide the
insecure intellectuals of his own generation, not with models, but with

inspirational figures whose main value is in building self-confidence rather than inspiring to action. But since "the kind of ego-building calisthenics Emerson performed ultimately produces the demand for a fit arena in which to practice them," he may be seen as contributing to "Teddy Roosevelt charging up San Juan hill" and, presumably, involvement in Vietnam.

Two articles in *Thoreau: Studies and Commentaries* (see section *ii* above) deal with Thoreau and India. Kamala Bhatia (pp. 117–32), claiming that Thoreau's life and writings have "a remarkable affinity with Indian thought," compares Thoreau's mysticism not only with the Hindu scriptures but also with such modern writers as Aurobindo Ghose and Rabindranath Tagore. Nissim Ezekiel (pp. 133–43) disputes the widely held view that Gandhi was a "disciple" of Thoreau's. In fact, Gandhi read "Civil Disobedience" years after he had formed many of his ideas of political action, and the philosophical bases of their lives were quite dissimilar.

Andrea Goudie in "Exploring the Broad Margins: Charles Ives's Interpretation of Thoreau" (*MQ* 13:309–17) claims that the "Thoreau" section of the American composer's *Concord Sonata* effectively reflects the spirit of the author of *Walden* because of its musical contrasts between "quiet thoughtfulness and volatile complexity." Another yoking of Thoreau and Ives, by Philip Corner (*Thoreau: Studies and Commentaries*, pp. 53–81), "puzzled" and "outraged" some of its hearers when it was first presented at the Thoreau Festival in Garden City in 1967, according to Walter Harding. It is easy to see why, since the essay is alternately hortatory and obscure.

A literary curiosity is reported by J. Edward Schamberger in "Grapes of Gladness: A Misconception of *Walden*" (*ATQ* 13:15–16). Schamberger describes a little-known booklet by Marshal V. Hartranft issued in 1939 as a rebuttal to Steinbeck's *Grapes of Wrath*, offering *Walden* as a solution to the problem of the Okies.

iii. Criticism: Poetry and Prose

There was more specifically literary criticism on Emerson than Thoreau, primarily because of a symposium on *Essays: First Series*, "Emerson's Strategies of Rhetoric," which occupied all of *ESQ* 18, iv. All of the essays except "The Over-Soul" are considered at least once. Three articles are devoted primarily to the study of images: LeRoy

Lad Panek deals with those of commerce, law, and physics in "Compensation"; William J. Scheick with those of the garden and the farm in "Prudence"; and David G. Hoch with those of the sphere in "History" and "Art." Two others discuss the imagery as related to structure in "Circles": Jack Null finds the structure to be based upon "central clusters or nodules of imagery" which radiate out into the essay and intersect with each other, while Albert H. Tricomi finds coherence through images of expanding circularity, paragraphs which develop by flashes of insight out of potential ideas in the preceding paragraph, and "religio-epic" diction. The other articles deal with disparate topics: William Bysshe Stein analyzes Emerson as "the vatic poet of cosmic consciousness" in "History"; William K. Bottorff considers the paradoxes in "Self-Reliance" both as rhetorical devices and as a mode of unconventional utterance; Brian C. Bond divides "Spiritual Laws" into a number of incremental sections; Mary E. Rucker examines the dialectical balance maintained in "Friendship" between the inadequacies of actual friendship and the spiritual reality which the concept adumbrates; and Carl Nelson finds numerous eastern echoes, especially from the *Bhagavad-Gita,* in "Heroism." One essay, "Intellect," is called by Sanford Pinsker "an anti-essay . . . which substitutes poetic technique for the usual modes of persuasive rhetoric in an attempt to express the inexpressible," and another, "Love," is considered by Carol Clancey Harter an embarrassing failure because of Emerson's "fundamental ambivalence . . . toward the subject itself, particularly toward its potential physicality and its social manifestation in matrimony."

According to Ralph C. LaRosa in "Invention and Imitation in Emerson's Early Lectures" (*AL* 44:13–30), Emerson's use of proverbial sentences in the lectures of the 1830s was designed to help him rediscover, or "invent" for himself, the preexisting truths of the universe and avoid the pitfalls of mere imitation. The proverbs, whether of the common folk variety or derived from literary sources, have a structure which, like experience itself, resists "absolute order, natural or approximated by rhetorical convention . . . in favor of variation." LaRosa examines a number of specific proverbs in detail, including some of Emerson's own, most of which mimic the form but lack the impact of common proverbs (e.g., "He that does nothing is poorer than he who has nothing").

Lawrence J. Buell in "Reading Emerson for the Structures: The

Coherence of the Essays" (*QJS* 58:58–69) rejects the traditional view that Emerson's essays are incoherent or that they are only very generally or abstractly patterned. He contends that Emerson had control over his topic "from section to section [and] paragraph to paragraph" and analyzes a number of passages in detail to demonstrate his point, including "History" and "Self-Reliance" in their entirety. The result is the kind of close reading to which Emerson is not subjected often enough. The article is solidly grounded in the currently appearing editions of the journals and lectures and shows what can be done in clarifying Emerson's creative technique by utilizing them.

R. A. Yoder in "Toward the 'Titmouse Dimension': The Development of Emerson's Poetic Style" (*PMLA* 87:255–70) distinguishes three phases in Emerson's poetry, linked to changes in Emerson's thought. In what Yoder calls the poems of 1834 (the year of Emerson's "poetic maturity") the style is characterized by neatness, gnomic compression, and spontaneity of intuited insight. The second phase, which lasted just a year or two centering on 1840, was patterned after the wild freedom of Anglo-Saxon poetry and demanded a looser poetic form and a more discursive manner closer to the actual processes of thought. In the third and longest phase, which began after 1841 and lasted the rest of Emerson's life, the poet, now primarily an observer rather than a hero, used oblique wit and understatement to express the limitations of insight and knowledge. Aware that Nature seldom answers our questions directly, Emerson became, Saadi-like, "the bard and sage mellowed by experience."

Charles C. Walcutt in "Emerson's 'The Sphinx'" (*Expl* 31:item 20) attempts to explain the poem by proposing that the Sphinx's question as to why man is out of harmony with nature is a misleading one, since it is based on the idea that a state of repose is the only proper view of reality. The poet refutes the Sphinx by answering that man is made not for repose but for quest, and her subsequent transformation into various natural forms confirms his insight. As with most explanations of the poem, the analysis seems logical except that there are certain passages in the poem it does not clarify.

The most substantial piece of criticism on Thoreau in 1972 was Stanley Cavell's *The Senses of Walden* (New York, Viking), a difficult, sometimes provocative book. Considering *Walden* akin to a piece of scripture, it attempts to analyze the way in which Thoreau imbues his language with a depth of rediscovered meaning, thus making possible the regeneration of both the writer and his readers. The book is divided into three sections, Words, Sentences, and Portions, but these headings are not to be taken as an accurate guide to contents. There are many stimulating passages in Cavell's book: his examples of the ways in which the actions in *Walden* are metaphors for the act of writing itself; his discussion of Thoreau's use of economic terms in the larger context of the lives of his contemporaries; his ability to shed new light on familiar passages by the emphasis given to certain words; his description of the reader's reactions in the act of reading. But the logical sequence of Cavell's discussion is not always obvious, as if it proceeded out of some sort of free association, and his style is frequently very dense, with a penchant for paradox that might give Thoreau himself pause. The discussion at the end of the philosophical implications of *Walden*, especially, is heavy going.

Two articles deal with the structure of *Walden*. In "Symmetry Out of Season: The Form of *Walden*" (*SAB* 37,iv:18–24) A. E. Elmore sees *Walden* as consisting of two unequal parts: the first twelve chapters deal with summer and fall, the last six with winter and spring. This "front-heavy or top-heavy symmetry" (!) parallels "Thoreau's philosophical method in his Walden experiment, which was to move from the pluralism of particulars to the unity of universals," i.e., from a practical, public life to one of private discovery. Raymond P. Tripp, Jr. (*TSB* 118:5–6) maintains that *Walden* can be read as a three-stage argument: the first six chapters are "negative" (eliminating unnecessary things); the middle six are "assertive" (seeing the world from a new perspective); and the last six are "integrative" (combining explorations of the internal and external world).

Robert D. Arner in "The Deserted Village of Walden Woods: Thoreau's Ruin Piece" (*ATQ* 14:13–15) links the depiction of the vanished villagers of Walden in the first half of "Former Inhabitants; and Winter Visitors" with the Romantic tradition of the pastoral ruin, noting that it shows Thoreau "in an uncharacteristic mood, . . . steeped in gloom," but that he is rescued by recognition of the "ongoing vitality" of nature, represented by the perennially blooming lilac.

In "Thoreau as Yankee in Canada" (*ATQ* 14:174–77) Sidney Poger defends the least successful of Thoreau's travel narratives, maintaining that it is "Thoreau's *Innocents Abroad*, in which he satirizes the traveler, his companions, and the country traveled through."

David L. James in "Movement and Growth in 'Walking'" (*TJQ* 4,iii:16–21) sees the polar images of the essay as the sun and the swamp, "a subtle blending of the lofty and the low."

iv. Criticism: Ideas

In the second chapter of *The Voice of the Folk: Folklore and American Literary Theory* (Amherst, Univ. of Mass. Press), Gene Bluestein considers Emerson as one of the two major nineteenth-century interpreters (Whitman is the other) of the no longer controversial idea that a country's literary tradition must be based upon the fables and language of its common people. Tracing this view to the German philosopher and poet Johann Gottfried von Herder, Bluestein links it to Emerson's belief in the "epiphanies" which may arise out of even the most ordinary things, the expression of which constitutes one of the major goals of the poet. Unfortunately, Bluestein says, Emerson's own poems usually fall short of the concreteness and immediacy which his literary theory demanded.

In "Democrat in Heaven—Whig on Earth: The Politics of Ralph Waldo Emerson" (*HNH* 27:123–40) George E. Carter selects evidence to show Emerson a thoroughgoing conservative whose hero was Daniel Webster—unaware that other evidence indicates early dislike of the Whigs and early criticism of Webster.

Stephen Railton in "Thoreau's 'Resurrection of Virtue!'" (*AQ* 24:210–27) discusses the gradual growth of Thoreau's awareness of the "offensive" elements of nature, which threatened his belief in nature's essential purity, and his resolution of the philosophical problem this presented. By the time of *Walden* Thoreau was able to see the "excrementitious" sand in the railroad cut in the spring as an example of the vital force of nature revealing itself in inorganic things as it shortly would in organic. The most meaningful metaphor for Thoreau, Railton says, was the water lily (developed too late for inclusion in *Walden*) which, growing in slime, represented "nature's ability to transmute its baser elements into virtuous (i.e., pure) ones."

In "Thoreau as Mythologist" (*RS* 40:195–206) Richard F. Fleck argues that Thoreau's concept of mythology is peculiarly modern because he believed "that nature lies at the core of myth and that primitive cultures create simple folktales and folkpoems, gradually evolving into a more sophisticated mythology which is universal in time and place." He notes that Thoreau was aware of the myth-making potential of the American experience, e.g., Columbus as Jason, Franklin as Prometheus. In *TJQ* 4,i:1–9, Fleck discusses the mythological implications Thoreau uncovers in such New England subjects as lumbermen, ice cutters, the telegraph and the railroad. In an article as poorly focused as its title, "Thoreau, Mythology, Simplicity and Self Culture," (*TJQ* 4,iii:1–15) James T. Jenkins claims that Thoreau misused the "myth" of simplicity, appropriate to the individual's attempt to attain greater self-awareness, when he applied it to the quite different demands of a profit-oriented society.

Kichung Kim in "Thoreau's Science and Teleology" (*ESQ* 18:125–33) shows that although Thoreau might have been expected to support the traditional views of the separate origin of species as set forth by Agassiz, he actually preferred the views of Asa Gray, Darwin's American disciple, on genetic continuity. The teleology of Thoreau's time was inspired by a need to have nature made significant to man in some philosophical way, and like Goethe, Thoreau discovered that "the [natural] fact will one day flower out in a [spiritual] truth" through flights of poetry, specifically in the passage about the thawing sand and clay in the railroad cut at the end of *Walden*.

In "*Walden* and Its Audiences: Troubled Sleep, and Religious and Other Awakenings" (*MLR* 67:756–62) Leslie D. Foster considers the "awakening" motif in *Walden* in the context of the various audiences Thoreau is addressing. To the John Farmers of the world, whose incessant labor prevents spiritualization, he speaks sympathetically; toward those caught up in the periodic revival movements of the early nineteenth century he is satiric; for those who, like himself, are fully committed to an interior rebirth, he humbly confesses the gap between the ideal and the actuality.

Finally, a criticism of Thoreau appears in, of all places, the bulletin of the Thoreau Society. Ray Gagnon in "Thoreau: Some Negative Considerations" (*TSB* 121:5–7) finds Thoreau frequently insecure, petty, and "far less able . . . to hold to his transcendental faith . . . than was Emerson, say."

v. Dissertations

Twenty-two dissertations wholly or partly concerned with Emerson, Thoreau, or Transcendentalism are listed in *Dissertation Abstracts*

International for 1972. Four deal exclusively with Emerson, linking him with the Hindu scriptures, Islamic literature, the associationist movement, and his reputation in Germany. In others he is studied in conjunction with Thoreau and Whitman, Shelley and Mill, Robert Frost, and Paul Tillich. For Thoreau, two dissertations touch on his prose style and two on his ideas, one analyzes *Cape Cod*, and one gives *Walden* a psychoanalytical reading. He finds himself in the unlikely company of Henry Adams, Gertrude Stein, and Norman Mailer in another. One dissertation examines the *Dial*, and one Bronson Alcott's reputation. Four touch on Transcendental writers in considering such topics as nature poetry, the familiar essay, the travel book, and Quakerism. One considers "transcendental naturalism" as one of three kinds of American literary naturalism.

vi. Miscellaneous

At present there are five separate publications devoted primarily or exclusively to the study of the Transcendentalists—as it turns out, an example of overkill. The most significant of these, the *Emerson Society Quarterly*, for so long under the direction of Kenneth W. Cameron, in 1972 appeared under a new editor and in a new format as *ESQ: A Journal of the American Renaissance*. It now consists entirely of critical articles. Cameron's current publication, the *American Transcendental Quarterly*, is very similar to the old *ESQ*, consisting not only of critical articles but of reading lists, excerpts from book catalogues, and miscellaneous reprinted matter. One unhappy feature of *ATQ* is that titles of articles are frequently misleading. One entitled "Thoreau on the Limitations of Great Circle Sailing" is a reprint of a nautical article in a 1903 encyclopedia, and another, "Death and Beyond in the American Renaissance," reproduces a medieval picture book of 1450! It would certainly be a service to scholars to omit listing of such material in bibliographies.

The study of Thoreau is served by the long-standing *Thoreau Society Bulletin* (founded in 1941). Not pretending to be primarily a critical journal, the *TSB*'s characteristic blend of information, gossip, and Concord-oriented enthusiasm makes it great fun to read, and its bibliography, appearing in every issue, does not hesitate to turn over the tiniest pebble of information relating to Thoreau. The *Concord Saunterer*, a small, chatty quarterly put out by the Thoreau Lyceum in

Concord, has a long way to go before it can compare with the *TSB*, but lately it has been printing significant short articles on manuscripts relating to Thoreau. The oddly named *Thoreau Journal Quarterly*, issued by the Thoreau Fellowship, Old Town, Maine, is a poorly printed publication most of whose short articles can best be described as amateurish. Readers with an aesthetic sense of language are advised to enter the prose thicket of the *TJQ* with care. A change of editorship beginning with the January 1973 issue may produce some salutary changes.

Two publications of Transcendental Books (Hartford, Conn.) appeared in 1972: *Emerson and Thoreau Speak* (reprinted from *The Massachusetts Lyceum*, an earlier volume from the same press) and an enlarged edition of *Emerson and Thoreau as Readers*. Issued as a Thoreau Society Booklet was *The Thoreau Collectors' Guide to Book Prices*, by Walter Harding (1971).

Finally, Richard J. Eaton, in "Thoreau's Herbarium" (*Man and Nature* Dec.:2–5), describes Thoreau's collection of pressed and dried plants, now in the Gray Herbarium at Harvard. The collection, built up primarily between 1856 and 1860, contains over 60 percent of the species known to occur in Concord, a remarkable achievement.

University of Vermont

2. Hawthorne

Nina Baym

In this year's chapter I refer to some eighty-seven published items, mostly from 1972 but including a few earlier pieces that escaped me previously. I have been unable to find some festschrift items, and I have omitted some foreign publications in languages that I cannot read or where past experience suggests that the work will be a restating of current critical approaches for an uninformed audience. I have also left out a few notes and omitted all the dissertations, of which nine are listed in DAI, none of a promisingly original nature.

If I had restricted myself to reporting on Hawthorne criticism of significance—work, that is, which is cognizant of and contributes to the body of approaches by which we attempt to understand this major writer—I would not have cited more than a dozen pieces of criticism. The great bulk of this year's critical output is thin, repetitious, and bland. Moreover, much of it is dismayingly amateurish, badly written and inadequately aware of current scholarship, if not of scholarship altogether. As a result, major issues are regularly ignored or rehashed unawares, while the author makes his or her "contribution"—but one wonders what these authors think they are contributing to. It seems to me that we are seeing here, in what should be a professional literature, the continuation of undergraduate pedagogy which encourages each student to ignore published research and think everything out for himself. Although I do believe that this is an appropriate undergraduate strategy, it would seem that in graduate school a transition must be made, and students must have it explained to them that their insights, if they are to be of value *to others*, must be brought into the context of an ongoing scholarly effort. We can and must fault the journals—some are especially blameworthy here—for publishing work of unprofessional quality; but the major source of our trouble, I think, is in graduate training. It is time for a backswing of the pendulum.

I'll let this stand as a generalization and try in the commentary that follows to point out work of particular excellence. A preliminary word is in order here about the welcome contribution being made to Hawthorne studies in general by C. E. Frazer Clark, Jr., the Hawthorne scholar and collector who is behind several Hawthorne events this year: reprinting of rare texts, the *Nathaniel Hawthorne Journal* (now in its second year of publication), and the fascinating Authors at Auction series initiated with a Hawthorne volume.

i. Texts, Life, Reputation, Bibliography

Three volumes of the Ohio State Centenary Edition of Hawthorne's work appeared with the 1972 copyright, although two of them didn't actually make the calendar year. Volumes 6 and 7 are the writings for children: *True Stories from History and Biography*, and *A Wonder Book* and *Tanglewood Tales*, respectively. The historical introduction by Roy Harvey Pearce, which discusses Hawthorne generally as an author for children, is found in Volume 6, while appropriate textual material appears in each volume. The texts of *Grandfather's Chair*, *Famous Old People*, and *The Liberty Tree* all use the first printed editions for their copy-texts, adopting some emendations from the revised versions printed a decade later. For *Biographical Stories* there exist holograph fragments dispersed among the Houghton, Berg, Rosenbach, and Historical Society of Pennsylvania collections, and these have been followed for copy-text. Where manuscript is wanting, the first edition is substituted. Printers' copy holograph survives for both *A Wonder Book* and *Tanglewood Tales*, the former at the University of Virginia, the latter at the Morgan Library, and are followed as copy-texts. The editing thus is straightforward and cruxes are at a minimum. Pearce's introduction is excellent, although perhaps a bit more interpretative than it should be for the context.

Volume 8 comprises *The American Notebooks* and runs with apparatus to 835 pages (price: $19.50). Since the American Notebooks run some 200,000 words, compared to 300,000 each for the English, and French and Italian Notebooks, we can anticipate volumes running well over a thousand pages and making even deeper inroads into our pocketbooks. The editing problems of the American Notebooks are very complex, and to the editor's credit (Claude M. Simpson) he has provided remarkably clear and succinct apparatus. There were origi-

nally eight manuscript notebooks, of which five survive, all in the
Morgan Library. These five, however, were mutilated in various ways
by Sophia Hawthorne when she transcribed passages from them for
publication in the *Atlantic*. Most of the lost readings were recovered
when Randall Stewart edited the Notebooks, but the surviving five
have been edited afresh and further restorations effected. For the
three missing books there are no choices but to leave them out or fall
back on the printed texts in full knowledge that they are corrupt, and
the latter course has been followed. Simpson provides, in additon to
the historical introduction, explanatory notes and an index. This is a
very pleasing volume despite its rather alarming bulk.

C. E. Frazer Clark, Jr., has published reprints of his copies of two
rare Hawthorne texts: *The Love Letters of Nathaniel Hawthorne*
(Washington, NCR/Microcard), a one-volume reprint of a two-
volume set privately published in 1907 in an edition of 62 copies; and
Letters of Hawthorne to William D. Ticknor, reprinted in one volume
from a private two-volume issue of 1910 in 100 copies (Washington,
NCR/Microcard). Both, in the absence of any scholarly or comprehensive edition of Hawthorne's letters—surely the single most extraordinary and incomprehensible gap in American literary scholarship
—are most valuable. Hawthorne's letters of courtship are unlike anything else in his life in their relaxation of reserve and surrender to
feeling; moreover during the courtship period he wrote little besides
these letters. Later letters to Sophia are less moving, but still important. Those to Ticknor cover the last fifteen years of Hawthorne's life
and are the only sustained correspondence from this late period. Not
being scholarly editions, these books transmit a great many errors.
The love letters, preserved in the Houghton, have been inked and
scissored by Sophia, and her corrupt versions were the basis for the
published volumes. In an introduction, Clark gives us some examples
of recovered readings and also corrects some mistaken dating in the
text, but this is a reprint and not an editing job. Until we get a full,
modern edition of the letters, however, we can be grateful to Clark
for making his rare items widely available in this way.

Sophia's censoring hand is in evidence, then, in both notebooks
and letters this year, and perhaps a word in her defense is appropriate.
What she did is shocking by our standards, but is perfectly in accordance with the public standards of editing and private standards of
decorum of her own age. The editors of nineteenth-century authors,

especially if they were friends or family, took considerable liberty with texts. If Hawthorne had been persuaded to publish his letters and journals during his lifetime, it is almost certain that he himself would have performed a bowdlerizing job on the text before he released it for public scrutiny.

Of course for many critics the fact that other editors did censor, and that Hawthorne himself probably would have, is only additional ammunition against Sophia, who begins to seem less a particular human being than the symbol of a repressive society which inhibited our great writers and consequently made them lesser artists than they might have been. This view of woman as emasculator is very popular in American thought and can be seen in fiction as well as in criticism. In fiction, however, where the author is responsible only to his own vision, it is of course legitimate; as an a priori critical assumption it is irresponsible. It is enlightening to contrast Hawthorne's own view of these matters, for Hawthorne made repression and inhibition of artistic and sexual energy one of his major themes. As he pictured it, repressive forces were codified into powerful social structures which were managed by older, authoritarian *males*. Women were generally victimized by these forces; when left to themselves, they were usually the ones who urged men overtly toward greater self-expression (Hester) or unconsciously released radical energies in them by virtue of the awakening of sexual attraction (Miriam). In *The Scarlet Letter* Hawthorne clarified his perception of the basic social arrangement: Hester, the woman, represents the passionate and self-expressive urge, while repression and inhibition are centered in the powerful males who are the executives and guardians of social order. Oddly enough, the same critics who fault Sophia for her censoring activities frequently also criticize Hester for her attempts to persuade Dimmesdale to uncensor himself. Of course the question here should not be what the general role of woman in society is, but specifically what the relationship was between Hawthorne and his wife. My point is that the first question is usually substituted, in the criticism, for the second; and that it is answered according to the critics' own mythology.

C. E. Frazer Clark, Jr.'s *Hawthorne at Auction* (Detroit, Gale Research Co.) is a sheer delight as well as a valuable piece of scholarship, collecting and reprinting the sales catalogues of all important auctions of Hawthorne material from 1894 to 1971. As Clark explains in his introduction (which is also a pleasure for its personal revela-

tions about collecting), all the great Hawthorne collections formed
before 1924 were broken up at auction, and the annotated catalogues
of these sales often provide information unavailable elsewhere. Collectors who had obtained material from the Hawthorne family or
other prime sources often make unique biographical or bibliographical identifications; and where material has disappeared or is of limited
access, catalogues are often the only record of an item's existence. The
book also may convey, to the majority of Hawthorne students who
work at a great distance from rare first editions and manuscripts,
something of the excitement of these items as tangible objects. The
Nathaniel Hawthorne Journal published transcriptions and facsimiles
of several Hawthorne items from Clark's collection, including letters
from Hawthorne to Samuel M. Cleveland, from Elizabeth P. Peabody
to Harriet Lathrop, from Franklin Pierce to Horatio Bridge, and from
Hawthorne to Joseph B. Boyd.

Minor contributions toward the primary record include John J.
McDonald, "The Old Manse Period Canon" (*NHJ* 2:13–39), a careful dating of all twenty-one of the magazine pieces Hawthorne wrote
while living at the Manse, with good explanations of the processes by
which decisions were reached; "New Light on the Editing of the
1842 Edition of *Twice-Told Tales*," by C. E. Frazer Clark, Jr. (*NHJ*
2:91–103, plus appendices), comparing a family copy possibly annotated by Hawthorne of the *Token* in which three pieces later collected
in 1842 appeared, with the 1842 printing itself; " 'The Whole is a
Prose Poem': An Early Review of *The Scarlet Letter*" by Benjamin
Lease (*AL* 44:128–30), reprinting a very perceptive review published in the Boston *Post* five days after the romance appeared; and
Edward C. Peple, Jr., "Three Unlisted Reviews of Hawthorne" (*ESQ*
18:146–47), reprinting three brief unnoted reviews from the *Dial*
of 1841, presumably Margaret Fuller.

Discussing "Needs in Hawthorne Biography" (*NHJ* 2:43–45),
Arlin Turner feels that little factual biographical information can
possibly be left to be discovered, and what is left can make little difference in the general picture. Three areas of promise remaining, in
his view, are (i) Hawthorne's reading and his response to what he
read, (ii) his personal and social relationships, and (iii) his responses
to events and ideas of his time. This list really goes to show that, facts
notwithstanding, the man as the responsive interacting human being
has still eluded us. And without a sustained act of imaginative sym-

pathy from a biographer of great talent and commitment, he will continue to. C. E. Frazer Clark, Jr., wrote on "Unexplored Areas of Hawthorne Bibliography" (*NHJ* 2:47–51). Besides the basic need for a comprehensive bibliography, there are three relatively unexplored bibliographical areas: Hawthorne in American newspapers (reviews, notices, and reprinting), Hawthorne in American periodicals, and Hawthorne in the English mass media. The last in particular offers a wide field of opportunity.

Nathaniel Hawthorne: A Reference Bibliography, 1900–1971 edited by Beatrice Ricks, Joseph D. Adams, and Jack O. Hazlerig (Boston, G. K. Hall) is meant to answer a clear research need, but is so ineptly done that it serves no purpose whatever, and one hopes that if other, more qualified persons have planned to produce such a work they will not now be deterred. Trying to understand the vast number of mistakes and inconsistencies in the handling of material, in the annotating, and in the subject index, I finally had to conclude that article titles were almost the sole source of information utilized by the compilers, and hence that this bibliography was put together by people who had read almost none of the material they indexed.

ii. Critical Books and General Articles

Neal Frank Doubleday's *Hawthorne's Early Tales: A Critical Study* (Durham, N.C., Duke Univ. Press) is a fine addition to Hawthorne scholarship, a sound, solid, reasonable book emphasizing Hawthorne's craftsmanship and tying him firmly into the literary context of his time. It is important to remember that Hawthorne began his career not as a purveyor of significance but as a teller of stories very much under the sway of contemporary influences, among which Scott, gothicism, and literary nationalism predominated. It is vital to keep these influences in mind so as not to confuse a literary convention for his personal voice. The book covers extant tales from the period 1825–1838, and if Hawthorne's essential mystery is outside Doubleday's scope, his work will still save many hunters of the "inmost Me" from foolish error. It's a model book, also, for scholarship, critical awareness, and clear, graceful writing.

The same cannot be said, alas, for two other book-length studies. One of these, *Hawthorne's Historical Allegory: An Examination of the American Conscience* (Port Washington, N.Y., Kennikat Press,

1971), by John E. Becker, is devoted almost entirely to *The Scarlet Letter* and argues that with a sufficiently generous definition of the term allegory we can call Hawthorne an allegorist. The book's second point is that *The Scarlet Letter* consists of two superimposed allegories: one forced upon the sinners by the Puritan typing of their deeds, and the other an authorial allegory which expands, contradicts, and finally transcends the first. This is a good point and would have made a fine article, but padded out with excessive quotation, elaborate digression, and unnecessary documentation (clear marks of an unretouched dissertation), it loses all its force. Robert H. Fossum's *Hawthorne's Inviolable Circle: The Problem of Time* (Deland, Fla., Everett/Edwards) looks like another unrevised dissertation rushed into print. Fossum considers the major romances and several better-known short stories from the vantage point of Hawthorne's preoccupation with "time," almost immediately redefined as "the past." Since, as Fossum's footnotes guilelessly confess, he has been anticipated in virtually every reading he presents, his sole contribution is the rather abstract intellectual scheme encompassing all Hawthorne's references to the past. But the schematization is carried forward at considerable distance from Hawthorne's concreteness, and the result is an impression of definitional sophistry rather than genuine engagement with the works talked about.

Without a good library and a good command of German, Hawthorne students will be unable to read Alfred Weber's *Die Entwicklung der Rahmenerzählungen Nathaniel Hawthornes: "The Story Teller" und andere frühe Werke 1825–1838* (Berlin, Erich Schmidt), but there is a good, detailed review by Christoph Lohmann (*NHJ* 2:267–70) suggesting that it is one of the more important books on Hawthorne recently to appear. The title translates roughly to "the development of the framed narratives of Nathaniel Hawthorne: 'The Story Teller' and other early works 1825–1838," and the book is described as an ambitious and learned attempt to reconstruct the early projected and completed series of tales and hence to recreate the earliest, missing phase of Hawthorne's career. Right or wrong in its reconstruction, the book is extremely important, according to Lohmann, for the connections it makes between Hawthorne and European Romanticism. This is the first of a projected three-volume study, and one would hope that an enterprising university press will soon go about getting it translated.

A dozen or so general articles of widely varying quality but no great importance appeared in 1972. Robert Penn Warren's 1970 acceptance speech for the National Medal for Literature at the Library of Congress was printed (*NHJ* 2:85–89), but despite its title, "Hawthorne *Was* Relevant," it is a general talk with almost nothing to say about the author. Anne Hildebrand's "Incomplete Metamorphosis in 'Allegories of the Heart'" (*ATQ* 13:28–31) says that Hawthorne's failure to absorb his symbols fully into the texture of his work is not really a failure, since it supports his technique of multifaceted insight. M. J. Ferrell's "Imbalance in Hawthorne's Characters" (*SDR* 10:45–59) runs through a number of Hawthorne's imbalanced characters (one paragraph for each) to conclude that such characters represent a failure of balance (sic). Jac Tharpe, "Hawthorne and Hindu Literature" (*SoQ* 10:107–15), points out some parallels in passages from "Rappaccini's Daughter" and "Roger Malvin's Burial" with certain Hindu literature faddish among the Transcendentalists. The dates of composition of the two stories make the Rappaccini parallel seem more likely to me than the other; but Tharpe's larger point, that in thinking of an author's reading we ought not to confine ourselves to lists of books borrowed from the library, is surely well taken. "Further Spenserian Parallels in Hawthorne" by Rod Wilson (*NHJ* 2:195–201) adds a couple of passages from *The Faerie Queene* to the accumulated body of Spenser sources for Hawthorne's work: Book VI for *Blithedale*, Book V for "Endicott and the Red Cross." This is the first note of Hawthorne's use of Book V. Wilson also reminds us that, for whatever reason, Hawthorne tried to conceal his borrowings from Spenser. Roger Howell in "A Note on Hawthorne's Ambivalence Towards Puritanism: His View of Sir Henry Vane the Younger" (*NHJ* 2:143–46) points out conflicting depictions of Henry Vane in the sketch of Anne Hutchinson, *Grandfather's Chair*, and "Howe's Masquerade."

Of somewhat more weight, Raymona E. Hull in "Hawthorne and the Magic Elixir of Life: The Failure of a Gothic Theme" (*ESQ* 18:97–107) surveys Hawthorne's uses of alchemical motifs throughout the canon. She argues that alchemy works well as a symbol but poorly as a central element of plot. Harry C. West in "Hawthorne's Editorial Pose" (*AL* 44:208–21) discusses Hawthorne's narrative habit of posing as the editor rather than author in his works. This pose makes possible his prevailing tone, that of one engaged like his readers in the search for significance in the material before them all. In "Hawthorne's Treatment of the Artist" (*NEQ* 45:65–80) R. K. Gupta characterizes Hawthorne's artist figures as gifted individuals who sustain the burden of their vision at the cost of immense suffering. Isolation is so terrible a calamity that nothing but the pursuit of art justifies risking it. The article is notable for the fact that it sees no ambiguities, ambivalences, or ironies in any of Hawthorne's portraits of artists; and equally notable for an apparent unawareness of all the criticism that has made a point of such complexities. There is a very brief look at Hawthorne's use of historical fact in "The Function of Historical Sources in Hawthorne, Melville, and R. P. Warren," by D. Nathan Sumner (*RS* 40:103–14). Sumner asserts that Hawthorne was less interested in depicting specific historical episodes than in creating a generalized awareness: to give readers a sense of the reality of Puritan America rather than actual historical knowledge.

Linda Ray Pratt speaks briefly of the Hilda-Miriam and Priscilla-Zenobia pairs in "The Abuse of Eve by the New World Adam" (*Images of Women*, pp. 155–74). Her context is the Adamic myth of Cooper, Hawthorne, and James wherein, she argues, the Adam figure condemns himself to a life of "self deception and moral infancy" when he refuses the embrace of the "post-lapsarian Eve." Another discussion of Hawthorne's view of women is Darrell Abel's "Hawthorne on the Strong Division-Lines of Nature (*ATQ* 14:23–31). The strong division lines are sexual, and the main point of Abel's disorganized discussion seems to be that Hawthorne judged women by different criteria from men both in real life and in his fiction. Hence, for example, Hawthorne is critical of Hester's radical speculation—that he *is* critical Abel does not doubt—not because it is radical, but because thinking is a masculine activity. The jolly tone of the article ("we're all male chauvinists together, ho ho") completes a performance that a Women's Caucus member might have invented for the purpose of demonstrating sexist criticism.

This year's article to argue for Hawthorne as a religious man is "Nathaniel Hawthorne and the Natural Desire for God" (*NHJ* 2:159–71) by Joseph Schwartz. Like many before him, Schwartz says that Hawthorne was clearly, if not dogmatically, a Christian; that a personal quest for God was "seminal" in his thinking; and that he has a "profound and easily observed reverence for the Christian mysteries." Hawthorne did not disguise his "deep innate sense of religion" and indeed often "boldly sentimentalized it." The first part of the overall assertion, that Hawthorne did not like dogmatic or institutional religion, is supported by many convincing quotations, although the effort here is surely superfluous. Evidence for Hawthorne's profound religious sense is given in the shape of many quotations expressing a vague, sentimental piety which hardly demonstrates respect for, let alone knowledge of, any "Christian mysteries." The point about the acknowledged sentimentality of Hawthorne's religious rhetoric would seem to be that while sentimentality may or may not be sincere, it is never "bold" and it is invariably unthinking. Hence, though Schwartz's quoted passages might show real religious emotion, they show nothing like a "personal quest" for God which would be "seminal" in Hawthorne's "thinking." This way of talking about Hawthorne proceeds, I suppose, from the strong conviction that an important writer *must* be religious, or at least the strong wish that he be so. But it is more than an inaccurate way to characterize Hawthorne; it leaves us with fewer tools of language to talk meaningfully about writers who really *are* religious, who are searching for God, who do respect the Christian mysteries, and in whose work the religious emotion is really seminal and the expression of it bold.

iii. Long Romances

Though roughly thirty articles appeared this year on the longer works, no more than four seem to me to be of first quality; another half-dozen perhaps have something to say, and the rest are filler. The only general article on the romances is Paul McCarthy's "A Perspective in Hawthorne's Novels" (*BSUF* 13,i:46–58); the other items are all devoted to single works. McCarthy considers the scenes which are literally elevated above the action in the four novels: the scaffold in *The Scarlet Letter*, the arched window in *The House of the Seven Gables*, Coverdale's bower in *The Blithedale Romance*, and the towers of *The Marble Faun*. He shows how these scenes, which are exercises in the literary representation of pictorial perspective, also provide moral and intellectual perspective on the characters' situations and are always scenes of summing up and emphasizing.

"Hawthorne's 'The Custom-House' and the Conditions of Fiction in America" by Donald D. Kummings (*CEA* 33,iii[1971]:15–18) is not scholarly, but provides a competent summary of the surface argu-

ment and structure of the essay, helpful to prospective teachers of the
piece. Peter L. Hays's note, "Why Seven Years in *The Scarlet Letter?*"
(*NHJ* 2:251–53) points out the extensive use of the seven-year inter-
val and relates it to the standard term of apprenticeship and inden-
tured service in the New World. A longer article which is still essentially a note is "Hawthorne and the Branding of William Prynne" by
Mukhtar Ali Isani (*NEQ* 45:182–95), which shows parallels between
the life of William Prynne and events in *The Scarlet Letter*. Prynne,
a persecuted man turned persecutor, resembles first Hester and then
Chillingworth. Another note, by R. B. Jenkins, "A New Look at an
Old Tombstone" (*NEQ* 45:417–21), proposes an interesting reading
of the last paragraph of *The Scarlet Letter*. Jenkins argues that only
the letter A is actually engraved on the stone, and the heraldic reading is the narrator's description of the device rather than the device
itself. Moreover, since Dimmesdale was buried long before Hester,
the A must have originally been meant for him and signified "Angel."

William R. Manierre points out "Some Apparent Confusions in
The Scarlet Letter" (*CEA* 33,iii[1971]:9–13). In the concluding chapters Hawthorne flatly contradicts himself about the success or failure
of Chillingworth's mission and is confusing about the success of
Pearl's. These "missions" are conceived of in theological terms—Chillingworth is to damn, Pearl to save. In my article "Passion and Authority in *The Scarlet Letter*" (see *ALS 1970*, p. 26) I argued that
Pearl and Chillingworth were not characters in their own right, but
fragments separated from the anguished psyches of Hester and Dimmesdale respectively. The conclusion of *The Scarlet Letter* represents
resolution for both these characters, as a result of which the fragments
lose their apparently autonomous power. This interpretation assumes
that the frame of reference in *The Scarlet Letter*, as in all Hawthorne's
work, is secular; and it becomes increasingly clear to me that the
opposition in the criticism of the gloomy to the cheerful Hawthorne
is far less a crux than the opposition of the religious and secular
writer. Here indeed, according to which kind of interpretation one
reads, are two entirely different writers: one concerned with salvation and the Divine Law, the other with relationships of one man or
woman to other human beings and to society.

Another article on Pearl, by John A. Andola, entitled "Pearl: Symbolic Link Between Two Worlds" (*BSUF* 13,i:60–67), is a competent
rehash. Since the article has no footnotes, it is just barely possible

that the author doesn't know that all his ideas have appeared in print before. A third article taking Pearl as its focus, is the year's loftiest theological piece ("Theology and Literature: *The Scarlet Letter,*" by Raymond Benoit, *BuR* 20:83–92). Benoit discusses Pearl as a union of spiritual and material, symbolizing the workings of both religion and art. The notion of art as a kind of divine incarnation seems to me very far from Hawthorne's view of his profession, and although such ideas were in the air in his day they represented the poets' attempt to claim significance for their enterprise rather than, as Benoit has it, the religionists attempt to claim significance for *theirs.* I think that a historically inappropriate reading is being presented here.

"Hawthorne's Concept of Tragedy in *The Scarlet Letter*" by Dan Vogel (*NHJ* 2:183–93) is a complexly wrought analysis of the romance as a tragic structure uniting the classical and Christian and culminating in catharsis. The formal discussion, however, is but a front for the author's contention that *The Scarlet Letter* is essentially a theological work in which Dimmesdale wins through to glory, ironically with Chillingworth's help and in spite of the temptings of his adversary Hester, who is "passive" and "morally dense" as well as "mindless of problems of guilt and morality" and "perfectly willing . . . to leave such matters to her beloved." Since Hester does integrate experience on the secular plane, she has always had her detractors, but I haven't before seen her characterized in terms so patently contradicted by what Hawthorne says and shows about her. Conversely, let us remember that Dimmesdale is chiefly characterized not by his faith, but by his conservatism: his need to think and live along the lines that society has already laid down. The underlying issue once again is whether the book has a theological or secular ambience. Two articles this year ingeniously attempt to bridge the chasm between secularity and theology, Betty Kushen's "Love's Martyrs: The Scarlet Letter as Secular Cross" (*L&P* 22:108–20) and Preston M. Browning, Jr.'s "Hester Prynne as Secular Saint" (*MQ* 13:351–62). Kushen points out the religious substratum of imagery employed in the secular situation of passionate love, while Browning develops a contemporary view of Hester in terms of the existentialist idea of secular sainthood in Camus, and Bonhoeffer's idea of "religionless Christianity."

Robert E. Todd studies Hester as an archetype in "The Magna Mater Archetype in *The Scarlet Letter*" (*NEQ* 45:421–29). The Magna Mater, or Great Mother, as developed by Jung and more extensively discussed by Erich Neumann, is a bipolar and immensely powerful figure, sometimes terrible and sometimes good. She originates either in the collective unconscious or (more likely) in the very young child's experience of the mother, and Hester is seen to play this archetypal role toward Dimmesdale, being both creative and destructive, the womb and the tomb. The study, though provocative, has the effect of turning Hester entirely into an aspect of Dimmesdale's dilemma and depriving her of existence and drama in her own right. My candidate for the best article on *The Scarlet Letter* in 1972 is Karl P. Wentersdorf, "The Elements of Witchcraft in *The Scarlet Letter*" (*Folklore* 83:132–53). This is a close study of events cohering around Mistress Hibbins and of references in the novel to the Black Man. Wentersdorf concludes that Hawthorne probably believed that there had been cultic witch meetings in seventeenth-century New England and meant the references to them to be taken literally. Mistress Hibbins is a real witch. References to the Black Man have both a metaphorical and historical reference: it is suggested that the community believed that the Devil actually appeared at these cultic meetings. Finally, since the Puritans attributed fiction to the Devil, the elements of witchcraft merge in a satire on the Puritan aesthetic. (The idea of art as covert or subversive activity, Wentersdorf might have added, is clearly enunciated in "The Custom-House" and is central to the thematic pattern of *The House of the Seven Gables*.)

On *The House of the Seven Gables* only two slight pieces appeared. One of these, "Ending the *Seven Gables*: Old Light on a New Problem" by Jerome Klinkowitz (*SNNTS* 4:396–401), argues against an earlier article by Frank Battaglia (see *ALS 1970*, p. 28) which, unfortunately, he misreads. Though its argument is valid, its occasion is invalid; whoever refereed it for the journal did not do his homework. The second article is by Edward Stone and is entitled "Hawthorne's Other Drowning" (*NHJ* 2:231–37). Stone compares Hawthorne's account of the real drowning of Miss Hunt in Concord to the literary drowning which presumably derived from it, that of Zenobia, to show that there is really very little similarity in these two events. He goes on to point out an interesting parallel between Miss Hunt, a young girl left adrift by rapidly changing social and economic conditions in America, and Hepzibah. Perhaps overingenious, the article is still intriguing.

This was the year of *The Blithedale Romance*, for ten articles appeared on it. I'll begin with a 1969 piece which, because it was published in a German festschrift, was regrettably overlooked for several issues of *ALS*. This is Hans-Joachim Lang's "*The Blithedale Romance*: A History of Ideas Approach," published in *Literatur und Sprache* (pp. 88–106). This essay demonstrates that understanding the common intellectual currents of Hawthorne's day as expressed in significant works (Godwin's *Caleb Williams*, Goethe's *Elective Affinities*, Swedenborg, and Fourier) shows *Blithedale* to be not a compendium of "phantasmagoric antics" but a timely work. The bulk of the article is given to background study because Lang feels that the controlling themes of *Blithedale* become immediately clear when the influences are known.

Donald Kay's "Five Acts of *The Blithedale Romance*" (*ATQ* 13:25–28) divides the novel into five acts and subdivides these acts into twenty-nine scenes. A more sophisticated formal discussion is Louis Auchincloss's "*The Blithedale Romance*: A Study in Form and Point of View" (*NHJ* 2:53–58), which talks about Coverdale as a fusion of character and technique. The shared ignorance of narrator and reader forces the reader to participate in Coverdale's voyeurism and hence to feel what it is like to be Coverdale, a man living a half-life incapable of intellectual or emotional commitment. C. E. Schorer discusses "Hawthorne and Hypnosis" (*NHJ* 2:239–44), trying to demonstrate that the hostility towards mesmerism seen in *Blithedale* derived from bad personal experience with Sophia's invalidism. But the evidence adduced actually shows that Hawthorne was horrified by the idea of hypnosis even before Sophia experienced it. The really interesting point in Hawthorne's attempts to dissuade Sophia from mesmeric therapy, so far as *Blithedale* is concerned, is his insistence that these were not spiritual but corporeal phenomena. This says much about his view of Priscilla and I think would tell against the interpretations given by two leading Hawthorne critics in talks delivered at the December MLA convention and printed in the *Nathaniel Hawthorne Journal*: Richard Harter Fogle, "Priscilla's Veil: A Study of Hawthorne's Veil-Imagery in *The Blithedale Romance*" (2:59–65), and Roy R. Male, "Hawthorne's Fancy, or the Medium of *The Blithedale Romance*" (2:67–73). Both of these take Priscilla to represent the pure essence of imagination. For Fogle, the veiled Priscilla is a Shelleyan image of cloudlike luminosity. With or without the veil, he says, "Priscilla is essentially true and beautiful, a touchstone for the perceptions of others"—including, of course, skeptical critics like myself who see her as vapid, conventional, inhibited, blighted: the product of a fallen world. Male says that once we realize that Hawthorne's theme is the relation of inner experience, particularly daydreaming, and the reality of ordinary life, we will see at once that Priscilla is the Fancy. Mesmerized in the city, she is removed to the country "to understand what might happen to man and woman in fresh circumstances." The article is peppered with frequent assurances that its approach is new, daring, cognizant of recent breakthroughs in psychology and philosophy, and appropriately light and fantastic enough for Hawthorne's own Barthian technique in this fiction. But when he does not make *Blithedale* seem like Priscilla's *Adventures in Wonderland*, Male is actually giving us familiar bad news: in fresh circumstances, woman (Zenobia) and man (Hollingsworth), for different reasons mess things up and end worse than they began, while intellect (Coverdale) can do nothing about it.

Gustaaf Van Cromphout's "Blithedale and the Androgyne Myth: Another Look at Zenobia" (*ESQ* 18:141–45) points out that Zenobia partly is, and partly advocates, an ideal of androgyny. But, he says, Zenobia's "fate" shows that for Hawthorne "the proud prophetesses of androgynous perfection were examples *par excellence* of strictly feminine vulnerability." There is no mention, and no apparent awareness, of recent writings by Baym (*ALS 1968*, p. 27; *ALS 1971*, p. 29), Marks (*ALS 1970*, p. 29), and Morgan (*ALS, 1971*, pp. 33–34) on Zenobia and feminist ideology.

To move from Priscilla and Zenobia to the political and economic dimensions of the book, we may first mention Allen Flint's " 'Essentially a day-dream, and yet a fact': Hawthorne's *Blithedale*" (*NHJ* 2:75–83), which claims that "while rejecting the wisdom and efficacy of reform, Hawthorne deemed progress to be inevitable" and that *Blithedale* is Hawthorne's major statement of these beliefs. While Flint can produce much evidence for Hawthorne's distrust of reform, he has not one quotation to support the claim of a belief in inevitable progress. And the article doesn't seem to know that the question of Hawthorne and reform, and of *Blithedale* and reform in particular, has been extensively treated in the criticism; it is, therefore, quite repetitious. I'll close my discussion with two strikingly similar articles, both very good: Nicholas Canaday, Jr., "Community and Identity at Blithedale" (*SAQ* 71:30–39), and John C. Hirsh, "The Politics of

Blithedale: The Dilemma of the Self" (*SIR* 11:138–46). These articles propose the same ideal of community as the purpose Blithedale should have had—in Hirsh's words, "to bring into society a group of individuals, each with his own identity, in such a way that their mutual interdependence will aid, not limit, their individual growth." As Canaday puts it, "the most important function of a true community of human beings . . . lies in the mutual establishment of the identity of each of its members." Both of these articles see Blithedale as failing to live up to this ideal of community, but Canaday judges it much more harshly. Hirsh feels that the Blithedale participants had this ideal in mind, but were unable to work out the interdependence of social and human relations. Too individualistic, they did not fully understand the social needs of human beings. Canaday too points out this confusion, among Blithedalers, of brotherhood with sociality, but argues that the motifs of masks, disguises, simplistic labels, and veils show that the idea of validating real identities was never held by the Blithedalers, and that the "community" was therefore sham from the first.

For *The Marble Faun* I report on four articles, one a 1970 piece from the Italian journal, *Studi americani,* by Marga Cottino Jones entitled "*The Marble Faun* and a Writer's Crisis" (16:81–123). The article theorizes that the falling off in *The Marble Faun,* the loss of Hawthorne's synthesizing powers which resulted in his "use of material not necessary to the plot itself," can be attributed as much to outer distraction as inner paralysis. She reminds us convincingly of the enormous increase in outer experience and stimuli that Hawthorne underwent as a resident of England and especially Italy. Since, however, I believe that the architectural, topographical, and artistic material is all saturated with significance for the plot, the major contention of the article strikes me as wrong. *The Marble Faun* is certainly Hawthorne's most ambitious and difficult book, but everything in it functions and, when the whole is grasped, the audacity of the imagination at work here is positively breathtaking.

Marjorie Elder ("Hawthorne's *Marble Faun*: A Gothic Structure," *Costerus* 1:81–88) applies Hawthorne's notebook characterizing of Gothic architecture as a blend of majesty and minuteness to *The Marble Faun* by asserting that the book has a majestic theme which it articulates through minute details. "Pre-Raphaelite Allegory in *The Marble Faun*" by Suzanne Blow (*AL* 44:122–27) claims however that the minute detailing of the emblematic scenes in the book resembles work of the Pre-Raphaelites, which Hawthorne knew and liked. Since, of course, the Pre-Raphaelites were imitating or reinterpreting medieval painting, these two views are compatible. Finally, Robert Emmet Whelan, Jr., contributed "*The Marble Faun*: Rome as Hawthorne's Mansoul" (*RS* 40:163–75) to his series of articles interpreting Hawthorne through Bunyan and reading all his works as "allegorical description[s] of the painful journey that an unregenerate soul takes from Paradise Lost to Paradise Regained." Rome is the Soul, and the characters are parts of it: Miriam the Will, Donatello the Flesh, Hilda the Spirit, and Kenyon the Intellect. The drama is the struggle between Hilda and Donatello for influence over Miriam, and Hilda wins. Whelan's work is certainly ingenious, but strikes me as about the farthest removed from Hawthorne's substance of any critic now working on the author.

One good article came out on the unfinished romances, Christoph K. Lohmann's "The Agony of the English Romance" (*NHJ* 2:219–29). Lohmann shows that Hawthorne was unable to carry out his original plan to write a light satirical story of confrontation between two worlds. As so often happened with him, the material caught him up and presented a darker aspect. The first determination to end the confrontation between England and America with a victory for the American side became impossible, because it involved (symbolically) giving up the past. The conflict began to appear irreconcilable, because we need the past and future both, and ought not to have to choose. "The work in which he tried to achieve his most mature synthesis of insights into the human condition turned out to be a virtually unread document of his agony."

iv. Short Works

The discrepancy between professional and amateurish work in Hawthorne studies is nowhere more obvious than in the articles published on Hawthorne's shorter works. A dismaying proportion of these are no more than intelligent term papers (no matter what their actual genesis may be). The few good pieces shine all the more brightly.

Four articles are general studies. In "Hawthorne and the Beautiful Impulse" (*ATQ* 14:48–54) Max L. Autrey argues as have many before him that since the supreme achievement of each artist figure (he cites

"Drowne," "The Snow Image," "Feathertop," and "The Artist of the Beautiful") is unsuccessful, Hawthorne stresses the effort, the impulse, the process in art rather than its results. Similarly old hat, the discussion in Paul A. Newlin's "'Vague Shapes of the Borderland': The Place of the Uncanny in Hawthorne's Gothic Vision" (*ESQ* 18:83–96) says that Hawthorne uses the uncanny (the gimmick in this article is a definition of the uncanny derived from Freud) to exemplify his concern with the effects of sin and hidden guilt. Carol McGinnis Kay tells us that "Hawthorne's Use of Clothing in his Short Stories" (*NHJ* 2:245–49) reveals character: ragged characters are apt to be isolated and out of touch with humanity, while brilliantly dressed characters are often vain and shallow—unless, on the contrary, they are tragic figures. "Jeremy Taylor and Hawthorne's Early Tales" by Frederick Asals (*ATQ* 14:15–23) is in fact a look at the marriage motif in "The Wedding Knell," "The Maypole of Merry Mount," and "The Minister's Black Veil," but it doesn't get very far in its investigation.

Taking the stories, for convenience, in alphabetical order, we begin with Mary Sue Schriber's "Emerson, Hawthorne, and 'The Artist of the Beautiful'" (*SSF* 8[1971]:607–16), which argues, without taking into account any previous scholarship on the story or on the interrelationships of Hawthorne and Transcendentalism, that Hawthorne's concept of beauty in the story participates in the Emersonian tradition. Owen Warland and his butterfly are accepted as unironic presentations of an ideal. Robert D. Arner has written a fine piece called "The Legend of Pygmalion in 'The Birthmark'" (*ATQ* 14:168–71), which argues briefly and convincingly that Hawthorne uses the legend to show what Aylmer is not. Aylmer is an ironic Pygmalion because Pygmalion, "having attained perfection in his art, finds that he prefers the imperfections of a mortal woman. . . . He prays to Venus to permit his creation to enter the realm of Nature, while Aylmer strives for just the opposite."

"The Bosom Serpent: A Legend in American Literature and Culture" by Daniel R. Barnes (*JAF* 85:111–22) is a general discussion of the uses of literature for the folklorist, and of folklore for the literary scholar. Barnes suggests that we can learn much about an artist's procedure when he utilizes folklore elements: chiefly, and specifically, Hawthorne's use of the bosom serpent is differentiated from folklore by his lack of concern with phenomenal reality and an unfolkloristic interest in signification. John McElroy ("The Brand Metaphor in 'Ethan Brand,' " *AL* 43: 633–37) hypothesizes that the name Brand is meant to be significant and discusses some possibilities. No previous criticism on this topic is acknowledged to exist. Ely Stock in "Witchcraft in 'The Hollow of Three Hills' " (*ATQ* 14:31–33) says that the story's witchcraft references show biblical knowledge. Jane Donahue Eberwein in "Temporal Perspective in 'The Legends of the Province House' " (*ATQ* 14:41–45) says that in Hawthorne's work the past is necessary to understand the present but drains away the life of the present, that the past can be neither successfully evaded nor used, and that there is no freshness or newness in the world.

" 'The Man of Adamant' and the Moral Picturesque" by Buford Jones (*ATQ* 14:33–41) is a rich article that resists summary. It talks about how Hawthorne worked toward his own aesthetic in regard to the treatment of landscape, how he rejected the conventions of the "sublime" in favor of the "moral picturesque," wherein picturesque refers both to aesthetic attractiveness and to the picturing forth of meanings. Jones's discussion of Hawthorne's techniques in painterly terms is both illuminating and appropriate. Edward Stone's "The Two Faces of America," *OhR* 13:5–11, uses "The Maypole of Merry Mount" as the first of a long series of American statements which characterize the nation as suspicious of joy and unable to distinguish harmful from harmless pleasure. Today, flower children and police reenact the drama of Merry Mount; Hawthorne had historical acuity as much for the future as the past. J. Gary Williams looks at this story in terms of its historical accuracy in "History in Hawthorne's 'The Maypole of Merry Mount' " (*EIHC* 108:173–89) and finds that in going beyond its Puritan sources the story is even more cognizant than these sources of the actual issues involved in the real event. Hawthorne's technique for showing the limitations of the sources is clearly to slip in and out of the Puritan viewpoint so that the reader can see how far it goes, or does not go.

Raymond Benoit proposes an existential reading in "Hawthorne's Psychology of Death: 'The Minister's Black Veil' " (*SSF* 8[1971]: 553–60). The veil, which means nothingness, symbolizes death or non-being, and in donning it the minister shows himself a fully living person, one who sees and accepts non-being in the center of being. The others in the story, denying death, are the dead in life. In " 'Mr. Higgenbotham's Catastrophe'—The Story Teller's Disaster" (*ATQ*

14:171–73) Thomas H. Pauly reads the tale as centering on a story-teller and thus extracts an autobiographical expression from it. A fine article on "My Kinsman, Major Molineux" is by E. B. England, called "Robin Molineux and the Young Ben Franklin: A Reconsideration" (*JAmS* 6:181–88). Drawing on previous work demonstrating the likelihood that Ben Franklin's account of his arrival in Philadelphia in the *Autobiography* was much in Hawthorne's mind as he wrote "My Kinsman," England shows that Hawthorne "sought implicitly to criticize the vision of reality which is embodied in the *Autobiography*." In that work, an "initially confusing world steadily becomes clear and coherent under the pressure of a decisive mind." Robin tries to act firmly and decisively, but "his behavior is shown to be inadequate to the task of bringing order out of the complex, mysterious world he confronts. Robin must submit to an ambiguous discontinuity which is in the nature of things. . . . Only when he becomes passive in this way does the secret of the 'mystery' reveal itself to him." This article is a model of scholarship, self-awareness, and good writing.

Another superior article, by M. D. Uroff, is on "The Doctors in 'Rappaccini's Daughter'" (*NCF* 27:61–70). The main point is that none of the three doctors in the story are good scientists or objective about their work, so that the story cannot be read as a critique of scientific objectivity but indeed is almost the opposite, a criticism of the *failure* of objectivity, an "unscientific attitude toward medicine." The three men are devoted above all to proving themselves right, and none takes a disinterested attitude toward Beatrice, victim of all of them. The article also contains clarifying information about the state of medical thought in Hawthorne's time. David J. Lytle in "Giovanni! My Poor Giovanni!" (*SSF* 9:147–56) suggests that the story is about Giovanni's sexual fantasy, which nearly destroys him but from which he is saved by common sense. Beatrice, the fantasy figure, is an adolescent projection of lust and holy love combined, an untenable mixture in real life and thus dangerous to Giovanni's further development. The article is spoiled by an overlong and demonstrably wrong discussion of the status of evil in Hawthorne's works; Lytle argues that since evil is the creation of the human heart, it therefore doesn't really exist. Practically, this view has the effect of removing any blame from anyone who harms another: since Beatrice is just a fantasy figure, and the whole fantasy is evil, nobody is to blame for killing her at the end, nor has anything "really" happened. More briefly,

Hubert I. Cohen in "Hoffmann's 'The Sandman': A Possible Source
for 'Rappaccini's Daughter' " (*ESQ* 18:148–53) suggests that E. T. A.
Hoffman's "The Sandman" (not directly but as summarized in an
article by Sir Walter Scott) was a source if not the source for Hawthorne. Scott's summary does have striking points of similarity, and
given Hawthorne's love of Scott, the suggestion seems likely.

Gloria Chasson Elrich in "Guilt and Expiation in 'Roger Malvin's
Burial' " (*NCF* 26:277–89) presents an interpretation of the dynamics
of that story that is much like Frederick Crews's but is more sympathetic to Reuben Bourne in its understanding of the reality of the
dilemma in which Bourne is placed by his father-in-law. In " 'Roger
Malvin's Burial'—A Parable for Historians?" (*ATQ* 13:45–49) Diane
C. Naples sees the story as commentary on the early frontier and
warning to frontier historians: the first settlers brought guilt and
entanglement with the past along with them, there is really no "New
World," etc. A similar point is made by Fred Erisman in " 'Young
Goodman Brown,' Warning to Idealists" (*ATQ* 14:156–58), where
the objects of Hawthorne's admonitions are the Transcendentalists.
Did Hawthorne really write in order to warn? It seems most unlikely.
In "The Summons of Young Goodman Brown" (*Greyfriar* 13:15–24)
Gordon V. Boudreau provides a good summary of the various critical
positions that have been taken toward this enigmatic story, and suggests that Hawthorne's failure to validate Brown's experience, and
especially to confirm or deny the reality of the pink ribbons, serves
the purpose of exercising the reader's moral imagination. Harry M.
Campbell, "Freudianism, American Romanticism, and 'Young Goodman Brown,' " (*CEA* 33,iii[1971]:3–6) argues in a simple-minded
way that the use of Freudian theory should be limited critically to
overt sexual matters and that to do otherwise is to distort literature.
The interpretations of the tale by Male, Hoffman, and Crews are
cited as bad examples.

Robert E. Morsberger in "Wakefield in the Twilight Zone" (*ATQ*
14:6–8) is under the misapprehension that the story has been slighted
by critics. He notes that Wakefield's is a life of meaningless detachment. Daniel R. Barnes in "Faulkner's Miss Emily and Hawthorne's
Old Maid" (*SSF* 9:373–78) proposes "The White Old Maid" as a
source for "A Rose for Emily." Two other notes discussing Hawthorne's influences on other writers—Melville, specifically ("Hawthorne and Melville's Enceladas" by Mildred K. Travis, *ATQ* 14:5–

6; and "The Minor Fiction of Hawthorne and Melville" by R. Bruce Bickley, Jr., *ATQ* 14:149–52)—are overingenious and trivial on a significant topic which requires sensitivity and tact.

University of Illinois

3. Melville

Hershel Parker

Now I know why some contributors to *ALS* write their chapters as a professional duty rather than an ebullient addition to the history of literary scholarship and criticism: the majority of studies published on Melville in 1972 are not worth reading. Factual errors abound: stories are misdated, characters are confused with others, events are misrepresented (one writer even counts fewer rapes than a story has). Writers blithely cite whatever text comes to hand, such as the Dell *Moby-Dick*, which William M. Gibson would not think of using, or the anglicized Constable *Pierre*. Writers revive long-exploded theories without knowing they are exploded, argue points which others had already made better, and routinely fail to acknowledge major commentary on their topics—all this despite the bounty of new bibliographical guides. As Michael Millgate said in *ALS 1971*, "To ignore in this manner what others are saying, or have said in the past, is not merely to be redundant: it is to deny the very principles embodied in the terms *scholarship* and *criticism* and to undermine all possibility of rational discussion and interchange." And whatever the prerequisites for publishing on Melville may be, aspiration toward stylistic felicity seems rarely to be one of them. Let us hope that contributors to *ALS* may soon find themselves celebrating a scholarship and criticism which honors American literature; meanwhile, a few writers like Kuklick, Wadlington, Higgins, and Tichi were not enough to rescue 1972 from triviality.

i. Bibliography and Editions

In the last paragraph of the Melville chapter for *ALS 1971*, Merton M. Sealts, Jr., praised Nathalia Wright's chapter on Melville in the revised *Eight American Authors*. Now that indispensable collection is photo-offset as a Norton paperback, handier than ever and still legible in reduced format. Perhaps in reprintings the publisher can correct some of the typographical errors which mar Wright's excellent work.

No volume in the Northwestern-Newberry edition was published in 1972, though three texts appeared which in one way or another derive from editorial work in that edition or by some of the NN editors. *Shorter Works of Hawthorne and Melville* (Columbus, Ohio, Charles E. Merrill), edited by Hershel Parker, provides the best available texts for most of the stories and sketches it reprints (including the first critical texts of "Bartleby" and "Benito Cereno"), despite some typos and a few failures of the editor to make necessary emendations. An editorial typing blunder on p. 2 may do more for Mrs. Melville's reputation than all her husband's Freudian biographers have done. The edition of *Typee* in the Penguin English Library contains a sensible introduction by George Woodcock which does more than usual justice to Melville's indebtedness to Defoe and Swift. The text is mongrel: Woodcock seems to imply that it was based upon the Northwestern-Newberry edition (the "most reliable"); if so, it departs from that source in many unspecified ways. Nor is it clear what served as printer's copy for the somewhat anglicized Penguin English Library edition of *Moby-Dick*, prepared by Harold Beaver. This edition attempts to synthesize the best features of two earlier editions. Though Beaver does not say so, his "A Note on the Text" derives primarily from the Norton Critical Edition, even to the reprinting of most of the Norton lists, somewhat altered and condensed but still in the Norton format. The upwards of three hundred pages of explanatory notes are profoundly indebted to the Mansfield-Vincent notes, to the point of silently following them in some of their errors. Not an exemplary specimen of bookmaking. In *Bartleby the Scrivener: A Casebook for Research* (Dubuque, Iowa, Kendall/Hunt), Stanley Schatt includes the *Putnam's* text of the story plus several standard modern essays and briefer comments. The format is clumsy (double-column $8\frac{1}{2} \times 11$ pages); the editorial prose is rough and ready ("Because of the Melville industry, a casebook on Bartleby [sic] will not please everyone."); and "The Controlled Research Text" is breezy to a fault ("Betty Coed" plagiarizes Richard Fogle in one memorable section). Still, it is good to have the essays gathered between two covers. Lawrance Thompson's *Benito Cereno* (Barre, Mass., Imprint Society) is a book for the general, if affluent, reader. He prints a somewhat modernized text of Melville's story and a similarly modernized text of chapter 18 from Amasa Delano's *Narrative of Voyages and Travels* (1817). The foreword reviews Melville's publishing career to "throw light on stylistic strategies" employed in Melville's story; the afterword treats the story as "a study in various modes of perception—various ways of looking, or of not looking, at evil."

ii. Books

The Melville Society of America issued *Melville Dissertations: An Annotated Directory*, compiled by Joel Myerson and Arthur H. Miller, Jr. This new *Directory* has more than twice the number of entries in the Hillway-Parker *Directory of Melville Dissertations* (1962). An annual supplement is to be printed in *Extracts*, the newsletter of the Melville Society (see section *xii* below). Thomas J. Rountree's *Critics on Melville* (Coral Gables, Fla., Univ. of Miami Press) includes substantial quotations from critical essays on most of Melville's books, beginning with Joseph J. Firebaugh on *Typee* and ending with Charles Weir, Jr., on *Billy Budd*. Any such collection is of some use, though Rountree's selections seem uncommonly arbitrary. The two-page "Selected Bibliography" is woefully inadequate and erroneous. A. Carl Bredahl, Jr.'s *Melville's Angles of Vision* (Gainesville, Univ. of Fla. Press), No. 37 in the University of Florida Humanities Monograph series, derives from his 1969 dissertation at Pittsburgh. Bredahl omits *Moby-Dick*, but in chapters on several other books holds that "Melville's angles of vision, his use of perspective, are central to his novels, and an understanding of them is essential to our appreciation of the author as artist. Perspective, since it has both psychological implications and physical representations, provided Melville with a basic concept upon which he could build his art; it provides the reader with an approach to the heart of that fiction." William B. Dillingham's *An Artist in the Rigging: The Early Work of Herman Melville* (Athens, Univ. of Ga. Press) is much more mature and graceful than Bredahl's monograph, but not entirely satisfactory. Any advantages in the order in which the books are discussed (*Typee, Redburn, White-Jacket, Omoo,* and *Mardi*) may be outweighed by the difficulty of dealing in that order with the development of Melville's craftsmanship and the growth of his mind. From "The Lee Shore"

Dillingham extracts "three basic ideas": the "nature of experience," "the thirst for psychological freedom," and "the paradox of Promethean heroism." He sees *Typee* and *Redburn* as dealing "with the nature of experience," while *White-Jacket* and *Omoo* "depict the hero in the act of acquiring and proving his independence"; *Mardi* is the most comprehensive treatment of all three themes. In a review, William Gilman has protested reasonably (*AL* 45:120–21) that like "much archetypal and impressionist criticism," this book "rides theses, substitutes something else for the text, or resorts to reductive generalization," but perhaps the worst weakness is a pervasive sobriety, if not an outright resistance to Melville's humor. *An Artist in the Rigging* will not evoke the extremes of praise and blame called forth by several of the books published in 1970; it is a gentlemanly book, to be consulted rather formally, learned from sedately, and disagreed with politely. For Aaron Kramer's *Melville's Poetry*, see section *x* below.

iii. General

Bruce Kuklick's "Myth and Symbol in American Studies" (*AQ* 24:435–50) is the most important theoretical article of the year, required reading for everyone in American literature and American studies. Kuklick defines the methodological premises which guide the "humanist" writers in American studies who have been inspired by Henry Nash Smith's *Virgin Land* (especially Leo Marx, but also others like R. W. B. Lewis, Charles L. Sanford, Alan Trachtenberg, and John William Ward), then assesses the plausibility of those premises and of the humanists' conclusions. *Moby-Dick* is the main example in Kuklick's challenge to "the humanist analysis of the relation between the great work of art and the culture in which it is written."

"Melville and the Idea of the City" by James Polk (*UTQ* 41:277–92) is a general survey of "urban imagery" in Melville's works from *Typee* to *Clarel*. Polk's observations are often unexceptionable, though they seldom shed new light; the same topic was treated with rather less complexity by Paul McCarthy in *RS* 38:214–29 (see *ALS 1971*, pp. 56–57). One boggles at some of Polk's comments, particularly the description of Celio as "the disaffected Catholic monk." Joyce Carol Oates's chapter on "Melville and the Tragedy of Nihilism" in *The Edge of Impossibility* (New York, Vanguard), pp. 59–83, is a very slightly expanded version of her 1962 article (*TSLL* 4:117–29) on "Melville and the Manichean Illusion." Passages on *Pierre* and some other works stand up well enough, but the work of Hayford and Sealts has outdated much of what she says about *Billy Budd*. Charles N. Watson, Jr., takes up a familiar subject in "Melville and the Theme of Timonism: From *Pierre* to *The Confidence-Man*" (*AL* 44:398–413), attempting to retrieve the notion of Melville's Timonism from "the status of an unscholarly myth" to which "the 'normalizing' biographical work of the early 1950's" relegated it. Watson's method of drawing "biographical conclusions" from Melville's fiction tends to trivialize both the life and the works, and instead of restricting himself to genuinely Timonized characters, he ends up attributing Timon-like feelings and actions to some who are distinctly unlike Timon. This article makes one eager to read a worthy study of the possibility that in the years after *Moby-Dick* Melville began projecting a role for himself as "Oblivion's volunteer." (Watson and the editorial board at *American Literature* ought to have known that "Bartleby" was published before *The Encantadas*; in a study of Melville's developing Timonism it is jarring to have "Bartleby" cited as continuing a pattern established in that "earlier" work.)

iv. From *Typee* to *White-Jacket*

Scholarship on Melville's early books was routine this year. Mukhtar A. Isani in "Melville's Use of John and Awnsham Churchill's *Collection of Voyages and Travels*" (*SNNTS* 4:390–95) establishes only that the book in question was available at the New York Society Library while Melville was a member, not that he used it for *Mardi* or *Moby-Dick*. *American Literature* should not have published a note by Keith Huntress, " 'Guinea' of *White-Jacket* and Chief Justice Shaw" (43:639–41), since it recounts an incident fully outlined in Anderson's *Melville in the South Seas* (1939)—a book Huntress does not mention. (Perhaps *American Literature* ought to start printing the names of editorial readers who recommend publication.) "Messianic Nationalism in the Early Works of Herman Melville: Against Perry Miller" by John Gerlach (*ArQ* 28:5–26) is a general survey with only brief discussion of Miller's claims in *The Raven and the Whale* about Melville's involvement with the New York "Young America" group. Gerlach does not define his differences with Miller clearly, despite his title, and notably fails to examine Melville's nationalism in the important context of his family's political commitments. He asserts that throughout his career "Melville used messianic national- ism to seek conventional approval, while at the same time having his own private joke about this characteristic American delusion"—a statement that any reading of *Clarel* would invalidate. No reference is made to carrying the discussion into Melville's later works.

v. Moby-Dick

This year's meatiest study is Warwick Wadlington's "Ishmael's Godly Gamesomeness: Selftaste and Rhetoric in *Moby-Dick*" (*ELH* 39: 309–31), an article which may rank not immeasurably below Be- zanson's classic "*Moby-Dick*: Work of Art" (1953) in permanent use- fulness. Wadlington argues that one "of the basic structural and rhetorical patternings of *Moby-Dick* is the repetition of . . . enchant- ment-like captivations or commitments and the subsequent releases from them, a cycle that generates Ishmael's self-being as both charac- ter and narrative consciousness." The "making of individual identity is of primary thematic importance," and Ishmael "offers his readers, insofar as possible within the limits of an aesthetic experience, what Ahab purports to offer to his 'audience'—selfhood." By way of demon- strating this last point, Wadlington offers the most sensitive reading of the first chapter yet published. So ambitious an article is bound to be unsatisfying at certain points. My own major objections are few— mainly a feeling that Wadlington sees Ishmael as a little more sane and normal than he is (perhaps Wadlington is overreacting against Brodtkorb's anachronistic view of Ishmael as an existential hero full of boredom, dread, and despair). Wadlington may also minimize the degree to which Ishmael as he tells the story is still drawn toward both Bulkington and Ahab. After all, Bulkington receives his apothe- osis in Ishmael's six-inch chapter, during the writing of the book, and Ishmael suggests that as "sleeping partner" of the narrative Bulking- ton puts up much of the emotional and intellectual capital even though he is not in sight. There are minor flaws: Wadlington quotes a passage from *The Confidence-Man* which gets the butterfly before the caterpillar, though Elizabeth S. Foster had discussed the error, and he ignores a suggestion in the Norton *Moby-Dick* which crucially affects a passage which he repeatedly refers to—the suggestion that

Ahab, not Ishmael, is the speaker of the famous "Ifs" paragraph in
"The Gilder." For all this, Wadlington's essay is probably the best
study to appear since Brodtkorb's book in 1965. With this article and
one on *The Confidence-Man* discussed below, *ELH* redeems itself
after the portentous, murky studies of Melville it published in the
1960s.

Three lengthy discussions can be surveyed together. "Melville:
One Royal Mantle of Humanity," Harold Kaplan's chapter in *Demo-
cratic Humanism*, is well timed for the nostalgia vogue, a diffuse, un-
Promethean, 1950s interpretation of Ahab which makes no mention of
the criticism of the 1960s, not even Brodtkorb's book. Edward J. Rose's
"Annihilation and Ambiguity: *Moby-Dick* and 'The Town-Ho's
Story' " (*NEQ* 45:541–58) is cryptic not through profundity so much
as lack of transitions. The author calls his study a "reinvestigation of
Melville's vision of the nature of man and of art." (Old legends die
hard. Rose says Melville warns us "not to read his novel as a 'hideous
and intolerable allegory' "; in fact, the passage in question refers to
the white whale and not the book.) The best of these three, Gordon
V. Boudreau's "Of Pale Ushers and Gothic Piles: Melville's Architectural Symbology" (*ESQ* 18:67–82) is a fresh and solid image study
(showing how consistently the whale is compared to a Gothic cathe-
dral), though marred by strained, Thompsonesque puns.

Five briefer studies can also be treated together. The title of Edward Stone's "The Other Sermon in *Moby-Dick*" (*Costerus* 4:215–22)
refers to Fleece's sermon in chapter 64; the article is an elaboration of
Vincent's observation that the "cook's sermon is the anti-masque (always satiric and parodic) to the masque (lyric and serious)" of
Father Mapple's sermon. Stone's guesses about the times at which
parts of *Moby-Dick* were composed strike me as improbable. In any
case, conjecture about the priority of composition of certain chapters
in the book has become a game which anyone can play because it
has no rules: otherwise could two critics (not including Stone) argue
that "The Town-Ho's Story" was (take your pick) the first and the
last chapter written? John O. Rees, Jr.'s "Spenserian Analogues in
Moby-Dick" (*ESQ* 18:174–78) finds evidence that "the much-
discussed 'gams' in *Moby-Dick*" (is there more than one true gam?)
"offer a pattern of omens, exemplary contrasts, and attempts to de-
flect Ahab from his quest which often recall Spenser's preliminary
incidents" in *The Faerie Queene*, Book II, Canto 12. There may be

no end to articles on "Zoroastrianism and the Fire Symbolism in *Moby-Dick*"; this one by Mukhtar Ali Isani (*AL* 44:385–97) holds plausibly enough that "it is in the context of Zoroastrianism that the fire symbolism of the novel reaches its fullest significance." Isani characterizes Ahab as the "rebel quester" and Fedallah as the "orthodox quester," an ironic team. After the historically improbable assertion that Melville "helped to mold the categories out of which emerged the philosophy called Existentialism," John Rothfork in "The Sailing of the *Pequod*: An Existential Voyage" (*ArQ* 28:55–60) compares and contrasts Ahab and Ishmael as "Existential voyagers." Elmer R. Pry, Jr., in "That 'Grand, Ungodly, God-like Man': Ahab's Metaphoric Character" (*Style* 6:159–77) concludes: "First, it is clear that Ahab's mind has both wholly irrational and wholly rational periods; second, Ahab obviously embraces an immense pride as one vital trait which operates in both the sane and the crazed Ahab; and finally, Ahab possesses a fierce soul which remains an enigma (both for the reader and for Ahab himself), because it is both an illogically concrete form and an authentically intense metaphoric inner force." After Pry's rigorous and somewhat mechanical survey, a review of Stanley Geist's ardent pages on the same subject might be refreshing (*Herman Melville: The Tragic Vision and the Heroic Ideal* (1939).

A 1971 item, "The Whale and the Panorama" (*NCF* 26:319–28) by Robert L. Carothers and John L. Marsh does not in fact deal with "a possible visual inspiration" for *Moby-Dick* "which has as yet gone unnoticed." The Russell-Purrington panorama they found is cited in the Mansfield-Vincent edition of *Moby-Dick* (1952), p. 693, and indexed on p. 853 under "Purrington and Russell's Whaling Voyage Panorama." Priority of discovery aside, Carothers and Marsh tell us rather more about the panorama than Mansfield and Vincent did. Hershel Parker's "Five Reviews not in '*Moby-Dick*' as Doubloon" (*ELN* 9:182–85) reprints in full the five reviews referred to; at least two are of considerable interest and should be consulted by anyone who needs to generalize about the reception of *Moby-Dick*. Herbert Rothschild, Jr., in "The Language of Mesmerism in 'The Quarter-Deck' Scene in *Moby Dick*" (*ES* 53:235–38) notes specific technical meanings in phrases such as "the Leyden jar of his own magnetic life." Janez Stanonik's answer to the question "Did Melville Ever See an Albino?" (*AL* 43:637–38) is that he had a chance to when a Negro albino child was exhibited in Albany during June 1837. Kenneth

Walter Cameron reprints in facsimile the Boston *Daily Evening Traveller*'s account on November 3, 1851, of the sinking of the *Ann Alexander*; his rather extravagant title is "Starbuck, Moby, and the Wreck of the Ann Alexander" (*ATQ* 14:99–100). No one should need to consult the two Melville items in *AN&Q* 10; one wonders why they were published. John B. Humma's unconvincing, pun-mongering "Melvillian Satire: Boomer and Bunger" (*ATQ* 14:10–11) delivers much less than the title promises. Carl Oglesby may have enjoyed writing his neo-Olsonian piece, "Melville, or water consciousness & its madness: *a fragment from a work-in-progress*," in *Literature in Revolution*, edited by George Abbott White and Charles Newman (New York, Holt, Rinehart and Winston), pp. 123–41. With any luck the work-in-progress will have a prolonged gestation. For an article by Julian C. Rice which is partly on *Moby-Dick*, see section *viii* below.

vi. Pierre

Most of the writing on *Pierre* did not rise to a level remotely worthy of the book. A left-over 1971 item, Sara Chapman's "Melville and Bellow in the Real World: *Pierre* and *Augie March*" (*WVUPP* 18: 51–57) makes very simple comparisons. Patricia Barber's gracelessly written "Melville's Self-Image as a Writer and the Image of the Writer in *Pierre*" (*MSE* 3:65–71) does not advance the state of knowledge on her important subject; indeed, by its innocent citation of well-refuted arguments it might actively retard knowledge. In "Echoes of Emerson in Plinlimmon" (*ATQ* 14:47–48) Mildred K. Travis makes some comparisons which seem more obvious now than when Elizabeth S. Foster made them three decades before. In the course of identifying, as the title says, "Hawthorne and Melville's Enceladus" (*ATQ* 14:5–6), Travis trivializes one of the greatest scenes in Melville. (This year Cameron was an outright menace with his *ATQ*.) Much of Margaret S. McCroskery's "Melville's *Pierre*: The Inner Voyage" (*StH* 2:1–9) is routine and tends toward summary rather than close analysis; despite its relevance to her topic, she does not mention E. L. Grant Watson's important essay. In *Pierre*, she says, "Melville courageously faces the possibility of nihilism and uncovers the paradoxical inseparableness of meaning and meaninglessness of which the twentieth century has become so painfully aware."

The year's first true grain of wheat on *Pierre* is Donald Phelps's "The Holy Family" (*Prose* 5:99–113). Phelps has not done all his homework (better to have read E. L. Grant Watson than Charles Olson) and he does not attempt much close analysis. Nevertheless, his observations are occasionally suggestive and his style is elegant. Several fine phrases will seep into more ponderous treatises: who could resist quoting "the pantomime of slaughter, the stereopticon *Hamlet*, which wraps up the narrative"? Even a routine page (and most of Phelps's main points are routine) yields nuggets like this passage: "while *The Confidence-Man* moves with a kind of loose artifice, a *boulevardier*'s gait, through its succession of dialogues, *Pierre* is a series of massive broken blocks, fragments of commentary or monologue, whereby Melville's own voice holds the book to the present; his voice supplanting Pierre's voice, his consciousness eventually becoming Pierre's consciousness." Still better is Brian Higgins's "Plinlimmon and the Pamphlet Again" (*SNNTS* 4:27–38). The title is foreboding enough, but Higgins vigorously shows that despite all that has been written the Pamphlet "has not received adequate recognition for the sustained and intricate piece of satire that it is." Now readers can temporarily put aside Floyd C. Watkins's exhaustive survey (see *ALS 1964*, p. 37); first they should go to Higgins for a thoughtful examination of Melville's "satiric strategies" and for revealing parallels with writings by Bacon and Swift.

vii. "Bartleby"

"Bartleby" continues to fascinate its readers without inspiring many of them to careful analysis. Two studies claim to have found sources. The first, Edward Stone's "Bartleby and Miss Norman" (*SSF* 9:271–74) does not make a plausible case for indebtedness to a story by Thomas Hood. George Monteiro's "Melville, 'Timothy Quicksand,' and the Dead-Letter Office" (*SSF* 9:198–201) is more interesting, though it mistakes a commonplace topic in Melville's time for a specific source. (As Hans Bergmann and I are finding, evocative articles about dead-letter offices had something of a vogue in the years just before Melville wrote "Bartleby.") David Shusterman's "The 'Reader Fallacy' and 'Bartleby the Scrivener'" (*NEQ* 45:118–24) is a point-by-point rebuttal to the article by Liane Norman (see *ALS 1971*, p. 50), whom he finds guilty of a variety of the "affective fallacy."

Shusterman would have done well to place his differences with Norman in the context of the larger argument over "double writing" in the tales. Nathan A. Cervo's "Melville's Bartleby—*Imago Dei*" (*ATQ* 14:152–56) perfunctorily sees the story as adumbrating many works of twentieth-century European art which portray men as doomed ghosts in a godless world. Central themes of "Bartleby" are said to be "the nature of man, the nature of God, and the relationship between the two." Daniel Stempel and Bruce M. Stillians in "'Bartleby the Scrivener': A Parable of Pessimism" (*NCF* 27:268–82) find the key to the story in an article on Schopenhauer in the April 1853 *Westminster Review*. In treating the narrator as an example of Schopenhauer's "just man" they ignore the way his ethics are foreshadowed in the Plinlimmon Pamphlet (how does the "just man" differ from the nominal Christian?). Indeed, the authors discuss the problem of when and where Melville saw the article on Schopenhauer rather than the prior question of whether or not he actually saw it. On the evidence at hand, I would guess not. Nicholas Ayo's "Bartleby's Lawyer on Trial" (*ArQ* 28:27–38) at the outset perpetuates the legend that the Harper's fire of 1853 destroyed the plates of Melville's books (and implies that the fire occurred in time to have been memorialized in "Bartleby"). After a general survey of critical opinion, Ayo places the narrator in the dock, indicting him on such grounds as his utilitarianism and his "short-lived" solidarity with the human condition. All this is to the good, but Ayo does not follow out the implications of his evidence: he accepts the last line of the story as the narrator's genuine recognition that Bartleby's aloneness suggests "the larger implications of the imperfect human condition." Harold Kaplan (see section *v* above) makes some general comments on the story, seeing Bartleby "as an inverted Captain Ahab." Again Kaplan seems not to have read much recent criticism, some of which might have incited him to more careful analysis. (Was Bartleby indubitably a victim of the spoils system?) Few readers will agree with R. Bruce Bickley, Jr.'s contention that Bartleby is a portrait of Hawthorne; for more on his article see the next section.

viii. Tales—Other Than "Bartleby"

Vida K. and O M Brack, Jr., collaborated on "Weathering Cape Horn: Survivors in Melville's Minor Short Fiction" (*ArQ* 28:61–73), a graceful survey, humane and literate, but finally not adding much to earlier surveys such as Leyda's (1949). The first paragraph seems to say that Melville "retreated to Arrowhead" after "the total failure of *Pierre*," and the violation of chronology in which some stories are discussed does not make the reader feel especially secure. But any article is worth looking at which says neatly that in "Poor Man's Pudding and Rich Man's Crumbs" the true foundation of human dignity is "subverted by the insistence of the Americans, rich and poor, on behaving as though the 'ideal of universal equality' were achieved, and of the British on behaving as though it were absurd." R. Bruce Bickley, Jr., surveys some resemblances in "The Minor Fiction of Hawthorne and Melville" (*ATQ* 14:149–52); many readers will actively dispute his belief that in "The Piazza" Melville was committing himself "to a Hawthornean vantage point," but all will agree that Melville's use of Hawthorne's minor stories needs fuller exploration. In "Sitting Up with a Corpse: Malthus according to Melville in 'Poor Man's Pudding and Rich Man's Crumbs'" (*JAmS* 6:69–83), Beryl Rowland reads that diptych as Melville's "bitter ironic image" of the relationship between the price of corn, procreation, and morality, and of "the pointless role of charity in a Malthusian world." Marvin Fisher in "'Poor Man's Pudding': Melville's Meditation on Grace" (*ATQ* 13:32–35) makes some interesting comparisons between that half of the diptych and writings by Irving and Emerson, though his attempt to put the story into a theological context seems less successful. Alan Shusterman's "Melville's 'The Lightning-Rod Man': A Reading" (*SSF* 9:165–74) is a sensible, straightforward reading very like earlier sensible, straightforward readings, some published in the same journal. Thomas Werge's "Melville's Satanic Salesman: Scientism and Puritanism in 'The Lightning-Rod Man'" (*NCCL* 21:6–12) takes up a topic critics discussed in the 1950s. Werge thinks that the "'religion' of Melville's satanic salesman" is "scientism." Much of the article is unexceptionable—but pretty much old news. (I notice a mangled quotation at 11.9.) Jesse Bier in "Melville's 'The Fiddler' Reconsidered" (*ATQ* 14:2–4) argues that most readings treat that story too simply as recommending "a work-a-day, happy obscurity" for one who "has tasted the bitter rewards of an ambitious but spurned talent." The real meaning, Bier believes, is that Helmstone wrongly learns the "lesson of facile self-abnegation," and tears up his manuscript when he should have torn up the hostile review of his poem. Bier's argu-

ment ignores the strong internal evidence that Helmstone's poem is
no great loss to posterity. In "Melville's 'The Bell-Tower' and Ben-
venuto Cellini" (*AL* 44:459–62) Robert E. Morsberger discusses the
possible influence of accounts of Cellini's career on that story. While
not primarily on Melville, Albert E. Stone's "A New Version of
American Innocence: Robert Lowell's *Benito Cereno*" (*NEQ* 45:
467–83) contains running comments on Lowell's uses of and depar-
tures from Melville's "Benito Cereno." Hershel Parker's " 'Benito Cereno' and *Cloister-Life*: A Re-scrutiny of a 'Source' " (*SSF* 9:221–32)
shows that H. Bruce Franklin was wrong to think that William Stirling's history of Charles V was a source for "Benito Cereno" (*see ALS
1963*, p. 34). For some of the parallels Franklin cites there are closer
parallels to "Benito Cereno" in Melville's own early works (written
before Stirling's studies) or else closer parallels in the known source,
Delano's *Narrative*; a few more of Franklin's parallels "must be dismissed because they are based on an imperfect report of what Stirling says." Julian C. Rice in "The Ship as Cosmic Symbol in *Moby
Dick* and *Benito Cereno*" (*CentR* 16:138–54) suggests that especially
in the second of the two works Melville employs the "world-as-ship
metaphor" with "a special awareness of its traditional use and meaning, thereby enhancing cosmic irony." Theodore L. Gaillard, Jr.'s
"Melville's Riddle for Our Time: 'Benito Cereno' " (*EJ* 61:479–87)
grows out of teaching the story to tenth graders at St. Mark's School.
Almost everything Gaillard says has been said many times before, but
one almost forgets that in the pleasure of encountering so graceful
and cogent an explication of the imagery. Howard Kerr's *Mediums,
and Spirit-Rappers, and Roaring Radicals: Spiritualism in American
Literature, 1850–1900* (Urbana, Univ. of Ill. Press), pp. 43–54, cheerfully puts "The Apple-Tree Table" against the background of the fad
for spiritualism.

ix. The Confidence-Man

Writing on *The Confidence-Man* was routine except for one admirable
article by Cecelia Tichi. In his rompish "The Last Word on *The
Confidence-Man?*" (*IllQ* 35:15–29) Lawrence Buell is rather cheeky
both toward the book and criticism on it (much of which he selectively
ignores), though he is indebted to criticism which holds that in this

book Melville meant no meanings unless that meaning itself is past finding out. Buell feels the book is too funny to have any serious meaning. Stanley Trachtenberg is even more derivative in "'A Sensible Way to Play the Fool': Melville's *The Confidence Man*" (*GaR* 26:38–52), which glances at some of Melville's comic strategies. In Chapter 2 of *Toward a New Earth* John R. May sets himself against R. W. B. Lewis's view that the book portrays a humorous apocalypse. May grimly sees in the book "the last loosing of Satan." The problem deserves fuller analysis than it has had, for the Devil-allegory critics like Shroeder have not adequately explained just what they mean by calling the book apocalyptic. Joyce Adler's "Melville on the White Man's War against the American Indian" (*S&S* 36:417–42) is a vigorous polemic mainly on the Moredock section of *The Confidence-Man*, a book she sees as Melville's urgent depiction of a United States rushing toward disaster because of its national sins, which include its mistreatment of Negroes and Indians. Like others from Roy Harvey Pearce onward, Adler cannot believe that Melville could express attitudes toward real Indians which are commendable by liberal twentieth-century standards yet use them as symbols of evil, as such critics as Shroeder, Foster, and Parker have thought. Adler ignores most commentary on the Moredock chapters and unkindly handles most of what she does mention, launching a formidable *ad hominem* attack on Shroeder which is not only impolite but downright wrong, in my judgment. Her failure to assimilate earlier criticism, and her excess of moral indignation toward the critics she does mention, keep her from developing some potentially fine insights, especially into the pattern of characters who sin by deputy (and perhaps want to be saved by deputy?).

The year's reward is Cecelia Tichi's "Melville's Craft and Theme of Language Debased in *The Confidence-Man*" (*ELH* 39:639–58). Tichi falls into the common practice of discussing even minor critical articles but neglecting Foster's long introduction and explanatory notes, and she has a couple of local confusions (such as making Pitch the teller of the Moredock story), but hers is the most original article on the book in several years. This passage suggests her approach: "By depersonalizing dialogue, divorcing speeches from speakers, and restraining visual evocation, Melville forces his reader to focus largely upon the entity of language, itself horrendously corrupted and debased. Neither does Melville permit aural inattentiveness to the woeful abuses of it. A close reader is taxed throughout to discern both blatant and subtle flaws in the rhetoric, and indirectly he is enjoined to deplore them. The debasement of language is, in fact, a salient theme in *The Confidence-Man*, and the one which very likely bound Melville to these eccentricities of craftsmanship" (p. 643). No previous critic had focused so minutely upon Melville's linguistic strategies; indeed, Tichi's article takes place with Sealts's 1967 study of geniality (see *ALS 1968*, p. 47) and Bowen's 1969 essay (see *ALS 1969*, p. 48) on Melville's tactics of indirection in a trend toward greater attention to Melville's satiric strategies in particular passages. All three of these critics are convinced that the book has meanings—and discernible ones at that.

x. Poetry

Aaron Kramer's *Melville's Poetry: Toward the Enlarged Heart* (Rutherford, N.J., Fairleigh Dickinson Univ. Press) is, the sub-subtitle says, "A Thematic Study of Three Ignored Major Poems." In this order, they are "Bridegroom Dick," "The Scout Toward Aldie," and "Marquis de Grandvin." Preceding them is a longish "introductory essay." The little book is an outgrowth of Kramer's exasperation with the way Melville's "few towering works of fiction" are "milked dry year after year in lectures, essays, and dissertations," while much evidence is neglected: "the bulk of Melville's poetic output is either altogether ignored by Melville specialists in their most ambitious commentaries, or apologized for in one or two condescending phrases based less on a study of the poems than on an inherited attitude." Kramer's book can only do good, but the academic world being what it is, we may now anticipate a spate of articles on "Bridegroom Dick" while other works like "Rip Van Winkle's Lilacs" continue to be ignored. The only other items on Melville's poetry were Safford C. Chamberlain's protest in "Melville's *Clarel*" (*PMLA* 87:103–04) against factual inaccuracies in Stanley Brodwin's article (see *ALS 1971*, pp. 53–54) and Brodwin's rebuttal, "Melville's *Clarel* Continued" (*PMLA* 87:310–12). In these exchanges nobody wins, but the truth is that misreadings of *Clarel* are now beginning to rival misreadings of *The Confidence-Man*.

xi. Billy Budd

Writing on *Billy Budd* was weak. Remarkably, critics refuse to recognize that the Hayford-Sealts textual discoveries, now a decade old, have interpretative implications: Vere's character is analyzed just as in the 1950s, with no inkling that such confident analysis of an unfinished, contradictory characterization might be out of place. Kenneth Walter Cameron (*ATQ* 14:167–68) reprints "Another Newspaper Anticipation of *Billy Budd*," which is not at all a direct anticipation of Melville's story but merely an account of an execution at sea in 1846. Like any such document, it is of interest, though not for any light it might shed on *Billy Budd*. In *Power and Innocence: A Search for the Sources of Violence* (New York, W. W. Norton), Rollo May simplistically attempts to relate Billy Budd and Allison Krause as innocents whose deaths are wholly unexpected. Passages from May's book are printed in *Psychology Today* (6:53–58). In "The Trial of Billy Budd, Foretopman" (*American Bar Association Journal* 58: 614–19), Jack W. Ledbetter takes a legal view of the guilt or innocence of Billy Budd and Captain Vere. Ledbetter's summary of the plot is error-ridden and his style is exclamatory, but by arraying precedents he gives plausible answers to such questions as whether or not Billy Budd was "properly charged, tried, convicted and sentenced according to the applicable laws of the time" or whether Vere's "drumhead court martial" was "legally constituted and conducted." He decides that though Billy was falsely accused of one crime, mutiny, he became guilty "of at least two crimes, striking a superior officer and murder, and possibly a third, mutiny," while Vere violated fundamental legal principles both in the trial and the execution. Since Ledbetter makes no attempt to determine what Melville thought the legalities of the case were, his study must be classed merely as a curiosity. In the chapter of *Democratic Humanism* cited in section *v* above, Harold Kaplan also approaches *Billy Budd* simplistically: "The necessitarian and abstract justice of Captain Vere cannot examine the heart and conscience of Billy, cannot distinguish deeper motives and values." Chronology is disregarded ("Cereno is an interesting variation on the theme of Vere"), and no understanding is shown that Melville's late revisions complicate any final judgment of Vere. Again, Kaplan seems to have stopped reading scholarship and

criticism about the time Eisenhower was reelected. Peter A. Stitt's
"Herman Melville's *Billy Budd*: Sympathy and Rebellion" (*ArQ*
28:39–54) should not have been published. How can anyone in 1972
discuss a "Preface" to *Billy Budd* which is not and never was a preface? Michael J. Kelly in "Claggart's 'Equivocal Words' and Lamb's
'Popular Fallacies'" (*SSF* 9:183–86) makes far too much ado about
finding one particular place where Melville might have encountered
the proverbial phrase "handsome is as handsome does." Robert Narve-
son in "The Name 'Claggart' in *Billy Budd*" (*AS* 43:229–32) makes
very tenuous suggestions about the reasons for Melville's choosing the
name of his master-at-arms. Maxine Turnage's title is promising:
"Melville's Concern with the Arts in *Billy Budd*" (*ArQ* 28:74–82); the
article turns out to be thin. She sees the story as "a study of the destiny
of wrongly estranged components of art: the satiric and the didactic
in Claggart from the esthetic in Billy." Above them both stands Vere,
a "just specimen of the patrons of art in Melville's day."

xii. Miscellaneous

A motley group of articles remains. In "'Evidences of Regard': Three
Generations of American Love Letters" (*BNYPL* 76:92–119) Alice
P. Kenney quotes extensively from many Gansevoort and Melvill
family letters, most of them previously unpublished. Among the correspondents are Melville's grandfather, Peter Gansevoort, and Catherine Van Schaick; Allan Melvill and Maria Gansevoort; Melville's
uncle, Peter Gansevoort, and his two wives; and Catherine Gansevoort (Melville's first cousin) and Abraham Lansing. The chief authority on the Gansevoort family, Kenney supplies invaluable personal
and historical background for the letters she prints. Her resolute
contrasting of Dutch and English patterns of communicating emotion
may smack of innocent nineteenth-century racism, but she is on safer
ground in citing parallels in English literary styles from the time of
Addison and Richardson to that of Thackeray and Trollope. Darlene
Mathis Eddy's "Bloody Battles and High Tragedies: Melville and
the Theatre of the 1840's" (*BSUF* 13:34–45) is necessarily conjec-
tural, devoted to sketching something of the kinds of theatrical con-
tacts Melville must have had, since he "lived in an age of innumerable

panoramas and dioramas and could have seen, almost simultaneous-
ly, spectacular Shakespearean productions and a variety of dioramic
subjects." She argues plausibly that "what Melville saw on the stage
often touched directly upon what he was discovering in Elizabethan-
Jacobean literature." Richard Colles Johnson, the Bibliographical
Associate of the Northwestern-Newberry edition, in 1971 (*ABC* 21:
7–8) gave a tentative survey of "Melville in Anthologies"—that is, the
known anthologizing of Melville during his lifetime. When Johnson
wrote, the Melville Collection at the Newberry Library contained
nearly six hundred literary anthologies which "chronicle Melville's
early (and sometimes later) neglect (as evidenced in some eighty
anthologies which contain no mention of him) and the subsequent
mushrooming of his popularity and reputation." Morris Star's "Melville's Markings in Walpole's *Anecdotes of Painting in England*"
(*PBSA* 66:321–27) sympathetically analyzes Melville's markings (he
made no annotations) in a book not mentioned in Sealts's *Melville's
Reading* (1966) but now held at the Newberry. In "Mather's Melville
Book" (*SB* 25:226–27) George Monteiro does some poignant homework that ought to have been done decades ago. Everyone knew that
the publisher to whom Frank Jewett Mather, Jr., proposed a biography of Melville was Houghton Mifflin, but to confirm that belief
Monteiro prints a reply to Mather from Ferris Greenslet, November 20, 1906. Greenslet's letter is to some extent predictable, but it
takes an important place among the scant documentary evidence
about Melville's reputation during the beginning of the century. Kenneth Walter Cameron prints an "Uncollected Melville Letter" (*ATQ*
14:111), a response to an autograph seeker dated Boston, December
4, 1857: "Dear Sir. Your Note is received and in accordance with your
request, I am Very Truly Yours H Melville." Monteiro's "Melville in
Portuguese" (*Serif* 9:23–24) is a checklist of translations of *Moby-
Dick* and a few others of Melville's works. Samuel Rosenberg's "Come
Out Herman Melville, Wherever You Are! (The Man Who Turned
to Stone)" originally appeared in his *The Come as You Are Masquerade Party* in 1970; now the book is reprinted in paperback by Penguin
and retitled *The Confessions of a Trivialist*. Rosenberg is an enthusiastic discoverer of commonplaces, and his essay is haphazard, slapdash, funny, ultrapersonal, and error-ridden, but proof that cultists
can still flourish despite the deadening weight of Academic Criticism.

Under Hennig Cohen's editorship, *Extracts: An Occasional News-letter* has begun to print notes running to two or three pages.[1]

The ragtag flotilla of books launched in 1970 evoked several essay reviews. Robert C. Ryan reviewed many of these books authoritatively in *SIR* 10[1971]:230–240. As the foremost student of Melville's poetic manuscripts, Ryan should be consulted on William Bysshe Stein's *The Poetry of Melville's Late Years*, especially. One rumor has it that "A Monument to Melville" (*TLS* 21 Jan.:53–55) is by a mordant-witted, red-bearded Fiedlerian, but the evidence is hardly conclusive. The "monument" of the title is the Northwestern-Newberry edition, about which thoughtful comments are made; the remainder of the article skewers several books, notably excluding *Melville: The Ironic Diagram*. Paul McCarthy's "Books on Melville in 1970" (*SNNTS* 4:98–111) does not have quite the authority of Ryan's review or the verve of the *TLS* review. Allen Hayman's indignant little review of Gay Wilson Allen's *Melville and His World* and Martin Leonard Pops's *The Melville Archetype* (*MFS* 18:286–88) should be read. Hershel Parker's "Trafficking in Melville" (*MLQ* 33:54–66) is a disheartened response to five books from 1970. As usual, the best reviewing was seldom found in *American Literature*.

University of Southern California

---

1. Anyone writing on Melville can pay the annual dues of five dollars to the Melville Society and get in return *Extracts* and assorted bonuses. Apply to the new editor, Donald Yannella, Department of English, Glassboro State College, Glassboro, N.J., 08028.

4. Whitman and Dickinson

Bernice Slote

Whitman studies still linger in the shadow of the great outpouring during and after his sesquicentennial in 1969. No new books have appeared except for collections and reprints, although dissertations thrive and, even for a career so well documented as Whitman's, new details of biography and publication continue to filter through. A couple of well-arranged collections of important criticism through the years have been published—*Critics on Whitman* and *Critics on Dickinson*, both edited by Richard R. Rupp (Coral Gables, Fla., Univ. of Miami Press). For both Whitman and Dickinson, recent critical effort seems to be directed more and more to the analysis and interpretation of individual poems. At least for writers on Whitman this tendency has a somewhat calming effect: there are fewer of the effusions which sometimes pass as criticism. Emily Dickinson has survived the psycho-analytical attacks of the last few years, and her critics, too, have quietly retired to her poetry. For both poets, however, the volume of critical work has temporarily declined.

i. Whitman

a. **Bibliography, biography.** Further clues to bibliographical problems involved in "The Case of the Whitman Notebooks" (see *ALS 1971*, pp. 59–60) are offered by the publication of microfilm prints of the inside front and back covers of Whitman's "earliest" notebook and an article by Esther Shephard ("The Inside Front and Back Covers of Whitman's Earliest Known Notebook: Some Observations on Photocopy and Verbal Descriptions," *PMLA* 87:1119–22). Disagreements on the dating of the notebook and confusion as to its whereabouts have been noted in earlier discussions by John C. Broderick, Edward F. Grier, Floyd Stovall, and Esther Shephard. The purpose of the current note is to point out that previous descriptions of Whitman's notations in the notebook have not been entirely accurate. Since some of the controversy about the date of Whitman's entries relates to when persons lived at given addresses, and supporting evidence is taken from Brooklyn city directories, I might observe—in the cause of accuracy—that such directories are often a year behind an actual residence, depending on when the names are gathered for the listing.

Bibliographical information in the *Walt Whitman Review* continues to be a mainstay for the student of Whitman. A more recent Whitman periodical is *Calamus* (Tokyo). It would serve the scholar better if reprinted articles were identified as such and the original publication cited.

In the last few years reprints of editions of Whitman's work and of early critical and biographical books about Whitman have proliferated. They have not generally been mentioned here because it is assumed that no new scholarly contributions are involved. However, a timely warning in Artem Lozynsky's "Irresponsible Reprint: Bucke's *Walt Whitman*" (*WWR* 18:104–06), a review of a reprint edition of Bucke, with an introduction by Harold Jaffe and published by the Johnson Reprint Corporation (1970), draws attention to possible trouble. Numerous errors and omissions in the handling of this reprint are pointed out, particularly that there is no statement as to which of several texts has been used. One is likely to take a scholarly reprint on faith, but obviously the too faithful may find themselves in a morass of inaccurate, incomplete, and unidentified texts.

Two new Whitman items have appeared. A previously unrecorded letter to H. H. Furness (Jan. 26, 1881) is reproduced in the *Walt Whitman Review*, with a note by William White (18:141–42). Professor White also presents a new biographical account in "Walt Whitman on Trial: A Clipping from His *Daybook*" (*PrS* 46:52–56). The clipping, marked "*From the New York World*" and printed in 1887, tells of an 1840 trial in which the youthful Whitman was vindicated.

The *Long-Islander* Whitman page of June 1, 1972, edited by William White, commemorates the one-hundredth anniversary of Whitman's visit to Dartmouth College, where he read "As a Strong Bird on Pinions Free" on June 26, 1872. The editor says that the page reprints Whitman's poem as he wrote it in 1872, three unsigned news stories by Whitman about his experience, Harold Blodgett's 1933 account of the Dartmouth visit, and photographs.

Studies of Whitman in his own time still yield some new material. One of the most valuable of the articles this year is Robert Scholnick's "Whitman and the Magazines: Some Documentary Evidence" (*AL* 44:222–46), in which are presented a number of previously unpublished letters to Edmund C. Stedman from the editors of *Atlantic*, *Scribner's*, *Galaxy*, and *Harper's* on their relationship with Whitman before 1880. The letters are from the Columbia University collection. The evidence is that Whitman did have grounds for the complaint of rude treatment by the magazines which he had inserted in the *West Jersey Press* for January 26, 1876. However, although Whitman attacked all four magazines indiscriminately, "the editors had widely different attitudes toward his work," and it was only *Scribner's* which was actually closed to Whitman.

Some accounts have been given of Whitman's 1879 trip to Missouri, Kansas, and Colorado, but Robert R. Hubach adds a helpful summary of views from that territory in "Western Newspaper Accounts of Whitman's 1879 Trip to the West" (*WWR* 18:56–62), citing over forty new short articles and notes about Whitman. Although news reports contained such satirical phrases as "the renowned cosmical poet of America" (Kansas City *Times*), the author concludes that Whitman's publicity shows that "he was regarded in the West as something of a celebrity even at that time"; it is also significant that a number of papers in small towns as well as in the cities commented on Whitman's presence.

b. **Criticism: general.** A fresh look at Whitman is Sarah Blacher Cohen's "Walt Whitman's Literary Criticism" (*WWR* 18:39–50), which focuses on the poet's miscellaneous comment on other writers, English and American. His evaluations of literature are seen as noteworthy but personal: the only two British writers he judged to be sufficiently democratic for America were Burns and Dickens. His critical tenets were often demanding: "Not only did he insist that literature be organic and concerned with nature, he also demanded that it be spontaneous, yet restrained; forceful, yet delicate; moral, yet optimistic; championing the hero, yet exalting the common man; and extolling the universal, yet magnifying America."

William M. White in "The Dynamics of Whitman's Poetry" (*SR* 80:347–60) sees sexuality and the oppositions (and union) of male and female elements central to Whitman's poetry. Though not a new idea, it is argued persuasively that "sex is Whitman's basic meta-phor," that all of his poems are love songs, and that there is not oppo-sition of the elements in his poetry but a merging to become a whole. A similar type of unity is discussed by Mary Ann Turner in "Recon-ciliation of Love and Death in 'Out of the Cradle' and Other Poems" (*WWR* 18:123–32): "Meaning is given to life, and a greater intensity is given to love, only after man understands the nature of death." In addition to "Out of the Cradle," other poems which demonstrate such a union of love and death include "As I Ebb'd with the Ocean of Life," "Scented Herbage of My Breast," "Dirge for Two Veterans," "When Lilacs Last in the Dooryard Bloom'd," "Song of Myself," and "Out of the Rolling Ocean the Crowd." Another kind of doubleness is suggested by Nancy Lenz Harvey's citing of repeated imagery in "Whitman's Use of *Arms* in the *Leaves of Grass*" (*WWR* 18:136–38) —"arms" taken to mean both "the physical limbs of the human body and the accoutrements of war," each meaning having its connotations of unity and disunity.

The problem of structure in Whitman is skillfully handled by V. K. Chari in discussing the catalogue poems ("Structure of Whitman's Catalogue Poems," *WWR* 18:3–17), which he sees as deliberately loose and fluid—"a unity of psychological impression rather than a well-wrought structure." Chari defines a "fluid form" as one whose thematic units are repetitive rather than sequential; it elaborates and amplifies rather than advances thought. In rejecting the traditional structuring devices of meters and stanzas, Whitman had to rely on other elements, defined here as (1) a "spinal idea," (2) thought and sound rhythms, and (3) "terminal devices that secure the effect of closure." Some of the major catalogue poems discussed are "Crossing Brooklyn Ferry," "The Sleepers," "Starting from Paumanok," "Song of Myself," "A Song of Joys," and "Spontaneous Me." "Song of My-self," for example, is described as "a mosaic of experience" in which parts are meaningful only when they are seen in the whole fabric of the poem "spread out before us like a canvas." The article is especially effective in the detail it presents in full support of an elusive concept.

c. **Criticism: individual poems.** Unlike previous years, those writ-ing on "Song of Myself" do not attempt structural patterns. G. S. Amur in "Whitman's Song of Man: A Humanistic Approach to 'Song of

Myself'" (*WWR* 18:50–56) looks at the poem as an organized exploration of questions as to the concept of man, his system of values, and a definition of human goals. Whitman's humanism is distinctively religious, but a product of human experience and not of supernatural revelation. Two short articles comment, though not very clearly, on section 52 of the poem. Adrianne Baytop examines the vertical and horizontal (cyclic) movements ("'Song of Myself' 52: Motion as Vehicle for Meaning," *WWR* 18:101–03), and Sally Ann Batchelor contributes definitions and examples of Whitman's "barbaric yawp" ("Whitman's Yawp and How He Yawped It," *WWR* 18:97–101).

Three approaches to "When Lilacs Last in the Dooryard Bloom'd" —the historical, the pastoral, the aesthetic—are helpfully reviewed and defined by Evelyn J. Hinz in "Whitman's 'Lilacs': the Power of Elegy" (*BuR* 20,ii:35–54). Examples of particular approaches are given from F. O. Matthiessen (historical), Richard P. Adams (pastoral), James E. Miller, Jr. (pastoral-elegiac), and Charles Feidelson, Jr. (aesthetic-process). All three approaches are considered inadequate to explain "the universal and popular appeal of 'Lilacs'"; another point of view is to stress the purely emotional and verbal qualities of the poem, whereby a necessarily negative conclusion about the reconciliation it offers is countered by "the rhetoric Whitman employs to prevent the listener from realizing what the speaker is really saying." "Lilacs," then, succeeds as an elegy because "the rhetoric holds the intellect in abeyance." Another article on the same poem, Jane A. Nelson's "Ecstasy and Transformation in Whitman's 'Lilacs'" (*WWR* 18:113–23), sees it as performing the function of elegy but not in a familiar form. In it is "an intense personal experience that at the same time performs the public function of explaining the meaning of death to a mourning community." One interesting suggestion in the article is that the experience of the poem follows the exercises of the shaman, whose function is to escort the dead to their resting place and to reveal to the community the significance of death. Many of the details of shamanism (the bird as the most important symbol, for example) are well drawn in parallels with Whitman's poem.

"A Reading of 'The Sleepers'" (*WWR* 18:17–28) by R. W. Vance is a thoughtful analysis of the structure of the poem. In the dream or vision framework the main theme—"the eventual transcendence of evil and death through sympathy and love"—is expressed through two

patterns of imagery: "the cyclical movement from birth to adolescence
to death" and "the sexual relationship between the poet and the
night." In a somewhat fuzzily written piece, "Time and Eternity in
'Crossing Brooklyn Ferry'" (*WWR* 18:82–90), Eugene R. Kanjo
explicates "Crossing Brooklyn Ferry" as "an interweaving of the
temporal and the eternal so that neither is independent of nor superior
to the other." Dale Doepke's "Whitman's Theme in 'Cavalry Crossing
a Ford'" (*WWR* 18:132–36) is an excellent article, lucid and suggestive. He sees the poem as not only a vivid description but also "a
reflection of Whitman's philosophy of a democratic society and an
affirmation of support for the cause of the Union." The scene delighted
Whitman, but it also became a symbol of "bravery, daring action, and
the self-expression of a free and proud spirit." It typifies "the tension
between man as an independent creation and man as a social being."
Another brief explication is R. Galen Hanson's "A Critical Reflection
on Whitman's 'The Base of All Metaphysics'" (*WWR* 18:67–70).
Here Whitman is a "gospel writer" whose theme is that "man is love
and love, man."

d. **Relationships.** Studies of various contexts of Whitman in his
world and ours include the traditional nods from poet to poet, trans-
mutations into new forms of words and music, wide-ranging responses
from those of different cultures, and—most modern of all—a linking
of Whitman's poetic techniques and purposes to those of contemporary "encounter groups" (Paul J. Ferlazzo, "Encounter: Whitman
and His Reader," *WWR* 18:138–40).

For Whitman and music we have Joseph Gerard Brennan's informative piece, "Delius and Whitman" (*WWR* 18:90–96), in which
he studies in some detail Delius's *Sea Drift*, with text from "Out of
the Cradle Endlessly Rocking"; *Idyll*, based on "Once I Pass'd
Through a Populous City"; and *Songs of Farewell*, based on Whitman's "Songs of Parting." There are also other relationships in Delius's
individualism and his work as a "song of himself." Delius, however,
celebrated the past; Whitman, the future. Another note by John S.
Wannamaker describes the musical setting by Robert L. Sanders for
"Song of Myself," premiered in New York in 1976 ("A New Musical
Setting of 'Song of Myself,'" *WWR* 18:28–31).

In "Whitman-Tennyson Correspondence: A Summary and Commentary" (*WWR* 18:75–82) John M. Ditsky reviews the known

letters between the two poets, interpreting the situation fairly as a meeting of "two men of enormous ability almost shyly, but certainly self-consciously, aware of their positions in respect to the tradition of poetry," and perhaps even in respect to those of a later century who might view them. Whitman made the overtures, but was reticent; Tennyson was polite and reserved, but fascinated. D. H. Lawrence and Whitman are considered, especially in terms of their understanding of "sympathy," by Marian L. Stein in "Affirmations and Negations: Lawrence's 'Whitman' and Whitman's Open Road" (*WWR* 18:63–67).

Ward B. Lewis writes on the links between Whitman and the German writer Johannes Schlaf (1862–1941) in "Walt Whitman: Johannes Schlaf's New Being ('Neuer Mensch')" (*Calamus* 6:22–34). Schlaf translated and edited *Leaves of Grass* and wrote both criticism and poetry that joined with Whitman.

Walt Whitman Today, edited by Roger Asselineau and William White (Detroit, Wayne State Univ. Press), presents sixteen essays on Whitman's reputation and relationships. Articles are on Spain, by Concha Zardoya; Germany, by Hans-Joachim Lang; Belgium, by Guillaume Toebosch; France, by Marcel Martinet, Jules Romains, Jean Guehenno, and Jean Marie Le Clezio; Italy, by Mariolina Meliadò Freeth; Czechoslovakia, by Ján Boor; Yugoslavia, by Sonja Bašić; Denmark, by Jørgen Erik Nielsen; Sweden, by Frederic Fleisher; Iceland, by Leedice Kissane; plus "My Relationship with Whitman," by Jorge Guillén; "The Shock of *Leaves of Grass*," by Léopold Sédar Senghor (of Senegal); two articles on Whitman in Russian by Kornei Chukovsky; "On Translating Whitman into French," by Roger Asselineau; and a final piece by Pablo Neruda, "We Live in a Whitmanesque Age." Some of these essays have previously appeared in the 1969 and 1971 Walt Whitman pages in the *Long-Islander* (though these are not all identified), but since that paper is hard to obtain, we are grateful for a convenient collection. The scope of the book was widened a bit for Chilean Neruda (whose essay first appeared in the *New York Times*, April 14, 1972), but he concludes the far-ranging view of Whitman abroad appropriately with the statement that "man's liberation may often require bloodshed, but it always requires song—and the song of mankind grows richer day by day, in this age of sufferings and liberation." The collection is useful. It also stretches the imagination.

ii. Dickinson

a. **Bibliography.** One of the rewards of scholarly enterprise is to find a lost work by a great writer—if, of course, its identity is clear. Charles Gullans and John Espey in "Emily Dickinson: Two Uncollected Poems" (*AL* 44:306–07) present poems found in the *Chap-Book* for October 15, 1895, and said by Herbert S. Stone in his literary column "Notes" to be Emily Dickinson's "orphic utterances." The first poem cited ("A clamor in the treetops") does have something of the Dickinson turn of metaphor and phrase, but the second one seems totally out of character. One should perhaps be cautious about accepting Stone's identification. For one thing, the poems were not included in *Poems: Third Series*. If Mrs. Todd had sent out poems from that collection to be printed in periodicals, as the authors note, it was uncommonly careless of her to ignore these altogether.

Since the publication of Willis J. Buckingham's *Emily Dickinson: An Annotated Bibliography* (see *ALS 1970*, pp. 70–71), bibliographers have been adding items to its more than two thousand titles. George Monteiro in a review, "Buckingham's ED Bibliography" (*EDB* 20:28–30), adds titles of dissertations, theses, and poetry about Dickinson, along with some corrections. F. L. Morey in "Miscellaneous Addendum to Buckingham" (*EDB* 21:75–77) lists twenty-two titles from Japanese, Slavic, Uralic, Hebrew, Yiddish, Korean, Vietnamese, Arabic, Indian, and Persian sources.

One shortcoming of the Buckingham listing, according to William White, is that it does not include bibliographical descriptions, and in "Emily Dickinson's 'Poems: Third Series': A Bibliographical Note" (*Serif* 9,ii:37–41) he supplies full details on the early printings of *Poems: Third Series* (1896). For the same volume, Josiah Q. Bennett adds notes on weights of paper used in a series of printings through 1906 ("A Footnote to Mr. White's Article on Emily Dickinson's *Poems: Third Series*," *Serif* 9,ii:41–42).

Much miscellaneous material on Dickinson continues to appear in the *Emily Dickinson Bulletin*, including current listings of reviews and publications (*EDB* 21:81b–87). It is reviewed by Carlton F. Wells in "*The ED Bulletin*. The First Four Years" (*EDB* 21:53–54). The first issue of a new publication, *Higginson Journal of American Poetry*, edited by F. L. Morey, appeared in 1972. The *Higginson*

Journal, though only peripherally connected with Dickinson, has occasional helpful notes and news items.

An extensive revaluation of the dating of certain Dickinson letters, as given in the 1958 *Letters* edited by Thomas H. Johnson and Theodora Ward, is in "The Dating of Emily Dickinson's Letters to the Bowles Family, 1858–1862" (*EDB* 20:1–28), by Myra Himelhoch and Rebecca Patterson. However, in the analysis of thirty-two letters in the Bowles series, only eleven have been substantially redated by several months or more. The main effect of the redating (which seems to have been carefully determined on the basis of handwriting and internal evidence) is to narrow the period of time for the correspondence. The first three letters (L189, L193, L196) are moved from 1858 to 1859, and two (L299 and L300) from 1864 to 1860 and 1861.

b. Criticism: general. In the aftermath of the publication of *After Great Pain* (see *ALS 1971*, p. 71), John Cody's psychiatric analysis of the inner life of Emily Dickinson, numerous reviewers have reacted to his portrait of a woman under emotional and mental stress whose poems in part emerged from that struggle. Two review articles serve as helpful guides to opinion: Eleanor Lyons in "A Psychiatric Look at Emily Dickinson" (*HSL* 4:174–79) centers on the problem of "what happens to Emily Dickinson the poet" through the approach to her work which Cody denies he is making but still uses when he interprets poems not as works of art but as biographical evidence. Professor Lyons also observes—fairly, it seems to me—that Dr. Cody sometimes wrenches "the impact of a poem to fit his preconceived theory," quotes out of context, and attributes imaginative experiences to the writer's personal life. The conclusion is that Cody's "impressive exploration of Emily Dickinson as a person may, in other words, have caused her irreparable harm as a poet." Cynthia Chaliff, who has also written on Emily Dickinson from a psychoanalytic point of view (see *ALS 1970*, pp. 72, 74), reviews the Cody book (*L&P* 22:45–47) and takes issue with Dr. Cody in spite of what she considers to be a "masterful accomplishment." She, too, suggests that he has chosen—and bent—poems to fit his thesis. He also "too easily makes the leap from the possible to the probable to the factual." The central thesis of the book —that Emily Dickinson was deprived in her relationship with her mother—is also questioned, with the suggestion that cultural factors have not been sufficiently considered: "The dominating father and weak mother were the paradigm for the Victorian world, and not peculiar to the Dickinson home."

To most critics the term "poetess" implies a kind of lesser breed than poet, a writer weakly feminine who attempts verse, in her fashion. In "Emily Dickinson Was a Poetess" (*CE* 34:63–70) Elsa Greene argues interestingly if not always clearly that the Amherst poet should indeed be evaluated in a feminine, not male, literary tradition: "She did not, in fact, inhabit the same milieu which influenced Ralph Waldo Emerson and his puritan male forebears, and it is a deadly favor to assume she did." In choosing her vocation, Emily Dickinson risked "psychic and social penalties" unknown to male poets. Yet we can learn from her writings something more of the nature of "female being" and of Dickinson's attempts "to define herself and to perceive truthfully the milieu in which she experienced life."

In "The Solitary Dissenter: A Study of Emily Dickinson's Concept of God" (*EDB* 20:32–48) Gary D. Elliott takes the view that Dickinson's withdrawal from the world was neither an abdication nor a denunciation; it was instead a Thoreauvian attempt to find in solitude "some answers to life." Her chief question was her search for a God she could accept—and not the Calvinist God of her father. The article reviews poems and passages in the letters which trace her meditative search, full of conflicting views of God but marked, too, by a continuing faith.

Unified themes and patterns in Emily Dickinson's poetry are subjects of several substantial articles. George Monteiro in "Emily Dickinson's Brazilian Poems" (*Inter-americana di Bibliografia* 22:404–10) reviews symbolic geographical references in five poems of the early 1860s ("I'll clutch—and clutch–," "Some such Butterfly be seen," "My first well Day—since many ill–," "A Moth the hue of this," and "I asked no other thing–"). Sources for some of the Brazilian themes are noted in *Exploration of the Valley of the Amazon* by William Lewis Herndon and Lardner Gibbon (1853–1854). The symbolism of Brazil is seen as "something desirable, beautiful, and exceeding rare." On some details (particularly that "Brazil" means red, not blue) this article disputes statements in Rebecca Patterson's "Emily Dickinson's Geography: Latin America" (see *ALS 1969*, pp. 73–74).

Another article by Rebecca Patterson worth noting is "Emily

Dickinson's Jewel Imagery" (*AL* 42[1971]:495–520). From tables analyzing comparative uses of jewel imagery by Dickinson and other writers (the Bible to Wallace Stevens) and showing the relative uses in Dickinson's poems from 1858 to 1885, Professor Patterson concludes that her poetry "contains as many instances of jewel words as the Bible" or all of Shakespeare, and that she increased her use of such allusions through the years. The favorite stones, according to the tables, seem to be amber and pearl ("the most sexually charged"). References to jewels and their meaning in both the poems and biographical incidents are discussed.

Jo Anne Neff in "The Door Ajar" (*EDB* 21:78–81a) notes that in seventy-seven poems there are door images, used especially "to draw vivid descriptions and comparisons between being outside and inside of certain situations." Chiefly, the images imply a house of the soul.

c. **Criticism: individual poems.** H. A. Bouraoui's reexamination of "Because I could not stop for Death" ("'Leaning Against the Sun': Emily Dickinson, the Poet as Seer," *RS* 37[1969]:208–17) is one of the best discussions we have of this poem, considering it in its complete version (and not the mutilated form with the fourth stanza omitted, used by Allen Tate and Yvor Winters in earlier explications) and in its relationship to other Dickinson poems about death and her feelings about immortality. Death, in the Dickinson poems, may be either "the final torture" or a kind and dashing lover. In the poem, Death is both natural fact and bridegroom, the conclusion the end of a wedding journey and the afterlife seen in domestic human terms. Rebirth is suggested, however, and the spiritual fact of Eternity is asserted with the upward movement of the last stanza. The linking of images in the poem is further seen as an evidence of Emily Dickinson's conscious, subtle craft, the images presenting the ideas: the movement is from descriptive and concrete to abstract, but also translating abstract ideas into concrete images.

In a number of short articles, single poems are given partial but perceptive readings. George Monteiro sees "I never lost as much but twice" as not autobiography but a transformation of the poet's personal losses "into the Jobean poetry of anguish" (*Expl* 30[1971]:item 7). Parallels with the book of Job are traced, but in the end Dickinson's poem borders on blasphemy: God is "Burglar" and "God-banker"

as well as "Father." W. Herget (*Expl* 30:item 55) suggests that the
term "Checks" in the last line of "I never saw a moor" might be a
gambling metaphor, denoting chips or counters used in playing certain games. Only at the end of the game ("As if the Checks were
given") does one know whether he has won or lost. Larry Rubin
(*Expl* 30:item 67) debates Elizabeth Bowman's explication of "The
Soul selects her own Society—" (see *ALS 1970*, p. 75) with his view
that the overall tone of the poem is stern, matter-of-fact, take-it-or-
leave-it, rather than the poet's disapproval of the shut door. Other
poems are cited to support this possible Dickinson mood. The distinction between Indian summer and June is crucial to the meaning
of "These are the days when Birds come back—," writes Robert L.
Berner (*Expl* 30: item 78). June is "the image of the Eden from which
we have fallen"; Indian summer is "a truer image of the human
condition." The sacramental imagery of the close leads us to see that
"we achieve a kind of immortality by an act of the imagination in
which we see in the objects of the natural world the emblems of the
spiritual reality of our condition." Charles J. Hauser, Jr., has a brief
note on the image of the poet as a wine-taster in "I taste a liquor never
brewed" (*Expl* 31:item 2). Previous criticism of "I started Early—
Took my Dog—" is reviewed by George S. Lensing (*Expl* 31:item 30),
who asserts that the poem's strength is that it sustains "seemingly
contradictory interpretations," that the main symbol may be the sea
as both lure and domination, as male-principle, as maturity, and as
death. The poem is structured on several polarities related to these
symbolic meanings.

Three articles deal with "There's a certain slant of light." George
Monteiro objects to some readings of the poem as either pro- or anti-
Emersonian (*Expl* 31:item 13), and suggests on the basis of contextual evidence that it be viewed not as a modern poem but as "the poet's
commitment to certain Puritan and Pauline ideas concerning the ways
of divine Grace." Dickinson "draws upon the Biblical idea of glory
('light') which has the literal meaning of *weight*," an idea derived
in part by the Puritans from Corinthians II, one of her favorite books.
Donald Eulert in "Emily Dickinson's Certain Slant of Light" (*ATQ*
14:164–66) sees that light as real and physical, one that comes and
goes, and stresses the emotional effect of details in language and
imagery, the poem's psychological movement. It begins with despair,

an internal hurt, but as that experience recedes it becomes impenetrable; it has "a look of distance." Donald Eulert's close reading of the poem as a movement of emotion and sense is commended by Kenneth W. Cameron in "Emily Dickinson and Hesperian Depression" (*ATQ* 14:184–85). He quotes a passage by William G. Niederland ("On Hesperian Depression") from the *Digest of Neurology and Psychiatry* (Jan. 1972), describing from case studies the mood depicted in "There's a certain slant of light."

Mario L. D'Avanzo comments on Emersonian connections to interpret two of the Dickinson poems. In "Dickinson's 'The Reticent Volcano' and Emerson" (*ATQ* 14:11–13) he considers Dickinson's tension between belief and skepticism as focused on the volcano, which suggests an uncommunicative God. He refers to Emerson's "The Problem" with its figure of an erupting volcano as the source of "canticles of love and woe," and to a similar use in *The American Scholar*. Dickinson's poem goes on to assert, ironically, that in the face of a "reticent volcano" man can also learn to survive without listeners. The second article by Mario L. D'Avanzo, " 'Unto the White Creator': The Snow of Dickinson and Emerson" (*NEQ* 45:278–80), discusses the poem "Publication—is the Auction" as "a statement on essential inspiration, or divinely sponsored creativity." True poetry and poets are related to the snow and the artist-creator of Emerson's "The Snow Storm." The "snow of poetry in her poem" is "the white soul" of organic form.

d. **Relationships.** One of the most interesting of Dickinson relationships is that with Japanese readers and scholars. A good summary of interest in Japan is given by Amy Horiuchi and F. L. Morey in "Japanese Evaluation" (*EDB* 21:57–60), noting that the Japanese criticism began only in 1958 and that elements usually stressed are Dickinson's succinctness, her paradoxical quality, and her themes of immortality. The work of Toshikazu Niikura is particularly mentioned. The Japanese review is partly bibliographical, as is F. L. Morey's summary of items in a checklist of criticism from "Miscellaneous Languages" (*EDB* 21:60–64), in which twenty-three items are discussed. The conclusion from these and previous surveys in the *Emily Dickinson Bulletin* (see *ALS 1970*, p. 71) is that Emily Dickinson is "well established in Italy, Germany, France, and Spain," with a growing acceptance in Japan and Teutonic countries of northern Europe. In other countries there is a smattering of translations and criticism. It may be an appropriate Dickinson paradox to find one of the most reticent of American poets reappearing even in Asia and the Orient.

University of Nebraska–Lincoln

5. Mark Twain

Hamlin Hill

After the lean year for Mark Twain in 1971, this year seemed something like an epic of gluttony: a new volume in the Mark Twain Papers, several interesting anthologies, a large number of articles and notes (but in increasingly elusive journals), and the first volume in the Iowa/California Edition, *Roughing It*. (It is only a rumor that a Star from the East settled over Virginia City when *Roughing It* appeared.) And during the year, *What is Man?*, *The Innocents Abroad*, and the first volume of the complete *Notebooks & Journals* moved toward publication; the apparent decline of 1971 turns out to have been only a pause for breath.

i. Textual and Bibliographical

There were two keepsake-texts of Mark Twain items in 1972. The Center for Editions of American Authors prepared an exhibit for the Folger Shakespeare Library on "The Author's Intention": its keepsake was a five-page facsimile of a hitherto unpublished segment of the autobiography called "Something About Copyright." The typescript, with longhand corrections by Mark Twain, is a plea for protection of the literature which is "a country's most valuable and most precious possession." The Friends of the Bancroft Library issued "The Great Landslide Case," edited by Frederick Anderson and Edgar M. Branch, as its twentieth keepsake (Berkeley, Univ. of Calif. Press). Three versions of the hoax—from the San Francisco *Call* of August 30, 1863, from the Buffalo *Express* of April 2, 1870, and from chapter 34 of *Roughing It*—are reprinted, together with an analysis of Mark Twain's revisions and exhaustive historical annotation.

Anderson has also provided a brief preface to a reissue of *The Family Mark Twain* (New York, Harper and Row)—that amazing 1462-page anthology which contains almost all the major writings of

Mark Twain's career and is one of the biggest bargains in print, even at $12.50. *A Pen Warmed-up in Hell: Mark Twain in Protest* (New York, Harper and Row) is Anderson's collection of political and social satire—divided into sections "On War" and "The Human Condition." Selections range from "Goldsmith's Friend Abroad Again" and "About Smells" in 1870 to the spectacular anti-imperialist essays of the last years of Mark Twain's life. The introduction balances the inconsistencies in Mark Twain's "radical" voice—his squeamishness, occasional illogic, and a limited sense of history—with the felicitousness of his modes of expressing his indignation at human viciousness. Such dated material as "King Leopold's Soliloquy" is omitted so that, without clutter, we "can share Mark Twain's perception of evil, feelings of guilt, and expressions of rage at the world's injustices."

Published so quietly as to be almost surreptitious was Ray B. Browne's 1970 anthology, *Mark Twain's Quarrel with Heaven* (New Haven, Conn., College and Univ. Press). The title is somewhat misleading: a complete text of "Captain Stormfield's Visit to Heaven" and the first publication of "The Reverend Sam Jones's Reception in Heaven" and "Mental Telegraphy?" (the latter from 1891–92 and 1907, respectively) make up the collection, together with a long and painstakingly researched introduction. Browne makes extensive use of the unpublished notebooks to chart the growth of the manuscript which fascinated and obsessed Mark Twain longer than any other in his entire literary career.

Janet Smith's new anthology, *Mark Twain on Man and Beast* (New York, Lawrence Hill) is a wonderful, crotchety, outrageous collection of forty-four selections Mark Twain wrote about animals with, as the editor says, "in the notes that precede each section . . . a condensed biography of Mark Twain." Foolish consistencies cannot daunt Mrs. Smith, though: if the mood strikes her to attack Van Wyck Brooks or Edmund Wilson or bullfighting or modern criticism, she pauses to attack. The "condensed biography" moves in erratic imitation of the Mexican plug in *Roughing It* (but Mrs. Smith provides a chronological chart of Clemens's life at the conclusion so that the reader can "put the bits together" for himself). Some of the selections are predictable chestnuts ("Baker's Blue Jay Yarn," "The Jumping Frog"), but many are extracted from inaccessible or unexpected sources (3,000 *Years Among the Microbes*, for example). There are mistakes in some of Mrs. Smith's facts; but I suspect that this subjective, opinionated, audacious, and impudent anthology is one Mark Twain would have enjoyed reading.

Contrasting with Mrs. Smith's lively and disorderly collection are two texts whose high seriousness is carried almost beyond the point of virtue. The seventh volume of the Mark Twain Papers is *Mark Twain's Fables of Man* (Berkeley, Univ. of Calif. Press), edited by John S. Tuckey with texts established by Kenneth M. Sanderson and Bernard L. Stein. The volume prints thirty-six hitherto unpublished writings, which Tuckey separates into three thematic categories: "The Myth of Providence," "The Dream of Brotherhood," and "The Nightmare of History." "Generally speaking," Tuckey explains, "these sections include, in the order given: (1) satirical writings on what Mark Twain saw as the outworn but still confining myths of an exploded, prescientific view of man and the universe, from which man's imagination needed to be freed; (2) representations of the dubious possibilities for a true brotherhood of man; (3) writings in which past and present conditions are seen as portending a darkened future in which a new religious myth would once more captivate and enslave man and in which still later equivalent myths, through the ages, would die and be recreated endlessly" (p. 3). The first section ranges through the full possibilities of Mark Twain's bitterness. The "Little Bessie" anecdotes question, through literal interpretation, many of the basic premises of fundamentalism; "The Second Advent" transplants the birth of Jesus to Black Jack, Arkansas, in the nineteenth century; "The Private Secretary's Diary" and "The Victims" are acrid attacks on the workings of Divine Order. In "The Dream of Brotherhood" a long story called "The Refuge of the Derelicts" is the major attraction—a hundred-page attempt, written in the summers of 1905 and 1906, to define the consequences of altruism. The final section, "The Nightmare of History," contains the murky and tediously convoluted mock history called "The Secret History of Eddypus" and Mark Twain's pageant of civilization's atrocities, "The Stupendous Procession." Three appendices and 245 pages of textual apparatus complete the volume.

Fables of Man will provide scholars with valuable insights into some of the basic philosophical constructs of Mark Twain's mind, especially in the later years of his life; but tracing the development of his thoughts would have been easier had the selections within each of the three main sections been arranged in chronological order.

The Iowa/California edition of *Roughing It* (Berkeley, Univ. of Calif. Press for the Iowa Center for Textual Studies) has an introduction and explanatory notes prepared by Franklin R. Rogers, with textual work by Paul Baender. The introduction and historical annotation present a workmanlike summary of the facts of composition, publication, and reception of the travel book and identify the factual contexts.

The text itself raises some fundamental problems. It is becoming increasingly clear, as the Center for Editions of American Authors passes its century-mark of authorized volumes, that the determination of a writer's "intention" is a much more subjective procedure than anyone originally thought. The problem becomes one of defining intention at a given point in time, to a particular audience, at a certain stage in the author's career. Already, Mrs. Hawthorne's "censorship" of passages in *The Blithedale Romance*, Howells's removal of anti-semitic passages from the magazine version of *The Rise of Silas Lapham* when it went to press as a book, and Stephen Crane's removal of the "huge fat man" from chapter 17 of the 1895 edition of *Maggie: A Girl of the Streets* have caused modern editors to have their choices of texts challenged. The rule seems to be "If you can't find a soiled fish, then soil one yourself."

To be sure, *Roughing It* involves no major problems. But normalizations in spelling are defended on the basis of "Mark Twain's preferred choice"—but that choice is in many cases the manuscript of *The Adventures of Tom Sawyer.* Changing *barrelled* to *barreled* because the humorist ordinarily did not double *l*'s is an especially unfortunate example, since he did write a short novel which he preferred to call *A Double-Barrelled Detective Story.* Altering *somersault* to *summerset* because the latter spelling occurs in a passage deleted in manuscript from *Tom Sawyer* raises, at the very least, the question of whether the word in the novel was spoken by the narrator or by the central character—dignified narrative or slangy, boyish dialogue? And removing several clauses from the text of *Roughing It* which refer to specific illustrations in the first edition seems a more violent solution than printing the illustrations in the new "definitive" text.

It is true that there are justifications for these changes and that the alternative readings are present in the textual appendices for the unpersuaded reader. But if *Roughing It* is an indication of the editorial policies of the Iowa Center for Textual Studies, there is a basic premise which I find bothersome. John Gerber pinpoints the attitude in his article on modern texts of *Tom Sawyer* and *Huckleberry Finn* (discussed below), when he says that Mark Twain "intended to eliminate in the galleys or expected his editor to change" misspellings, errors, and inconsistencies in his own manuscripts. But, so far as I know, the American Publishing Company, publisher of both *Roughing It* and *Tom Sawyer*, had no editors on its staff; certainly no record of one survives, and the idea of a room full of copy editors with stacks of blue pencils is completely incongruous with the style, the mercantilism, and the aggressive sales philosophy of that organization. Indeed, when *Innocents Abroad* was being readied for the printer, Elisha Bliss, president of the American Publishing Company, had to suggest hiring an outside proofreader to go over the manuscript, indicating pretty clearly that none was in Bliss's employ. Mark Twain replied to this offer, by the way, on February 14, 1869: "I don't much like to entrust even slight alterations to other hands. It isn't a judicious thing to do, exactly." It sounds like a useful injunction for future volumes in the Iowa/California Edition; tinkery texts fill at least one reader with apprehension, and especially so for a writer as inconsistent and idiosyncratic in spelling and punctuation as Mark Twain was.

The article by John C. Gerber mentioned above, "Practical Editions: Mark Twain's *The Adventures of Tom Sawyer* and *Adventures of Huckleberry Finn*" (*Proof* 2:285–92), is a survey of the available paperback editions of the two Mark Twain novels most often used in classrooms, and at the same time a summary of the textual problems in those texts which the Iowa/California edition proposes to correct. *Tom Sawyer* suffers from major corruptions in all available paperbacks, with the Bantam and Penguin Puffin texts the most unreliable. For *Huck*, several present-day paperbacks follow the first American edition which Gerber prefers as copy-text to the Buffalo Public Library manuscript fragment; but most of the classroom-oriented volumes, based on the Author's National or other later editions, contain as many as 2600 unauthorized variants.

In "Mark Twain in Knee Pants: The Expurgation of *Tom Sawyer Abroad*" (*Proof* 2:145–51) O M Brack, Jr., shows how Mary Mapes Dodge censored the typescript used for printing *Tom Sawyer Abroad* in her *St. Nicholas*, a magazine for children, by correcting verb forms, double negatives, and similar inelegancies of Huck's language. She removed references to drunkenness, the words *sweat, scab, slobbered*, and comic allusions to Catholicism and the Sunday School. Most unfortunate was the fastidious editor's removal of references to death—especially the deletion of several sentences describing the members of a caravan suffocated by a sandstorm. Two-thirds of the American edition was set from the *St. Nicholas* copy (the first nine chapters), but the English (Chatto and Windus) version was prepared from another typescript and therefore is substantially closer to Mark Twain's intention.

Philip C. Kolin in "Mark Twain's *Pudd'nhead Wilson*: A Selected Checklist," *BB* 28[1971]:58–59,48 collects sixty-one items, ranging from unpublished dissertations to chapters in books, all dealing with *Pudd'nhead* and all "studies which stay well within the mainstream of useful criticism." More useful is Joseph B. McCullough's "A Listing of Mark Twain's Contributions to the Buffalo *Express*, 1869–1871" (*ALR* 5:61–70). This checklist of 134 items—some signed "Mark Twain," some "Carl Byng," and some unsigned—is divided into the categories "Sketches," "Sketches and Poems Signed Carl Byng," "Editorials," "People and Things," and "Miscellaneous" (items in each of the headings, in the order listed: 60, 8, 32, 31, and 3). This preliminary checklist is a prolegomenon to an edition of the *Express* contributions now being prepared by McCullough and Martin B. Fried.

ii. Biographical

In one of the most provocative articles of the year, Howard G. Baetzhold, "Found: Mark Twain's 'Lost Sweetheart'" (*AL* 44:414–29), there is a detailed survey of the major influence of Laura Wright, the fifteen-year-old with whom Clemens fell in love in 1856. After a brief courtship, the couple abruptly separated—presumably at the instigation of Laura's mother. But throughout his life (and throughout his fiction), the memory of Laura Wright stalked Mark Twain relentlessly. She was the subject of lifelong dreams and of lifelong notebook entries—including several written in code. Late in Clemens's life, the two corresponded (in 1906), and Clemens aided Laura's handicapped son with $1000. Laura provided many of the attributes of Becky

Thatcher in *The Adventures of Tom Sawyer,* of Laura Hawkins—as a girl—in *The Gilded Age,* of Hello-Central in *A Connecticut Yankee,* and of the girl in "My Platonic Sweetheart," as Baetzhold convincingly documents; that she also explains in part Clemens's obsessive fascination with other fifteen-year-old girls in the last years of his life seems equally probable.

In "Mark Twain and the Civil War" (*BSUF* 13:53–61) Elmo Howell admirably confirms his opening sentence—"Not much is known with certainty about Mark Twain's involvement in the Civil War"—by allotting only the first three paragraphs of his nine-page article to that topic. Then there are paragraphs about Clemens's lack of success as a pilot, about Missouri in the 1830s, about *Huckleberry Finn* and *Which Was It?*. In concluding, Howell suggests that Clemens's desertion from Marion's Raiders after three weeks as a Confederate "volunteer," "left a wound that did not heal. It planted a doubt . . . and laid the foundation for misanthropy and dissociation in his last years."

Harold Aspiz's "Mark Twain and 'Doctor' Newton" (*AL* 44:130–36) fills in some blanks in the story of Olivia Langdon's cure by a faith healer when she was seventeen. Having suffered spinal paralysis from a fall on the ice, she was "cured" by James Rogers Newton. Aspiz compares the account by Mark Twain in his *Autobiography* with the one in the promotional tract *The Modern Bethesda* (1879), which specifically mentions the healing of Olivia. In addition, Aspiz notes similarities in both physical description and inflated rhetoric between Newton and the Dauphin in *Huckleberry Finn.*

Three articles focus on the Clemens's Hartford years. Joseph S. Van Why, in a descriptive catalogue for the Stowe-Day Foundation's exhibit *Hartford as a Publishing Center in the Nineteenth Century* (Hartford, 1971), discusses the phenomenon of the subscription-book industry in relation to Mark Twain's career (pp. 1–6) and catalogues a number of subscription volumes by other authors intent upon reaping the spectacular profits from this mode of publication. Barbara Lamkin Barnes' "Mark Twain's Family Christmas" (*Yankee* 36:106–09, 136, 139–41) provides a slight summary of the various activities of the Clemens family members during typical holiday seasons—company dinners, the visit from Santa Claus, plays, reading Christmas stories, and tobogganing in the snow. The most impressive part of the article is a spectacular color photograph of the Hartford house in the snow. Robert Bush's "Grace King and Mark Twain" (*AL* 44:31–51) traces the long friendship between the New Orleans novelist and the Clemens family, beginning with her visit to Hartford in the summer of 1887 and extending on to the end of the nineteenth century. Included are lengthy extracts from Miss King's notebooks and letters and three previously unpublished letters of Clemens, all of which provide some revealing glimpses of the Hartford household.

"How Samuel Clemens Became Mark Twain's Publisher: A Study of the James R. Osgood Contracts" (*Proof* 2:117–43) by Frederick Anderson and Hamlin Hill is at least distinguished by being the longest eight-page article of the year. Accompanied by eighteen plates which reproduce in facsimile the publishing contracts for *The Prince and the Pauper, Mark Twain's Cyclopaedia of Humor, The Stolen White Elephant,* and "Old Times on the Mississippi" (later to become *Life on the Mississippi*), the article argues that Osgood served merely as a distributor-agent for the manufacturing and marketing of those volumes of Mark Twain's which bore the Osgood imprint. Since Clemens provided the capital for the publication and earned the lion's share of the profits, his brief association with Osgood was a transitional phase which led to his founding the publishing house of Charles L. Webster and Company.

Dr. Walter J. Friedlander's "Mark Twain, Social Critic, and His Image of the Doctor" (*AIM* 77:1007–10) is, in spite of its comprehensive title, nothing more than a collection of Mark Twain's comments on specific physicians—whom he generally praised—and on the profession collectively—which he found to be avaricious, incompetent, and usually lethal.

Ben M. Vorpahl's "'Very Much Like a Fire-Cracker': Owen Wister on Mark Twain" (*WAL* 6[1971]:83–98) is basically concerned with Wister's 1935 "appreciation" at the humorist's centenary celebration—which was equivocal praise at best. The historical background of Wister's acquaintance with Mark Twain is hastily sketched; a look at Wister's letter to Clemens of November 27, 1900, a telegram of January 10, 1901, and letter of November 26, 1906 and at the mentions of Wister in Clemens's notebooks (December 19, 1900 and June 2, 1902), all in the Mark Twain Papers, would have provided additional foundation for the slight friendship, including at least three dinner invitations.

iii. General Criticism

In "Mark Twain's Requiem for the Past" (*MTJ* 16,ii:3–10) Stanley
R. Harrison undertakes the chore of divorcing Mark Twain from that
biographical criticism which explains his increasing misanthropy and
cynicism on the basis of personal disaster and innate temperament, by
charting a movement from the "youthful exuberance" of *Tom Sawyer*
through a "moment of awareness" in "Old Times on the Mississippi"
to an "emotional testament to the sobering awareness of maturity" in
Huckleberry Finn. Mark Twain's own literary growth parallels the
emotional change of the United States in the nineteenth century; and,
according to Harrison, "surely such a thesis is more attractive and
satisfying than one that seeks external biographical data in an attempt to account for the shifting vision of an artist." Since he admits
that the example of Poe in the early part of the century (the exuberant,
youthful part, you will remember) contradicts his thesis, one of his
readers, at least, is more puzzled than satisfied.

Even more puzzling, and more disappointing, is Robert Penn
Warren's "Mark Twain" (*SoR* 8:459–92). Those of us who would
welcome a New Critical look at Mark Twain will find nothing to satisfy us in this 33-page collection of misinformation and generalizations
that seem too elemental even for a junior-high-school workbook. Warren traces "the key image of Twain's work, that of the journey,"
through the major works, concluding that in *A Connecticut Yankee*
that journey, into the self, "gets as close to the heart of darkness as he
ever could—or dared—get, and all subsequent works represent merely
additional notes and elaborations of detail of that shocking experience." Plot summaries and biographical inaccuracies corrupt what
could have been a major statement by a critical position that has too
often scorned Mark Twain. A critic who identifies Will Bowen as
three separate friends of Mark Twain does not convince me of his
control over his facts.

Lynn W. Denton surveys Mark Twain's references to the American Indian in *Roughing It, Innocents Abroad, Life on the Mississippi*,
and several minor works in "Mark Twain and the American Indian"
(*MTJ* 16,i:1–3). He concludes, with oversimplification, that Mark
Twain's attitude changed from one of revulsion to idealization as he
became "convinced that the white-oriented civilization must receive
the blame for the introduction of evil into an otherwise sinless society."

Alan Gribben in "Mark Twain, Phrenology and the 'Temperaments': A Study of Pseudoscientific Influence" (*AQ* 24:45–68) undertakes a major examination of Clemens's lifelong interest in and utilization of phrenology, most significantly in his concept of "temperaments" which "not only shaped his self-concept, but also influenced his choice of language in expressions of his later deterministic philosophy." Clemens first learned about phrenology from the Reverend George Sumner Weaver's *Lectures on Mental Science According to the Philosophy of Phrenology*, and echoes of its argot appear in *Innocents Abroad, Roughing It, Life on the Mississippi, The Adventures of Tom Sawyer, Adventures of Huckleberry Finn*, and *A Connecticut Yankee in King Arthur's Court*. In spite of his ambivalence toward phrenologists and his use of them for comic purposes, Mark Twain's discussions of innate temperament in his later writings —"In Defense of General Funston," *What Is Man?*, and "The Turning Point of My Life," for example—prove the durability of the fundamental concepts of phrenology in his thought.

Robert Taylor, Jr., in "Sounding the Trumpets of Defiance: Mark Twain and Norman Mailer" (*MTJ* 16,iii:1–14) proposes in an overlong biographical generalization about the two writers that both serve as social gadflies to their generations, speaking out in favor of unpopular causes and questioning the values of dominant American culture.

iv. Earlier Works

Very little interest was generated by the works preceding *Huckleberry Finn* in 1972. Louis J. Budd in "Did Mark Twain Write 'Impersonally' for the *New York Herald?*" (*LibN* 43:5–9) suggests that in spite of his claim that he had a contract to write "2 impersonal letters a week" for the *Herald*, there are only three possible Mark Twain communications to that paper in early 1868: "Gossip at the National Capital" (printed on February 3), and two columns headlined "Washington Gossip" (published on February 10 and 18).

Without suggesting concrete indebtedness, Robert L. Coard in "Mark Twain's *The Gilded Age* and Sinclair Lewis's *Babbitt*" (*MQ* 13:319–33) explores and compares the satiric methods in the two novels: indictments of corruption, poorly constructed plots, and a similarity of technique ("a fondness for slapdash but exuberant irony;

a love for mocking bloated rhetoric; an enthusiasm for exhibiting illit-eracies; a glee in creating grotesque proper nouns; and a general delight in twisting, clipping, and telescoping words"), and similarities in the personalities of Sellers and Babbit are the points of agreement. In "Tom Sawyer's Mock Funeral: A Note on Mark Twain's Religion" (*MTJ* 16,iii:15–16) Elmo Howell suggests that the scene of the boys' return to their own funeral is an affirmation of religious values rather than a mockery of them, because it affirms "love, loyalty, compassion, and deep humility before the Divine will."

In "Two American Bumpkins" (*RS* 41,i:61–63) Hollis L. Cate notes parallels in Sarah Kemble Knight's description of a rustic in her *Journal* and the brief depiction of Nicodemus Dodge in *A Tramp Abroad*. And Joe David Bellamy ("Two Eras, Two Epitaphs: Steamboating Life in the Works of Mark Twain and Richard Bissell," *BSUF* 13,iv:48–52) looks superficially at *Life on the Mississippi* and *A Stretch on the River* as elegies to the two eras of the packet and the steam towboat.

Carl L. Anderson's "Strindberg's Translations of American Humor" (*Americana Norvegica* 3:153–94) examines more thoroughly than Bergholz (see *ALS 1971*, p. 81) the material in *Amerikanska humorister*. Anderson argues that Strindberg's "arbitrary and sometimes drastic revision" shows in the translations of "The Loves of Alonzo Fitz Clarence and Rosannah Ethelton" and "About Magnanimous Incident Literature," while many of the translations of other humorists were probably made by others. A table of sample variants (p. 182–84) provides a useful index of Strindberg's license with Mark Twain; and Anderson concludes with a convincing suggestion that "the purgative value of Twain's irreverent humor" was more important to Strindberg's own thought than that of any other American humorist.

v. Huckleberry Finn

As usual, *Huckleberry Finn* drew more attention than any other work, and as usual the commentary ranged from the ridiculous to the profound.[1] Four studies in 1972 dealt with the influence of *Huck*

1. Perhaps this is as good a spot as any to point out to authors of articles and editors of journals that it is a disservice to readers, present and future, to use cheap paperback reprints for reference and footnotes. If Gerber's article about

on other literature or its parallel to more recent writing. In "Twain's
Finn and Alger's Gilman: Picaresque CounterDirections" (*MarkhamR* 3:53–58) Thomas N. Walters explores the possibilities of
picaresque form in *Huck* and Horatio Alger's *Jed, the Poorhouse Boy*
(1900). As young men without homes, parents, or money, Huck and
Jed are similar; but the differences in morality, language, and comic
methods underscore the essential dichotomy in the two books. Jed
compromises and joins society, while Huck remains outside—a rebel.
David M. Andersen ("Basque Wine, Arkansas Chawin' Tobacco:
Landscape and Ritual in Ernest Hemingway and Mark Twain," *MTJ*
16,i:3–7) is concerned more substantially with *The Sun Also Rises*
than with *Huck Finn*, noting some similar uses of trivial detail for
verisimilitude. Joseph Brogunier ("An Incident in *The Great Gatsby*
and *Huckleberry Finn*," *MTJ* 16,ii:1–3) notes the similarity of the
long lanky man who recreates Sherburn's murder of Boggs with the
old man who Nick Carraway supposes will retell the events of Myrtle
Wilson's death. And in "*The Adventures of Huckleberry Finn* and
Intruder in the Dust: Two Conflicting Myths of the American Experience" (*BSUF* 13,i:4–13) Philip J. Skerry compares the two novels
on four levels ("the basic narrative level, the psychological level, the
sociological level, and the symbolic level"), concluding that Huck
embodies the Adamic myth by escaping from history and time into
the frontier, while Chick "accepts experience, realigns himself with
history and tradition, and exists not only in space, but in time."

Two short notes explicate specific passages in *Huck*. Stuart Lewis's
"Twain's *Huckleberry Finn*, Chapter XIV" (*Expl* 30:item 61) argues
that in the debate between Huck and Jim over Solomon's wisdom,
Jim's is the more persuasive argument—based on a slave's awareness
of the debased value of human life. And Robert D. Arner ("Acts
Seventeen and *Huckleberry Finn*: A Note on Silas Phelps' Sermon,"
MTJ 16,ii:12), suggests that verse 29, about the worship of money,
provides an ironic comment on the tragic materialism in the novel
and notes that one of the men who accompanies Paul to Athens in the
chapter is named Silas.

Three articles focus on specific characters in the novel. Judith

---

their unreliability is not convincing enough in itself, then the argument of their
ephemeral nature ought to persuade any self-respecting scholar, critic, or editor
to utilize a standard, widely available, hardbound edition for his apparatus.

Fetterley's "Disenchantment: Tom Sawyer in *Huckleberry Finn*" (*PMLA* 87:69–74) is a major examination of Tom's character. In *Huck*, Tom assumes some dimensions which were absent from his personality in his own novel: he becomes a practical joker whose pranks are always cruel ones; his "obsession with rules becomes the index to his unreality and makes him the butt rather than the agent of exposure"; and Tom has reversed his role as a leader who makes play out of work by making work out of what should be play in *Huckleberry Finn*. In the final chapters of the later novel these changes are most obvious: his pleasure in causing discomfort to others is almost sadistic; his rigid obedience to the "rules" for freeing Jim makes an "uncontrollable" character; and instead of exposing the hypocrisy of the adult community (as he had in *Tom Sawyer*), Tom's actions in *Huck* expose only the defects in his own character.

Joseph R. Millichap's "Calvinistic Attitudes and Pauline Imagery in *The Adventures of Huckleberry Finn*" (*MTJ* 16,i:8–10) is in fact a filtering of the Presbyterianism of the Missouri frontier through Pauline imagery, focusing almost exclusively upon Pap Finn as the equivalent of the Satanic "old man." And Andrew Solomon ("Jim and Huck: Magnificent Misfits," *MTJ* 16,iii:17–24) marshals all the predictable, unglittering generalities about the pair. Any article whose first sentence is "Both Jim and Huck in Mark Twain's *Adventures of Huckleberry Finn* are extremely real" is my nominee for a *New Yorker*-style column, "Scholarly Essays We Never Finished Reading."

Several studies of *Huckleberry Finn* undertook to place it within ethical and philosophical frameworks. Bruce E. Miller in "*Huckleberry Finn*: The Kierkegaardian Dimension" (*IllQ* 34,i:55–64) attempts to plot Huck's growth in the context of Kierkegaard's concept of "knights of the faith"—the confrontation with a morally shocking demand, acceptance of the requirement, and final preservation of "the right order of things." Huck's crisis in chapter 31 follows this pattern, and his lighting out for the territory is his act of retirement "from social intercourse in order to take up another communion." Alan Ostrom, in "Huck Finn and the Modern Ethos" (*CentR* 16:162–79), writes a lucid and engagingly phrased statement of a traditional view of the novel: Huck, torn between impulses as an asocial individual and as a member of his culture, finally and necessarily fails to overthrow the conventions that Tom Sawyer embodies. Old wine in an attractive new bottle, Ostrom's article imposes no external theories upon the novel, as Miller's does.

J. R. Christopher's "On the Adventures of *Huckleberry Finn* as a Comic Myth" (*CimR* 18:18–27) applies Northrop Frye's myth criticism to *Huck*. Appropriate ingredients present in the novel include the doubling of heroes, ritual deaths, a recognition, and the basic comic types—*alazon* (Tom), *eiron* (Huck, the Duke and the Dauphin), *bomolochos* (Jim), and *agroikos* (Huck, Sherburn). The specific pigeonholes which Christopher offers are Quixotic comedy (in which the comic hero leaves, rather than changes, his society) and picaresque satire. Divorcing the questions of freedom from Frye, Roy Harvey Pearce argues in "Huck Finn in His History" (*EA* 24[1971]:283–91) that, unlike most protagonists of nineteenth-century fiction, who are "ready to accommodate themselves to their society" after their struggles with it, Huck "gains no sense of his own history and has no future." Huck's central function is as a role player and a passive witness to the events of the novel; he is unable to reconcile the conflict between conscience and truth and "exists not as an actuality but a possibility" only.

Finally, an article that only tangentially concerns itself with questions of escape, freedom, and lost or preserved individuality: Graham Burns's "Time and Pastoral: *The Adventures of Huckleberry Finn*" (*CR* 15:52–63). Like Ostrom (above), Burns builds basically upon earlier criticism—Henry Nash Smith and Leo Marx, most directly—in attempting to define and capture the essential pastoral nature of life on the raft (predominantly in the chapters between Jackson's Island and the Grangerfords'). He examines the ways that Mark Twain creates a sense of timelessness through the lyric and elegiac qualities of Huck's descriptive prose and through the implicit tragedy at the end of the journey: "There are throughout the central sections subtle intonations of elegy: intonations that imply an experience that is not for everybody, and one that cannot ultimately last. . . . The timelessness of the river is paradoxically end-stopped by time. The duration of the journey downstream is an imaginative analogue for the duration of boyhood, and . . . in a way of America's innocence itself. Huck's childhood is American literature's last succumbing to the high attraction of the pastoral ideal; and the pathos of it, felt within the work itself, is that it *is* the last" (p. 53). Such generalizations, accompanied by sensitive analyses of the rhetoric of some of Huck's descriptions of scenes on the River, capture more vitally and effectively than all the Eliots and Trillings the evocative emotional power of *Huckleberry Finn.*

vi. Later Works

Don W. Harrell's "A Chaser of Phantoms: Mark Twain and Romanticism" (*MQ* 13:201–12) combines biographical and critical interests. "If escape from reality is a part of Romantic sensibility," he argues, then Mark Twain has close parallels to Romanticism. That is a substantial *if*, however; and Harrell's catalog of factual and fictional escapes might just as easily derive from laziness, hedonism, boredom, or fear. Descriptions of nature, memories of the past, and dream visions constitute the modes of escape that Harrell examines. I have chosen to include the article here, however, because the brief discussion of the dream vision turned nightmare in three later works —"The Enchanted Sea Wilderness," "An Adventure in Remote Seas," and "The Great Dark"—is a helpful one which might properly be expanded further.

The only article of the year on *A Connecticut Yankee* was John S. Dinan's "Hank Morgan: Artist Run Amuck" (*MSE* 3:72–77), which argues that Hank is "more naive than cynical," but nevertheless a coldly calculating artist, like Miles Coverdale in *The Blithedale Romance*, whose artistry is ultimately apocalyptic and suicidal. Indirectly, George Fortenberry's "The Unnamed Critic in William Dean Howells' Heroines of Fiction" (*MTJ* 16,i:7–8) is concerned with "Fenimore Cooper's Literary Offenses." The unnamed critic to whom Howells refers in regard to Cooper's heroines was obviously the Mark Twain of that critical essay.

Pudd'nhead Wilson continues to attract more attention than any work except *Huck.* Two source studies, neither of them very convincing, deal with the novel. Mario L. D'Avanzo ("In the Name of Pudd'nhead," *MTJ* 16,ii:13–14) proposes that Benjamin Franklin's mention in *Poor Richard's Almanac* of "*solid Pudding*" provides the source of the nickname, with the Franklinesque connotation reinforced by the Calendar aphorisms and Wilson's traits of "patience, industry, studiousness, frugality." Robert Rowlette offers another candidate in "Mark Twain, Sarah Grand, and The Heavenly Twins" (*MTJ* 16,ii:17–18). Madame Grand's novel, which Mark Twain read and annotated, contains a set of twins whom the humorist criticized as "tiresome creatures supposed to be funny." Possibly, in spite of a fuzzy chronology, it was the evidence of Madame Grand's failure which persuaded Mark Twain to remove his extraordinary Siamese twins from *Pudd'nhead*, Rowlette argues. His source for the annotations is the Anderson Auction Catalog of Mark Twain's Library (1911); a fuller, more precise, and possibly more convincing argument might have resulted from an inspection of the actual copy of *The Heavenly Twins* which Clemens annotated, now in the Henry W. and Albert A. Berg Collection of the New York Public Library.

In the contexts of *Pudd'nhead Wilson*, what is worse than beating a dead dog is beating the dead half-a-dog. It is true that Marvin Fisher and Michael Elliott go beyond the earlier explications of the joke that cost David Wilson his reputation in "*Pudd'nhead Wilson*: Half a Dog Is Worse Than None" (*SoR* 8:533–47), with an extended catalogue of all the dogs (and even most of the cats, for good measure) in Mark Twain's writing. They argue that the half-a-dog joke is "the most important iconographic clue to the meaning of the novel," because the dog evolves into "the long-suffering victim of callous and complacent cruelty" and becomes emblematic of Middle American culture. The Wilson who makes the joke is the perceptive cynic of the Calendar aphorisms rather than the character in the novel, however; for the remark contains "bitterly ironic wisdom—an exposure of what seems at best human folly and at worst the ineradicable evil in man's nature." I find the authors' notion of dichotomy in the personality of David Wilson a more provocative issue than the half-a-dog one; and Frank C. Cronin in "The Ultimate Perspective in *Pudd'nhead Wilson*" (*MTJ* 16,i:14–16) moves tentatively in the same direction. He identifies the omniscient narrator (who is also nominated as the author of the Calendar chapter-mottoes) as the center of the novel. But Cronin fails to pursue the possibilities of the topic; there are no quotations from this implied author's language or descriptions of his attitudes toward the material he relates.

An ingenuity reminiscent of Edwin Fussell's in *Frontier: American Literature and the American West* marks John M. Brand's "The Incipient Wilderness: A Study of *Pudd'nhead Wilson*" (*WAL* 7:125–34). "From the beginning of his novel, Twain traces the inexorable process by which the lawlessness of the wilderness slowly permeates the settlement," Brand argues. The loss of law—the old Virginia code—occurs as David Wilson settles, significantly, on "the western fringe of town." When Wilson reveals the truth of the fingerprints, he initiates "the momentous step Dawson's Landing has taken back East, away from the chaos of the wilderness." In "Pudd'nhead Wilson's Fight for Popularity and Power" (*WAL* 7:134–43) Eberhard Alsen focuses upon Wilson as the central concern of the novel—his growth from pariah to mayor. Deviousness, an urge for self-aggrandizement, and hypocrisy ultimately gain Wilson the popularity and power he has sought; but since he "finds himself at the head of an unenlightened community whose values he despises but cannot change," he is ironically "a pudd'nhead after all."

Jack Scherting in "Poe's 'The Cask of Amontillado': A Source for Twain's 'The Man That Corrupted Hadleyburg'" (*MTJ* 16,ii:18–19) suggests that the unspecified insult, the delayed vengeance, and the exploitation of human vanity to achieve revenge all indicate an indebtedness to Montresor in Mark Twain's story. More substantial is Helen E. Nebeker's "The Great Corrupter or Satan Rehabilitated" (*SSF* 8[1971]: 635–37). Elaborating upon Henry B. Rule's argument that the stranger in "Hadleyburg" is Satan (see *ALS 1969*, p. 87), Nebeker argues that even Satan is unable to corrupt further an already debased humanity. God, who orders all the events, is the Great Corrupter, capable of turning even Satan's attempts to reward "virtue" into destruction.

Two separate studies note parallels between "A Double-Barrelled Detective Story" and Sherlock Holmes. Jeanne Ritunnano's "Mark Twain vs. Arthur Conan Doyle on Detective Fiction" (*MTJ* 16,i:10–14) points out that *A Study in Scarlet*, with its specific mention of a character who became "a human bloodhound," is the direct target of satire in the "Detective Story," and "unrealistic artificiality and naive optimism" on Doyle's part are the more general targets. W. Keith Krause ("Mark Twain's 'A Double-Barreled Detective Story': A Source for the Solitary Oesophagus," *MTJ* 16,ii:10–12) suggests that Mark Twain's descriptive opening paragraph, containing the famous "bird," parodies Doyle's description of a Southwestern landscape in the middle of *A Study in Scarlet*.

Two slight studies of later works appeared in 1972. Robert Rowlette ("Mark Twain's Barren Tree in *The Mysterious Stranger*: Two Biblical Parallels," *MTJ* 16,i:19–20) notes the relationships of Philip Traum's miracle in chapter 10 to Jesus's feeding of the five thousand

and the cursing of the fig tree. Wendy A. Bie ("Mark Twain's Bitter Duality," *MTJ* 16,ii:14–16) explicates the duality in man's nature as expressed predominantly in *Letters from the Earth*. Bie believes that "the *Letters* represent a stylistic shift from the narrative to the epistolary, and, unavoidably, to first person," but there is unfortunately no elaboration of the lapses in point of view in the *Letters*.

Much more solid is Stanley Brodwin's "The Humor of the Absurd: Mark Twain's Adamic Diaries" (*Criticism* 14:49–64). Brodwin studies the diaries of Adam, Eve, and Satan in order to show "that humor is a theological element that binds God's creation to man's fall. Humor is both a cause and effect of the fall." In "Adam's Diary" and "Eve's Diary" the humorist achieved a playful irony by humanizing the two characters until all vestiges of their mythical dimensions are lost: Adam and Eve fall because of their naïveté, their love, and their large senses of humor. In "That Day in Eden," Brodwin argues, the events, reported by Satan, are deterministic, the tone pessimistic; although there is a bittersweet humor in the story, its major thrust is to "show the inability of innocence to cope with the moral demands of which it can have no conception." Finally, the postlapsarian concerns of "Papers of the Adams Family" point out the dilemma of a human race in which death and war accent the "cold grotesqueness" and philosophically absurd in Mark Twain's view of the Adamic myth. Brodwin's article is perceptive and assimilative—unlike most of the articles this year.

I must report, with a relief that approaches hysteria, my inability to find the *Journal of the Otto Rank Association* in any accessible library; and, therefore, I am unable to record my impressions of Virginia P. Robinson's "The Double Soul: Mark Twain and Otto Rank" in that journal (6,i:32–53). Any reader whose sense of disappointment is too uncontrollable can read Lewis P. Simpson's "Mark Twain and the Pathos of Regeneration: A Second Look at Geismar's *Mark Twain*" (*SLJ* 4,ii:93–106), which, in the guise of a reexamination of Geismar's "biography," is in fact a sophisticated and elaborate study of the Rankian elements in Mark Twain's fiction and life. Finally, and belatedly, I cannot neglect Louis D. Rubin, Jr.'s "How Mark Twain Threw Off His Inhibitions and Discovered the Vitality of Formless Form" (*SR* 79[1971]:426–33). A review of Geismar's *Mark Twain: An American Prophet*, and at the same time a parody of "Fenimore Cooper's Literary Offenses," it probably does not belong here at all.

But after making my way through the Mark Twain scholarship for 1972, with all its vicissitudes, I looked up this review; and expecting never to smile again, I laughed so raucously at the devastating ridicule and the vitriolic satire that a librarian asked me to leave the Periodical Room. In a year marked by tediously lengthy and ultimately disappointing scholarship on Mark Twain, Rubin's pastiche was an adroit performance worth a special trip to the campus!

University of Chicago

6. Henry James

William T. Stafford

The reputation of Henry James throughout 1972 was a subject for public print in a way probably unequaled since the year he died, possibly never before equaled. The occasion was the February publication of Leon Edel's *Henry James: The Master, 1901–1916* (Philadelphia, Lippincott), the fifth and final volume of his monumental Life, the first volume of which, *The Untried Years, 1843–1870*, had appeared nineteen years earlier, in 1953. Widespread and controversial reaction to the now completed Life also became widespread and controversial attention to James himself, and attention to that reaction is as much the proper subject of this chronicle as is the biography itself.

Dominating and pervasive though that comprehensive subject was, other Jamesian criticism continued to appear—to appear, moreover, in some new configurations that might well stand as some new beginnings in Jamesian scholarship, even as the completion of Edel's Life could be seen as signaling the end of the old, although distinctions in these matters can never be precisely indicated. Whether old or new, attention to James continues to be profuse—six new book-length studies during 1972 (three by English scholars, one by a German, and two by Americans); a complexly arranged and significant anthology of James's comments on the theory of fiction; a book-length comparative study of James and Meredith; and long, long chapters on James in books with subjects as varied as the English country house, spiritualism in American literature, the novel of manners in America, and distances from consciousness to conscience in the works of Goethe through those of Camus. Periodical criticism is even more radically different, with source studies, parallels, and influences usurping space that in the past has been so freely given to explication, the latter represented this year by only three studies of individual tales and by little more than that in studies of individual novels.

General criticism, also more voluminous this year than in the past, encompasses such disparate fields as sociology, politics, feminism, sexism, and prophecy. James's relation to his cultural milieu appears to be on the edge of almost microscopic analysis. All in all, it was thus a bumper year for Jamesian scholarship—but the big news is Edel's Life.

i. Biography and Reputation—The Edel "Life": Reaction

The most blatant, if by no means the most telling, attack on Edel and on James provoked by the biography, among those I have seen, is Philip Rahv's "Henry James and His Cult" (*NYRB* 10 Feb.:18–22). Probably the most uncritically laudatory is that by Joseph Epstein, whose very title, "The Greatest Biography of the Century" (Chicago Tribune *Book World*, 6 Feb.:1,3,6), is indication enough of his attitude. The more important reviews probably fall between these two extremes.

Rahv's curious attack deserves more than a word or two, for it was also *at least* curious to Norman Podhoretz, who himself responded to Rahv, in a piece in *Commentary* ("A Minor Cultural Event," 53,iv:7–10), charging him with political opportunism. Rahv's "change of mind about James," says Podhoretz, "is blatantly political in inspiration." And his current attitude toward James is marked, he continues, with "an animus . . . so fierce and the wish to belittle . . . so relentlessly in control" that Podhoretz himself feels compelled to detail Rahv's various previously published (and generally favorable) attitudes toward the novelist. The gist of Podhoretz's charge, I think it fair to say, is that Rahv is guilty of currying favor with the young because Rahv now feels, writes Podhoretz, "that James is 'patently deficient' in the qualities 'young people' allegedly want from literature." (Rahv had specified "immediacy, spontaneity, and sensuality" as precise qualities James lacked.) Podhoretz then goes on to tout a longer piece on James in that same issue of *Commentary* by a critic who *is* under thirty (Edward Grossman's "Henry James and the Sexual-Military Complex," see below). Rahv's other points are generally those of a kind one might have expected from Maxwell Geismar several years ago: that Edel "makes too much of James, . . . overestimates his importance in the most extravagant manner possible, . . . is much too expansive," and so on. William James is described as more right than the cult will admit in his objections to Henry's late style; the Prefaces are often misread under the mistaken assumption that James practiced what he preached; the international fables are said to involve values from which "at this late date one recoils with bewilderment"; the three last great novels are each seriously flawed; Edel himself is said to be "far too staunch an adherent of the James cult, which he assumes is destined to last forever," not realizing that James's reputation is "seriously on the wane," that his "greatness" is merely on "a national scale." It is indeed a curious piece. Rahv's attack a few weeks later in the Letters column of *NYRB* ("Digging James," 6 April:37–38), in reply to Adeline R. Tintner's objections to some of his views, is no less relentless.

Much more telling, it seems to me, is Quentin Anderson's careful reluctance, in his "Leon Edel's 'Henry James'" (*VQR* 48:621–30), to use the word *biography* in referring to Edel's work. His provocative point appears to me to be that Edel, throughout, has so exclusively related James's imaginative faculty to the works he created that the so-called Life itself, Edel's total narrative, "becomes the analogue of a Jamesian fiction whose plot is the sequence of his contentions with the persons of the family romance, and in which James acts by producing his fictions—his responses to the inward demand for 'self-analysis.'" That is to say, as I understand it, everything is so drawn to and through and *for* the works that James's supposed "life" is ultimately seen only as one vast compendium of all the fiction, the life existing, as it were, only for the purposes of making the fiction, the fiction, for making the life. The result, I suppose one could say, is a kind of onanism, thereby precluding the successful "placing" of James in a literary tradition. At the same time, Anderson concludes, in this most important essay, Edel's very method is that which James's work most insistently demands, a command, as it were, not to write "biography" at all. Whatever its limitations, Edel's "narrative" is thereby "engrossing," and that he should have become "his deed's creature is no wonder." In our "joint preoccupation" with James, so, in a way, have we all.

A more conventional kind of reservation about the work is Joseph Wisenfarth's review in *Commonweal* (98,11:44–45), which charges that the Life is "too long to sustain interest, too warped by a 'high selectivity' to be believable overall, and too negligent of scholarship on James not to be shortsighted." Oscar Cargill (in *AL* 44:

330–32) raises some of the same questions, although believing *The Master* to be "unquestionably the best volume in the series." Cargill sees some limitations in Edel's psychological approach to fiction, but the "impressionistic" methods have, for him, some virtues; and he ends with general praise for the volume.

Among the plethora of favorable and sometimes even extravagantly ecstatic reviews are those appearing in *TLS* ("The Matter of the Master," 18 Aug.:957–59), in *NYTBR* (Hilton Kramer's "Henry James," 6 Feb.:1, 32–33), in the *New Yorker* (Naomi Bliven's "Home James," 29 April:137–40), and in *SatR* (John Aldridge's "The Anatomy of Passion in the Consummate Henry James," 12 Feb.:65–68). The *TLS* reviewer, for example, sees Edel's greatest achievement in the Life in his humanizing James, in his "special talent" for demonstrating one James tactic or another to have been "the plausible reactions of a living rather than the diagrammatic outcome of some abstruse theory of 'form' and 'mode.'" Hilton Kramer emphasizes the same point, adding that Edel "has also offered us a model of what the biography of a writer should ideally be—not a mere compendium of facts and undigested documents, but a literary form that makes us *see* its subject in all its inward complexities as well as its worldly comings and goings." It is, for him, a "*most* extraordinary" biography, perfectly worthy of "the greatest of American writers," and "in its narrative force perhaps indicative of the fact that narrative itself, as a viable mode of literary discourse, may have passed from the hands of the novelists and historians to those of the biographer." Both Naomi Bliven and John Aldridge have nothing but the highest praise for Edel's success in this last volume in bridging the gap between James's private or writing self and his public or worldly self in ways that bring profound understanding to both those selves. "We may wonder how soon," Aldridge concludes, "the two will come together in such perfect union in such a monumental talent and an exemplary human being."

It is Aldridge, finally, in this for me most eloquent of tributes to James and to Edel that most appropriately sits beside my point of departure, Rahv's debunking. I have space for a single example, James's attitude toward and treatment of sex. Rahv had described James's late-life homoerotic attitudes toward such young men as Hendrik Andersen and Hugh Walpole as appearing to him "to be no more than pathetic symptoms of senile sexuality." He later expressed his feeling that James "was deeply and irretrievably offended by the grossness of the flesh," had long exploited this limitation into an "obsessive, . . . a veritable delirium of refinement," and elsewhere said that James's "scrupulosities, whatever their cultural, social, or psychic origin, are far too readily pressed into service." For Aldridge, however, it is the very absence of the explicitly sexual that gives such implicit force to James's treatment of the topic. "Whether by wisdom or by prudery," he writes, "what he called the great relation between men and women is carried on most interestingly, perhaps even most passionately, when the parties involved cannot or dare not take each other to bed. . . . The news of orgasm has long since reached us. The inexhaustible mystery, the drama that is forever refreshed because it is nowhere ever the same, is to be found in the nature of the people in the relationship being consummated." Whatever liberalized James "from localized phallic sexuality, it may have enabled him to create in his work an image of the erotic which, just because it transcended the limits of the copulative act, became symbolic of the most uni-versalized passion operating at every level of human loving and consciousness."[1]

For me, Edel's *The Master* is in some ways the least engrossing of the five volumes. The James of these years, to be sure, is a twentieth-century James and as such a more public, more available James than he had ever been in the nineteenth century—the "facts" of his life and their configurations much more widely disseminated than had ever been the case previously, the documents available to the biographer, Edel himself tells us, quite the equal of all the material available for the first four volumes. But *The Master* may also be the least dramatic of the five volumes, as if preparation for these culminating years were somehow more exciting than the culmination itself. Even so, it is an appropriate biographical culmination, to the fascinating volumes which precede it no less than to the magisterial literary stature of its subject.

Edel's by now well-known method has its own rich if complacent familiarity. And the major "events" of these last years are predictable enough: the three great novels; the "affairs" of sorts with Jocelyn

1. For the record, additional reviews of the Edel volume also appeared in the following: *Booklist* 1 May:746; *Choice* 9:212; *Economist* 5 Aug.:48; *Nation* 24 April:539; *New Statesman* 4 Aug.:162; *America* 20 May:551; *American Libraries* 3:681; *Guardian Weekly* 12 Aug.:18; *Listener* 17 Aug.:213; *New Leader* 3 April:14; *Spectator* 5 Aug.:213; *Newsweek* 14 Feb.:92; and *Time* 14 Feb.:70.

Persse and Hugh Walpole; the return visit to America and its results in *The American Scene*; the preparations for and disappointments in reactions to the New York Edition; the domestic and professional "arrangements" (servants *and* amanuenses); the Edith Wharton connection in rich and fulsome detail; the death of his brother William and paradoxically stronger ties with his brother's family; his comings and goings; his multitudinous friendships; the breaking-out of the First World War; his illnesses; his death.

Much more is likely to be written about James's death-bed dictations associating himself with Napoleonic power in spite of the fact that the pertinent documents of that dictation were first published four years ago (see *ALS* 1968, pp. 87–88), but those ramifications are almost the only ones in this volume likely to stir the kind of occasional critical outcry provoked by the first volume and its contentions of intense sibling rivalry between the philosopher brother William and the novelist, or that in Volume 3 and James's curious relations with Constance Fenimore Woolson, or that audaciously central thesis of Volume 4 linking the fiction of the late 1890s to James's psychic needs to relive his childhood, adolescence, and coming of age in order to combat the destructive elements of the dramatic fiasco during the early years of that decade.

But my wish here, finally, is in no sense an intention to belittle. Quite the contrary. It is to describe an impression, in fact, to commemorate the completion of this biographical endeavor; for, *as biography* (Anderson's studied reluctance to use the term notwithstanding) it must be considered—in scope and in dedicatory zeal—a literary event of the first order, commensurate to nothing less, whatever the scholarly disagreements about methods or parts or indeed the quality of mind that produced it, than the indelible impact that the total œuvre of Henry James has itself made on the imagination of the modern world. However justified the scores of complaints Jamesians have made about Edel's indifference over the years to their considerable contributions to our knowledge of the novelist and his works, the simple truth of the matter is that very few of them have themselves been able to ignore Edel's work, whatever their disagreements with it. Even fewer, I predict, will be able to do so in the future.

One mini-tempest quickly following the publication of the biography surfaced, not surprisingly, in the Letters column of *TLS* (15 Sept.:1060) when Jacques Barzun reprinted William James's entire letter refusing membership in the National Institute of Arts and Letters to refute Edel's reading that William had rejected membership because his "younger and shallower and vainer brother" was already a member. Edel immediately replied (*TLS* 13 Oct.:1227), admitting the facetious tone of William's remark but also pointing to the "daggerside of wit and humor" that "Freud initiated us to . . . long ago." The last word comes from Lionel Trilling (*TLS* 20 Oct.:1257), whom Edel had quoted for support and who dissassociates himself from Edel's reading in order to support Barzun. More substantive interpretive controversies about the biography are sure to follow in the future.

Additional biographical material appearing during the year is exceedingly slim. H. Montgomery Hyde, in "Henry James and Theodora Bosanquet" (*Encounter* 39,iv:6–12), reprinted some previously unpublished excerpts from Miss Bosanquet's diary which recount personal family details surrounding James's death and funeral. And Francizek Lyra in "Correspondence of Helena Modrzejewska (Modjeska) to Henry James" (*KN* 19:89–96) makes available seven unimportant letters (in a mixture of French and English) the Polish actress wrote the novelist between May 1879 and September 1891.

A final word should be given over here to Jay B. Hubbell's "placement" of James in his delightfully informative *Who Are the Major American Writers?* (Durham, N.C., Duke Univ. Press) for its compact and accurate and lively account (pp. 122–35) of James's literary reputation.

ii. Criticism, Essays, Drama

James E. Miller, Jr.'s *Theory of Fiction: Henry James* (Lincoln, Univ. of Nebr. Press) may well be the most important anthology yet made among those numerous volumes that have collected in one way or another James's essays or comments on special subjects. It is clearly one of the most useful, in part because the subject matter itself, the theory of fiction, is patently among the most important of the various literary heritages James left us, in part because it is so conveniently and thoroughly arranged—arranged, moreover, from sources scattered throughout his vast body of work, his stories about writers, his critical and speculative essays, his *Notebooks*, Prefaces, and letters. Its opening and closing essays ("The Art of Fiction" and "The Future

of the Novel") are elsewhere available enough, but the 250 interven-
ing selections which span the half-century that marks James's creative
career gives even them a kind of enriched meaning never before quite
so apparent. The selections are grouped under fifteen major headings,
with two levels of various subdivisions incorporated into each chapter, and all conveniently titled and cross-indexed so that easy reference to one another and to their original context is possible. Chapter
V, for example, consists of three parts—A: Novel, Poem, Play; B:
Picture, Anecdote, Short Story, Nouvelle; C: Allegory, the Extraordinary, Romance, Fairy Tale, Ghost Story—with each part having
from five to ten separate comments by James on each, usually arranged chronologically, but not slavishly so, thereby presenting and
developing James's collective attitudes on each aspect of his subject.
It is an imaginative and useful scheme. A fine twenty-five-page introduction outlines the volume as a whole. Brief forewords to each chapter summarize the major points. And it concludes with a Bibliography
of Sources, an Index to authors and works referred to, and a long list
of critical terms that are as much glossary as index. Leon Edel is
surely correct in describing it as "a permanent addition to the Jamesian shelf."

Other attention to James's criticism during the year pales by contrast. Herwig Friedl's *Die Funktion der Bildlichkeit in den kritischen
und theoretischen Schriften von Henry James: Ein Entwurf seiner
Literaturtheorie* (*BzJA*) may be an exception, although my understanding of its author's statement of purpose (I have seen only an
English translation of it)—how the images in James's critical and
theoretical writings become a key to the "ever-changing interest of
the theoretical consciousness in the phenomena of artistic creation,"
this theoretical consciousness to be understood "as an equivalent to
the implicit narrator in fiction"—somehow does not persuade me to
believe so. Michael D. Patrick's "Henry James's Literary Criticism"
(*IllQ* 35,ii:21–33) is a conventional overview of James the critic that
adds very little to what we already know.

In the broader area of "social reportage and impressionistic sociology," as Milton A. Mays defines it in his good study, "Down-Town
with Henry James" (*TSLL* 14:107–22), is revealed James's very sharp
insight into the dilemma of the American male who has had opened
to him in American society only moneymaking and politics. Mays's
sources are the early travel sketches of America, the much later

American Scene, and the short satiric sketches in his American-set fictions of the 1870s and '80s. James's late prophecies for the American male ever escaping this limitation are said to be only "thoughtfully pessimistic." L. Moody Simms, Jr.'s "Henry James and the Negro Question" (*AN&Q* 10:127–28) is an inconsequential note taking Maxwell Geismar to task for oversimplifying James's attitudes toward the American Negro on the basis of Geismar having cited a single passage in *The American Scene*.

David K. Kirby covers familiar ground in his "Henry James's *The Other House*: From Novel to Play" (*MarkhamR* 3:49–53) in recounting how both versions of the work came to be written, their similarities and differences, and how the technique of foreshortening contributes to the long-recognized superiority of the dramatic over the novelistic version.

iii. Sources, Parallels, Influences

Michael Egan's *Henry James: The Ibsen Years* (London, Vision Press), the most recent account among the many accounts of James's relation to Ibsen, may well be the last word on this great connection, however exaggerated it is in spots on James's use of Ibsen. Egan obviously knows James's and Ibsen's work extremely well—knows, for example, the great variety of Jameses revealed by his fiction, although his focus is properly on those Jameses who appear following his introduction to the works of the Norwegian dramatist in 1889, on the impact of that knowledge on James's own playwriting attempts, and, more importantly, on the fiction that followed it—that of the last great period no less than that of the late 1890s. What James first learned from Ibsen, says Egan, was that it was "possible to heighten a realistic effect through the interaction of image and physical fact." What the connection finally led to was James's ability "to synthesize the dramatic and narrative arts."

Egan's account of this developing thesis is impressive—not, of course, in the many ties he sees between the two Henrys in the play *The Reprobate* and in *The Other House*, wherein the Ibsen influence has long been recognized—but in *Covering End* and *The Spoils of Poynton*, at one stage of development, and a good deal more audaciously, in *The Turn of the Screw* and *The Wings of the Dove*, at another. He breaks down all of the works into scenes and acts, and reads them as if they were Ibsen plays, but also makes important distinctions and is never really blind to other forces at work on them and the fact that they are, after all, fictions. Unlike the "prompt-book" novels (*The Spoils*, for example), *The Wings* is seen as employing "to great effect the technique of scenic disguise." Egan is led through Ibsen, moreover, to see—correctly, I think, whatever James may have intended—that in effect Kate is more important to the subject of that novel than is Milly. He goes on to link Kate to Hedda Gabler, and Kate's father Lionel to John Gabriel, ending up, for me at least, with a strange, rich reading of the novel as a consequence. The book as a whole perhaps rides its thesis too hard. The ties between *The Turn of the Screw* and *Ghosts*, for example, are much too explicitly and exclusively made; *Hedda Gabler* is perhaps not *the* main source for *The Wings*. Still, this is a readable book throughout, and Ibsen indeed was, I am also convinced, "a liberating factor in James's artistic evolution, . . . showing him how to resolve many of the technical problems of his later development."

Egan's reference to James and Ibsen in his "Introduction" to *Henrik Ibsen: The Critical Heritage* (London, Routledge and Kegan Paul) is a brief recap (pp. 16–18) of his book, but attention should be given here also to parts of three previously unpublished letters from James to Edmund Gosse about Ibsen which Egan reprints in his anthology, especially the first letter (January 29, 1889) recounting James's first comments in writing on the playwright: "I have perused your very interesting acct. of Ibsen, as I always peruse you when I find you. You must tell me more about I. This is not in this case female-American for *me*."

Matthew Arnold and his famous distinctions between Hebraism and Hellenism are the sources seen by Edward Engelberg as a major influence on James in his chapter "The Tyranny of Conscience: Arnold, James, and Conrad's Lord Jim" (*The Unknown Distance: From Consciousness to Conscience: Goethe to Camus* [Cambridge, Harvard Univ. Press], pp. 154–72). Although noting throughout James's work the problem of how to transform a destructive Conscience into a redeeming Consciousness, Engelberg's major emphasis here falls under the rubric of Arnold's distinctions, especially as they help define the contrasting roles of Rowland Mallet and Roderick Hudson in James's first novel. The results support the general concern of Engelberg's book well enough, and he also clearly establishes James's use and knowledge of Arnold's formulations, but one does not thereby learn much about James's fiction that he did not know before.

One perhaps does, on the other hand, in a remarkable series of five articles by Adeline R. Tintner, who explores in a variety of ways the pervasive influence of Balzac (and occasionally others) on James's fiction. Her "Hyacinth at the Play: The Play Within the Play as a Novelistic Device in James" (*JNT* 2:171–85), for example, after seeing some ties with *Hamlet* following James's own lead in the Preface to *The Princess Casamassima*, goes on to demonstrate persuasively how James's "reading of Balzac gave him examples of performances which prefigure and parallel the action of the drama." Her "'The Old Things': Balzac's *Le curé de Tours* and James's *The Spoils of Poynton*" (*NCF* 26[1971]:436–55) presents firm evidence of similarities between the two works in plot, in some names, in descriptions, even in novelistic rhythms. James's deep and abiding knowledge of the Balzac novel is clearly established, a psychological case is made for the appeal of the situation of the novel at the time James wrote it, and even his death-bed hysteria is appropriately made to bolster her case. Her "The Influence of Balzac's *L'Envers de l'histoire contemporaine* on James's 'The Great Good Place'" (*SSF* 9:343–51) is another persuasive case of that story's "clear-cut dependence on Balzac's work." Her "Balzac's *Two Maries* and James's *The Ambassadors*" (*ELN* 9:284–87) points out that the "Two Maries" in *Une Fille d'Eve* are the much more likely source for the two Marys in *The Ambassadors* than the more often pointed-to Virgin Mary; for in Balzac, as in James, "the religious duality had already been secularized," as had "the metaphor of salvation." Finally, in a slightly different direction, her "James's Mock Epic: 'The Velvet Glove,' Edith Wharton, and Other Late Tales" (*MFS* 17:483–99) presents a compelling and elaborate study of how the mythological understructure of "The Velvet Glove" and its views of Edith Wharton open new vistas of understanding to six other tales of James's late years, "Crappy Cornelia," "Mona Montravers," "Julia Bride," "The Jolly Corner," "The Bench of Desolation," and "A Round of Visits."

In attention to another French source, Lyall H. Powers in "James's Debt to Alphonse Daudet" (*CL* 24:150–62) follows pretty much the general thesis of his recent *Henry James and the Naturalist Movement* (1971) in his restating of the pervasive debt to *L'Evangéliste* in *The Bostonians* and how Daudet generally became such a strong element in James's whole middle "naturalistic" period. Anthony D. Briggs in "Alexander Pushkin: A Possible Influence on Henry James" (*FMLS* 8:52–60) is properly cautious in his speculation that James, especially through Turgenev, *could* have gained some elements of his "The Aspern Papers" from the Russian's *Yevgeniy Onegin, The Queen of Spades*, and *The Bronze Horseman*. And Charlotte Goodman's "Henry James's *Roderick Hudson* and Nathaniel Parker Willis's *Paul Fane*" (*AL* 43:642–45) is a brief demonstration of the many similarities between the two novels and the fact that James was familiar with Willis's work before he wrote his own novel.

In the equally numerous parallel or comparative studies that appeared during the year, one might first return to Balzac via Peter Brooks's provocative "The Melodramatic Imagination" (*PR* 39:195–212) wherein the French novelist and James are his prime exempla as users of melodrama as a way "of perceiving and imaging the spiritual world where there is no longer any clear idea of the sacred, no generally accepted societal moral imperatives." For the "melodramatic imagination," he continues, "things are necessarily all in the nature of metaphor because things are not simply themselves, but refer to, speak of, something else." That something else reveals their insistence that "life does contain . . . a moral occult which is the realm of eventual value," all of which is ultimately "more nourishing than mere 'behavioristic' novelists would have us believe."

Also important is Donald D. Stone's *Novelists in a Changing World: Meredith, James and the Transformations of English Fiction in the 1880's* (Cambridge, Harvard Univ. Press), a fresh view of the fiction of the decade that should certainly invite attention from those, such as Lyall H. Powers, who have held that James's so-called middle-period, at least in its major thrust, was a "naturalistic" period with primary ties to the sons of Balzac. Stone contends instead that the Victorian milieu was the more important of the contexts in which James then wrote and that, moreover, the major works of that period, beginning with *The Portrait* and continuing through *The Bostonians, The Princess*, and *The Tragic Muse*, represent the major portion of James's fictional accomplishment. His major thesis appears to be how James, during this period, "shifted his personal allegiance from the world as picturesque material for the novelist to the artist's own world of consciousness, which can transform any impressions into the stuff of art." Early mockings of this "Pateresque sensibility" shifted into dogmatic assertion of it in such works as *The Princess* and *The Tragic Muse*; but "in Dr. Sloper, Gilbert Osmond, and Ralph Touchett, he showed the harm that such sensibilities cause others whom they treat in the light of [this] aesthetic spectacle" so that the work in which these three appear, in thus showing "limitations of the individual point of view left to itself," becomes for Stone (with *The Bostonians*) "three of James's four best novels." Most of his later work reversed that lesson, to its detriment, although also transforming "Pater's dictum that the world exists at best as an aesthetic spectacle . . . into a formula for the author of novels and the hero of fiction." Stone's argument is of course considerably more complex than I have here indicated, in its attention to Jamesian prototypes that were to appear pervasively in modern fiction, in its contrasts to Meredith (for whom, he says, "the novel existed for the sake of the world, while for James the world existed for the sake of the novel"), and in its intricate final view of James as one who, "by shifting his values from the world to his own inner world and his own artistic standards, successfully salvaged the writing of fiction—and the need for fiction—for the modern world." It is a curious book, worthy perhaps to be set beside those recent ones by Philip Weinstein and Charles T. Samuels (see *ALS 1971*, pp. 93–95) in its thoughtful questioning of received opinion about the precise nature of James's values.

Other parallel studies of British examples include Roger Ramsey's "The Available and the Unavailable 'I': Conrad and James" (*ELT* 14[1971]:137–45) and Nan B. Maglin's "Fictional Feminists in *The Bostonians* and *The Odd Woman*," in *Images of Women*, pp. 216–36. Ramsey's is an amusingly expressed comparative study of *The Turn of the Screw* and *Heart of Darkness* with a special emphasis on the two "I's" of the two famous tales and the crucial difference that results in the fact that the narrative "I" disappears after the Introduction in James's example but is present throughout in Conrad's. Ramsey also provides some amusing speculation on James as a possible source for Marlow and other Conrad narrators. Nan Maglin's is an insignificant contrast of the alleged pro-feminist attitudes in Gissing's novel to the purported anti-feminist one in James's. She appears to be totally blind to the fact that *The Bostonians* is as much anti-Ransom (that is, anti-male) as it is anti-female.

Another feminist study is Judith H. Montgomery's much more important "The American Galatea" (*CE* 32[1971]:890–99), a view of

Hawthorne's Zenobia, James's Isabel Archer, and Edith Wharton's
Lily Bart as examples of archetyping and idealizing American women
and thereby not only reflecting but consolidating and perpetuating
a restrictive and demeaning stereotype. Such a thesis leads her, of
course, to a very negative and thus oversimplified view of Isabel's
return to Osmond. Two other parallel studies with American writers
are Joel Salzberg's "The Gothic Hero in Transcendental Quest: Poe's
'Ligeia' and James' 'The Beast in the Jungle'" (*ESQ* 18:108–14) and
J. R. McElrath's "Thoreau and James: Coincidence in Angles of
Vision" (*ATQ* 11[1971]:14–15). Salzberg's illuminating comparison
maintains that, whatever their difference, both authors present a
"transcendentally aspiring protagonist" in whom "the sensibilities of
a visionary, his homage to other-worldly experience, and the aftermath of his obsession establish a similar thematic design." McElrath's
much less important note merely finds in *The Portrait* a description
by Gilbert Osmond of Lord Warburton that makes a point much like
one of Thoreau's in *Walden*.

Finally, Frederick Y. Yu's "Andrew Lytle's *A Name for Evil* as a
Redaction of 'The Turn of the Screw'" (*MQR* 11:186–90) is a brief
contention that Lytle's book is much more important as "an analysis
of the failure of the Agrarian movement" than it is for its ties to James,
however unmistakable and manifold those ties are.

iv. Criticism: General

Of the three book-length studies of James to be cited in this section
this year, first mention, I suppose, might well go to John Goode's
collection, *The Air of Reality: New Essays of Henry James* (London,
Methuen) in the light of the editor's claim "that a critical confrontation with James must call in question the prevailing stance of literary
studies." Unhappy with most Jamesian criticism since "the mid fifties"
and finding "severely limited" those few books since then for which
he has been "grateful," Goode, I assume, sees this volume as some
sort of corrective. In view of this view, from which the editor carefully
disassociates the other contributors to the volume, I at least expected
from the nine essays that follow (almost all by British academicians)
something quite different from what I got: the single unifying suggestion from the editor that each contributor "might profit most by
asking questions about the relationship of the work to the world it

takes account of" and the result, in the essays themselves, of nothing more unifying than a strong and consistent sense of cultural history. My views of the essays themselves I have recorded elsewhere (*AL* 45:618–19) and refer interested readers there. For the record here, let me only list the contributors and their subjects: R. W. Butterfield, "*The American*"; John Lucas, "*Washington Square*"; David Howard, "*The Bostonians*"; D. J. Gordon and John Stokes, "The reference of *The Tragic Muse*"; Juliet Mitchell, "*What Maisie Knew*: portrait of the artist as a young girl"; Margaret Walters, "Keeping the place tidy for the young female mind: *The Awkward Age*"; Bernard Richards, "*The Ambassadors* and *The Sacred Fount*: the artist *manqué*"; John Goode, "The pervasive mystery of style: *The Wings of the Dove*"; and Gabriel Pearson, "The novel to end all novels: *The Golden Bowl*."

Martha Banta's *Henry James and the Occult: The Great Extension* (Bloomington, Ind. Univ. Press) also displays a strong historical sense, although on a much more specialized subject: the various "spiritualistic" movements of the nineteenth and early twentieth centuries and James's relation to them. Her thesis is succinct: although James "repudiated—with wit and bite—the inanities, the absence of style, and the self-imposed limitations of scientific empiricalism and spiritualist vaporizing, he took note of what they said about the human consciousness. He took warning of their follies; occasionally, he took fire over the possibilities for his art that they offered to his probing artistic eye." The matter of the book is given in three parts— the first devoted to "the intellectual and emotional milieux" of then-current supernatural concerns, William James's various interests and involvements, and Henry's highly sceptical but nonetheless curiously expedient attention to the movement; the second, to his uses of traditional supernatural motifs in his own fiction; the third, to the extensions and aesthetic results of this lifelong interest in the occult into his themes of consciousness that are not necessarily "extraordinary" ones. Most readers, I suppose, will accept most easily the second of these matters, will view most sceptically the third, although some marvelously suggestive ties are made in that last chapter, as in *The Wings of the Dove* and "The Beast in the Jungle," for a single example, and the parallels between Densher's attitude toward the dead Milly and Marcher's toward the dead May Bartram. Other groups are also freshly suggestive, as in her chapter on "The Vampire Breed," which not only establishes links among the early "Professor Fargo," *The Bostonians*, and *The Sacred Fount* but also picks up along the way meaningful parallels in Hawthorne's *The Blithesdale Romance* and in Howells's *The Undiscovered Country*. And of course there is a lengthy and sensible, if in no way startling, analysis of "The Turn of the Screw," properly attuned to the belief that "the story's howness ought to be the way one comes to . . . [its] whyness." An uneven book, *Henry James and the Occult* is also an original book, with demonstration aplenty of how solidly James, whatever his various transcendencies, was also a man of his times.

Howard Kerr's much broader concern with this same subject, in *Mediums, and Spirit-Rappers, and Roaring Radicals: Spiritualism in American Literature, 1850–1900* (Urbana, Univ. of Ill. Press), a title taken from *The Bostonians*, is evidence enough of this level of occult activity during the late nineteenth century in America. His concern with James is much more limited than Banta's, focusing as he does primarily on a single novel in the chapter, "The Young Prophetess: Memories of Spiritualism and Intimations of Occult Consciousness in Henry James's *The Bostonians*" (pp. 190–222), although some attention is also given to "The Turn of the Screw," "Maude-Evelyn," and "The Friends of the Friends." What he so clearly establishes is James's knowledge and uses of specific mesmerists and mediums in *The Bostonians*, especially Cora Hatch, an actual "trance maiden" with a "background of occult reform" for the "great deal of attention" he paid to Verena's "charismatic effect on her audiences and to her peculiar mode of consciousness." Additional sources, occult and otherwise, are also brought into his analysis, as well as some concern for how *The Bostonians* anticipate "the studies of psychical consciousness which lay ahead in James's supernatural fiction."

The reader of the third new book to be cited here, Seymour Chatman's *The Later Style of Henry James* (Oxford, Blackwell), a stylistic study, should not be too hastily put off by either the title or the highly technical and imposing chapter titles with such words and phrases as "Obliquity," "Deixis," and "Cleft Sentences and Related Forms." Although highly technical, the book in fact is also highly readable. I am not equipped to question Chatman's methods, but his results appear to be eminently sensible, if hardly surprising, in the demonstrated recognition of how closely appropriate to James's general artistic purpose are the various elements of his style. An example: "What has been said about the register of verbs of mental action is equally true of the nouns: they do not represent a desire for narrowly exact and professional nomenclature, but rather an attempt to catch the mind at work, in all its uncertainty, indeed, assuming uncertainty to be its ordinary lot, experience to be essentially fluid, and so the narrative task is necessarily approximative." The book concludes, moreover, with a stylistic analysis of two parodies, Max Beerbohm's "The Guerdon" and W. H. D. Rouse's "The Enchanted Copse," both reprinted, to show how his method distinguishes a good one (Beerbohm's) from a bad one. Neat. In contrast, an article such as Barry Menikoff's "The Subjective Pronoun in the Late Style of Henry James" (*ES* 52[1971]:436–41) appears to be very small, however correct he is in seeing the functional use of that device in selected later stories.

Two additional books devote long chapters to James, both setting him in still other traditions (one American and the other English), and one of them at least (Richard Gill's *Happy Rural Seat: The English Country House and the Literary Imagination*, New Haven, Yale Univ. Press), so far as I know, breaking totally new ground in its comprehensive placing of James among the high creators. Gill's long chapter, "The Great Good Place: Henry James and the Country House" (pp. 19–93), is remarkably wise, thorough, and perceptive in seeing what that English institution stood for in James's own life no less than in his fiction. The number of houses he knew and created, their carefully chosen names, and their symbolic resonances are all analyzed in the context of biographical detail, the important travel sketches, the notebooks, and of course the fiction itself, early and late. Although his extended focus is on *The Portrait, The Princess*, and *The Spoils of Poynton*, brief attention is also given to much, much more—almost every work, I would say, in which a house has symbolic value—and in a manner so provocative and rich that one wishes additional space were available. A useful brief appendix, "Tradition and the Individual Talent: The Literary Background of the Country House in James's Fiction" (pp. 253–59), discusses literary users of the house as symbol that James might be expected to have known—Hawthorne, to be sure, but also Balzac, the gothic novel itself in various manifestations, and, finally, English Victorian fiction generally.

James W. Tuttleton's "Henry James: The Superstitious Valuation of Europe," in his *The Novel of Manners in America* (Chapel
Hill, Univ. of N.C. Press, pp. 48–85), is less impressive. James is said
to be America's most impressive novelist of manners simply because
he is our most impressive novelist, for reasons of "his sense of character in relation to society, his commitment to civilization, his artistic
intelligence, his command of language, the particular felicity of his
style, the characteristic comedy of his phrasing and diction." Some
nice contrasts and comparisons are drawn with Howells, and James's
"complexity of manners" in the early novels is meaningfully tied to
the "complexity of style" in his later ones.

Remaining general studies are a grab bag. James M. Cox, in
"Henry James: The Politics of Internationalism" (*SoR* 8:493–506),
is concerned with illustrating the much stronger political imagination he finds in a work like *The Golden Bowl* than in *The Bostonians*
or *The Princess Casamassima*, especially in its political parable of
"Americans as invaders and redeemers of Europe." And if American
expansion, he says, is now more than we can stand, nothing has yet
come along in the way of an art form "which offers the possibility of
withdrawal as powerfully as James offered the possibility of expansion." Judith Chernaik in "Henry James as Moralist: The Case of the
Late Novels" (*CentR* 16:105–21) offers a good analysis of how in
late James "the real and the romantic . . . infiltrate and subvert each
other so thoroughly that every absolute becomes relative, every good
an evil or a source of evil, evil itself a possible good." Yet, she continues, relativism is not the final ethical measure, for James recognizes that although "no formulated response is adequate to the reality
which is finally known," his recognition of the absolute that *is* "there"
is embedded in his definition of the romantic as that which "we never
can directly know." Manfred McKenzie in "Communities of Knowledge: Secret Society in Henry James" (*ELH* 39:147–68) constructs
an elaborate "generic" situation for three of James's works, the early
"Adina," *The Portrait*, and *The Golden Bowl*, in order to develop a
rubric under which exclusion from European society leads a protagonist first to accept and then occasionally to transcend his acquired
demeaned nature. *The Golden Bowl*, predictably, becomes his great
example. Evelyn J. Hinz in "The Imagistic Evolution of James's Businessman" (*CRevAS* 3:81–95) singles out the recurrent images of appe-

tite that consistently mark his businessmen, in the earliest stories
through *The Ivory Tower*, in original and revised examples. Barbara
Martineau in "Portraits Are Murdered in the Short Fiction of Henry
James" (*JNT* 2:16–25) traces the convention of the slashed portrait
in three of James's tales ("The Story of a Masterpiece," "The Liar,"
and "The Beldonald Holbein"), sees some interrelations among them,
and ultimately sees the convention itself reflecting James's uneasiness
at "the destructive potential of the artist's role." And Edward Grossman in "Henry James and the Sexual-Military Complex" (*Commentary* 53,iv:37–50) presents an amusing autobiographical essay, of a
kind we used to call the *New Yorker* "type," that recounts some experiences of the author here and in Paris that he finds illuminated
through associating himself first with Basil Ransom of *The Bostonians* and his and James's attitudes toward Verena and Olive. He later
associates himself exclusively with James through later works and
the fact that James had missed the Civil War just as Grossman had
missed the Vietnam one. More about Grossman here than James, but
it is provocative enough in the variety of ways James speaks to this
well-read young man.

J. Don Vann's *Critics on Henry James* (Coral Gables, Fla., Univ.
of Miami Press) is a needless collection of less than 90 pages of reprinted criticism, almost three-fourths of which is readily available
in book form elsewhere.

v. Criticism: Individual Tales

Although, as we have seen, James's short fiction received voluminous
attention in various special categories throughout 1972, it was subjected to "pure" explication in a surprisingly small number of cases.
John Griffith in "James's 'The Pupil' as Whodunit: The Question of
Moral Responsibility" (*SSF* 9:257–68) rereads the tale as "black
high comedy," sees the Moreens as "laughable" (which is not to say
that they are "laudable"), and points out that "ironic inevitability" is
not necessarily "an instance of human malevolence." M. D. Uroff in
"Perception in James's 'The Real Thing'" (*SSF* 9:41–46) cites "per-
ceptual hazards" as the subject of the story. "The basic problem," he
says, "is optical." And Charles A. Nicholas in "A Second Glance at
Henry James's 'The Death of the Lion'" (*SSF* 9:143–46) finds in it
a "curiously prophetic attack on those post-Eliotic critics who . . .

avoid the author at all cost because of their veneration for his work."
The author-worshipping narrator and his girl friend are said to be
the real butt of the satire.

vi. Criticism: Individual Novels

Studies of individual novels during the year, like those of the tales,
are in relatively short supply, although attention aplenty was given
them in those categories already discussed, which, of course, supplement what follows.

Treatments of *The American* are, as usual, uneven. John V. An-
tush's "The 'Much Finer Complexity' of History in *The American*"
(*JAmS* 6:85–95), for example, is broadly speculative in seeing embodied in Newman the myth of what it is to be a rich American at
the same time that James sees myth per se as often an escape from
the truths of historical reality. But Joseph M. Backus in "'Poor Val-
entin' or 'Monsieur le Comte': Variation in Character Designation
as Matter for Critical Consideration in Henry James's *The American*"
(*Names* 20:47–55) is much too obvious in discussing the variety of
ways names and other character designations convey meaning in
the novel.

Four novels were subjects of only single studies each. Elsa Net-
tels's "Action and Point of View in *Roderick Hudson*" (*ES* 53:238–
47) is another of those studies of Rowland's role as a Jamesian observer but here one that emphasizes how "Roderick's deterioration is
not the kind of action which permits the fullest development of
James's method," unlike later "observed" subjects. Anthony J. Maz-
zella's "James' *The Portrait of a Lady*" (*Expl* 30:item 37) is a neat
little note establishing how, in preparing a two-volume edition of the
novel, James provided a revised final scene to Volume 1 to parallel
that at the end of Volume 2. Theodore C. Miller's "The Muddled Politics of Henry James's *The Bostonians*" (*GaR* 26:336–46) sees Basil's
characterization as somewhat chaotic, reflecting thereby James's own
indecisiveness about the relation of his art to his own political views.
And Joel Salzberg's "Love, Identity, and Death: James' *The Princess
Casamassima* Reconsidered" (*BRMMLA* 26:127–35) very knowl-
edgeably maintains that this novel, when "reduced to its essence, . . .
emerges as a study of how love galvanizes Hyacinth into being and
how lovelessness destroys [him]."

Ronald Wallace's lengthy "Comic Form in *The Ambassadors*" (*Genre* 5:31–50) is an elaborate demonstration of the various ways comedy informs the structure of the novel, controls Strether's final vision of what he himself is, and predicts some directions the form will later take in such works as Forster's *Where Angels Fear to Tread* and Joyce's *Ulysses*. Albert A. Dunn in "The Articulation of Time in *The Ambassadors*" (*Criticism* 14:137–50) examines the novel in the light of its temporal and spatial perspectives *and* forms. Theme and method are thus seen to be one, providing such neat turnabouts as Strether's recognition at the end that his "old past" might well now become "his problematic future."

Three of the four articles on *The Wings of the Dove* are more or less conventional ones. The last is quite something else. Bill D. Mc-Dowell's "The Use of 'Everything' in *The Wings of the Dove*" (*XUS* 11,i:13–20) is another of those recent studies that trace the function of a single word throughout a particular work. Sister Stephanie Vin-cec's "A Significant Revision of *The Wings of the Dove*" (*RES* 23: 58–61) is a misnamed note on a factual correction James made in a revision of the novel, replacing a described statue of St. Mark with one of St. Theodore. And Milton Kornfeld's "Villainy and Responsi-bility in *The Wings of the Dove*" (*TSLL* 14:337–46) is a not very persuasive reading of the novel that defends Densher as finally em-bodying a kind of "heroism that can go beyond guilt toward mean-ingful and decisive action," possessing as he finally does a vision of that good that "can redeem evil." This leads Kornfeld into a much too harsh view of Kate, and, indeed, into a view of the novel as a whole that sees in it "a staunch form of optimism and human possi-bility in a world on the verge of dissolution."

But the arresting explication of the year is Robert C. McLean's "'Love by the Doctor's Direction': Disease and Death in *The Wings of the Dove*" (*PLL* 8sup.:128–48), a long, involved case emphasizing Milly's illness and death as the crux of the novel's action (as it is). He goes on to define her disease as "mental, not organic" and her death literally as a suicide, "most probably by leaping . . . from the balcony of the Palazzo Leporelli." He of course sees many ties be-tween Milly's death and the suicide of Constance Fenimore Woolson, between Milly and Alice James. Milly's illness is said to be a kind of hysteria growing out of sexual repression; she is said to be diabolic and crafty throughout, jealous, lustful, self-pitying, and pathological.

The dove, he concludes, "has practiced the wisdom of the serpent." At the time "of her Christmas death, her wings spread across a continent to hang heavy upon the man she loved and the rival she hated." Each reader will have to decide the merits of this view for himself. I can only suggest that it ultimately might well take a place in interpretations of this novel comparable to that held by John A. Clair's "*The American*: A Reinterpretation" (*PMLA* 74[1959]:613–18) as the most distinguished odd-ball interpretation of that earlier work.

Purdue University

7. Faulkner

Michael Millgate

Though the distribution of items naturally shifts from year to year, there is a discouraging sameness about each new crop of Faulkner books and articles. The particular phenomenon of four more articles on "A Rose for Emily" in 1972 is but an index of a general tendency to dwell on the familiar rather than venture into the unexplored, to engage with previous critics rather than with Faulkner himself, to launch into the analysis of individual works without first acquiring familiarity with the Faulkner canon as a whole, to make portentously and at length critical points which are already sufficiently familiar or self-evident. The need now is not for restatements and mild modifications of accepted critical commonplaces but for rigorous and detailed studies—drawing upon the widest possible range of interpretative, stylistic, textual, genetic, biographical and other approaches—not only of the best-known works but of those which remain virtually untreated, among them most of the earlier and later novels, most of the short stories and sketches, and almost all of the poetry and the non-fiction prose. Why go back over the too well-trodden ground of "A Rose for Emily" when so many really first-rate Faulkner stories deserve attention? Perhaps a moratorium should be declared on articles on "Emily" until we have at least an equal number on "Mountain Victory."

i. Bibliography, Editions, and Manuscripts

James B. Meriwether's "A Proposal for a CEAA Edition of William Faulkner," delivered as an address at a Toronto editorial conference in November 1969, has at last been published in *Editing Twentieth Century Texts* (Univ. of Toronto Press, pp. 12–27) edited by Frances G. Halpenny. It describes how a definitive Faulkner text might ideally be prepared, and suggests ways in which, given the copyright and other conditions actually prevailing at the present time, it should at least be possible to achieve "practicable" editions by completing and separately publishing the editorial *apparatus* for definitive texts, with corrections and emendations keyed to the best available commercial texts by the standard method of page-line references. Meriwether gives examples of specific problems involved in editing *Go Down, Moses*, and in a final footnote he records that the CEAA has subsequently agreed to award a seal to "An Approved Textual Apparatus" on the model of the seal already awarded to approved texts.

John Bassett's *William Faulkner: An Annotated Checklist of Criticism* (New York, David Lewis) sets out to provide a complete listing of Faulkner criticism in English (including books, articles, dissertations, and contemporary reviews) up to the beginning of 1972—a large ambition which has come respectably close to being achieved. The book has its weaknesses: its arrangement is occasionally irritating, its cross-referencing sometimes faulty, and there are, inevitably, points at which it falls short of comprehensiveness. But it is nonetheless much more complete and useful than any previous checklist and must be reckoned to have established itself as a necessary tool for the Faulkner critic and scholar for some time to come. Designed as a continuation of Maurice Beebe's checklist in the Spring 1967 issue of *MFS*, James Barlow Lloyd's "An Annotated Bibliography of William Faulkner, 1967–1970" (*UMSE* 12[1971]:1–57) has now been superseded by Bassett's much larger project. Lloyd does, however, include some foreign-language and other items which Bassett omits, and his summaries are generally longer.

A major event of 1972 was the first appearance of the full text of the important and, by Faulknerian standards, highly personal introduction written by Faulkner for a projected new edition of *The Sound and the Fury* which was announced by Random House in 1933 but never published. "An Introduction for *The Sound and the Fury*" (*SoR* 8:705–10) is edited by James B. Meriwether, who also supplies a rich historical commentary. See also the article by Carl Ficken listed under *Light in August*.

ii. Biography

The one major item is Thomas L. McHaney's "The Falkners and the Origin of Yoknapatawpha County: Some Corrections" (*MissQ* 25:

249–64). Offered as a corrective to common biographical errors about Faulkner and as a summary of "the salient facts about the Falkner family," the article meticulously sets out and documents a great deal of information about Faulkner's background, focusing especially on Colonel W. C. Falkner and his railroad and on the geographical "prototypes" of Jefferson and Yoknapatawpha County. McHaney's article listed under *The Wild Palms* is also of considerable biographical significance. Other articles contribute minor points of interest. In "William Faulkner—The Young Poet in Stark Young's *The Torches Flare*" (*AL* 43:647–49) Hubert McAlexander, Jr., points to resemblances in appearance and background between the young Faulkner and Eugene Oliver, a minor character in Young's novel of 1928, which had a setting apparently based on Oxford, Mississippi. Elmo Howell's "William Faulkner's Graveyard" (*NMW* 4:115–18) quotes and comments upon some of the inscriptions on tombstones (Faulkner's among them) in the Oxford cemetery, while in "Auntee Owned Two" (*SoR* 8:836–44) Faulkner's nephew Jim Faulkner recounts a family anecdote about the events which led to the erection in Oxford of two statues of Confederate soldiers, one on the university campus and the other on the town square. Glimpses of Faulkner in his later years are provided by Dorothy B. Commins, the widow of Faulkner's editor Saxe Commins, in "William Faulkner in Princeton" (*JHS* 2[1969]: 179–85) and by Ted Olson in "Faulkner and the Colossus of Maroussi" (*SAQ* 71:205–12). The latter contains recollections of Faulkner's visit to Athens in 1957 and particularly of an occasion when Faulkner, engaged in competitive tale-telling with George Katsimbalis (Henry Miller's "Colossus of Maroussi"), told as if it had happened to himself what sounds to this reviewer very much like a reworking of the unpublished and highly romanticized World War I flying story "With Caution and Dispatch," now among the Faulkner papers at the University of Virginia.

Of quite a different kind is Andrew H. Pfeiffer's "Eye of the Storm: The Observers' Image of the Man Who Was Faulkner" (*SoR* 8:763–73), an attempt to bring together the varying testimony at present available about Faulkner the man. Interesting enough as a reminder of what has been said, the essay suffers from its lack of curiosity about the sources cited (Robert Coughlan, for example, is described as Faulkner's "friend and neighbor") and its failure to attempt any assessment of their likely authenticity. Also to be listed here: Clayton

Robinson's "Memphis in Fiction: Rural Values in an Urban Setting" (*Myths and Realities*, pp. 29–38), which briefly summarizes the Memphis references in some of Faulkner's works; Redding S. Sugg, Jr.'s "John Faulkner's Vanishing South" (*AH* 22,iii[1971]:65–75), which reproduces in color, with brief commentaries, several of John Faulkner's "primitive" paintings, two of them illustrations to the work of his more famous brother.

iii. Criticism: General

a. **Books.** In *Faulkner's Women: Characterization and Meaning* (Deland, Fla., Everett/Edwards) Sally R. Page rightly emphasizes the individuality of Faulkner's female characters, too often dismissed as stereotypes. But while her study is suggestive, its overall effect is disappointing: too much space is devoted to conventional recapitulations of plots, characters, and themes; the concentration on particular figures tends to blur the complex interrelationships which may exist among several women characters within a single novel; and instead of the special perspective provoking new questions and insights, the analyses fall for the most part into familiar patterns. This last reservation must also be made about Michaela Ulich's *Perspektive und Erzählstruktur in William Faulkners Romanen von "The Sound and the Fury" bis "Intruder in the Dust"* (*BzJA* 34), a study of point of view in *The Sound and the Fury, As I Lay Dying, Absalom, Absalom!*, "The Bear" (in isolation from *Go Down, Moses*), and *Intruder* in terms of the approaches developed by such critics as Wayne Booth.

Several new books are only partly concerned with Faulkner. Louis D. Rubin, Jr., for example, has some brief observations in the course of the more general argument developed in *The Writer in the South: Studies in a Literary Community* (Athens, Univ. of Ga. Press), while Merrill Maguire Skaggs in *The Folk of Southern Fiction* (Athens, Univ. of Ga. Press) comments sensibly on such novels as *Absalom, Absalom!* and *The Hamlet*, in which Ratliff is seen as "the plain man as hero." In *Circles Without Center: Paths to the Discovery and Creation of Self in Modern Literature* (Cambridge, Harvard Univ. Press) Enrico Garzilli considers how the various narrators—and, indeed, readers—of *Absalom, Absalom!* pursue knowledge of themselves in their quest for the truth about Sutpen. His concern in *As I Lay Dying* is with "the relationship between the experience and the word," which he links with the problem of identity, but while his approach to both novels is interesting he seems ill at ease with detailed analysis, and the readings of quoted Faulkner passages sometimes seem highly arbitrary. In *The Thing Contained: Theory of the Tragic* (Bloomington, Ind. Univ. Press, 1970) Laurence Michel praises and attempts to define Faulkner's achievement as a tragic writer; though his overall argument seems oblique and inconclusive, the comments on particular novels, especially *Go Down, Moses*, are sometimes worthwhile. Also to be mentioned here are the appearance (New York, Frederick Ungar) of Eleanor Hochman's translation of Claude-Edmonde Magny's *The Age of the American Novel: The Film Aesthetic of Fiction Between the Wars*, first published in French in 1948, and the inclusion of previously published Faulkner essays in C. Hugh Holman, *The Roots of Southern Writing: Essays on the Literature of the American South* (Athens, Univ. of Ga. Press).

b. **Articles.**   Sorin Alexandrescu's "William Faulkner and the Greek Tragedy" (*RoR* 24,iii[1970]:102–10)—translated from his book, *William Faulkner* (see *ALS 1970*, p. 118)—pursues analogies between tragic aspects of Faulkner's writings and the patterns of Greek drama: in Faulkner's world, for example, a rigidly defined social hierarchy is seen as operating restrictively upon individuals in ways comparable to the controlling roles played by the gods in Greek tragedy. John M. Ditsky's concern in "Uprooted Trees: Dynasty and the Land in Faulkner's Novels" (*TSL* 17:151–58) is to insist that "the concept of dynastic establishment, especially as the saga of 'great families,'" figures less importantly in Faulkner's work than has sometimes been argued. Unfortunately, the article attempts too much in too brief a space and suffers from the inadequacy of its summarizing and discussion of any given work.

iv. Criticism: Special Studies

a. **Ideas, influences, intellectual background.**   J. Robert Barth, S.J., is the editor of *Religious Perspectives in Faulkner's Fiction: Yoknapatawpha and Beyond* (Notre Dame, Ind., Univ. of Notre Dame Press), a collection of essays, all but one of them previously published, which deal in one way or another with the presence of religious themes or images in Faulkner's work. Though it is good to be reminded of some of the individual essays, the volume as a whole seems not to add up to anything very substantial: the editor, in an introduction, an epilogue, and intercalated commentary, attempts to sustain a continuing line of inquiry and speculation but can claim little more at the end than that Faulkner's vision is "broadly religious." In *Kierkegaard and Faulkner: Modalities of Existence* (Baton Rouge, La. State Univ. Press) George C. Bedell explains that he has "sought to produce a kind of conceptual collage by juxtaposing the works of Søren Kierkegaard and William Faulkner and by interfering as little as possible with the new shapes that emerge." He does not suggest that Kierkegaard influenced Faulkner, but rather that Faulkner's characters will be "elucidated" by subjection to "the Kierkegaardian analysis." I am not competent to comment on the readings of Kierkegaard which emerge, but so far as Faulkner is concerned the approach seems unproductive, since the resulting discussions of *The Sound and the Fury, Sanctuary, Light in August, Pylon,* and *The Wild Palms* stay well within the bounds of the familiar.

Three papers on Faulkner and history were given at an SCMLA symposium in New Orleans in October 1971 and printed in a special supplement to *MissQ* 25. In "Faulkner and History" (pp. 3–14) Cleanth Brooks explores the dramatization of alternative attitudes towards history in such novels as *Absalom, Absalom!* and *Go Down, Moses* and concludes that Faulkner, who seems to have distrusted all abstract theories of human existence, had a sense of history which was fundamentally at odds with the characteristically American millennialist and gnostic enthusiasms. In "Faulkner's 'Mississippi'" (pp. 15–23) James B. Meriwether discusses Faulkner's use of historical material in terms of that "undeservedly neglected little masterpiece," the "Mississippi" essay published in *Holiday* magazine in 1954. Meriwether brings out the way in which the essay's intricate blend of fact and fiction makes it not only a self-portrait of the artist but a demonstration of the degree to which Faulkner's own fictional world had itself become historically factual: "his novels have as real an existence as do those battles which he lists in his essay." In the final paper, Michael Millgate's "'The Firmament of Man's History': Faulkner's Treatment of the Past" (pp. 25–35), Faulkner's concern in *Go Down, Moses* and *Absalom, Absalom!* is taken to be not so much with history as fact as with history as the stuff of legend and the object of interpretative effort. In *Requiem,* as to some extent in all the Yoknapatawpha novels, his aim in filling out the historical background of his characters and his county was "the realisation of his world on paper, in fiction, with all the fullness and absolute solidity it had long achieved in his imagination." A valuable essay on the same general topic is Ursula Brumm's "Forms and Functions of History in the Novels of William Faulkner" (*Archiv* 209:43–56), which notes that Faulkner habitually viewed history from the standpoint of the present and "personalized it into relation and reception," and that in making Ike McCaslin and Quentin Compson the "historical consciousness" of, respectively, *Go Down, Moses* and *Absalom, Absalom!* he achieved his deepest insights into the "reciprocal relationship between character and history" and especially into the way in which the activity of mind "converts the past into an imaginative present." Perhaps this is also the place to mention Lewis A. Lawson's essay on Faulkner in *The Politics*, pp. 278–95. Though Lawson is concerned rather with Faulkner's social attitudes in general than with his specifically political beliefs, he has brief but sensible comments on several of the major works and suggests that, because of Faulkner's willingness in his later years to sacrifice privacy in order to achieve direct expression of his beliefs, there is a sense in which "the most important character he created in the forties and fifties was his own."

In "A Housman Source in *The Sound and the Fury*" (*MFS* 18: 220–25) Joseph Brogunier usefully surveys what is at present known of A. E. Housman's influence on Faulkner, even while his specific assertion of a link between the Quentin-Caddy "suicide pact" and poem LIII of *A Shropshire Lad* appears rather unconvincing. Elmo Howell's "Faulkner and Scott and the Legacy of the Lost Cause" (*GaR* 26:314–25) opens with some valid comparisons between Scott and Faulkner, but the article as a whole seems chiefly concerned to berate the latter for his "errant attitude towards the Old South." Faulkner's own influence upon a later writer is discussed by Dean McWilliams in "William Faulkner and Michel Butor's Novel of Awareness" (*KRQ* 19:387–402), which offers some suggestive comments on Faulknerian techniques, especially in *Absalom, Absalom!*, to which Butor has acknowledged his indebtedness.

b. **Language and style.** Though it touches upon much else, the specifically Faulknerian content of M. E. Bradford's "Faulkner's Last

Words and 'The American Dilemma'" (*ModA* 16:77–82) consists of
a primarily rhetorical analysis of the last of Faulkner's speeches, made
before the American Academy of Arts and Letters. In "William
Faulkner: The Novelist as Oral Narrator" (*GaR* 26:183–209) Helen
Swink surveys the techniques by which Faulkner so often creates "an
illusion of 'voice,' . . . of an oral storyteller." It is a useful article, and
would have been far more so had fuller bibliographical references
been provided for its many allusions to previous criticism and to
Faulkner's own works.

c. Race. The potential usefulness of Charles D. Peavy's *Go Slow
Now: Faulkner and the Race Question* (Eugene, Univ. of Ore. Books,
1971) is indicated by its placing of Faulkner's non-fiction statements
on racial issues within their historical contexts. But those statements
themselves are not closely examined, the comments on Faulkner's
fiction are often simplistic and highly questionable (Gavin Stevens
is taken to be an authorial mouthpiece in *Intruder*, the racial complexities of *Go Down, Moses* are scarcely touched upon), the bibliography seems sadly outdated, and several relevant works by Faulkner
himself (e.g., *Sartoris* and *The Reivers*) are not even mentioned. All
in all, this must be judged a disappointing piece of work which fails
to make any substantial contribution to understanding its important
—and undeniably difficult—subject. In "Faulkner's Curse" (*ArQ* 28:
333–38) Walter Taylor attributes much too absolutely to Faulkner
himself an obsession with "the curse of slavery" which is more properly to be associated with his characters. Taylor also comes to the
surprising conclusion that Ike McCaslin transcends that curse to
become the first Faulkner "hero . . . who can in some degree solve the
personal problem of his own relationship to Negroes."

v. Individual Works to 1929

There was no article on *Soldiers' Pay*, and *Mosquitoes* was discussed
only by Glenn O. Carey in "Faulkner and *Mosquitoes*: Writing Himself and His Age" (*RS* 39[1971]:271–83), an article concerned chiefly
to summarize the objects of satire in the conversations between Fair-
child and Julius and to relate them, in rather aimless fashion, to
Faulkner's non-fiction statements on similar themes in the 1950s.

Sartoris provides the chief but by no means the exclusive subject of Walter R. McDonald's "Sartoris: The Dauntless Hero in Modern American Fiction," in *Modern American Fiction*, pp. 107–20. Apart from an insufficiently developed hint at the possibility of a highly critical valuation of Miss Jenny as a kind of priestess of violence, the comments specifically on *Sartoris* are not especially innovatory. In "Faulkner's Idiot Boy: The Source of a Simile in *Sartoris*" (*AL* 44: 474–76) Calvin S. Brown suggests that a phrase about "pipes blown drowsily by an idiot boy" may have derived from the figure of Will o' the Woods in a 1916 novel, *The House of Luck*, by Harris Dickson.

Apart from the printing of Faulkner's introduction (see section *i* above), the items devoted to *The Sound and the Fury* are all of minor importance. William E. Grant in "Benjy's Branch: Symbolic Method in Part I of *The Sound and the Fury*" (*TSLL* 13:705–10) insists upon the importance of "the paradoxical, as well as the obvious Christian implications" of the symbolism, particularly of ritual cleansing, which he identifies in the Benjy section and in the novel as a whole, while in "Quentin's Responsibility for Caddy's Downfall in Faulkner's *The Sound and the Fury*" (*NMW* 5:63–64) Jackson J. Benson argues—rather unexpectedly in view of his title—that Caddy's fate was her own responsibility and not Quentin's. William V. Davis's "*The Sound and the Fury*: A Note on Benjy's Name" (*SNNTS* 4:60–61) comments rather unilluminatingly on the Hebrew meanings of Benjamin; Michael Millgate's "Faulkner and Lanier: A Note on the Name Jason" (*MissQ* 25:349–50) briefly discusses Faulkner's possible awareness of a passage about a cotton-speculating Jason in Sidney Lanier's poem "Corn"; and Roger Ramsey's "Faulkner's *The Sound and the Fury*" (*Expl* 30:item 70) makes an unhelpful suggestion about the source of Benjy's capacity to "smell" death. See also under Brogunier in section *iv.a* above.

vi. Individual Works, 1930–1939

David M. Monaghan develops, in "The Single Narrator of *As I Lay Dying*" (*MFS* 18:213–20), an ingenious but highly tenuous argument which seems to raise just as many difficulties as it claims to resolve. His suggestion, briefly, is that Addie acts as the novel's ultimate narrator in that "the whole action is a product of Addie's conscious stream, liberated as it must inevitably be, from the limitations of time and place." In "The Old Testament Vision in *As I Lay Dying*," the new essay (pp. 107–16) in the collection edited by Barth (see section *iv.a* above), Philip C. Rule, S.J., points out some interesting Old Testament echoes and analogies but does little to enlarge understanding of the novel. A similar judgment must be made of Eulalyn W. Clark's "Ironic Effects of Multiple Perspective in *As I Lay Dying*" (*NMW* 5:15–28), a straightforward account of various ironic effects achieved by Faulkner's manipulation and juxtaposition of the novel's many points of view, and of Alan D. Perlis's "*As I Lay Dying* as a Study of Time" (*SDR* 10,i:103–10), which adds nothing of significance to Robert Hemenway's *MFS* article of 1970 (see *ALS 1970*, p. 123).

Gerald Langford's *Faulkner's Revision of "Sanctuary": A Collation of the Unrevised Galleys and the Published Book* (Austin, Univ. of Tex. Press) follows much the same pattern as his study of the manuscript of *Absalom, Absalom!* (see *ALS 1971*, pp. 115–16), and many of the faults of that earlier work unhappily persist: no account is taken of other pre-publication states of the text (e.g., the manuscript and the revised galleys), while the use of the 1962 reset edition for collation purposes ignores changes made since first publication (Langford seems unaware of James B. Meriwether's 1961 *PBSA* article on the text of *Sanctuary*). On the other hand, the volume does in effect make the unrevised galleys accessible to all students of Faulkner, and its introduction argues—interestingly but perhaps too strenuously—for the superiority, in many respects, of this version of the novel. In "The Last Scene of *Sanctuary*" (*MissQ* 25:351–55) Giliane Morell discusses various aspects of the novel's close, especially its setting and its relationship (more strongly emphasized in pre-publication versions) to the preceding scene, in which Popeye awaiting execution appears as bored and as concerned merely for his personal appearance as Temple sitting in the Luxembourg Gardens. Joanne V. Creighton's "Self-Destructive Evil in *Sanctuary*" (*TCL* 18:259–70) is loosely argued—Popeye's sexual incapacity is seen as rendering him automatically incapable of "any expression of love" and hence of "the choice of moral behavior"—and shows little familiarity with the accumulated criticism and scholarship on the novel.

In "The Opening Scene of William Faulkner's *Light in August*" (*Proof* 2:175–84) Carl Ficken considers evidence for revision of the very beginning of the novel which has been preserved in the two pages of printed text which constitute (together with a titlepage) the

salesman's dummy of *Light in August.* The article includes photographs of the binding and contents of the dummy, which is now at the
University of Virginia. The most interesting of the critical articles is
perhaps J. F. Kobler's "Lena Grove: Faulkner's 'Still Unravish'd Bride
of Quietness'" (*ArQ* 28:339-54): although it does not quite substantiate its case that the use of the "Ode on a Grecian Urn" in *Light
in August* constitutes a "startling and successful" exception to the
rule that Faulkner does not sustain symbolic patterns throughout a
whole novel, this is nonetheless an intelligent extension of the perceptions presented in Norman Holmes Pearson's *Shenandoah* essay
of 1952. In "Polarity and Paradox: Faulkner's *Light in August*" (*CEA*
34,ii:26-31) Jeff H. Campbell points out that Hightower provides
essential links in terms both of narrative and of imagery between the
contrasted stories of Lena Grove and Joe Christmas, and that as the
one "reflective consciousness" of the novel he indicates possible reso-
lutions of its ambiguities. Caroline Borden's "Characterization in
Faulkner's *Light in August*" (*L&I* 13:41-50) launches a savage if not
very coherent attack on Faulkner as "bourgeois propagandist" and
on this particular novel as an attempt to persuade American workers
to eschew class struggle and follow Lena Grove's passive example.
One's sympathy for the author's approach is not enhanced by the imprecision of her allusions: e.g., "Max McEachern and his wife adopt
Joe at the age of five and try to bring him up by the Bible and the
whip." M. Thomas Inge's "Faulknerian Light" (*NMW* 5:29) is a
simple reminder—should one still be needed—of what Faulkner himself said about the title of *Light in August* in *Faulkner in the University,* while "*Light in August*" *and the Critical Spectrum* (Belmont,
Calif., Wadsworth, 1971), edited by John B. Vickery and the late
Olga W. Vickery, is a useful if slightly unadventurous collection of
fifteen previously published articles or book chapters dealing with
the novel.

There were no articles on *Pylon* (see, however, under Bedell in
section *iv* above), but *Absalom, Absalom!* prompted several items,
most notably Elisabeth S. Muhlenfeld's "Shadows with Substance
and Ghosts Exhumed: The Women in *Absalom, Absalom!*" (*MissQ*
25:289-304), a careful and suggestive analysis of the novel's nine
female characters designed to bring out their intense individuality
and at the same time their common need to "communicate the simple
fact of [their] humanity." Frank R. Giordano, Jr., in "*Absalom, Ab-*

salom! as a Portrait of the Artist" (*From Irving to Steinbeck*, pp. 97–107) engages in a somewhat inconclusive discussion of Quentin as "the artist-hero in Faulkner's variant of the Künstlerroman," shaping the raw materials of the Sutpen story in his ivory tower of a Harvard room but failing to discover through his art the meaning and clarification to which he aspires. In "Flem Snopes and Thomas Sutpen: Two Versions of Respectability" (*DR* 51:559–70) Duane Edwards's initial perception of basic similarities between the careers and ambitions of Sutpen and Flem is valid enough, but the article as a whole becomes overextended and repetitious. More substantial if perhaps pursued a little too far is Thomas H. Adamowski's argument—in "Dombey and Son and Sutpen and Son" (*SNNTS* 4:378–89)—for the closeness of *Absalom, Absalom!* and *Dombey and Son* as critiques of "the depredations of extreme individualism" and for a possible influence of Dickens's novel on Faulkner's. Also concerned with influences are Beth B. Haury's "The Influence of Robinson Jeffers' 'Tamar' on *Absalom, Absalom!*" (*MissQ* 25:356–58), which suggests that Faulkner's handling of the novel's characterization is closer to Jeffers's poem in important ways than to 2 Samuel, and D. M. Monaghan's "Faulkner's *Absalom, Absalom!*" (*Expl* 31:item 28), which rather unpersuasively sees the episode in the novel in which Sutpen's sister is forced from the road by a carriage as "clearly derived" from an episode in *Oedipus Rex* in which King Laius's slaves and then the king himself try to beat Oedipus out of their way. It seems worth noting here that "The Manuscript of *Absalom, Absalom!*" (*MissQ* 25:359–67), Noel Polk's excellent essay-review of Langford's *Faulkner's Revision of "Absalom, Absalom!"*, contains some useful additional information about the manuscript itself.

The chapter (pp. 106–42) on *The Unvanquished* in Forrest L. Ingram, *Representative Short Story Cycles of the Twentieth Century* (The Hague, Mouton, 1971) argues for the seriousness and coherence of the book not as a "traditional" novel but as "a short story cycle" whose unity is that of "discrete pieces juxtaposed in such an order that the significances of each story deepen and expand as the reader moves from story to story." Some attention is given to the revisions made between magazine and book publication but in this as in other aspects of the study the initial promise of the approach is not in the end fulfilled.

Thomas L. McHaney's "Anderson, Hemingway, and Faulkner's

The Wild Palms" (*PMLA* 87:465–74) is an important article both
for the thoroughness and scope of its treatment of the novel itself
and—though its conclusions here are largely speculative—for Faulkner biography. Especially valuable is the light thrown on Faulkner's
relationships, personal and literary, with Sherwood Anderson and
Ernest Hemingway. Another significant contribution is Cleanth
Brooks's "The Tradition of Romantic Love and *The Wild Palms"*
(*MissQ* 25:265–87), an analysis of the relationship between Harry
Wilbourne and Charlotte Rittenmeyer in terms of the concept of romantic or chivalric love as defined by Denis de Rougemont in *Love
in the Western World*. The article incorporates an edited transcript of
a discussion in which various aspects of the novel are pursued further
by Cleanth Brooks himself and by several other participants, among
them Morse Peckham, James B. Meriwether, and Thomas L. Mc-
Haney. The miscellaneous comments in P. G. Rama Rao's "Faulkner's
Old Man: A Critique" (*IJAS* 1,iv[1971]:43–50) need not be sought
out, while Lewis A. Richards's "Sex under *The Wild Palms* and a Moral Question" (*ArQ* 28:326–32) is worth looking at only as a curious
throwback to the Faulkner criticism of an earlier day: its argument,
dependent upon serious misreadings of this and several other novels,
is that Faulkner's world is devoid of love and morality and, in particular, that his leading female characters "indulge in carnality illicit-
ly and shamelessly, while at the same time they lack sympathy, understanding, warmth, and decency."

vii. Individual Works, 1940–1949

No articles dealt primarily with *The Hamlet*. The Snopes trilogy as a
whole provoked only an unimportant article, P. P. Sharma's "The
Snopes Theme in Faulkner's Larger Context" (*IJAS* 1,iv[1971]:33–
41).

My reasons for disappointment in James Early's *The Making of
"Go Down, Moses"* (Dallas, So. Methodist Univ. Press) have been
set out in a review already published (*AL* 43[1973]:134–35): essentially, Early seems to me not to have tackled his subject in sufficient
depth or even with a sufficient sense of the stature and complexity of
Go Down, Moses itself. Precisely the same shortcoming characterizes
the second edition of *Bear, Man, and God: Eight Approaches to Wil-*

liam Faulkner's "The Bear" (New York, Random House, 1971), edited by Francis Lee Utley and others. The changes from the first (*Seven Approaches*) edition are considerable and generally for the better, but the volume still does a disservice to Faulkner and to students of his work by perpetuating the notion that it is possible to talk sensibly about the *Go Down, Moses* text of "The Bear" in isolation from *Go Down, Moses* as a whole. Viola Sachs, *Le Sacré et le profane: "The Bear" de William Faulkner* (Paris, Département Anglo-Américain, Université de Paris, 1971), is an analysis (in English) of parts 1, 2, 3, and 5 of "The Bear" carried out as a class project by twenty-eight French undergraduates: though it cannot really be recommended as a critical contribution, it has interest as a pedagogical exercise.

There are also several articles on *Go Down, Moses*, none of major significance. Though interesting for its quotations from the diary (published 1910) of a Mississippi plantation owner, Joseph Brogunier's "A Source for the Commissary Entries in *Go Down, Moses*" (*TSLL* 14:545–54) fails to offer convincing evidence of specific indebtedness on Faulkner's part. Lewis M. Dabney's " 'Was': Faulkner's Classic Comedy of the Frontier" (*SoR* 8:736–48) is an appreciative if not especially innovatory article which draws out the omnipresence of the hunt as action and theme and the affinities with traditional tall-tale patterns. Walter Taylor's "Faulkner's Pantaloon: The Negro Anomaly at the Heart of *Go Down, Moses*' (*AL* 44:430–44), on the other hand, attacks Faulkner for his "failure" to create in Rider, the central figure of "Pantaloon in Black," a character who will illustrate and justify the attitudes towards Negroes expressed by Ike McCaslin in part 4 of "The Bear": one has only to see Ike as something less than Faulkner's hero and spokesman for the entire argument of the article to seem irrelevant. A similar caveat needs to be entered in respect of the three remaining articles: Gorman Beauchamp's "The Rite of Initiation in Faulkner's 'The Bear' " (*ArQ* 28:319–25), which speaks of Ike's initiation as not simply an awakening to the existence of evil but as a specific formal ritual conforming to universal archetypal patterns; James Walter's "Expiation and History: Ike McCaslin and the Mystery of Providence" (*LaS* 10[1971]:263–73), which sees "Go Down, Moses," the novel's concluding section, as an essentially comic demonstration of "the agency of Providence in the working out of history" and hence as supportive of Ike's belief in an ultimate "redemption occurring in time"; and Walter R. McDonald's "Faulkner's 'The Bear': Part IV" (*CEA* 34,ii:31–32), an unimportant note on Hubert Beauchamp's "legacy" to his godson, Ike McCaslin.

In "Faulkner's Relationship to Gavin Stevens in *Intruder in the Dust*" (*DR* 52:449–57) David M. Monaghan argues—cogently, if at somewhat unnecessary length—that while Faulkner has some sympathy with Stevens's ideas, he nonetheless satirizes the lawyer's tendency to abstraction and his failure to apply his ideas in concrete situations. Philip J. Skerry in "*The Adventures of Huckleberry Finn* and *Intruder in the Dust*: Two Conflicting Myths of the American Experience" (*BSUF* 13,i:4–13) follows an even more elaborate and roundabout route to the assertion of valid but quite straightforward points of comparison and contrast between the two novels, Twain's tending towards repudiation of society, Faulkner's towards reintegration into society.

viii. Individual Works, 1950–1962

Requiem for a Nun provides the material for two articles, both of genuine interest. Noel Polk's "Faulkner's 'The Jail' and the Meaning of Cecilia Farmer" (*MissQ* 25:305–25) is a closely argued analysis of the three-part structure of the prologue to Act III of *Requiem* and of the way in which it moves towards the humanistic assertion implicit in the story of Cecilia Farmer, the frail girl who innocently ensures the preservation of her own memory and in so doing demonstrates "that what man can not, will not, 'relinquish,' is not his past: it is his sense of himself as a human being, his hopes for himself as an Individual, his terrible awareness of the basic, irresolvable *I*, immutable in history, which, despite all the anxieties of modern mass living, is still his commitment to life." Though one must surely question the final emphasis of Panthea Reid Broughton's "*Requiem for a Nun*: No Part in Rationality" (*SoR* 8:749–62)—that Faulkner achieves, most notably through Nancy, "a vision of transcendence inaccessible to the merely rational mind"—she offers a sensible reading at least of the narrative prologues and of the way in which they assign a positive valuation to those symbols (such as the courthouse) which serve to embody human dreams and bind men into communities.

Faulkner's last four novels attracted only three articles between them. Glenn O. Carey's "William Faulkner: Man's Fatal Vice" (*ArQ* 28:293–300) is a somewhat superficial consideration of Faulkner's treatment of war in his fiction, and particularly in *A Fable*: because the Corporal is viewed in wholly positive terms, Faulkner's ideas about the human predicament inevitably emerge as far more simplistic than they really are. There was nothing on *The Town*, but in "The Dilemma of the Human Heart in *The Mansion*" (*Renascence* 25:35–45) Joanne V. Creighton expresses more admiration for Linda Snopes —as one who "attests to the courage, dedication, involvement, and self-sacrifice needed to give substance to empty ideals"—than most critics have done. The emphasis is a useful one, although the article otherwise breaks little fresh ground. Finally, in "*The Reivers*: Readings in Social Psychology" (*MissQ* 25:327–37) Albert J. Devlin very interestingly argues that the central initiation experience of the novel does not occur in a sociological vacuum but is precisely and closely linked to changes within the structure of the Priest family and of society at large: "Lucius will achieve social maturity, but Faulkner implies that the process is shaped by impersonal forces. . . . One can almost speak of Lucius condemned to a promising future."

ix. The Stories

"A Rose for Emily" continues—exasperatingly and, it seems, ineluctably—to attract more attention than any other Faulkner short story. The most ambitious item this year, Norman N. Holland's "Fantasy and Defense in Faulkner's 'A Rose for Emily'" (*HSL* 4:1–35), develops an extended psychological analysis—bringing out what Holland sees as "the dominant unconscious mode of the story, the anal" —which then becomes the starting point for a more general discussion of the role of psychoanalysis in literary criticism. Though it is too long and too leisurely, Terry Heller's "The Telltale Hair: A Critical Study of William Faulkner's 'A Rose for Emily'" (*ArQ* 28:301–18) does offer useful observations on the technique of the story and on the way in which it focuses on the reactions of the town quite as much as on Miss Emily herself. Daniel R. Barnes, in "Faulkner's Miss Emily and Hawthorne's Old Maid" (*SSF* 9:373–77), points to some rather unremarkable similarities between Faulkner's story and Hawthorne's "The White Old Maid," while G. R. Wilson, Jr., in "The Chronology of Faulkner's 'A Rose for Emily' Again" (*NMW* 5:56,44,58–62), makes yet another vain attempt to force precision upon a time-scheme which Faulkner seems *not* to have worked out in detail.

In "Faulkner's 'That Evening Sun' and Mencken's 'Best Editorial Judgment'" (*AL* 43:649–54) Leo M. J. Manglaviti draws upon material—a typescript of the story and letters by both author and editor —now in the New York Public Library for a discussion of the ways in which Faulkner modified the story at H. L. Mencken's instigation before its publication in the *American Mercury*. Scottie Davis's "Faulkner's Nancy: Racial Implications in 'That Evening Sun'" (*NMW* 5:30–32) seems oddly titled in that it apparently seeks to argue that Nancy's fate is the consequence not of white racial attitudes but of her own weaknesses of character. More substantial is Robert W. Funk's "Satire and Existentialism in Faulkner's 'Red Leaves'" (*MissQ* 25:339–48), which sees the first three sections of the story as essentially satirical—working through the ridiculousness of the difficulties in which the Indians find themselves as a result of their adoption of slavery and other customs of the white man—and the subsequent narration of the Negro's flight as attaining almost mythic stature as a projection of man's universal "rage to live." Another worthwhile study, not least as an example of the kind of close scrutiny Faulkner's short stories urgently need but all too rarely receive, is François L. Pitavy's "A Forgotten Faulkner Story: 'Miss Zilphia Gant'" (*SSF* 9:131–42). It seems a pity, however, that in pursuing points of comparison with other Faulkner works, notably *Light in August*, Pitavy should have omitted to develop a really comprehensive analysis of the story itself. There is also a brief note by Bernard Knieger—"Faulkner's 'Mountain Victory,' 'Doctor Martino,' and 'There Was a Queen'" (*Expl* 30:item 45)—which simply quarrels with the plot summaries of these stories given in *Crowell's Handbook of Faulkner*.

University College, University of Toronto

8. Fitzgerald and Hemingway

Jackson R. Bryer

The two noteworthy characteristics of the year's work on Fitzgerald and Hemingway are a substantial drop in the number of pieces on Fitzgerald and a refreshingly large number of essays which focus on the texts themselves rather than using the fiction as a point of departure for excursions into speculations on biography, cultural history, and the like. Floyd C. Watkins's several excellent essays on Hemingway's style in his *The Flesh and the Word* are, hopefully, symptomatic of a turning directly to the writings of these two critically much abused authors. The reduction in material on Fitzgerald perhaps indicates a long overdue realization on the part of serious critics that his work simply does not and cannot support the volume of comment which it has received in the past twenty years. That much of the valuable work on Fitzgerald continues to be in the area of bibliography and texts—with the single most important publication on either writer in 1972 being Matthew J. Bruccoli's Fitzgerald bibliography—is a healthy sign, for this is where the needs are. And finally, as in 1971, much of the best work to be mentioned below appeared in the pages of the 1972 *Fitzgerald/Hemingway Annual*.

i. Bibliographical Work and Texts

Simply stated, Matthew J. Bruccoli's *F. Scott Fitzgerald: A Descriptive Bibliography* (Univ. of Pittsburgh Press) is surely the most significant piece of Fitzgerald research since Arthur Mizener's 1951 critical biography. While Mizener's book is certainly more readable, Bruccoli's may well be more indispensable. It is not only a volume which every student of Fitzgerald must own; it is a model for anyone planning a scholarly author bibliography. Even to anticipate the many ways in which it may prove useful is unfairly to suggest its limitations. It is the result of fifteen years' work as scholar, collector, compiler, and bibliographer; and its thoroughness is staggering. The volume is divided into nine major sections (covering such areas as full-length works by Fitzgerald; contributions by Fitzgerald to collections edited by others; first appearances of Fitzgerald pieces in magazines and newspapers; manuscript and typescript material by Fitzgerald quoted in auction, bookdealer, and library-exhibition catalogues; published interviews with Fitzgerald; dust jacket blurbs by Fitzgerald; and a bibliography of Zelda Fitzgerald's publications) and ten appendices. The latter include lists of Fitzgerald moviewriting assignments, Fitzgerald works available in Braille, facsimiles of Fitzgerald's book contracts, unpublished plays by Fitzgerald, mimeographed film scripts by Fitzgerald (with the locations of these noted), and unlocated clippings found in Fitzgerald's scrapbooks.

Such a rapid description of the book's contents, however insufficiently it covers the wealth of material made available, does suggest the wide range of Bruccoli's scholarly net and the incredible diligence with which he has pursued his task. Much new information is provided, and numerous textual problems in the study of Fitzgerald are here resolved. Finally, and perhaps most important, Bruccoli's work demonstrates that a bibliography can be far more than a dreary catalogue; it can clearly be creative scholarship, settling some issues and stimulating interest in others. It sets a standard which future scholars will find difficult to match; and it does for Fitzgerald studies what Audre Hanneman's definitive bibliography has done for Hemingway.

Bruccoli displays the same sort of thoroughness and scholarly expertise in " 'A Might Collation'—Animadversions on the Text of F. Scott Fitzgerald," in *Editing Twentieth Century Texts*, ed. Francess G. Halpenny (Univ. of Toronto Press). The focus here is on the highly corrupt texts of *The Great Gatsby* and *Tender Is the Night* now in wide circulation; and Bruccoli provides rather frightening collations of the major editions of both novels to show just how bad the available texts are. On a more modest scale, Robert P. Weeks in "Cleaning Up Hemingway" (*FHA 1972*:311–13) points out two typographical errors which have persisted through successive printings of "My Old Man" and "Fifty Grand." Both significantly alter the meaning.

Among the other textual pieces on Fitzgerald, Alan Margolies unearths Fitzgerald's plans for a prison play (*PBSA* 66:61–64) as disclosed in material available in the Princeton University Library;

and Jennifer McCabe Atkinson complains in convincing fashion about the text of Fitzgerald's story "Lo, the Poor Peacock" which appeared in the September 1971 issue of *Esquire* (*FHA 1972:* 283–85). Margolies also locates and describes three stories listed as lost by Atkinson in the 1971 *Annual* (*FHA 1972:335–36*); and the editors of the 1972 *Annual* present a special lyric which Fitzgerald wrote for a song from *Safety First!*, for a St. Paul friend, Ruth Sturtevant (pp. 19–23). The 1972 *Annual* also reprints Fitzgerald's 1923 list (pp. 67–68) of "10 Best Books I Have Read," which he compiled for the North American Newspaper Alliance; and a list of his own works which Fitzgerald sent in 1937 to scholar Fred B. Millett for the latter's use in his *Contemporary American Authors* (pp. 39–41). "F. Scott Fitzgerald's Copy of *Ulysses*" (*FHA 1972:5–7*) presents a facsimile of a note from Joyce to Fitzgerald and a list of the annotations Fitzgerald made in his copy of Joyce's novel (most of these consist of his identifications of the parodies in Chapter 14, "The Oxen of the Sun").

The enumerative checklists in the 1972 *Annual* are headed by extensive listings of the year's work in Fitzgerald (pp. 341–46) and Hemingway (pp. 347–67) studies. These are extremely full and detailed (although unannotated) compilations and include much very elusive material such as local newspaper articles. Briefer lists in the *Annual* are those by Linda Berry and Patricia Powell of Fitzgerald in translation (pp. 69–80); the editors' catalogue of Zelda Fitzgerald's paintings based on a 1934 exhibition (pp. 35–37); and C. E. Frazer Clark, Jr.'s checklist and notes on "Pre-Publication Printings of Hemingway" (pp. 195–206).

The only significant new Fitzgerald or Hemingway material to appear in 1972 is contained in *The Nick Adams Stories* (New York, Scribner's). This collection of twenty-four pieces is not only arranged in chronological sequence (previously the Nick Adams stories had appeared in various collections in jumbled sequence) but also includes eight new items. The latter vary in length, significance, and intention. Three are little more than vignettes; two are full stories; one is the opening of an unfinished novel; and two are fragments. But one of the fragments, "The Indians Moved Away," is a gem, while the longest piece, "The Last Good Country," is rather discursive and rambling. In the end, though, it is good to have all this material assembled in one volume. The only regret is that Philip Young, who apparently is responsible for putting the collection together, provides such a brief and superficial preface. Young has, however, done a detailed examination of the new collection in " 'Big World Out There': *The Nick Adams Stories*" (*Novel* 6:5–19), where he combines background information about their publication with a systematic analysis of the stories. Scribner's ought to include this essay in subsequent editions of the book.

ii. Letters and Biography

As further indication that additional Fitzgerald letters exist which should be published, Matthew J. Bruccoli and Jennifer M. Atkinson have edited *As Ever, Scott Fitz-:Letters Between F. Scott Fitzgerald and His Literary Agent, Harold Ober, 1919–1940* (Philadelphia, Lippincott). While this collection does not contain the kind of entertaining literary gossip and occasional literary criticism to be found in Fitzgerald's correspondence with Maxwell Perkins, it provides us with a picture of a man who probably played an even more important role in Fitzgerald's life than Perkins did. Harold Ober was Fitzgerald's only literary agent and, as the person responsible for marketing his writings to magazines, literally sustained the author. The collection centers squarely on money and on the difficulties inherent in being a professional writer in the '20s and '30s. It is, moreover, a meticulously edited volume. Bruccoli and Atkinson have somehow convinced a commercial publisher to print manuscript materials exactly as found—mistakes, typos, cross-outs, and all. Their footnotes and interlinear comments are, in themselves, an encyclopedic compendium of information about Fitzgerald's life and career. A dividend is the delightful reminiscence of Ober which Fitzgerald's daughter provides as a foreword.

Ring Around Max:The Correspondence of Ring Lardner and Max Perkins, edited by Clifford M. Caruthers (DeKalb, No. Ill. Univ. Press), contains much material about Fitzgerald, in Caruthers's foreword and in the texts of the letters themselves, and some about Hemingway. The 1972 *Annual* prints facsimiles of two letters—one (pp. 81–83) to Scribner's editor Roger Burlingame in 1925, thanking Burlingame for his praise of *Gatsby*; and the other, Edith Wharton's famous letter to Fitzgerald about *Gatsby* (pp. 85–87). More important than either of these is a Fitzgerald letter about the genesis of

"The Ice Palace," which originally appeared in a 1920 issue of the *Editor* and is reprinted by the editors of the 1972 *Annual* (pp. 59–60). Also of interest are R. L. Samsell's gathering of six letters Fitzgerald wrote to Hollywood producer Hunt Stromberg, with whom he worked on *Infidelity* and *The Women* (*FHA* 1972:9–18); and a previously unpublished note Fitzgerald wrote to publisher Bennett Cerf in 1932, supporting *Ulysses*, then the subject of a court case. The only letter materials related to Hemingway are two letters written by his mother to a friend (*FHA* 1972:301–02), of marginal interest only.

Biographical interest in both Fitzgerald and Hemingway continues to be strong, although this year there are only two largely biographical pieces on Fitzgerald, while there are several on Hemingway. Arthur Mizener's *Scott Fitzgerald and His World* (New York, Putnam's) does not, in its text, go much beyond the information already readily available; but it brings together a large number of photographs—of Fitzgerald, of places lived or visited, and of persons and places typical of the period about which Fitzgerald wrote—which give a unique flavor to the volume. Anthony Buttitta in "Scott: One More Emotion" (*FHA* 1972:25–34) reminisces about meeting Fitzgerald in Asheville, North Carolina, in 1935, at a time when Fitzgerald was very down on himself and very morose. It is a depressing but undoubtedly accurate portrait.

Coincidentally, three of the recent biographical books on Hemingway focus on his prowess as a fisherman. *Out Fishing with Hemingway* (Pocatello, Idaho State Univ. Press) is a charming thirty-three-page reminiscence by Norwegian Harald Grieg (here translated with a brief introduction by Charles H. Kegel) of a 1950 visit with Hemingway in Cuba. *Fishing with Hemingway and Glassell* by S. Kip Farrington (New York, McKay, 1971) is far less reminiscence and far more fishing lore. To be sure, there is considerable incidental information about Hemingway; but much of the book concerns fishing as a sport. More worthwhile for literary scholars is James McLendon's *Papa: Hemingway in Key West* (Miami, Fla., E. A. Seemann), which centers on the years 1928–1940. This is an entertainingly written yet informative book by a man who, unlike most of those who write Hemingway biography, never knew his subject. It provides some interesting side-glances at the writing of the twelve-year period with which it is concerned. It is also largely free of the adulatory tone which dominates so many biographical

books on Hemingway. The same cannot, unfortunately, be said for
Vernon (Jake) Klimo's and Will Oursler's *Hemingway and Jake: An
Extraordinary Friendship* (Garden City, N.Y., Doubleday). Although
again, the careful reader will find useful tidbits between the lines—
especially regarding Hemingway's opinions on other writers—the
hyperbolic and chatty nature of the book dominates.

Bertram D. Sarason's collection, *Hemingway and "The Sun" Set*
(Washington, NCR Microcard Eds.), is intended to be both biographical and critical; but its main effectiveness seems to be in the
biographical area; hence its inclusion here. The volume basically
brings together pieces which convincingly suggest that *The Sun Also
Rises* is a *roman à clef*. Editor Sarason's long introductory essay is a
fascinating and detailed description of his own efforts to track down
many of the real-life counterparts of Hemingway's characters and
establish beyond doubt their relationship to the events of the novel.
Part II of the book contains essays (several reprinted from the *Connecticut Review*) on and interviews with the persons whom Hemingway fictionalized. Part III consists of essays and other materials
relating to the novel (these are also mainly reprints and include
Fitzgerald's famous letter to Hemingway about the first draft of the
novel). This third section is somewhat more diffuse in its focus than
the first two; but the effect of the book as a whole is to show how
closely Hemingway did work with his real-life models. If at times
Sarason and his interviewers and interviewees show an unfair ani-
mosity towards Hemingway, who was, after all, writing fiction, it is
one of the ironies here that, despite their protestations, Hemingway
seems to have been more accurate in his portraits than they are.

Donald St. John, who contributes two of the interviews to Sarason's volume, continues his probing of the real-life basis of Hemingway's fiction in "Hemingway and Prudence" (*ConnR* 5, ii:78–84).
Here St. John's concern is with Petoskey, Michigan, where Hemingway spent his summers and which served as the setting for *The Tor-
rents of Spring* and six short stories. He tells of visiting places described in the novel and traces the history of Prudence Boulton, the
model for the Indian girl in "Ten Indians" and "Fathers and Sons."

In "The Importance of Knowing Ernest" (*Esquire* 77, 11:98–101,
164–70) nine persons who knew Hemingway—ranging from critics
Malcolm Cowley and Carlos Baker through journalists like A. E.
Hotchner, George Plimpton, and Lillian Ross to Truman Capote and

John and Mary Hemingway—are interviewed and comment on their impressions of him. The result is a fascinating kaleidoscope, for each person comments on the view of the person just prior to and just after him or her. One of the interesting conclusions to be drawn from this piece is that each person knew a different Hemingway.

The 1972 *Annual* contains three biographical pieces on Hemingway. The most important of these is the text of an MLA panel discussion on Hemingway in Oak Park, Italy, and Chicago (pp. 113–44). The panelists included three friends from Oak Park High School and two men who sailed on the S.S. *Chicago* with Hemingway in 1918; and their reminiscences are wonderfully informal and informative. Similarly unscholarly are Ralph Church's memories of Hemingway and Anderson in Paris (pp. 145–56) and translator Victor Llona's reminiscences of meetings with Hemingway (pp. 159–71).

More a combination of biography and criticism is Harold M. Hurwitz's excellent discussion of the Hemingway-Pound relationship in "Hemingway's Tutor, Ezra Pound" (*MFS* 17:469–82). Hurwitz begins by tracing in great detail the close and enduring friendship between the two writers, accounting for it on both literary ("Hemingway was looking for criticism and appreciation, and Ezra provided both") and non-literary grounds. He then deals extensively with Pound's literary influence on Hemingway, which he sees as most apparent in the early work which Pound helped to make "tighter and sharper" by "eliminating superfluous adjectives and adverbs and by tutoring him in techniques of economy and precision." Hurwitz also feels that Hemingway learned a great deal about rhythm and images from Pound and from Pound's poetry. Altogether, this is a well-researched and convincing essay on a subject often alluded to by earlier critics but never studied in such depth before.

iii. Criticism

a. **Collections.** Aside from Bertram D. Sarason's volume of materials relating to *The Sun Also Rises* discussed above, the only new collection on Hemingway and Fitzgerald is one which was published in 1971 but overlooked in last year's survey, John Graham's *Merrill Studies in "A Farewell to Arms"* (Columbus, O., Charles E. Merrill, 1971). Graham reprints reviews and essays and contributes a rather brief preface and a useful bibliography.

b. **Full-length studies.** There continues to be a dearth of worthwhile full-length works on Fitzgerald and Hemingway, no doubt because their writings have already provoked so much criticism and scholarship that relatively little ground is left uncovered. The result is that those books which do appear for the most part deal with either very limited aspects of their subject or approach the material from a very narrow or thesis-bound point of view.

This last is the major criticism to be made of the one full-length study of Fitzgerald published in 1972, John F. Callahan's *The Illusions of a Nation:Myth and History in the Novels of F. Scott Fitzgerald* (Urbana, Univ. of Ill. Press). Callahan continues a trend in Fitzgerald studies of recent years, seen most effectively in Milton R. Stern's *The Golden Moment* (1970), of dealing with the fiction in the context of the American experience. But where Stern stayed quite close to the writing, Callahan ranges far more into examining Fitzgerald's work in terms of what can only be seen as quasi-literary standards. An openly interdisciplinary study as its title implies, *The Illusions of a Nation* begins with the short-lived but representative presidential aspirations of Eugene McCarthy and proceeds to Fitzgerald, a "novelist who captured the complexity of the American idealist, the frailty of his historical and psychic awareness together with his 'willingness of the heart.'" An opening section on "The Creation of an American Mythos" places Fitzgerald in the context of the American experience, while succeeding chapters deal with *Gatsby* and *The Last Tycoon* (briefly) and with *Tender Is the Night* (for well over two-thirds of the book). There are valuable insights and helpful readings throughout; but Callahan's consideration of literature as history all too often neglects it as literature. The last sentence of the book makes clear just how far from the novels themselves Callahan's messianic political fervor has taken him: "For all their pain and loss his novels with their moral sympathy and historical intelligence put contemporary Americans in touch with ourselves and maybe even move us toward a society whose values, language, and politics will harmonize in democratic forms."

The four full-length books on Hemingway fall into two groups: two are quite general in their approach and two more narrow. To deal with the latter group first, Chaman Nahal's *The Narrative Pattern in Ernest Hemingway's Fiction* (Rutherford, N.J., Fairleigh Dickinson Univ. Press, 1971) is built around the thesis that Hem-

ingway's novels begin with the forward movement of the action—
one event leading naturally to another—but then they seem to relax
so that the forward movement comes to a pause. It is during this
pause, Nahal feels, that the "individual returns to a deep mystery
within himself through passivity" and makes himself ready for the
next move. Describing this pattern in terms of the human heartbeat—
"systolic, the active action, and diastolic, the passive action"—Nahal
works his way quite persuasively through the novels and the short
stories. While, as with any such thesis, there is an occasional show of
critical gymnastics in order to fit a particular work into the pattern,
Nahal does seem to have found a valid approach and his book is
valuable.

Of far less popular appeal and actually, as its title indicates, only
secondarily concerned with Hemingway is Christopher Rudston
Longyear's *Linguistically Determined Categories of Meaning—A
Comparative Analysis of Meaning in "The Snows of Kilimanjaro"*
(The Hague, Mouton, 1971). Longyear aims in his study "to find
evidence of correlation between *effect* on a reader of a literary work
of art on the one hand and, on the other, types of *meaning* employed
in the language out of which the literary document is constructed."
In pursuit of this goal, he compares the 1938 text of Hemingway's
short story with the 1950 German translation by Annemarie Horschitz-
Horst. Although the study which results contains some worthwhile
insights on Hemingway's style and themes, it is very difficult reading
and involves the non-specialist in a great deal of technical linguistic
terminology.

Of the two general studies of Hemingway, one, Carlos Baker's
Hemingway—The Writer as Artist (Princeton, N.J., Princeton Univ.
Press), is actually the revised fourth edition of one of the two or
three indispensable books on its subject. Baker indicates in his preface that approximately one-quarter of this volume is new material.
He has revised the two opening biographical chapters, incorporating
material discovered since the publication of his biography in 1969,
and has added separate chapters on *A Moveable Feast* and *Islands
in the Stream*. The first of these deals primarily with the circumstances
of the composition of *A Moveable Feast* and relates the sketches in
the book to the facts of Hemingway's relationships with the persons
he portrays. Baker concludes, "In spite of its value as a personal
record by a very well-known writer about the days when his career

was just getting started, and in spite, too, of the interest which such a memoir must always have for future generations, the question of the truth of Hemingway's report hovers over the whole book." The chapter on *Islands in the Stream* also gives a detailed and valuable history of the novel's composition—surely the last word on this subject—and then proceeds to a consideration of the autobiographical aspects of the hero, what Baker calls "the Narcissus principle," and to a careful explication of the various episodes and events in the book. This chapter stands as the best to date on this novel.

Arthur Waldhorn's *A Reader's Guide to Ernest Hemingway* (New York, Farrar, Straus and Giroux) is much more than its modest title suggests. Beginning with useful succinct chapters on the life, the major themes of the work, and the Hemingway style, Waldhorn then offers brief and sensible readings of all the major writings, with a chapter devoted to each book and separate ones on the Nick Adams stories, on Hemingway as journalist, poet, satirist, and dramatist, and on "The Snows of Kilimanjaro" and "The Short Happy Life of Francis Macomber." The book also includes a selective and judicious annotated bibliography, a listing of films based on Hemingway's work, a chronology of the Nick Adams stories, and a comparison of the contents of *in our time* (1924) and *In Our Time* (1925). While specialists may find some of Waldhorn's readings unoriginal, most readers will use the book as probably the best available general introduction to all of Hemingway's writing.

c. **General essays.** The trend, noted in last year's chapter, away from good general essays on Fitzgerald and Hemingway continues this year, with relatively few such pieces to be found. Two items deal with Hemingway's critical reception. Yuri Prizel in "Hemingway in Soviet Literary Criticism" (*AL* 44:445–56) summarizes and analyzes what Russian critics said about Hemingway from 1955 to 1970. He finds that they set him apart from other contemporary Western writers, connecting him with the realists; and they increasingly directed their attention away from the political side of his art and toward the aesthetic aspects of it. Prizel sees Hemingway's great popularity in the Soviet Union as attributable to his "powerful, fast-moving prose," his treatment of love, and his anti-fascism. This is a well-researched and important essay. Of less significance but interesting nonetheless is Frank M. Laurence's study of "Hollywood Publicity and Hemingway's Popular Reputation" (*JPC* 6:20–31). Laurence shows how Hollywood misrepresented Hemingway and his work by attributing "to his writing those qualities of entertainment that the mass audience most highly valued"; and thus played a large role in making him a cultural hero "even across the broadest stratum of American society."

W. J. Kimball's "Hemingway and the Code" (*Ventures* 6 [1970]: 18–23), a not very original piece, specializes in wordy clichés like the following: "The code hero . . . offers up and exemplifies certain principles of honor, courage and endurance which in a life of tension make a man a man, and enable him to conduct himself well in the losing battle that is life." In a much more provocative essay Leo Hamalian, writing on "Hemingway as Hunger Artist" (*LitR* 16:5–13), points out the prevalence in Hemingway's work of "gustatory images and scenes." This implies that "appetite was for Hemingway something more than itself, that Hemingway attached a metaphysical meaning to the act of breaking bread and taking wine." Hamalian defines the meaning thus: "the act of appeasing the appetite is a way of knowing the self and those with whom hunger is consummated. The place where it is consummated assumes a special significance; it becomes a place of security in the middle of the darkness, a kind of altar towards which men turn instinctively for such consolation as faltering human communication can offer." Hamalian then convincingly traces this motif through eleven of Hemingway's major short stories.

There are two other essays on the short stories, both refreshingly close to the texts and both quite original. In "The Structure of Hemingway's Short Stories" (*FHA* 1972:173–93) Sheldon Norman Grebstein defines two dominant and recurring structural designs: a design based upon the movement from outside to inside or vice versa; and a pattern which uses a movement toward and away from a place or destination. Grebstein traces the first of these through "The Doctor and the Doctor's Wife," "Che Ti Dice La Patria?", and "A Day's Wait"; and discusses the second one in "Indian Camp," "A Way You'll Never Be," and *The Old Man and the Sea*. Approaching Hemingway's fiction in this way, Grebstein feels, answers the persistent complaint that it is "narrow in range and intellectually thin," because "the very structure or pattern of Hemingway's stories comprises a form of thought, perhaps for an artist the most cogent kind: form *as* thought."

B. A. Hauger focuses on another structural feature in "First Person Perspective in Four Hemingway Stories" (*Rendezvous* 6,i[1971]: 29–38). Noting that, unlike other writers who use first-person narrative as a means of explaining character motivation, Hemingway does so to emphasize theme, Hauger examines "My Old Man," "Fifty Grand," "Now I Lay Me," and "An Alpine Idyll" in detail. This is a well-written and well-thought-out piece of analysis.

One of the two general essays on Fitzgerald, Ruth Prigozy's "Gatsby's Guest List and Fitzgerald's Technique of Naming" (*FHA 1972*: 99–112), extends study of this technique to its use in Fitzgerald's other fiction. Prigozy finds that he first used the catalog of names in "Bernice Bobs Her Hair" (1920) to describe a young crowd at a country-club dance, used it again in *The Beautiful and Damned* (1922) in the list of suitors Gloria records in her diary, and then used it in *Tender Is the Night* (1934) when he listed tourists on the Riviera. Claiming that Fitzgerald "used names throughout his literary career as a major fictional device to direct and control the reader's response to character and action," Prigozy then glances at the individual names in the fiction, pointing out how often a character's name is suggestive of the author's attitude towards him. Her conclusion, that "names in Fitzgerald's novels and stories often serve as compressed yet acute analyses of social class and caste, cameo studies of shades and nuances in the manners and morals of his fictional social world," seems indisputable, based on the careful and detailed amassing of evidence which precedes it.

Alan Casty's "'I and It' in the Stories of F. Scott Fitzgerald" (*SSF* 9:47–58) uses the existential psychology and ethics of Sartre and Martin Buber as "a valuable perspective from which to view Fitzgerald's insights into the problems of self-recognition and fulfillment." Casty defines Buber's concept of the "I and It" as one in which one person "lets the other exist only as his own experience, only as a part of himself," that is, another person becomes an object, a thing, an It to be used. This concept is then applied to the short stories, with specific discussions of "May Day," "Absolution," "The Diamond as Big as the Ritz," "Winter Dreams," "The Bridal Party," "Basil and Cleopatra," "A Woman with a Past," "The Rich Boy," "Babylon Revisited," "Crazy Sunday," and "Outside the Cabinet Makers." Casty's essay is as convincing as it is original.

d. Essays on specific works: Fitzgerald. Even more than in past years, *Gatsby* receives the lion's share of the critical attention given to specific Fitzgerald fiction. Katherine B. Trower in "Visions of Paradise in *The Great Gatsby*" (*Renascence* 25:14–23) attempts "to uncover the flaws inherent in Gatsby's idea of the terrestrial paradise and in his dream of Daisy, rather than to emphasize his lack of self-knowledge, even though this latter limitation contributes to his downfall and to that of his dream." Gatsby's mistake, Trower contends, is in trying to translate his dream into reality. Although much of this seems obvious, the essay is nonetheless clearly and sensibly written.

More original in its approach is David Stouck's "White Sheep on Fifth Avenue: *The Great Gatsby* as Pastoral" (*Genre* 4[1971]:335–47). Stouck contends that it is through a sense of the pastoral that the true dialectic of the novel comes into focus, because there is an imaginative identity between Gatsby and Nick based on the facts that "their struggle derives from the same imaginative source and that their actions represent two alternative responses to what is at bottom the same dilemma." Thus, it is Gatsby's choice "to pursue the pastoral dream and attempt the impossible by giving it flesh and blood form"; while Nick "recognizes the truth of the American adage, 'you can't go home again,' and withdraws from the self-destructive holocaust at the end."

Laurence E. MacPhee examines the automobile motif in the novel as it applies to Jordan Baker, in "*The Great Gatsby's* 'Romance of Motoring': Nick Carraway and Jordan Baker" (*MFS* 18:207–12). In a piece which is ingenious and convincing, MacPhee sees Jordan as embodying the type of disorder and disarray which the automobile symbolizes in the novel and points to the fact that her name is compounded from two of the best-known trade names in motoring—the Jordan "Playboy" and Baker "Fastex" Velvet, a luxury upholstery fabric for automobiles. He then quotes the advertisements for both products, noting several fascinating links with the novel—the persistent use of golfers in the ads for the Jordan "Playboy," for example.

While Kermit W. Moyer's "*The Great Gatsby*: Fitzgerald's Meditation on American History" (*FHA* 1972: 43–57) begins with the intention of "a reading of the novel which clearly articulates the way Fitzgerald has worked out his historical theme," it contains a goodly number of close readings touching on a variety of aspects of the book. Among these are the images of circularity and the technique of circularity employed, the persistent flower metaphor which "reveals the essential materiality at the core of Gatsby's transcendentalism," and, most central to Moyer's thesis, the basic opposition in the novel between materiality and transcendental vision. Moyer does an effective job of relating characters and scenes in *Gatsby* to one or the other of these two forces.

In two brief notes in the 1972 *Annual*, Edward Stone (pp. 315–16) and Robert Emmet Long (pp. 307–09) deal with the guest list and "The Allusion to Gilda Gray" in the novel, respectively. Stone sees connections between the guest list and passages in *The Aspern Papers* and *Look Homeward, Angel*. Long claims that the mention of Gilda Gray "supplies a connection between the mislocations of value and deceptions of Gatsby and those of his age."

There are, as in past years, several influence studies and essays linking *Gatsby* with other works without a specific claim of influence. In "An Epistle to Gatsby: On the Use of Riches" (*FHA 1972*:61–65) Harry Williams compares the novel to Pope's two *Moral Epistles* on riches, finding "a strikingly similar approach . . . to the use of money, to the user, and to the inherent moral question and its inevitable resurrection in terms of nature, society, and the individual." For both Fitzgerald and Pope, Williams contends, "paper credit is the source of society's ills, or simply the source of its waste." George Monteiro (*FHA 1972*:291–94) sees *Gatsby* "in the broadest sense" as "an ironic version" of Keats's "The Eve of St. Agnes" and focuses on a comparison of two scenes: Gatsby's display of his shirts for Daisy and the rich feast of "cates and dainties" with which Porphyro courts Madeline.

Joseph Brogunier's suggestion in "An Incident in *The Great Gatsby* and *Huckleberry Finn*" (*MTJ* 16,ii:1–3), that the scene in Fitzgerald's novel in which Nick passes the spot where Myrtle Wilson died and imagines a crowd gathered there derives from the Colonel Sherburn episode in Twain's novel, seems far-fetched. D. B. Graham is on firmer ground when he links the Valley of Ashes passage to a description at the beginning of Chapter 16 of *Vandover and the Brute* in which Frank Norris describes the "blighted urban landscape" of San Francisco (*FHA 1972*:303–06). James Ellis adds to the controversy regarding the reference to the "Stoddard lectures" in *Gatsby* by suggesting that it is not Theodore Lothrop Stoddard who is referred to but John Lawson Stoddard whose "stereoptically illustrated travelogues of primarily European cities" were very popular in the late nineteenth century (*AL* 44:470–71). Finally, Robert Emmet Long (*FHA* 1972:325–28) looks forward rather than backward by linking Gatsby with Jay Livingston in Louis Auchincloss's *A World of Profit* (1968) and George Dethriffe in C. D. B. Bryan's *The Great De-thriffe* (1970).

There are two 1972 essays on *Tender Is the Night*. In much the better of the two, John Stark (*FHA* 1972:89–95) does a stylistic analysis of the three opening paragraphs of the 1934 edition, considering such elements as sound, adjectives, imagery, allusiveness, and sentence and paragraph construction. Stark's detailed explication lends credibility to his conclusion: "It is possible to deduce from Fitzgerald's style his method of organizing experience, which is perhaps the most important thing that style can reveal." We need more studies of style in Fitzgerald, and Stark's piece is a good, albeit brief, model. The other essay on *Tender Is the Night*, Takashi Tasaka's "The Ethic and Aesthetic Aspects in *Tender Is the Night*" (*Studies in American Literature* [Chu-Shikoku American Literature Society] 8:15–21), offers little that is new, and it is confusingly written.

e. **Essays on specific works: Hemingway.** *The Sun Also Rises* dominates discussions of specific Hemingway works this year, with seven pieces. Three of these appear in the 1972 *Annual*. In "Hemingway, Money and *The Sun Also Rises*" (pp. 257–67) Richard P. Sugg deals with the same motif as is covered by Scott Donaldson (see *ALS 1971*, pp. 136–37) Starting with the premise that "Man's varied relationships with and participation in a life grounded in the senses is the subject of the novel, and money is a major symbol of both the literal and spiritual dimensions of the relationship," Sugg suggests that money imagery indicates character—"all of the people in the book are revealed by their relationship to money and their consciousness of what constitutes 'your money's worth.' " But, more importantly for Sugg, money also symbolizes the "exchange of values" on all levels of human action.

Carole Gottlieb Vopat (*FHA* 1972:245–55) in "The End of *The Sun Also Rises*: A New Beginning" provides an excellent discussion of the changes she sees in Jake's personality through the novel, changes which she feels are "summed up concisely and symbolically in the final pages of Book III." She examines these pages in great detail and makes a very convincing case. Similarly careful is Gerald T. Gordon's study of "Hemingway's Wilson-Harris: The Search for Values" (*FHA 1972*:237–44). A character pretty much ignored by previous critics, Wilson-Harris is seen by Gordon as a complement to Jake and Bill who is constantly being "tested for 'code' values." Further, "he serves to express the fact that the code can be attained by anyone, if he simply gives of himself, takes a chance, and periodically removes himself from work and responsibilities." As with both the other 1972 *Annual* essays on *Sun*, this one presents a concise and persuasive close reading of the text.

Linda W. Wagner also works closely with the text of the novel in "*The Sun Also Rises*: One Debt to Imagism" (*JNT* 2:88–98). Drawing upon her extensive knowledge of Imagist poetry, Wagner makes an eloquent and convincing case for Hemingway's debt to Pound and Imagism, a debt which she sees as most clearly evident in this novel: "In using the methods of suggestion, compression, and speed within the outlines of traditional novel form, Hemingway achieved a lyric evocation of one segment of life in the 1920's." Wagner uses a very effective technique in the essay: she examines several passages from the novel and she prefaces each such examination with an Imagist axiom which that passage follows, such as "Compose in the sequence of the musical phrase, not that of the metronome," or "Go in fear of abstractions."

Floyd C. Watkins's recent study *The Flesh and the Word* (Nashville, Tenn., Vanderbilt Univ. Press, 1971) contains several valuable chapters on Hemingway's style. Among these is one on *The Sun Also Rises* (pp. 95–108) which begins by contrasting the splendid rhetoric of Milton's Satan and Shakespeare's Lear with the non-rhetoric of Jake Barnes. "Exalted rhetoric in Hemingway's novel would be inappropriate by its very nature," Watkins points out, because the modern tragic hero "knows not why or by what rules he has fallen," and thus Hemingway's unique style "is an almost perfect vehicle to express the futility of those who have discovered the failure of meaning and language." In this connection, Watkins argues for the overworked influence of *The Waste Land* on Hemingway's novel.

In one of the two brief notes on the novel, David M. Andersen's "Basque Wine, Arkansas Chawin' Tobacco: Landscape, and Ritual in Ernest Hemingway and Mark Twain" (*MTJ* 16,i:3–7), argues, with neither a great deal of persuasiveness nor much significance, that the two wine-sharing scenes in Hemingway's novel can be compared with the "tobacco chawin'" scene in *Huckleberry Finn*. The other note, J. M. Linebarger's "Symbolic Hats in *The Sun Also Rises*" (*FHA* 1972:323–24), focuses intriguingly on Brett's hat as a "symbol of assumed masculinity" illustrating "her unladylike desire to dominate men" and traces mentions of that hat through the novel.

Of the five pieces on *For Whom the Bell Tolls*, the most worthwhile is Robert O. Stephens's "Language Magic and Reality in *For Whom the Bell Tolls*" (*Criticism* 14:151–64). Stephens sees Hemingway's characters as "concerned, even obsessed, with language magic —with the tendency to presume necessary connections between words and things or actions and to assume control over events and feelings by the power of words." Robert Jordan, through Hemingway's use of mythic language, tries to "realize the action in terms of words and by this act to reconceive his world." This is a complex essay to follow, but it rewards careful reading.

Colin S. Cass and Michael J. B. Allen center their attention on two other patterns in the novel. Cass's concern (*FHA* 1972:225–35) is with the love story. He feels that, unlike in *A Farewell to Arms*, "idyllic love" in *For Whom the Bell Tolls* "becomes an adequate counter-balance to war." Both love and war, Cass argues effectively, "contribute to the definition of Jordan as a complete man, without ignoring or contradicting one another." Allen's "The Unspanish War in *For Whom the Bell Tolls*" (*ConL* 13:204–12) deals with what he calls the "metaphysical violence" in the novel, which goes beyond the "historical violence" of the Spanish Civil War. Hemingway uses war symbolically, "as a frame or correlative, for the inner crisis that springs from the recognition of the self, its existence and its annihilation." Thus, according to Allen, the Spanish war becomes "the experience of total violence encompassing the self . . . the recurring ordeal that each individual must undergo in order to 'die well' and paradoxically to attain a sense of what it means to 'live well.'" At times Allen seems to be stating the obvious, but his argument is clearly stated.

Like his section on *The Sun Also Rises*, Floyd C. Watkins's discussion of *For Whom the Bell Tolls* in his *The Flesh and the Word* is an absorbing study of style. Watkins sees Hemingway's problem in the novel to have been "the finding of a style in which to embody the theme of universal brotherhood and of the supremacy of mankind over the individual." The results are uneven, Watkins claims plausibly, because "the style and the language are not great enough to indicate the depth of the theme and the tragedy. The book is often sentimental and shallow in its failure to find images and languages for its great theme."

Paul Delaney's note on "Robert Jordan's 'Real Absinthe' in *For Whom the Bell Tolls*" (*FHA 1972*:317–20) looks at the symbolic use of drink in the novel. Specifically, Delaney is concerned with how Jordan's fondness for "real absinthe" sets him apart from the other characters.

Floyd Watkins continues his discussion of style and meaning, this time with respect to *A Farewell to Arms*, in "World Pessimism and Personal Cheeriness in *A Farewell to Arms*" (*The Flesh and the Word*, pp. 109–26). Watkins finds that this novel presents the ideal conjunction of style and meaning: "style and the major subjects of the novel (war, love, religion) form an almost perfect harmony in the rejection of the general and vague and the acceptance of only the particular, the things of the senses, the knowable."

Forrest D. Robinson's "Frederick Henry: The Hemingway Hero as Storyteller" (*CEA* 34,iv:13–16) deals, as its title suggests, with Frederick Henry as the first-person narrator of the novel, who, contrary to what previous critics have assumed as the passive protagonist figure, is in reality an active force through his reenactment of the action. He resolves a conflict through his role of storyteller. Robinson's essay is really too brief to be able to make a convincing case.

In a carefully argued essay on *The Old Man and the Sea*, John Bowen Hamilton (*Renascence* 24:141–54) considers the fish as the "organic, symbolic center" of the novel. Hamilton feels that Hemingway's answer to *nada* can be seen in this novel "in the tragedy of an old man who almost unknowing discovered in a great fish the great paradox of suffering and grace; who, enduring almost intolerable pain, experienced the awe, the mystery of existence in a few moments of insight into the loneliness of the hostile forces in a cruel and unyielding ocean." Floyd C. Watkins (*The Flesh and the Word*, pp. 152–66) considers *The Old Man and the Sea* as the single exception in Hemingway's decline because it is a return to the style of his early works. "Style, not situation," Watkins argues, "is the difference between the good novels and the bad ones, the early and the late."

Watkins also has an excellent discussion of Hemingway's non-fiction (pp. 127–36). Focusing primarily on *Death in the Afternoon* and *Green Hills of Africa*, he offers the view that Hemingway's style in his non-fiction of the 1930s represents a dramatic contrast with and falling-off from the careful writing of his earlier fictional works. This falling-off has further significance because "it anticipates a fundamental change in the fiction" which is made manifest in *For Whom the Bell Tolls* and *To Have and Have Not*.

There is the usual year's supply of explications of the short stories. Most of these are superficial, dealing, as they invariably do, with an image pattern or an influence or a source. Such studies have a certain kind of interest; they often satisfy our need for rational ordering of fiction or for an explanation of where an author gets his ideas. But they seldom offer major illumination of the writing itself. So we get pieces like Michael S. Reynolds's "Two Hemingway Sources for *In Our Time*" (*SSF* 9:81–86), which gives detailed descriptions of two actual incidents which may or may not lie behind two chapters of Hemingway's book. The results are convincing, albeit not very startling or helpful to readers of the fiction.

Of the four essays on "The Short Happy Life of Francis Macomber," the most worthwhile is Anne Greco's "Margot Macomber: 'Bitch Goddess' Exonerated" (*FHA* 1972:273–80). Greco does a good job of proving her thesis that "Margot Macomber is not the destructive 'bitch goddess' who shatters her husband's manhood and then intentionally cuts short his newly found life. On the contrary, . . . her verbal attacks are an attempt to force her husband into recognizing his disgrace so that he might work out some means of atonement." In three short notes on the story, J. F. Peirce (*SCB* 32:230–32), Allen Shepherd (*FHA* 1972:297–99), and J. F. Kobler (*FHA* 1972:295–96) deal respectively with the car as a symbol in the story, Hemingway's sudden shift into the mind of the lion, and "shit" as the word Wilson has in mind when he calls Francis a "four-letter man."

James Twitchell's "The Swamp in Hemingway's 'Big Two-Hearted River'" (*SSF* 9:275–76) offers the intriguing suggestion that there is no swamp in the story—"at least not outside the imagination or

memory of Nick Adams." Twitchell supports this opinion by noting
that what Nick says about the swamp is not characteristic of a swamp,
especially in the Michigan woods. But, in a good example of the ir-
responsibility often found in pieces such as this, Twitchell offers no
speculation as to why the imaginary swamp appears in the story.

In a far more plausible and full reassessment of a Hemingway
story, Scott MacDonald in "Implications of Narrative Perspective in
Hemingway's 'The Undefeated'" (*JNT* 2:1–15) feels that the few
previous critics of the story have distorted its thematic emphasis.
MacDonald's major point is that Zurito, not Manuel, is the true hero;
for at the end, "While Manuel lies on the table, defeated as a matador
and stubbornly unwilling to admit the truth about himself, Zurito
stands above him, victorious both as a picador and as a man, unbowed
and undefeated in every way." In proving this thesis, MacDonald
carefully and convincingly makes his way through the text, showing
how subtle shifts in narrative perspective reveal Manuel's true status. This is the best 1972 essay on a Hemingway short story.

George Monteiro's essay on "God Rest You Merry, Gentlemen,"
"Hemingway's Christmas Carol" (*FHA* 1972:207–13), sees a triple
focus in the story: the story of a "God-ridden boy in extremis"; two
surgeons' personal and professional conflicts; and—directly—the narrator's story. He also notes the Biblical allusions and the various attitudes towards Christianity expressed in the story. His conclusion is
that "having built his story around perspectives, Hemingway fails to
weld the narrator's to the others" and that the structure of the story
"sets up expectations that are not satisfactorily fulfilled."

As a footnote to Emily Stipes Watts's 1971 book on Hemingway
and the arts, Barbara S. Groseclose in "Hemingway's 'The Revolution-
ist': An Aid to Interpretation" (*MFS* 17:565–70) interprets the story
through "an analysis of the details relating to trecento and quattro-
cento painters, particularly Andrea Mantegna." Hemingway's use of
Mantegna and the painters with whom he is contrasted exemplifies
the theme of "optimism (which is the affirmation of immortality in
the Christian religion and the belief in a continuing world revolution in Marxism)" as opposed to "skepticism and cynicism." This
opposition is personified in the figures of the youth and the narrator.

Finally, in "A Note on 'One Reader Writes'" (*FHA* 1972:329–
31) Mark Edelson offers a detailed brief explication of this little-
studied story.

f. **Foreign criticism.** Foreign comment on Hemingway continues steadily, while Fitzgerald continues to be almost completely ignored by foreign critics. Tamara Denysova's *Ernest Hemingway: Žyttja i tvorčist* (Kiev, Dnipro) is apparently the first Ukrainian monograph on Hemingway. We also have *Hemingway Tempo, Vida e Obra* by Otto M. Carpeaux (Rio de Janiero, Bruguera, 1971), a volume in Portuguese; *Hemingway-Geijitsu to Byori* (Tokyo, Kongo Shuppan), by Komao Ito; and Georges Bonneville's *Pour qui sonne le glas* (Paris, Hatier, 1970), a study guide to *For Whom the Bell Tolls* in French. Among the many shorter pieces on Hemingway are these: A. M. Vásquez-Bigi, "Introducción al estudio de la influencia barojiano en Hemingway y Dos Passos" (*CHA* 265–67:169–203); N. Anastas'ev, "Posle legendy" (*VLit* 16,i:119–34); Ángel Capellán, "El ciclo vital del héroe hemingweiano" (*Arbor* 318:31–57); Fujio Nakano, "E. Hemingway and His Nihilism" (*HSELL* 18,ii:35–49) in Japanese; Christian W. Thomsen, "Liebe und Tod in Hemingways *Across the River and Into the Trees*" (*NS* 20[1970]:665–74); Friedhelm Güntert, "Zum Thema der Kreuzigung in Hemingways Einakter 'To-day Is Friday!' " (*NS* 21:538–43); Klaus-Dieter Gottschalk, "Verkehrte Welt in Hemingway's 'The Doctor and the Doctor's Wife' " (*NS* 21:285–93); and Owen J. Miller, "Camus et Hemingway: pour une évaluation méthodologique" (*RLM* 264–70[1971]:9–42).

g. **Dissertations.** Graduate research interest in Fitzgerald and Hemingway waned somewhat in 1972, after 1971's all-time high level. Of the four dissertations on Fitzgerald, James L. W. West III's "Materials for an Established Text of F. Scott Fitzgerald's *This Side of Paradise* (*DAI* 32:5754A–55A) breaks significant new ground and will, hopefully, be published—in part or in full. The three other Fitzgerald dissertations, while they do not excite the interest of West's, seem to be opening new areas as well. They are Thomas K. Bloom, "The Style of F. Scott Fitzgerald" (*DAI* 33:746A), Dan E. Bronson, "Vision and Revision: A Genetic Study of Scott Fitzgerald's Short Fiction with Some Excursions into His Novels" (*DAI* 33:2362A), and John B. Durrell, "The Other Side of Paradise" (*DAI* 32:5784A–85A). Durrell's rather vaguely titled study deals with Fitzgerald's attempts at "formal tragedy."

The three Hemingway dissertations seem rather less promising of future original scholarship: Charles W. Dunn, Jr., "Ironic Vision in

Hemingway's Short Stories" (*DAI* 32:5225A), John A. Shtogren, Jr., "Ernest Hemingway's Aesthetic Use of Journalism in His First Decade of Fiction" (*DAI* 32:6454A–55A), and Glen J. Wiese, "Moral Vision in Hemingway's Fiction" (*DAI* 32:5811A).

University of Maryland

    This chapter could not have been completed without the research assistance of Joanne Giza and a summer grant from the General Research Board of the University of Maryland.

Part II

9. Literature to 1800

J. A. Leo Lemay

The major interests of scholars writing on early American literature continue to be Puritanism, Edward Taylor, and the fiction of Charles Brockden Brown. The most neglected areas are the writers of the Southern and Middle Colonies, Enlightenment ideas, and eighteenth-century writers other than the novelists. Because of the imminence of the Bicentennial of the American Revolution, there is a renewal of interest in the Revolutionary writers, which should become more pronounced as we approach 1975–1976.

Two important collections of essays appeared in 1972. *Major Writers of Early American Literature* (Madison, Univ. of Wis. Press), edited by Everett H. Emerson, contains a series of original, splendid essays on William Bradford, Anne Bradstreet, Edward Taylor, Cotton Mather, William Byrd, Jonathan Edwards, Benjamin Franklin, Philip Freneau, and Charles Brockden Brown. One may lament the absence of Crèvecœur and Paine—but, these two figures excepted, the authors chosen are undoubtedly the standard fare of early American literature. The other collection, edited by Sacvan Bercovitch, *Typology and Early American Literature* (Amherst, Univ. of Mass. Press) contains a series of important articles on the history and varieties of typology and on typology in the works of various early American authors. Since most of these essays are re-printed, only the excellent original essays by Ursula Brumm and Jesper Rosenmeier, together with Bercovitch's own much expanded bibliography, will be noted below.

Highlights of 1972 are a fundamental article on colonial intellectual history by Norman S. Fiering, a perceptive and fresh survey of a single subject in seventeenth-century New England writings by Roger B. Stein, a sensitive reading of "The Hasty Pudding" by Robert D. Arner, *Men of Letters in Colonial Maryland* by J. A. Leo

Lemay, and editions of writings by Thomas Shepard, Eliza Lucas
Pinckney, Jonathan Edwards, and Benjamin Franklin.

i. Edward Taylor

Donald E. Stanford's eminently sound essay ("Edward Taylor,"
Major Writers, pp. 59–91) emphasizes Taylor's use of rhetoric,
shrewdly accounting for the poet's fascination with amplification and
paradox. Stanford analyzes the usual meditative structure of the
Preparatory Meditations (using 1.33 and 1.39 as typical examples),
considers Taylor's use of typology (taking 2.78 as a model), and
justifies the inconsistent imagery. Stanford takes up several aspects
of *Gods Determinations*: the structure and contents are briefly but
clearly sketched; the possible relationship of the poem to Taylor's
quarrel with Solomon Stoddard over communion is considered; the
influence of secular drama on the poem is rejected; the styles of the
various parts are described; and finally the whole poem is judged
to be lacking as a "coherent composition." Although Stanford also
briefly considers the miscellaneous poems and sermons of Taylor, he
concludes that it is because of the *Preparatory Meditations* that Taylor "can stand comparison with major poets like Donne, Herbert, and
Crashaw." In a detailed examination of the ways that Taylor uses
typology, Ursula Brumm ("Edward Taylor and the Poetic Use of
Religious Imagery," in *Typology*, pp. 191–206) maintains that Taylor "neglects esthetic niceties" because "meaning is the primary concern" in his poetry; and in a splendid commentary on meditation
1.10, she shows how Taylor uses typology esthetically to present his
"one theme"—"God's glory and man's redemption through grace."

Taking up the question of Taylor's mysticism, William J. Scheick
("Man's Wildred State and the Curious Needlework of Providence:
The Self in Edward Taylor's *Preparatory Meditations*," TSL 17:129–
37) convincingly argues that Taylor was not a mystic in the proper
sense of the term, but that the poems are essentially a record of Taylor's "self wrestling for true identity in Christ," an issue that theologically had to be left unresolved, "since a sense of confidence might
testify to damning presumption." In an examination of an issue that
Donald E. Stanford has treated, Reid Maynard concludes that Taylor's sacramental and devotional views, like his use of imagery and
attitudes towards the elect, are all typically Puritan ("The Poetry of

Edward Taylor: A Puritan Apologia," *Caliban* 9:3–17). Alan B.
Howard's ambitious essay (which won the Foerster award as the
best article in *AL* for 1972) argues that Taylor's poetry is not "metaphysical" but emblematic, that the emblematic method breaks down
the unity of symbol and form expected in great poetry, and that the
emblematic method even fails to state an enriching relation between
theology and life. Howard ("The World as Emblem: Language and
Vision in the Poetry of Edward Taylor," *AL* 44:359–84) implies that
Taylor's artistic achievement is less than that of either William Bradford or Anne Bradstreet. Although Taylor was, on occasion, an em-
blematist (others have previously shown this, though with less thoroughness than Howard), this is but one strain in his meditative
poetry. Although I do not consider Taylor a metaphysical, those who
categorize him as such need not be convinced to the contrary by this
article, for Howard does not deny that Taylor possesses those characteristics of style which are usually said to define metaphysical
poetry. And I find myself in complete disagreement over the implication that Taylor is a lesser artist than Bradford or Bradstreet: Taylor
is more complex, almost always briefer, and often (*contra* Howard)
unified.

Three pieces by Mukhtar Ali Isani are complementary. In "Edward Taylor and the 'Turks'" (*EAL* 7:120–23) Isani surveys Taylor's
knowledge of the Orient and his metaphoric use of it. In "The Pour-
ing of the Sixth Vial: A Letter in a Taylor-Sewall Debate" (*PMHS*
83[1971]:123–29) he prints Taylor's letter of September 29, 1696,
wherein Taylor gave the reasons for his orthodox opinion that Rev.
16.12 referred to the decline of the Ottoman Empire (i.e., to the
"Turks"), in opposition to the singular opinion of Samuel Sewall, who
maintained that it referred to the decline of Catholicism and of the
Spanish Empire in America. And in "The Growth of Sewall's *Phae-
nomena Quaedam Apocalyptica*" (*EAL* 7:64–75) Isani traces the development of Sewall's interpretation of Rev. 16.12 as an aspect of his
patriotic and millennial thought, with interesting asides on Sewall's
characteristic habits of thought, methods of composition, and opinion concerning the origin of the American Indians.

The texts of more Taylor writings are made available in two other
articles. Thomas M. Davis ("Edward Taylor's 'Valedictory' Poems,"
EAL 7:38–63) prints three of Taylor's poems "preparatory to Death,"
and his poem "Upon my recovery out of a threatening Sickness in

December Ano Dmi 1720." From the Church Records at Westfield, Mass., Thomas M. Davis and Virginia L. Davis print a long passage concerning the Day of Judgment ("Edward Taylor on the Day of Judgement," *AL* 43:525–47), which is "clearly part of an early sermon, probably preached at Westfield." A final note on Taylor is John Higby's "Taylor's 'Huswifery' " (*Expl* 30:item 60), explaining that a fulling mill "not only cleanses newly woven fabric but changes its very quality by giving" it "full body."

ii. Puritanism

In a fundamental article for colonial intellectual history, Norman S. Fiering ("Will and Intellect in the New England Mind," *WMQ* 29: 515–58) sketches the argument over the nature of the will in sixteenth- and seventeenth-century Western thought, distinguishing the Protestant intellectualist position (which maintained, in effect, that the will was an aspect of the intellect), the illuminationist position (or Cameronianism, which tended to be identified with both Arminianism and Pelagianism and which tended to deify reason), and Augustianian voluntarism (whose adherents believed that the will was capable of defying the intellect, and who, in some cases, tended to "a fideism which divorced the religious life from both reason and natural morality"). Fiering shows the vitality of these positions (especially the intellectualist and voluntarist) in seventeenth-century New England and argues that an underlying aspect of the debate in the Great Awakening consisted in Jonathan Edwards' commitment to the voluntarist position and in Charles Chauncy's to the intellectualist position. A book that, like Fiering's article, would seem to promise much illumination on the intricacies of colonial Puritanism is Keith L. Sprunger's *The Learned Doctor William Ames: Dutch Backgrounds of English and American Puritanism* (Urbana, Univ. of Ill. Press); but, perhaps because it attempts to do too much, it is a better introduction to Puritanism than an exposition of Ames's role in the underlying issues of theology and of intellectual history. The three parts of the book are an interesting biography of Ames, a cursory survey of his theological writings (e.g., Sprunger mentions that Ames is a voluntarist, but he doesn't say what voluntarism is or what this means in Ames's thought, nor do we find any "inconsistency" in Ames's voluntarism as presented by Sprunger—cf. Fiering, p. 535—nor are we

told how "revolutionary" Ames's thinking was—cf. Fiering, p. 537),
and a brief survey of his enormous influence on later Puritanism. It is
a good book for a beginner to read, for it clearly and precisely (and,
unfortunately, repeatedly) tells us what the influence of Ramism
meant for Puritans—but this will not enlighten students who have
read Walter J. Ong or Wilbur Samuel Howell. Lee W. Gibbs in
"William Ames's Technometry" (*JHI* 33:615–24) gives a slightly
more detailed survey of a subject well treated by Sprunger. Gibbs
discusses the major sources of technometry, its definition and structure, and its function (a "meta-discipline which systematically inte-
grates the whole body of knowledge").

A perceptive and fresh view of some well-known Puritan writings
is set forth by Roger B. Stein ("Seascape and the American Imagination: The Puritan Seventeenth Century," *EAL* 7:17–37), who shows
that the sea is usually a symbol of "a lost coherence, a lost cosmology"
and of a meaning of ultimate significance. With discerning remarks
about William Bradford, Thomas Tillam, Edward Johnson, Anne
Bradstreet, John Fiske, Philip Pain, Edward Taylor, John Josselyn,
and Richard Steere, Stein surveys the seventeenth-century New England writers and finds them rewarding. This is one of the few appreciative essays that makes one want not only to read the works
discussed but also to read the complete work of which this essay will
evidently form a part.

The Governor of Plymouth Colony is the subject of two general
essays and one specialized article. Jesper Rosenmeier ("'With My
Owne Eyes': William Bradford's *Of Plymouth Plantation*," *Typology*, pp. 69–105) sketches the background in Separatist writings of
some of Bradford's dominant views and images (e.g., the Separatists
as pilgrims and the parent-child metaphor), shrewdly examines the
composition of *Of Plymouth Plantation* (called "a work of retrospection"), points out the functions of the character sketches, presents
the metaphoric structures of the book as a reenactment of Christ's
Passion, and suggests the reason for Bradford's study of Hebrew in his
last years. Isidore S. Meyer's "The Hebrew Exercises of Governor
William Bradford" (in *Studies in Jewish Bibliography, History, and
Literature In Honor of I. Edward Kiev*, edited by Charles Berlin [New
York: KTAV Publishing House, 1971], pp. 237–88) is a learned and
richly documented monograph on Bradford's (and on other Puritans') interest in Hebrew, interpreting the background and causes of

Bradford's late compositions (including the poetry and the *Dialogues*), containing facsimiles of the first five and last nine pages of Bradford's "Dialogue or 3d. Conference," with identifications of the Hebrew. David Levin's "William Bradford" (*Major Writers*, pp. 11–31) claims that Bradford's history "gives the best picture that I know of Puritan piety in action in the New World, and it owes much of its success to the obligations imposed on every believer by that piety: to search faithfully for an understanding of God's revealed will in the ambiguous evidence of the historical world." Inter alia, Levin characterizes the pattern of Bradford's organization, not as lament and decline, but as "perennially dialectical, cyclical, alternating," and calls attention to the scenes of confrontation as a repeated motif. Implicitly objecting to Samuel Eliot Morison's edition (which relegates the letters to appendices), Levin evaluates the functions of the letters that Bradford incorporated into the history.

J. H. Dorenkamp ("The *Bay Psalm Book* and the Ainsworth Psalter," *EAL* 7:3–16) demonstrates the influence of Henry Ainsworth's *The Booke of Psalmes: Englished* (Amsterdam, 1612) upon a number of the translations in the *Bay Psalm Book* and makes me wonder if it may be possible to carry further Zoltán Haraszti's work in identifying the authors of particular translations, for those most heavily influenced by Ainsworth may all be by the same author. Maxine Turner's "Three Eighteenth-Century Revisions of the *Bay Psalm Book*" (*NEQ* 45:270–77) does not, despite the title, discuss revisions, but completely new versions of the psalms by Cotton Mather, John Barnard, and Thomas Prince. One wonders why just these three of the several versions of the psalms written by eighteenth-century Americans (Thomas Cradock published an English as well as an American version) are selected for mention.

Ann Stanford's essay on "Anne Bradstreet" (*Major Writers*, pp. 33–58) surveys the life and writings of Bradstreet, pointing out that the long poem "The Four Seasons" contains an early portrait of America as homeland, and that "A Dialogue Between Old England and New . . . 1642," defends the New England Puritans from the charge of a cowardly forsaking of their fellow Puritans in England. Stanford particularly praises several poems: "As loving Hind that (Hartless) wants her Deer," "As spring the winter doth succeed," "Upon my dear and loving husband his goeing into England, Jan 16, 1661," "Contemplations," "The Flesh and the Spirit," and "As weary pilgrim." Stanford also charts Bradstreet's progressive acceptance of religion and of the judgments of God, but fails to convince me that the letter concerning religious doubts is "one of the finest pieces of colonial prose" or that the elegy "In memory of my dear grandchild Elizabeth Bradstreet" is "one of the finest elegies in American literature." Although most of Neil H. Keeble's "Anne Bradstreet: The First Colonial Poet" (*LHY* 13,i:13–28) is a popular and familiar appreciation, the piece attains some interest for the colonialist when Keeble finds the basis in Puritanism of "our present surfeit of flesh," when he lists some of Bradstreet's poetic faults, and when he argues that Puritanism rather than the American experience was important to Bradstreet's poetry.

John Cotton has traditionally been the most studied of the three greatest puritan ministers who emigrated to New England in the 1630s, but with Michael McGiffert's edition of the autobiography and journal of Thomas Shepard and with a spate of articles on Thomas Hooker, the other two (both more interesting literary artists than Cotton) may be experiencing a modest revival. On Cotton himself, there is only Richard Etulain's "The New Puritan: Recent Views of John Cotton" (*Rendezvous* 7,i:39–51), which examines especially the opinions and contributions of Larzer Ziff, Emery Battis, Everett H. Emerson, and Darett B. Rutman—all of whom are basically sympathetic to the personality of this paradoxically mild, accommodating, and warm intellectual. McGiffert's edition, *God's Plot: The Paradoxes of Puritan Piety: Being the Autobiography & Journal of Thomas Shepard* (Amherst, Univ. of Mass. Press), has an excellent introduction and notes. The autobiography (along with Increase Mather's, Jonathan Edwards's and John Woolman's) is one of the classic spiritual autobiographies of colonial America and thus familiar to most colonialists—but Shepard's journal—which reveals him constantly worrying that theologically sound subject for Puritan neuroses, the state of his grace—is here printed in full for the first time and should become a key document in the future study of Shepard's thought and of American Puritanism. Perhaps I might voice my two complaints: several pages are wasted on a Series Editor's Preface, and the abbreviation for *Christ* (X^t) is expanded as *Lord* (p. 31).

In "Thomas Hooker and the Westminster Assembly" (*WMQ* 29: 291–300), Sargent Bush, Jr., plausibly argues that two of Hooker's publications were written and sent to England in an attempt to influence the Westminster Assembly. Winfried Herget ("Preaching and Publication—Chronology and the Style of Thomas Hooker's Sermons," *HTR* 65:231–39), points out some of the difficulties of determining the best text when the printed sermons are based upon notes made by an auditor. And from a seventeenth-century notebook, Everett H. Emerson prints a Thanksgiving sermon that Hooker delivered on October 4, 1638 ("A Thomas Hooker Sermon of 1638," *RALS* 2:75–89).

No literary works dealing with Roger Williams appeared, but Theodore Dwight Bozeman ("Religious Liberty and the Problem of Order in Early Rhode Island," *NEQ* 45:44–64) shows that Roger Williams believed in civil order and that he counteracted effectively the reality (and the reputation) of Rhode Island as an anarchic government. A brief survey of the American career of George Keith, who is presented as a Quaker version of Roger Williams, was written by Edward J. Cody ("The Price of Perfection: The Irony of George Keith," *PH* 39:1–19), remarking that Keith left the Quakers because they were too impure and attacked the Quaker magistrates for partaking in government. The poet, classicist, and Harvard president, Urian Oakes, is the subject of another of Leo M. Kaiser's splendid editions ("The Unpublished *Oratio Secunda* of Urian Oakes, Harvard, 1675," *HL* 21:385–412), giving hundreds of notes documenting Oakes's classical allusions in his commencement address of 1675.

B. Richard Burg ("A Letter of Richard Mather to a Cleric in Old England," *WMQ* 29:81–98) edits a letter of the founding Mather from his massive (and still unpublished) manuscript "A Plea for the Churches of Christ in New England" (1645–46). The letter of 1636 reveals Mather's thinking on church doctrine during the crucial and formative years when the Massachusetts ministers were dealing with the troublesome Roger Williams and the Antinomian Anne Hutchinson. Sacvan Bercovitch's "Cotton Mather" (*Major Writers*, pp. 93–149) is clearly the best overall appreciation yet written of the writings and the significance (though this is overstated) of the most famous of the Mathers. Bercovitch surveys his diaries in order to assess Mather's character, presenting him as a Henry Adams of his day while showing that he viewed himself as the latest antitype of John the Baptist and as a type of the Gethsemaneic Christ. Bercovitch interprets Mather's enormous literary productivity as a frantic rhetoric of wish fulfillment—an attempt to create an imaginative world different from the disappointing one he inhabited, while forever crying up his provincial situation in chauvinistic hyperboles as God's cynosure. Mather's orthodox Puritanism and his pietism are viewed as coordinate parts of his efforts to do good, best portrayed in his popular *Bonifacius* (1710). Other works that receive more than passing characterization are *Psalterium Americanum, The Christian Philosopher*, and the "epic" *Magnalia Christi Americani*.

Two articles appeared on special aspects of Mather. Thomas Steele, S.J. ("The Biblical Meaning of Mather's Bradford," *BRMMLA* 24[1970]:147–54) points out that in the *Magnalia* sketch of Bradford, Cotton Mather portrays the governor as an antitype of Paul. He notes that Bradford himself had supplied Mather with this typological interpretation by implicitly comparing the description of the Pilgrim Fathers' escape by sea with the Pauline "perils by sea," Acts 27. And Richard H. Werking ("'Reformation Is Our Only Preservation': Cotton Mather and Salem Witchcraft," *WMQ* 29:281–90) argues that Mather was involved in the witchcraft crisis primarily because he wanted to confirm the existence of the spiritual world; and Werking emphasizes that, while Mather endeavored to keep up a due respect for the judges, he always attempted to protect those who were actually accused of witchcraft.

Several publications bear upon the important Mather-Taylor-Stoddard controversy. E. Brooks Holifield ("The Renaissance of Sacramental Piety in Colonial New England," *WMQ* 29:33–48) questions the significance of the publication of a number of communion manuals in New England between 1690 and 1738, arguing that two opposing motives were responsible: the anguish of the religiously scrupulous concerning their possible unworthiness, and the ministers' attempt to influence the indifferent and irreligious. Holifield points out that these manuals are the background for (and were influenced by) the Stoddardian controversy. Arguing for the importance of the distinction between conversion and regeneration in Solomon Stoddard's interpretation of the qualifications of those who could receive the Lord's Supper, Robert Lee Stuart ("'Mr. Stoddard's Way': Church and Sacraments in Northampton," *AQ* 24:243–53) claims that Jonathan Edwards was closer to Stoddard's position than he himself recognized and that Stoddard's *The Doctrine of the Instituted Churches Explained* (1700) is the key work in Stodard's theological position. Another article by E. Brooks Holifield ("The Intellectual

Sources of Stoddardeanism," *NEQ* 45:373–92) traces the background of the origin and development of Stoddard's doctrine of the Lord's Supper in Continental and English theology, particularly in the writings of William Prynne and John Humfrey. Holifield also traces the course of Solomon Stoddard's quarrels with Increase and Cotton Mather, as well as with Edward Taylor. New light will be shed on this famous controversy by the publication of "Increase Mather's Confutation of Solomon Stoddard's Observations Respecting the Lord's Supper, 1680," in *PAAS* for 1973.

Finally, I should notice two popular treatments of Puritan authors. Barbara McCrimmon ("John Winthrop's Journal," *MSS* 24:87–96) recapitulates some of the familiar contents of the journal, with attention to the history of its editing and the transmission of the text. And Zdeněk Vančura, "Bringing the Gospel to the Indians of New England" (*PP* 14[1971]:81–90), tells the story of the seven Eliot Indian tracts, with particular attention to the "cultural and psychological material" therein.

iii. The South

J. A. Leo Lemay's *Men of Letters in Colonial Maryland* (Knoxville, Univ. of Tenn. Press) is in three parts. "The Wilderness" contains essays on Andrew White, S.J., whom Lemay believes to be the author of the first three Maryland promotion tracts and a major contributor to a fourth; on George Alsop, emphasizing his satire of English society as the natural converse of his praise of edenic America and attempting to identify this unknown but talented author; and on John Hammond, stressing his love for America and his contribution to the American Dream. The second part, "The Planter," deals with Ebenezer Cook, showing how his Hudibrastic satire of America, *The Sot-Weed Factor*, also mocks English attitudes toward America and how this "Poet Laureate" of Maryland used popular English songs about America and American oral anecdotes, in addition to such characteristic American motifs as the initiation of the tenderfoot; with William Parks, whose printing press and personal encouragement were responsible for a minor flourishing of belles-lettres; and with Richard Lewis, a poet who celebrated the New World in memorable verse and who pondered philosophical questions (if this chapter were being written today, the implied religious satire in "A Journey from Patapsco to Annapolis" would be pointed out). The last part, "The Club," contains essays on Jonas Green, printer, poetaster, and clubman; on the Rev. James Sterling, poet, playwright, and opposer of the Rev. George Whitefield; on that engaging author Dr. Alexander Hamilton, giving an account of the various mock literary wars he inspired, his active club life, and his humorous masterpiece (still unpublished) "The History of the Tuesday Club"; and on the Rev. Thomas Bacon, a typical cultivated litterateur of the mid-eighteenth century.

In "A New Edition of the Works of Captain John Smith," Wesley Frank Craven (*WMQ* 29:479–86) announced the forthcoming edition from the expert Philip L. Barbour. And Barbour, in the second installment (see *ALS 1971*, p. 157) of a technical study of the Indian words recorded by Smith ("The Earliest Reconnaissance of the Chesapeake Bay Area: Captain John Smith's Map and Indian Vocabulary, Part II," *VMHB* 80:21–51), continues his meticulous preparation for the edition. The master of Southern colonial literature, Richard Beale Davis ("Neglected 'Literary' Materials for Writing an Intellectual History of the Colonial South," *From Irving to Steinbeck*, pp. 29–44) points out that the wills, sermons, and letters of the early South are an "expression and guide" to its literary achievement and cultural life, proving his point by quotations from the wills of William Fitzhugh (d. 1701) and Sir John Randolph (d. 1738). A careful article on "Agricultural Propaganda in Lawson's *A New Voyage to Carolina*" by W. H. Lindgren III (*NCHR* 49:333–44) shows that Lawson exaggerated the figures on grain production in North Carolina with a view to the potential limits of gullibility of his audience: for he exaggerated only within the limits of credibility the supposed yield on the planting of wheat, which English farmers were familiar with—but his claims for the productivity of corn and of rice would have been unbelievable to anyone familiar with the raising of those grains; English farmers were not.

The essay on "William Byrd: Taste and Tolerance" by Richard Beale Davis (*Major Writers*, pp. 151–77) begins with a survey on Byrd's life, emphasizing his American identity, his typicality, and his adherence to the classical virtue of the golden mean. Davis then examines Byrd's lesser-known writings, his political and legal tracts, character sketches, and verse, before moving to the diaries and letters, singling out particular anecdotes, attitudes, and ironies in the letters for comment. The characterization and appreciation of the *Secret History* and of *The History of the Dividing Line* are judicious and contribute such information as the approximate dates of composition. Robert D. Arner's excellent discussion of the "Monitor" essay series in the *Virginia Gazette* of 1736–1737 ("The Short, Happy Life of the Virginia 'Monitor,'" *EAL* 7:130–47) demonstrates the influence of Petronius's *Satyricon* on the series and sensitively and critically reads the individual essays. But the evidence presented for two authors of the essays is, like the discussion of the authorship, inconclusive. Unfortunately the survey of students (as possible authors) at William and Mary College did not make use of the only resources worth consulting—the Archives of William and Mary, where references to alumni have been steadily collected—so that Arner overlooks even such a well-known man and writer as Benjamin Waller (1716–1786).

The Letterbook of Eliza Lucas Pinckney, edited and annotated by Elise Pinckney (Chapel Hill, Univ. of N. C. Press), consists of a delightful series of letters, from the earliest ones of the young maiden refusing a match to a wealthy man she despised ("the riches of Peru and Chili if he had them put together could not purchase a sufficient Esteem for him to make him my husband") to those of the mature woman informing her young children of the death of their father. She mentions reading John Locke (who is supposed to be practically unknown in America before 1750 but who was recommended to the young girl by Charles Pinckney) in 1741, Samuel Richardson's *Pamela* in 1742, and his *Grandison* in 1754 and alludes to or quotes from Nicholas Malebranche, Virgil, Plutarch, Cervantes, Addison, Milton, Robert Boyle, Thomas Parnell, James Thomson, Richard Glover, and Edward Young—and paraphrases Richard Lewis on the mockingbird. How I wish that scholars who consider what books were known in colonial America would not confine themselves to a few booklists, but would read, among other works, the whimsical, playful letters of this delightful woman. I also wish that the other extant letters of Pinckney had been published. An article "Eliza Lucas Pinckney: Portrait of an Eighteenth Century American" by Sam S. Baskett (*SCHM* 72[1971]:207–19) emphasizes her developing American identity, her growing interest in Col. Charles Pinckney, and the "inescapably second-class status" of colonial Americans in England. The writings of another Charlestonian, Henry Laurens, are progressing well. *The Papers of Henry Lucas, Volume Three: January 1, 1759–August 31, 1763*, edited by Philip M. Hamer and George C. Rogers, Jr. (Columbia, Univ. of S. C. Press) contains the long, interesting "Letter Signed Philolethes," replying to Christopher Gadsden's newspaper essay and pamphlet of 1761 and 1762, in which Laurens attempts to justify Col. James Grant's slurs on the "cowardly" American rangers as opposed to the "brave" British regulars.

Phinizy Spalding ("Oglethorpe and Philanthropos," *GHQ* 56:137–45) prints the poem by "Philanthropos," complimenting James Edward Oglethorpe, which appeared in John Peter Zenger's *New York Weekly Journal*, December 20, 1742. Two mock wills from southern colonial newspapers are printed by Jack D. Wages ("Mock Wills: Parody in the Colonial South," *SNL* 9:192–94), one from the *Virginia Gazette* of July 29, 1737, and the other from the *Maryland Gazette* of March 20, 1760. Neither compares with the most famous mock will of colonial America, John Seccomb's "Father Abbey's Will." David C. Skaggs and F. Garner Ranney report ("Thomas Cradock Sermons," *MHM* 67:179–80) that approximately a hundred manuscript sermons by Cradock have been added to the five already deposited at the Maryland Historical Society. And Richard K. MacMaster ("Arthur Lee's 'Address on Slavery': An Aspect of Virginia's Struggle to End the Slave Trade, 1765–1774," *VMHB* 80:141–57) reprints a pseudonymous essay by Lee against slavery with a long introduction concerning the antislavery movement in pre-Revolutionary Virginia.

iv. Franklin and the Enlightenment

Annus Mirabilis! The new editors of *The Papers of Benjamin Franklin* (New Haven, Yale Univ. Press) have produced two volumes (15 and 16) in one year. Under the editorship of William B. Willcox, the volumes now have a brief introduction commenting on the contents (a questionable procedure in a great edition, as it suggests an "established" attitude toward the contents); minimal explanatory comments are made in those cases where Verner Crane has explicated the situation in his *Franklin's Letters to the Press* (thus the *Papers* does not supersede Crane but supplements him); Willcox introduces the policy of giving résumés of some letters to Franklin and of some documents concerning him (thus making a judgment concerning the interests of future scholars); and, most pernicious, Willcox reprints

texts from Crane when the originals are readily available (see 16:22).
Volume 15 is devoted to Franklin's papers during 1768 and includes
several splendid letters (e.g., to Lord Kames, February 28, anticipating a passage in the *Autobiography*; to William Franklin, March
13, on that "venal nation," England); his pro-American journalism
(especially the brilliant "Causes of the American Discontents Before
1768"); an example of his omnivorous scientific interest in the lucid
letter to Sir John Pringle on the effect of the depth of water in canals;
his experiments with a phonetic alphabet (downplaying the religious
impudence of "A new Version of the Lord's Prayer," the editors argue
that his phonetic experiment underlies this spoof); his famous letter
on early marriage (p. 182), really a public essay; and his splendid
hoax, "The Captivity of William Henry." Although the totality of the
evidence that Franklin wrote "The Captivity" is overwhelming—
there is even a manuscript portion of a draft—the editors nevertheless doubt its authenticity because they find its irony "too subtle and
indirect" and even suggest another extraordinarily improbable candidate as the author. Volume 16, for the year 1769, contains less belletristic material, though there are letters to George Whitefield on
religion, to Mary Stevenson and to Jane Mecom on reason (satirized
as inferior to instinct), and a brilliant letter to William Strahan on
American politics. Both of these volumes of the *Papers* print Franklin's
marginalia from political pamphlets, which are of special value, for
here is one of the few times when it is not necessary to consider
Franklin's opinions in the light of the audience for whom they were
written or of his sensitive public position.

In the only general essay devoted to Franklin in 1972, J. A. Leo
Lemay ("Benjamin Franklin," in *Major Writers*, pp. 205–43) argues
for the American influences in the style and content of the Silence
Dogood essays and points out the vicious satire therein on Cotton
Mather and Samuel Sewall; claims that Franklin's pointed satire of
his once prospective in-laws was the cause of Thomas Godfrey's
taking his almanac to another printer and thus the reason that he was
forced to start his own almanac; examines *The Way to Wealth* as a
rhetorical tour de force; writes a rather long appreciation of the incredible variety of the voices, tones, and contents of Franklin's personal letters; surveys the voluminous public writings, tracing the
origin of "An Edict by the King of Prussia" and commenting on its
persona and irony; and chronicles the contemporaneous reputation

of Franklin's bagatelles before examining the structure and themes of "The Ephemera." The brief remarks on the *Autobiography* point up the book's fictions, its use of other genres, the American Dream theme (both as metaphor for the history of America and as "archetypal recapitulation of the development of every individual"), and Franklin's main persona in the book, the *amicus humani generis.*

Ross Miller's largely theoretical essay, "Autobiography as Fact and Fiction: Franklin, Adams, Malcolm X" (*CentR* 16:221–32), examines vanity as a chief problem of the genre of autobiography, the autobiographer's story as a microcosm of a historical period; autobiographies as "sensuous histories" of their eras; the autobiographers' personae as representative of a group of mankind; the autobiographer as creator of—or, at least, as one who imposes a pattern on—his life; the genre as "an attempt to make history into a novel," thus casting Franklin's autobiography as the literary ancestor of such "new journalism" as Truman Capote's *In Cold Blood*; and the autobiography as a psychological investigation of the limits of self-knowledge. Focusing on "Some Thematic Patterns in Franklin's *Autobiography*" (*ECS* 5:421–30), A. B. England argues that the central theme of the book is the conflict between order and chaos; he gives examples of ways this conflict is presented in the structure of the *Autobiography*, in the character sketches, in anecdotes, in the imagery, in the style, and in the personality of Franklin. England also, in "Robin Molineux and the Young Ben Franklin: A Reconsideration" (*JAmS* 6:181–88) comments on the differences between Franklin's and Hawthorne's stories. Martha Banta's essay ("Benjamin, Edgar, Humbert, and Jay," *YR* 60[1971]:532–49) finds a dichotomy in American literature between Franklinian fable and Poesque dream, and comments on this dichotomy in Fitzgerald's *The Great Gatsby* and in Nabokov's *Lolita*.

Alfred Owen Aldridge's "Polly Baker and Boccaccio" (*AION-SR* 14:5–18) notes the similarity between the tale told by Philostratus, "Lady Filippa Against the Statute of Prato," in the *Decameron* and Franklin's "The Speech of Miss Polly Baker"; but after a brief survey of the known copies of the *Decameron* in colonial America, Aldridge concludes that it was unlikely that Franklin read the book, though he may well have been indirectly influenced by it. Examining the old mystery of where Franklin got the Thomas Hutchinson and Andrew Oliver letters (which discredited the two Loyalists in 1773), Bern-

hard Knollenberg ("Benjamin Franklin and the Hutchinson and
Oliver Letters," *YULG* 47:1–9) contends that Thomas Pownall was
his source. And Richard E. Amacher, on internal evidence, argues
that a short anonymous satire on slavery that appeared in the *American Museum* for July 1788 is probably by Franklin ("A New Franklin
Satire?" *EAL* 7:103–10), but P. M. Zall has pointed out to me that
this appeared earlier in the Philadelphia *Independent Gazetteer* of
May 29, 1787, p. 3, in a slightly different text, and Zall considers it
most unlikely that Franklin would have submitted a piece to this
paper, for the *Independent Gazetteer* was generally the opposition
(i.e., the anti-Franklin) paper of this period. M. E. Grenander has
written an appreciation of "Benjamin Franklin's String Quartet"
(*EAL* 7:183–86), but W. Thomas Marrocco believes, with good evidence, that it is not by Franklin ("The String Quartet Attributed to
Benjamin Franklin," *PAPS* 116:477–85). Sheldon Sloan shows (what
we would all assume) that Mason Locke Weems made up the story
of Franklin gazing at a picture of Christ as he died ("Parson Weems
on Franklin's Death," *PMHB* 96:369–76), and traces the appearance
of this nonsense in later biographies of Franklin.

Harriet Rose ("Towards the Pleasure Principle: Character Revelation in Benjamin Franklin's *To the Royal Academy*," *Paunch* 35:16–
25) finds that the supposed orderliness of Franklin reveals "a cluster
of traits which Freud associated with the anal personality" and that
these traits are suppressed "in such semi-fictional works as the *Autobiography* or *Poor Richard*," but apparent in the "less inhibited form
of the bagatelle." With such a premise (one knows, of course, that
all but one of his bagatelles will be ignored), Franklin's scatological
jeu d'esprit "To the Royal Academy"—which is, of course, a splendid
example of the common scatological spoofs so familiar to all students
of eighteenth-century literature, an age some psychological critic
will no doubt label the Anal Age of Literature—"gives us a unique
glimpse into the psychic impulses underlying his personality." Perhaps my opinion—a four-letter word rhyming with *rap*—will be
thought revealing of my own complexes. Perhaps the worst article
that I have read for this year's survey is Robert K. Dodge's "Didactic
Humor in the Almanacs of Early America" (*JPC* 5[1971].592–605),
which makes the obvious point that most of the humor in the seven-
teenth- and eighteenth-century American almanacs was didactic. Of
Franklin's great "The Way to Wealth," we read "This preface is also

worthy of remark as it showed the great popularity of Franklin's proverbs." Specialists in seventeenth-century New England should not miss the concluding sentence, supposedly explaining the reason for the popularity of didactic humor (which, of course, is typical of the humor of eighteenth-century English almanacs, as well as American, and which is a natural concomitant of the Joseph Addison and Richard Steele philosophy of trying to educate and to improve the lot of the vast majority of eighteenth-century mankind): "Puritanism was still popular and the didactic humor reflected a belief in the Puritan virtues of hard work, sobriety and frugality, not only as virtues, but also as the way to wealth."

In a fine examination of "The 'Reasonable' Style of Tom Paine," Evelyn J. Hinz (*QQ* 79:231–42) shows that Paine, despite claiming to appeal to the reason, is actually a sourcebook for seemingly unconscious logical fallacies. Alfred Owen Aldridge ("Thomas Paine, Edmund Burke, and Anglo-French Relations in 1787," *SBHT* 12 [1971]:1851–1861) supplies the background for Paine's pamphlet *Prospects on the Rubicon* (1787), which attempted to promote friendly relations between England and France. Two articles deal with the replies to Paine's *The Age of Reason*: Franklyn K. Prochaska ("Thomas Paine's *The Age of Reason* Revisited," *JHI* 33:561–76) briefly analyzes the two parts of the book, surveys the four categories of replies (by Unitarians, Anglicans, Methodists, and politicians), and argues that "the French revolution created the furor over Paine's pamphlet in England." With a much smaller focus, James H. Smylie ("Critical Perspectives on Deism: Paine's *The Age of Reason* in Virginia," *ECS* 6:203–20) also finds four strategies of replies (different from Prochaska's) to Paine. The total substance of Armand Barotti's contribution to Paine studies ("Tom Paine's Class Outlook," *L&I*, 12:31–36) is adequately summed up in its labeling of Paine as "an international bourgeois lackey."

A learned and suggestive essay by Henry Steele Commager ("The American Enlightenment and the Ancient World: A Study in Paradox," *PMHS* 83[1971]:3–15) contrasts the use of classical history by John Adams (who believed that human nature and government were essentially everywhere and always the same) with Thomas Jefferson (who believed that history suggested a philosophy of progress). Jefferson's interest in Spanish language, literature, and in the teaching of Spanish—which he viewed as an aspect of American patriotism—is traced by R. Merritt Cox ("Thomas Jefferson and Spanish: 'To Every Inhabitant Who Means to Look Beyond the Limits of His Farm,'" *RomN* 14:116–21), who notes that both Franklin and Jefferson subscribed to the works of Tomás de Iriarte (Madrid, 1787). And John M. Werner ("David Hume and America," *JHI* 33:439–56) briefly documents the relations of Franklin and Hume, as well as the knowledge of Hume's writings revealed by Charles Carroll of Carrollton, Josiah Quincy, Jr., Thomas Paine, Alexander Hamilton, James Madison, John Adams, and Thomas Jefferson.

v. Jonathan Edwards and the Great Awakening

The fourth volume in the Yale edition of "The Works of Jonathan Edwards" has appeared: Jonathan Edwards, *The Great Awakening: A Faithful Narrative; The Distinguishing Marks; Some Thoughts Concerning the Revival; Letters Relating to the Revival; Preface to "True Religion,"* edited by C. C. Goen (New Haven, Yale Univ. Press). Although the text is modernized (a mistake, for the primary audience for these volumes is scholarly), it has been prepared with greater care than the preceding volumes in the edition and is generally excellent (but see the few corrections by David D. Hall, *NEQ* 45: 455–57). Besides setting the works within their historical contexts, Goen's nearly one-hundred-page introduction points out the crucial scholarly questions in such sections as "The Arminian Threat" and "The Morphology of Conversion." Some scholars have already disagreed with Goen's analyses (notably William J. Scheick in *Thought* 48:309–11), but every future student of Edwards will find his introduction, text, annotations, and indexes indispensable.

Daniel B. Shea, Jr., in an excellent general essay on the thought and writings of "Jonathan Edwards: Historian of Consciousness" (*Major Writers*, pp. 179–204) calls his various works on the Great Awakening psychological interpretations of history and claims them as major contributions "to the history of the American consciousness." Shea begins with a consideration of Edwards' early writings on philosophy and science, treating his permutations of Isaac Newton and John Locke. The examination of *Images or Shadows of Divine Things* finds more unity and recurrent themes than are readily apparent, pointing out that Edwards, like Emerson and Thoreau, is concerned with "the real through material shadows." In the sermons,

Shea emphasizes the effect on the audience of "kinesthetic trepida-
tion," together with Edwards's own "Swiftian pessimism" and his
perception of the "absurd figure" of man. Shea's sympathetic and persuasive interpretation of *Freedom of the Will* and *The Great Doctrine of Original Sin* is appropriately presented in chilling terms for
the modern reader, for the notion of Original Sin in Edwards is
compared to a "single community's guilt, even by those who never
fired a shot or whipped a slave." Considering the "Imagery in the
Sermons of Jonathan Edwards" (*EAL* 7:172–82), Annette Kolodny
argues that in every one of Edwards's sermons (as in each of the
three briefly examined: *Sinners in the Hands of an Angry God, God
Glorified in Man's Dependence,* and *The Peace Which Christ Gives
His True Followers*), the "aggregate of images" forces "the listener
to go through very specific and analyzable emotional responses."

David Lyttle ("Jonathan Edwards on Personal Identity," *EAL*
7:163–71) shows that by positing an immaterial thinking substance,
Edwards adapted the Lockean position of personal identity in his
argument on Original Sin and that this addition to Locke's notion
of the continuity of idea/consciousness caused yet "another example
of the tension" in Edwards's thought "between the ideas of monism
and the utterly sovereign and transcendent God." Of the attempts to
find a single key to Edwards's thought there are no end. Leonard R.
Riforgiato ("The Unified Thought of Jonathan Edwards," *Thought*
47:599–610) believes he has found "the essential key to Edwardian
ontology which later merged into his mature theological reasoning":
Riforgiato thinks that the influence of Newton and Locke led to
Edwards's youthful formulation of a cosmology which in turn supported his ontology and, influenced by the Trinitarian model (in
which "the interaction between the three Persons is the consent of
being to itself"), is the basis of his theology. In a careful essay on the
basis of Edwards's theory of the imagination, Sang Hyun Lee ("Jonathan Edwards's Theory of the Imagination," *MichA* 5:233–41) finds
that Edwards, developing Locke's notion of the association of ideas,
came to regard the "habit of mind" as the "mind's power to imaginatively relate its ideas according to certain patterns," patterns which
could, for a sanctified person, be similar to God's patterns of reality.
After finding that the major sources of Edwards's representations of
the devil are from the Bible, the writings of John Flavel, and Milton's
Paradise Lost, Christopher R. Reaske ("The Devil and Jonathan

Edwards," *JHI* 33:123–38) unconvincingly claims that Edwards had "a mild preoccupation with the devil" in the 1730s, that this "turned into a monomania during the Revival," and that Edwards had "a subdued awareness of him even in later life."

Stephen J. Stein believes that "A Notebook on the Apocalypse by Jonathan Edwards" (*WMQ* 29:623–34) will document Edwards's religious prejudices (especially his anti-Catholicism) and is of central importance for his millennialism. Henry Abelove has edited "Jonathan Edwards's Letter of Invitation to George Whitefield" (*WMQ* 29:487–89) of February 12, 1739/40. And Christopher R. Reaske claims that Edwards's views on sanctification were influenced by his tutor ("An Unpublished Letter Concerning 'Sanctification' by Elisha Williams, Jonathan Edwards' Tutor," *NEQ* 45:429–34), but the evidence is too scanty for judgment, even if it were shown that Williams's position was different from that of his contemporaries. On the other side of the argument over the Great Awakening, a letter that Charles Chauncy wrote in 1743, just after the publication of his anti-enthusiastic *Seasonable Thoughts*, is published by Edward M. Griffin ("Chauncy and *Seasonable Thoughts*: A New Letter," *AN&Q* 11:3–5).

There are no surprises in Barbara A. Larson's analysis of "Samuel Davies and the Rhetoric of New Light" (*SM* 38[1971]:207–16), unless it be that the piece is not grounded in the psychology and rhetoric of the eighteenth century but in the elementary commonplaces of rhetorical theory of the twentieth. A more informative approach is taken by Eugene E. White's *Puritan Rhetoric: The Issue of Emotion in Religion* (Carbondale, So. Ill. Univ. Press), but it is aimed toward undergraduates in the discipline of speech. Although the long introductory essay and notes trace the history of Puritan rhetoric and the structure of the sermon, too frequently there are summaries of what is well known (e.g., George Whitefield's popularity) in an emotionally heightened style ("Whitefield's tour had also established the archetype of emotionalism and of ministerial practice which shaped the Epitasis and made inevitable the Catastrophe of the Great Awakening"). Finally, Henry J. Cadbury reports finding another manuscript of John Woolman's important essay, "A Word of Remembrance and Caution to the Rich" ("Another Woolman Manuscript," *QH* 61:16–23).

vi. The Revolutionary and Early National Periods

The master of Freneau studies, Lewis Leary ("Philip Freneau," *Major Writers*, pp. 245–71), returns for a splendid assessment. One section is devoted to an appreciation of Freneau's unfamiliar poetic characterizations, such as "The New England Sabbath Day Chase" and "Elijah, the New England Emigrant." To Freneau's Revolutionary poems Leary gives short shrift, judging only "To the Memory of the Brave Americans" as more than competent. Predictably, there is a fine appreciation of "The Wild Honeysuckle" and of "To a Caty-Did"; but surprisingly, Leary prefers the almost sentimental "Dying Indian" (certainly a hackneyed topos) to the more ambitious "Indian Burying Ground." There are appreciations of the almost unknown "A Moral Thought" and of "Stanzas Written on the Hills of Neversink." Freneau's prose is flatly condemned as inferior to that of a number of his contemporaries, though Leary finds the increasing Americanization of Freneau's major personae worthy of comment. Leary concludes that Freneau is a poet of four, or five, or possibly six poems that are not great and that he is comparatively insignificant insofar as his influence is concerned—but that we would not want to be without those few fine poems. In passing, Leary calls for someone to do the "difficult and lengthy task of preparing" a definitive edition of the poetry.

In "Two Last Poems of Freneau" (*EAL* 7:111–19) John F. Collins prints the concluding stanza of "Winter" (the last four lines have hitherto been unpublished), which is generally regarded as Freneau's last poem, and, on internal evidence, attributes the anonymous poem "The Vale of Obscurity" (which appeared in the *Monmouth Enquirer*, July 7, 1829) to Freneau. Charles L. Batten, Jr. ("A Newly Discovered Poem by Philip Freneau on the Death of General Moreau," *AL* 44:457–59) prints a brief poem on the death of General Jean Victor Moreau (d. 1813), written in a copy of Patrick Brydone's *Tour Through Sicily and Malta*. Gerald L. Grotta credits Freneau's editorials in the *National Gazette* in 1791–93 with a major role in gaining admission for the public and the press to the sessions of the U.S. Senate ("Philip Freneau's Crusade for Open Sessions of the U.S. Senate," *JQ* 48[1971]:667–71).

One of Freneau's opponents and favorite foils throughout the

Revolution is the subject of a short, interesting, life-and-times biography by Alfred Lawrence Lorenz, *Hugh Gaine: A Colonial Printer-Editor's Odyssey to Loyalism* (Carbondale, So. Ill. Univ. Press). This thoroughly researched, valuable portrait of the literary scene in pre-Revolutionary and Revolutionary New York especially describes the contents of the *New York Mercury*, the newspaper that Gaine edited from 1752 to 1783. A Southern conservative is the subject of Anne Young Zimmer and Alfred H. Kelly's "Jonathan Boucher: Constitutional Conservative" (*JAH* 58:897–922), which points out that Boucher in his early Virginia career "was an American Whig patriot" and that it was only in his later Maryland and English career that he expounded the conservative doctrines with which he is completely identified. The authors demonstrate that his collection of American sermons preached between 1763 and 1775 and published in 1797 were rewritten (perhaps only from notes) after the Revolution and that Boucher was not a throwback follower of Filmer, as is usually claimed, but a constitutional conservative, similar in political philosophy to Thomas Burke. The essays of a Southern patriot are surveyed in Don Higginbotham's "James Iredell's Efforts to Preserve the First British Empire" (*NCHR* 49:127–45). S. F. Roach, Jr. ("The *Georgia Gazette* and the Stamp Act: A Reconsideration," *GHQ* 55[1971]:471–91) notes that the *Georgia Gazette* espoused a patriotic position during the Stamp Act controversy, though the printer was later a loyalist. In "A Note on the Canon of Alexander Martin" (*EAL* 7:92) J. A. Leo Lemay points out two additional poems by the Governor of North Carolina (see *ALS 1971*, p. 159). And Durward T. Stokes contributes an article on the publisher of the *Cape-Fear Mercury*, 1769–1775 ("Adam Boyd, Publisher, Preacher, and Patriot," *NCHR* 49:1-21), an editor who wrote occasional verse.

Michael Kammen's now standard edition of William Smith, Jr., *The History of the Province of New York*, (2 vols., Cambridge, Harvard Univ. Press) presents an excellent text, with the manuscript additions made by Smith in his own personal copy; but the annotations and indexing (except for information relating to New York politics, narrowly conceived) are inadequate. The great Indian leader "Garrangula" is not identified as "Otreonti" ("Garrangula" is a corruption of the French nickname for him, "La Grande Gueule," literally "The Big Mouth," but more appropriately "The Great Voice"), nor is the best brief account (in the *Dictionary of Canadian*

Biography, 1:525–26) referred to; so that one could still, as I did over a decade ago with the nineteenth-century edition of Smith's *History*, search in the Library of Congress until exhausted, without turning up any information whatsoever about "Garrangula," whose truly grandiloquent speech takes up three pages of the *History*.

Information about the method of composition of two contemporary historians of the American Revolution has appeared. George William Pilcher in "William Gordon and the *History of the American Revolution*" (*Historian* 34:447–64) shows that Gordon's supposed plagiarisms were typical of the practice of the day, that Gordon himself acknowledged his sources, that he was forced to revise the original manuscript because his English publishers judged it too favorable to the Americans, and that Gordon's published *History* is of value partially because of its comparative impartiality. (Incidentally, I wish that Gordon's letters on the American Revolution, published in the American newspapers while the conflict was in progress, were gathered, edited, and published.) And Paul H. Smith prints Charles Thomson's letter of November 4, 1786, to David Ramsay on his manuscript history of the American Revolution ("Charles Thomson on Unity in the American Revolution," *QJLC* 28[1971]:158–72). In addition to casting light on Ramsay's carefulness, this letter perhaps reveals why Thomson himself never wrote a history of the American Revolution; for he urged Ramsay to "travel through the several states, to view the scenes of actions & converse with the people who were near them in order to obtain the fullest information & to form a right judgement"—a course that would have taken at least several years—and this *after* Ramsay had completed his manuscript.

Although Robert D. Arner does less with the political and religious implications in "The Hasty Pudding" than the poem calls for, he nevertheless has written the best appreciation yet of the rhetorical artistry, comic elements, metrical and rhyming effects of the poem ("The Smooth and Emblematic Song: Joel Barlow's *The Hasty Pudding*," *EAL* 7:76–91). Arner overstates Barlow's originality in the use of the Indian maiden, for she is the traditional seventeenth- and eighteenth-century symbol for America, commonly found on maps and other visual representations. A similar though less ambitious article is Alessandra Contenti's *"The Hasty Pudding* di Joel Barlow" (*SA* 16[1970]:9–24), which catalogues the rhetorical and structural devices (according to Cicero's *De Oratore*) used in the poem. In

"Joel Barlow's Poetics: 'Advice to a Raven in Russia'" (*ConnR* 5,ii: 38–43) Arner examines the structure and style of the poem, commenting particularly on the alliteration, diction, and assonance, explicates the major symbols, and notes allusions to Goethe's *Faust* (though this is not entirely convincing) and to *Paradise Lost*. The discussion of "The Hasty Pudding" in Arthur L. Ford's *Joel Barlow* (TUSAS 193) is mainly quotation and summary, with little analysis and no surprises. The concluding comments on the structure, "forward" movement, metrics, and syntax are commonplace. Approximately half of the discussion of "Advice to a Raven in Russia" is taken up by quotation of the poem, nor is the commentary enlightening. The rest of the book is, unfortunately, on a par with these sections, with errors of fact (even of the date of birth in the chronology) and clichés in abundance.

The poetry of the period is also studied in Eugene L. Huddleston's "Sense and Sensibility in Early American Poetry: The Case of Matilda's 'Elegy Supposed to be Written on the Banks of Detroit River'" (*NOQ* 44,ii:18–25), in which "Matilda" (a New York poet of the 1780s) is defined as a sentimentalist. Huddleston argues that his poetry is of dubious excellence because he was trapped between a "genteel intellectual milieu and the vulgar experience of real life." This echoes an argument advanced by Leon Howard that the problem with American literature of the late eighteenth century is that the forms and conventions of contemporary English poetry were unsuited to American (frontier) experience—but arguments concerning the taste and prevailing *weltanschauung* of any age explain neither the greatness of a great poet nor the inferiority of an inferior poet like "Matilda." The influence of Shakespeare's sonnets on a satirical song written by James Harvey of North Carolina before February 1, 1775, is claimed by Robert M. Calhoon and Susan C. Griswold ("The Bard of Avon and Some Carolina Pop Song Lyrics (1775)," *NCarF* 16[1968]:12–14).

Not always cogently, R. Lynn Matson ("Phillis Wheatley—Soul Sister," *Phylon* 33:222–30) argues, contrary to the usual interpretation, that the poems of Wheatley show "that she protested slavery . . . often implicitly through the use of various escape themes in her poetry." Roger A. Bruns ("Anthony Benezet and the Natural Rights of the Negro," *PMHB* 96:104–13) points out how the Quaker Benezet used the philosophical arguments of the American revolutionaries in his writings against slavery. Berta Grattan Lee demonstrates how the naturalist and poet William Bartram ("William Bartram: Naturalist or 'Poet'?" *EAL* 7:124–29) adapted the famous alligator scene in the *Travels* from a description he had earlier reported to Dr. John Fothergill. Robert H. Elias and Michael N. Stanton ("Thomas Atwood Digges and *Adventures of Alonso*: Evidence from Robert Southey," *AL* 44:118–22) point out that in a draft of his reminiscences, Robert Southey mentioned Digges as the author of *Adventures of Alonso*. Sargent Bush, Jr., notes that the mock references to the reviews in the introduction to the third volume of *Modern Chivalry* reveal that Hugh Henry Brackenridge had read the reviews that appeared in William Young's *Universal Asylum and Columbian Magazine* ("*Modern Chivalry* and 'Young's Magazine,'" *AL* 44:292–99).

Norman Philbrick's welcome anthology, *Trumpets Sounding: Propaganda Plays of the American Revolution* (New York, Benjamin Blom), contains seven plays, including two of my favorites from the period, *The Fall of British Tyranny: Or American Liberty Triumphant* and Robert Munford's *The Patriots*. The other plays included, with excellent annotations and competent introductions, are *A Dialogue, Between a Southern Delegate and His Spouse, on His Return from the Grand Continental Congress* (the author-persona is the "Spouse," so Philbrick, lost in circular reasoning, argues that the author must have been a woman); *The Blockheads: Or, The Affrighted Officers*, and *The Motley Assembly*, both generally attributed to Mercy Otis Warren; and *The Battle of Brooklyn* and *The Death of General Montgomery*, both by Hugh Henry Brackenridge. John J. Teunissen's fine article, "Blockheadism and the Propaganda Plays of the American Revolution" (*EAL* 7:148–62), discusses Jonathan Sewall's *A Cure for the Spleen* (1775), Mercy Otis Warren's *The Blockheads* (1776), and the anonymous *The Blockheads* (1782), which Teunissen attributes, on internal evidence, to General John Burgoyne. Teunissen (who does not seem to know the best modern treatment of Sewall—Clifford K. Shipton's sketch, in *Harvard Graduates*, 12:306–25) believes that Sewall has been neglected because he was a Loyalist—but it seems to me that Patriots and Loyalists are about equally neglected. In a final piece on the early theater, David Ritchey ("The Baltimore Theatre and the Yellow Fever Epidemic," *MHM* 67:298–301) argues

that the attempt by William Godwin and Christopher Charles Mc-
Grath to establish a permanent theatre in Baltimore failed because
of the yellow fever epidemic.

As usual, there are a number of good articles on Charles Brockden
Brown. Donald A. Ringe views "Charles Brockden Brown" (*Major
Writers*, pp. 273–94) as a successful precursor of the great American
prose writers from Poe and Hawthorne to James and Faulkner, since
Brown uses the trappings of the gothic novel as psychological symbols
of the state of the heroes. Ringe also argues that Brown combines the
intellectual traditions of the novel of purpose with a psychological
and pragmatic study of the actual operation of intellectual positions
in the lives of his characters, who consequently act within complex
situations that adumbrate the fictions of Melville. For Ringe, Brown
is essentially a psychological novelist interested in ideas. Like Ringe,
Robert D. Hume ("Charles Brockden Brown and the Use of Gothicism: A Reassessment," *ESQ* 18:10–18) uses a critico-literary historian's technique of deciding upon the genre of Brown's novels in
order to say what they are essentially about. Hume briefly defines the
traditions of the eighteenth-century English novel and demonstrates
that within the definition, Brown was not a gothic novelist. Unlike
gothic novelists, "Brown is not principally an affective writer"; when
he employs gothic gimmicks, "his object is to produce a reaction in
the character, not the reader." And so Hume too concludes that Brown
is chiefly a psychological novelist.

With a shifting focus on the novels as parables of ideas, Paul
Witherington ("Benevolence and the 'Utmost Stretch': Charles Brockden Brown's Narrative Dilemma," *Criticism* 14:175–91) surveys *Wieland, Edgar Huntley, Jane Talbot*, and *Arthur Mervyn*, implicitly
concluding that Brown failed as a writer because he did "not trust
the 'utmost stretch' of imagination." David Lyttle's psychological
reading of *Wieland* ("The Case Against Carwin," *NCF* 26[1971]:
257–69), which Lyttle calls "Brown's finest work," argues that "Carwin is above all the rebellious son who seeks revenge against the
father; he is the antiauthoritarian psychotic, the deadly little boy,
the homocidal [sic] innocent." Lyttle maintains that Wieland is
Carwin's father figure and that Clara is his mother surrogate; further,
that the oedipal theme is found in Brown's life and in his other
works. In "Charles Brockden Brown's 'Portrait of an Emigrant'"
(*CLAJ* 14[1970]:87–90), Charles E. Bennett presents a little-known

Brown story of a French couple living a "Bohemian life-style." That
the aristocratic Frenchman and his part-black wife may represent
an antithesis to one idea of the late-eighteenth-century American
ethic seems reasonable; that they represent an artistic as opposed to
pragmatic/practical ethic seems feasible; but that idleness and self-
indulgence make this couple an heir of John Woolman and a fore-
father of Thoreau and Whitman seems farfetched. Cecelia Tichi
shows ("Charles Brockden Brown, Translator," *AL* 44:1–12) that
Brown's translation of C. F. de Volney's *A View of the Soil and Climate of the United States* was nationalistic and speculates that he
undertook it as a preparation for his proposed American geography.
And Richard F. Fleck argues that the forest scene in *Edgar Huntley*
is symbolic of Huntley's state of mind ("Symbolic Landscapes in
Edgar Huntley," *RS* 39[1971]:229–32).

Marius B. Péladeau, who formerly edited *The Verse of Royall
Tyler* (see *ALS 1968*, p. 124), has now performed the labor of editing *The Prose of Royall Tyler* (Rutland, Vt., Tuttle). The valuably
annotated text features Tyler's "The Bay Boy," an unfinished semi-
autobiographical novel (which began as an attempt to rewrite his
early, not unsuccessful novel *The American Captive*) of life in pre-
Revolutionary Boston. I might note that Tyler's misspelling of the
name of the American defender Col. Isaac Barré as "Col. Barry"
causes Péladeau (p. 167) to identify him as Col. Henry Barry, who
was, in fact, a loyal British soldier and a talented parodist of American patriotic songs. Péladeau also includes the Spondee essays, i.e.,
Tyler's part in the Colon and Spondee series written with Joseph
Dennie; miscellaneous essays and manuscript drafts; and even some
law cases. Scholars need not consult the impossibly strained article
by William Gribbin ("The Legacy of Timothy Dwight: A Reap-
praisal," *CHSB* 37:33–41), which finds in Dwight's verse both "the
heart of Romantic America" and the reason why "the weakened faith
of one era was preserved and amplified for a later time," nor the
popular biographies by Thomas F. Jones, *A Pair of Lawn Sleeves:
A Biography of William Smith (1727–1803)* (Philadelphia, Chilton)
and by David F. Hawke, *Benjamin Rush: Revolutionary Gadfly*
(Indianapolis, Bobbs-Merrill, 1971). Howard R. Marraro's "Views
on America and the American Revolution in Contemporary Italian
Reviews," (*FI* 5[1971]:67–81) summarizes the articles (including
reviews of books by William Robertson, Jonathan Carver, and Wil-

liam Stork) about America that appeared in two of the leading
Italian journals during the Revolutionary period, noting that they
were generally pro-American.

vii. Books, Bibliography, Libraries

Typology and Early American Literature, edited by Sacvan Bercovitch (Amherst, Univ. of Mass. Press) contains his expanded annotated bibliography (see *ALS 1970*, p. 155) of typological studies from
the Bible and the Church Fathers to twentieth-century criticism.
J. A. Leo Lemay's *A Calendar of American Poetry in the Colonial
Newspapers and Magazines and in the Major English Magazines
Through 1765* (Worcester, Mass., American Antiquarian Society) is
a separate printing, with a few additions and corrections, of the
bibliography that appeared in the Society's *Proceedings* (see *ALS
1969*, p. 140; *ALS 1970*, p. 173). And Roger P. Bristol in "American
Bibliographical Notes" (*PAAS* 82:45–53) gives a number of additions
and corrections to Evans and to Bristol's *Supplement to Evans*.

Norman S. Fiering's article "Solomon Stoddard's Library at Harvard in 1664" (*HLB* 20:255–69) adds to our knowledge of books in
seventeenth-century America and to Stoddard's intellectual history.
Joyce Ketcham gives an interesting account of "The Bibliomania of
the Reverend William Bentley, D.D." (*EIHC* 108:275–303), together with an explanation of how he came to leave half of his library
to Allegheny College and half to the American Antiquarian Society.
Ketcham notes the need of publishing the complete manuscript catalogue of Bentley's books. The story of Thomas Jefferson's library sold
to the Library of Congress is briefly told by Frederick R. Goff ("Jefferson the Book Collector," *QJLC* 29:32–47). And Edwin Wolf 2d,
the master of early American books, briefly describes the libraries of
twelve major book collectors ("Great American Book Collectors to
1800," *Gazette of the Grolier Club*, 16[1971]:3–70). Those whom
Wolf believes the greatest collectors are Increase Mather (along with
Cotton Mather and Mather Byles), Thomas Prince, James Logan,
Thomas Jefferson, Benjamin Franklin, John Adams, John Winthrop
(along with John Winthrop II and IV), Isaac Norris II, William
Bentley, Thomas Wallcut, and William Mackenzie. In addition, Wolf
mentions more than another dozen early Americans who possessed
splendid libraries.

The first American use of Faust, according to André Dabezies ("The First American *Faust* (1720)," *CLS* 8[1971]:303–09), is Thomas Walter's attack on John Checkley, *A Choice Dialogue Between John Faustus, a Conjurer, and Jack Tory, His Friend* (Evans 2194). Josiah Q. Bennett notes that the Lilly copy of John Gerar William De Brahm's *Time an Apparition of Eternity* (1791) (Evans 23319) has a detachable covering that served as a dust jacket (". . . and Other Detachable Coverings . . . ," *Serif* 8, iv[1971]:31–33). And two articles deal with travel literature. Oral S. Coad, "Some Traveler's Eye Views of the Jerseyman" (*JRUL* 25:41–66) surveys early opinions of New Jersey in travel accounts, and Lawrence S. Thompson, "German Travellers in the South from the Colonial Period Through 1865" (*SAB* 37,ii:64–74) gives a brief account, with a valuable bibliography.

viii. Other Studies

Two prolific translators of Spanish travel accounts of the New World "helped to keep the theme of overseas expansion" before the English public in the five years after Richard Eden's last work and before Richard Hakluyt's first translation (Loren E. Pennington, "John Frampton and Thomas Nicholas: Two Sixteenth-Century Propagandists for English Expansion," *ESRS* 20:5–23). Four articles appeared on the captivity narratives. Kathryn Whitford traces the "patterns of mutations and interpretation" in Cotton Mather's three versions of the story of Hannah Dustin, who killed her Indian captors, before surveying the later appearances of the story in Thomas Hutchinson, Timothy Dwight, John Greenleaf Whittier, Thoreau, and Hawthorne ("Hannah Dustin: The Judgement of History," *EIHC* 108:304–25). In the first of three essays by Richard VanDerBeets on the captivities ("A Surfeit of Style: The Indian Captivity Narrative as Penny Dreadful," *RS* 39[1971]:297–306) the development of sensationalism in the captivities is followed from its rise with the flourishing of sentimentality in the mid-eighteenth century to its culmination "in the travesty of the pulp thriller." In " 'A Thirst for Empire': The Indian Captivity Narrative as Propaganda" (*RS* 40:207–15) VanDerBeets notes the anti-French and anti-Catholic propaganda in the captivities during the colonial period, the anti-English sentiments during the Revolutionary period, and (not surprisingly) the anti-Indian sentiments thereafter. And in "The Indian Captivity Narrative as Ritual"

(*AL* 43:548–62), VanDerBeets argues that the captivities generally conform to an archetypal pattern of initiation, including "Separation (abduction), Transformation (ordeal, accommodation, and adoption), and Return (escape, release, or redemption)" and maintains that this pattern, together with "such ritual practices as cannibalism and scalping," accounts for the emotional strength of these former best sellers.

Volume 16 of Clifford K. Shipton's *Biographical Sketches of Those Who Attended Harvard College . . . 1764–1767* (Boston, Mass. Historical Society) includes sketches of the poets Oliver Whipple and Nathaniel Niles (whose "The American Hero" was one of the most popular songs of the Revolution), the author Asa Dunbar, and the intellectual and Harvard president Joseph Willard. Lodwick Hartley's "The Dying Soldier and the Love-Lorn Virgin: Notes on Sterne's Early Reception in America," (in Arthur H. Cash and John M. Stedmond's *The Winged Skull: Papers from the Laurence Sterne Bicentenary Conference*, Kent, Ohio, Kent State Univ. Press, 1971, pp. 159–69) traces Sterne's role in America, not only his popularity with individual figures like Franklin and Jefferson but also his influence on such genres as the sentimental novel and the Shandean drama, and includes a checklist of the American editions of Laurence Stern to 1800 (pp. 311–12). Finally, David C. Humphrey, in "Colonial Colleges and English Dissenting Academies: A Study in Transatlantic Culture," (*HEQ* 12:184–97) cogently rejects the received opinion that the English dissenting colleges were important influences on colonial education.

University of California, Los Angeles

10. Nineteenth-Century Fiction

M. Thomas Inge

In sheer quantity, the amount of material published on the authors covered in this chapter decreased slightly during 1972 in comparison with the last two years. It is a pleasure to report, however, that the quality of the scholarly effort and critical judgment exercised has been quite high and often distinguished. This is especially true of book-length studies by Jay B. Hubbell, John P. McWilliams, Donald A. Ringe, James W. Tuttleton, Benjamin Lease, Merrill Maguire Skaggs, and Howard Kerr. One hopes that this indicates a new period of higher standards in scholarly inquiry and publication.

i. General Topics

The rise and fall of literary reputations and answers to the question "Who are the best American writers?" are fascinating subjects of inquiry for literary historians because they tell us so much about the intellectual climate of the times and the relationship of literature to popular and critical sentiment. One of our finest literary historians, Jay B. Hubbell, has spent almost two decades studying the subject and has produced a remarkable survey of the ups and downs in the rankings of American writers in *Who Are the Major American Writers?* (Durham, N.C., Duke Univ. Press). The first half of the book is concerned with the nineteenth century, during which "Americans kept looking hopefully for the great American writer whom the British insisted that the new nation must produce to prove its intellectual greatness." In addition to the writers given full chapters in this volume elsewhere, Hubbell provides interesting commentary on the reputations of Irving, Cooper, Simms, Howells, Crane, and numerous other minor figures, although the wealth of material included is made less accessible by a selective index.

Like the other useful Goldentree Bibliographies, Harry Hayden

Clark's *American Literature: Poe Through Garland* (New York,
Appleton-Century-Crofts, 1971) contains selective checklists on
Cooper, Crane, Garland, Howells, Norris, and many lesser nineteenth-
century fiction writers. Numerous such writers are also covered in
the checklists in *Western American Literature: A Bibliography of
Interpretive Books and Articles* by Richard W. Etulain (Vermillion,
Univ. of South Dakota), which also has a general section on local
color and regionalism. Another item of bibliographic interest is the
"Index and Author Guide to the *Family Companion* (1841–43)" by
Robert A. Rees and Marjorie Griffin (*SB* 25:205–12), which locates
pieces in that Georgia publication by William A. Caruthers, Caroline
Lee Hentz, John Neal, William Gilmore Sims, and William Tappan
Thompson, among others.

In "Frivolity to Consumption: Or, Southern Womanhood in
Antebellum Literature" (*CWH* 18:213–29) John C. Ruoff's intent is
to test William R. Taylor's contentions that women became a central
force in the plantation legend and that the plantation became a
matriarchy, through an analysis of novels, romances, and sketches
published in the North and South between 1832 and 1861 by such
writers as Stowe, Kennedy, Paulding, Simms, John Esten Cooke,
Caroline Lee Hentz, Emma D. E. N. Southworth, St. George Tucker,
Maria J. McIntosh, Caroline E. Rush, and Emily C. Pearson. Ruoff
finds no evidence to support Taylor, although his essay is too cursory
to be entirely convincing. More satisfactory and informative is Kenneth M. Roemer's "Sex Roles, Utopia and Change: The Family in
Late Nineteenth-Century Utopian Literature" (*AmerS* 13,ii:33–47),
which finds that the descriptions of love affairs and family life found
in the flood of utopian novels between Edward Bellamy's *Looking
Backward* in 1888 and 1900 "provide revealing insights into American
attitudes about sex roles, and, furthermore, illuminate the complex
mixture of 'radicalism' and 'conservatism' that characterizes many
American reform movements."

Although I have seen only the first of two installments, Limin
Chu's "Mirror of Darkness: The Images of China and the Chinese in
the Fiction of the *Overland Monthly*" (*TR* 2[1971]:15–49) reviews
and categorizes eighty-one stories published in the San Francisco
magazine with interesting results. Part 1 deals with tales in the categories of Chinese invasion, opium, oriental vengeance, and "Dark
Ways and Vain Tricks." "The Image of the Negro in Popular Maga-

zine Fiction, 1875–1900" by George R. Lamplugh (*JNH* 57:177–89) examines several popular magazines (*Atlantic, Harper's, Scribner's*) for black images in short stories and not unexpectedly finds further examples of the well-known stereotypes which dominated fiction of the era.

ii. Irving, Cooper, and Their Contemporaries

Lewis Leary's "The Two Voices of Washington Irving" (*From Irving to Steinbeck*, pp. 13–26) is a sensible and concisely written essay which distinguishes between the characters, styles, and humor of Geoffrey Crayon and Diedrich Knickerbocker, Irving's two personae. It is easily one of the best assessments of Irving's comic spirit in print. An engaging study in international cultural relations is found in "Washington Irving's Hispanic Literature" by C. A. Baiocco (*Américas* 24,iv:2–11), a heavily illustrated survey of the influence of Spain on the literary and intellectual development of Irving. An interesting manifestation of his interest in Spanish culture is his unpublished eighteen-page autograph manuscript, apparently a translation from Ambrosio de Morales's *La Crónica General de España* (1586), which William J. Scheick has edited in " 'The Seven Sons of Lara': A Washington Irving Manuscript" (*RALS* 2:208–17). The occasion for the thin volume of essays compiled by editor Andrew B. Myers, *Washington Irving: A Tribute* (Tarrytown, N.Y., Sleepy Hollow Restorations), was the sesquicentennial of the publication of *The Sketch Book*. Considering the impressive list of contributors—Haskell S. Springer, William L. Hedges, Carl H. Woodring, Lorman A. Ratner, Herbert L. Kleinfield, Joseph T. Butler, William M. Gibson, and Myers—it is a pity they were so severely limited to such brief, superficial statements. The illustrations, however, make the book an attractive collectors' item.

Of less consequence are the other Irving items: Benjamin Lease provides further information about Irving's being proposed as a member of a committee to construct a monument to Shakespeare in 1823 and the controversy it caused in "*John Bull* Versus Washington Irving: More on the Shakespeare Committee Controversy" (*ELN* 9:272–77); Bruce Granger writes a brief appreciation of "The Whim-Whamsical Bachelors in *Salmagundi*" (*Costerus* 2:63–69); and Ben Harris McClary publishes the suppressed portion of an 1823 letter demonstrating that at least once Irving procured a manuscript for the plagiaristic purposes of a friend, John Howard Payne, in "Irving's Literary Pimpery" (*AN&Q* 10:150–51). The first general anthology of American short stories, Mary Russell Mitford's *Stories of American Life* (London, 1830), has been reprinted in facsimile, with an introduction by Clarence Gohdes (3 vols., New York, MSS Information Corp.). Interestingly enough, Irving was excluded, said Miss Mitford, because "his writings are essentially European, and must be content to take their station amongst the Spectators and Tattlers of the mother country."

Cooper was the subject of an extremely thorough study of political values in his writing by John P. McWilliams, Jr., *Political Justice in a Republic: James Fenimore Cooper's America* (Berkeley, Univ. of Calif. Press). McWilliams takes Cooper at his own word, that he was "a gentleman who is the reputed author of a series of tales, which were intended to elucidate the history, manner, usages, and scenery, of his native land" (*Notions of the Americans*, 1828), and examines his work as a defense and proclamation of the political truths of his fledgling nation. Setting aside artistic and biographical considerations, McWilliams engages in a series of exhaustive political analyses of selected fiction and non-fiction to outline Cooper as the consistent republican he remained until 1850. The result is a fine example of intellectual history that informs and clarifies. In his comprehensive study of *Democratic Humanism* (pp. 103–13) Harold Kaplan discusses some of the political reasons why D. H. Lawrence reacted so strongly to Cooper and placed him at the center of his thesis on American culture and values. Cooper also figures prominently in Edward K. Spann's impressive historical study of shifting personal, moral, and intellectual relationships of a group of cultural leaders in *Ideals and Politics: New York Intellectuals and Liberal Democracy, 1820–1880* (Albany, State Univ. of N. Y. Press).

Both Irving and Cooper are approached from a unique point of view in *The Pictorial Mode: Space and Time in the Art of Bryant, Irving and Cooper* by Donald A. Ringe (Lexington, Univ. of Ky. Press), one of the year's most inspired and original studies. On the assumption that literature and painting are analogous arts, Ringe details the affinities that exist between the aesthetic theories of the Hudson River School painters and the literary practice of Bryant, Irving, and Cooper, especially the emphasis on visual perception and

the belief that knowledge of the external world derives from sensation. With focus on the concepts of space and time, Ringe earns his
conclusion that an understanding of the pictorial style would appear
essential for an accurate interpretation and just estimate of the
authors' artistic success. The book represents interdisciplinary criticism at its best and suggests the need for more studies of writers
within their total cultural contexts. "It may seem surprising to begin
a study of novelists of manners in America with James Fenimore
Cooper," says James W. Tuttleton in *The Novel of Manners in America* (Chapel Hill, Univ. of N.C. Press), pp. 28–47, but he does so in
an effort to prove that "Cooper was *first*, if not foremost, a novelist of
manners" through his urgent concern over "the relationship of manners to morals and the interplay of social classes." Clearly Cooper's
first and inferior novel *Precaution* (1824) was modeled after the
British novel of manners, and Tuttleton goes on to display convincingly how these matters remained central to his artistic concerns. In the
process he throws an interesting light on Cooper's fiction. " 'But the
Penalty of Adam': Cooper's Sense of the Subversive" (*CRevAS* 3:21–
32) by Geoffrey Rans makes out a case for Cooper's awareness of the
meaning of the spoliation of the virgin forest and the consequences
of man's war against his natural environment.

A now forgotten novelist who threatened to become Cooper's
chief rival in the 1820s was John Neal, a startling and sensational
figure now accorded a full-length biographical-critical assessment by
Benjamin Lease in *That Wild Fellow: John Neal and the American
Literary Revolution* (Univ. of Chicago Press). According to Lease's
well researched and written account, Neal must have led the most
tempestuous and fascinating life of a man of letters in the nineteenth
century, and while his accomplishments were minor, his influence on
and anticipations of Poe, Hawthorne, Melville, Whitman, and Twain
should be recognized. Poe called him a genius, others called him a
madman, but Hawthorne paid the most interesting tribute in 1845:
"How slowly our literature grows up! Most of our writers of promise
have come to untimely ends. There was that wild fellow, John Neal,
who almost turned my boyish brain with his romances; he surely has
long been dead, else he never would keep himself so quiet." Lease's
study is that rare thing—an entertaining piece of scholarship. Other
contemporaries of Irving and Cooper were given some attention this
year: Doreen Hunter perceptively analyzed "America's First Ro-

mantics: Richard Henry Dana, Sr., and Washington Allston" (*NEQ* 45:3–30); Michael Fellman discussed "Sexual Longing in Richard Henry Dana, Jr.'s American Victorian Diary" (*CRevAS* 3:96–105); and Joyce Henry discovered "Five More Essays by James Kirke Paulding?" (*PBSA* 66:310–321), that is five anonymous satiric "Leaves from Mrs. Trollope's Journal" which clearly appear to have come from his hand.

William Gilmore Simms was the subject of a considerable amount of critical attention, especially in the pages of the *Southern Literary Journal*, where six essays appeared. James E. Kibler makes clear "Simms' Indebtedness to Folk Tradition in 'Sharp Snaffles'" (4,ii:55–68) by relating three events in the story to well-established folk parallels, and John C. Guilds's "Simms as Editor and Prophet: The Flowering and Early Death of the Southern *Magnolia*" (4,ii:69–92) details an important chapter in Simms's career as editor of the *Magnolia; or Southern Monthly* from July 1842 until its demise in June 1843, because of difficulties which he himself predicted would doom any Southern magazine. "Of Time and the South: The Fiction of William Gilmore Simms" by Simone Vauthier (5,i:3–45) is an extensive and revealing examination of the importance of "time" as a concept in the fiction. The strategies elucidated by Vauthier enhance our respect for Simms and demonstrate that he had a view of "time" which was then novel in American fiction. Annette Kolodny's discussion of "The Unchanging Landscape: The Pastoral Impulse in Simms's Revolutionary War Romances" (5,i:46–67) carefully explicates the historical romances in an effort to understand Simms's attitudes towards nature and his pastoral inclinations. Mary Ann Wimsatt makes out a good case for "Simms as Novelist of Manners: *Katharine Walton*" (5,i:68–88) by analyzing his "social life novel" of 1845 mentioned in the title, although he once disparaged the form. Finally, "From Notes to Novel: Simms's Creative Method" (5,i:89–107) by Miriam J. Shillingsburg describes how Simms reused his own materials in his writings and reveals that "he can often be praised for taking particular care with his style in order to produce the kind of dramatic excitement he found effective in fiction and which he praised in his contemporaries." An authoritative critique of Simms as a writer of short stories, a form in which he apparently had considerable skill, is found in John C. Guilds, "The Achievement of William Gilmore Simms: His Short Fiction" (*Spectrum* 2:25–35).

Simms and a variety of his contemporaries are subjected to a series
of concise and sensibly focused essays on views of blacks in American
prose from the Declaration of Independence to the Emancipation
Proclamation in Jean Fagan Yellin's *The Intricate Knot: Black Figures in American Literature, 1776–1863* (New York, N.Y. Univ.
Press). The figures covered are Thomas Jefferson, George Tucker,
James Kirke Paulding, John Pendleton Kennedy, William Gilmore
Simms, Richard Hildreth, Harriet Beecher Stowe, William Wells
Brown, Nat Turner, and Martin Robison Delany. She then concludes
with an analysis of Melville's "Benito Cereno" and certifies it as per-
haps the nineteenth century's most profound response to racism in
creative literature.

iii. Local Color, Humor, and Popular Fiction

The best single piece of scholarship on the local-color writers as a
group to appear in some time is Merrill Maguire Skaggs's *The Folk
of Southern Fiction* (Athens, Univ. of Ga. Press). Comprehensive in
its grasp and sensitive in its perceptions, she proves that the Southern
plain folk have been an important presence in literature beginning
with the Southwestern humorists and extending through the local
colorists; that their life was recorded and preserved in all its details;
and that according to this picture, "the defining characteristics of
lives lived by plain folk in the South are isolation, a generous hospi-
tality offered strangers, an indulgence in gossip, a consuming interest
in romance, an intolerance of differing opinions, and a propensity for
violence." Mrs. Skaggs demonstrates how effectively fiction can be
used to recapture facts of the past, but in addition she takes the time
to speak about the art of a host of major and minor regional writers
and provides a fine analysis of their stylistic techniques as well.

One of the early titles in the new Western Writers Series is *Bret
Harte* by Patrick Morrow (WWS 5), who tries to rescue him from
both "the amateur enthusiasts and the moral elitists" by surveying in
a balanced perspective his initiation of the local color movement, his
achievements as a comic writer, and his contributions as a critic and
editor of American letters. The concise pamphlet is a fine introduction
to a writer who is much misunderstood and undervalued. A useful
tool for future reassessments has been provided by Linda D. Barnett
in the form of an extensive, two-part checklist, "Bret Harte: An An-

notated Bibliography of Secondary Comment" (*ALR* 5:189–320 [1865–1904] and 331–484 [1905–1971]), helpfully indexed and with an introduction by Patrick Morrow on "The Predicament of Bret Harte" (5:181–88). This apparently brings into print the major portion of Mrs. Barnett's dissertation, "The Critics of Bret Harte: An Annotated Bibliography" (*DAI* 33:1713A). The Kate Chopin revival has slacked off, although there were two good articles and two dissertations. "The Romantic Imagery in Kate Chopin's *The Awakening*" by Donald A. Ringe (*AL* 43:580–88) attempts to open the novel to a broader interpretation than is usually made by reading it in terms of the transcendental concept of the soul's emergence into a new life, and "Pride and Prejudice: Kate Chopin's 'Désirée's Baby' " by Robert D. Arner (*MissQ* 25:131–40) finds that often anthologized but misjudged story one of Mrs. Chopin's most successful efforts.

Several other local colorists received brief attention. In "Craddock's Girls: A Look at Some Unliberated Women" (*MarkhamR* 3:74–77), Mary Nilles surveys Mary Noailles Murfree's shallow, uneducated, and submissive females for curious reasons. She should be reminded that there were many women like that in the pre-liberation days and that Miss Murfree would in fact have been dishonest to her experience to have depicted them otherwise. She was no Kate Chopin nor pretended to be. Perhaps a hundred years from now, someone will read Ms. Nilles's essay and think how obvious and silly some female literary criticism could be in the twentieth century. Doris Lanier's "Mary Noailles Murfree: An Interview" (*THQ* 31:276–78) reprints an article published in the Macon (Ga.) *Telegraph*, November 15, 1885, reporting a conversation with the author about her writing habits. Susan Allen Toth ("Sarah Orne Jewett and Friends: A Community of Interest," *SSF* 9:233–41) discusses literary relations between Miss Jewett and three other contemporaries—Rose Terry Cooke, Mary Wilkins Freeman, and Alice Brown. Arlin Turner has edited an 1882 open letter by "George W. Cable on Prison Reform" (*HLQ* 36:69–75), and in an essay-review on "Lafcadio Hearn in Cincinnati" (*New Republic* 167, 7 Oct.:32–33) John F. Szwed and Carol Parssinen comment on Hearn's early years as a typical muckraking journalist in Cincinnati of the 1870s. Although Hearn earned the unfair label of a youthful sensationalist, he "descended into the depths of urban life to revel in its unseen glories and to unmask humanity in its apparent ugliness." Useful bibliographical materials are

Jean Nosser Biglane's "Sherwood Bonner: A Bibliography of Primary and Secondary Materials" (*ALR* 5:39–60) and Susan Allen Toth's "Alice Brown (1857–1948)" (*ALR* 5:134–43).

Another pamphlet in the Western Writers Series is devoted to an Easterner who came west armed both with sketch pad and pen, *Mary Hallock Foote* by James H. Maguire (WWS 2). Mrs. Foote was one of the first women to portray the West in fiction; and while recognizing her weakness, Maguire recommends her for her sensitivity and candor in her portrayals of frontier life. Richard W. Etulain has contributed a bibliographical essay, "Mary Hallock Foote (1847–1938)" (*ALR* 5:145–50). Another Easterner who settled in Michigan and set about preserving in frank prose the raw aspects of life on that Midwestern frontier is assessed in *Caroline M. Kirkland* by William S. Osborne (TUSAS 207). Though heavily dependent on excerpt and summary, since Mrs. Kirkland's works are largely unknown and unavailable, Osborne clarifies the reasons for her success in her own day when she earned the respect of Poe and the American reading public.

The third volume in the Harvard English Studies entitled *Veins of Humor* and edited by Harry Levin (Cambridge, Mass., Harvard Univ. Press) is a miscellaneous collection of essays united only by their general concern with humor, but four concern specifically American topics. In "Transcendental Antics" (pp. 167–83) Joel Porte decidedly proves that "the comic impulse is a significant component of Transcendentalism" and provides an engaging view of the lighter side of sombre old Emerson and a few others caught at play. The dean of scholars in American humor, Walter Blair, with his usual authority and gentle wit, traces the persistence of the comic narrative modeled upon the oral tale through more than a century and a half in " 'A Man's Voice Speaking': A Continuum in American Humor" (pp. 185–204). Bruce Jackson's "The *Titanic* Toast" (pp. 205–23) examines variants of the black oral narrative poem called the "toast" about the sinking of the Titanic, and Roger Rosenblatt's "The 'Negro Everyman' and His Humor" (pp. 225–41) is an incisive appreciation of Langston Hughes's character Jesse B. Semple. Also, W. M. Frohock's "The Edge of Laughter: Some Modern Fiction and the Grotesque" (pp. 243–54) incorporates comments about humor in Ralph Ellison, and if you want to catch pop novelist Erich Segal on stage as a serious scholar, he has an essay here on comedy in Christopher

Marlowe (pp. 69–91). Other general pieces on American humor in the periodicals include John Q. Anderson's interesting study of "Some Migratory Anecdotes in American Folk Humor" (*MissQ* 25:447–57) and James L. W. West III's valuable survey and checklist of "Early Backwoods Humor in the Greenville *Mountaineer*, 1826–1840" (*MissQ* 25:69–82). Two significant anthologies in the development of nineteenth-century American humor have been reprinted in facsimile (New York, MSS Information Corp.): *Polly Peablossom's Wedding* (1851), edited by T. A. Burke, and *Mark Twain's Library of Humor* (1888), edited by Clemens, Howells, and Charles Hopkins Clark, with a new foreword by Clarence Gohdes outlining the book's history.

The best study of an individual humorist this year is John A. Reed's *Benjamin Penhallow Shillaber* (TUSAS 209), who created the enormously popular female character Mrs. Partington. Reed's intent is "to analyze the techniques and values of his humor, to relate it to the native comic tradition, and to show that he possessed more versatility as a humorist than has generally been assumed." He largely succeeds, although the nature of the material has required heavy quotation, almost an anthology approach. Perhaps, however, that's one of the best ways to construct a study of a humorist, as illustrated by Louis Hasley's edition of *The Best of Bill Nye's Humor* (New Haven, Conn., College and Univ. Press). Hasley's biographical and critical introduction and his selection of eighty-two excerpts may do more for Nye's reputation, once nearly rivaling that of Mark Twain, than a dozen evaluative essays. This is not to say that a humorist's accomplishment cannot be enhanced by a judicious and well-written appreciation, such as that on George Washington Harris by Eugene Current-Garcia, "Sut Lovingood's Rare Ripe Southern Garden" (*SSF* 9:117–29), a comprehensive statement of what makes Harris's writing so compelling for both his admirers and denigrators, the best since Milton Rickels' study for the Twayne series (see *ALS 1965*, p. 134). Gerald L. Smith ("Augustus Baldwin Longstreet and John Wade's 'Cousin Lucius,'" *GHQ* 56:276–81) not unexpectedly finds parallels between the central figure in Wade's contribution to *I'll Take My Stand* (1930), "The Life and Death of Cousin Lucius," and Longstreet, on whom Wade wrote an authoritative biography in 1924. "Josh Billings and His Burlesque 'Allminax'" by David K. Kesterson (*IllQ* 35:6–14) describes the popular comic almanacs produced by Henry Wheeler Shaw from 1870 to 1879. Clarence L. Mohr's "Candid Comments from a Mississippi Author" (*MissQ* 25:83–93) publishes two letters by sometime humorist Joseph B. Cobb; and James C. Austin's "Charles Farrar Browne (1834–1867)" (*ALR* 5:151–65) is a thorough bibliographical essay.

A fascinating study in popular culture, excellent for its thorough research and scholarly style, is Howard Kerr's *Mediums, and Spirit-Rappers, and Roaring Radicals: Spiritualism in American Literature, 1850–1900* (Urbana, Univ. of Ill. Press). In studying the development of spiritualism during what Hawthorne dubbed the "Epoch of the Rapping Spirits," when Kate and Margaret, the famed Fox sisters, were the talk of people everywhere, he has outlined a popular cult which touched the American literary imagination at all points. As Kerr amply demonstrates, the spiritualist movement profoundly influenced Melville, Hawthorne, Howells, James, Twain, and a host of lesser lights, and from *Pierre* to *Huckleberry Finn*, their writings reflect this influence. As entertaining as it is informative, this study clearly establishes the importance of popular culture in understanding the art and literature of any given era. This service, unfortunately, is not performed by the disparate group of essays gathered by James C. Austin and Donald A. Koch in *Popular Literature in America* (Bowling Green, Ohio, Bowling Green Univ. Popular Press). There seems to be no working definition of popular literature uniting the essays or principle of organization behind the anthology. The best pieces are Arlin Turner's "The Uncertainties of Authorship in the South After the Civil War" (pp. 184–98) and Lewis Leary's "The Lovingoods: Notes Toward a Genealogy" (pp. 112–28, collected earlier in his *Southern Excursions*; see *ALS 1972*, p. 178). The remaining thirteen essays, on everything from dialect sermons to television, were written by Margaret P. Ford, C. Hugh Holman, Wilton Eckley, John T. Flanagan, Lee Coyle, George W. Linden, Sylvia Kluth, John T. Flautz, George Kummer, Alma J. Payne, Harry M. Brown, and editors Austin and Koch. The book is a festschrift in honor of Lyon N. Richardson.

In "The American Railroad Novel" by Dorothy J. Smith (*MarkhamR* 3:61–71;85–93) a comprehensive survey is provided of both nineteenth and twentieth century examples of this genre of popular fiction. Michael Zuckerman's perceptive analysis of "The Nursery Tales of Horatio Alger" (*AQ* 24:191–209) makes the interesting discoveries that in Alger's formulaic novels, "Beneath his explicit emphasis on striving upward ran a deeper desire for stability and security; beneath his paeans to manly vigor, a lust for effeminate indulgence; beneath his celebration of self-reliance, a craving to be taken care of and a yearning to surrender the terrible burden of independence." That makes quite a difference in how we calculate the influence of "our rhapsodist of rags-to-riches." Also, Bruce E. Coad finds that there is less idealism and more blatant materialism operating behind the typical protagonist of these novels in "The Alger Hero: Humanitarian or Hustler?" (*CCTET* 37:21–24). Brita Lindberg-Seyersted's "Three Variations of the American Success Story: The Careers of Luke Larkin, Lemuel Barker, and Lemuel Pitkin" (*ES* 53:1–16) traces the success myth from Alger's *Struggling Upward* through Howells's *The Minister's Charge* to Nathanael West's *A Cool Million* to find respectively "the full acceptance of the myth, a sincere questioning of it, and a total rejection." Although it holds no surprises for American readers, foreign students will find it a sensible introduction to the theme in these three novels.

Ralph D. Gardner has published a revised edition of his thorough *Road to Success: The Bibliography of the Works of Horatio Alger* (Mendota, Ill., Wayside Press, 1971). George Lippard, that popular scandalous novelist of the 1840s, has been given an intelligent assessment which effectively designs for him a unique place in American letters, by Heyward Ehrlich, "The 'Mysteries' of Philadelphia: Lippard's *Quaker City* and 'Urban' Gothic" (*ESQ* 18:50–65).

iv. Howells, Realism, and Post-Civil-War Fiction

Jay B. Hubbell's chapter on Howells in *Who Are the Major American Writers?*, pp. 115–22, is a concise survey of the rise and fall of his reputation from the "laying on of hands" by the New England Brahmins to the Howells revival of the 1950s. Hubbell quotes Carl Van Doren, writing only three years after Howells's death, "Where else, indeed, may be found another representation of American life during half a century as extended and accurate as that in Howells's total work?" This too is the reason offered by James W. Tuttleton on why Howells deserves to be read in the chapter on Howells in *The Novel of Manners in America* (pp. 86–121): "Few writers of his time brought to life so vividly the social experience of nineteenth-century America or dramatized so convincingly the problems of middle-class existence in fiction." Moving from *Their Wedding Journey* (1872) through *The Rise of Silas Lapham* (1885), Tuttleton expands upon his argument in graceful prose. It is an expanded, revised, and improved version of an earlier essay (see *ALS 1970*, p. 193).

Sam B. Girgus's intriguing reading of "Bartley Hubbard: The Rebel in Howells' *A Modern Instance*" (*RS* 39[1971]:315–21) finds that while Howells condemned Bartley's character, behavior, and honesty, it is also possible to view him as a born rebel who almost without conscious intention challenges the middle-class values, standards, and power structure of his world and thus becomes something of an early existential anti-hero. Paul A. Eschholz remains more on the surface in his reading of the novel as an important "initial attempt to seriously understand and interpret the rapidly changing conditions of American society": "Howells' *A Modern Instance*: A Realist's Moralistic Vision of America" (*SDR* 10:91–102). A bit more specialized and carefully researched is Nathalia Wright's "The Significance of the Legal Profession in *A Modern Instance*" (*From Irving to Steinbeck*, pp. 57–70), in which she finds the practice of law a touchstone in the characterization and a key to the central theme—"the problem, inherent in the democratic system, of insuring the liberty of the individual without the forfeiture of social responsibility."

In a second essay, "The Moral World of Silas Lapham: Howells' Romantic Vision of America in the 1880s" (*RS* 40:115–121), Eschholz interprets *The Rise of Silas Lapham* as an effort of Howells to "reassure himself that industrialism, economic progress, and the influx of immigrants into the United States had not tainted or harmed the security of Jeffersonian morality," in the wake of the change and chaos portrayed in *A Modern Instance*. It is a sensible reading of the novel's social comment. Ralph Behrens emphasizes the importance of recognizing the character of Bromfield Corey in *The Rise of Silas Lapham* as "Howells' Portrait of a Boston Brahmin" (*MarkhamR* 3:71–73), and Herbert V. Fackler finds in the novel a graphic portrayal of "the evils of estrangement from the native soil" in "Sticking to the Roots: The Deracination Motif in *The Rise of Silas Lapham*" (*MarkhamR* 3:73–74). John W. Crowley's "The Length of Howells' *Shadow of a Dream*" (*NCF* 27:182–96) discusses the philosophical questions raised in that novel where "Howells confronted the threat to his vision of moral order posed by his growing awareness of sub-

conscious motivation in human behavior. Does suffering, particularly
in the form of psychological anxiety, serve any moral purpose? Is
morality itself psychologically relative?" George Fortenberry identifies "The Unnamed Critic in William Dean Howells' *Heroines of
Fiction*" (*MTJ* 16,i:7–8) as his friend Mark Twain.

Several items of bibliographical interest appeared. Ulrich Halfmann and Don R. Smith completed "William Dean Howells: A
Revised and Annotated Bibliography of Secondary Comment in
Periodicals and Newspapers, 1868–1919" (*ALR* 5:91–121), which
corrects and expands a portion of an earlier checklist in the journal's
special number on W. D. Howells (see *ALS 1969*, p. 173). Ulrich
Halfmann also has located some hitherto unknown periodical writings
by Howells as a literary critic and social commentator in "Addenda
to Gibson and Arms: Twenty-Three New Howells Items" (*PBSA*
66:174–77). Scott Bennett, "David Douglas and the British Publication of W. D. Howells' Works" (*SB* 25:107–24), details the publication history of the works in Britain and the efforts of Howells and
his Edinburgh publisher, Douglas, to protect the literary property
from piracy. In one paper from an MLA Seminar on "Practical Editions" (*Proof* 2:293–300), Don L. Cook examined the Howells texts
available in anthologies, hardcover books, and paperbacks and found
a dreary representation of anthology excerpts, outrageously priced
hardcover reprints, a few efforts at responsibly edited paperbacks,
and general textual corruption among them all (except for the CEAA
texts). Hershel Parker has written a thorough and responsible review
essay on "The First Nine Volumes of a Selected Edition of W. D.
Howells" (*Proof* 2: 319–32) and finds the project a great success. Of
incidental interest is a reprinting of a piece from the Boston *Journal*
of March 1, 1890, by "J. P." about the principal characters in *A Hazard
of New Fortunes* (*ALR* 5:74–77).

George Perkins's textbook *Realistic American Short Fiction* (Glenview, Ill., Scott, Foresman) provides a concise survey of the history
and meanings of realism in the introductory essay. An anthology
edited by Hans Bungert, *Die amerikanische Short Story: Theorie und
Entwicklung* (Darmstadt, Wissenschaftliche Buchgesellschaft) collects some critical essays not easily accessible and includes an original
one by Paul Goetsch, "Die Begrenzung der Short Story" (pp. 368–87).
Of the twenty-three essays by Americans and Germans, sixteen are
in English. Edwin H. Cady's effort last year to define realism in *The*

Light of Common Day: Realism in American Fiction (see *ALS 1971*, pp. 167–68) occasioned a seminar discussion at the MLA convention in December. The papers prepared by the three panelists—Louis J. Budd, Marjorie Dew, and David E. E. Sloane—were published in *American Literary Realism* (5:485–91).

Sibley S. Morrill has completed an intriguing piece of detective work in *Ambrose Bierce, F. A. Mitchell-Hedges and the Crystal Skull* (San Francisco, Cadleon Press) which provides another solution to the reason for Bierce's presence in Mexico in 1913 before his mysterious disappearance—that he was sent there as a government intelligence agent to gather information on Japanese and German threats to American interests. Though too complicated to summarize here, Morrill's argument is long on speculation and short on material evidence, but readers should judge its merits on their own. One Mexico City newspaper found it of sufficient interest to publish an abridged translation of the brief book in serial form: "El Misterio de la Calavera Maya de Cristal" (*Excelsior* 21 Dec.: 4A; 22 Dec.: 4A; 23 Dec.: 4A; 24 Dec.: 4A, 18A; and 26 Dec.: 4A), and there was some talk of a movie version. Highly sensitive to the unexpected depths of Bierce's fiction, William Bysshe Stein explicates one of his stories in "Bierce's 'The Death of Halpin Frayser': The Poetics of Gothic Consciousness" (*ESQ* 18:115–22), and Joseph J. Comprone makes suggestions for taking "A Dual-Media Look at 'An Occurrence at Owl Creek Bridge'" (*EE* 17:14–17).

John William DeForest was the subject of a brief study by Frank Bergman, *The Worthy Gentleman of Democracy: John William De-Forest and the American Dream* (Heidelberg, Carl Winter, 1971), which concentrates on the author's thought and moral imagination rather than the historic and artistic importance of his fiction (the usual approaches) to interpret it against his growing conception of the American Dream. The result is a carefully researched and solid piece of intellectual history which clarifies DeForest's intent as a writer, although the extensive documentation and footnotes sometimes threaten to outweigh the text. George Monteiro, "John Hay's Fiction" (*SSF* 8[1971]:543–52), surveys the brief fictional work of a promising writer of the 1860s who would earn distinction as a biographer of Lincoln, and Ronald L. Baker notices another forgotten writer in "An Annotated Bibliography of Works about Rowland E. Robinson" (*VH* 40:67–72).

v. Stephen Crane

Partly as a result of celebrating the centennial of Stephen Crane's birth (November 1, 1871) and the increasing vigor of Crane scholars, a great variety of materials appeared this year. The one book-length study is *Cylinder of Vision: The Fiction and Journalistic Writing of Stephen Crane* by Milne Holton (Baton Rouge, La. State Univ. Press), which attempts to clarify the paradox of Crane's complex commitment to both naturalism and impressionism by exploring his use of vision and his control of the way the characters, the author, and the reader see things. Rather than take a radical departure from the existing body of Crane criticism, Holton's stated intention is to build his critical position upon it. This is both the book's value and weakness—that is, the book all too often reads like a synthesis and summary which would be useful to the beginning Crane scholar, but Holton's own contributions are buried in it. Its originality might have been rendered more serviceable in a slender volume excluding the summaries. I would also question Holton's decision to omit attention to the poetry because of its "idiosyncratic nature"—all the more reason to study it in relation to the rest of Crane's work.

Stephen Crane in Transition: Centenary Essays (Dekalb, No. Ill. Univ. Press) is a collection of ten original pieces edited, with an introduction, by Joseph Katz. Moving systematically over Crane's work, Bernard Weinstein writes on "Stephen Crane: Journalist" (pp. 3–34), Marston LaFrance on "*George's Mother* and the Other Half of *Maggie*" (pp. 35–53), Jean Cazemajou on "*The Red Badge of Courage*: The 'Religion of Peace' and the War Archetype" (pp. 54–65), E. R. Hagemann on " 'Sadder Than the End': Another Look at 'The Open Boat' " (pp. 66–85), Max Westbrook on "Whilomville: The Coherence of Radical Language" (pp. 86–105), and Lillian B. Gilkes on "*The Third Violet, Active Service,* and *The O'Ruddy*: Stephen Crane's Potboilers" (pp. 106–26). The more general essays are "Stephen Crane: Style as Invention" by James B. Colvert (pp. 127–52), "Stephen Crane as a Collector's Item" by Matthew J. Bruccoli (pp. 153–73), and "Theodore Dreiser and Stephen Crane: Studies in a Literary Relationship" by Katz (pp. 174–204). Every single essay speaks with the authority of a large acquaintance with the Crane canon, and collectively they constitute a significant contribution to criticism, but special mention should be made of Katz's "Afterword: Resources for the Study of Stephen Crane" (pp. 205–31), a valuable point of departure for future scholarship. Thomas A. Gullason has assembled a rich variety of types of reprinted material in *Stephen Crane's Career: Perspectives and Evaluations* (New York, N.Y. Univ. Press): documents regarding Crane's family, eighteen brief estimates-reminiscences from the 1890s to the 1960s, five essays on the sources of Crane's art, six essays representing different critical approaches to his work, and twenty-two essays on specific novels, stories, and the poetry. To this Gullason has added two original essays of his own, several introductions to units, a biographical chronology, and a lengthy selective bibliography. The collection is a good representation of types of scholarship published on Crane and will be of value to students and scholars, although the absence of an index is regrettable. Also noteworthy are Joseph Katz's general reader's edition of *The Complete Poems of Stephen Crane* (Ithaca, N.Y., Cornell Univ. Press), based on his earlier critical edition (see *ALS 1967*, pp. 145–46), an excellent piece of editing; and R. W. Stallman's *The Stephen Crane Reader* (Glenview, Ill., Scott, Foresman), in which the editor unfortunately chose not to include the best available texts from Fredson Bowers's edition in progress.

What should have been the signal publication of the year turns out to be a massive monument to critical arrogance and scholarly revenge. Robert Wooster Stallman's formidable *Stephen Crane: A Critical Bibliography* (Ames, Iowa State Univ. Press) is of value only as an exhaustive checklist of writings by and about Crane. The needed descriptive and annotated bibliography remains to be done according to sound scholarly practice; hopefully next time it will elucidate Crane. In other bibliographical publications, Joseph Katz examines the sorry state of available paperback texts for teaching or reading Crane's best known novel in "Practical Editions: Stephen Crane's *The Red Badge of Courage*" (*Proof* 2:301–318); Fredson Bowers contributes four notes on editing procedures used in the Crane edition under way at the University of Virginia to *The Author's Intention* (Columbia, S.C., CEAA), a publication issued on the occasion of an exhibition for the CEAA at the Folger Shakespeare Library, February 14 to March 10, 1972; Lewis H. Fine comments on one of Crane's unfinished dramas, published last year (see *ALS*

1971, p. 185), in " 'The Fire-Tribe and the Pale-Face': An Unfinished
and Unpublished Play by Stephen Crane" (*MarkhamR* 3:37–38);
and John W. Ferstel provided a brief list of 1970–1971 additions to
"Stephen Crane Bibliography" (*Thoth* 12,iii:39–40). The issue of
the *Stephen Crane Newsletter* published this year (dated Vol. 5, no.
i, 1970) contained royalty figures on sales of *The Red Badge of Courage* from 1911 to 1923, a note on the age of Jimmie Trescott in "The
Monster" by Carl Ficken, a checklist of notices and reviews about
Crane in the weekly *Public Opinion* from 1895 to 1903 by George
Monteiro, a similar list of items in *The Argonaut* from 1895 to 1901
by E. R. Hagemann, and other items. Bernice Slote provides a textual
note on the reproduction of a manuscript version of the poem "War
Is Kind" in "Crane's 'Lines': A Manuscript Facsimile" (*PrS* 46:95).
Through an oversight, I failed to mention last year Stanley Wert-
heim's thorough and useful annotations on over one hundred pieces of
scholarship about Crane in his contribution to *Hawthorne, Melville,
Stephen Crane: A Critical Bibliography* (New York, Free Press; pp.
203–301).

Robert H. Elias's brief "Stephen Crane: Encore" (*EA* 24 [1971]:
444–48) surveys the difficulties confronting Crane biographers in the
course of reviewing Jean Cazemajou's *Stephen Crane (1871–1900):
écrivain journaliste* (1969), the published version of his French dissertation. Noting that little has been said about Crane's relationship
to the myth of the West as outlined by Henry Nash Smith, R. W. B.
Lewis, Leslie A. Fiedler, and others, Robert Glen Deamer has analyzed "Stephen Crane and the Western Myth" (*WAL* 7:111–23)
and argued that "Crane was, perhaps, not as obsessed with the consequences of the vanishing of the American wilderness as were
Cooper, Twain, or Faulkner; but his writings show that he did have
an intense awareness of the American myth of the West and that his
essential attitude toward 'The Passing of the West' was not parodic,
not satiric—but serious, sympathetic, and even tragic." "Stephen
Crane and the Antinomies of Christian Charity" by George Monteiro
(*CentR* 15:91–104) finds that perhaps his family religious influence
was the reason for the conflict between an uncongenial determinism
and his emotional response to life by examining "Crane's stubborn
preoccupation, as a person and a writer, with the Christian ideal of
charity as a possible and practicable antidote to man's predatory

instincts." Both Deamer's and Monteiro's essays are lucid and well-argued. Walter Sutton makes brief and inadequately developed comparisons between Crane, the Imagists, Whitman, and Emily Dickinson in "The Modernity of Stephen Crane's Poetry: A Centennial Tribute" (*Courier* 9[1971]:3–7), which raises more problems than it resolves; and the English summary of Yoshie Itabashi's "New York City Sketches—Crane's Creed and Art" (*SELit* (Eng. No.): 208–09) indicates that it deals with Crane's honesty and concern with human relations.

The mixture between colloquial and literary language in *The Red Badge of Courage* is subjected to careful analysis in "Crane and the Colloquial Self" by Neil Schmitz (*MQ* 13:437–51), one of the best studies of dialect and diction in Crane I have read, although there is much more to be said on the subject. Jean G. Marlowe's "Crane's Wafer Image: Reference to an Artillery Primer?" (*AL* 43:645–47) finds another source for the most debated image in American letters in an explosive device called a "wafer" used to fire a Civil War cannon. "Two Soldiers: A Comparative Study of Stephen Crane's *The Red Badge of Courage* and Tayama Katai's 'One Soldier' " by Margaret Frances Loftus (*SAmL* 9[1971]:67–79) compares two war stories told in the naturalistic manner by Eastern and Western contemporaries unaware of each other's existence. "The Logic Beneath 'The Open Boat' " by George Monteiro (*GaR* 26:326–35) has another go at that much-explicated story by arguing logically that the "detailed representation of life is actually the sketching in of the archetypal image of man sheltered from natural forces by the 'egg-shell' of a life-boat" and going into Crane's Christian background again, especially Protestant hymns about lifeboat salvation. A thorough explication of another favorite story, in German, is Franz H. Link's "Stephen Cranes 'The Blue Hotel': eine Interpretation" (*LWU* 5:22–32).

Of biographical interest are David E. E. Sloane's "Stephen Crane at Lafayette" (*RALS* 2:102–05), which gathers available evidence about his short and unpleasant term at Lafayette College in 1891, and R. W. Stallman's "How Stephen Crane Got to Crete" (*AL* 44:308–13), which disagrees with an earlier article by Lillian Gilkes on the direction from which Crane approached Crete to cover the Greek war.

vi. Naturalism and the Late Nineteenth Century

A valuable anthology for studying late-nineteenth-century literary, social, and philosophical forces has been assembled by Donald Pizer in *American Thought and Writing: The 1890's* (Boston, Houghton Mifflin). Arranged thematically, selections from the work of forty-eight writers, philosophers, historians, journalists, theologians, and political figures help delineate the major problems and crises of a transitional decade in American intellectual life.

All of the criticism on Norris this season appears to focus on his perpetually controversial novel, *McTeague*. In "*McTeague*: The Imagistic Network" (*WAL* 7:83–99) Suzy Bernstein Goldman moves beyond the previously examined images of gold, animals, and machinery, to consider the functions of food, liquid, fights, teeth, hands, prisons or bonds, and music to demonstrate that the often criticized ending of the novel grows integrally out of the imagistic structure. What she observes is convincing, although it doesn't alleviate the melodramatic effect of Norris's conclusion. "*McTeague*: A Probe Into Man's Dualism" by Masao Tsunematsu (*SAmL* 7[1971]:57–66) outlines the already clear dualisms in human nature depicted by Norris. Charles S. Watson finds "A Source for the Ending of *McTeague*" (*ALR* 5:173–74) in Dante's *Inferno* and details striking parallels to prove his point. Mukhtar Ali Isani in "Frank Norris on the Purpose of *McTeague*" (*AN&Q* 10:118) reprints an unnoticed statement in the Philadelphia *Book News* of May 1899 by Norris that his chief object was first "to produce an interesting story" and second to protest and revolt against "elegant" and "decadent" contemporaneous fiction. In his effort to assemble the dispersed pages of the manuscript of the novel for the forthcoming Centenary Edition of the Works of Frank Norris, Joseph Katz provides a report on where he stands in "The Manuscript of Frank Norris' *McTeague*: A Preliminary Census of Pages" (*RALS* 2:91–97). There is a general note by John E. McCluskey on "Frank Norris' Literary Terminology: A Note on Historical Context" (*WAL* 7:148–50), which discusses why he "designated Zola and Howells representatives of opposed literary movements and associated the fiction of Zola and himself with romance rather than realism." The reason has to do with the literary terminology of the times rather than a lack of logic in Norris.

Increasing interest in Chesnutt continues with several critical essays. Walter Teller's "Charles W. Chesnutt's Conjuring and Color-Line Stories" and John Wideman's "Charles W. Chesnutt: *The Marrow of Tradition*" (*ASch* 42:125–27 and 128–34) are two essays in the Reappraisals series, the first a superficial survey of his life and career and the second an admirable analysis of Chesnutt's most successful and complex novel; "Chesnutt's Conjure Tales: What You See Is What You Get" by David D. Britt (*CLAJ* 15:269–83) succeeds in elucidating the carefully contrived double structure which underlies those stories required by the racial climate in which they were written; William M. Andrews ("Chesnutt's Patesville: The Presence and Influence of the Past in *The House Behind the Cedars*," *CLAJ* 15: 284–94) reads his first novel as "an illustration of the social effects and moral consequences of a particular people's imperviousness to the passing of time and the changes which supposedly accompany it"; and Cary D. Wintz's "Race and Realism in the Fiction of Charles W. Chesnutt" (*OH* 81:122–30) is another general survey of his career, inadequate as criticism and generally out of touch with the latest assessments of Chesnutt.

Just as the figure of the artist plays an important part in the works of Poe, Hawthorne, Melville, Howells, and James, in "The Artist in *The Damnation of Theron Ware*" (*SNNTS* 4:432–41) A. Carl Bredahl, Jr., finds him a central figure in Harold Frederic's novel, if the artist is defined as "the person who is able to organize creatively the meaning and form of his existence." The essay is especially interesting for its examination of the part music plays in the novel. Allen F. Stein's "Evasion of an American Dream: Structure and Theme in *The Damnation of Theron Ware*" (*ALR* 5:23–36) demonstrates "just how carefully the plot structure of *The Damnation of Theron Ware* is set up to be the key means of conveying the prevalent tone of derision. Indeed, it is only when we see that this novel in fact delineates a whole series of 'fresh starts' for Theron, recurring at virtually equidistant intervals in the plot line, that we perceive the full ironic nature of Theron's damnation and of Frederic's treatment of several basic motifs in nineteenth-century American romantic literature," especially the theme of the initiation of the innocent. Jean Frantz Blackall provides a perceptive assessment of a less frequently studied novel in "Frederic's *Gloria Mundi* as a Novel of Education" (*Mark-*

hamR 3:41–46), and Robert H. Woodward has gathered, edited, and introduced "A Selection of Harold Frederic's Early Literary Criticism, 1877–1881" (*ALR* 5:1–22). There are two brief essays on Hamlin Garland: John H. Irsteld's "The Use of Military Language in Hamlin Garland's 'The Return of a Private'" (*WAL* 7:145–47) and Barbara Martinec's "Hamlin Garland's Revisions of *Main-Travelled Roads*" (*ALR* 5:167–72).

Two writers given book-length critical examinations for the first time this year are E. W. Howe and Edgar Fawcett. S. J. Sackett's *E. W. Howe* (TUSAS 195) includes a biography, followed by studies of Howe's fiction (especially his pioneer psychological/deterministic novel *The Story of a Country Town*), his aphorisms, the travel books, and his autobiography. In *Edgar Fawcett* (TUSAS 201), Stanley R. Harrison discusses the achievements of a minor writer whose realistic and naturalistic novels influenced the work of Garland, Crane, Norris, London, and Dreiser, and whose international novels continued a tradition established by James. Both volumes are welcome for their attention to neglected figures, but the study of Fawcett is written in a stilted, pretentious style that should have been more rigorously edited. Richard D. Walter's *S. Weir Mitchell, M.D.–Neurologist: A Medical Biography* (Springfield, Ill., Charles C Thomas, 1970) is a plodding account which relies more on excerpt and quotation than ingenuity, but perhaps it will serve a purpose for medical students interested in Mitchell as a clinical neurologist rather than as novelist and man of letters. However, Kelley Griffith, Jr.'s "Weir Mitchell and The Genteel Romance" (*AL* 44:247–61) is a fine study of the novelistic tradition in which his fiction belongs.

A few other minor figures were given some attention. Allan M. Axelrad, "Ideology and Utopia in the Works of Ignatius Donnelly" (*AmerS* 12,ii[1971],47–65), is another reassessment of Donnelly's utopian vision as a Populist through his fictional and non-fictional writing which concludes that he "stands at the beginning of what was to become an honorable twentieth-century literary tradition of forecasting technological wastelands." John Patterson, "From Yeoman to Beast: Images of Blackness in *Caesar's Column*" (*AmerS* 12, ii[1971],21–31) clarifies the meaning of Donnelly's use of images of blackness and individual transformation in that novel. George Spangler's "Robert Herrick's *Waste*: Summary of a Career and an Age" (*CRevAS* 2[1971]:26–36) is an informative discussion of one of Herrick's last works, a revealing autobiographical novel. Finally, the meaning of Henry Adams's pseudonymous novel of New York society is competently explicated by David S. Barber in "Henry Adams' *Esther*: The Nature of Individuality and Immortality (*NEQ* 44:227–40).

Virginia Commonwealth University

11. Poe and Nineteenth-Century Poetry

G. R. Thompson

Poe was the subject of two books, by Stuart Levine and Daniel Hoffman, and one festschrift, *Papers on Poe: Essays in Honor of John Ward Ostrom*, edited by Richard P. Veler (Springfield, Ohio, Chantry Music Press at Wittenberg University). The first two will be discussed at an appropriate point below, but since individual articles in the Veler collection will be noticed by subject matter, it may be proper to observe here that the book well represents the interests of contemporary Poe scholars. As E. Arthur Robinson observes in a review article (*PoeS* 5:57–59), the seventeen essays, considered as a whole, offer implicit debate between those who view Poe as a Romantic idealist whose characters seek transcendental vision and those who view him as an absurdist whose characters are isolated in an incomprehensible universe. Although few new hard facts have been turned up, Poe biography has received recent attention with a pamphlet on Poe's army years, rediscovered reminiscences, and essays on Poe's relations with his contemporaries. General articles on Poe's philosophical and literary vision were plentiful, though of greatly uneven quality. An area of special interest in the year's work was the examination of Poe's fiction in relation to the gothic tradition. Good studies of Poe's comic and satiric side meanwhile continue to increase. Compared with the fiction, the poetry attracted little notice, though Poe as a poet fared generally as well as other minor poets of the nineteenth century. Despite a fair number of items of various kinds, however, few studies of the minor poets besides the continuation of the Longfellow correspondence by Harvard seem of great moment though thanks to the TUSAS program we have two new books, on Paul Hamilton Hayne and Sidney Lanier, while South Carolina has issued a combined biography and edition of James M. Legaré.

i. Poe

a. **Biography.** J. Thomas Russell's *Edgar Allan Poe: The Army Years* (USMALB 10) is somewhat misleadingly titled. Although Russell briefly surveys the general conditions of Poe's association with the United States Army, no new material is presented until section three, which deals with the 1831 cadet subscription to Poe's *Poems*. Russell has found in the USMA Archives Treasurer's ledger a list of deductions from Cadet accounts of $1.25 each rather than the 75¢ or $2.50 as variously reported in biographies of Poe. He reprints the complete list and notes that a canceled check made out to Poe in the USMA collection is for $170, whereas the total raised by the 135 subscribing cadets was $168.75, suggesting that one of the officers at the academy must have contributed as well. Poe's severance pay was a separate transaction of $36.72, as recorded in the USMA Archives Treasurer's Office Cash Book, 1830–49.

Several articles deal with Poe's Philadelphia years, both directly and indirectly. In "An Attack on Poe in 1864" (*Papers on Poe*, pp. 161–64), William Coyle reprints a section from John Frankenstein's *American Art: Its Awful Altitude* (1864) in which Frankenstein, a sculptor and painter, reviles the dead Poe for his supposed criticisms of the author's paintings years before. Heyward Ehrlich's "The 'Mysteries' of Philadelphia: Lippard's *Quaker City* and 'Urban' Gothic" (*ESQ* 18:50–65), though devoted primarily to an examination of George Lippard's most famous novel, surveys in its opening sections the relations of Lippard and Poe during Poe's residence in Philadelphia. Lippard defended Poe's reputation during these years and is, according to Ehrlich, the real author of "The Spermacetti Papers" and of "The Walnut-Coffin Papers," which appeared in *The Citizen Soldier* in 1843. These two works have been erroneously attributed to Poe by Charles F. Heartman and James R. Canny in their *Bibliography of First Printings of the Writings of Edgar Allan Poe* (rev. ed., Hattiesburg, Miss., Book Form, 1943), a point made independently by Emilio DeGrazia in "Edgar Allan Poe, George Lippard and the 'Spermacetti and Walnut-Coffin Papers'" (*PBSA* 66:58–60). J. Albert Robbins in "Edgar Poe and the Philadelphians: A Reminiscence by a Contemporary" (*PoeS* 5:45–48) reproduces passages from an anonymous series of articles published in the *Philadelphia Sunday Dispatch* in 1850, apparently written by a native Philadelphian well acquainted with the literary scene. Poe is portrayed as sensitive to both real and imagined affronts, as inordinately proud of being a Virginian, as possessing a combination of maturity and naïveté, as impractical, and as a winsomely obnoxious inebriate. There is a suggestion that Poe wrote for the *"Daily Seasons,"* which Robbins believes from various internal references to be a code name for the Philadelphia *Spirit of the Times.*

In "Poe and Thomas Dunn English: More Light on a Probable Reason for Poe's Failure to Receive a Custom-House Appointment" (*Papers on Poe,* pp. 165–93) William H. Gravely, Jr., adduces two principal reasons why English may have interfered with Poe's Philadelphia appointment in 1842–43. First, English was associated with the dominant Whig splinter group supporting President John Tyler in Philadelphia and would not, as a political man, have seen any advantage to a non-political appointment. Second, English was at this time an active temperance writer, and in a state of drunken excitement at a party in Washington, Poe had made fun of the hypersensitive English's mustaches and figure. Gravely points out that Poe's reference to joining "the Washingtonians" in his letter to F. W. Thomas after his disgrace in Washington refers not to politics but to the Washington Temperance Society, which had chapters in more than one seaboard city, including Philadelphia. These very temperance societies, to one of which Poe gave his pledge, seem to have been instrumental in the blackening of his name so quickly after his death, as Burton R. Pollin's "The Temperance Movement and Its Friends Look at Poe" (*Costerus* 2:119–44) reveals.

Poe's imp of the perverse is well illustrated in another anecdote of his later period. He had managed to get on as a copy editor for the *New York Mirror* in 1844, and he dramatized his arrival with his successful balloon hoax in the *New York Sun.* In "Thomas Low Nichols, Poe, and the 'Balloon Hoax'" (*PoeS* 5:48–49), Doris V. Falk describes Nichols's account of the publication of the tale in his *Forty Years of American Life, 1821–1861.* According to Nichols, Poe stood outside the door where the papers were on sale and announced to the eager customers that the story was a hoax, while Moses Y. Beach, the publisher of the *Sun,* watched the crowd of potential buyers disperse. Arlin Turner's "Poe and Simms: Friendly Critics, Sometimes Friends" (*Papers on Poe,* pp. 140–60) is a chronicling of both the development of a literary relationship between the two Southern writers and the causes of its eventual decline, as Simms became increasingly disturbed by Poe's personal behavior. Turner corrects the impression that Poe's earliest reviews of Simms in 1836 and 1839 were unremittingly severe and outlines how in 1845 Poe and Simms "in effect collaborated in the current literary debate and made occasions each to bolster the literary reputation of the other" (p. 148). Despite his several defenses of Poe, Simms considered him a man of "sudden and uneven impulses of great nervous susceptibility," who wrote "in jerks and spasms only, and in the intervals of passion or drink, contended for fugitive performances," ending up "one of the most morally wretched of gifted men" (p. 158).

John E. Reilly, in "Ermina's Gales: The Poems Jane Locke Devoted to Poe" (*Papers on Poe*, pp. 206–20), gives us yet another perspective. He reviews the circumstances of Poe's acquaintance with Mrs. Jane Ermina Locke. After giving an account of Mrs. Locke's trip to Fordham, New York, to see Poe (in June of 1848) and of his trip to Lowell, Massachusetts, to see her (in July 1848), Reilly discusses the six poems Mrs. Locke wrote about Poe between December 1846 and July 1850. Her six "gales"—sentimental poetic outbursts—describe, according to Reilly, a circular emotional route: before meeting Poe in person, she shows rather detached admiration for the "suffering genius" of the "true poet"; after meeting him, she writes a frenzied and almost sexually explicit account of the transport she felt while in the "clasp" of this "god," "as lip to lip he pressed" before down she sank "throbbing" to "rest" in a *trance divine my heart upon his own!"* (pp. 211–12); then, after Poe's death the next year, she again exhibits detached compassion for the late, great "poet."

b. **General critical estimates.** Although some interesting, broadly speculative assessments of Poe emerged during the year, Poe studies were also plagued by the kind of article that exhibits no awareness on the critic's part of the scholarship behind, on, or around his subject. An egregious example of the kind is James Blish's elliptically titled "The Climate of Insult" (*SR* 80:340–46). Blish defends Poe from the strictures of Paul Elmer More and Yvor Winters as if nothing further had been discovered or thought for thirty or forty years. The article is platitudinous and unoriginal. A better essay, but also one that fails properly to place the subject in the perspective of previous scholarship, is John N. Serio's "From Edwards to Poe" (*ConnR* 6:88–92).

Without reference to the work of major Poe scholars, he argues that
Poe reflects the Puritan mystical strain (leading to the Transcendentalists); yet, by depiction of guilt and the dark underside of experience, Poe is allied to the darkness of Hawthorne and Melville. Specific parallels between Jonathan Edwards and Poe would in fact give
the formulation new interest, but as presented the demonstration is
not convincing. As to landscape aesthetics, George E. Mize with "The
Matter of Taste in Poe's 'Domain of Arnheim' and 'Landor's Cottage'"
(*ConnR* 6:98–99) "discovers" a source previously recorded by Jeffrey
A. Hess (see *ALS 1970*, pp. 212–13).

A reorganization of William Goldhurst's "Poe-esque Themes"
(*Papers on Poe*, pp. 126–39) in the light of previous scholarship might
have helped to make his essay read less like a series of disconnected
lecture notes. But Goldhurst's discussion has many glancing insights,
presumably to be more fully developed in a future study. For the
present, we have his preliminary identification of seven major themes:
The Devil on the Loose, Compulsive Self-Betrayal, Appearance and
Reality, Plastic Space and Time, Buried Alive, Supernal Oneness,
The Novel Experience.

As mentioned, several general essays in *Papers on Poe* outline
what presently seems to be the major critical debate among informed
Poe scholars. The position of those critics who see Poe as seriously
involved in the occult mysticism and pseudoscience of his day is
stated, yet modified, in Eric W. Carlson's "Poe's Vision of Man" (*Papers on Poe*, pp. 7–20). The central theme in Poe's works, he maintains, is not death and annihilation but "rediscovery of the psychal
power" of man. He divides Poe's works into three categories. The
first he calls "Paradisaical" writings, in which the Poe hero feels an
"acute sense of loss" of a former, Neoplatonic, ideal existence. The
second he calls "Existential" writings, in which the Poe hero meets
the indifference of the universe with "something other than terror,
resignation, or hopelessness." The third he calls "Psycho-Transcen-
dental" writings, in which the Poe hero, through reintegrated poetic
sense or while in a "sleep-waking" state, expands his consciousness
beyond ordinary limits. The three categories correspond to the past,
the present, and the future. For Poe, man "may again become whole
by tapping the powers of his spiritual preconscious or psyche" and
thereby become one with God. Carlson has to modify some of his
claims in order to make a story like "Eleonora" (which he calls a

"partial" realization of Poe's grand theme) fit the formula, and he does not at all persuade one that "Usher" and "Ligeia" present unification and beatitude rather than disintegration and horror. But his position is worth attention, describing as it does one thematic thread in Poe's works, despite his surprising assertion that Poe's principal vision is as transcendental as Emerson's.

The opposite position is forcibly stated by Sidney P. Moss in "Poe's Apocalyptic Vision" (*Papers on Poe*, pp. 42–53). He maintains that "Poe carried the theme of alienation and victimization to its ultimate conclusion—that man is totally helpless in a universe he has abandoned all hope of understanding" (p. 47). Moss argues that although alienation is the basic condition of man, the great "touchstones" of world literature finally reaffirm a harmonious world order. But Poe's characters, who are "all of them more or less interchangeable like mechanical parts, seem the most diminished in all literature, driven atoms in a universe void of hope, meaning, and volition" (pp. 50–51). Moss's argument is a well-stated modification and elaboration of, among others, the views of D. H. Lawrence and Allen Tate; but he becomes hesitant and apologetic at the end, especially when he comes to "Ligeia" and "Usher," which he (properly, in my view) regards as delusive dialogues of the mind with itself.

My own essay holds a middle position between these two extremes taken by Carlson and Moss. Although in "Poe and 'Romantic Irony'" (*Papers on Poe*, pp. 28–41) I affirm a species of Transcendentalism in Poe, it is in a radically different perspective than Carlson's, and ultimately the conception of Poe is closer to Moss's. The essay is an attempt to evidence the claim that in the air and known to Poe were Romantic theories of "irony" as the highest act of philosophical and artistic "reason." "Romantic irony" is the simultaneous investment of belief in and detachment from any subject—whether a single literary work, art in general, a philosophical point of view, or life itself. Laughter becomes a defense against a world that one also takes seriously; the element of the comic is therefore much more important in understanding the "serious" side of Poe than most critics will admit. Seen in the perspective of international Romanticism, the concept of the arabesque in Poe's time was much more complex and a good deal richer than is generally realized, implying both a technique of intricate manipulation of narrative frames and a philosophical view of the ironies of human existence. By achieving ironic vision through arabesque techniques, the artist can occasionally "soar free-ly" over the contradictions of earthly existence. This fleeting "trans-cendental" irony, however, is the only hope man has in an illusory and possibly malevolent universe.

Advertised as the "best book by anybody on Poe," Daniel Hoff-man's eccentric and breezy *Poe Poe Poe Poe Poe Poe Poe* (Garden City, N. Y., Doubleday) has an impossible advance billing to live up to. Hoffman's basic approach is old hat, reaching back through Allen Tate to Marie Bonaparte and Joseph Wood Krutch toward a simple Freudian understanding of Poe and overlaying this with Jung. He presents at least seven fragmented images of Poe—including Oed-gar, Idgar I AM Poet, Edgar Élan Poet, Hoaxiepoe, Poe the Pundit, Edgar the Metaphysician, and so on—fragmented images that do not coalesce into the single "Edgarpoe" he constantly refers us to. Hoff-man's Edgarpoe achieves coherence and unity almost as consequence of his madness, manifested in his quest for the ultimate archetype— the End of Everything—in his seeking some unearthly other realm out of space and time where he would not have to suffer the loss of mother, lover, sister, or cousin.

Nearly the entire first chapter concerns the impact of Poe not on the general reader but on Hoffman; and so the book continues its mad and maddening way, combining occasionally brilliant sub-jectivity with irritating irrelevancies. Chapter 2 considers the poetry (the poetic soul preyed on by Time); 3, the critical theory (empha-sizing the importance of the mathematical); 4, the poet-mathemati-cian Dupin and the ratiocinative tales; 5, "Voyages": "Going down" (such as "A Descent into the Maelström"), "Sent up" (such as "Hans Pfaall"), "Counter clockwise" (such as "Valdemar"), "Beyond apoca-lypse" (such as "Monos and Una"); 6, such "dull realities" as money, politics, the social order. Chapter 7, on "grotesques" and "arabesques," argues that such tales as "William Wilson" and "Amontillado" are allegories of "pseudo-suicide," in which the violent act is both itself and its opposite, all directly related to Poe's vision of cosmological unity. Chapter 8, "The Marriage Group," treats what at first seems an unlikely series of stories ("The Black Cat," "Berenice," "The Spec-tacles," "Loss of Breath," and "Ligeia"). The concluding chapters deal with *Pym*, *Eureka*, "Usher," and Poe's mind as a "haunted palace." But in a work that strives so hard to be idiosyncratic, the specific readings are curiously unoriginal—blind to much previous scholarship. What virtue the book has for the student of Poe is the general shape Hoffman gives to Poe's corpus, suggesting new groupings of works under provocative subtitles. But even in the final chapters, where Hoffman attempts to join the themes of his book, the effect is anticlimactic and blurred.

It is disappointing to find a similar garrulousness and overpersonal tone in Stuart Levine's more conventionally academic *Edgar Poe: Seer and Craftsman* (Deland, Fla., Everett/Edwards), especially since Levine has made a serious attempt to address himself to major critical problems in the proper understanding of Poe: the consistency of Poe's aesthetic theories, the romantic uses of horror, the biographical interpretation of Poe's works, the magazine environment in which Poe worked, the occult as a theme in Poe, and the moral element in Poe's tales. (Levine deals only with the tales, dismissing the poems without explanation.) As his title indicates, Levine seeks a unitary key to the apparently bifurcated Poe, whom he regards as both a romantic seer and a crafty calculator of popular appeal. The seeming contradiction in Poe's aesthetic theory—in which writing is at one time viewed as a lightning bolt of inspiration and at another time as a mechanical process—is in Levine's view a consistent "artistic code . . . at once pragmatic and romantic" (p. 8). Taking up two central documents, he argues that "The Poetic Principle," which deals with the source and nature of inspiration, the deep human instinct for supernal beauty, is only one half of Poe's theory. The other half is embodied in "The Philosophy of Composition," which deals with the technical means by which "the beauty perceived by this inspiration may be effectively set down on paper" (p. 14). Levine asserts that Poe conceived of the romantic artist as a sort of holy man using his stories to show, through his characters' "acts of perception, what the universe is all about" (p. 10). The "process of perception" becomes Levine's main subject, and what is perceived, he argues, even in the horror tales, is a form of "supernal beauty-in-unity." Moreover, the "form which each of the tales took was a function of the nature of the perceptive process. . . . It can be said to determine both the personalities of his characters and the manner of their insight" (p. 10).

Discussions of many tales are thin and disappointing, but with "The Imp of the Perverse," for example, what strengths there are to Levine's book come nicely together. Not only does he approach a story from an interdisciplinary point of view but he also demonstrates here, by careful consideration of the structure of the story, that Poe's narrator initially dupes us, that the "perversity" the narrator describes is not the impulse to murder, but his impulse to confess. At the beginning of the tale, the narrator calmly persuades us that he is the victim of some external evil force; but it is gradually revealed that he is "incapable of seeing that the murder itself is an evil thing," and we come to see that the story dramatizes "a perfect moral inversion" (p. 211). Levine also suggests that while Poe here is experimenting with the connections between "creativity, sexuality, and the death-wish" and with "an almost universal human fear of and fascination with a fatal fall" (p. 209), he also is coolly "utilizing" a moral theme.

Levine's book as a whole, however, is not uniformly illuminating, and like Hoffman's, it ends anticlimactically: Levine's discussion of *Pym* is weak, and I believe him ill-advised to have reprinted his rambling discussion of the *Journal of Julius Rodman* as the final analysis before an insufficiently synthesizing "Epilogue" concludes the book.

c. Gothic tales: "Ligeia" and "The Fall of the House of Usher." Poe's two most famous tales form the locus of special interest in Poe's fiction in the context of the gothic tradition. Clark Griffith, for example, in "Poe and the Gothic" (*Papers on Poe*, pp. 21–27) briefly argues that Poe modulated the technique of gothic fiction by shifting the terrifying from external phenomena to the internal mind. In this Griffith observes a difference between the eighteenth-century mentality and the romantic, especially as demonstrated by Poe's narrator in "The Fall of the House of Usher." Griffith's point that the gothic tales are projections of the mind is similar to but not so broadly inclusive as Sidney Moss's in the article discussed earlier. The larger critical implications are more fully developed in the Poe essays of Richard P. Benton's edited symposium, "The Gothic Tradition in Nineteenth-Century American Literature," in two parts (*ESQ* 18: 1–66,67–123). Benton's own introductory essay, "The Problems of Literary Gothicism" (pp. 5–9), though brief, is useful for its bibliographical survey of studies of the gothic, for its questions about the relation of "high" gothic writing to popular literature, for its observation of the black American writer's almost obsessive employment of the gothic, and for its indication of differences between British and American gothic modes.

One of the symposium essays is cast as a corrective to psychoanalytic criticism. In "Poe and the Gothic Tradition" (*ESQ* 18:19–29),
Maurice Lévy rejects certain biographical, Freudian interpretations
of Poe's tales especially popular in France but also current in American criticism. He suggests instead that Poe was perfectly aware of
a variety of traditional gothic techniques and that, moreover, his
imagery reflects psychological archetypes embodied in the gothic
genre rather than Poe's own sick soul. One of the most useful implications of Lévy's article, though not fully developed, is that there
are three kinds of "psychological" approaches to Poe (indeed, to
literature) that must be carefully differentiated: (1) a biographical,
"psychoanalytic" approach in which Poe himself is the subject; (2)
a "psychological" interpretation of the characters and their actions
and perceptions in the dramatic world of the tale; (3) an "archetypal"
approach which sees certain universal human responses embedded in
gothic works. This distinction I also try to observe in my contribution
to the symposium, " 'Proper Evidences of Madness': American Gothic
and the Interpretation of 'Ligeia' " (*ESQ* 18:30–49). The question
of the narrator's veracity is reexamined in the perspective of literary
history. The central question of whether the narrator actually wit-
nesses an attempt at reincarnation, or this occurrence is merely the
product of his opium-soaked brain, is resolved when we see "Ligeia"
in the context of the development of gothic fiction from Germany to
England to America. In the American mode of gothic, clues to the
real psychological (and frequently absurdist) action of a seemingly
supernaturalist tale are patterned much like that of a detective story,
and the vision of the human mind that emerges is one of despair over
the ability of the mind ever to know anything with certainty. The
narrator is a totally unreliable reporter of events (as a number of
important statements in Poe's letters, essays, and reviews further
corroborate), so that, ultimately, "Ligeia" is a tale of existential
absurdity.

Joel Salzberg's "The Gothic Hero in Transcendental Quest: Poe's
'Ligeia' and James' 'The Beast in the Jungle' " (*ESQ* 18:108–14)
presents the thesis that in Poe and James the sensual gothic hero of
the later eighteenth century and the earlier nineteenth is romanticized into a transcendental idealist. But both writers make the new
hero as "ruthless" in his idealism and commitment to the world of the
spirit as the earlier gothic hero was in his erotic excesses. Not all the

parallels between the two stories that he presents are of equal force, but Salzberg does manage to make the two tales mutually illuminating as dramas of "unchecked solipsism." Daniel Hoffman's vigorous essay, "I Have Been Faithful to You in My Fashion: The Remarriage of Ligeia's Husband" (*SoR* 8:89–105), makes a similar point about the narrator's love of the abstracted Ligeia for her "boundless mind." The narrator tries to possess an archetype of "forbidden knowledge" by possessing the flesh-and-blood woman, but he is interested in the latter only because she is the channel to the former. Hoffman then shifts into a psychoanalysis of the "impotent" Poe, consistent with the themes of his book, in which this article is reprinted as a subchapter. When Hoffman takes up the question of whether Ligeia wills her own reincarnation or whether her husband wills it—noting that the bridal bower is an "externalization" of the narrator's mind—the circularity of his approach becomes manifest. He observes that death is a frequent "mythic" metaphor of sexual consummation and remarks that the "prototypes" of the tale clearly come out of the author's psychological experience, especially the loss of various women in his life.

In any event, no matter what the critical orientation, one thing that characterizes recent discussions of "Ligeia" is implicit agreement that the key to the experience embodied in the tale is the narrator's state of mind. The same implied agreement does not obtain for discussions of "The Fall of the House of Usher," however. Thomas J. Rountree, for example, in "Poe's Universe: The House of Usher and the Narrator" (*TSE* 20:123–34) sees the role of the narrator in a very special way. Emulating Richard Wilbur, he draws parallels between the tale and Poe's theories in *Eureka* that the universe is composed of a series of cyclical expansions and contractions and that every work of divine creation must expire by returning to "original unity." Inverting the argument of Maurice Beebe, Roundtree asserts that the universe is in its contractive phase as the tale opens. The narrator from the outside world notices the pattern of unity between the house, its surroundings, and its inhabitants; by witnessing this accelerated progress toward unity, he increases his awareness of the universal collapse and thus exemplifies Poe's remarks in *Eureka* that all individual consciousnesses will eventually be "merged in the general consciousness."

The roles of the narrator, Usher, and the house are seen differently in the half-dozen articles comprised in a small symposium on "The Fall of the House of Usher" in the first number of *Poe Studies* during 1972. In "The Psycho-Sexual Reading of 'The Fall of the House of Usher'" (*PoeS* 5:8–9), John L. Marsh essentially ignores the presence of a narrator and recapitulates a number of Freudian arguments by suggesting that Poe's story is a drama of cognition in which sexual guilt is the major theme. Usher is governed by a perverse sensuality that causes him to violate his sister's seemingly lifeless body. Madeline returns, blood upon her robes, for a last "mad trist," symbolic of the coming together of those dark forces that make man so pitifully vulnerable. Colin E. Martindale in "Archetype and Reality in 'The Fall of the House of Usher'" (*PoeS* 5:9–11) takes a modified Jungian approach that reemphasizes the role of the narrator and the importance of "The Mad Trist." He argues that the story may be read as the narration of Usher's attempt to escape from a regressive state of consciousness. By breaking Usher's isolation, the narrator allows him to escape momentarily, as symbolized by the burial of Madeline, through repression of the feminine, unconscious element of his personality. An archetypal interpretation of the dream symbols of "The Mad Trist" suggests a way of escape from his limbo state; Usher, however, is unable to act, and the tale ends with the final overwhelming of the ego by the unconscious. In an unusual gothic reading, combining the Freudian with the supernatural, "Roderick Usher: Portrait of the Madman as Artist" (*PoeS* 5:11–14), Gerald M. Garmon attempts to dismiss the narrator as unimportant to the interpretation of the tale. He proposes instead Roderick Usher's conception of art and his function as an artist as the unifying key to the various problems the story presents, for it is Usher's debilitating artistic "hypersensitivity" that embodies the paradox of his personality. Since Roderick can no longer play a dominant male role, the house, which is specifically said to have become sentient or sensitive through long and intimate union with the family of Usher, takes on that role, imprisoning Roderick and Madeline together in an effort to preserve its own life energies. In his art works and poems, Roderick attempts to work out his subconscious awareness of his situation and to communicate it to the narrator; but the narrator, failing to understand Roderick's struggle to free himself from the house, considers him a madman.

It is hard to evaluate these varying approaches to the tale without letting one's own reading get in the way. Suffice it to say that these articles are uneven in clarity and persuasiveness. My own essay in the symposium, "The Face in the Pool: Reflections on the Doppelgänger Motif in 'The Fall of the House of Usher'" (*PoeS* 5:16–21), argues that a gothic tale by Poe is a complicated system of interpenetrating structures and simultaneous effects, so that, as in a Hawthorne story, we are presented with a kind of multiple choice. We find on one level a series of supernatural events, on another level a rational explanation of these, on another level a psychological explanation, and on yet another level an insinuated burlesque. The whole system of interpenetrating structures leads ultimately to Poe's mockery of the ability of the human mind ever to know anything with certainty, whether about the external reality of the world or about the internal reality of the mind. The primary structure of "Usher" is generated by that progressive subjectivity of the narrator first hinted at by Darrel Abel. This basic structure is paralleled by the motif of the double and its redoubled manifestations, further redoubled by the imagery of the face or skull which inverts back on the self as a symbol of the totally subjective reality seen from the inward perspective of characters caught in a mental labyrinth.

G. S. Amur addresses himself to some related points. Although his "'Heart of Darkness' and 'The Fall of the House of Usher': The Tale as Discovery" (*LCrit* 9[1971]:59–70) does not to my mind consistently develop a clearly stated thesis, I yet find some precisely articulated insights, as when Amur observes that the "structure of these stories . . . is determined by the pattern of the experience of the narrators but this experience itself . . . is a result of their encounters with the central characters [Kurtz and Usher] and with the matrix of *their* experience."

Perhaps the most boldly original of the several essays on "Usher" is Barton Levi St. Armand's "Usher Unveiled: Poe and the Metaphysic of Gnosticism" (*PoeS* 5:1–8). St. Armand observes that Poe's writings are frequently condemned for their apparent lack of a coherent metaphysic. Yet if a story like "Usher" is examined in the light of ancient Gnostic thought, particularly the school of Hermeticism, or philosophy of alchemy, one finds a richly allusive if not allegorical system of symbols of the prison-house world, the hidden god of unity, and an escape through a transcendent act of knowing. St. Armand attempts to show that a series of details in "Usher" correspond with the alchemical progression of planetary metals, the mortification of the dragon, the Hermetic vessel or vault, the hermaphroditic marriage, and the conjunction of elements. Thus Roderick can be seen in the tradition of the questing alchemist, or hierophant of Hermetic mysteries, who conducts an experiment in spiritual transmutation which risks both his mind and his soul.

d. Other gothic tales and *The Narrative of Arthur Gordon Pym.*
Lee J. Richmond offers a supernaturalistic reading of "Morella" as an example of Poe's "controlled dramatic irony." In "Edgar Allan Poe's 'Morella': Vampire of Volition" (*SSF* 9:93–94) Richmond argues that, contrary to the usual interpretations, Morella did not want the narrator's love but instead drained him of his power of will so that she could submerge his identity in her own and thereby assure her metempsychosis. The narrator has sealed his own destiny through his weakness and is doomed to live forever a death-in-life existence, whereas she has "achieved life-in-death." This interesting theory has unfortunate gaps in it, the major of which perhaps is Richmond's failure to show how his reading can be accommodated to the conclusion of the tale: the second Morella dies, and in the tomb the narrator finds "no traces" of the first Morella. Richard C. Frushell's " 'An Incarnate Night-Mare: Moral Grotesquerie in 'The Black Cat' " (*PoeS* 5:43–44) is a provocative essay that suffers from some imprecision in developing its argument. Frushell attempts to detail the "ironically shifting meanings" of the two cats "in an investigation of the 'moral' undercurrent implicit in the narrator's degeneration by stages into the condition of grotesque perversity." The murder of the first cat (animal instinct) combined with the murder of his wife (human instinct and rationality) equals the murder of self. The second cat is at the end of the tale emblematic both of his diabolic brute passion and of his walled-up moral sense, so that he is a moral grotesquerie of his former self.

Two notes on "The Cask of Amontillado" make each approximately the same point as the other and are mutually illuminating. James E. Rocks in "Conflict and Motive in 'The Cask of Amontillado' " (*PoeS* 5:50–51) suggests that Poe made use of traditional anti-Catholic themes in the gothic fiction of the late eighteenth and early nineteenth centuries. And Kent Bales in "Poetic Justice in 'The Cask of Amontillado' " (*PoeS* 5:51) writes: "A Roman Catholic aristo-

crat takes revenge on his Freemason enemy by walling him into a
corner of the family catacombs, thus destroying his life . . . by ma-
sonry. To most readers this is an audacious pun, but to anti-Masonic
readers it is poetic justice as well." But Poe gives the tale a further
twist: the narrator confesses the secret murder to his priest as he
prepares to die and thinks himself now safe from retribution; yet in
a Christian universe no private vengeance can be exacted with im-
punity; a mortal sin unrepented will bring damnation from a higher
tribunal.

Ian V. K. Ousby's source note " 'The Murders in the Rue Morgue'
and 'Doctor D'Arsac' " (*PoeS* 5:52) corrects some oversights of Arthur Hobson Quinn, who had misdated a series entitled "Unpublished Passages in the Life of Vidocq," by one "J.M.B.," published in
Burton's Gentleman's Magazine between September 1838 and May
1839. Although other sources have been cited, Poe seems not only
to have borrowed the names Dupin and Vidocq from this series but
also a detail or two from "Doctor D'Arsac," the second of the tales.
Donald Barlow Stauffer in "Poe as Phrenologist: The Example of
Monsieur Dupin" (*Papers on Poe*, pp. 113–25), draws attention to
Poe's omission in later printings of the original first paragraph of
"The Murders in the Rue Morgue," wherein he discussed man's reasoning powers in terms of such phrenological categories as "primitive
faculty," "ideality," "causality," and "comparison." Stauffer contends
that "M. Dupin himself can be fully understood only when we see
him in the light of these terms and in the light of Poe's other writings
about phrenology . . ." (p. 114).

J. V. Ridgely's announced purpose in "The End of Pym and the
Ending of *Pym*" (*Papers on Poe*, pp. 104–12) is to "modify and extend some of the conclusions set forth" in an earlier article (see *ALS
1966*, p. 132). In the present article, Ridgely speculates that three
narrative lines were in turn aborted, superseded, and left open-ended
for a final effect of mystification. Showing how Poe abandoned J. M.
Reynolds's polar narrative for Benjamin Morrell's *A Narrative of Four
Voyages*, Ridgely argues that Poe conceived of the people of Tsalal
as deriving from the dispersion of tribes in Old Testament days and
still ruled by "Tsalemon" or "Psalomoun," an idea derived from
Morrell. There are also in Morrell discussions of an ancient race of
Patagonians once physically tall and now much diminished. From

this a "faintly detailed" story emerges, according to Ridgely. "Gigantic white ancients . . . following some prophecy, have gone on forever, leaving behind them a people destined to deteriorate, to become 'shady,' and to fear whiteness"; and in the huge white figure at the pole, Pym and Peters encounter one of the original settlers of Tsalal. Ridgely's argument is plausible, though critics inclined to see *Pym* as more tightly integrated and possessing more serious meaning than he does will surely feel resistance to accepting fully a hypothesis that tends to reduce the work to the level of science fiction or fantasy.

In fact, Grace Farrell Lee in a remarkable essay, "The Quest of Arthur Gordon Pym" (*SLJ* 4,ii:22–33), opposes the view that because Poe composed the work in several stages it does not have any "structural principal underlying the successive stages of the story." Instead, *Pym* "revitalizes an archetype found throughout religious mythology, the descent into Hell, and utilizes the structure of a sea voyage, a familiar post-Jungian image of the collective unconscious, to voyage into the recesses of the human psyche and to journey backward in time to the origins of creation." With Pym there is a "surging inward upon himself," a series of archetypal returns or rebirths. Lee observes many parallels in folklore and biblical lore and explains how Tsalal may be seen as a portrayal of hell. She concludes that, if black and white symbolize anything in this story, "it must be the basic forces of attraction and repulsion of which the universe consists," as articulated in *Eureka*.

A complication not addressed in Lee's essay is the humorous, satiric, hoaxical aspect of *Pym*. Although William Peden's "Prologue to a Dark Journey: The 'Opening' to Poe's *Pym*" (*Papers on Poe*, pp. 84–91) is rather truncated and does not build cumulatively on some recent studies of the satiric element in the work, Peden nevertheless performs a useful service in calling attention to the incredible number of absurdities in the first chapter (which is not, however, precisely the "opening" of *Pym*). The most blatant of these is the sequence in which Pym is pinned to the hull of the *Penguin* by a bolt through his neck, is submerged for well over five minutes, and then shows up for breakfast the next morning with no visible signs of his ordeal. Peden suggests that all this is a deliberate indication to the wary reader that Pym is an "Existential non-hero" and that the whole book is absurdist, an "existentialist trip from nothingness to nothingness."

e. **Humor and satire.**   In two pieces Alexander Hammond gives us important new insights into Poe's intentions in the *Tales of the Folio Club*, never published as a group. In "Poe's 'Lionizing' and the Design of *Tales of the Folio Club*" (*ESQ* 18:154–65) he argues that the 1835 form of the story is a satiric imitation of Disraeli's *Vivian Grey*, that "Thomas Smith" is Disraeli himself, that it is read by the narrator of the entire collection in his effort to join the current literary establishment, and that the tale is the capstone tale of the entire series. In "A Reconstruction of Poe's 1833 *Tales of the Folio Club*: Preliminary Notes" (*PoeS* 5:25-32) Hammond attempts, like others before him, to assign tales to Club members and to establish the ordering and function of the stories in the framework. Both of Hammond's essays are characterized by precise and thorough scholarship and brilliant argument; and it is to be hoped that, as indicated in the second article cited, he will soon produce an annotated scholarly edition of this reconstructed series of stories—though any such work is destined to be hotly debated by Poe scholars.

In fact, William Goldhurst's "Poe's Multiple King Pest: A Source Study" (*TSE* 20:107–21) begins with an attack on what he considers an overemphasis on the *Tales of the Folio Club*. Goldhurst observes that we do not know certainly that the Folio Club stories were "intended as lampoons, nor do we know the extent or degree of satire" Poe meant to embed in each one. As to "King Pest," Goldhurst does not deny its comic and satiric level, but he believes that "deeper impulses must have taken over." His argument is quite tenuous, however, relying on a chain of associations he never fully evidences in the tale. During the course of his discussion, Goldhurst observes that wine is often a means of insight in Poe's works—*in vino veritas*—and that Poe's characters frequently do not stop to think at all, but, inspired by their inebriation, see straight through to "reality." L. Moffitt Cecil in "Poe's Wine List" (*PoeS* 5:41–42) makes a more reasonable assessment. He writes that although some famous wines serve as motivating agents in some of Poe's stories, he never wrote about them in the way a connoisseur would. Characters like Bibulus O'-Bumper, Bon-Bon, and Fortunato make fools of themselves when they pretend to connoisseurship, and Poe generally used wine as a metaphor for man's pretenses and failings.

Bernard A. Drabeck in " 'Tarr and Fether'—Poe and Abolitionism" (*ATQ* 14:177–84), by adding the element of abolitionism, presumably intends to extend Richard P. Benton's theory that Poe's story of the insurrection of the inmates of a madhouse is a comic allegory of the North and the South. The narrator thus is "the ignorant, intrusive Northerner who has entered into a situation that is entirely beyond him; the superintendent is the aberrant Southern Abolitionist, a fanatic who sides with the inmates of the Southern institution and in effect becomes one of them; and the insane are the slaves, pathetic creatures whose worst impulses are unleashed by the freedom they gain" (p. 181). This statement is clear enough, but it comes so late in the argument and there has been so much contradiction and bad writing that few readers will be persistent enough to come to it.

Burton R. Pollin's examination of the sources and allusions in several of Poe's comic stories may be considered as a group. In "Poe's Tale of Psyche Zenobia: A Reading for Humor and Ingenius Construction" (*Papers on Poe*, pp. 92–103), Pollin denies that "How to Write a Blackwood Article" and "A Predicament" (earlier titled "Psyche Zenobia" and "The Scythe of Time") were aimed at Margaret Fuller, but instead suggests that "Poe was using buckshot rather than a bullet" in his satire. Pollin reconsiders a number of comic allusions and surveys rhetorical devices. In "Poe's Mystification [*sic*]: Its Sources in Fay's *Norman Leslie*" (*MissQ* 25:111–30), Pollin surveys Poe's literary battle with Theodore S. Fay in an attempt to show that Fay was one of the main satiric targets of both "Mystification" and "The Literary Life of Thingum Bob." In "Light on 'Shadow' and Other Pieces by Poe; or, More of Thomas Moore" (*ESQ* 18:166–73), Pollin maintains that not only did an episode in Moore's *The Epicurean* (about a corpse attending an Egyptian feast) furnish the plot and background for "Shadow" but also that the tale presents a burlesque of Moore in a manner similar to the style of other *Folio Club* tales. Moore also figures as a satiric target in several other of Poe's works. Particularly useful is Pollin's identification of Poe's "Fum Fudge" references as a comic allusion to a series of satiric letters published by Moore in 1818 as *The Fudge Family in Paris* and a sequence of parodies and imitations in England and America. (These were eventually followed with a sequel by Moore in 1835, *The Fudges in England.*)

William H. Gravely, Jr., in "New Sources for Poe's 'Hans Pfaall'" (*TSL* 17:139–49) demonstrates that Poe's most significant sources for the tale were "scientific rather than fictional." George Tucker's

A Voyage to the Moon (1827) was less the immediate source than Sir John Herschel's *A Treatise on Astronomy* (1833) and two scientific accounts of balloon ascensions: Vincent Lunardi's *An Account of the First Aërial Voyage in England* (1784) and Thomas I. M. Forster's *Annals of Some Remarkable Aërial and Alpine Voyages* (1832). Although he admits the possibility that Poe's intention may have shifted to some satirical poking at Tucker, Gravely feels that Poe's first intention was to write a moon-journey account that excelled in the very quality that he thought Tucker's lacked—verisimilitude—which explains his heavy reliance on these works.

As the frequent references noted so far in the year's work on Poe bear out, the design of the universe as conceived in *Eureka* has come to seem central to an understanding of the shaping force behind Poe's other works. Yet only three critics, to my knowledge, have seriously addressed themselves to the principal critical problem that *Eureka* presents—its complexity of tones. One of these critics, Harriet R. Holman, has now extended her earlier investigation of what she calls the "encyclopedic" satire of *Eureka* (see *ALS 1969*, p. 194) with an examination of another set of allusions that Poe has worked into the book. In "Splitting Poe's 'Epicurean Atoms': Further Speculation on the Literary Satire of *Eureka*" (*PoeS* 5:33–37), Holman argues that a crucial question is how Poe meant his statements on the atom to work as a literary device. In densely allusive language, Poe remarked that Lord Rosse's telescope had scientifically established the correctness of the atomic theory Epicurus had evolved by intuition (that a nebula is composed of atoms attracted to each other in an increasingly narrow orbit in the process of forming new worlds). But this was precisely the reverse of contemporary telescopic findings according to Holman. Poe develops this allusion as a complicated conceit which has three directions: he moves from Rosse's studies in exact science to the "explosive" volcano of Aetna in the "Rossi" Mountains; from the nebula of "Orion" to his own review of R. H. Horne's epic *Orion*; and from "nebulae," "narrow orbits," and "miasma" to his foes in the Boston coterie with their "satellite" metaphysicians and "cloudy" Transcendentalists. Use of an obscure scientific theory discredited in the first century is, Holman argues, characteristic of Poe's hoaxing in general and of the heavy attack he directed throughout *Eureka* against both pedantry and arm-chair science.

Two Canadian scholars see the *Journal of Julius Rodman* as a satiric attack on the two-faced moral code of white civilization embodied in American western narratives and offer the opinion that Rodman's hypocritical speeches to the Indians present "a perfect paradigm of contemporary American history" (p. 335). Whether this last is true or not, John J. Teunissen and Evelyn J. Hinz, in "Poe's *Journal of Julius Rodman* as Parody" (*NCF* 27:317–38), perform a valuable service in reconceiving what Poe (if, indeed, Poe is the author of this work, an issue the authors do not address) may have been up to in his heavy borrowings from Jefferson, Lewis and Clark, Mackenzie, Townsend, and Irving. Their argument goes beyond those who regard the work as another Poe hoax. "What has not been appreciated," they write, "is that the *donnée* of the *Journal* is that it is the work not of Poe but of Rodman and that the seeming plagiarisms are the means to a satiric end."

f. Poetry. Except for the discussion in Hoffman's book, study of the poetry was confined to a handful of articles and notes. Lewis Leary in "Edgar Allan Poe: The Adolescent as Confidence Man" (*SLJ*, 4,ii:3–21) offers an appreciative overview of "America's first great writer of the second rank" by attempting to describe the Romantic vision of poetry found in Poe's works from "Al Aaraaf" to the prose-poem *Eureka*. In the course of his discussion, Leary makes several observations on the uses of incantatory verse both to invoke a visionary "other" world and also to suggest that words themselves become traps to ensnare listeners or readers; thus Poe's poem on the nature of poetry, "Al Aaraaf," is a kind of invocatory "halfway house" for those who desire a better world than can actually be had. This metaphor, however, is typical of those Leary employs throughout in an effort to make Poe "relevant." In "Edgar Poe and the New Knowledge" (*SLJ*, 4,ii:34–40), George Monteiro takes issue with those who have seen "Sonnet—To Science" as merely a conventional Romantic lament over the destruction that scientific knowledge has wrought "in killing the myths once so meaningful to poets." Rather, he says, the narrative voice of the poem resists the statement it must make, so that the very poet who creates the effective images of the defeated Romantic vision at the end of the poem is not himself a defeated poet. "Sonnet—To Science" thus becomes a key to understanding Poe's "internalization of the demonic quest romance," in which, from the "ashes of his indignation," the "poet himself" emerges as "his own ideal hero." This is an argument deserving of far greater development than Monteiro gives it.

John Timmerman's mistitled "Edgar Allan Poe: Artist, Aesthetician, Legend" (*SDR* 10:60–70), after an unpromising opening, settles down into an interesting sketch of Poe's "aesthetic of poetry" in an effort to show "the affinities of this aesthetic with the spirit of English Romanticism." Although he neglects the earlier work of George Kelly and others, Timmerman does offer several provocative suggestions. He points out that Poe thought the task of the poet was to capture some ineffable ideal beauty and to re-create it, thereby awakening in other men a sense of the eternal, since the poem is incomplete if it does not produce the effect in other men of the "excitement of soul." This effect is accomplished by allying "beauty" and "truth" with "sadness" in a symmetrical, rhythmic pattern of verse that parallels the rhythmic symmetry of the universe as described in *Eureka*. Certain "excellences" enhance this process— particularly what Poe calls "complexity" and "suggestiveness." In his emphasis on feeling, emotion, music, and movement, rather than on philosophy, morality, or utilitarian value, Poe's aesthetic parallels Romantic aesthetics in general. The "inevitable result of finite hearts longing for infinite goals will be despair"—especially since Poe's "concern was not for human feelings but rather for the poet's conception of the feelings necessary to best provoke a sense of beauty" as he conceived it.

Glen A. Omans in "Poe's 'Ulalume': Drama of the Solipsistic Self" (*Papers on Poe*, pp. 62–73) argues that in Poe's poems and stories death of the beloved represents the loss of the vision of the ideal other world and thus is an impingement of external reality upon the hero's mind, which has sought its own closed system of meaning. " 'Ulalume,' " Omans argues, "goes one step farther. The introverted imagination can no longer experience even a hallucination of the ideal." Psyche fears that any portent or symbol the speaker encounters will lead back inevitably to Ulalume's tomb, thereby causing the anguish of confronting either the nothingness of the external universe or the "terrors of solipsism" in his own being. Oman believes that, in the poem, we witness a grim situation in which a skeptical Poe, outside the poem, has created an optimistic narrator-Poe inside the poem."

The impulse to read Poe's poems biographically has resulted in an interesting speculation by Miles D. Orvell. In " 'The Raven' and the

Chair" (*PoeS* 5:54) Orvell suggests a psychological source for the power that the figure of the raven may have held for Poe—John Allan's dining chair with a carved ebony bird strongly resembling a raven mounted on its back—which may still be seen in the Poe Museum in Richmond, Virginia. In a very private way, then, the raven suggested alienation or separation to Poe. Two other notes on the poem, however, emphasize the larger significance of the raven figure. In "Classical Raven Lore and Poe's Raven" (*PoeS* 5:53) John F. Adams observes that in classical mythology, the raven was a messenger and Pallas Athena its first master; in Ovid the raven was originally white; in Suetonius the raven represented hope; and the sound the raven makes that we transcribe "caw" the Greeks transcribed as *cras*, their word for "tomorrow." Poe reverses this call into "nevermore" and transforms hope into black despair, giving ironic dimension to a seemingly private symbol. Byrd Howell Granger in "Devil Lore in 'The Raven'" (*PoeS*, 5:53–54) similarly attempts to broaden the significance of the raven figure by reference to tradition. In folklore, he claims, the raven has long been known as a guise of the devil; thus its appearance may be in response to a half-conscious summons from the student, who has been dabbling in black magic at midnight. The merging of the student's shadow with that of the raven parallels the loss of one's shadow in a pact with the devil and suggests the reason why he shall not be reunited with Lenore in heaven.

Thomas Ollive Mabbott notes in the introductory matter to "Eldorado" in his edition of Poe's *Poems* (see *ALS 1969*, pp. 182–83) that the meter of the poem resembles that of "A Tom-a-Bedlam Song" in Isaac D'Israeli's *Curiosities of Literature* and that of Charles Lever's drinking song, "The Man for Galway," from Lever's novel, *Charles O'Malley*. This novel Poe reviewed, calling some of the songs "doggerel verses," as Burton R. Pollin notes in "Poe's 'Eldorado' Viewed as a Song of the West" (*PrS*, 46:228–35). Pollin then asks an important question: "If 'Eldorado' is to be termed one of Poe's noblest works [Mabbott's judgment], why did he choose the 'doggerel' meter of a drinking song as a model?" (p. 230). Pollin's answer, however, somewhat avoids the critical question. He argues that Poe was seeking both a topical subject matter and a topical form to reestablish his popularity; "Eldorado" is merely an effort to cash in on the current California craze by attempting a popular song of the Gold Rush

genre. Instead of exploring the complexities of the serious played off
against the satiric, Pollin is content to suggest that Poe was attempting to imitate the strategy of "a repetend in a changing last line context" so "successful" in "The Raven" four years earlier.

Alice Moser Claudel, in her economical essay "Mystic Symbols
in Poe's 'The City in the Sea'" (*Papers on Poe*, pp. 54–61), gently
demonstrates how arrogance can trip up even the best of scholars.
"Absurd" and "inept" were Mabbott's judgments on the speculations
of Killis Campbell and Louise Pound that Poe's city in the sea was
modeled on Babylon. Mabbott pointed out that Poe's phrase "Baby-
lon-like walls" indicates that the city described in the poem is other
than Babylon, that Babylon was far from any sea, and that Poe's
earlier title, "The City of Sin," clearly identified the place as one of
the cities of the plain, Sodom or Gomorrah. Claudel observes, however, that Poe's very allusion makes Babylon part of the background
of the poem and that a number of obscurities can be cleared up by
reference to Babylonian legend. She notes also that Mabbott himself
had noticed similarities of phrasing in the poem to Isaiah 14.9, but
for some reason did not mention that Isaiah was here referring to
Babylon, that Isaiah compared its prideful king to Lucifer (14.12),
and that Isaiah predicted that Babylon would become the possession
of pools of water (14.23). In the more speculative portion of the
article, Claudel refers us to Pieter Breugel the Elder's famous painting of the "proud tower" of Babel, lopsided and crumbling, and
bathed in a hellish glare, with the Euphrates made to look more like a
luridly lit sea than a river. She suggests that much of the confusing
imagery of the poem is explained if we see that the city is reflected
in the water rather than actually submerged and that the imagery of
wind, water, and light merges to imply a point between life and
death, beginning and ending. Claudel then proceeds to explain the
references to ivy, the violet, the viol, and the vine, diamonds, Astarte,
and the like in terms of Babylonian myth; she notes, for example, that
the Babylonian king was said to have been suckled at the breasts of
Ishtar (Astarte) and that Hammurabi, the Babylonian ruler, declared
that the insignia of royalty were conferred on him by the god *Sin*.
Two other notes attempt to expand the allusive richness of the poem
further. Christopher P. Baker, in "Spenser and 'The City in the Sea'"
(*PoeS* 5:55), suggests that Poe adapted a phrase about a "proud
towre" from the *Faerie Queene* (2.9.45) to convey the imminence of

death. Daniel Driskell in "Lucretius and 'The City in the Sea' " (*PoeS* 5:55), argues that the 1805 John Mason Good translation of *De Rerum Natura* contains a number of parallels not only with "The City in the Sea" but also with *Eureka* and other works; he points especially to the images of intertwined light and liquid, of turrets, fanes, and altars crumbling under corrosive time, of a huge, elevated figure of death and superstition that looks down from a gigantic tower, and of the simultaneous sinking down of the doomed city and the rising up of a fiery hell.

ii. Bryant, Whittier, Legaré, Hayne, Lanier, Longfellow

Bryant's poetry was totally neglected during the year. Kenneth Walter Cameron's "Bryant's Correspondents—A Checklist" (*ATQ* 13:37–45) is merely an alphabetical listing of letters from Bryant to various contemporaries in the "Bryant-Godwin deposit" in the New York Public Library. "A Bryant Letter with Poem (1825)" (*ATQ* 14:81–82) merely reprints the 1971 catalogue advertisement of Kenneth W. Rendell, Inc. Whittier fared a little better. Notley Sinclair Maddox's "Whittier's *Ichabod*" (*Expl* 30:item 59) carries further the discussion of Whittier's use of the Bible and of Milton's Satan to characterize Daniel Webster by correcting errors in Wayne R. Kime's essay (*Expl* 28[1970]: item 59). George Carey's "John Greenleaf Whittier and Folklore: The Search for a Traditional American Past" (*NYFQ* 27 [1971]:113–29) calls attention to Whittier's use of "both historical records and active nineteenth-century oral traditions" in *Legends of New England, The Super-Naturalism of New England*, and "Narrative and Legendary Poems." Country born and country bred, Whittier was the "first real spokesman for New England folklore." Remembered almost solely as a poet, however, Whittier, one may forget, also wrote a novel. Donald Ringe, in "The Artistry of Whittier's *Margaret Smith's Journal*" (*EIHC* 108:235–43) argues that critics who see the novel as disunified mistake Whittier's intent and miss his manipulation of point of view: "Margaret Smith is the central consciousness of the work and the means through which the various elements of the book are successfully unified." Ernest J. Moyne's "John Greenleaf Whittier and Finland" (*SS* 44:52–62) documents Whittier's interest in not only the literature but also the people of Finland.

Aside from Jay B. Hubbell, there would seem to be only two

experts on the Southern poet James Mathewes Legaré. One is Curtis Carroll Davis, who in *That Ambitious Mr. Legaré: The Life of James M. Legaré of South Carolina, Including a Collected Edition of His Verse* (Columbia, Univ. of S. C. Press) attempts to present final versions of all the known poems—forty-nine in all, nineteen more than in the collected volume of 1848. Davis also includes elaborate textual commentary and bibliographical appendices. The other Legaré scholar is James E. Kibler, who offers a critical appraisal (*GaR* 26:385–89) of Davis's textual methodology, along with the titles and locations of two poems Davis overlooked. The first half of Davis's volume (about 150 pages) is a biography of the little-known Legaré compiled from nearly thirty years' patient research in antebellum journals, annuals, newspapers, family records and recollections, and various archival deposits. Legaré turns out to have been not only a poet of some note but also a novelist and short-story writer, a painter, an inventor, and a lawyer, who at one time earned the dislike of William Gilmore Simms for his "ambition" to break into the Northern literary cliques presided over by Lewis Gaylord Clark and the *Knickerbocker* group. As a poet, according to Davis, Legaré frequently exhibits a terser style than that associated with most Romantic antebellum Southern poetry and also makes greater use of exact observation of the actual natural scenery of his area.

Legaré was often compared by Southern contemporaries with the South Carolina poets Timrod and Hayne. Rayburn S. Moore's study of the latter, *Paul Hamilton Hayne* (TUSAS 202), is an informed and critically astute assessment of a minor poet who has, Moore persuades one, been undeservedly neglected in this century. Not that Moore is blinded by enthusiasm for his subject. On the contrary, in his summing up, Moore catalogues Hayne's weaknesses: he uncritically accepted English poetic traditions and a "sentimental" and "sterile" Romanticism; he was unduly influenced by Romantic orientalism and (like Legaré) wrote bad imitations of Leigh Hunt; he overused emphatic rhyme; his poetry generally gives the impression of being divorced from life and lacks intellectual content. But Moore observes, after granting these weaknesses, that Hayne is yet, "in the scope, versatility, and bulk of his production, . . . the most substantial Southern poet of the nineteenth century." This is a startling statement. Moore elaborates in an illuminating comparison with Poe, Timrod, and Lanier.

Hayne did not write any one poem which comes near the perfection of Poe's "To Helen" or Timrod's "Ode," but he wrote
more passably good verse than Poe or Timrod or Lanier. . . .
Hayne lacked Poe's sense of art and critical acumen, Timrod's
theme and control, and Lanier's inventiveness and fertility;
but he could, on occasion, be as musical as Poe, as eloquent as
Timrod, and as lush as Lanier. Poe and Timrod are better poets
than Hayne, if only their best work is selected to compare with
his. This is not necessarily the case with Lanier, for his best is
in many ways very much like Hayne's: in few instances is the
promise fulfilled in the performance. Still, Hayne's canon is
rounded in ways that Poe's or Timrod's or Lanier's is not. It
reflects the full scope of a striving for expression in a spectrum
of poetic types and structures, and it suggests therefore a range
and completeness which are missing in the output of the
three other nineteenth-century Southern poets of consequence.
[pp. 168–69]

Moore also treats another aspect of Hayne's career, the decline of his
reputation ("The Old South and the New: Paul Hamilton Hayne and
Maurice Thompson," *SLJ* 5,i:108–22), by chronicling the strains and
rifts in the friendship of the two men over their interpretations of
each other's works and of the postwar South. Although Hayne sought
to reconcile the regions after the war, he was basically a defender of
the Old South; and he saw in Thompson's novels of the early 1880s
elements of a willingness on the part of Southerners "to forget or
ignore the past and to accommodate their views to an explanation . . .
which condemned everything the Old South had stood for." Thompson's three articles on Hayne after Hayne's death became each in
turn increasingly critical and helped greatly to diminish the reputation of a man who was once considered by many throughout the country (including Longfellow, Lowell, Bryant, Whittier, Howells, and
Lanier) "the poet laureate of the South."

C. H. Edwards, Jr., in "Lanier's *The Symphony*, 64–84" (*Expl*
31:item 27) tries to demonstrate that "though no one has been able
to show that Sidney Lanier's 'The Symphony' actually has a symphonic structure," parts of it, including lines 64–84, are "analogous to
musical modulation." Jack De Bellis, however, comes very close to
demonstrating the symphonic form of the poem, despite his own dis-

claimer, in his fine *Sidney Lanier* (TUSAS 205). He attempts in this book to defend Lanier from the criticisms of the New Critics, especially Tate and Warren, by examining the "esthetic and moral complexity" of Lanier's canon. De Bellis reveals Lanier to be extraordinarily complicated, widely read, intellectual, philosophical, scholarly, and intense. Lanier's early reading of Goethe, Kant, and Carlyle and his reading of chivalric romances provided the matrix for the conflict between realist and Romantic impulses in his works. In his poetry of social consciousness during Reconstruction, these conflicting impulses are held in artistic tension by various symbols of opposition, just as they are in his novel *Tiger-Lilies*, eventually to be resolved in his later works in a final theme of forgiveness. De Bellis argues that in his major poems, such as "Corn," "The Symphony," "The Marshes of Glynn," Lanier is not addicted to obscurity, illogical symbolism, and bad metaphor as his critics have maintained, but instead exhibits a richly suggestive symbolic and metaphoric technique. De Bellis is in fact successful in showing the coherencies not only of Lanier's style but also of his moral vision and aesthetic conception in his total work, including his studies of the novel and the "science" of verse—though it is surprising that nowhere does De Bellis mention Edd Winfield Parks's *Sidney Lanier: The Man, the Poet, the Critic* (see *ALS 1969*, p. 198).

Longfellow complained frequently in his journal of how great a personal burden was the massive correspondence he felt obliged as a "man of letters" to conduct. "I am plagued to death," he wrote, "with letters from all sorts of people, and of course about their own affairs." (May 15, 1855). This constant letter-writing pressed on him by others robbed him, he felt, of time and energy that might be put to better use. Volumes 3 and 4 of Andrew Hilen's impressive edition of *The Letters of Henry Wadsworth Longfellow* (Cambridge, Mass., Belknap Press of Harvard Univ. Press), covering the years 1844 to 1856 and 1857 to 1865, print 1,500 surviving letters from the more than 4,000 Longfellow is known to have written during this twenty-two year period. The correspondents represented in these volumes number 425, and each volume is over 500 pages long. As with the first two volumes of the edition (see *ALS 1967*, pp. 159–60), the format is open and readable, the volumes are conveniently divided into periods and subperiods with helpful titles by the editor, and the letters are well annotated. Moreover, Hilen provides clear and concise introductions to each volume and to each subperiod of Longfellow's life and correspondence. The letters themselves, however, as Hilen observes, are disappointing:

> In general, the letters of 1844–1865, apart from those to his family and intimate friends, are characterized by brevity, formality, and perfunctoriness ... [for] many of the letters in Volumes III and IV are little more than polite responses, conventionally phrased and straightforward in content. Their value lies merely in annotating the poet's biography. ... even those letters to which Longfellow devoted more time, energy, and thought have only moderate intellectual or narrative interest. Perhaps this is because he remained at home for most of the twenty-two years following his marriage to Frances Appleton. ... He had become a member of the establishment, and most of his letters from this period, in their politeness and reserve, reflect this new social status. [p. 3]

Hilen notes that the letters suggest that Longfellow participated more actively than is generally suspected in the political dramas of his day and that he was ever a shrewd and practical businessman. But principally he "preserved a solid defense against disclosing the more intimate, emotional, and spiritual events of his life." For this reason, Hilen remarks, "it is doubtful that the discovery of more letters from this period will alter the picture of Longfellow that emerges from these volumes."

Elizabeth Evans in "The Everett-Longfellow Correspondence (*ATQ* 13:2–15) prints twenty-eight letters in the Harvard College Library by Alexander Hill Everett, editor of the *North American Review* from 1830 to 1836. His letters to Longfellow cover the period 1830 to 1846 and "remind us that Longfellow was once a critic and a reviewer, contributing eleven articles to the *North American Review*, the five during Alexander Everett's tenure as editor reflecting his linguistic and poetic interests."

Donald A. Sears, in "Folk Poetry in Longfellow's Boyhood" (*NEQ* 45:96–105) calls attention to the probable impact of Longfellow's early reading of local ballads of shipwrecks, accidental deaths, family tragedies, events from the Revolutionary War, and the like by Thomas Shaw, Ebenezer Robbins, and other Maine writers, along with satiric ballads against the temperance faction of Portland and rhymed

street-greetings by the town barber and the local fishermen. Such
works, especially those combining grief, religion, and hymnals, reveal the "popularity of the ballad form in the early United States . . . .
By tapping this ballad audience a few years later, such a poet as
Longfellow was able to earn a comfortable living."

Two articles appeared on Longfellow's conception of the American Indian in *Hiawatha*. Joseph S. Pronechen's "The Making of
Hiawatha" (*NYFQ* 28:151–60) merely re-surveys what is known of
Longfellow's use of his sources. Gordon Brotherston in *"Ubirajara,
Hiawatha, Cumandá*: National Virtue from American Indian Literature" (*CLS* 9:243–52) discusses three American works about the Indian in terms of J. G. Herder's doctrine of national folk literature and
Chateaubriand's role as mediator between Indian and "white" literature. Both the Brazilian writer José de Alencar in his *Ubirajara* (1874)
and the Ecuadorian writer Juan Léon Mera in his *Cumandá* (1871)
made their Indians sound like Europeans. Longfellow in *Hiawatha*
is closer to the actual oral traditions of Indian culture; but his conception of the Indian, for all its sympathy, is still that of an outsider—
"white" to the extent that it is "elegiac." "More than access to Original
America," Brotherston writes, "Hiawatha gave a sense of its end . . . .
With the arrival of the Europeans, Hiawatha moves obligingly westward 'into the fiery sunset.' " Thus, like the two South American
writers, the North American writer unknowingly expresses the paradox of Herder's conception of "die Wilden" and of a national literature "uncontaminated by the 'künstliche wissenschaftliche Denkart,
Sprach und Letternart' of metropolitan Europe."

Washington State University

Once again I am obliged to thank my department for a summer grant-in-aid;
this grant allowed Mr. Gherry Hedin to help me collect materials for this review.
I might add that in an effort to maintain objectivity on those essays that I had
any connection with as editor or publisher, I have sometimes had recourse to
abstracts prepared by the authors, as yet unpublished, but in my possession; as
will be evident, however, I do not always agree with these critics.

12. Fiction: 1900 to the 1930s

Warren French

The absence during 1972 of general studies of the fiction of the first four decades of this century, the preponderance among books about individual authors of non-committal biographies, and the lack of fresh and provocative insights in analytical articles—except those concerning a few perplexing and long-neglected works like Jean Toomer's *Cane*—offer strong evidence that those novels and short stories that we still label "modern," sometimes even "contemporary," are becoming a part of history and that if they are to survive except as museum pieces, they must begin to meet tests of universal significance rather than immediate relevancy. Ingenious but hermetic explications must be supplanted by appraisals of these works in broad cultural contexts. Until the slow machinery of publication is able to catch up with a rapid shift of focus in criticism, scholarship may remain at a standstill while the careful editions and reference materials necessary to the efforts of a freshly oriented generation of scholars are readied.

i. Inheritors of the Genteel Tradition

The three women who best bridged in fiction the gap between the fading gentility of the late nineteenth century and the vulgar materialism of the early twentieth have no doubt benefited greatly from the increased emphasis upon women's studies, even though all three novelists were marked by an individualism and an integrity that make them of continuing interest as social and critical fashions change.

A new book about Willa Cather proves less interesting than a special issue of *Western American Literature* (Spring 1972) devoted to her, testifying once again to her importance as a regional author. The most general of five articles, Patrick J. Sullivan's "Willa Cather's

Southwest" (*WAL* 7:25–37), summarizes five novels concerned with
the region and concludes that the Southwest played a crucially liberating role for Miss Cather in finding herself and developing her
fiction. Evelyn J. Hinz's "Willa Cather's Technique and the Ideology
of Populism" (*WAL* 7:47–61) describes the novelist's "artistic theory
and practice" as "exactly suited to express the ideology of populism,"
because she presented from her personal experience "the world of the
farm and the view of the farmer as the natural man in harmony with
his environment." Yet she transcended provincialism, because she
realized, too, that "to give her stories 'glory' the realistic must be
made to shadow forth the eternal."

Other articles deal with individual novels about the Southwest.
David Stouck's on *The Professor's House* is described below with a
group of other studies by the same author. Patricia Lee Yongue's
"*A Lost Lady*: The End of the First Cycle" (*WAL* 7:3–12) describes
Niel Herbert's disillusionment as "suggestive in many ways of the
story of Nick Carraway's loss of wonder in *The Great Gatsby*." The
novelist, this critic feels, "drained the optimism from the earlier
pioneer novels, much as the new generation of 'shrewd young men'
was draining the spirit of optimism from the Old West." A counter-
balancing note of optimism is sounded in James M. Dinn's "A Novelist's Miracle: Structure and Myth in *Death Comes for the Archbishop*" (*WAL* 7:39–46), which argues that "very much like Thoreau,
Willa Cather begins on the most prosaic level but offers a gradual
initiation into lyrical flights of the spirit," so that "if one allows full
scope to her structural hints, and if her underlying myth makes its
presence felt, the reader may be initiated into a much richer dimension [than the solidly historical] which can invert his usual orientation" (p. 45).

These essays provide a much more stimulating introduction to
this author, whose work remains vital as we approach her centenary,
than Dorothy T. McFarland's *Willa Cather* (New York, Frederick
Ungar), a "reconsideration" which sees the fiction as a metaphor of
the conflict which Miguel de Unamuno referred to as "inward tragedy"—the conflict between the world as scientific reason shows it
and "as our religious faith affirms it to be." Sketchy summaries of the
novels stress their religious and idealistic aspects and the novelist's
view of the world after 1922 as "spiritually impoverished."

Most of the makings of a book developing a less familiar thesis are found in a group of articles by David Stouck. His most strained argument is presented in *"O Pioneers!*: Willa Cather and the Epic Imagination" (*PrS* 46:23–34), which develops the position that while it is popularly held that the epic is "restricted to the earliest imaginative expressions of each culture" and that "modern society seldom produces an outlet for the epic imagination," Willa Cather in writing about the settling of the Midwest "chose her subject, as Melville had earlier, from the classical matter for American epic—the struggle of man against nature." (One is inclined to agree with Miss Cather's own description of the novel as "a pastoral," because it lacks the panoramic sweep of a work that attempts to forge a group consciousness through the embodiment of a heroic ideal.) Stouck is much more convincing when he develops one of this highly self-conscious novelist's own terms, as he does in "Willa Cather's Unfurnished Novel: Narrative in Perspectives" (*WascanaR* 6,ii:41–51), which calls for a criticism of fiction that "illuminates something of its organic nature" by tracing through *A Lost Lady* and *My Mortal Enemy* the way in which a "central consciousness" of a detached observer manages to "transcend personal frustration and disillusionment not through involvement but through imaginative perspectives which [lead] to a contemplative state of awareness and acceptance."

Collaborating with his wife Mary-Ann, Stouck also makes a strong case for "Hagiographical Style in *Death Comes for the Archbishop*" (*UTQ* 41:293–307), pointing out that in this novel Willa Cather uses the mode of the saint's legend, reflecting the lack of concern in medieval literature for causal relationships, so that a narrative consists of a series of scenes each complete in itself. Finally in "Willa Cather and *The Professor's House*: 'Letting Go with the Heart'" (*WAL* 7:13–24), Stouck argues that the world broke apart for the novelist in the early 1920s "because she could no longer endorse the pursuits of a materialistic and competitive society which reflected her own fruitless and false ambitions"; Stouck further maintains, however, that this fracture did not end her imaginative life, because in *The Professor's House* and subsequent novels "there is a sustained dialectic between the desire for power and the transcendence of individual ambition."

Elsewhere Clive Hart in "*The Professor's House*: A Shapely Story" (*MLR* 67:271–81) reinforces Stouck's view of the novel by reading it not as "a story of imaginative escape from the unsatisfactory mod-

ern world into a vision of past but irrecoverable beauty and harmony," but rather as a story of "fallen man's failure to integrate his
visions of harmony with the realities of his emotional nature." William J. Stuckey also attacks the superficiality of some previous criticism of another favorite novel in "*My Ántonia*: A Rose for Miss
Cather" (*SNNTS* 4:473–83). Charges that the focus in the novel is
divided between Ántonia and Jim Burden can be resolved, Stuckey
thinks, by reading the novel not as the story of Ántonia's agrarian
success but rather as the story of Jim's success as an artist in convert-
ing the woman into an artistic symbol of a way of life that he approves.

Ellen Glasgow has attracted fewer recent analytical defenders
than Cather, but as we approach also the centenary of her birth, two
substantial publications provide solid background for further interpretive study. E. Stanly Godbold, Jr.'s *Ellen Glasgow and the Woman Within* (Baton Rouge, La. State Univ. Press) is a biography
based on personal papers that emphasizes only those aspects of her
novels that touch upon her life. It provides an impeccable, impersonal
account of a remarkably self-sufficient woman; and it is ideally com-
plemented by Edgar E. MacDonald's "Ellen Glasgow: An Essay in
Bibliography" (*RALS* 2:131–56), a comprehensive survey of the
state of Glasgow scholarship. Blair Rouse's brief "Ellen Glasgow:
Manners and Art" (*Cabellian* 4:96–98) attributes present neglect of
the novelist to her refusal "to exploit violence or sentimentality for
the sake of sensation," though "she did not hesitate to come to grips
with unpleasant subjects."

Recent commentators on Edith Wharton display no such scholarly reserve as those writing about Glasgow, but are rather vigorously
partisan in their claims. James W. Tuttleton's "Edith Wharton: The
Archeological Motive" (*YR* 61:562–74) argues for the possible creative use that can still be made in troubled times of Mrs. Wharton's
belief that "very little of distinctively human nature can exist independently of society and its forms"—a theme which she treated in
two ways: by dramatizing "the web of culture, manners, and mores"
which enclose men and warning of the danger of alienating oneself
from it, and also by reconstructing "archeologically" the social world
of her youth. Focusing on a more limited target, James W. Gargano
argues with equal force in "*The House of Mirth*: Social Futility and
Faith" (*AL* 44:137–43) that the triumphant secret—residing in an
undisclosed word—that Lily Bart and Lawrence Seldner possess in

the final chapters of the novel has to be "faith," which Mrs. Wharton defined as "an almost mystical assurance that only moral action can save the ever-threatened continuity of human existence."

The word "respectful" understates the attention that Owen Wister is beginning to receive after having long been thought merely popular. A most impressive example of the kind of archetypal criticism that examines a work in its mythological context, as called for in Northrop Frye's *The Critical Path*, is Joseph F. Trimmer's *"The Virginian:* Novel and Films" (*IllQ* 35,ii:5–18), which exemplifies the benefits that may accrue to both literary and cinematic criticism through an intelligent combination of them. Trimmer traces the changes from the novel in two film versions, observing that "what is surprising is the way in which this alteration documents significant changes in the character of the Western myth and our attitude toward it." He reads Wister's novel as making the symbolic point that the country is "revitalized by strong, rugged men bred in the West and polished by contact with Eastern culture." In the first film (1929), however, the protagonist remains essentially the same character and does not need to change "his cultural allegiance to the West" to win an Eastern bride. Finally, the second film (1945) ends "not with a synthesis of East and West but a capitulation in favor of the East," as the disillusioned protagonist exchanges the virtues of the West "for the love of Victorian seriousness, cultural rigidity and the emergence of the corporate executive."

After his success with *The Virginian,* Wister himself abandoned the West for the South. His second highly successful novel, *Lady Baltimore* (named not for an aristocractic character, but a popular cake), is a defense of the genteel society of Charleston, South Carolina. Julian Mason traces the history of Wister's family connections with traditional Charleston society and the boost that his once-popular work gave the tourist trade in two articles: "Owen Wister, Champion of Old Charleston" (*QJLC* 29:162–85) and "Owen Wister and the South" (*SHR* 6:23–34). Both stress that Northern critics— including Wister's friend President Theodore Roosevelt—were annoyed by what they considered a too harsh treatment of Northerners and a too kindly treatment of Southerners.

Useful biographical studies have been provided also of two of the final representatives of New England's fading genteel tradition. Stephen Birmingham's *The Late John Marquand: A Biography* (Philadelphia, Lippincott) focuses on the subject's marriages, divorces, and family quarrels, but contains the insightful generalization that Marquand wrote "novels of defeat and compromise, where the 'system' or set of systems is always, in the end, too much for the individual" (p. 241). Barton L. St. Armand's "Facts in the Case of H. P. Lovecraft" (*RIH* 31:3–19) describes the "intellectually fascinating and factually boring" life that this man whom European critics have described as the "greatest American master of supernatural fiction" led in his native city of Providence. St. Armand protests that even today the city does not seem to know "the man who identified himself so completely with its uniqueness and its traditions."

ii. The Redskins

The University of Minnesota Pamphlets on American Writers, which have provided such efficient introductions to our literature to readers at home and abroad, has terminated with its 103d number. Surprisingly, in view of the many younger, less renowned novelists already honored, one of the last group of pamphlets to appear is W. H. Frohock's *Theodore Dreiser* (UMPAW 102). This series from a great Midwestern public institution has always been less hospitable to accounts of Midwestern "Redskins" than to representatives of the Eastern genteel tradition. Facing directly this frequent cultural bias of American literary critics, Frohock opens his discussion with an acknowledgment that "we have only recently begun to concede what Europeans have told us for years"—that Dreiser was a major writer, whose originality lay in his constitutional inability "to say he saw what he did not in fact see, what wasn't there to be seen" (p. 5). Frohock then attributes changed attitudes today to our finding it hard to believe that "the so-called Genteel Tradition was not a cynical conspiracy among an established elite to legitimize their fortunes and justify the society they headed" (p. 6). He concludes an unexceptionable account, drawing on the most useful recent criticism and strongly defending Dreiser's often underrated craftsmanship, with the observation that Dreiser's novels offer not "a picture *of* American life so much as pictures *from* American life," written by "a native of the area," who could write about it "without sounding as if he had gone on a slumming expedition" (p. 46).

Another vigorous defense of Dreiser is John J. McAleer's "An

American Tragedy and *In Cold Blood*" (*Thought* 47:569–86), which argues that despite numerous parallels between the books, Dreiser's has a social urgency that Capote's lacks, since the former was not written simply "to establish a literary method, with murder incidental to the author's purposes." McAleer feels that Capote's effort to create a "non-fiction novel" bogged him down in petty facts; whereas Dreiser's fictionalizing his material liberated him from details so that he might make his story an attack upon the consequences of the American dream.

In a comprehensive assessment of "Dreiserian Tragedy" (*SNNTS* 4:39–51) William L. Vance maintains that the novels convey "a sense of fatality that is more than naturalistic determinism," which does imply the possibility of eventual control, because Dreiser does not believe that social reform can ever get at man's tragic condition, for which unknowable supernatural forces are responsible.

Sister Carrie remains unagingly seductive to interpreters. In "Dreiser's Hurstwood and Jefferson's Rip Van Winkle" (*PMLA* 87: 514–16), John R. Byers, Jr., adds to Hugh Witemyer's earlier speculations about the influences of Dreiser's theatre-going experiences (see *ALS 1971*, p. 217) the argument that it is "ironic and portentous" that Carrie, Hurstwood, and Drouet watch Joseph Jefferson's famous production of *Rip Van Winkle*, a play about "a once prosperous man locked out of his home," and that Dreiser may have seen "the tragic possibilities in the usually comic Rip for the development of Hurstwood." Speculating on the influence of another art, Robert J. Griffin explores in "Carrie and Music: A Note on Dreiser's Technique" (*From Irving to Steinbeck*, pp. 73–81) the way in which the power of music constitutes a major motif in the novel in three aspects—music's expressive and affective powers and "the musiclike power of other phenomena which similarly succeed in effective communication or exerting strong influences on responsive persons." In his study extending over two centuries of "Sin and the City: The Uses of Disorder in the Urban Novel" (*CentR* 16:203–20), Alan Rose points out that Carrie never really experiences "evil and corruption" in the way that most migrants from the country to the city do, so that her view of experience is "as immature at the end of *Sister Carrie*, when she has wealth, as it was at the beginning."

A further souvenir of the celebration in 1971 of the centenary of Dreiser's birth is an issue of the University of Pennsylvania's *Library*

Chronicle (Winter 1972) containing the 1971 A. S. W. Rosenbach
Fellowship lectures in bibliography and other pieces. In one lecture,
"Dreiser's Novels: The Editorial Problem" (*LC* 38:7–24), Donald
Pizer examines these works "as an excellent example of the futility
of applying copy-text principles to the editing of much twentieth-
century fiction," since all editions have been printed from the same
stereotyped plates and the editorial problems are encountered in
"messy" pre-publication material; in the other lecture, "Bibliography
and the Biographer" (*LC* 38:25–44), Robert H. Elias shows how
changes in manuscript versions of *The "Genius"* over a number of
years present actually the story of Dreiser's own "progressive self-
knowledge." Joseph Katz's "Theodore Dreiser's *Ev'ry Month*" (*LC*
38:46–66) shows how Dreiser's attempt in the mid-nineties to create
a magazine for the whole family resulted in one that was snapped up
by women. In "Dreiser's Debt to *Jay Cooke*" (*LC* 38:67–77) Philip
L. Gerber traces the novelist's use of Ellis Paxson Oberholtzer's *Jay
Cooke: Financier of the Civil War* (1907) in describing Frank Cow-
perwood's early years in *The Financier*, because of lack of information about this period in the life of Charles T. Yerkes, Jr., the principal
model for Dreiser's character. Finally Richard W. Dowell's "Dreiser's
Notes on Life: Responses to an Impenetrable Universe" (*LC* 38:78–
91) presents material gathered from seventy-eight bundles of Dreiser's ruminations to reach the conclusion—sharply opposed to William
L. Vance's, described above—that these "workshop" notes make clear
that to Dreiser life was not "a cruel brutal procedure" and show how
he gave "poetic meaning to the entire universe."

The *Jack London Newsletter* continues to provide a wealth of
biographical and bibliographical information about the works of the
author it honors, as well as some critical articles. Its most ambitious
offering so far is Ronald Gower's "The Creative Conflict: Struggle and
Escape in Jack London's Fiction" (*JLN* 4[1971]:77–114), two portions of a longer study which present exhaustive evidence to support
the conventional view that London's work displays an impressive
amount of information gathered from a wide range of reading, but
that this material is unassimilated and disordered and "never suggests
to the reader the strong consistent view of life evident in the greatest
writers."

Two London novels continue to attract most attention. N. E.

Dunn and Pamela Wilson in "The Significance of Upward Mobility in *Martin Eden*" (*JLN* 5:1–8) soundly rebuke many critics' assumptions that the title character's suicide is inadequately prepared for by arguing that "the structural development of the novel is not governed by the expected literary convention but derives from a sociological pattern—that of the person frustrated in a movement of upward social mobility." Forrest W. Parkay's "The Influence of Nietzsche's *Thus Spoke Zarathustra* on London's *The Sea-Wolf*" (*JLN* 4[1971]: 16–24) points out that while both writers "depict men aspiring to that ultimately unattainable goal, the superman," *The Sea-Wolf* attacks the Nietzschean ideal because London was "searching not for the superman, but for the 'super-society,' where all will live in a state of utopian harmony, devoid of harmful individualism."

An obscure work has provoked a lively controversy. (American literary criticism seems marked by an almost fatiguing politeness.) Donald R. Glancy explains in "'Anything to Help Anybody': The Authorship of *Daughters of the Rich*" (*JLN* 5:19–26) that the play, edited by James E. Sisson (Oakland, Calif., Holmes, 1971) is not London's work as claimed by Sisson, but a vaudeville sketch by an audacious actress named Hilda Gilbert, who prevailed upon London to allow her to trade upon his reputation in order to try to improve her position in the theatre. Sisson attempts to refute Glancy's well-documented arguments in "Jack London and *The Daughters of the Rich*" (*JLN* 5:27–32), but fails to explain away statements in Ms. Gilbert's correspondence with both Jack and Charmian London.

Howard Lachtman's "Man and Superwoman in Jack London's 'The Kanaka Surf'" (*WAL* 7:101–10) remarks a curious relationship between two other obscure works by suggesting that except for a happy ending "The Kanaka Surf" tells the same story of domestic conflict as the tragic *The Little Lady of the Big House*, suggesting that when London transplanted material from Sonoma to Hawaii, "he could move from negation to affirmation." These last two terms are also the subject of James I. McClintock's "Jack London: Finding the Proper Trend of Literary Art" (*CEA* 34,iv:25–28), which argues that the view of many critics that London "wanted to dramatize man's insignificance" but unintentionally portrayed his capacity affirmatively is backwards, because really "London wanted to dramatize a new version of human dignity but unintentionally drifted toward the pessimism which is undeniably present in his stories, partly because he was more skillful at creating his powerfully suggestive landscapes than his characters."

Somewhat exaggerating London's influence at home, Horst Ihde argues from East Germany in "Jack London als sozialistischer Schriftsteller" (ZAA 20:5–23) that the novelist was the first proletarian writer in the United States and that The Iron Heel was his most important socialist work.

The relationship between two of California's pyrotechnical literary giants is traced in "Upton Sinclair to Jack London: A Literary Friendship" (JLN 5:49–76), Charles L. P. Silet's editing of thirty-nine letters written between September 1905 and August 1916. The scattered articles about Sinclair also continue to provide principally notes for what must eventually be one of the most voluminous American biographies; but Judson Grenier's "Upton Sinclair and the Press: The Brass Check Reconsidered" (JQ 49:427–36) has implications for an understanding of Sinclair's literary techniques. It traces the history of Sinclair's sensational attack on the American press, pointing out that "not in spite of its faults but because of them" the book stimulated others to undertake more scholarly and objective examinations of newspaper practices that did help to establish in the 1920s new standards of professional decency.

Other "Redskin" novelists remain little noted. Robert McIlvaine's "Robert Herrick and Thorstein Veblen" (RS 40:132–35) briefly points out similarities between Veblen and a Dr. Norden in Herrick's novel Together and also the similarities in the same work of Dr. Renault's analyses of the faults of modern society to Veblen's.

iii. The Iconoclasts

The most provocative responses in 1972 to the still relevant idol smashers of the 1920s are two studies of the unduly neglected Ring Lardner that arrive at diametrically opposed conclusions. Allen F. Stein maintains in "This Unsporting Life: The Baseball Fiction of Ring Lardner" (MarkhamR 3,ii:27–33) that Lardner "missed an opportunity to make significant use of sports material" because his "thoroughly rootless characters . . . with poorly defined goals and weakly conceived means of attaining them" are never "of sufficient weight to necessitate the establishment of a readily perceivable code" for purposes of evaluation. Leverett T. Smith, Jr., argues, however, in the heavily documented " 'The Diameter of Frank Chance's Diamond': Ring Lardner and Professional Sports (*JPC* 6:133–56) that although after Lardner moved to New York in 1919 he wrote with decreasing frequency about professional sports, in the baseball stories he did write he "was concerned with attacking the new style of play"—which emphasized pleasing the grandstands rather than displaying the intelligence and teamwork of the pre-World-War-I game —and attacking also "the fans for their stupidity in enjoying" this degraded and degrading spectacle.

Perhaps the permanent value of Lardner's work remains equivocal because he never thought of himself as an artist. In his foreword to *Ring Around Max: The Correspondence of Ring Lardner and Max Perkins* (DeKalb, No. Ill. Univ. Press), editor Clifford M. Caruthers brings out that Lardner looked upon himself principally as a newspaper columnist and did not even retain copies of his stories after they appeared in popular periodicals. Perkins was surprised that he had to dig the stories out for himself to edit the collections and that he never could prevail upon Lardner to write a novel.

Winesburg, Ohio continues to fascinate critics increasingly intrigued by problems of thematic unity in fiction. Ralph Ciancio's " 'The Sweetness of the Twisted Apples': Unity of Vision in *Winesburg, Ohio*" (*PMLA* 87:994–1006) defends against attackers Anderson's prologue, in which an aged writer attributes the characters' grotesqueness to fanaticism. Ciancio maintains that the work is "unified by Anderson's philosophical vision if not by a sometimes errant formal instinct" and that the fanaticism the characters exhibit in social crises is simply the external and metaphysical counterpart of their struggle "to transcend the innate finitude that circumscribes their dreams." Douglas G. Rogers's "Development of the Artist in *Winesburg, Ohio*" (*Studies in the Twentieth Century* no. 10:91–99) presents George Willard's history as that of "a developing artist," whose departure at the end of the book signifies the maturing of his attitudes through his confrontations with the "grotesques." Carlos Baker's "Sherwood Anderson's Winesburg: A Reprise" (*VQR* 48: 568–79) maintains more simply that "deprivation, search, release, and repression" are the key terms for understanding the recurrent patterns that unify the book.

A truly delightful reading experience that non-specialists may miss is provided by Ray Lewis White's editing of *Sherwood Anderson/Gertrude Stein: Correspondence and Personal Essays* (Chapel Hill, Univ. of N.C. Press), a handsome presentation of existing letters between the pair (many referred to are lamentably missing), along with reprintings of the published statements each made about the other. The result is an extraordinary account of the surprising friendship between "a sophisticated, highly educated esthete like Gertrude Stein and a comparatively uneducated, naïve, midwestern ex-businessman like Sherwood Anderson" (p. 3)—a friendship that these documents make clear was based on the mutual loneliness of two writers who dedicated their lives to very different kinds of literary experiments that could not be appreciated by their immediate circle of friends.

It is disheartening to report that the Spring 1972 issue was the last of *The Cabellian*, the most ambitious and tasteful of several recent journals to be focused on the work of a single author. (Editor Julius Rothman provides, incidentally, "A Short History of *The Cabellian*" in *NR* 2,iv[1973]:59–64). This last issue contains material not only on Cabell but on some important contemporaries as well. The lead articles are two of the longest to appear in the journal. Joe Lee Davis's "Cabell and Santayana in the Neo-Humanist Debate" (*Cabellian* 4:55–67) contrasts attacks the two writers launched separately on the Neo-Humanists in the 1930s. Cabell's praise in *Some of Us: An Essay in Epitaphs* (1930) challenges the subordination of aesthetic to ethical criteria in evaluating literature and winds up suggesting that critic Irving Babbitt and Sinclair Lewis's George Babbitt really had much in common, because "Neo-Humanism is nothing more nor less than the same conformity that spiritually gelded Lewis' immortal realtor but on the presumably highest level of American culture"; Santayana's *The Genteel Tradition at Bay* (1931), on the other hand, challenges the Puritan foundation and character of Neohumanist ethics. Louis Cheslock's "*The Jewel Merchants*, an Opera: A Case History" (4:68–84) is an account by the composer—reprinting correspondence and reviews—of his turning Cabell's one-act play of that name into a one-act opera that was premiered in Baltimore in 1940.

Margaret Anne Schley's "The Demiurge in *Jurgen*" (4:85–88) argues that Cabell's purpose in the novel resembles Joyce's in *A Portrait of the Artist as a Young Man*—"to show the evolution of the artist, particularly . . . a romantic writer." Hugh J. Ingrasci's "The

Cabellian Picara as Women's Liberationist" (4:89–95) proves actually to be an account of Claire Myers Spotswood's *The Unpredictable Adventure* (1935), an allegorical novel about a woman seeking liberation in which both Cabell and his character Jurgen appear as characters and in which the heroine Tellectina's independence of thought is somewhat paradoxically attributed to Cabell's influence.

The Cabellian was, in fact, just beginning with this final issue to broaden its coverage of Cabell's contemporaries. Abe C. Ravitz's "Assault with Deadly Typewriter: The Hecht-Bodenheim Vendetta" (4:104–11) describes the way in which Ben Hecht exploited bizarre details of Maxwell Bodenheim's life in *Count Bruga* and Bodenheim retaliated with a picture of Hecht as an unscrupulous parasite in *Duke Herring*. Meanwhile one of Cabell's most provocative works continues to excite attention elsewhere. James Blish's "The Long Night of a Virginia Author" (*JML* 2:393–405) argues that not until *The Nightmare Has Triplets* did the novelist write a book that was "truly dreamlike in detail, in structure, and even in the systematic omission of the senses of taste and smell."

Two articles make large claims for major iconoclastic novels of the 1920s. Robert L. Coard's "Mark Twain's *The Gilded Age* and Sinclair Lewis's *Babbitt*" (*MQ* 13:319–33) argues that while Lewis was apparently not specifically influenced by Twain, the two express similar views of the corruption of American business, politics, and religion during similarly turbulent postwar eras. James B. Lane's "*Manhattan Transfer* as a Gateway to the 1920s" (*CentR* 16:293–311) finds, however, that this theme of "spiritual decay in the midst of illusory material progress" is best reflected by the "indecisive, impotent, and anemic" characters of Dos Passos's novel.

What writer was the most honored by annual anthologists of the best short stories during the decades that saw Faulkner, Hemingway, Lardner, Fitzgerald, Steinbeck, Katherine Anne Porter produce their best works? Wilbur Daniel Steele—all of whose separate books are now out of print, although some of his famous stories are retained in anthologies. Steele knew many of the iconoclasts of the '20s and would have been one of the group considered in this section of this essay, except that he never tore down any icons. Instead he churned out popular melodramas, employing two chief literary stratagems—intricate plots and surprise endings. The story of his life and work is told in Martin Bucco's *Wilbur Daniel Steele* (TUSAS 198). Since

Bucco is obliged to admit that readers sensed even in Steele's heyday that "his illusory hold on the *lived* life was flaccid—that the *real* seemed to elude his technical brilliance" (p. 74), the historian can do little more than provide plot summaries of out-of-print works, including several novels that never enjoyed the success of Steele's stories. While one may speed through these summaries, the book provides illuminating material of a kind not frequently offered about the differences between a commercially successful writer and a literary artist.

iv. The Harlem Renaissance

Interest in Black fiction of the 1920s continues to flourish to an extent that demands the recognition of its writers as a distinctive subject for critical appraisal. Michael L. Lomax's "Fantasies of Affirmation: The 1920's Novel of Negro Life" (*CLAJ* 16:232–46) deals, in fact, with comparatively overlooked writers like Jessie Fauset, Nella Larsen, and Rudolph Fisher, who concerned themselves with what they called the "advanced element" of urban black society. Lomax shows how this "new elite" sought almost hysterically to disassociate itself from the black masses in order to win acceptance into the general American social order. One aspect of this effort is explored in Richard K. Barksdale's "Symbolism and Irony in McKay's *Home to Harlem*" (*CLAJ* 15:338–44), which points out that this novel was originally disparaged by black critics because of its repugnant realism that might confirm white prejudices against blacks as sexual animals. Barksdale argues, however, that the novel is not just a naturalistic exposé of the black urban ghetto in the 1920s, but a study in symbolic conflict on two levels between "order and disorder," with Jake, the protagonist, "a wise primitive . . . blessed with an intuitive sense of order" in a world in which he "can never truly find a home."

Eugenia Collier's "The Endless Journey of an Ex-Coloured Man" (*Phylon* 32[1971]:365–73) also describes as "amazing" James Weldon Johnson's sometimes attacked novel, because of its uncommon realistic and compassionate treatment of the Afro-American torn between two cultures with conflicting views. (The whole Winter 1971 issue of *Phylon* is devoted to Johnson, but only this article deals with his fiction.)

A quartet of articles in the *CLAJ* shows that Jean Toomer's puzzling *Cane* remains the principal focus of critical interest in the black art of the 1920s. W. Edward Farrison's "Jean Toomer's *Cane* Again" (*CLAJ* 15:295–302) argues again that the book cannot be called a novel and that it is unlikely that it has had the influence some critics have said it has. Younger critics fail, however, to support the older black scholar. Patricia Watkins answers her question "Is There a Unifying Theme in *Cane*?" (*CLAJ* 15:303–05) by finding it in Toomer's despairing message that man is "a creature alone and apart" and that men's souls "whimper in low, scared voices, lonely and calling out for someone to let them in, to cover them so that they will not shiver"—a call that no one will answer. Catherine L. Innes insists somewhat less comprehensibly that "The Unity of Jean Toomer's *Cane*" (*CLAJ* 15:306–22) lies in Toomer's negation of the theories in P. D. Ouspensky's *Tertium Organum* that through the development of "cosmic consciousness" the hidden meaning of all things will be realized. *Cane* depicts a failure to achieve this consciousness because of "the perversion of religion and art when they are deprived of the conscious effort to cultivate and grow toward a higher form." Finally Bowie Duncan's "Jean Toomer's *Cane*: A Modern Black Oracle" (*CLAJ* 15:323–33) views the book as "a definite break with traditional linear thought about composition" and compares it to an elaborate jazz composition that lays down themes and performs variations upon them "without defining a rigid progression," thus producing "a composition that is continually in process."

Charles W. Scruggs's "The Mark of Cain and the Redemption of Art: A Study in Theme and Structure of Jean Toomer's *Cane*" (*AL* 44:276–91) presents evidence from Toomer's papers and correspondence that the title makes a punning reference to the biblical Cain and that Toomer "wanted to depict black experience in mythic terms, using the myth of Cain to explain the uprootedness of the American Negro as American whites used the myth of Adam to suggest the antithetical experience of a return to primal innocence." Looking at only one aspect of the book, Frank Durham in "Jean Toomer's Vision of the Southern Negro" (*SHR* 6:13–22) finds that *Cane* is a protest novel, but that this aspect of Toomer's vision has often been overlooked because his subtle presentation of "the oppression and brutality which the Negro must endure as a result of white fear, bigotry, injustice, and violence" lacks "the shrillness and overt propaganda" of the work of other black writers of the period.

Tackling an even subtler work than *Cane* that has still not received proper recognition, Johnnine Brown Miller argues in "The Major Theme in Langston Hughes's *Not Without Laughter*" (*CEA* 32,vi[1970]:8–10) that the hero Sandy—whom some critics have found colorless—"like the hero that he is, blends the two worlds of materiality and intellect in appropriate proportions" and in so doing "neither wholly rejects nor accepts the models provided by the other characters in the novel."

v. The Expatriates

A main source of information about those who fled the American wasteland of the 1920s and 1930s remains Richard Centing and Benjamin Franklin V's lively quarterly *Under the Sign of Pisces: Anaïs Nin and Her Circle*, which contains many biographical and bibliographical notices, as well as Bruce Woods's "On the Question of Miller's Anarchy" (3,iii:7–10), an indignant response to Peter L. Hays's "The Danger of Henry Miller" (see *ALS 1971*, p. 229), explaining that the world Miller seeks to alter is not that of politics, "which is incapable of changing men," but "the world of self."

The indomitable Ms. Nin herself is used by Ellen P. Killoh in "The Woman Writer and the Element of Destruction" (*CE* 34:31–38) as an extreme example of "the problem of the writer as an agent of destruction," because, while according to the novelist's theories "constructive female art would concentrate on the building of connections between people," her own stories "concentrate on the other side of the coin—on the missed connections and the parties no one really attends."

A great expatriate lady is far more kindly treated in Earl Fendelman's "Gertrude Stein Among the Cubists" (*JML* 2:481–90), which argues that although *The Autobiography of Alice B. Toklas* outraged many artists, "they often expressed more wounded pride than solid disagreement," because, although Stein may have misinterpreted cubism, she—like Braque and Picasso—"wished to express the paradox that restructuring individual perspectives might lead to the possibility of shared vision that would empower the artist to escape his isolation."

vi. The Cosmogonists

Interest in Katherine Anne Porter continues to focus on her connections with Latin America. Joan Givner's "Katherine Anne Porter and the Art of Caricature" (*Genre* 5:51–60) traces her serious interest in caricature in expounding her moral philosophy to her acquaintance in the early 1920s with the Mexican artist Covarrubias and argues that she insisted that any distortion resulting from the use of this technique is "inherent in the people themselves and is not the result of the author's exaggeration."

Steinbeck studies flourish. A special double number of the *Steinbeck Quarterly* (Summer-Fall 1972) is devoted to new studies of nine of the stories collected in *The Long Valley*. (A supplementary analysis of *The Red Pony* cycle follows in 1973.) Almost all the articles explicate individual stories as studies of frustration. Franklin E. Court's "A Vigilante's Fantasy" (5:98–101) argues that Mike joins the mob in "The Vigilante" because "the world of home and cut lawns does not fulfill him." John M. Ditsky's "Steinbeck's 'Flight': The Ambiguity of Manhood" (5:80–85) finds Pepé's attainment of manhood "clouded with ambiguity" because of "the contradictions inherent in a situation in which a man gains his life only to lose it." Joseph Fontenrose's "'The Harness'" (5:94–98) rejects the theory that there are "two Peters" in the story, for though the man we first meet may free his shoulders of the harness, "he cannot free his soul." Reloy Garcia's "Steinbeck's 'The Snake': An Explication" (5:85–90) theorizes more elaborately that for the frustration in each story, there is compensation—as in "The Snake," for example, a young man's introduction into evil is compensated by his "growing awareness of a new dimension of meaning and knowledge." Pursuing a familiar tack, William V. Miller argues in "Sexual and Spiritual Ambiguity in 'The Chrysanthemums'" (5:68–75) that Elisa remains unfulfilled because her misdirected efforts to requite her sexual needs through "an imagined participation in a romantic experience" fails. Arthur L. Simpson, Jr.'s "'The White Quail': A Portrait of the Artist" (5:76–80) advances the more arresting theory that the story "portrays the humanly destructive effects of an absolute commitment to what M. H. Abrams would term an expressive aesthetic"—"the personal and social effects of a subordination of life to an art which takes its sole value and reason for being as a unique expression of the artist's private vision."

Three essays strike out in new directions. Peter Lisca's "'The Raid' and *In Dubious Battle*" (5:90–94) discusses Steinbeck's first use of the Christian allusions that he would draw upon heavily in later novels. Warren French's "'Johnny Bear'—Steinbeck's 'Yellow Peril' Story" (5:101–07) discusses reflections in the story of the anti-Oriental sentiments that affected much thinking and writing in California from the end of the Civil War to World War II. Tackling one of Steinbeck's least studied tales, Sanford E. Marovitz in "The Cryptic Raillery of 'St. Katy the Virgin'" (5:107–12) advances the complicated and persuasive argument that "Steinbeck changed the emphasis and direction of his story as he wrote, and the religious allegory became the controlling idea only after he had already worked his way well into the satire."

The Red Pony stories have also been the subject of two studies. Howard Levant's "John Steinbeck's *The Red Pony*: A Study in Narrative Technique" (*JNT* 1[1971]:77–85) sees these stories as set off from much of Steinbeck's work by "a relative absence of extraneous devices intended to force order into a work of art," since "the major themes are always kept in view and focus the organic development of the narrative." Howard D. Pearce's "Steinbeck's 'The Leader of the People': Dialectic and Symbol" (*PLL* 8:415–26) reads the story as about "being and knowledge"—the frontier is not merely a phenomenon (ontological) but also an unknown which spurs the desire to know (epistemological). Jody's parents fear frontiers which threaten their security. They must know the answers to all questions; but Jody is a romantic figure who is able to absorb a concept of past glory and vitality "in the face of stifling motionlessness, powerlessness, and disillusion."

Richard C. Bedford presents a somewhat similar argument in "The Genesis and Consolation of Our Discontent" (*Criticism* 14:277–94), arguing that Steinbeck in his last novel weaves together "the naturalistic and the metaphysical," abandoning determinism for a concept of the individual human being "freely willing what he will think of as his destiny." Peter Lisca's "The Dynamics of Community in *The Grapes of Wrath*" (*From Irving to Steinbeck*, pp. 127–40) traces a similar interweaving in the much earlier novel, finding that "seemingly inherent biological drives toward community" are "sup-

ported and given authority through a continuum of historical and religious reference" (p. 133).

Steinbeck's work continues to be compared with classics of British
literature. Joan Steele's "A Century of Idiots: *Barnaby Rudge* and
Of Mice and Men" (*StQ* 5:8–17) shows how both authors "through
the portrayal of an idiot's relationship to society" reveal their social
attitudes, which promote reform rather than revolution. John L.
Gribben's "Steinbeck's *East of Eden* and Milton's *Paradise Lost*: A
Discussion of *Timshel*" (*StQ* 5:35–43) argues even more grandilo-
quently that both authors in their own ways "affirmed the doctrine of
man's free will, and the responsibility of every man to stand account-
able for his own actions in choosing between right and wrong." Reloy
Garcia's *Steinbeck and D. H. Lawrence: Fictive Voices and the Ethical Imperative* (SMS 2) finds these two seldom associated authors
alike in their strengths and weaknesses. They developed strikingly
similar concepts of the nature of art and the function of the artist,
based on their impelling conviction that "art was moral" (p. 4).
"Their ostensibly unrelated declines," Garcia also finds, "derive from
the central paradox in esthetics: art must be of its time and personal,
but transcendent." Either "absolute withdrawal" or total immersion
in the world will break the artist's prophecy and destroy his art
(p. 35).

The only general analysis of Steinbeck's work in 1972 was Todd
M. Lieber's insightful "Talismanic Patterns in the Novels of John
Steinbeck" (*AL* 44:262–75), which points out the recurrence of structural patterns based on "man's continual need for a talisman"—a
symbol "to which the deeper portion of the mind . . . attaches significance and value."

Irving Malin's *Nathanael West's Novels* (Carbondale, So. Ill.
Univ. Press) is—as the author suggests—basically a long chapter appended to his *New American Gothic*, since he finds that his characterization of important post-World-War-II novels well fits West's
work. Pointing out that West shies away from "the full-bodied, substantial materials used by George Eliot or Jane Austen," Malin argues
that "by emphasizing dreams," West "compels us to realize that ra-
tionalism, sanity, and daylight thinking are less important (and
creative) than the irrational dreams we share" (p. 7). Because Malin
limits himself to an explication of the texts—especially their symbols—
he does not elaborate upon his perceptive comment that "West is the

spiritual father (or brother)" of the writers discussed in the earlier book; but he does make clear why West—unlike many of his contemporaries—is not fading into history, but just beginning to find his most appreciative audience.

There are more varied comments in *Nathanael West: A Collection of Critical Essays* (Englewood Cliffs, N.J., Prentice-Hall, 1971), which draws upon not just academic critics but other novelists as well and West himself to illuminate his techniques. Editor Jay Martin's conclusion that "West never attempted to correct society through satire or abandon it through irony" clashes oddly with his further assertion that the artists with whom he must be compared are "Persius, Rabelais, Johnson, and Dickens" (p. 10). More helpful is Dieter E. Zimmer's comment in "Nathanael West, oder Warnungen vorm Tag der Heuschrechen" (*NRs* 82:287–302) that *A Cool Million* failed to attain popularity when it appeared in the 1930s because the audience was frightened away by its "terrorized wit."

Thornton Wilder's novels were neglected in 1972, but Thomas Wolfe continued to recruit admirers. Nancy Lenz Harvey's "*Look Homeward, Angel*: An Elegiac Novel" (*BSUF* 13,i:29–33) presses the point that brother Ben stands in the novel in the same position as Edward King in Milton's poem "Lycidas," from which Wolfe takes his title, and that the bulk of each work is . . as much "the poet's own ambitions and disappointments as it is the praise of his dead friend." Richard H. Cracroft's "A Pebble in the Pool: Organic Theme and Structure in Thomas Wolfe's *You Can't Go Home Again*" (*MFS* 17:533–53) rejects charges that the novel is formless and sees it as structured—in Wolfe's own words—"as a series of concentric circles," like those emanating from a pebble thrown in a pool; these circles then connect as in another favorite image, a spider's web. Lawrence J. Dessner's "Thomas Wolfe's Mr. Katamoto" (*MFS* 17:561–65) sees the Japanese sculptor in the same novel as a witty parody of George Webber/Thomas Wolfe's own literary career, since, though George condescends to the sculptor, both produce "larger-than-life works which purport to express a facet of the American ethos."

In the most comprehensive recent study of Wolfe's work, "Thomas Wolfe and the Family of Man" (*Spectrum* 2:47–54) Paschal Reeves maintains that George Webber reflects a different view of "the family of earth" from Eugene Gant, because Wolfe did achieve maturity in his social thinking near the end of his life, as the center of his interest shifted from the individual to the society which shapes him.

vii. Richard Wright and the Tough and Tender Thirties

Again our most celebrated black writer nearly merits a chapter to himself as the many tributes published in 1972 include the best book-length study so far of his career. Several issues of journals were dedicated or almost entirely devoted to him. Much of this material, however, emphasizes the importance of biographical material to an understanding of Wright's work.

Keneth Kinnamon's *The Emergence of Richard Wright* (Urbana, Univ. of Ill. Press) opens with this statement: "The childhood and youth of Richard Wright were filled with obstacles to a career of literary distinction more formidable than those faced by any other major American writer. That a novelist rather than a criminal emerged from the racial prejudice, poverty, family disorganization, and inadequate education that afflicted his early years is a phenomenon not easy to explain" (p. 3). Kinnamon attempts, however, to explain this phenomenon more thoroughly and convincingly than anyone else so far, following Wright's artistic development from his first encounter as a child with fiction in the form of a whispered story to the international acclamation of *Native Son*. The strongest clue to the extraordinary achievement, Kinnamon believes, is Wright's intense childhood reactions to fiction despite his fanatically religious family's and his oppressive community's disapproval of his reading and writing. "Perhaps the significant fact about Wright's early reading," Kinnamon theorizes, "is not that it consisted of subliterary pulp fiction by such writers as Zane Grey and Horatio Alger, but that any reading at all provided an emotional release from the pain of his life" and became for him "a tactic for survival" (p. 37).

Wright is the subject of the Winter 1971 issue of *New Letters* (vol. 38), which grew out of a two-week institute at the University of Iowa. The issue, introduced by Robert Farnsworth, is largely biographical, containing letters, essays, song lyrics and haiku by Wright himself, personal impressions by nine friends, Daniel Aaron's "Richard Wright and the Communist Party" (pp. 170–81), Michel Fabre's "Wright's Exile" (pp. 136–54), and a lengthy bibliography. Two arti-

cles are of special interest to literary historians: Thomas Cripps's
"*Native Son* in the Movies" (pp. 49–63), which relates the difficulties
of attempting to bring to the screen the film that has rarely been exhibited since it was finally shot in Chicago and Argentina with Wright
himself portraying Bigger Thomas, and John Houseman's "*Native
Son* on Stage" (pp. 71–82), which relates the less well publicized
difficulties attendant upon the development of a playscript from the
novel because of the alterations that consultant Paul Green insisted
upon and that are still preserved in the published version of the play,
making it radically different from what was performed. Only two contributions are primarily literary criticism: Edward A. Watson's "Bessie's Blues" (pp. 64–70), which argues that Wright makes "subtle
yet powerful imaginative" reference to Negro music through Bessie
Mears, Bigger's girl friend, "whose speech and life-style embodies in
no simple way the spirit of the *blues*," and Katherine Spandel's "*The
Long Dream*" (pp. 88–96), a reading of this novel as the story of a
young hero whose initiation closely resembles Wright's own and who
is finally left up in the air, because Wright himself had rejected both
religion and existentialism, but could find little support for the philosophy of love that he was trying to develop near the end of his life.
Material in a later issue of *New Letters* (39,i:61–75) presents the
young Richard Wright as writer of a term paper on "Ethnographical
Aspects of Chicago's Black Belt," accompanied by a "Bibliography
on the Negro in Chicago, 1936."

Wright remains of special interest to journals devoted primarily
to black writers. Lewis Leary's "*Lawd Today*: Notes on Richard
Wright's First/Last Novel" (*CLAJ* 15:411–20) sees this apprentice
work as providing "a powerful and terrifying insight into what it is to
be black in America," but also "insidiously" presenting "what it means
to be white, colorless, ubiquitous." If Wright's hero is a caricature, he
caricatures "the white world which tempts with more than it dares to
offer." Looking at Wright's handling of black and white worlds in
another perspective, Phyllis R. Klotman and Melville Yancey argue
in "Gift of Double Vision: Possible Political Implications of Richard
Wright's 'Self-Consciousness' Thesis" (*CLAJ* 16:106–16) that white
social outcasts can develop the same kind of "double vision" that
lawyer Ely Houston in Wright's *The Outsider* describes as characteristic of Negroes who are outcasts by birth and must therefore be
"both *inside* and *outside* our culture at the same time." Seeking a

metaphysical dimension in a novel usually regarded as Naturalistic, Eugene E. Miller points out in "Voodoo Parallels in *Native Son*" (*CLAJ* 16:81–95) resemblances between Haitian rites and the scene in which Bigger kills Mary Dalton. Such parallels, Miller believes, enable us to see that while on one level the murder speaks of psychosocial realities, on another it shows Bigger's entry into "a cosmic unity, even though he cannot explain that entry very clearly or distinctly in philosophic terms."

Less controversially, R. B. V. Larsen explains in "The Four Voices in Richard Wright's *Native Son*" (*NALF* 6:105–09) that the novelist skillfully manipulates the dominant voice of a third-person narrator, the inarticulate voice of Bigger, the biased voice of the "objective" white establishment, and the humane voice of lawyer Boris Max. Turning to an earlier work, Carole W. Oleson discusses in an accompanying article, "The Symbolic Richness of Richard Wright's 'Bright and Morning Star'" (*NALF* 6:110–12), the way in which Wright contrapuntally manipulates rain as a symbol of the pressure of adversity and an airplane beacon flashing through the wet darkness as a symbol of hope. Raman K. Singh's more comprehensive "Christian Heroes and Anti-Heroes in Richard Wright's Fiction" (*NALF* 6:99–104,131) outlines the novelist's movement from "a selection of the best in Christian teachings" in the stories of the 1930s to a "condemnation of everything Christian in *The Outsider*," to at last a probing of the nature of God that comes up with a negative answer in the late story, "Man, God Ain't Like That." In another general study, "Richard Wright: The Expatriate as Native Son" (*AL* 44:97–117), Harold T. McCarthy maintains that although Wright's fictional treatment of the American scene "spluttered out" after his expatriation, his visits to foreign lands made him realize that all oppressed minorities anywhere could be included in the American category of "Negro."

In view of Wright's break with the Communist Party, Marxist interpretations of his work are of special interest. From East Germany comes Friederike Hajek's "*American Tragedy*—Zwei Aspekte . . ." (*ZAA* 20:262–79), which considers the similar treatment in two powerful American novels of young men driven to death in a capitalist society and finds that Dreiser's presents the resigned, dejected viewpoint, whereas *Native Son* presents a rebellious, warlike one. Back home in an issue of *College English* devoted to the Marxist interpretation of literature, James G. Kennedy views "The Content and Form of *Native Son*" (*CE* 34:269–83) as expressing "the consciousness of the militant stratum of the working class as to the dehumanizing material and social relations imposed upon workers" and finds Wright a better Marxist than his Communist characters, "since he shows, even in Bigger's destructive purposefulness and in his delusory vision, the potentialities for inventiveness and for social consciousness in a most thwarted American worker." Annette Conn comments briefly in an afternote that Kennedy may confuse "class oppression" and "national and social oppression," because Bigger's limitations are thrust upon him by a racist society.

Long ignored because of the continuing attention to Wright, his contemporary Zora Neale Hurston is beginning at last to find critics who treat her more sympathetically than Darwin T. Turner did in *In a Minor Chord* (see *ALS 1971*, p. 240). Marion Kilson points out in "The Transformation of Eatonville's Ethnographer" (*Phylon* 33: 112–19) the influence on Ms. Hurston's fiction of her training in ethnography, particularly in her dispassionate depiction of her characters' difficulties in attempting to achieve fundamentally bourgeois ideals. James R. Giles discusses the frustration of one such effort, pointing out in "The Significance of Time in Zora Neale Hurston's *Their Eyes Were Watching God*" (*NALF* 6:52–53,60) that the "major underlying theme" of the novel is the contrast between characters "so white-oriented that they measure time in a rational, materialistic way" and "those whose blackness is so intact that they view time emotionally and hedonistically." The latter group, Giles maintains approvingly, triumphs.

The reasons why an objective study of the writings of Edward Dahlberg has been so long arriving are set forth in the preface to Fred Moramarco's astute and judicious *Edward Dahlberg* (TUSAS 206), the first book-length study of a cryptic figure who eludes categorization. Dahlberg's personal unusual severity "on those commentators who have written about his work with anything less than almost total adulation" and the resultant polarization of critics into those who see him "either as the most neglected genius of our time or as an arrogant pedant" make it difficult for one to pursue a middle course. Moramarco, nevertheless, enjoys remarkable success; yet his determined efforts only make one aware of the difficulties of dealing with Dahlberg in a critical survey like *ALS*. Where does he "belong"? Although his early novels and activities link him with the tough-guy

writers of the 1930s, his best works (Moramarco argues that these
are *Can These Bones Live?* and *Because I Was Flesh*) are neither
novels nor tough-guy writings. Dahlberg, as Moramarco also points
out, seems "distant" to critics, "out of touch with the main literary
currents of the day" (p. 26). Moramarco questions whether Dahlberg
is moved to his merciless outbursts against contemporaries by "malevolence or moralism" (p. 27). Reading the analyst's careful summaries of Dahlberg's varied and uneven works, however, one finds
both terms inadequate and irrelevant. Dahlberg's subject has always
been his own astonishing sensibility that makes other people bearable
only as projections of himself. The value of Moramarco's painstaking
labors is limited because no outsider can hope to tell us much about
a man who has himself become the principal explicator of the image
that he projects to the public.

Lewis Fried's "James T. Farrell: Shadow and Act" (*JA* 17:140–
55) enables us to see why this now somewhat eclipsed novelist has
protested the "Naturalistic" label often bestowed upon him. Fried
reads Farrell's fiction as a "sustained meditation upon the shaping of
individual and social destinies" based upon the philosophies of C.
Judson Herrick, George Herbert Mead, and John Dewey. Farrell's
characters are not, Fried contends, "passive creatures who are en-
meshed in circumstances beyond personal control"; rather, Farrell's
"functional conception of character and environment" is based upon
the idea that the terms of man's freedom are "formal and effective"
and that "he can realize the potential of his self" (p. 147).

Fried also reconsiders the work of another "proletarian writer" of
the 1930s—Jack Conroy—in an issue of *New Letters* (Fall 1972) dedicated to this "Sage of Moberly, Missouri" and containing reminiscences and some pictures of him. In *"The Disinherited*: The Worker
as Writer" (*NewL* 39,i:29–40), Fried finds Conroy's novel "hardly
typical of radical fiction" and discusses it "like its urban, and
American-Jewish counterparts, *Bottom Dogs*, *From Flushing to Cal-
vary*, and *Jews Without Money*" as "about the growth and allegiances
of the writer," struggling to reconcile the claims of his past with those
of the present. In an accompanying "Conversation with Jack Conroy"
(pp. 41–56), Fried records the novelist's recollections of the 1930s.

More romantic regionalists than Conroy still attract defenders.
Although not directly attacking or even contradicting Floyd C. Watkins's *"Gone with the Wind* as Vulgar Literature" (see *ALS 1971*,

p. 243), Jerome Stern argues in "*Gone with the Wind*: The South as America" (*SHR* 6:5–12) that "the Southern myth is the American myth" and its popularity is due "not to its accuracy as a history of the South, but to its accuracy as a dramatization of American attitudes." (The argument would carry more weight if Stern extended his last phrase to read "those anti-intellectual American attitudes especially prevalent in the South.") Still in the South, Mrs. Sylvia Gibbs traces in "Jesse Stuart: The Dark Hills and Beyond" (*JLN* 4[1971]:56–69) the career of the prolific writer from his departure from his native hills in search of education until his return; and James E. Rocks's "T. S. Stribling's Burden of Southern History: The Valden Trilogy" (*SHR* 6:221–32) finds the Mississippi novelist important as an early Southern propagandist for improved racial relations, though his trilogy becomes "so harsh and ruthless that it is perhaps overly partisan."

There is another point of view in the study of the North Carolinian *James Boyd* (TUSAS 199) by David E. Whisnant, for "in his stories and novels the New South represents the viable ideal, but the Old South remains a way of life that has at least an esthetic appeal" (p. 39). Whisnant argues that Boyd's mediatory consciousness sought "not so much to take a stance as to find legitimate grounds for sympathy" (p. 141)—perhaps the reason he is less well remembered as a novelist than as the organizer of the Free Company of Players, who presented a series of broadcasts on civil rights by prominent authors and actors in 1940–41.

T. M. Pearce's *Oliver La Farge* (TUSAS 191) treats that author as one "who sought to write about an environment alien to his own upbringing" in New England and to defend minority cultures against "the invasion of mass social patterns." Only two chapters—about a quarter of the book—are devoted to LaFarge's novels and short stories as related to his experiences as scientist and historian.

Paul Reigstad's *Rölvaag: His Life and Art* (Lincoln, Univ. of Nebr. Press) is a long delayed tribute to another displaced artist. Reigstad draws extensively upon Rölvaag's autobiographical writings and, in fact, adds little to them in his sympathetic study. Rölvaag was an author with the limited aim of fostering the Norwegian immigrants' adjustment to the New World. He knew himself very well, and he understood exactly what he was trying to do. He was not, therefore, the kind of cryptic or visionary writer whose works challenge the insights of an interpreter.

Rölvaag's work lends itself less well to intensive, isolated analysis than to illustrative use in a discussion like Frank L. Stallings, Jr.'s "The West: The Perpetual Mirage in Literature" (*Myths and Realities*, pp. 39–49), which points out the way in which "the mirage-like quality of the American West is clearly revealed" in a literature in which "perpetually characters *see* one thing, are charmed into *believing* what they see, only to be disillusioned by the reality just below the surface."

Indiana University–Purdue University at Indianapolis

13. Fiction: The 1930s to the Present

James H. Justus

The year's work shows few surprises, either in substance or methodology. There is still the lamentable tendency toward repetitiveness (a result primarily of slack scholarship) and a flailing about for critical approaches to replace the much-abused New Critical ones. Among individual writers, interest continues highest in O'Connor and Mailer. A few trends are apparent: (1) for the first time more attention is being paid to black writers other than Baldwin and Ellison—much of it significant; (2) descriptive and evaluative pieces on what Barth calls "irrealism" are showing up more frequently, both as traditional analyses and as criticism which attempts, with varying success, to be as experimental as its subject; and (3) there is considerable interest, especially evident in completed dissertations, in studying little-known, once-popular, and rediscovered authors.[1] In the nearly seventy completed dissertations reported, nearly a third are studies of multiple authors, themes and topics (the grotesque; the estranged and self-aware protagonists; war fiction; the presidency), and black literature.

i. General Studies

a. **Overviews.** In *Shriven Selves: Religious Problems in Recent American Fiction* (Philadelphia, Fortress Press), Wesley A. Kort explores the interrelationship of selected confessional fiction and the "pluralistic" religious sensibility. Despite a strong anticlericalism in all of his authors, Kort sees religion as an important element in the

1. Among individual authors who were the subjects of dissertations, O'Connor and Nabokov lead the list (5), followed by Warren (4), Mailer (3), and Vonnegut, Malamud, Styron, and McCullers (2 each). But also appearing were John Hawkes, Peter Taylor, William Gaddis, and Hortense Calisher.

struggles of their confessional narrators, who find themselves caught in a "provocative middle position between the private and the public or the religious and the nonreligious realms, between the language of mystery and the language of problem-solving." Kort's specific readings will be noted in appropriate places below.

"Compassion in Contemporary Fiction" is the final chapter of a study of mostly nineteenth-century novels, *Harvest of a Quiet Eye: The Novel of Compassion* (Bloomington, Ind. Univ. Press, 1971), in which James Gindin discusses the trend away from what he calls the "compassionate novel" toward fictional concepts and practices involving the frank use of artifice, autonomous modes of reality, and fable. Gindin's definition is mostly negative: compassionate fiction posits no God, no metaphysic, no framework of ethical values or pietistic judgments; it is not likely to be allegorical, futuristic, incantatory, or apocalyptic; rather, it tends to "extend its terms historically, to depict a greater quantity of experience instead of distilling experience to derive lessons from it." Barth's characteristic work is too self-consciously autonomous to qualify as compassionate; but, strangely enough, Pynchon's *V.*, because it avoids easy moral judgments, comes close. In the work of Donald Barthelme and John Hawkes, fable is "intellectualized evasion"; Updike's *Couples* "reads like a morality play"; and recent works by Mailer "suggest an attitude of compassion negatively." Although Gindin insists that his key term is neutral, customary connotations invariably tend to make "compassionate" works more desirable than "non-compassionate" ones.

Bruce Cook's earnest bias and reportorial vignettes, not his barely manageable style, make *The Beat Generation* (New York, Scribner's, 1971), worth reading. This pop history is filled indiscriminately with trash and treasure: a valuable unscrambling of Jack Kerouac's chronology, a persuasive contention that Mailer introduced violence into the Beat ethos, and sidelights on such lesser-known figures as John Clellon Holmes and Chandler Brossard rest cheerfully alongside a mindless paean to William Burroughs, casually remembered and undocumented interviews, and a generally hazy sense of discrimination among the talents in that movement. Cook's anti-academic querulousness with the "critical mafia" which conspired to ignore the Beats becomes more than a bit tiresome.

Charles I. Glicksberg's *The Sexual Revolution in Modern American Literature* (The Hague, Martinus Nijhoff, 1971) is a shrill critical history of those writers who "go the whole hog," hiding "nothing that pertains to the *vita sexualis*." The patron saints of the "Beat Generation" are said to be Henry Miller, Dylan Thomas, Wilhelm Reich. One strange chapter (pp. 143–70) includes commentary on John O'Hara, Vance Bourjaily, and Katherine Anne Porter as well as Kerouac, Brossard, and others associated with that movement. Glicksberg devotes one chapter, "The Death of Love" (pp. 185–213), to the "literature of erotica," samples of which come from Mary McCarthy, Nabokov, Styron, Leslie Fiedler, and others, all purporting to show the "changing Sex-*Anschauung* of our times." One entire chapter (pp. 214–22) is an analysis of James Jones's *Go to the Widow-Maker*, "the novel to end all sex novels." Were it not for the citing of recent works, this study might well be mistaken for one written in the 1940s.

Like the King and the Duke who knew what would fetch Arkansaw, Gerald B. Nelson thinks he knows how to fetch us all with his *Ten Versions of America* (New York, Knopf): a swinging style, outrageous pronouncements, a wise-ass ennui, and a dependable theme to trot out for yet another round—the death of the American Dream. Nelson builds his book around homogenized "biographies" (Jake Barnes, Humbert Humbert, Eliot Rosewater, etc.), which he then develops by escalating thesis sentences into instant sententiae. The kind of personal criticism offered here might have been revolutionary had it been written before D. H. Lawrence, but Nelson tosses off such generalizations as "Americans are killers" as if Lawrence had never existed; similarly, "Puritans" are flogged as if Nelson had never heard of H. L. Mencken. Reading the "biographies" of Yossarian, Tommy Wilhelm, and Hazel Motes is not going to benefit those who want to know more of Heller, Bellow, or O'Connor—most of us have been there before.

"The Jew's Complaint in Recent American Fiction: Beyond Exodus and Still in the Wilderness" (*SoR* 8:41–59) is as much cultural analysis as it is literary criticism, with Alan Warren Friedman's concentration on the Jewish tendency to reject stasis and fixity and to embrace chances in which "beginnings are still possible." Friedman glances briefly at Bellow and Malamud, but his central text is *Portnoy's Complaint*—in some ways the most intelligent piece yet done on Roth's book. Allen Guttmann's "The Conversion of the Jews" (*The Cry of Home*, pp. 245–67) is on acculturation, the Jews' "metaphoric conversion to America," with attention paid to the fiction of Myron Kaufmann and Neal Oxenhandler as well as that of better-known figures.

For the Critical Idiom series, Philip Thomson has written *The Grotesque* (London, Methuen), an exercise in extended definition as well as a succinct historical survey, which will be of interest to critics of several contemporary American authors. More specialized is "A Theory of the Grotesque in Southern Fiction" (*GaR* 26:426–37), in which Alan Spiegel argues that *grotesque* refers not to mode, mood, or quality of a fiction but to a character type—a physically or mentally deformed figure who often transcends his grotesquerie to become a *pharmakos* character. This figure is an essential part of the typology of Southern literature; in contrast, classic gothic fiction is Northern, in which authors such as Purdy, Hawkes, and Heller view the world as "nightmare fantasy."

An important and provocative essay, Lewis P. Simpson's "Southern Spiritual Nationalism: Notes on the Background of Modern Southern Fiction" (*The Cry of Home*, pp. 189–210), posits the image of the South as a "metaphysical nation," a special "redemptive community" parallel with that of New England earlier, in which its artists act as both prophets and priests. The fact of slavery blocked the impulse to "divinize" Southern civilization in the nineteenth century, says Simpson; only after World War I were Southern writers fully conscious of their sensibility as modern American as well as regional writers, an awareness that the Southerner was a part of the "apocalypse of modern civilization."

Walter Sullivan, in *Death by Melancholy: Essays on Modern Southern Fiction* (Baton Rouge, La. State Univ. Press), has brought together eight previously published essays which are indispensably corrective for those critics of recent Southern writing who tend to be overly sanguine about both its ethical integrity and its aesthetic quality. Insights into an even younger generation of Southern authors can be gleaned from John Carr's collection of interviews, *Kite-Flying and Other Irrational Acts: Conversations with Twelve Southern Writers* (Baton Rouge, La. State Univ. Press), including Jesse Hill Ford, Reynolds Price, and Marion Montgomery.

"The Faculty Novel" (*GaR* 25[1971]:41–50) is a sketchy and superficial survey by Irving A. Yevish, who makes the fairly obvious distinction between the "undergraduate novel," with its typical protagonist's search for freedom, and the "faculty novel," with its depressing array of security-obsessed academics who fall short of both "enchantment" and disillusionment. The "undergraduate novel" is still a promising subgenre, as is evident in Maurice E. Coindreau's "College Life and the American Novel," a two-part essay originally published in 1946 and 1963 and now reprinted, along with other essays, in *The Time of William Faulkner: A French View of Modern American Fiction* (Columbia, Univ. of S. C. Press, 1971) in a translation by George M. Reeves.

b. **The new fiction: theories and modes.** Frustrated by ordinary assumptions about reality, the newer writers are seeking the freedom "to represent as reality the images in their minds and the relations among these images that satisfy them." This is Arthur Mizener's generalization about "The New Romance" (*SoR* 8:106–17), whose practitioners include Barth, Heller, Barthelme, and Pynchon. Although this piece is neither as comprehensive nor as theoretical as its title suggests, it nevertheless makes useful connections between the new fiction and the older romance conventions. Despite his title, Alfred Kazin's essay "The World as a Novel: From Capote to Mailer" (*NYRB* 16, 8 April[1971]:26–30) is really about the competition of facts with and the pressure of actuality upon fiction. The "reason" for a non-fiction novel, says Kazin, is that it "points to events that cannot ever be discharged by a writer's imagination." Only the journalist feels able to set down the world "as our common experience," a confidence that fictionists do not feel, "for if the 'world' is not an experience held in common, still less is it a concept on which all can agree."

More thoroughgoing is Raymond M. Olderman's *Beyond the Waste Land: A Study of the American Novel in the Nineteen-Sixties* (New Haven, Conn., Yale Univ. Press), a study of representative novels which reveal how the "traditional devices of romance are now being employed as a way of capturing the absurdity of ordinary life." If the older forms are marked by myth and allegory, the irresolution of tensions, and the emphasis on plot rather than character, the new romance uses the modes of fable and black humor and surface action for its own sake, and exploits comic-book identities and jokes arising out of a sense of entrapment in the "fabulous nature of fact." Olderman believes this newer fiction reflects a vision different from the visions of writers most often associated with the 1950s (Mailer, Bellow, Malamud, Styron), with their dependence upon the iterated search for identity, the recurring journey, and existential underpinnings. Although we may be getting a little weary of the waste land as handy catch-phrase, Olderman for the most part is convincing in showing how vital that controlling metaphor is for these newer romancers who are radically modifying received patterns and conventions.

A similar but more restricted thesis can be found in Charles B. Harris's *Contemporary American Novelists of the Absurd* (New Haven, Conn., College and Univ. Press, 1971), which also focuses on novels of the 1960s. It was not until this "Decade of the Absurd," argues Harris, that novelists matched their absurdist themes with absurdist techniques (burlesque, parody, innovative language). The older notion of art as an ordering discipline which makes sense out of nature and reality turns in upon itself, and Barth, Pynchon, Heller, and others burlesque not only life but also the very vehicle for examining life. If such works as Barthelme's *Snow White* or Purdy's *Malcolm* adapt pop art and camp forms, they do so not to create "anti-art" (as Susan Sontag would have it) but to make artifice a means of rejuvenating the traditional romance.[2] Segments on specific authors in both Olderman's and Harris's books will be noted in relevant places below.

"Innovative Short Fiction: 'Vile and Imaginative Things'" is the essay which introduces a collection of recent fiction by both the famous (Barth, Vonnegut, LeRoi Jones) and the still-obscure (James Giles, Ronald Sukenick, Thomas Glynn): *Innovative Fiction: Stories for the Seventies*, edited by Jerome Klinkowitz and John Somer (New York, Dell). The essay is a brief for the new forms which articulate a kind of initiation rite that is imaginatively an "absorption," an "annihilation of the ego in a vision of the world that the ego has created." This formula covers Barthelme's "trash phenomenon," Brautigan's efforts to wrench the world from its own banality into fresh, magical perceptions; the new epistemologies of Coover and Hawkes; and the breakthroughs into new levels of rapport with "reality" seen in

---

2. Carl R. Dolmetsch analyzes " 'Camp' and Black Humor in Recent American Fiction" (*Amerikanische Literatur*, pp. 147–74) and finds that burlesque, parody, travesty, literary allusion, even historical romance are all "vehicles and concomitants" of both modes in post-modern fiction.

Sukenick and Glynn. Though these apologists for the new fiction occasionally make excessive claims for the rationale behind it, their own perceptions of the unity in all the variety are fresh and coherent.

Sukenick's *Up* is also cited as a skillful tour de force of authorial fantasies by Howard M. Harper, Jr., in "Trends in Recent American Fiction" (*ConL* 12[1971]:204–29), a useful and admittedly tentative assaying of fiction more recent than that covered by Harper's fine *Desperate Faith* (see *ALS 1967*, p. 191). The technical competence and virtuosity have never been higher, Harper declares, especially in Coover, Vonnegut, Barth, and others; and even the more traditional narrative techniques of Roth, Malamud, Dickey, Oates, and others are impressively used. The dominant mood, seen in the "current obsession with craftsmanship," is the felt sufficiency that "aesthetic form in itself is enough" for recording the vagaries and urgencies of individual consciousness. Harper appends a "Selected Checklist of American Fiction, 1968–1970." In a Scandinavian perspective, Brita Lindberg-Seyersted discusses "American Fiction Since 1950" (*Edda* 71[1971]:193–203) and concludes by remarking three major trends now to be found: the writing of Negro novelists, documentary fictionists, and "fabulators-black humorists."

An ambitious and committed study is *Space, Time and Structure in the Modern Novel* (New York, N. Y. Univ. Press, 1971) by Sharon Spencer, who places great faith in the aesthetic integrity of the new "architectonic" novel, which she defines as a fiction which absorbs, as a structural feature, the possibilities released by our knowledge of dreams and by the evolving concepts of time and space. The architectonic novelist must battle the natural tendency of the genre "to consist of a series of flat surfaces arranged sequentially so as to body forth" its subject. What is important in such fiction is not characterization or narrative per se, but the expression of the author's view of reality, and Spencer sees this phenomenon occurring in novels with structures that are both closed (the deliberate restriction of perspective for creating autonomous worlds) and open (the use of multiple perspectives for attacking a subject from many angles, the aim of which is diffusion). Although she is often captious about unsympathetic readers and critics whose sensibilities and values "reflect the social and political ambience of the 1930s," Spencer produces a theoretical book that is commendably clear, without the formal disjunctions she prefers in fiction.

More historically oriented, Naomi Lebowitz's *Humanism and the Absurd in the Modern Novel* (Evanston, Ill., Northwestern Univ. Press, 1971) contrasts the temperaments associated with newer absurdist fiction and the traditional "humanist" novel: the absurdist imagination tends to see art conquering life; the humanist supports life. This brief, intense, and frankly biased book is especially good in recounting the origins of the conflict and in describing the alternative attitudes toward language and man's fictions. Like Spencer, Lebowitz uses specific works to illustrate her broadly conceived ideas.

In a theoretical piece which seeks to refurbish Marxist criticism, "The Great American Hunter, or, Ideological Content in the Novel" (*CE* 34:180–97), Fredric Jameson explores, as sample works, *Why Are We in Vietnam?* and *Deliverance*. His rarefied thesis is that both novels are covertly preoccupied with class conflict, class hatred, and "post-industrial distortions of the human spirit." The enemy which Dickey's heroes go forth to meet is not natural or human violence but "the Thirties," so they may settle their accounts with the great radical tradition; and the hillbilly figures are a displacement for "the peoples of the Third World, of the Blacks, of the intransigent and disaffected young." The real subject of Mailer's novel is the machismo cult and its major expression—competition; rather than repudiating the society's dominant values, Mailer adopts them with the "fanatical exaggeration of the newly converted."

In "Faction: Tendenzen zu einer kritischen Faktographie in den USA" (*Amerikanische Literatur*, pp. 127–46), Dietmar Haack proposes a new term, faction, to replace the cumbersome non-fiction novel, traces its impulses back to Upton Sinclair and Ida Tarbell, and gives separate readings of Capote's *In Cold Blood*, Hersey's *The Algiers Motel Incident*, and Mailer's *The Armies of the Night*. Although he discriminates among these texts in authorial aims and techniques, Haack sees a common urgency behind their form—false information in the public media.

ii. Norman Mailer

In his frankly partisan *Mailer* (London, Fontana/Collins) Richard Poirier recounts one writer's struggle to find appropriate forms for rendering a "conspiratorial" and embattled imagination. He suggests

(1) that war was pivotal for Mailer long before his experiences in World War II resulted in *The Naked and the Dead*, (2) that his "combative eagerness" has been a continuing response to anything that would limit his power to affect history, (3) that "sexual creativity and the creative effort to shape history" are related in Mailer's efforts to "seize control of the links of social cause and effect," and (4) that the crucial texts which reveal these patterns are "The Metaphysics of the Belly," "The White Negro," and "The Political Economy of Time."

A similar combativeness, more epicene than Mailer's, pervades this chic little book. Hip honorifics ("daring," "extravagance," "intellectual savvy") predictably vanquish square pejoratives ("deadening academic-literary-intellectual-social commitment," "washed out wastes of the humanistic tradition"). Poirier's assertion that the substance of *Why Are We in Vietnam?* derives from our major works of the last century and a half is a half-truth. Other judgments are even more stylishly self-indulgent: *Death for the Ladies* is a "quite good volume of poems"; Mailer's mastery of competing styles may well be "unequalled since the parodic brilliance of Joyce in *Ulysses*." In short, *Mailer* is very personal criticism, by turns finely intelligent and irresponsible, and should be balanced by older criticism in the humanistic tradition which Poirier scorns.

Robert Alter calls Mailer the "most stubbornly political of living American novelists," and his "Norman Mailer" (*The Politics*, pp. 321–34) is only one of several essays exploring the nature of Mailer's politics. Alter suggests that *An American Dream* and *Why Are We in Vietnam?* strain to imagine politics "as a part of everything else in life" through ritualistic acts and symbolic bouts. In "Norman Mailer's Civil War" (*War and Society*, pp. 153–68), Paul Levine traces the novelist's political metamorphoses. In *The Naked and the Dead*, the terms of the dialectic are a dying liberalism and a nascent fascism; in later works, as Mailer's vision becomes more apocalyptic, his heroes "abandon politics for imagination, liberalism for hipsterism, and Marxism for existentialism."

In "Norman Mailer: The Writer as Radical" (*Amerikanische Literatur*, pp. 92–100), which is more summary than criticism, Allen Guttmann concludes that Mailer is too eccentric to be the spokesman for any single ideology. More firmly, Matthew Grace contends that Mailer's historical perspective is essentially private, and the political arena is a "vast metaphor for the psychic conflicts within the man and the artist." In "Norman Mailer at the End of the Decade" (*EA* 24 [1971]:50–58) Grace's thesis is that Mailer distrusts both communists and fascists because they pretend to know the course of history, which is dialectical and inconclusive.

"Multiplicity," which provides Mailer's later work with its contemporary relevance, is praised by James Gindin in "Megalotopia and the Wasp Backlash: The Fiction of Mailer and Updike" (*CentR* 15[1971]:38–52). Throughout a purely arbitrary contrast, Mailer receives higher marks than Updike because of his commitment to "actual experience without prescriptive formulation," and as a "megalotopian" he has faith in a better, more equitable society that can embody vast diversity.

Charles I. Glicksberg's chapter on Mailer in *The Sexual Revolution in Modern American Literature* (pp. 171–81) is rigorously judgmental. The energy of vision "that should go into the making of his books," charges Glicksberg, "is dissipated in evangelical exhortation" for sexual license, an obsession which becomes a self-imposed restriction and thus mars most of Mailer's work.

There were fewer pieces devoted to individual works, and they were generally less interesting than the more comprehensive essays. In "The Naked, the Dead, and the Machine: A New Look at Norman Mailer's First Novel" (*PMLA* 87:271–77), Randall H. Waldron concentrates on the informing influence of the machine in *The Naked and the Dead*, in which structure, character, imagery, and symbolism are shaped by metaphors representing the machine age. "Faulkner, Mailer, and Yogi Bear" (*CRevAS* 2[1971]:69–71) is a casual little piece by Ralph Maud, who believes the title of *Why Are We in Vietnam?* is unironic: D. J. and Tex are successfully initiated into a "blood brotherhood in the cause of callousness and violence. The voice of God in the Northern wilderness is no more than the common will of normal vicious America."

"Witness and Testament: Two Contemporary Classics" (*NLH* 2[1971]:311–27) is Warner Berthoff's stately salute to *The Autobiography of Malcolm X* and *The Armies of the Night*. The first he calls a latter-day version of the "Political Testament," while the second is a reinvention of the personal testament—a description, like *Walden*, of the writer's transformation of his own life "into a practical moral experiment." Armin Paul Frank's "Literarische Strukturbe-

griffe und Norman Mailers *The Armies of the Night*" (*JA* 17:73–99)
is a meticulous application of New Critical theories of structure to a
non-poetic text. Not only is Mailer's book primarily illustrative; the
results are disappointing. Even Frank seems not entirely happy with
his findings, though he finds a place for Mailer's book somewhere
between *Walden* and *The Education of Henry Adams*.

Leo Braudy has edited *Norman Mailer: A Collection of Critical
Essays* (Englewood Cliffs, N. J., Prentice-Hall), comprising an interview and eleven articles, all previously published. Although his introduction, "Norman Mailer: The Pride of Vulnerability" (pp. 1–20),
emphasizes generally the range and variety of a long literary career,
Braudy makes the perceptive point that Mailer's protagonists, who
are frustrated writers (or only partially successful ones), orphaned,
impotent, and "bottled up," are a major link with Hemingway, with
whom Mailer has for so long been obsessed.

Those who are interested in Mailer's tiff with women's liberation-
ists may find something useful in Annette Barnes's "Norman Mailer:
A Prisoner of Sex" (*MR* 13:269–74). In a personal essay, "American
War Novels: Yesterday, Today, and Tomorrow" (*YR* 61:517–29),
Stanley Cooperman observes that the only war which Mailer has
always been fighting is the sexual one and that war in *Why Are We
in Vietnam?* is a phallic, not a moral, phenomenon. Finally, Douglas
H. Shepard contributes "Norman Mailer: A Preliminary Bibliography of Secondary Comment, 1948–1968" (*BB* 29:37–45).

iii. Flannery O'Connor

With four new books (and several more on the way), the usual spate
of articles and notes, and the founding of the *Flannery O'Connor
Bulletin*, the O'Connor industry now promises to rival that of Salinger fifteen years ago.

In *The Eternal Crossroads: The Art of Flannery O'Connor* (Lexington, Univ. Press of Ky., 1971), Leon V. Driskell and Joan T. Brittain announce their concern with the fiction "as form, not as regional
or sectarian formulations," but their real interest lies precisely with
those formulations—"sacramental elements" in the fiction, especially
in those stories which show a "considerable doctrinal gain" over
earlier attempts—or with influences primarily regional or religious:

the Bible, Teilhard, Pope John, Mauriac, Faulkner (Hawthorne's impact is "largely technical" and Nathanael West's is "exclusively superficial"). They charge that critics who fail to understand this author "as a Georgian or as a Catholic" are in fact part of what O'Connor called her "hostile audience." It may have been hostile during O'Connor's lifetime, but a glance at Driskell and Brittain's own bibliography will show that since 1964 she has been overwhelmingly, even suffocatingly, admired—and not all the perceptive criticism has come from Georgia Catholics. Despite its narrowness, however, this book contains valuable insights: on the Christian *malgré lui* of the novels, on connections between *The Violent Bear It Away* (her "greatest single accomplishment") and "The Lame Shall Enter First," on the decision to replace "The Partridge Festival" with "Parker's Back" in the posthumous collection of stories, and on the anagogical significance of travel and travelers in the fiction.

While he acknowledges the important doctrinal quality of O'Connor's work, Miles Orvell incorporates this element in other contexts in *Invisible Parade: The Fiction of Flannery O'Connor* (Philadelphia, Temple Univ. Press). He suggests the writer's kinship with the Southwestern humorists and the great American romance writers (even Poe, whose *Pym* proceeds like an O'Connor work, in that "naturalistic observation, culminating in decisive, violent action, gives way to a visionary conclusion"). Even when he relates her to European Catholic authors, he stresses differences rather than similarities. *Invisible Parade* is stronger on unified segments, even within chapters, than on overall coherence; but Orvell has a knack for generalizing on the qualities of the fiction as well as giving acute, evaluative readings of specific works. Her best fiction, he says, reveals "a constantly felt tension between the pull of reality and the pull of Reality, between surface and depth, between fact and mystery." When the "true country" exercises "untoward suzerainty over the countryside," that loss of tension makes for obviousness, a fiction of statement. In the novels Orvell sees the defining dramatic image as "an *act* performed *by* the hero," but in the stories the defining image is "an *intrusion* of some outside figure *upon* the protagonist." He is the first critic to pay great attention to the book reviews (1956–1963) which O'Connor wrote regularly for a Catholic journal—not only confirming an orthodoxy we have come to expect of her but also revealing an insistence upon the need for reason as well as revelation. Orvell ends his study with a discussion of the relationship between belief and O'Connor's kind of fiction.

In her brief foreword to Kathleen Feeley's *Flannery O'Connor: Voice of the Peacock* (New Brunswick, N. J., Rutgers Univ. Press), Caroline Gordon announces the subject as "the theological background of Flannery O'Connor's work," and so it is; but Sister Kathleen herself warns us that O'Connor is neither a "tractarian" nor a "Catholic apologist" and that in her lifetime she scorned those who would "use" fiction for "any pragmatic purpose, no matter how commendable." This book benefits from the critic's study of O'Connor's personal library, although her practice of glossing marked passages in the books she read with parallel "illustrations" from the books she wrote finally becomes restrictive and mannered—a forced convergence. Sister Kathleen traces the "home" theme in *Wise Blood*, with its mixture of comic tones and Hawthornesque romance: O'Connor's ability to deal with both mystery, "the touchstone of romance," and manners, " the raw material of comedy," is brilliant; but its very comedy makes the novel unequal "to the demands of the theme of alienation." She cites the "paradigmatic aspect of biblical history" as an important surrogate for O'Connor's lack of a classical education; and she may be the most helpful critic yet to discuss Teilhard's much-discussed influence on the novelist—especially fine is the discussion of the sacredness of matter.

"Flannery O'Connor once remarked that the most memorable event in her life prior to the publication of *Wise Blood* was the featuring of a bantam chicken which she had trained to walk backwards by Pathé newsreels." This is the grotesque opening sentence of Gilbert H. Muller's *Nightmares and Visions: Flannery O'Connor and the Catholic Grotesque* (Athens, Univ. of Ga. Press), and both its image and its syntax participate astonishingly in the subject. It is nevertheless a valuable book for understanding "the most graphic of postwar American writers." Muller insists that grotesque is neither romantic nor realistic, but a unique aesthetic. He stresses the distinctions between gothic romance fiction and the grotesque, using the function of violence as a touchstone. He also traces the connections between "existential dislocation" (which is at the core of the grotesque vision) and spiritual dislocation (which explains why most of O'Connor's characters can be evaluated according to their attitude toward Christianity). Although she affirms the contradictory aspects of the unregenerate world and its irrationality, often through grotesque tricksters, her fiction embodies a transcending principle of order: correctives to man's desperate condition are the foundations of nature and grace. Like Driskell and Brittain, Muller devotes considerable space to O'Connor's metaphor of the journey, but whereas their emphasis on the novelist's anagogical method forces them into an upbeat mood which sees transformation and enlightenment everywhere, Muller emphasizes the iconographic nature of the quest metaphor and makes the healthy point that precious few of the questers emerge at the end of their journey "transformed by their confrontation." Muller believes that the grotesque, whose vagaries O'Connor was committed to exploring, inhibits the possibility of Christian tragedy, but it does not "expunge the possibility of making a Christian statement about the nature of reality."

Melvin E. Lorentzen's "A Good Writer Is Hard to Find" (*Imagination and the Spirit*, pp. 417–35), a relentlessly amplified argument that O'Connor is indeed a Christian writer, suggests that her grotesques can be neither explained nor understood: their meaning lies in their embodiment of "the mystery of iniquity and the mystery of redemption." In "Flannery O'Connor and the Home Country" (*Renascence* 24:171–76) Elmo Howell argues briefly against making the author's fictive settings too dependent upon verisimilitude, but observing that O'Connor was "proud to be a Georgian" falls short of substantive explanation.

A frank confrontation with the reality of violence and a respect for steadying institutions and manners are the antidotes to spiritual decay, according to Marion Montgomery in "Flannery O'Connor's Transformation of the Sentimental" (*MissQ* 25[1971]:1–18). Sentimentality is a state which assails man with vague humanitarian impulses and promotes an excessively high regard for man's "natural condition." In his explication, "On Flannery O'Connor's 'Everything That Rises Must Converge'" (*Crit* 13,ii:15–29), centering on Julian's point of view, Montgomery says that to read the story only in the light of Teilhard is to see nothing of original sin on which the story is premised. "Convergence" is not that of one person with another, but of Julian with the world of guilt and sorrow; his tragedy is, he recognizes, that he has destroyed what he loved through blindness. C. R. Kropf links this story with another highly regarded one in

"Theme and Setting in 'A Good Man Is Hard to Find' " (*Renascence* 24:177–80, 206). The "true country" is more than a spiritual abstraction; the confrontation of the Misfit and the grandmother is a reinforcement of the two major themes, "the nature of the mythic past and the problem of sin."

Richard Pearce is one of those critics who place a higher value on the novels than on the stories, but unfortunately his discussion of O'Connor (*Stages of the Clown*, pp. 67–83) goes no further than an appreciation of the "humanity" of her grotesques. Albert Sonnenfeld detects, as others before have pointed out, that for O'Connor the essential strategy of salvation involves "a return to the stormy principles of the prophet in the wilderness"—a supposedly fundamentalist position, though this critic's understanding of Southern Baptists is simplistic ("Flannery O'Connor: The Catholic Writer as Baptist," *ConL* 13:445–57). According to J. C. Keller's "The Figures of the Empiricist and the Rationalist in the Fiction of Flannery O'Connor" (*ArQ* 28:263–73) O'Connor developed these two character types in order to satirize a secular humanism; the empiricist is represented by Hazel Motes, the rationalist by George Rayber.

In "Hazel Motes in Transit: A Comparison of Two Versions of Flannery O'Connor's 'The Train' with Chapter 1 of 'Wise Blood' " (*SSF* 8[1971]:287–93), Margaret Harrison traces the changes made from the 1947 thesis story and the beginning of the 1952 novella, which include nuances of themes and such matters as characterization and indirect discourse. David R. Mayer investigates "the phenomenon of shaman spirit possession" as it relates to Tarwater's struggle, in "*The Violent Bear It Away*: Flannery O'Connor's Shaman" (*SLJ* 4,ii:41–54). He finds several elements (trance behavior, dissociation, healing) in many incidents in the novel which are said to have "shamanistic counterparts somewhere in the world."

The first volume of the annual *Flannery O'Connor Bulletin* features critical essays, a reminiscence, and a survey by the curator, Gerald Becham, of the O'Connor collection in Georgia College at Milledgeville (pp. 66–71). Charles M. Hegarty traces the evolution of one of the writer's most mysterious protagonists in an impressive textual study of "The Life You Save May Be Your Own"—"A Man Though Not Yet a Whole One: Mr. Shiftlet's Genesis" (pp. 24–38). In "A Note on Flannery O'Connor" (*SSF* 9:409–10), Hegarty also comments on a disputed passage in "The Church and the Fiction

Writer." Stuart Burns's "Freaks in a Circus Tent: Flannery O'Connor's Christ-Haunted Characters" (pp. 3–23) makes distinctions between those characters who are grotesque because of the situations in which they get caught and those whose actions appear to be grotesque because they stem from a "violent view of reality." Ted R. Spivey oddly argues that O'Connor's atmospheric landscapes are more important than the characters who stand out against them, in "Flannery's South: Don Quixote Rides Again" (pp. 46–53), a characteristic which may be the residual "spirit of the Spanish Catholicism of an earlier day." This half-meditation, half-reminiscence precedes Rosa Lee Walston's "Flannery: An Affectionate Recollection" (pp. 55–60). In "The Lessons of History: Flannery O'Connor's 'Everything That Rises Must Converge'" (pp. 39–45) John F. Desmond discusses the relationship of Julian and his mother as the central focus. Those characters who resist convergence ("the universal drive toward spiritual union among men, through love") thus require an apocalyptic-like violence to break them.

Finally, Louise Blackwell's analysis of "Flannery O'Connor's Literary Style" (*AntigR* 10:57–66) is really a discussion of the author's use of religious symbols. In most respects, says Blackwell, O'Connor is neither an innovator nor an experimenter.

iv. Saul Bellow, Bernard Malamud, and J. D. Salinger

Robert R. Dutton's *Saul Bellow* (TUSAS 181) may be the first study to relegate Bellow's Jewishness "to the incidental" in favor of his "universal intentions." By measuring his subject against a modified Renaissance notion—man as subangelic—Dutton is reasonably successful in stressing the broadly moral and humanistic aspect of Bellow's career. But the most interesting segments in this book have only tangential connection with a thesis—drawing the ethical patterns of *Gulliver's Travels* in *Henderson the Rain King*, seeing a disguised Faust legend in *Herzog*, and discovering that *The Adventures of Augie March* can be read as a parodic capsule history of American literary styles and fashions.

The implications of Dutton's fine phrase concerning *Henderson*, "spiritual malaise in an environment of sufficiency," are richly explored in *Saul Bellow* (New York, Frederick Ungar) by Brigitte Scheer-Schäzler, who sees *Henderson* as the melancholy record of a

man "who remains an undaunted adorer of life." She perceptively
insists upon the sadness beneath all the exuberance in *Augie March*,
a predominant note stemming from Augie's inability to define the
"chosen thing" for which he quests. This critic also makes explicit
what everyone has suspected for some time, the closely autobiographical nature of *Herzog* (adduced from Bellow's speeches, interviews, and essays). And while Dutton believes *Mr. Sammler's Planet*
to be Bellow's finest achievement because of its integration of form
and content, Scheer-Schäzler is more perfunctory in her admiration;
she asserts that its language surpasses that of *Herzog*, though we are
unfortunately given no demonstration of that judgment. Despite excessive plot summary and occasional errors of fact (three years, not
nine, separate *Augie March* and *Seize the Day*), Scheer-Schäzler's
book, like Dutton's, manages to make its voice heard among the more
ambitious studies of Bellow.

Three different cultural influences behind *Henderson* are suggested. In "Bellow's Henderson as American Imago of the 1950's"
(*RS* 40:296–300), L. Moffitt Cecil believes Henderson to be Bellow's
counterimage to the Ugly American type, anticipating attitudes which
emerged explicitly a decade later. Byron D. Hull, in " 'Henderson the
Rain King' and William James" (*Criticism* 13[1971]:402–14), argues
that "all the chapters dealing with Henderson, Dahfu, and Atti are
explicable in terms of Jamesian psychology." In a careful use of textual allusions, Hull sees Dahfu as a Jamesian psychotherapist whose
program to rehabilitate Henderson depends upon a dynamic interaction of mind and body. Richard Pearce (*Stages of the Clown*, pp.
102–16) sees Henderson and Skipper of John Hawkes's *Second Skin*
as Harlequin figures, who thrive in chaos to build rather than destroy
and whose creations, though evanescent, are a source of pleasure for
the human spirit. Whereas Skipper is a variant of the *eiron* of classical
comedy, Henderson is a variant of the *miles gloriosus*, with traces of
Gargantua, Natty Bumppo, and the Lone Ranger also evident.

In "The Letters of Moses Herzog: A Symbolic Mirror" (*StH* 2,
ii[1971]:40–45), John S. Hill posits a fellowship of Bellow protagonists who struggle to impose themselves on their environments rather
than permitting themselves to become products of them, culminating
in Herzog, who is "a victim of his inability to master environment."
Bellow's problem was to hold that environment stable long enough

to put it in perspective, and his solution was to update the epistolary method for dramatizing man's ability to realize self.

If Herzog ends with an ethical faith, Artur Sammler ends with "infinite yearning," says James Neil Harris, in "One Critical Approach to *Mr. Sammler's Planet*" (*TCL* 18:235–50). As Bellow's first major work to use "sardonium as a *major* thematic technique," *Mr. Sammler's Planet* is an ironic work which aspires toward myth; it is also, says Harris, a "mythical oracular pronouncement analogous to the revelation of the Logos of God which permits the poet in the mythic tradition to consider himself as a prophet through whom God is acknowledged, *without irony.*" Some valuable insights are embedded in this overly long and pretentious essay.

Andrew Waterman's "Saul Bellow's Ineffectual Angels" (*On the Novel*, pp. 218–39) is a once-over-lightly survey which concentrates on *Herzog* and *Mr. Sammler's Planet*. Although Bellow has consistently pictured the follies of romantic subjectivism in characters faced with alternative dangers (alienation and compromise), they are also consistently unable to express their values in action.

Of all contemporary American novelists, only Bellow is substantial enough as an author of "compassionate" fiction to earn a segment (pp. 305–36) in James Gindin's *Harvest of a Quiet Eye*. Augie March moves without direction through dense, unstructured experiences and survives by his resilience; our interest in him lies not in any coherent message but in the elaborate details of Augie's adventures themselves. *Henderson* is less successful because its "fabulistic form suggests an intellectual and thematic tightness, a coherent structure for human experience, that the novel itself does not fully develop." *Mr. Sammler's Planet*, while its view of man is "more inflexibly deterministic," still insists upon the suspension of "salient moralities" and thus qualifies as a novel of compassion. Predictably, Gindin is less persuasive when he deals with Bellow's more tightly structured works such as *Dangling Man* and *The Victim*.

Chirantan Kulshrestha is the latest to hold "A Conversation with Saul Bellow" (*ChiR* 23,iv–24,i[double issue]:7–15), who disclaims any special identity as a "Jewish writer." Since "no good literature is parochial," he says, it should be available to "non-communicants."

The key term in Robert Warburton's "Fantasy and the Fiction of Bernard Malamud" (*Imagination and the Spirit*, pp. 387–416) has a

kind of Lewis Carroll solidity: "fantasy" here means Malamud's capacity "to marvel and wonder at the enigmas of human existence."
This piece is a compound of confident dryness, peculiar to the taxo-
nomic method, and pulpit oratory in which syntax itself is transcen-
dentalized. Warburton says that fantasy shapes the interaction between "the frustration of desire and the redemption of spirit within
the context of absurdity."

William Sharfman's "Inside and Outside Malamud" (*Rendezvous*
7,i:25–38), a discussion of images of enclosure and exclusion as
stages of the moral progress of Malamud's characters, never quite
clarifies the connections between situational problems (characters
"who are outside trying to get in or inside trying to get out") and
their larger meaning (abstract notions of "historical alignment," in
which Jewish identity comes to fruition in historical time). Sharfman's major text is *The Fixer*, in which Yakov Bok comes to grips
with both personal and historical time. The interrelationship of
Jewish identity and history is also the subject of Wesley A. Kort's
treatment of Malamud (*Shriven Selves*, pp. 90–115). The example
is Bok: convinced that history is antagonistic to Jewish identity, he
resolves to resist. Kort relates the theme of the loss of God in the
midst of gratuitous suffering not to the fashionable Death of God
theology of the 1960s, but to Rabbi Richard Rubenstein's idea that
"the only creative response to the evil history is the cultivation of
sacred place."

Although overargued, William J. Handy's essay on *The Fixer*
(*Modern Fiction: A Formalist Approach*, Carbondale, So. Ill. Univ.
Press, pp. 131–58), which includes a careful examination of several
crucial scenes in *The Assistant* and *A New Life* as well, demonstrates
that Malamud's focus in each work is not on the objective event but
on the "knowing subject," and the reader's experience parallels the
fictive process of the "discovery of the free self."

Alvin Greenberg muses on the extent to which the anti-heroes,
cripples, *schlemiels*, and victims of fiction since Dostoevsky "stand
for us" allegorically, in "A Sense of Place in Modern Fiction: The
Novelist's World and the Allegorist's Heaven" (*Genre* 5:353–66).
The novelist moves away from the abstractive and ideational (the
allegorical end of the fictional spectrum) and toward the phenomenal sense of things, the arena of the experienced and the possible
for man-in-the-world. Greenberg cites *The Natural* as specifically

anti-allegorical, since allegory, like ritual, is infinite and cyclical; in Malamud's novel, everything is over when the baseball season ends.

"The Nature and Interpretation of Symbolism in Malamud's *The Assistant*" (*CentR* 16:394–407) is a superficial, reductive, and patronizing essay by S. V. Pradhan, who presumes first to lecture Malamud on his "unsophisticated and naive symbolism" and then to suggest that this artlessness may be an overreaction to earlier experimentalism in the modern American novel. John Griffith details the implicit and explicit allusions to St. Francis of Assisi (*Expl* 31: item 1), suggesting finally that Frank Alpine's "glow of religious triumph" is a reflection of the saint's beatitude.

Using data from ethnology, history, and religion, Peter Freese produces three books in one, with *Die Initiationsreise: Studien zum jugendlichen Helden im modernen amerikanischen Roman* (Neumünster, Karl Wachholtz Verlag, 1971)—(1) a dizzying survey of authors from Charles Brockden Brown to Philip Roth who have written examples of the initiation novel, (2) an exhaustive exercise in taxonomy, and (3) a detailed analysis of *The Catcher in the Rye*, which Freese regards as the culmination of the type. At least ten characteristics are required of the "Initiationsreise-Roman," but there are some variants: Cooper and Faulkner work from "wilderness" patterns, and Wolfe and Fitzgerald from "undergraduate" ones. This study will be more useful for general scholars than for Salinger specialists.

The Catcher in the Rye is one of the twentieth-century novels cited by Alan H. Rose in "Sin and the City: The Uses of Disorder in the Urban Novel" (*CentR* 16:203–20). Though the "urban obsession" began, says Rose, as a means for opportunity, fortune, and maturity, it has gradually turned into a journey toward crime and degradation. Antolini's warning to Holden about a "special kind of fall" encapsulates the "subjectively shrunken state of the urban archetype."

In a minor piece, "The Suicide of Salinger's Seymour Glass" (*SSF* 9:243–46), Frank Metcalf suggests that Seymour's "sublimated pedophilic desires" are behind both his erotic trifling with Sybil and his suicide. Bernice and Sanford Goldstein in "Ego and 'Hapworth 16, 1924'" (*Renascence* 24:159–67) contend that Salinger's portrait of his guru at age seven shows Seymour already enlightened but also humanized: he displays instability and humility, marks of limitation. Gordon E. Slethaug discusses the Laughing Man, Franny, and Sey-

mour, whose varied responses to the tensions of ego and social forms
constitute an important understanding of "Form in Salinger's Shorter
Fiction" (*CRAS* 3:50–59). Considered as a single work, *Raise High
the Roof Beam, Carpenters* and *Seymour: An Introduction* assert
structurally the paradoxical affirmation of both forms and formless-
ness, society and ego.

v. Robert Penn Warren, William Styron, and Walker Percy

The Warren number of *Four Quarters* (21,iv) is a miscellany of critical essays, reminiscences, and "A Conversation with Robert Penn
Warren" (pp. 3–17), who tells Ruth Fisher of his varying degrees of
personal engagement when he writes fiction and poetry, as well as
his opinions on such topics as propaganda art, the influence of *The
Waste Land* on his generation, and college courses in contemporary
literature. Cleanth Brooks ("Brooks on Warren," pp. 19–22) remembers the earliest years with Warren in the 1920s and 1930s; Arthur H.
Scouten, a former student of Warren's at LSU, gives his version of
the genesis of Warren's third novel ("Warren, Huey Long, and *All
the King's Men*," pp. 23–26); and in "Right On! *All the King's Men*
in the Classroom" (pp. 69–78), Earl Wilcox cites the pedagogical
strengths of the novel for the present generation: Burden as "an
Everyman archetype" and Stark as the exemplar of power politics.
Victor Strandberg, the most perceptive critic of Warren's poetry,
contributes an addendum to his *A Colder Fire* (1965) with a fine
survey, "Robert Penn Warren: The Poetry of the Sixties" (pp. 27–44).
James H. Justus, taking some of his illustrations from the poetry,
writes on "Warren and the Doctrine of Complicity" (pp. 93–99)—
the recurring theme of "comprehensive human relatedness," with its
working premise that none is without guilt and none can survive
meaningfully without love.

"The Fictional Voices of Robert Penn Warren" (pp. 45–52) is a
suggestive but sketchy piece by Robert Frank Cayton, whose thesis
is that the novelist's diverse narrative voices are not only "thematic
agents" for communicating intellectual and moral truths but also
technical means for maintaining control of the fictive structures. Reality, according to Warren, is the validation of one's existence which
comes only through love, and D. G. Kehl explicates the various terms

of the dialectic in Warren's most recent novel in "Love's Definition: Dream as Reality in Robert Penn Warren's *Meet Me in the Green Glen*" (pp. 116–22). Although Kehl demonstrates how that novel is explicitly a dramatized definition of love, his leap in equating love's definition and self-definition is a little murky. Leonard Casper's "Ark, Flood, and Negotiated Covenant" (pp. 110–15) is needlessly elliptical, but beneath the mannered rhetoric is a densely packed argument which admirably comes to terms with a frequently misunderstood novel about the discovery of true selfhood among multiple characters. Curtis Whittington, Jr., in "The Earned Vision: Robert Penn Warren's 'The Ballad of Billie Potts' and Albert Camus' *Le Malentendu*" (pp. 79–90), first examines the interrelationship of Warren's 1942–1944 essays and the poem and then compares "Billie Potts" to Camus' play of 1944. The ballad and the play share both the archetypal journey of flight and return and the ironic method; what is not demonstrated is the assumption that Warren's vision of the human condition is absurdist in the same way as Camus'. H. D. Herring's "Madness in *At Heaven's Gate*: A Metaphor of the Self in Warren's Fiction" (pp. 56–66) discusses the plethora of incomplete selves in the second novel, but focuses on Slim Sarrett. Madness, says Herring, is the greatest threat to the individual because it corrodes the very meaning of self: the coherence of diverse components in a unified being. Allen Shepherd contends that *Band of Angels* is the only one of Warren's novels to deal specifically with forgiveness. In "Carrying Manty Home: Robert Penn Warren's *Band of Angels*" (pp. 101–09) he emphasizes the affirmative but unsatisfactory resolution (Warren's attempt to "carry off a black tragedy with a white joke").

Warren imposes a tragic pattern onto the facts concerning Huey Long, says R. Gray, in "The American Novelist and American History: A Revaluation of *All the King's Men*" (*JAmS* 6:297–307); and his ordering idea "creates a new shape and meaning from both" the facts and the pattern. Robert C. Slack argues that Stark is not just a crafty manipulator, but a "full-fledged exponent of Pragmatism," in "Willie Stark and William James" (*In Honor of Austin Wright*, pp. 71–79), a reductionist and overstated piece ("Now, Willie has no respect for the Law") which ignores previous discussions of this subject. Richard F. Bauerle discusses "The Emblematic Opening of Warren's *All the King's Men*" (*PLL* 8:312–14), the "nexus of dirt and death" of the first paragraph which announces the major motifs of the novel (power, death, love) and anticipates the stylistic modulations to come.

Dennis M. Dooley offers a substantial essay with "The Persona RPW in Warren's *Brother to Dragons*" (*MissQ* 25[1971]:19–30). The three digressions in this work mark the significant stages in the spiritual growth of the narrating voice, says Dooley, and that progress parallels a similar growth in Jefferson. Of marginal value is D. Nathan Sumner's "The Function of Historical Sources in Hawthorne, Melville, and R. P. Warren" (*RS* 40:103–14); it may be true that in *Brother to Dragons* Warren triumphantly forges a "radical redefinition of the role of historical data," but Sumner seems unaware that considerable earlier work renders his own contribution gratuitous. In making "The Case for Robert Penn Warren's Second Best Novel" (*CimR* 20:44–51) Allen Shepherd takes into account both the melodramatic aspects of *The Cave* and the authorial narrative voice, which is responsible for the intrusive statements of ideas. In another piece, "The Poles of Fiction: Warren's *At Heaven's Gate*" (*TSLL* 12[1971]:709–18), Shepherd considers the extensive relationship between "history" and "idea" in Warren's second novel, which, though more satisfactorily rendered than *Night Rider*, is still best read as the immediate precursor to *All the King's Men*.

Styron's chief concern is "the tragic condition of man's ancient feud with his own nature and destiny," according to Marc L. Ratner in *William Styron* (TUSAS 196); rather than being environmentally determined, his characters are allowed the necessary freedom to struggle against their egoism. Ratner's best illustration of his thesis is *The Long March*: through rebellion, Mannix finds the evils of a system within himself, slices through his self-delusions, and exorcises his personal devils to become mature. Ratner also emphasizes Styron's poetic sensibility, arguing convincingly that his forte is description. One catch-all chapter covers the novelist's modest knack for satire, his treatment of sexuality and violence, his religious attitudes, and a recapitulation of the black resistance to *The Confessions of Nat Turner*. (Earlier versions of Ratner's readings have already been noted: those on *Nat Turner* [ALS 1969, p. 299] and *Set This House on Fire* [ALS 1971, p. 264].)

The widely disseminated charge that Styron is guilty of distorting the facts of history in *Nat Turner* is disputed in an exceptionally thorough study, "History, Politics and Literature: The Myth of Nat Turner" (*AQ* 23[1971]:487–518), by Seymour L. Gross and Eileen Bender, who suggest that Thomas R. Gray's 1831 document, the "reliable" source of what is known about Turner, is itself political— an "exercise in reassurance" for whites who feared that the Turner insurrection was not purely local.

Donald W. Markos in "Margaret Whitehead in *The Confessions of Nat Turner*" (*SNNTS* 4:52–59) believes that the sexual attraction between the white woman and Turner is psychologically valid: she is Nat's most powerful reminder of his emasculation and the source of his greatest torment. Wesley A. Kort (*Shriven Selves*, pp. 116–40) relates Styron's fiction to the "theology of hope" so influential in the late 1950s because of its stress on social, economic, and political revolution. Kort sees three basic figures of the earlier novels—the observer, oppressor, and rebel—transmuted to a "more mythic vision of revolution" in *Nat Turner*.

Teut Andreas Riese in "Geschichtsverständnis und Geschichts-dichtung im Amerika des 20. Jahrhunderts" (*Amerikanische Litera-tur*, pp. 73–91) includes *Nat Turner* in his discussion of the centrality of history in those modern American works which focus upon the past in order to understand the present. In "Nat Turner and Black History" (*IJAS* 1,iv[1971]:1–6) Jimmie L. Franklin gives a summary of the Styron controversy for an Indian audience.

Of limited value are Marisa Bulgheroni's "William Styron: il romanziere, il tempo e la storia" (*SA* 16[1970]:407–28), a general account which also treats the novelist's fictional use of history; Mel-vin J. Friedman's "William Styron" (*The Politics*, pp. 335–50), which has little to say about the author's politics except the establishment of Styron's liberal credentials; and Daniel Halpern's "Checking in with William Styron" (*Esquire*, Aug., pp. 142–43), a chatty and trivial profile.

In "Walker Percy: Sensualist-Thinker" (*Novel* 6:52–65), William Dowie contends that the author's protagonists are both passive sen-sation-seekers and intellectuals seeking a balance between the ex-tremes of sensation and thought. In a piece of creative scholarship, "Mysteries and Movies: Walker Percy's College Articles and *The Moviegoer*" (*MissQ* 25:165–81) Scott Byrd examines the novelist's student reviews in the *Carolina Magazine*, arguing that Percy's understanding of the artifacts of popular culture reverberates in the first novel alongside the more serious echoes of Kierkegaard.

Lewis A. Lawson traces the physician figure in *The Moviegoer* and *The Last Gentleman* in "Walker Percy: The Physician as Novelist" (*SAB* 37,ii:58–63), concentrating on the reconciliation of layman and scientist who jointly acknowledge an area of existence answering only to subjective explanations. Ted R. Spivey ("Religion and the Reintegration of Man in Flannery O'Connor and Walker Percy," *Spectrum* 2:67–79) believes that the work of Percy and O'Connor should be read in the light of comparative myth and ritual as well as existentialism; he studies two works by each author which show their characters' awareness of the need for psychic reintegration.

Paul L. Gaston in "The Revelation of Walker Percy" (*ColQ* 20: 459–70) places *Love in the Ruins* in the apocalyptic tradition. More is a "straightforward surrogate" of Percy, a "sick diagnostician in a world too far gone even to care about its terminal illness." Gaston suggests that Percy's hometown, Covington, La., is to the novelist what second-century Rome was to St. John.

vi. Eudora Welty, Carson McCullers, and Truman Capote

Though many writers of the Southern Renascence once cast a jaundiced eye on the regional assumptions of the nineteenth-century local-color tradition, the relationship between the two literatures is significant, according to a solid study by Merrill Maguire Skaggs, *The Folk of Southern Fiction* (Athens, Univ. of Ga. Press). Faulkner, Welty, and O'Connor especially, like their predecessors, reveal that while their works are shaped by a culture, the works in turn shape the culture "by providing myths and metaphors and stereotypes with which [it] perceives and orders its particular experience." Skaggs's contextual approach works impressively with Welty, whose sources of humor are often stereotyped characters—old maids, matriarchs, dowagers—expressing their inner selves at public meetings—concerts, political rallies, funerals. Welty's short stories, says Skaggs, best reveal the continuities with the local colorists, although *The Ponder Heart* taps most completely "the possibilities inherent in forms, techniques, and targets" of the earlier literature.

Welty seems an unlikely author for having her works ransacked for evidence of characters plagued by the "face-breast equation"—a "hypnagogic hallucination" in which the eyes are imaginatively fused with the nipples of the breast—but Raymond Tarbox finds plenty of these sufferers. As he explains it, the phenomenon is an unfailing sign that the character, with a devouring oral rage, is in "dire need of being absolutely free of intense separation anxiety or persecutory fear." Tarbox focuses on "Death of a Traveling Salesman" and "Clytie" and gives his study the misleading title "Eudora Welty's Fiction: The Salvation Theme" (*AI* 29:70–91).

In "Vision and Perception in the Works of Eudora Welty" (*MarkhamR* 2,v[1971]:94–99) Ronald E. McFarland traces the progress of several protagonists from the mere limits of sight toward a more transcendent vision associated with human understanding. Charles E. May in "Le Roi Mehaigné in Welty's 'Keela, the Outcast Indian Maiden'" (*MFS* 18:559–66) argues that Little Lee Roy, not the former carnival barker, is the center of the story. As a "mythical outcast figure forced to serve as scapegoat for the bestiality of society itself," he is a holy innocent—in romance, the maimed king.

The ability to see things without editorial evaluations defines the quality of reality in the writings of both Sherwood Anderson and Welty, says Robert S. Pawlowski in "The Process of Observation: *Winesburg, Ohio* and *The Golden Apples*" (*UR* 37 [1971]:304,293–98). In each work the sense of place is important not for its geographical site, but for its usefulness in depicting a "species of social organization," the small town which entraps individuals in their solitariness. Elmo Howell's rambling appreciation, "Eudora Welty and the Use of Place in Southern Fiction" (*ArQ* 28:248–56), adds little to Welty's own comments on this subject.

"A Time Exposure" (*NMW* 5:11–14), another appreciation, is on Welty's book of photographs (*One Time, One Place*) by Daniel Curley, who perceptively sees links between Welty's foreword and her pictures. Charles T. Bunting contributes "'The Interior World': An Interview with Eudora Welty" (*SoR* 8:711–35), which contains especially interesting insights into the writing of *Losing Battles*. Linda Kuehl also offers an interview—"The Art of Fiction XLVII: Eudora Welty" (*ParisR* 55:72–97). Charles E. Davis suggests in "Welty's 'Old Mr. Marblehall'" (*Expl* 30:item 40) that the title character derives from Alfred Bunn's romantic escapist poem, "I Dreamt I Dwelt in Marble Halls."

Carson McCullers never affirms society, only the individual liv-

ing precariously in that society: this is Irene Skotnicki's observation
in "Die Darstellung der Entfremdung in den Romanen von Carson
McCullers" (ZAA 20:24–45)—and the alienation is exacerbated because the author is interested in psychological phenomena among
men of different levels of society. Remarking the conspicuous absence of working-class characters in McCullers's fiction, Skotnicki
suggests that such characters might have lessened the overpowering
sense we get in her work that men are bound together only by existential meaninglessness.

In "The Moral Function of Distortion in Southern Grotesque"
(SAB 37,ii:37–46) Delma Eugene Presley contends that grotesque
characters are used "to bear witness about human possibilities in
the light of God's grace as well as the inhuman possibilities of lives
lived without that light." Cripples thus suggest the wholeness of
man. Since this is a theological view of the grotesque, O'Connor is
a prime example, but the vision is similar, says Presley, in the work
of McCullers and Tennessee Williams, where there is a view of man
"informed by the redemptive potential of love."

Dawson F. Gaillard, writing on "The Presence of the Narrator in
Carson McCullers' The Ballad of the Sad Café" (MissQ 25:419–27),
attributes the power of this novella to the human voice of a townsman who is both biased and perceptive, whose mythmaking imagination dramatizes the process by which temporal events are meta-
morphosed into timelessness.

Dale Edmonds discusses a New Yorker story of 1942 in "'Correspondence': A 'Forgotten' Carson McCullers Short Story" (SSF 9:
89–92) which, though never collected, shows the author's gift for
light comedy. James W. Grinnell gives a brief reading of a more
familiar story in "Delving 'A Domestic Dilemma'" (SSF 9:270–71).
Supplementing Stanley Stewart's checklist (BB 22[1959]:182–85)
and Robert S. Phillips's checklist (BB 24[1964]:113–16), William
T. Stanley's "Carson McCullers: 1965–1969: A Selected Checklist"
(BB 27[1970]:91–93) lists new and previously unlisted writings and
a selection of reviews of Oliver Evans's The Ballad of Carson McCullers (1966).

In The New Journalism: The Underground Press, the Artists of
Nonfiction, and Changes in the Established Media (Lawrence, Univ.
Press of Kan., 1971), Michael L. Johnson devotes one chapter (pp.
45–84) to three non-fiction artists, Capote, Tom Wolfe, and Mailer, al-

though the account is more descriptive than critical. John J. McAleer is less enthusiastic about Capote's non-fiction novel in his comparison of "'An American Tragedy' and 'In Cold Blood'" (*Thought* 47:569–86). Because he was preoccupied with form, shackled by commitments which permitted him "neither to release fully the potentials of his materials nor to concentrate their power for maximum effectiveness," Capote produces a book considerably weaker in "truth of nature" than Dreiser produced with his old-fashioned fictionalizing.

Along with the usual items in "Truman Capote: 1943–1968: A Critical Bibliography (*BB* 27[1970]:57–60,71), David L. Vanderwerken includes newspaper and popular-magazine articles.

vii. James Agee and John Updike

Erling Larsen's *James Agee* (UMPAW 95) is a well-paced survey of a writer excessively described as "a Puritan who both despised and was 'sized' by Puritanism, a mystic divided against himself." Most of the coverage is devoted to the three long prose pieces which recount the education of a consciousness. Although *Let Us Now Praise Famous Men* and the two novels show the most agonizing self-examination, their aesthetic and philosophic ambivalences Larsen also sees in Agee's film scripts, which reveal the dilemma between Agee's doubts about the validity of art and his simultaneous feeling that the "artist is better and more important than the ordinary man."[3] Larsen mentions the poetry perfunctorily, but he gives generous space to the puzzling short fiction, notably "A Mother's Tale."

Victor A. Kramer continues his impressive work on Agee with four pieces. In "Agee and Plans for the Criticism of Popular Culture" (*JPC* 5:755–66) he brings together from the letters, fellowship applications, and other sources all of Agee's statements and projects for the systematic study of popular culture—twenty-five years prior to the founding of the journal in which this essay appears. In "Agee's *Let Us Now Praise Famous Men*: Image of Tenant Life" (*MissQ* 25:405–17), Kramer is particularly acute to the writer's sometimes distracted struggle to render precisely the Gudgers house and cloth-

---

3. Patrick Samway agrees that Agee's quest for aesthetic form and his abiding interest in family life were vitally related, but he sees little tension in that relationship. "James Agee: A Family Man" (*Thought* 47:40–68) is a general but graceful account which traces in the several genres in which he worked Agee's concern for remaining faithful to nuances of experience.

ing; despite the dominating authorial presence, the focus of that book is upon "a particular culture" capturable only through evocation and memory.

Kramer also publishes the first section of a crucial chapter (omitted from the book) as "The Complete 'Work' Chapter for James Agee's *Let Us Now Praise Famous Men*" (*TQ* 15,ii:27–48). What Agee emphasizes in this segment is not the particular nature of cottonfield work, but the "reiterative quality of *any* physical labor." In "James Agee's Unpublished Manuscript and His Emphasis on Religious Emotion in *The Morning Watch*" (*TSL* 17:159–64) Kramer uses drafts of the manuscript and passages from an alternative conclusion to support his claim that the core of the novella (as well as the source of its static quality) is the hero's effort to sustain a religious emotion, a doomed effort, since that emotion is intruded upon by other concerns—sex, skepticism, and what Agee terms a "sense of beauty and a sense of science."

Roger Ramsey nevertheless argues for a special tension and ambiguity in that static novella, created by the juxtaposition of a tripartite symbolic and a concentrated narrative structure. "The Double Structure of *The Morning Watch*" (*SNNTS* 4:494–503) is the first defense of the long middle section, and Ramsey does it well, using the analogy of the triptych in which the central panel is always visually and symbolically the most important.

In "Thematic Counterpoint in *A Death in the Family*: The Function of the Six Extra Scenes" (*Novel* 5:234–41) J. Douglas Perry, Jr., makes a case for the unity of the manuscript (though not necessarily of the editors' arrangement of it), which is not so much a record of a death in the family as it is a "moving image of that family before, as well as after the loss." The extra scenes function as "loving retrospection" to reinforce the novel's movement "from protection to exposure," similar to *The Morning Watch*.

Excluding the non-fiction and poetry, Robert Detweiler in *John Updike* (TUSAS 214) explicates the major works through *Rabbit Redux*, showing how "their mythic (and post-mythic) patterns relate to a disjunctive modern reality." Detweiler believes that the characteristic tone, especially when Updike's subject is the Protestant middle class, is elegiac and that one of his strengths is his deployment of unobtrusive technical skills. The discussion of the short stories seems notably fresh. Detweiler finds the image of the door, literal and symbolic, uniting all the stories in *The Same Door*; discovers a "marriage group" in *Pigeon Feathers*; and attributes the relative failure of *The Music School* to Updike's heavy sense of telling.

Wesley A. Kort (*Shriven Selves*, pp. 64–89) relates the theocentric doctrine of vocation, Luther's attempt to "rescue daily work from meaninglessness," to Updike's characters' vulnerability and their sacramental understanding of work. The problem of vocation, especially evident in *The Centaur*, is an inclusive concern which comprises a vast range of responsibilities to family and friends, personal integrity, and the awareness of the gap between what one wants to be and what he does. On the other hand, G. F. Waller in "Updike's *Couples*: A Barthian Parable" (*RS* 40:10–21) goes no further than Karl Barth's "compassionate neo-orthodoxy" as the undergirding source for the search for alternative values in a post-Christian Tarbox.

Robert H. Sykes contributes "A Commentary on Updike's Astronomer" (*SSF* 8[1971]:575–79), arguing that Walter is "The Astronomer" rather than the famed Bela. Alison Lurie's "Witches and Fairies: Fitzgerald to Updike" (*NYRB* 17, 2 Dec.[1971]:6–11) is a trivial piece which dips casually into fairy-tale patterns in arbitrarily chosen novels.

viii. Vladimir Nabokov and I. B. Singer

Despite a special segment on Nabokov in *Russian Literature Triquarterly*, no. 3, criticism of both Nabokov and Singer seems to have reached a plateau in both quantity and quality.

The *RLT* contributions range from a ponderous discussion of aesthetic exotica (D. Barton Johnson's "Synesthesia, Polychromatism, and Nabokov," pp. 378–97) to a breezy second look at Nabokov's commentary to his translation of *Eugene Onegin* (Larry Gregg's "Slava Snabokovu," pp. 313–29). Ludmila A. Foster's chronological survey of "Nabokov in Russian Emigré Criticism" (pp. 330–41) is useful scholarship, although the survey reveals that there was no significant shift in émigré attitudes toward Nabokov after World War II. Four pieces deal with specific books, including the self-explanatory ones by Kevin Pilon, "A Chronology of *Pale Fire*" (pp. 370–77), and Carl R. Proffer, "*Ada* as Wonderland: A Glossary of Allusions to Russian Literature" (pp. 399–430). Anthony Olcott in "The Author's Special Intention: A Study of *The Real Life of Sebastian Knight*" (pp. 342–59) shows that Nabokov's first novel in English uses the same devices that were to be made famous in later works: chess images, recurrence of details in unrelated contexts, games. Perhaps the most interesting of all these contributions is Paul Grams's "*Pnin*: The Biographer as Meddler" (pp. 360–69), a study of the liberties which "Nabokov" takes in order to "fictionalize" Pnin's biography. The impersonations of Pnin by his biographer are "literary counterparts of that obsessive imitation by which Cockerell himself is made a victim."

Despite his well-known disparagement of "Old Dusty," Nabokov makes his Humbert Humbert suffer from the Dostoevskian affliction of pedophilia, according to Melvin Seiden's "Nabokov and Dostoevsky" (*ConL* 13:423–44). The art and life of the older novelist lurk behind Nabokov's "buffoon," whose perversion reduces Dostoevsky to "the shabby status of a Russian Irving Wallace."

"The Editing Blinks of Vladimir Nabokov's *The Eye*" (*UWR* 8:5–30) is an exhaustive, precisely detailed reading by Susan Fromberg Schaeffer, who shows that the protagonist's desperate remedy to a failure of a sense of self is to split his consciousness into the "eye" who reflects and the "I" who acts, thus becoming both actor and audience, reflection and reflector. The difference between reality and imaginative creation, a theme which Schaeffer finds in *The Eye*, is never very clear-cut in the major texts of what John Barth calls the "literature of exhaustion," as John Stark demonstrates with commendable brevity in "Borges' 'Tlon, Uqbar, Orbis Tertius' and Nabokov's *Pale Fire*: Literature of Exhaustion" (*TSLL* 14:139–45). Stark, who examines the layers of "reality" in both works, finds a paradox: that this kind of artist, whose working premise is that the imaginary realm of fiction is exhausted, creates works of literature that "assert the primacy of the imagination and add to the total number of fictional works."

In his segment on William Burroughs and Nabokov in *Stages of the Clown* (pp. 84–101), Richard Pearce praises the improvising vitality of the *sotie* fools in *Naked Lunch* and *Lolita*. Though he thinks the latter is the more accomplished "devil's view of the world," his remarks on Burroughs are considerably fresher and more enlightening.

In *Isaac Bashevis Singer* (New York, Ungar) Irving Malin makes some useful distinctions between what he calls Singer's "open novels" (those of historical sweep and scope, with events treated comprehensively) and "closed" ones (those treating the "detailed, symbolic event" in a tight, even claustrophobic way). Malin prefers the short stories and the closed novels because he thinks Singer is more "at home in confined space," one of his links with Kafka, Gogol, and Poe. No innovator, Singer is a writer who uses traditional fable, folktale, and sermon as appropriate forms for a vision which celebrates the tension between the matter-of-fact and the miraculous. Despite an ungainly style—characterized by simple declarative sentences more elliptical than economical, a plethora of italicized phrases, and a fondness for exclamations—Malin's book is valuable for its sensible approach to a writer too often touted by critics overburdened with ethnic pieties. Especially recommended is the segment on the stories, which is not so much explication as a series of suggestive patterns laid out and remarked on through the citation of significant detail.

Elaine Gottlieb's "Singer and Hawthorne: A Prevalence of Satan" (*SoR* 8:359–70) is an exercise in comparison-contrast which because of its oversimplification (of Hawthorne) and its obviousness (about Singer) is of marginal value for serious readers of either author. Gottlieb does not pursue the implications of her inert remark that Singer recently (in *The Séance*) has moved closer to Hawthorne's practice of making Satan a symbolic rather than a literal character.

Paul Rosenblatt and Gene Koppel have compiled *A Certain Bridge: Isaac Bashevis Singer on Literature and Life* (Tucson, Univ. of Ariz. Press, 1971), an interview during which the novelist comments on a variety of topics: religious dogma and fiction, his audience, the relationship of his journalism and his serious writing, his faith in the "story" element in both poetry and fiction, and his notion of the child as the kind of uncorrupted consciousness which he likes to reach through his work.

ix. John Barth, Thomas Pynchon, and John Hawkes

Critique (13,iii) contains a Barth checklist and three essays, the most interesting of which is "Barth's Refutation of the Idea of Progress" (pp. 11–29) by Gordon E. Slethaug, who believes that Ebenezer's life in *The Sot-Weed Factor* disproves his earlier faith in inevitable progress. In *Giles Goat-Boy* the Law of Cyclology is realistically based on imperfection as well as aspiration, and the varied

characters in *Lost in the Funhouse* essentially repeat the development of Ebenezer and Giles. All betray Barth's view that the individual, society, and the cosmos are inherently chaotic.

James L. McDonald, in "Barth's Syllabus: The Frame of *Giles
Goat-Boy*" (pp. 5–10), argues that the front- and end-matter is not a
mere Nabokovian diversion, but a functional element which enables
Barth to surround his artifact (the sacred book *R.N.S.*) with commentary and analysis to register an account of the creative process
involved, an account which gives the sacred book only a hazy authenticity. Carol A. Kyle sees *Lost in the Funhouse* as a "microcosmic
anatomy of criticism" comprising two forms of prose fiction, the
absurd and the autobiographical, but the "The Unity of Anatomy:
The Structure of Barth's *Lost in the Funhouse*" (pp. 31–43) is stronger
when it becomes a guide through the separate stories. Joseph N.
Weixlmann contributes "John Barth: A Bibliography" (pp. 45–55),
including some of the more important book reviews and the tape and
disc recordings of Barth's work.

In *Giles Goat-Boy* Barth responds to two of Eliot's major indictments against the waste land—"the failure to believe in a mythology
and the psychological failure to unify our sensibilities"—says Raymond M. Olderman (*Beyond the Waste Land*, pp. 72–93). In the
context of the campus setting, an apt symbol for the waste land because of the academy's reliance upon rational consciousness and its
denial of mysteries, George's quest for maturity is measured by his
comprehension of the forces that control his life, a progress which
also provides the double structure (mythological and psychological).

Barth's often heard preferences for the writers of "irrealism"
(Borges, Hawkes, Barthelme) and his belief that realism is an "aber-
ration in the history of literature" are repeated in "Having It Both
Ways: A Conversation Between John Barth and Joe David Bellamy"
(*NAR* 15:134–50) and corroborated by Charles B. Harris (*Contemporary American Novelists of the Absurd*, pp. 100–20). Beginning
with *The Sot-Weed Factor* and continuing with *Giles*, Barth, says
Harris, eschews decadence and innovation in favor of ironic, even
farcical, imitations of fictions with connected tales and built-in artificial frames. His burlesque novels become extended metaphors for
his deepest concerns: a protean world plagued by discontinuity, incongruity, and an elusive reality. Harris unfortunately does not dis-

cuss the later work. D. Allan Jones's "The Game of the Name in Barth's *The Sot-Weed Factor*" (*RS* 40:219–21) is an exploration of the denotations and connotations of *Burlingame*.

Raymond M. Olderman's treatment of Pynchon (*Beyond the Waste Land*, pp. 123–49) is remarkably lucid in the explication of what often seem cryptic correspondences in *V*. ("the private individual does in microcosm what the public governments do in macrocosm, thereby raising an individual foible to a public, and perhaps universal, metaphysical principle"). Although a "communal dream of annihilation" is symptomatic of all events in *V*., Olderman convincingly shows that belief in Malta is affirmative because it produces a sense of communion and human endurance. In *The Crying of Lot 49*, Tristero is a metaphor for the narrow range of possibilities; the novella ends, despite the "persistence of terror," on a potentially life-affirming revelation—the coming of a new mystery.

The content of that anticipated revelation is ambiguous, says John R. May, in "Loss of World in Barth, Pynchon, and Vonnegut: The Varieties of Humorous Apocalypse" (*Toward a New Earth*, pp. 172–200). Though Oedipa, like Oedipus, discovers evil within the self, the auction-room apocalypse is humorous, presumably because it suggests that "our worst fears may not materialize." Robert Murray Davis's "Parody, Paranoia, and the Dead End of Language in *The Crying of Lot 49*" (*Genre* 5:367–77) concentrates on Pynchon's rich use of device (parody) and theme (paranoia) in their relation to such key words as *hieroglyphic* and *hieratic* (with their associations of the sacred).

Recently more and more critics agree that one of the basic themes of *V*. is entropy, and Charles B. Harris (*Contemporary American Novelists of the Absurd*, pp. 76–99) identifies the systematic use of entropy as metaphor as Pynchon's most important technique, since that leveling process, translated into social terms, means the "dedifferentiation" of both man and his creations and the shifting of animate man into inanimate automaton. As a secondary metaphor, the quantum theory, translated into fictive terms, means that the principle of uncertainty becomes the rule, never the exception.

In "Nightmare and Fairy Tale in Hawkes' 'Charivari'" (*Crit* 13, i:84–95), James L. Green sees this "satiric epithalamion," with its obsessive mythic-literary parallels, anticipating modes which Hawkes is to perfect in later novels. Despite the happy ending, traditionally associated with the innocence of fairy tale, the self-conscious and malicious narrator finally affirms "the reality of nightmare."

In a superb reading of *The Lime Twig*, Raymond M. Olderman (*Beyond the Waste Land*, pp. 150–75) finds the narrative and thematic center in Banks, whose pursuit of his own image is literalized in the racehorse. The terrorizing conspiracy between man's unconscious desires and the brutal facts of the external world "makes his life a dream of death"—although Banks's final act is redemptive, an example of Hawkes's notion of "cleansing" violence.

One of the most impressive volumes in the Merrill Studies is John Graham's compilation, *Studies in "Second Skin"* (Columbus, Ohio, Charles E. Merrill, 1971), a sampling of reviews, excerpts from the novelist's comments and interviews, some reprinted essays, and five previously unpublished pieces. In "Awakening Paradise" (pp. 52–63) Lucy Frost sees "violent discordance" as a distinctive Hawkesian device which in *Second Skin* accounts for a narrative coherence based on juxtaposition and recurring action, especially that of the voyage, both literal and metaphoric. After making a dispensable catalog of literary modes comprising *Second Skin*, William R. Robinson ("John Hawkes's Artificial Inseminator," pp. 63–69) draws an interesting parallel between Skipper's technological duties and Hawkes's self-conscious artifice, which bends technology to human purposes. If the "miraculous incarnation of spirit in body" is the end to which Hawkes devotes his living art, Skipper must be seen as an affirmative embodiment. Anthony C. Santore, however, takes an uncompromising anti-Skipper position in "Narrative Unreliability and the Structure of *Second Skin*" (pp. 83–93), stressing the ways that the protagonist's self-deception (his second skin) makes him a lying menace instead of a victim or scapegoat, and that the source of the self-deception is impatience and latent homosexuality. Other kinds of coherence, verbal and psychological, depend upon Hawkes's systematic exploitation of some poems by Edwin Honig (to whom *Second Skin* is dedicated), argues Stephen G. Nichols, Jr., in his fine "Vision and Tradition in *Second Skin*" (pp. 69–82). The mingling of realism and fantasy is possible because of the "visionary eye," a technique which Nichols also attributes to Hawkes's use of such ambitiously diffuse works as *The Tempest* and *The Odyssey*. One of the novelist's earliest champions, Albert J. Guerard, suggests some of the sources of the "new tonalities" which he thinks make this novel more accessible than the earlier works. In "*Second Skin*: The Light and Dark Affirmation" (pp. 93–102) Guerard distinguishes between the nuanced, suave, and exquisitely managed rhythms (out of Nabokov, Proust, and Delmore Schwartz), which he likes, and a staccato prose for accommodating the crowded details and "tough talk" (out of Bellow and Mailer), for which he is less enthusiastic.

Norman Lavers finds that "The Structure of *Second Skin*" (*Novel* 5:208–14) follows a parodic Great American Novel, configurations of which derive from Richard Chase and Leslie Fiedler, by paralleling Arcadian romances by Longus and Apuleius; "pastoral" chapters alternate with "melodramatic" ones to suggest the eternal conflict between life-giving love and annihilating hate.

"A Conversation on *The Blood Oranges* Between John Hawkes and Robert Scholes" (*Novel* 5:197–207) reveals the generative importance of *Twelfth Night* for Hawkes's recent novel, which stresses lyricism and idealism, but like most of his fiction still sets a high value on the "capacity to enjoy ugliness and to take a benign interest in the horrible."

x. Joseph Heller, Ken Kesey, and Kurt Vonnegut, Jr.

Wayne Charles Miller uses *Catch-22* and Cozzens's *Guard of Honor* throughout his survey, *An Armed America*, as his examples of opposing fictive expressions of the "divided stream" of war fiction created by World War II. *Catch-22* sums up a tradition which sees a military setting as a microcosm of a larger, often totalitarian, social order.

While Miller sees the source of its distinction in satire, Charles B. Harris (*Contemporary American Novelists*, pp. 33–50) views *Catch-22* as the first novel of the 1960s to match its absurdist themes with appropriate techniques, such as the ironic use of rational language, comic reversals, modulations of the cliché, and anticlimax—all suggesting a culture's inverted values. But Harris believes the ending to be optimistic, and Heller's "non-reflexive burlesque" signals his faith in the power of art to bring about change.

That ending is not quite optimistic, however, for Raymond M. Olderman, who focuses on Yossarian's realization that the killing absurdity of a bureaucratic institution can be conquered only by escape (*Beyond the Waste Land*, pp. 94–116). Although it is true that Yossarian anticipates the later passive hero "who has lost power over his life to something so vague he can only call it a conspiracy," his resolution to go to Sweden seems too hedged by ambiguities to be called "heroic departure." No particularly fresh insights emerge from Lucy Frost's "Violence in the Eternal City: 'Catch-22' as a Critique of American Culture" (*Meanjin* 30[1971]:447–53). Although the evils are social (dehumanization and bureaucratic abstraction), Yossarian's journey through Rome's "underworld of the doomed" reveals truths that had been hidden because of a personal spiritual flaw.

"In Defense of the Grim: A Personal View of the Film Version of *Catch-22*" (*StH* 2,ii[1971]:10–13) contains some pertinent commentary by Thomas Allen Nelson on shifts in cultural sensibility which occurred between the publication of the novel and the making of the movie. His observation that the novel "does not visualize as well as it intellectualizes" is partly corroborated in Richard B. Sale's "An Interview in New York with Joseph Heller" (*SNNTS* 4:63–74), in which we learn that Heller, with great faith in "form" and "aesthetic terms," organized his novel around three combat missions, a scheme established a full year before he began writing. "It takes a lot of planning," says Heller, "to make things seem unplanned."

In his segment on Kesey in *Beyond the Waste Land* (pp. 35–51) Raymond M. Olderman sees *One Flew Over the Cuckoo's Nest* as a romance of the here and now, formally linked to other new romances by the emphasis on caricatures, archetypes, and cartoons in characterization. McMurphy, the redheaded Grail Knight of pop culture, teaches the inmates to be black humorists to fight the desperate sterility of their institutionalized waste land. If the essential shock in traditional American romance, he observes, has been a character's discovery "that deep down he too is capable of evil," the shock in the 1960s is his discovery that "deep down he may be a source of unrelenting insanity."

But McMurphy's role, according to Nicolaus Mills, is to show the men—through laughter—the arbitrariness of the categories *sane* and *insane*. In "Ken Kesey and the Politics of Laughter" (*CentR* 16:82–90) Mills points out that Bromden learns to laugh before he relearns to speak, and does so by directing laughter at himself. McMurphy's modest politics of laughter is not intended to eliminate flaws among his fellows, but to show "that death and failure need not prevent them from acting."

A more specialized study is *"One Flew Over the Cuckoo's Nest* and the Comic Strip" (*Crit* 13,i:96–109). The narrative encourages anti-intellectualism, says Terry G. Sherwood, since it asserts the value of cartoons and TV Westerns as media for transmitting a vision of moral values over a code which asserts moral complexity. "Psychedelic Stimulation and the Creative Imagination: The Case of Ken Kesey" (*SHR* 6:381–91) is James O. Hoge's dispassionate scrutiny of the novelist's commitment to "unrestricted sensorial life" and his dedication to the "ecstasy of the present moment" to account for his celebrated rejection of further verbal communication. Unlike the Romantic poets and the *fin de siècle* Decadents, Kesey proposes sensation as the only standard for experience, and perpetual fantasy as preferable to reality; what results, says Hoge, is a "pitiful, self-defeating demand for protracted sensual euphoria."

Peter J. Reed's *Kurt Vonnegut, Jr.* (New York, Warner) is a first-rate assessment which also provides intelligent summaries of and continuities among the novels. Reed sees in *Player Piano* the most dated of the works because of its curious mixture of dystopian satire and local criticism in the Sinclair Lewis vein; *The Sirens of Titan* is "existential science fiction," which is less concerned with social commentary than with man's relationship to the universe and his own inner being. His chapter on *Mother Night* may be the most perceptive in the book: Reed stresses the function of role playing and the problem of identities in relation to Vonnegut's "Introduction." For all its ambiguities, says Reed, this book of dark dangers is a "morally determinate work." *Cat's Cradle*, which "glories in its own artifice," is called an entertainment; the weakness of *God Bless You, Mr. Rosewater* stems from an overreliance upon the conventions of the traditional novel; and Billy Pilgrim holds *Slaughterhouse-Five* together through his various roles as Everyman, Adam, Christ, and Gulliver.

In contrast to Reed's book, which is meant for beginners and faddists alike, David H. Goldsmith's less ambitious and more nebulous *Kurt Vonnegut: Fantasist of Fire and Ice* (Bowling Green, Ohio, Bowling Green Univ. Popular Press) seems directed at faddists only. In a chapter on "Vonnegut's Cosmos" we are told that the novelist's "teleological tug-of-war" should dispel any lingering urges to slap on him the "disreputable title of science-fiction writer"; in a desultory chapter on "Vonnegut's Technique" Goldsmith grapples inconclusively with style ("fresh" but not "innovative") and narrative patterns which are said to culminate in each book in epiphanies.

Most critics of Vonnegut concentrate on the moral vision behind the satire, and their comments on his technical and formal art are less than stringent. Raymond M. Olderman (*Beyond the Waste Land*, pp. 189–219) is convinced that the power of Vonnegut's fables lies in the deceptively simple way contemporary fact is used. While admitting to a certain want of craft in Vonnegut, Olderman urges us to read him with "different criteria" from other (and better?) novelists, a line disturbingly similar to that of certain liberal white critics of the 1960s who refused to judge black writing; invoking Vonnegut's "passionately honest heart and mind" is not sufficient.

Charles B. Harris (*Contemporary American Novelists*, pp. 51-75) shows some worry about Vonnegut's two-dimensional characters but seems unable to decide whether they burlesque our received notions about realism in the novel or whether they simply mask a frail talent. He is firmer in his discussion of two kinds of illusion treated in the novels: those which contribute to human despair and those which help us to prevent that despair.

L. J. Clancy says bluntly what others suggest gingerly—that Vonnegut has always been happier with ideas than with characters. In "'If the Accident Will': The Novels of Kurt Vonnegut" (*Meanjin* 30[1971]:37–45) he shows the range of this writer's themes to be small and consistent—the dehumanizing effects of war and overpopulation, distrust of government, the personal difficulty of loving, and the complexity of the father-son relationship. Vonnegut's talents, says Clancy, lie in the exploration of social problems, not in the creation of fantasy worlds. Clancy also contributes "'Running Experiments Off'" (*Meanjin* 30[1971]:46–54), an interview with Vonnegut, who discusses the inadequacy of Bruce Jay Friedman's term *black humor* as it applies to him; he prefers *gallows humor*, which more accurately denotes "a response to hopeless situations."

In "*Cat's Cradle* and Traditional American Humor" (*JPC* 5:955-63), W. John Leverence identifies sixteen aspects of American humor (some shaggily overlapping) which he finds in Vonnegut's novels, including Negro minstrelsy, grotesque naturalism, and the device of the humorless narrator. John R. May's "Vonnegut's Humor and the

Limits of Hope" (*TCL* 18:25–36) is primarily on *Cat's Cradle* and is incorporated in *Toward a New Earth*, pp. 172–200. Alfred Kazin finds the Indochina war lurking behind *Slaughterhouse-Five* in "The War Novel: From Mailer to Vonnegut" (*SatR* 54, 6 Feb.[1971]:13–15,36), a nicely done and suave retelling of changes in this genre which everyone else has perceived.

Vonnegut's use of science fiction is of increasing interest. G. K. Wolfe declares, in "Vonnegut and the Metaphor of Science Fiction: *The Sirens of Titan*" (*JPC* 5:964–69), that this second novel thematically and stylistically is related more to his later work than to his first, *Player Piano*, and that *Sirens* is more an "extended allusion to science fiction" than the real thing.

Though he disparages most science fiction, Vonnegut is still not beyond using its psychic, fictional, and philosophical rhetoric, says Gerard W. O'Connor in "The Function of Time Travel in Vonnegut's *Slaughterhouse-Five*" (*RQ* 5:206–07). Gail Landsman agrees, in a more extensive essay, "Science Fiction: The Rebirth of Mythology" (*JPC* 5: 989–96), which focuses primarily upon Vonnegut's treatment of the incomprehensibility of suffering, especially in *The Sirens of Titan* and *Slaughterhouse-Five*: "Our vision of what humanity may become in the *future* helps us to recognize what man is now, just as mythology's depiction of the *past* relates primitive man to his present condition."

Betty Lenhardt Hudgens has compiled *Kurt Vonnegut, Jr.: A Checklist* (Detroit, Gale Research Co.), which includes some juvenilia and the first magazine publication of forty-nine short stories in addition to books, interviews, and blurbs. Vance Bourjaily contributes a personal appreciation of Vonnegut.

xi. Ralph Ellison, James Baldwin, and Other Black Writers

In a kind of semantic meditation, *Black American Literature: Notes on the Problem of Definition* (Muncie, Ind., Ball State Monographs, 1971), Joseph F. Trimmer counters both an "integrationist" aesthetic (art as universal expression) and a "separatist" aesthetic (art as restricted ethnic expression). The values to be affirmed, he says, lie in the process of defining, not the static definition itself, a pattern akin to the real subject of America's literature in general. Though his pamphlet is primarily theoretical, Trimmer uses the writing of several authors as illustration, and one illuminating segment is his explication of LeRoi Jones's aesthetic.

Themes in Sherley Anne Williams's *Give Birth to Brightness: A Thematic Study in Neo-Black Literature* (New York, Dial Press) turn out to be shaggy ("the clash between the old and the new, the past and the future") and obvious ("racial conflict"). Despite its title, this is another study in black character types (here focusing on the "streetman," the heroic version of the trickster). In the course of her book, Williams makes interesting comments on black English, the relation of black streetmen to European picaros, and the need for a more vital kind of criticism of black literature than has yet appeared. Amiri Baraka (LeRoi Jones), James Baldwin, and Ernest Gaines are studied in detail.

Black Portraiture in American Fiction: Stock Characters, Archetypes, and Individuals (New York, Basic Books, 1971) is a sociocultural study by Catherine Juanita Starke based on a wide sampling of both popular and serious literature. Starke seems not to be aware of Sterling Brown's book on Negro stereotypes (though she cites a 1933 essay of Brown's) or of Nancy Tischler's more recent book. This kind of study would seem to be exhausted if we add James M. Mellard's essay on the formulaic aspects of black portraiture in popular fiction and their genesis in the originating culture ("Racism, Formula, and Popular Fiction," *JPC* 5[1971]:10–37) and Floyd C. Watkins's *The Death of Art* (see *ALS 1971*, p. 248).

In an important essay, O. B. Emerson stresses the shaping effects of the Harlem Renaissance on black culturalism, analyzes the ideological ambiguities in Richard Wright, traces the sources of Ralph Ellison's impressionism to Negro "folk identity," and discusses the significance of one important aspect of that identity—the blues—in the works of Ellison and Baldwin. Emerson concludes "Cultural Nationalism in Afro-American Literature" (*The Cry of Home*, pp. 211–44) with the convincing reminder that a new "Negro Renaissance" is now being spearheaded by John A. Williams, Ishmael Reed, and others who have gone beyond anger in order to cultivate a concern for craft.

Although William R. Mueller's thesis in his discussion of *Invisible Man* (*Celebration of Life*, pp. 50–68) improbably equates "identity" with "vocation," the essay itself is pretty standard insofar as it emphasizes Ellison's efforts to dramatize the difficulty of a young Negro to express what he feels rather than what a majority culture encourages him to feel. Sharon R. Weinstein's "Comedy and the Absurd in Ralph Ellison's *Invisible Man*" (*SBL* 3,iii:12–16) views the novel as a man's "education in laughter."

The most substantial piece on Ellison is "Ralph Ellison and the Metaphor of Invisibility in Black Literary Tradition" (*AQ* 24:86–100), in which Todd M. Lieber distinguishes between two metaphors with which black writers have apprehended the dilemma of invisibility: that of "innate or inherent invisibility" (an involuntary tack created by cultural patterns) and that of "mask-wearing" (the conscious adoption of false identities for protection). Through examination of a little-known story of a black flier in World War II, Joseph F. Trimmer calls for a detailed, systematic evaluation of all of Ellison's short fiction, now available only in periodicals ("Ralph Ellison's 'Flying Home'" [*SSF* 9:175–82]). Michael G. Cooke's Twentieth-Century Views volume, *Modern Black Novelists* (Englewood Cliffs, N.J., Prentice-Hall, 1971), contains previously published essays on U.S. writers as well as African and West Indian ones.

Neither Ellison nor Baldwin "sees politics as central to the condition of life," says Donald B. Gibson ("Ralph Ellison and James Baldwin," *The Politics of Twentieth-Century Novelists*, pp. 307–20). *Invisible Man* suggests first radicalism, then anarchy, before ultimately denying both; and in his novels, Baldwin, affirming a belief in a system of values "antecedent to politics," becomes an "institutionalist" who thinks problems can be solved by returning to the moral imperatives inherent in institutions.

David E. Foster argues, in "'Cause My House Fell Down': The Theme of the Fall in Baldwin's Novels" (*Crit* 13,ii:50–62), that man's fall from innocence figures as the important theme in Baldwin's first three novels (though not in *Tell Me How Long the Train's Been Gone*). Redemption by means of Christian grace in *Go Tell It on the Mountain* turns to an ambiguous musing of "fleshly grace" in *Giovanni's Room*; and it shows up in disjointed ways in *Another Country*, where the incoherent mastery of the theme indicates Baldwin's failure to discover an adequate secular alternative to the religious pattern. Fred L. Standley's "*Another Country*, Another Time" (*SNNTS* 4:504–12) is a solid and detailed structural analysis of Baldwin's most ambitious novel. Its plot, which interweaves four narratives in complex relationships through its three sections, makes this work a parable of reconciliation centering on Vivaldo and Ida.

"James Baldwin's Message for White America" (*QJS* 58:142–51) is a textbook exercise in rhetorical analysis by Gregory Mowe and W. Scott Nobles, who trace themes traced earlier by others and belabor the obvious: that Baldwin eschews traditional logic for persuasion.

The inability of Chester Himes, who began his career as a protest writer, to assimilate imaginatively his European phase in fiction is the subject of Edward Margolies's "Experiences of the Black Expatriate Writer: Chester Himes" (*CLAJ* 15:421–27). Instead, Himes re-created Harlem in eight detective novels (1958–1969), which are analyzed in Raymond Nelson's excellent "Domestic Harlem: The Detective Fiction of Chester Himes" (*VQR* 48:260–76). Each novel in the series focuses on a particular "institution" (gambling, numbers, evangelistic Christianity), and one purpose of the series is to evoke "a particular place at a particular moment of history, its customs, speech, topography, occupations, even its food—and record it for posterity." Nelson is particularly fine in his discussions of Himes's "iconographic" violence and the two protagonists, who are symbols of defiance and masculinity for a community forced to play compliant roles. This year also saw the publication of the first volume of Himes's autobiography, *The Quality of Hurt* (Garden City, N.Y., Doubleday).

A new interest in the black naturalist Willard Motley (1912–1965) is almost sure to follow the uncovering of his letters, documents, manuscripts, and memorabilia described in two pieces. "The Willard Motley Papers at the University of Wisconsin" (*RALS* 2:218–73), by Jerome Klinkowitz, James Giles, and John T. O'Brien, is a detailed listing of the materials covering 1957–1963; Klinkowitz and Giles also describe briefly the remainder (mostly uncatalogued) and reprint some relevant correspondence concerning *Knock on Any Door*, in "The Emergence of Willard Motley in Black American Literature" (*NALF* 6,ii:31–34). And in examining an unpublished novel from the latter materials, Charles Wood ("The *Adventure* Manuscript: New Light on Willard Motley's Naturalism," *NALF* 6,ii:35–38) finds a less sordid and deterministic view of man than that suggested in the published work.

Nancy Y. Hoffman, in "The Annunciation of William Demby" (*SBL* 3,i:8–13), sees the black artist as a symbol of human redemption in *The Catacombs*, a novel of exploration and process. John

O'Brien's "Interview with William Demby" (*SBL* 3,iii:1–6) reveals something of this novelist's sources (Virginia Woolf, Camus, Ellison) and interesting first-hand information on *The Catacombs*.

Interest in John A. Williams is increasing. In *"The Man Who Cried I Am*: Crying in the Dark" (*SBL* 3,i:24–32) Ronald Walcott sees Williams's hero enamored of the truth of his individuality in a context of the "obscenely political decade" of the 1960s. The political thrust, however, is that revolution cannot be undertaken for its own sake; it must emerge out of an "affirmative vision of the new world of human community." Robert E. Fleming's " 'Playing the Dozens' in the Black Novel" (*SBL* 3,iii:23–24) is a suggestive note on this cultural practice in *The Man Who Cried I Am* and *Invisible Man*. The protagonist's sense of identity, however, has its substance only in pain (hemorrhoids, rectal cancer), says Anneliese H. Smith in "A Pain in the Ass: Metaphor in John A. Williams' *The Man Who Cried I Am*" (*SBL* 3,iii:25–27).

Phyllis R. Klotman discusses the recurrent figure of the "Running Man" in three writers (William Kelley, Douglas Turner Ward, and Ronald L. Fair) and concludes that his apparently evasive action is a social rather than a solitary act ("The Passive Resistant in *A Different Drummer, Day of Absence* and *Many Thousands Gone*," *SBL* 3,iii:7–12). Jerry H. Bryant surveys two little-known writers—one, who since 1948 has virtually disappeared from bookshelves and histories, in "Individuality and Fraternity: The Novels of William Gardner Smith" (*SBL* 3,ii:1–8). Then in *"From Death to Life*: The Fiction of Ernest J. Gaines" (*IowaR* 3,i:106–20) he finds a sense of depth, humanity, and honesty in the work of a writer who began his career in 1963; Bryant believes Gaines's superbly sustained control of black Southern dialect is unmatched by his contemporaries. Stanley Schatt compiles "LeRoi Jones: A Checklist to Primary and Secondary Sources" (*BB* 28[1971]:55–57), part 2 of which is an annotated survey of secondary materials.

xii. Donald Barthelme, Richard Brautigan, and Others

In "Donald Barthelme's City: A Guide" (*TCL* 18:37–44) Francis Gillen claims that Barthelme's importance lies in his exploration of pop culture transmitted through mass media. Because of the "barrage of equally accentuated 'nowness,' " which reduces everything to trivia, man is caught between "undifferentiated fact and equally meaningless abstractions," and this in-between area is Barthelme's bailiwick.

"Thoughts on the Principle of Allegory" (*Genre* 5:327–52) is a pretentious and inconclusive essay by Gayatri C. Spivak, who discusses allegory in Rilke, Lawrence, Claude Simon, and Barthelme. *Unspeakable Practices, Unnatural Acts* falls into the "socially didactic" category, but even Spivak acknowledges that Barthelme has an "aggressively anti-allegoric" side. "From Breton to Barthelme: Westward the Course of Surrealism" (*Proceedings* 22[1971]:208–14), George Wickes's account of American acculturation of the French aesthetic of the 1920s, names Barthelme among the practitioners of the post-modern American authors.

Wickes also believes Richard Brautigan to be one of the "ubiquitous" surrealists currently writing, but for Kenneth Seib, Brautigan's is simply "a hipster's view of America's square-world ethics." In "*Trout Fishing in America*: Brautigan's Funky Fishing Yarn" (*Crit* 13,ii:63–71), Seib praises the unified structure, but he still sees it mostly as a hip collage of Rod McKuen, Franklin, Gatsby, Natty Bumppo, Hemingway, and Richard Chase. "Some Observations on *A Confederate General from Big Sur*" (*Crit* 13,ii:72–82) is an accurately titled, halfhearted little piece by Gerald Locklin and Charles Stetler, whose remarks fall somewhere between the level of trendy aphorisms and study guide questions for sophomores. *A Confederate General* may well be "a very funny, very sad, and very important novel," but these critics fail to demonstrate that judgment.

Raymond M. Olderman devotes space in his *Beyond the Waste Land* to two lesser-known authors, Stanley Elkin (pp. 52–71) and Peter S. Beagle (pp. 220–42). The first segment is a detailed study of Elkin's *A Bad Man*, whose protagonist is a supersalesman who neither hates nor loves before he is led to a love of all things in a "song of himself," which catalogues familiar human activities in a gesture of affirmation. Olderman's segment on Beagle concentrates on *The Last Unicorn*, an allegory of tenuous compassion focusing on both the wonder of the imagination and the wonder of the world.

Daniel J. Cahill's "Jerzy Kosinski: Retreat from Violence" (*TCL* 18:121–32) tries to show that however unrelieved the darkness and irrationality of his world, Kosinski's "acute cultural and spiritual dramatizations are reflective of hope"; despite some bolstering from the writings of Erik Erikson, the point is not persuasive. Metal Lale and John S. Williams cite Anna Freud for their rather simple thesis in "The Narrator of *The Painted Bird*: A Case Study" (*Renascence* 24:198–206)—that while Kosinski's young protagonist bears psychic wounds from his ordeal, the prognosis for his adulthood is good.

William V. Davis's "Fathers and Sons in the Fiction of Edward Wallant" (*RS* 40:53–55) is self-explanatory, but its brevity is a disservice to its subject. A bit more substantial is Davis's "The Renewal of Dialogic Immediacy in Edward Lewis Wallant" (*Renascence* 24: 59–69), which cites the major themes of the four novels (search for faith and love, the meaning of suffering, and the quest for "fatherhood and sonship"), one of which, *Children at the Gate*, is "almost a Christian parable." Both Davis and Robert W. Lewis, in "The Hung-up Heros [sic] of Edward Lewis Wallant" (*Renascence* 24:70–84), announce that *The Tenants of Moonbloom* is Wallant's masterpiece. Lewis places the other novels in the Dreiserian naturalistic tradition, but Moonbloom as hero is endowed with mythic and symbolic attributes.

"*The Onion Eaters* and the Rhetoric of Donleavy's Comedy" (*TCL* 18:167–74) is a perceptive essay by Thomas LeClair, who feels that J. P. Donleavy's sympathetic treatment of vulnerability repels rather than attracts the reader's sympathy, primarily because he fails in this novel to establish a climate of psychological realism. Henrietta Ten Harmsel's comparison of "'Young Goodman Brown' and 'The Enormous Radio'" (*SSF* 9:407–08) is adequate without being very original: John Cheever, like Hawthorne, deals basically with the "universal dilemma of maintaining a balanced humanity in a world where evil seems to overwhelm the good."

Mark Taylor's "Baseball as Myth" (*Commonweal* 96:237–39) is on Robert Coover's *The Universal Baseball Association*, which "demythologizes the sacred by exploring its profane sources." Coover, says Taylor, suggests that the cosmos is man's creation, another evidence of man's imaginative transcendence over his banal existence. Gordon Weaver conducts "An Interview with Charles East" (*NMW* 4:87–108), the author of *Where the Music Was*; and L. Moody Simms, Jr., contributes a biographical and critical sketch of the little-known "Edward Kimbrough: Mississippi Novelist" (*NMW* 4:109–14).

Leonard Lutwack believes that Ross Lockridge's single novel, like *The Octopus* and *The Sot-Weed Factor*, contains an "epicising poet who fails" in his grand efforts but whose creator goes on to write a novel fulfilling the requirements of the epic. He describes the intersecting of historical and mythical planes in *"Raintree County* and the Epicising Poet in American Fiction" (*BSUF* 13,i:14–28), a process both Homeric and Joycean. Lutwack's is a painstaking and fascinating analysis of a novel that deserves more attention.

Jerome Klinkowitz's "Getting Real: Making It (Up) with Ronald Sukenick" (*ChiR* 23,iii:73–82) is an introductory appreciation of the author of *Up*, which recounts the fictive process of a "Ronald Sukenick" toward a supreme fiction "which adequately handles the real." For this young author, seeking rapport with the real (as for Wallace Stevens, whose work he knows well) is "a way of making it through life," and that way is still the imagination. Sukenick makes his own case for giving up "that business about illusion" and suspending disbelief in fiction in Joe David Bellamy's "Imagination as Perception: An Interview with Ronald Sukenick" (*ChiR* 23,iii:59–72).

Wesley A. Kort's fine discussion of Peter DeVries (*Shriven Selves*, pp. 36–63) notes the shaping influence of Dutch Calvinism on the novelist's later protagonists, who accept the fact that transcendent power is insensitive to or even hostile toward them; in fact, says Kort, DeVries's work in the 1960s is consistent in method and vision with that of Heller, Barth, Hawkes, and Kesey.

Alfred S. Shivers's *Jessamyn West* (TUSAS 192) is the first full-length assessment of this "unconventional Quaker," and it emphasizes her fidelity to physical detail and historical accuracy in both the Indiana and California novels. In the course of his study, which is both scholarly and original, Shivers suggests that the Birdwell stories of *The Friendly Persuasion* (1945) and *Except for Me and Thee* (1969) should be combined into one collection and offers a chronological sequence of the twenty-five stories. Shivers also contributes a West checklist, "Jessamyn West" (*BB* 28[1971]:1–3). In analyzing "The Fiction of Jessamyn West" (*IMH* 67[1971]:299–316), John T. Flanagan finds her chief strengths to be the mastery of colloquial diction, the psychology of adolescence, and a firm sense of place.

Agnes Sibley's *May Sarton* (TUSAS 213) is a straightforward and useful introduction to both the poetry and the fiction, the latter which deals with the Belgium-born writer's interest in the impact of

European and American cultures and the related themes of detachment and exile. The need for love, not passion, is a consistent concern, says Sibley—a love which Sarton describes in *The Bridge of Years* as "positive detachment." Similarly, Dawn Holt Anderson characterizes "May Sarton's Women" (*Images of Women*, pp. 243–50) as "models" who require solitude for realizing their own identities and comes to the chilling conclusion that for Sarton sexual relationships are "debilitating" to personal growth.

Bernard Wolfe (TUSAS 211) is a study of the author of *The Great Prince Died* by Carolyn Geduld, who aptly describes it and earlier works as "political novels rationalized by psychoanalysis." This eccentric and eclectic writer is also adept, says Geduld, at satire and parody and a complex form of science fiction. In "Erich Segal as Little Nell: or, The Real Meaning of *Love Story*" (*JPC* 5: 782–98), Mark Spilka calls the heroine "Erich Segal in drag" and finds the novel laced with "homoerotic fears and revulsions." Fans of Seymour Krim will be interested in his "An Enemy of the Novel" (*IowaR* 3,i:60–62) in which he calls his work "personal, political, critical, journalistic, evangelistic."

Finally, several checklists should be noted. George E. Bush's "James Purdy" (*BB* 28[1971]:5–6) comprises works from 1956 "to the present"; Margaret S. Grissom's "Shirley Ann Grau" (*BB* 28 [1971]:76–78) is a primary checklist which includes some of the author's college contributions; and Lynda Lee Rushing's "William S. Burroughs: A Bibliography" (*BB* 29:87–92) begins with 1958 and includes the category-defying "Burroughs' creations."

Indiana University

14. Poetry: 1900 to the 1930s

Alvin H. Rosenfeld

i. General

There continues to be substantial scholarly and critical interest in American poets of the early decades of this century, an interest whose scope would be more impressive still if it were possible to include T. S. Eliot in this chronological grouping. With his exclusion, Pound appears the poet of greatest prominence, followed by Frost and Crane. In general, however, the tenor of much of this work is fragmentary and constrictive, as poems and authors tend to be treated individually and within the compass of closely defined critical aims rather than in more encompassing ways. A broader-ranging, more integrative effort is clearly in order but does not seem imminent. There is also a noticeable lack of evaluative criticism, with the result that the canon of our early-twentieth-century poets is already well established, albeit by standards of judgment that are no longer clearly apparent and perhaps no longer even consciously operative.

Doctoral dissertations were fairly widely distributed: five each on Pound and Frost, three on Crane, two each on Cummings and Aiken, and one each on Robinson, Jeffers, Ransom, Davidson, Stephen Vincent Benét, and Adelaide Crapsey; there were also two dissertations on poetry published in American magazines between 1912 and 1922.

The Explicator (Vols. 30–31) published seven items on Frost, four on Cummings, two on Robinson, and one on Ransom. (For brief notes of explication on Pound, see the commentary on *Paideuma* below).

Modern American Poetry, edited by Guy Owen (Deland, Fla , Everett/Edwards) reprints essays on seven poets of this period. David R. Clark's *Lyric Resonance: Glosses on Some Poems of Yeats, Frost, Crane, Cummings and Others* (Amherst, Univ. of Mass. Press) is mostly a gathering of the author's published criticism on modern poets, including Frost, Crane, and Cummings; however, the Crane section introduces some new material, which will be noticed below.

ii. Ezra Pound

Donald Davie concludes his review of Hugh Kenner's *The Pound Era*, "The Universe of Ezra Pound" (*Paideuma* 1:263–69), with an appeal that his fellow Poundians are almost certain to ignore: "From now on, there ought to be fewer books about Pound; and those few, if they are to justify themselves, will have to be very good." This is a necessary and understandable plea, but, as this year's scholarly production shows, it is not one that is likely to persuade: 1972 brought three new books on Pound (following three last year) and five dissertations (following last year's seven). In the last half-dozen years we have had some twenty-five books on Pound and hundreds of articles, essays, notes, and reviews. Whether the early decades of this century can properly be called "the Pound Era," as Hugh Kenner has designated them, is a debatable point, but there is no question that in the area of literary scholarship covered in this chapter we are deep into a "Pound Era" and one that shows no signs of soon tapering off.

Sister Bernetta Quinn's *Ezra Pound: An Introduction to the Poetry* (New York, Columbia Univ. Press), while written ostensibly for the non-specialist, is better suited for students of modern poetry who are already more than casually familiar with Pound's life and work. The biographical chapter suffers from a tendency to idealize the man and whitewash his politics; in this respect, the author continues that line of sentimentalism prominent in Pound scholarship that insists on treating Pound as a maligned and grossly mistreated moral genius. The chapter on Pound as preceptor is better for being less obviously partisan, but it does not go beyond being a light survey of the prose writings. A study of the early lyrics is more substantial and offers some helpful commentary on the technical and religious aspects of selected poems; this chapter is noteworthy for the dissenting opinion it takes on "Hugh Selwyn Mauberley." An informative chapter is devoted to Pound's translations from the Chinese, Japanese, Latin, Greek, Provençal, Tuscan, and Old English. The feature of the book, however, is its last two chapters, which are devoted to the Cantos. The author's wide knowledge of Pound is put to fruitful use here, and her treatment of *Thrones* is especially enlightening; specialists as well as those new to the poetry will benefit from Sister Quinn's explication of some of the more recondite historical material in the Cantos.

A more specialized book is Stuart Y. McDougal's *Ezra Pound and the Troubador Tradition* (Princeton, N. J., Princeton Univ. Press), a brief but admirably well focused study of Pound's relationship to the troubadors of medieval Provence—especially Arnaut Daniel, Bertran de Born, Arnaut de Mareuil, and Peire Bremon lo Tort. McDougal successfully pursues Pound's interests in these poets from the period of his earliest involvement with them as a young student and shows how he progressed from literal translations through more inventive translations to original poems that adapt Provençal themes and forms. The chronological scope of this study embraces in the main those works published by Pound between 1909 and 1919, but in a final chapter the author touches on some of the Cantos as well. He is especially good at discussing against their original sources such poems as "Marvoil," "Piere Vidal Old," "Sestina: Altaforte," "Na Audiart," "Near Perigord," and "Homage à la Langue d'Oc" and in demonstrating how, under the influence of the troubadors, Pound discovered new poetic forms and helped to free his language from the diction of the Pre-Raphaelites. A chapter on Pound's love ethic as derivative of values from medieval Tuscany and Provençal is also helpful.

Critics on Ezra Pound, edited by E. San Juan, Jr. (Coral Gables, Fla., Univ. of Miami Press), reprints excerpts from the work of twenty-three authors and publishes for the first time the editor's article "Ezra Pound's Craftsmanship: An Interpretation of *Hugh Selwyn Mauberley.*" The reprinted criticism, consisting chiefly of brief fragments (some no longer than a single page), is clearly meant for undergraduates; on the other hand, the editor's own contribution (which is seriously hampered by a penchant for an excessively abstract prose) is a full-length attempt at studying the "Mauberley" poem in terms of its formal structure and is obviously meant for another kind of readership, thus making for a strangely incongruous book.

A major addition to Pound studies is *Paideuma: A Journal Devoted to Ezra Pound Scholarship* (edited by Hugh Kenner and Eva Hesse, with the further editorial collaboration of Donald Davie, Donald Gallup, Lewis Leary, and Carroll F. Terrell). Two numbers appeared in 1972, and plans are to have three or more numbers appear annually hereafter. The journal will publish full-length scholarly and critical articles, smaller notes of explication, biographical information, documentary material, reviews, photographs, and notes and queries. Featured in the first number are John Peck's lengthy descriptive article on "Pound's Lexical Mythography" (pp. 3–36), a comparative study by Walter B. Michaels of "Pound and Erigena" (pp. 37–54), Donald Davie's historical and topographical guide, "The Cantos: Towards a Pedestrian Reading" (pp. 55–62), and John Espey's study of classical sources, "Towards Propertius" (pp. 63–74). Explications are offered by Hugh Kenner ("The 5 Laws and *Che Funge*," p. 83), Eva Hesse ("Frobenius as Rainmaker," pp. 85–88), and William M. Chase ("The Canto as Cento: A Reading of Canto XXXIII," pp. 89–100); Donald Gallup presents a small selection of "Letters to Viola Baxter Jordan" (pp. 107–11) and rounds out the first number with "Corrections and Additions to the Pound Bibliography" (pp. 113–25).

Paideuma no. 2 features Eva Hesse's learned "Books Behind *The Cantos*, Part One" (pp. 137–51), Lewis Leary's commentary on the correspondence concerning *Motive and Method in the Cantos of Ezra Pound*, "Pound-Wise, Penny-Foolish" (pp. 153–59, reprinted with additions from *StAR*; see *ALS 1970*, p. 285), and Daniel Pearlman's detailed source study, "Alexander Del Mar in *The Cantos*: A Printout of the Sources" (pp. 161–80). Included as well are several notes of explication, the most suggestive of which is Gary R. Libby's "Image or image: An Unnoticed Allusion in 'Hugh Selwyn Mauberley'" (pp. 205–06); Richard Stern's brief but revealing biographical sketch, "A Memory or Two of Mr. Pound" (pp. 215–19); some interesting documentary material, especially Robert A. Corrigan's extensive annotated checklist of critical responses to Pound's early verse, 1904–1917 (pp. 229–60; this supersedes the author's earlier version, "The First Quarter Century of Ezra Pound Criticism," *RALS* 2:157–207); and Davie's review of *The Pound Era* (pp. 263–69). *Paideuma* has already established itself as the major periodical exclusively devoted to Pound scholarship, and while its appeal is clearly to specialists, it will have to be consulted by all serious scholars in the field.

The debate over Pound's merits as a poetic spokesman for his age and the extent to which these may have been seriously compromised by his political behavior during World War II revived in 1972 with

a flurry of personal testaments, belletristic essays, and letters to the
editors of prominent newspapers. The issue was generated, at least
in part, by a campaign to secure the Nobel Prize for the aging poet
(who was to die in the fall of 1972), and voices were heard on each
side. Thus Henry Regnery, in a biographical essay marked by exaggerated claims, "Eliot, Pound and Lewis: A Creative Friendship"
(*ModA* 16:146–60), reviews the careers of the three authors, whose
primary aims, as he sees and extols them, were "to defend civilized
values." Contrastingly, a sterner, more vigorously argued, and far
more persuasive view is presented by Irving Howe in "The Return
of the Case of Ezra Pound" (*World* 1,ix:20–24). Howe offers a sober
review of Pound's Fascism and anti-Semitism, in the poetry itself as
well as in the infamous radio broadcasts, and concludes that the poet
was "a generous man committed to a murderous ideology."

A new and most valuable study of Pound's career as a broadcaster,
propagandist, and popularist is Robert A. Corrigan's "Ezra Pound
and the Italian Ministry for Popular Culture" (*JPC* 5:767–81). Working from U.S. Justice Department transcripts of Pound's broadcasts
over Radio Rome, Corrigan amply documents Pound's involvements
as a Fascist broadcaster with lengthy quotations from these radio
texts, the majority of which have remained unpublished and unknown to date. The material that Corrigan presents, filled as it is
with the poet's rantings against Roosevelt and the Jews, bears out
the author's point that "on the basis of such material, the government
had a better case against Pound than has ever been made public."

The same author documents a further dispute involving Pound
in "*What's My Line*: Bennett Cerf, Ezra Pound and the *American
Poet*" (*AQ* 24:101–13). The issue this time involved the exclusion
of Pound from a Modern Library anthology of British and American
poetry; the controversy, which developed late in 1945 and foreshadowed the storm that was to develop over the awarding of the
1949 Bollingen Prize, is skillfully reconstructed by Corrigan in another eminently readable piece of literary and cultural history. On
the basis of these two articles, Corrigan's book in progress on Pound's
turbulent relationship with America during World War II and the
decades immediately following promises to be a major study.

Pound defined an epic as a long poem containing history, and it
is not surprising that much recent criticism has been concerned with
excavating the various layers of history within the Cantos. In "The

Historical Pattern in Ezra Pound's Cantos" (*HAB* 22,iii[1971]:11–21),
P. L. Surette opposes the view (initiated by Yeats and carried on
principally by Kenner) that the Cantos represent a radical form of
modernist art and one that makes the poem barely accessible to the
traditional ways of literary criticism. To Surette the poem has a discernible and significant content ("history structured in terms of the
paradigmatic history of Troy") which will "yield its meanings by
the ordinary methods of literary analysis." Surette shifts away from
a concentration on technique, therefore, and offers an outline for
such an historical reading of the poem.

In an informative and highly readable article, "The City of Dioce,
U.S.A.: Pound and America" (*BuR* 20,ii:13–34), the same author
examines Pound's efforts to incorporate aspects of American history
in the cantos; the major focus is on the ten-year period 1924–34 and
hence on *Eleven New Cantos*. Not surprisingly, Pound's search for
an American hero resulted in the emergence of a figure far closer to
Pound's image of himself than to the historic Jefferson or Adams.

Pound's connection to his Victorian predecessors continues to attract scholarly attention and is the subject of two new articles. Jacob
Korg's "The Music of Lost Dynasties: Browning, Pound and History"
(*ELH* 39:420–40) is a densely written study of the ways in which the
two poets attempted to redeem "the inarticulate turmoil of history
. . . through the ordering power of art." The focus is on *Sordello*,
The Ring and the Book, and the Cantos. Ron D. K. Banerjee's principal interest in "Dante Through the Looking Glass: Rossetti, Pound,
and Eliot" (*CL* 24:136–49) is Eliot, and more specifically "La Figlia
che Piange," but students of Pound will also profit from this learned
comparative study of Dante's influence on the three poets; Banerjee
discusses Pound's "Donzella Beata," "Ballatetta," and "Francesca"
against Rossetti's "Blessed Damozel," a poem that served both Pound
and Eliot as a bridge back to Dante.

In an interesting essay that is as much a philosophical meditation
and personal testament as it is a study of Pound ("Notes on the Cantos of Ezra Pound," *HudR* 25:51–70), Richard Pevear directs attention to the complexities of time, history, epic, vision, cosmos, Christianity, and tradition as subjects germane to a consideration of the
Cantos. Pevear confesses that "a feeling of wholeness in the Cantos
. . . is very hard to explain," but nonetheless insists on the existence of
artistic coherence in Pound's long poem, a coherence owing to

Pound's "attentiveness to the existence of poetry in image and embodiment." As here, the language of this essay is frequently vague
and private, but Pevear is highly suggestive and merits reading all
the same.

Louis Dudek writes with a fellow poet's admiration for the linguistic richness and variety of Pound's poetry in "Exotic References in
the Cantos of Ezra Pound" (*AntigR* 11:55–66) and asks for more
learning and patience on the part of readers who are puzzled or re-
pelled by the poet's heavy use of foreign languages. Dudek, who
admits that much of the Cantos may be parody or macaronic farce,
nevertheless finds great nobility in Pound's work, which expresses
to him the elements "of a mystery religion," an idea that he unfortunately does not pursue further in this article.

In a valuable essay, "Ezra Pound and George Antheil: Vorticist
Music and the *Cantos*" (*AL* 44:52–73), William Walter Hoffa studies
Pound's interests in the American composer, whose musical achievements he greatly exaggerated but whose ideas he obviously felt close
to. Hoffa presents a comprehensive review of Pound's relationship to
Antheil and argues persuasively that the music of the Cantos should
be appreciated in terms of the rhythms and tensions of twentieth
century music rather than against the musical forms of the past.

Some miscellaneous articles remain to be mentioned. William
Fleming ("The Melbourne Vortex," *AntigR* 9:73–77) offers a brief
but engaging account of a Poundian "underground" in Melbourne in
the mid-1950s and of three periodicals (*New Times, Edge,* and
Meanjin) that were publishing material by and about Pound during
these years. Fleming reveals that Pound used a variety of pseud-
onyms in publishing "innumerable paragraphs, notes and features" in
these periodicals, but he is of the opinion that "it would today be an
impossible (and useless) task to extricate the Pound material from
that of his imitators." In "Ezra Pound's Relationship with Fenollosa
and the Japanese Noh Plays" (*MarkhamR* 3:21–27), Nobuko T.
Keith examines Pound's occasional references to the Noh plays in
the Cantos and concludes that although Noh "never became a major
influence on Pound," the poet may have "found the validity and
justification of his theory of the Imagisme in the Noh plays." G.
Singh's "Meeting Ezra Pound" (*DA* 46.403–09) records some of the
poet's conversation, including a few passing judgments on literary
figures, but otherwise does not provide any pertinent biographical

information. Maurice Hungiville in "Ezra Pound, Educator: Two Uncollected Pound Letters" (*AL* 44:462–69) prints two minor letters that Pound wrote to Joseph Brewer, president of Olivet College, in 1938; these are written in Pound's familiar and cranky epistolary style, but, in themselves, are not substantial enough to reveal much about Pound as educator.

iii. Frost and Robinson

With the exception of a Japanese study, Shichinosuke Anzai's *Robert Frost no Shi* (Tokyo, Taigenshobo), this year saw no new critical books on Frost, but Arnold Grade's edition of the *Family Letters of Robert and Elinor Frost* (Albany, State Univ. of N. Y. Press) is a worthy addition to the biographical literature. The volume brings together 182 previously unpublished letters written by Frost and his wife to their children and grandchildren between 1914 and 1963; Elinor Frost is the author of fifty of these; the rest belong to the poet. Editorial apparatus has been kept to a minimum, but brief notes are appended to most letters, and these, plus a Frost family chronology and an index featuring subject subheadings, help the reader find his way with little difficulty. Lesley Frost, the family's eldest daughter and the recipient of some three-quarters of the letters, has written a brief foreword, and Grade has added an afterword. The letters themselves offer a valuable interior view of the Frosts' family life and touch on a variety of subjects, including literary ones. Of particular interest are two letters to Lesley Frost in which the poet discusses the skills of expository prose writing (letter of 17 February 1919) and offers some detailed remarks on the origins and contributions of the imagist movement in poetry (undated letter of 1934, pp. 160 ff.). The volume, the fourth collection of Robert Frost letters to appear, adds substantially to the biographical record and should be welcomed by scholars.

Of lesser merit is Robert Francis's *Frost: A Time to Talk* (Amherst, Univ. of Mass. Press), which tells us far more about the author than it does about Frost himself; consequently, the scholarly value of this collection of "conversations and indiscretions" must be deemed slight. Francis knew Frost intermittently during the 1930s and 1950s and writes about the meetings he had with him during these years, but except for offering a few memorable snatches of Frost's conversation, this volume makes little contribution to our knowledge of either the poet or the man. Remembrances of Frost that seldom rise above the merely anecdotal tend to seem trivial and self-serving and should be discouraged.

Another example of this vein of writing is Wade Van Door's "In Robert Frost's Rubbers" (*MQR* 11:122–26). This brief essay, expressing an unabashed hero worship of Frost on the one hand and, on the other, some nasty *ad hominem* attacks against his biographer Lawrance Thompson, is reminiscent of some of the early sycophantic "defenses" of Walt Whitman written in the nineteenth century. Frost does not stand in need of any such "defense" as this, and one hopes that those among his numerous acquaintances still alive will realize as much and relax from publishing their loyalist testimonies.

"A Trip to Currituck, Elizabeth City, and Kitty Hawk, 1894" (*NCarF* 16[1968]:3–8) is a transcription of a tape-recorded conversation of March 3, 1961, at the University of North Carolina, in which Frost reflects on a trip he had made to Kitty Hawk, N. C., in 1894. His impressions of these events some sixty-five years later are still remarkably vivid, but Frost was unable to remember anything about his time in Kitty Hawk that might have influenced his poem by that title.

The most enlightening critical article on Frost published this year is Donald T. Haynes's "The Narrative Unity of *A Boy's Will*" (*PMLA* 87:452–64). Haynes returns to the original version of the text to study the narrative cycle of Frost's first published book; later versions eliminated the poet's prose gloss on thirty of the original thirty-two poems and eliminated as well the division of the volume into three parts; three poems were also omitted and one added. Haynes offers a close scrutiny of the text in light of the restorations he makes and concludes that it comprises "a series of lyrics arranged into a narrative cycle which traces the development of a youth from initial withdrawal to final return to society, and from initial interest in, to final, mature acceptance of his poetic vocation." In addition to presenting this narrative scheme and placing numerous poems within it, Haynes argues that a symbolic landscape and seasonal cycle are basic to the book's design, that flower picking and mowing are recurrent acts of specific symbolic importance, and that moments of dreaming are consistently identified with creativity. Despite the intricate presence of these elements within the book, it "does not succeed as narrative," in Haynes's view, and must be considered "a false start." The article is a major effort at studying the early Frost, and its methods and conclusions should pose significant challenges to other Frost scholars.

John Morris in "The Poet as Philosopher: Robert Frost" (*MQR* 11:127–34) explores some of the ways in which Frost demonstrated philosophical problems in his poetry; Morris offers an intriguing Biblical interpretation of "Maple" and an interesting Bergsonian gloss on "The Road Not Taken."

Eban Bass ("Frost's Poetry of Fear," *AL* 43:603–15) reviews a large number of poems in which fear plays a role as either a private experience or an intruder on marriage, but the author oddly comes to no new conclusions about his subject; this article promises far more than it finally delivers, for at the end the only knowledge we are left with is that which we already knew at the start, namely, that Frost's poetry is frequently shadowed by fear.

Laurence Perrine, making effective use of Biblical sources, probes the moral question of accepting or turning away a stranger in his brief but persuasive explication, "The Dilemma in Frost's 'Love and a Question'" (*CP* 5,ii:5–8); Perrine offers both a literal and a semi-allegorical reading of the poem and shows how the fundamental dilemma of moral choice in "Love and a Question" foreshadows the basic situation of "The Death of the Hired Man" and "Two Tramps in Mud Time."

Frank Lentricchia offers a belabored reading of the poem in "Experience as Meaning: Robert Frost's 'Mending Wall'" (*CEA* 34,iv:8–12); the author works out his explication in an effort to show the continuing value of New Critical method, but his exhibit is too petite to support his rather heavy labors, and the references to Kant are out of place for the poem at hand.

In an unexpected but informative article, "A Poulterer's Pleasure: Robert Frost as Prose Humorist" (*SSF* 8[1971]:589–99), C. W. Geyer calls attention to the eleven pieces of short comic fiction that Frost wrote for New England poultry journals during the years 1900–1909. (These have been collected in *Robert Frost: Farm-Poultryman*—see *ALS 1964*, p. 181—but have been overlooked in the main by other scholars.) Geyer shows that the eleven stories can be revealing of

Frost's knowledge of native humor, that they draw upon traditions of oral folklore, and that there are thematic parallels with some of Frost's early poetry.

In a brief note, "Longfellow's 'Sleep' and Frost's 'After Apple-Picking'" (*AN&Q* 10:134–35), Kenneth T. Reed suggests Longfellow's sonnet 'Sleep' as a prime source for Frost's poem and notes some of the similarities between the two poems. Richard Dillingham's "The Value of Social Conservatism According to Robert Frost" (*SAB* 37,iv:61–65) briefly explores Frost's attachment to holding opposing forces in equilibrium, an act of personal balance which the author sees somewhat too insistently in social terms.

There were no book-length studies of Robinson published in 1972, but the *Colby Library Quarterly* devoted the whole of its spring number (ser. 9, no. 9) to the poet. In "Robinson's Poets" (pp. 441–55), Nancy Joyner, acknowledging that Robinson left behind no comprehensive prose statements about his vocation, goes to the poems themselves in an attempt to clarify some of the bases upon which Robinson constructed his art. The largest part of her study is devoted to consideration of the satirical poems "Captain Craig" and *Amaranth*, but Joyner also reviews a number of Robinson's poems on poetry and on other poets and shows how these express Robinson's significant, if unsystematic, attitudes about poetry.

"The Man Against the Sky" remains a pivotal poem in Robinson's canon, and its central concerns with religious faith and the problems posed to faith by the modern world have attracted numerous critics. Robert S. Fish strangely ignores these in his dramatic and rhetorical analysis of the poem, "The Tempering of Faith in E. A. Robinson's 'The Man Against the Sky'" (pp. 456–68); some attention to the studies of H. H. Waggoner and David Hirsch in particular would have challenged and enhanced the author's argument.

Celia Morris, contending that Robinson is more a reflective than a narrative poet, explores the use of Arthurian material in *Merlin* and *Lancelot* in her clarifying study, "Robinson's Camelot: Renunciation as Drama" (pp. 468–81); the author finds Robinson close to Henry James in his interest in exploring the limitations and failures of human relationships and shows, through detailed examination of *Merlin*, how Robinson drew parallels between his characters' love affairs and the fall of the kingdom; the final, characteristic note of these poems is renunciation.

In a biographical essay, "Mowry Saben About Edwin Arlington Robinson" (pp. 482–97), Richard Cary establishes the ambivalent terms that marked the long friendship between Saben and Robinson and reviews the former's mixed opinions ("an amalgam of warts and worship") on Robinson as man and poet; five new letters from Saben to Denham Sutcliffe about Robinson are brought to light.

Another of Robinson's long friendships, that with his fellow poet and townsman from Gardiner, Maine, Mrs. Laura E. Richards, is described by Robert J. Scholnick in his informative article, "The Shadowed Years: Mrs. Richards, Mr. Stedman, and Robinson" (*CLQ* 9:510–31). Mrs. Richards regarded Robinson as "a kind of adopted son" and attempted to aid him in various ways, including numerous appeals to Edmund Clarence Stedman, the New York critic and anthologist, to take an interest in Robinson. Scholnick presents and helpfully comments on a gathering of previously unpublished letters between Mrs. Richards and Stedman in defining this three-sided friendship.

Charles A. Sweet, Jr., offers a novel explication of "Richard Cory" as a poem less about suicide than about "regicide" ("A Re-examination of 'Richard Cory,'" *CLQ* 9:579–81); Sweet reaches his startling conclusions as a result of shifting attention away from the courtly protagonist and to the "unreliable, unaware narrator," who, as a representative of the common, biased crowd of "people on the pavement," helps to bring down the "Promethean" figure of Richard Cory; the poem is thus to be taken not as "a painting of a gentleman, but a portrait of the portraiteer." Sweet's interpretation challenges all other readings of this poem and should be considered by Robinson scholars.

Another of Robinson's most frequently anthologized poems is examined by Mordecai Marcus in "E. A. Robinson's 'Flammonde': Towards Some Essential Clarifications" (*MarkhamR* 3:77–80); this is not an attempt at a full reading of the poem but rather a probe into some tantalizing details, specifically the analogies of Flammonde to Christ and Satan. Laurence Perrine in "The Sources of Robinson's *Merlin*" (*AL* 44:313–21) argues that the poet's chief source for Merlin was neither Malory nor Tennyson but the Vulgate *Merlin*, a twelfth-century prose romance which Robinson found conveniently summarized in S. Humphreys Gurteen's *The Arthurian Epic* (1895). Perrine quotes from this work and draws parallels between it and

Robinson's poem. Finally, in a detailed and well-documented brief article, "E. A. Robinson's Concessions to the Critics" (RS 40:48–53), Nancy Joyner chronicles the poet's reactions to critical reviews of his poetry and speculates on how his career may have been significantly shaped by the critical reception of his work.

iv. Hart Crane

Major desiderata in Crane scholarship have been filled in the last two years with the publication of valuable bibliographical works by Joseph Schwartz and Robert C. Schweik. Schwartz's *Hart Crane: An Annotated Critical Bibliography* (New York, David Lewis, 1970) lists and describes 568 critical items published between 1921 and 1968. Since the author's aim has been to be inclusive of all works published between these dates, the material covered includes not only books and articles exclusively devoted to Crane but also those that may make only passing reference to him or his work. The annotations, which are clearly and fairly presented, range from comments of just a sentence or two to précis that frequently run to one or two pages. The book also includes a rather full Hart Crane chronology, a list of his published writings, a descriptive account of the bibliographical studies of earlier scholars, and a useful chronological index of works about Crane arranged by year of publication. Schwartz's book is the first full-length, annotated critical bibliography of Crane and obviously will be of help to scholars in the field.

A second major bibliographical aid and something of a companion volume to the work just cited is *Hart Crane: A Descriptive Bibliography* (Univ. of Pittsburgh Press), by Joseph Schwartz and Robert C. Schweik. Once again, this publication fills a long-felt need, for it now provides a full and accurate descriptive bibliography of Crane's work. The major part of the book is devoted to presenting comprehensive bibliographical information on Crane's separate publications and on the poetry, prose, and letters not published separately. The entries in the section on separate publications are accompanied by illustrations of title pages or sample pages from the body of the text. There is also a photographic illustration of "C 33," Crane's first published poem, with the poet's name misspelled as "Harold H. Crone." Also included are briefer chapters on Crane's drawings (a line drawing of Slater Brown is reproduced), on translations (eight languages are covered), adaptations (including a reference to a musical setting for "Voyages III" by Elliott Carter), and doubtful attributions. Separate appendices are devoted to a chronology of Crane's life, a chronology of the publication of his poems, and a list of periodicals in which the poetry and prose first appeared. The book, handsomely produced and easy to work with, also includes a full index.

As *Hart Crane: A Descriptive Bibliography* was going to press, a gathering of ten previously unknown Crane poems and fragments of verse was published by Kenneth A. Lohf (*Antaeus* 5:17–21); these range in length from two to eighteen lines each and were composed at various times between 1920 and 1932. They are only minor pieces but students of Crane's poetry will want to take note of them, if only in passing.

Lohf has also assembled a group of six previously unpublished or uncollected prose manuscripts ("The Prose Manuscripts of Hart Crane: An Editorial Portfolio," *Proof* 2:1–60). Reproduced in facsimile and meticulously annotated, these include typescript or holograph drafts of the following: (1) "Note on the Paintings of David Siqueiros" (Siqueiros was the Mexican painter who had done an oil portrait of Crane); (2) "A Pure Approach to Any Art" (a fragment that foreshadows some of the ideas in the published essay, "Modern Poetry"); (3) Reviews of James Whaler's *Green River* (published in *Poetry* [April 1932]) and Phelps Putnam's *The Five Seasons* (never completed or published by Crane); (4) "Vocabulary" (a notebook, listing words, phrases, images, and quotations from Walt Whitman and Joseph Conrad); (5) "Title" (eighteen humorous titles, all relating to Indians, and perhaps intended as titles for songs); (6) "Note Book" (including a foreign review copy list for *White Buildings* as well as a financial record and miscellaneous notes). Lohf's descriptive notes on these items helpfully indicate their separate features and suggest their possible usefulness to Crane scholars.

Another 1972 publication by Schwartz and Schweik too late to be noted is a new edition of *White Buildings* (New York, Liveright), Crane's first published book, with a new foreword by John Logan accompanying Allen Tate's original introduction.

In "Hart Crane, Louis Untermeyer, and T. S. Eliot: A New Crane Letter" (*AL* 44:143–46) Richard Allan Davison brings to light a previously uncollected letter (dated January 19, 1923), which is interesting chiefly for the remarks it carries on T. S. Eliot, whose "The Waste Land" had only recently appeared; Crane felt himself challenged by the pessimism of Eliot's poem and sent to Untermeyer a manuscript copy of "For the Marriage of Faustus and Helen," remarking that he regarded his own poem as being of "an almost antithetical spiritual attitude" to Eliot's.

Mention should be made of a brief article by Schwartz and Schweik, "The Literary Manuscripts of Hart Crane" (*PBSA* 66:64–65), which calls attention to two entries in Kenneth Lohf's *The Literary Manuscripts of Hart Crane* (1967) that stand in need of correction.

The major critical study this year is Sherman Paul's *Hart's Bridge* (Urbana, Univ. of Ill. Press), an ambitious book that sets out to examine all of Crane's poetry. Paul reads Crane as a poet within the broader currents of Romanticism (the references to Blake, Emerson, Thoreau, and Whitman are pervasive), but he shows little concern for the problems that confronted such a late Romantic as Crane was. The critical vocabulary is eclectic, but derives chiefly from the New Criticism (especially I. A. Richards) and the phenomenologists (especially Bachelard); these approaches serve the author well in discussing Crane as a poet of consciousness and in explicating those interior moments of dream, reverie, and memory that are frequent in Crane's work. A finely detailed scrutiny of individual lines, words, and images is the book's strength, but it lacks the framework of ideas or controlling point of view necessary to establish major critical argument; it is not until the final chapter, in fact (where Paul contends with Crane's earliest and most negative critics—Tate, Winters, and Blackmur), that the author provides a sustained sense of Crane as a "cubist" poet whose private "journey to love" (*The Bridge*) was unfairly received by critics of the Eliotic school. The book has its uses as a critical guide (although it would have meant more ten years ago, before the critical studies of Lewis, Leibowitz, Butterfield, and others), but its narrowly focused method of explication and its heavy prose style (the more than six hundred footnotes only hint at the unusually dense employment of parenthetical statement, associational reference, quotation, and citation) make it a book that one will more readily consult than read.

Close examination of four Crane poems—"Repose of Rivers," "At Melville's Tomb," "For the Marriage of Faustus and Helen," and

"The Dance"—is offered by David R. Clark in *Lyric Resonance* (pp. 148–84). "Repose of Rivers" receives the author's most original interpretation: "the speaker of the poetry is not Crane but a river. . . . The poem is an account, by a river, of the river's cycle of existence." This is a startling reading of the poem, and, as Clark works it out, a consistent one, but there is little precedent for it elsewhere in Crane's work, and one is left with the feeling that the poet's meaning may have been sacrificed for the critic's novelty of approach. Clark is more traditional in his interpretation of "At Melville's Tomb," an elegy that he helps to explicate through citations from *Moby Dick* that seem to find their echo in Crane's lines. "For the Marriage of Faustus and Helen" is studied in Yeatsian terms as a poem driving towards a mature vision of tragic gaiety, and "The Dance" is examined chiefly in terms of its images, particularly as these fuse the identities of the Indian and his native culture of earth and sky with those of the white man and his world of industrialization. All of Clark's readings demonstrate close feeling for Crane's language, especially for his images, and deserve the attention of other scholars.

In a tightly argued article that dissents from all other scholarly opinion on "Voyages" ("Hart Crane's 'Voyages' Reconsidered," *ConL* 13:315–33) Evelyn J. Hinz returns to "Poster" and "Belle Isle" to grasp the genesis ideas for Crane's set of poems; her largest quarrel is with Crane's "affirmative critics," who have consistently willed a "positive" reading for the conclusion of "Voyages," a position that she considers inappropriate and strongly contests in her own study.

Bruce Bassoff's "Rhetorical Pressures in 'For the Marriage of Faustus and Helen'" (*CP* 5,ii:40–48) presents a detailed examination of the peculiarities of diction and unusual grammatical shifts in the first part of "For the Marriage of Faustus and Helen"; Bassoff's suggestive study, which draws upon some of the categories of Roman Jacobson, demonstrates how close attention to Crane's language can reveal much about the groping quality of the poet's explorations; such a linguistic approach seems to hold good promise for a fuller reading of the complete poem.

K. Ayyappa Paniker, "Myth and Machine in Hart Crane" (*LCrit* 9[1971]:27–41) is a carefully considered, if familiar, attempt to evaluate the poet's efforts at integrating the mythical and the mechanical.

In a biographical essay, "A Boat in the Tower: Rimbaud in Cleve-

land, 1922" (*Renascence* 25:3–13), Alfred Galpin, who was acquainted with Crane in Cleveland during the summer of 1922, attests
that the poet knew more French than is generally acknowledged.
Galpin describes Crane's interests in the French poets and his attempts at translating Laforgue; Galpin's own translation of Rimbaud's
Le Bateau Ivre, done under the influence of Crane, is reproduced in
its 1922 version, which Crane knew.

v. Cummings, Jeffers, Sandburg

The most noteworthy publication on Cummings this year is *E. E.
Cummings: A Collection of Critical Essays* (Englewood Cliffs, N.J.,
Prentice-Hall), edited by Norman Friedman; the fourteen essays
(all reprinted criticism) sample three decades of opinion on Cummings and treat the major prose books as well as the poetry. Friedman's introduction (pp. 1–14) argues, a little late in the day, that
the New Criticism has never been hospitable to Cummings's Romantic
vision and that other approaches are needed to clarify the transcendental dimensions of the poet's lyric and satiric worlds. A selected
bibliography of works by and about Cummings is included.

Cummings's well-known fondness for burlesque and other forms
of popular entertainment is examined by Patrick B. Mullen in "E. E.
Cummings and Popular Culture" (*JPC* 5[1971]:503–30). Mullen
reviews some of Cummings's prose essays on the circus, popular amusement parks, comic strips, animated cartoons, and Charlie
Chaplin and finds that the qualities singled out for special praise—
"the juxtaposition of opposites, incongruity, movement, and surprise"
—are observable in Cummings's poetry as well. Mullen has little
trouble finding poems that reveal these qualities, yet his argument
is not able to advance much beyond the exhibits themselves, leaving
one in doubt as to the value of a literary criticism established on
parallels between poetry and popular culture.

Otherwise, the published work on Cummings consists of brief
articles of explication. John W. Crowley's "Visual-Aural Poetry: The
Typography of E. E. Cummings" (*CP* 5,ii:51–54) describes some of
the ways in which the poet sought to gain tactile as well as oral-aural
effects in his poetry; as an occasion for his study, Cowley offers brief
commentary on the functional use of typography in "(b el l s?". In
"Cummings's '(Ponder, Darling, These Busted Statues,'" (*SAB* 37,iv:

66–69) G. R. Wilson, Jr., offers an explication of the poem, which he sees as deriving possibly from Marvell's "To His Coy Mistress." And a parallel to some of the lyrics of John Donne is suggested by G. J. Weinberger, who offers a new reading of "E. E. Cummings' 'the people who'" (*RS* 39[1971]:313–15); Weinberger focuses on the relationship between religious and love motifs in an attempt to explain the poem's method of transcendence.

John R. Alexander brings an admirable degree of critical balance to his study of "Conflict in the Narrative Poetry of Robinson Jeffers" (*SR* 80:85–99). This perceptive and carefully organized article is a major attempt to explore the conflict between Jeffers's philosophical commitment to the doctrine of Inhumanism on the one hand and his aesthetic commitment to narrative realism on the other; the first "clearly advocates a rejection of all that can be considered human," while the second "prescribes detailed attention to it." Alexander briefly examines four of Jeffers's plays and then concentrates on seven of the mature long poems. He concludes that although Jeffers never unequivocally managed a fusion of philosophy and aesthetics, the poetry at its best is characterized by a deep integrity of poetic imagination.

In "Jeffers' 'Cawdor' and the Hippolytus Story" (*WAL* 7:171–78) Robert J. Brophy draws upon the methods of archetypal criticism for his study of the myth-pattern behind Jeffers's long poem; the article offers a structural analysis as well as an examination of theme-images.

Beth B. Haury examines the literary connection between Jeffers and Faulkner in "The Influence of Robinson Jeffers' 'Tamar' on *Absalom, Absalom!*" (*MissQ* 25:356–58); through a study of the affinities between Faulkner's characterization, linguistic repetitions, and imagery in the novel and those of Jeffers's poem, the author concludes that Faulkner drew upon "Tamar" (as well as upon the Biblical account of King David and his children) in writing *Absalom, Absalom!* The myth of Tamar is further pursued, this time in connection with the Spanish poet Lorca, in J. R. LeMaster's "Lorca, Jeffers and the Myth of Tamar" (*NLauR* 1,i[1971]:44–51).

Carl Sandburg is one of the poets considered in John T. Flanagan's "Three Illinois Poets" (*CentR* 16:313–27). Flanagan outlines the career of Sandburg and compares the poet to Edgar Lee Masters and Vachel Lindsay, noting that "the reputations of all three poets have seriously shrunk since their peak of recognition." In Sandburg's case, the decline of the poet's appeal may be owing to serious objection to his optimism, a quality of spirit that does not easily fit the mood of the times but which the author feels can still be persuasive.

William A. Sutton offers an account of Sandburg's family background and the poet's trips to Sweden in "The Swedishness of Carl Sandburg" (*ASR* 60:144–47); the author notes that although Sandburg never lost sight of his ancestral heritage, his impulse was universalistic and his career was not deeply rooted in Swedish materials.

vi. Ransom, Aiken, and Others

Miller Williams's *The Poetry of John Crowe Ransom* (New Brunswick, N.J., Rutgers Univ. Press), although intended as a critical study of the poet, is, by default, a kind of selected anthology of Ransom's poetry with introductory and concluding notes by the author-editor. Fully half of the book's 120 pages are taken up with the poems themselves; in one case, a single poem ("The Vanity of the Bright Boys") is reproduced in nine different versions, with seven of these printed twice each. While the intention here is to allow us to study the changes that occurred in the poem during the forty-five years that Ransom worked on it, surely more is required of Williams than the half-page commentary he appends to this extended, thirty-page exhibit of the poem in all of its variations. His best pages are those devoted to discussion of Ransom's religion, a Southern adaptation of Calvinism and Christian stoicism, as he usefully explains it; the explication of Ransom's color symbolism may also be deemed helpful; but the rest of the book, when not taken up with citing numerous poems, offers only minimal and familiar treatment of the subjects (irony, symbolism, metaphor, dissociation of sensibility) it introduces.

In a biographical essay, "In His Own Country" (*SoR* 8:572–93), Thomas Daniel Young recounts in great detail the campaign led by Allen Tate and Andrew Lytle to keep Ransom from leaving Vanderbilt and taking up a position at Kenyon College. Young's account helps to point up once more the central importance of Ransom to the movement in Southern letters, so much of which revolved around Vanderbilt. The same author discusses "Necrological" as an example of Ransom's intentionally "restricted" but "near-perfect" lyrical art ("John Crowe Ransom: A Major Minor Poet," *Spectrum* 2:37–46).

Young acknowledges the severe limitations that Ransom has placed on both his form and subject matter, but finds him excelling as a stylistic master and, in this respect, an important "minor" poet. In an attempt to define "minor" poetry and to further his general argument, Young quotes from some interesting and previously unpublished letters of Allen Tate and Donald Davidson.

In an essay that is more an affectionate tribute than a piece of critical biography ("Conrad Aiken: Resident of Savannah," *SoR* 8: 792–804) Ted R. Spivey discusses the return of Conrad Aiken to Savannah; the author asserts but does not substantially support the claim that "the Savannah environment has been important to Aiken's development both as a poet and as a man." It is amusing to learn of Aiken and his wife drinking their martinis in one of the local cemeteries, but the student of Aiken's poetry will not discover very much that is pertinent in this essay. The same author discusses Aiken's autobiography in "Conrad Aiken's *Ushant*: Record of a Contemporary Poet's Quest for Self-Knowledge" (*SAB* 36,iv[1971]:21–28).

Maurice Duke prints eight minor letters of Sterling in "Letters of George Sterling to James Branch Cabell" (*AL* 44:146–53). And Jack Scherting discusses Ferril as a nature poet in "An Approach to the Western Poetry of Thomas Hornsby Ferril" (*WAL* 7:179–90).

Indiana University

15. Poetry: The 1930s to the Present

Linda Welshimer Wagner

i. General

Like the two previous years, 1972 showed the increasing academic respectability of the study of contemporary letters. In the poetry covered by this essay, thirty dissertations were completed, three each on William Carlos Williams, Wallace Stevens, and Richard Wilbur; two each on Robert Lowell, James Dickey, Marianne Moore, and Theodore Roethke; single studies of Sylvia Plath, John Berryman, Charles Olson, Gary Snyder, Robert Duncan, Allen Tate, and Randall Jarrell; and several others on various combinations of modern poets.

The quality of essays on the work of these poets was also generally high, and an increasing number of scholars seem to be attempting comparisons and correlations. Several excellent journals devoted exclusively to poetry—*Parnassus* and the *American Poetry Review*—made their appearance during the year, complementing the comparatively new *Boundary 2, New York Quarterly*, the *Ohio Review, Modern Poetry Studies*, and the *Iowa Review*.

The major critical study of American poetry during this period was Kenneth Rexroth's *American Poetry in the Twentieth Century* (New York, Herder and Herder, 1971). Admittedly idiosyncratic, the book generally is written with all the wisdom of Rexroth's long experience as practicing writer and translator. Filled with interesting theses, the book reminds one of Pound's prose: references are made as givens; explanations are few. Rexroth writes for the initiated reader.

Contending that Whitman was the only great American poet, both in terms of his philosophy and his thoroughly individual prosody, Rexroth sees the modern period as clear proof of the "great man" theory of art. Among the figures he sees as formative are Edgar

Lee Masters, Ezra Pound, Laura Riding, William Carlos Williams, the early Carl Sandburg, Alfred Kreymborg, Gertrude Stein, Kenneth Patchen, James Laughlin, and Lawrence Ferlinghetti.

Rexroth traces modern poetics to *Spoon River Anthology*, Sandburg's *Chicago Poems*, and Pound's *Des Imagistes* anthology, these three assisted probably by *Reedy's Mirror* and *Poetry*. (Frost and Robinson he considers the end of the previous period, not the beginning of this one.) But Rexroth is also quick to acknowledge that artists are often fed by currents and art forms other than the apparent ones, so he includes French, Russian, German, and Indian influences, among others.

He is surprisingly harsh on both Pound and Eliot, claiming that Pound's energy ran out too soon and that the writings of both poets too often "slip into rhetoric." In contrast, "Williams never slips . . . he doesn't talk about experience; he reveals it with humility." But for Rexroth, Williams's real greatness lies in his prosody, his trust of American English. Rexroth closes with chapters on black poets, on American poetry since 1955, and on the contemporary world scene. The lack of an index is regrettable.

Another important book is Paul Goodman's *Speaking and Language: Defense of Poetry* (New York, Random House). In addition to usefully surveying theories of language, the book states reasonably many givens about modern poetry. The modern emphasis on the concrete, on the use of image and scene as the best way to convey meaning, Goodman sees as related to the belief that speech also is a physical action. The poem—or any act of speaking—is not "imitation," nor is it "representation." It is its own act. Goodman has much recourse to linguistics. He also describes the process of writing; defines the audience for poetry; and surveys the whole bugaboo of organic form, adding a valuable measure to it with his term "literary probability."

In *Organic Form: The Life of an Idea* (London, Routledge and Kegan Paul) G. S. Rousseau, as editor, presents three essays by G. N. Giordano Orsini, Philip C. Ritterbush, and William K. Wimsatt. The book economically presents the long history of the concept, and its applications in both life sciences and literature. Rousseau includes a useful bibliography.

Martin Heidegger's *Poetry, Language, Thought* (essays given as lectures from 1935 to 1951) is now available in a translation by

Albert Hofstadter (New York, Harper and Row). The striking point about these essays is that, given their parallels with the Goodman poetics, Heidegger's emphasis throughout is on the moral function of poetry. A man writes as a way to know—to build or perhaps to find—his spirit.

Cleanth Brooks's varied essays in A Shaping Joy (New York, Harcourt Brace Jovanovich, 1971) deal less directly with poetics; but his observations on the role of the poet, the uses of metaphor, and formalist criticism as apt method in both prose and poetry are sage. In "Poetry Since 'The Waste Land,'" Brooks points out that the central principle of the "new" poetics has been juxtaposition, an alogical structure which is also found in many Romantic poems. Brooks's points about the artist as part of his community are also germane; he feels the writer who is more dependent on a literary clique than on a genuine community is in danger of losing his sense of reality.

One of the major assessments of post-modern poetry appeared in the new critical journal Boundary 2. David Antin's "Modernism and Postmodernism: Approaching the Present in American Poetry" (1: 98–146) surveys the "stable" critical attitudes during the period of transition—the late '40s and '50s—and shows how far criticism was from the real vitality of the practicing writers. Summarizing, Antin sees Schwartz, Lowell, Snodgrass, and others as the end of the moderns; and Olson, Creeley, Ignatow, Zukofsky, and Ginsberg as the beginning of the post-moderns.

Antin makes the observations that a collage structure has been basic to modernist art; that some critics still tend to equate the form of a poem with its philosophical stance; that Olson's Projective Verse is really psycholinguistic; that Pound remained provincial, never noticing the European or Southern writers at work before 1920. Considering contemporary poetry, Antin sees the many changes of the past century leading to the idea that the written poem is a "notation," the beginning of the process of the poem, not the final, codified thing. As a result of this changed perspective, the '60s saw much interest in both Concrete Poetry and tape recording. The influence of John Cage, Gertrude Stein, and the European Dadaists and Surrealists superseded that of even Pound and Williams; and interest in the poetry of non-literate and partially literate cultures was also high.

Antin closes by reaffirming the healthy state of contemporary poetry and the new excellence of the young poets.

The best description of Concrete Poetry is Mike Doyle's "Notes on Concrete Poetry" (*CanL* 46[1970]:91–95). Doyle sees the form as an entirely serious "verbivocovisual play," and describes the impulse for such poetics as a concern with "words, letters, syllables involving a conscious preoccupation with linguistics and semantics." He dates the actual movement to 1955, making it "parallel in time with the activity of the Black Mountain poets, Beat poetry and 'found' poetry, sharing with all a sense of the poem as thing-in-itself rather than representation or copy."

Of the essay-reviews and omnibus treatments, Fred Moramarco's "A Gathering of Poets" is representative of the best (*WHR* 26:189–96). He sees the newest collections as taking that "voyage of discovery" the post-modern artists have been interested in for a decade, and is impressed particularly with Carolyn Kizer's *Midnight Was My Cry* for its skillful craft reinforcing theme and James Tate's *The Oblivion Ha-Ha* for his use of surrealistic tactics to involve the reader. Moramarco's highest praise, like that of many other reviewers in 1972, was reserved for Galway Kinnell's *The Book of Nightmares,* a ten-poem sequence (ten poems of seven parts each) which may be the strongest long poem published since *Paterson.* He describes it as "simply a stunning work, rich in its imagery, haunting in its rhythms, evocative and terrifyingly accurate in its insights."

Louis L. Martz makes some acute comments in "Recent Poetry: Berryman and Others" (*YR* 61:410–22). He stresses Berryman's affinities with Wordsworth, and says that *Love & Fame* is the " 'Growth of a Poet's Mind,' but done in a mode of frankness impossible for the nineteenth century." Martz points out too that the collection has a heavily religious strain (in addition to the "Eleven Addresses to the Lord") and that perhaps Berryman's other work did also, had readers only looked for it.

Martz has high praise for Jon Silkin as being perhaps the best British poet writing today, for David R. Slavitt's "Eclogues," for Warren Slesinger's poetry, and for Anne Sexton's *Transformations.* Martz sees that Sexton's versions of the tales are actually personal poems—that the collection is a woman's lyric view of the world; and that Sexton manages to give each tale its wider implication through her deft interplay between a childlike vocabulary and a pattern of darker, adult asides.

In *Nietzsche in Anglosaxony* (New York, Humanities Press) Patric Bridgwater surveys Nietzsche's impact on both English and American literature. He concludes that many writers were indebted to the philosopher, especially at the turn of the century. His comments on Wallace Stevens are of interest here, as is his bibliography.

ii. Wallace Stevens

Three major books in Stevens criticism were published in 1972. Edward Kessler's *Images of Wallace Stevens* (New Brunswick, N. J., Rutgers Univ. Press) provides a method of reading the poetry. By working through the dominant image patterns, Kessler finds harmony in what seem to be contradictions within the poems. Kessler defends his methodology because he feels that, unlike the writing of Yeats or Eliot, Stevens's poetry shows little linear development; "rather, the poems eddy around certain fixed ideas revealed in a recurring pattern of imagery." Imagery does not, however, become symbolic; and Kessler points out repeatedly that Stevens's reference remains flexible, that he uses images for their "import" rather than for their literal meaning. Kessler further sees Stevens's use of abstract philosophy as primarily a means of knowing his physical scene more intimately. For Stevens, he feels, the human imagination and not reason is man's supreme asset.

Michel Benamou's *Wallace Stevens and the Symbolist Imagination* (Princeton, N. J., Princeton Univ. Press) basically complements Kessler's study, but the reading here is enriched through comparisons with painting and with the writing of Laforgue, Baudelaire, Mallarmé, Apollinaire, and others. Benamou's survey of Stevens's poetry is less complete; indeed, this book consists of six separate essays. Unlike Kessler, however, Benamou sees Stevens's poems falling into four stages of development, distinguishable chiefly by the kind of language and imagery used. Since the essays themselves do not dwell on these classifications, it is a minor difference. What Benamou does provide is interesting and valuable comparative material, and much new insight about Stevens's art.

The most comprehensive study of the three books is A. Walton

Litz's *Introspective Voyager: The Poetic Development of Wallace Stevens* (New York, Oxford Univ. Press). Litz studies closely Stevens's poetry written from 1914 to 1937, both the poems collected in *Harmonium* and those Stevens omitted, because Litz feels that critics have inadvertently misunderstood Stevens's development by considering *Harmonium* a typical "first book." Since Stevens was forty-four when it was published and had been writing poems since his college days—but particularly for the previous decade—he had gone through many changes of aesthetic theory before publishing the book. Litz's study is valuable not only for its sound judgment but also because it reprints significant previously uncollected poems. The new insights help us see Stevens picking his way through contemporary poetic enthusiasms, using what seemed germane to his own aims and attitudes. In the latter sections of the book, Litz also considers the later work, neither as simply a culmination of the early nor as an absorption of it, but as a new kind of equally effective poetry. And thematically, as Litz says, the final work "is neither eccentric nor private. It is built upon the central reality of our age, the death of the gods and of the great coordinating mythologies, and in their place it offers the austere satisfactions of a 'self' dependent on the pure poetry of the physical world, a 'self' whose terrifying lack of belief is turned into a source of freedom" (p. vi).

Peter L. McNamara's *Critics on Wallace Stevens* (Coral Gables, Fla., Univ. of Miami Press) reprints essays by Samuel French Morse, George McFadden, George Lensing, Marjorie Perloff, Frank Doggett, and others.

Several essays this year are of some interest. R. D. Ackerman's "Wallace Stevens: Myth, Belief, and Presence" (*Criticism* 14:266–76) attempts to redefine "myth" as a functional method within the poems. Through his use of myth, Ackerman feels, Stevens could provide "an atmosphere" in which physical detail and spiritual life could join. H. W. Burtner writing in "The High Priest of the Secular: The Poetry of Wallace Stevens" (*ConnR* 6:34–45) shares Kessler's view that Stevens used philosophical approaches only as a way to reach physical reality. Examining Helen Vendler's *On Extended Wings* in "Interpreting Stevens: An Essay on Poetry and Thinking" (*Boundary 2* 1:79–95), Joseph N. Riddel objects to her formalist methods and her choice of poems.

iii. William Carlos Williams

No new books on Williams were published this year, but the essays appear to be moving in comparatively new directions. Williams as novelist, as prose and prose-poem writer, and as aesthetician—these are the subjects of most of the published work.

Jesse D. Green in "Williams' *Kora in Hell*: The Opening of the Poems as 'Field of Action'" (*ConL* 13:295–314) sees the 1917 *Kora* as the beginning of his theoretical position fully presented in *Spring and All*. Art which grows from "the day's happenings" becomes Williams's aim. Neil Myers studies another of Williams's theories in "Decreation in Williams' 'The Descent'" (*Criticism* 14:315–27). Tracing the poet's use of the descent-ascent imagery in his poems, particularly "The Descent," Myers finds that for Williams "wilfully touching bottom is a process of gaining strength."

Some critical activity has no doubt been prompted by the newest of the Williams reissues, the 1970 *Imaginations* (Norfolk, Conn., New Directions), edited by Webster Schott. This book contains five works written from 1917 to the early '30s: *Kora in Hell*; *Spring and All*; *The Great American Novel*; *The Descent of Winter*; and *A Novelette & Other Prose*. Schott's introductions, to the collection and to the separate pieces, are capable and informative. They are also somewhat messianic, as he speaks of Williams as "an American original" and "the instrument of change."

Ron Loewinsohn, in his "Tracking W.C.W.'s Early Development" (*Sumac* 3[1971]:128–41), considers much of the material collected in *Imaginations* essential for any understanding of the poet. Loewinsohn concentrates on the composition of *The Tempers*, Williams's second book of poems, giving probable sources for many of the poems included in this 1913 collection.

Perhaps the most important contribution to Williams criticism this year was Anthony Libby's " 'Claritas': William Carlos Williams' Epiphanies" (*Criticism* 14:22–31). Libby relates the effect of Williams's short poems to Joyce's "epiphany," and in following Joyce's original definition of the term in *Stephen Hero* points out that epiphany works as a logical exercise, not an emotional one. Libby relates Joyce's definition to Aquinas's requirements for beauty (integrity, symmetry, and radiance or *claritas*), as Joyce himself had. "*Claritas* is *quidditas*. After the analysis which discovers the second quality the mind makes the only logically possible synthesis and discovers the third quality. This is the moment which I call epiphany."

Libby points out also that Williams uses many images of brightness, flame, and the radiance of precious metals. He also discusses the aesthetics of *Spring and All.* But primarily he refutes the usual view that the pre-*Paterson* poems operate like haiku. Libby sees Williams working "through a rather surprising rigorous process of logical analysis . . . [he] fits a characteristically modern pattern, but it is a pattern that develops out of traditional Western aesthetic philosophy, rather than out of a rebellion against tradition." If we can come to agree with this dimension to Williams's poems, perhaps we will have located one reason for the diverse "followers" of Williams's poetics.

In 1971 *Profile of William Carlos Williams,* Jerome Mazzaro's edition of reprinted essays, appeared from Charles E. Merrill Co., Columbus, Ohio. It includes for the first time Philip L. Gerber's "So Much Depends: The Williams Foreground" (pp. 5–24). Useful for his survey of the graphic art contemporary with Williams's early poems, Gerber's essay concentrates on the '20s and before.

iv. Black Mountain Poets and Others

A good deal of Martin Duberman's exhaustive *Black Mountain: An Exploration in Community* (New York, Dutton) is a history of the college from 1933 to 1956, but there is interesting information about Robert Creeley, Robert Duncan, and particularly Charles Olson, who came to be "unquestionably the heartbeat of Black Mountain during its last five years." It is useful for background and facts (though there are inaccuracies), but not for critical judgment (Olson's poems are dismissed as "ludicrous shorthand"). One of the best brief descriptions of the relationships at Black Mountain is Gilbert Sorrentino's "Black Mountaineering" (*Poetry* 116 [1970]:110–20). In Sorrentino's view, the people associated with the *Black Mountain Review* were continuing the direction of many unacknowledged writers: "the viability and energy of that work done by Pound, Williams, Zukofsky, Oppen, H. D., Dahlberg, et. al., *surfaced* in the *Black Mountain Review* in the verse and prose of a generation of writers . . . who felt themselves to be disenfranchised." Adding Louis Zukofsky, Edward Dahlberg, George Oppen and, by association, such poets as Kenneth Rexroth, Carl Rakosi, and Charles Reznikoff is a long-overdue move; and recent criticism seems to be aware of the fallacy of jumping from Pound and Williams to Robert Creeley.

An important collection for emphasizing this group of writers is *The Contemporary Writer: Interviews with Sixteen Novelists and Poets* (Madison, Univ. of Wis. Press). Edited by L. S. Dembo and Cyrena N. Pondrom, the book includes spirited and meaty interviews with Rexroth, Oppen, Rakosi, Reznikoff, and Zukofsky, all taped in 1968. Dembo's essay on the latter, "Louis Zukofsky: Objectivist Poetics and the Quest for Form" (*AL* 44:74–96), is a helpful survey of the chief importance of the poet, his affinities to other poets, and his use of collage and typographical experiments. Dembo has also written "The Existential World of George Oppen" (*IowaR* 3:64–90) to provide an important corrective to the view of Oppen as "Objectivist." The poet's method was imagistic, but even in his earliest poems he used the image as a means of knowing larger truths.

Edward Dahlberg (TUSAS 206) by Fred Moramarco is the first book-length treatment of the versatile Dahlberg. Moramarco credits him with not only incisive views of literature but also much seminal experimentation in crossing genre lines. Important as Dahlberg's writing has been in the last thirty years, the reader could hope for more discussion by the author about genre, and more examples from Dahlberg's writing itself; but this is a good and accurate book. Also of interest is the special Dahlberg issue of *Tri-Quarterly* (19 [Fall 1970]) containing essays by Jonathan Williams, Eric Mottram, Jules Chametzky, Anthony Burgess, and Kay Boyle; tributes from nearly forty other poets and scholars; selections from Dahlberg's letters to Jonathan Williams from 1955 to 1967; and various checklists.

A new book, *Kenneth Rexroth* (TUSAS 208), is also lively and perceptive. Morgan Gibson gives us some sense of where Rexroth's aesthetic places him in the wide continuum of modern poetry, emphasizing that for Rexroth the sense of spoken voice, of poem as spoken communication, is primary. Gibson also deals with Rexroth's "visionary aesthetics," his stance that the poem has an active responsibility for all mankind's suffering (and joy), and it is this part of Rexroth's belief that led to his involvement in the San Francisco Renaissance, in its early stages.

Of the poets usually connected with the Black Mountain area, Robert Creeley and Charles Olson have received the most comment during 1972. Aside from various reviews of *A Day Book*, there was a twenty-page checklist of criticism by Mary Novik and Douglas Calhoun (*WCR* 6:51–71) and Charles Altieri's essay "The Unsure Egoist: Robert Creeley and the Theme of Nothingness" (*ConL* 13: 162–85). Altieri bases his reading of the poems on Creeley's fear of "emptiness," the void, as recurring threat in any man's life. So pervasive is this fear to Creeley, says Altieri, that he strains particularly hard to make his verbal connections work. Many of his word choices, his persistent ambiguities, his shifts in expected linguistic order, his puns, are used to force the reader to respond. Altieri also sees Creeley's use of limited vocabulary and set of images as his attempt to create a truly personal speech. During his early poems the poet was content to make these connections on a personal level, through family and love relationships. But in *Words*, Altieri feels, Creeley is more interested in his own sense of being, defined variously as "place"; by *Pieces*, his interest lies in the extra-personal emptiness. *Here* and *there* become key words, simply, perhaps punningly, suggesting the enormity of his search for contact. See also Joel Oppenheimer, "The Inner Tightrope: An Appreciation of Robert Creeley (*Lillabulero* 8[1970]:51–53) and Russell Banks, "Notes on Creeley's *Pieces*" (pp. 88–91).

Several good essays on Olson's work also appeared. Surprisingly similar in intent, J. B. Philip's "Charles Olson Reconsidered" (*JAmS* 5[1971]:293–305) and L. S. Dembo's "Charles Olson and the Moral History of Cape Ann" (*Criticism* 14:165–74) stress that Olson's use of the history of Gloucester and Cape Ann is his means of reaching moral truth. Although Olson, like Pound, can be critical of America, "with his contrast between *polis*, the ideal society, and *pejorocrasy*, the debased world," he is also proud enough of his origins to use them as the basis for his poetic mythology (see also Ann Charters's introduction to *Charles Olson: The Special View of History*, Berkeley, Calif., Oyez, 1970). In "Charles Olson: Materials for a Nexus" (*Open Letter* 2:21–40) Matthew Corrigan describes Olson's poems as runes and makes valuable connections between Olson's theory of the poem as "the configuration of its creation" and his moral philosophy. Corrigan points out that for Olson, language was "vital speech," but it was also "forerunner of consciousness," man's way of finding what he knew. Corrigan also illustrates, convincingly, the similarities between Olson's poetic rhythms and Melville's later prose.

L. S. Dembo's interview with Paul Blackburn just a few months
before his death in 1971 has also been published in *ConL* 13:133–43.

v. Warren and Tate

Essays on and by Robert Penn Warren were plentiful in 1972. Sister
M. Bernetta Quinn traced one pervasive theme in "Robert Penn
Warren's Promised Land" (*SoR* 8:329–58). She sees his use of imagery of real places like Guthrie, Kentucky, as a way of reaching the
broader implications of his "promised land," a moral universe. Free
of nearly all contemporary influences, Warren operates of and from
his own interior terrain.

The April 1972 issues of both the *Hollins Critic* (9,i) and *Four
Quarters* (21,iv) were devoted to Warren. The latter included essays
by Cleanth Brooks, Robert Cayton, James Justus, Allen Shepherd,
Arthur Scouten, Victor Strandberg, and others. The former publishes
a single essay by Louis D. Rubin (pp. 1–10). "Dreiser and *Meet Me
in the Green Glen*: A Vintage Year for Robert Penn Warren" surveys
Warren's career, his most recent novel, and his *Homage to Theodore
Dreiser*. Rubin is amazed at Warren's perception for a novelist apparently so unlike himself, saying that Warren's study of *An American Tragedy* "is simply the best treatment it has yet received."

Following his literary biography of Tate, Radcliffe Squires has
edited *Allen Tate and His Work: Critical Evaluations* (Minneapolis,
Univ. of Minn. Press), reprinted pieces by thirty-five poets and critics.
Complete with bibliography of works by and about Tate, the book
includes Squires's biographic introduction and essays by John Crowe
Ransom, Andrew Lytle, Malcolm Cowley, Robert Lowell, Frank
Kermode, Arthur Mizener, Denis Donoghue, Cleanth Brooks, R. P.
Blackmur, and others.

Robert Dupree, writing in "The Mirrors of Analogy: Three
Poems of Allen Tate" (*SoR* 8:774–91), sees Tate as searcher, man
continually seeking in his culture the kind of "vital forms" his ances-
tors could find in theirs. Dupree uses "The Cross," "The Mediterra-
nean," and "The Last Days of Alice" to substantiate his thesis. (See
also Tate's reminiscence, "A Lost Traveller's Dream" in *MQR* 11:
225–36).

John T. Fain and Thomas D. Young have edited letters of Tate
and Donald Davidson for "The Agrarian Symposium" (*SoR* 8:845–

82). Written from 1928 to 1930, the letters record Tate's impressions of Eliot, Herbert Read, Hemingway as he was meeting them abroad, but they also consistently continue a dialogue that led to the 1930 *I'll Take My Stand.*

vi. Ignatow, Merton, Burke, Wheelwright

The first issue of the *American Poetry Review* features David Ignatow—poems, prose-poem, and lengthy excerpts from his *Notebooks.* Aside from the special Ignatow issue of *Tennessee Poetry Journal* (3,ii[1970]), Ignatow has seldom received attention in established journals. As Robert Bly says in "Some Thoughts on *Rescue the Dead*" (pp. 17–21), "it has been men younger than Ignatow who have insisted that his work be reviewed and published. He is the only poet in his generation to whom this has happened." Other items in the *TPJ* include Linda Wagner's "On David Ignatow" (pp. 41–45) and David Verble's "On Articles About Ignatow" (pp. 46–47).

Several items on John Wheelwright, who died in 1940, were published this year, as were his collected poems. A good introductory essay, surveying his life and the poems as masterpieces of metaphysical art, is "John Wheelwright: New England's Colloquy with the World" by Alvin H. Rosenfeld and S. Foster Damon (*SoR* 8:310–28). Rosenfeld also edits Wheelwright's 1925–1926 notebooks, as well as describing his "Bostonian" life, his associations at Harvard with other poets, his connections with *Secession* and various other little magazines ("The New England Notebooks of John Wheelwright," *NEQ* 45:568–77). *Collected Poems of John Wheelwright,* also edited by Alvin H. Rosenfeld (Norfolk, Conn., New Directions), includes 275 pages of Wheelwright's poetry, Robert Fitzgerald's poem "Portrait," and Austin Warren's revised essay from 1956, "Introduction: John Brooks Wheelwright" in which he terms the poet "a master of metaphysical poetry."

Interest in the poetry and prose of Thomas Merton, who died in 1968, is also growing. Three adequate essays describe his contributions as poet: Ralph D. Sturm's "Thomas Merton: Poet" (*ABR* 22:1–20); John D. Boyd's "Christian Imaginative Patterns and the Poetry of Thomas Merton" (*Greyfriar* 13:3–14); and "Thomas Merton's *Cables to the Ace*: A Critical Study" (*Renascence* 24:3–32). Flaherty describes Merton's use of allusion and symbol, his humor, and his difficult surrealist juxtaposition and relates Merton's literary methods to those of Alain Robbe-Grillet.

Merton's other voluminous writing (nearly fifty books besides uncollected essays and papers) is summarized and correlated in an impressive first study, *Thomas Merton, Social Critic*, by James Thomas Baker (Lexington, Univ. Press of Ky., 1971). Baker combines biography and thematic analysis in this readable book, with his emphasis on Merton's changing views as he matured within the monastic life. Judging Merton to be a true humanist, a man whose interest in social issues was never limited by prejudice, Baker predicts that on his later books will rest his eventual fame.

Armin Paul Frank's *Kenneth Burke* (TUSAS, 1969) serves as a necessary corrective to those who see Burke as primarily a literary critic. Frank devotes much of his study to a discussion of Burke's own poetry, short stories, and an anti-novel, and then moves to his criticism, finally attempting to "turn Burke's own methodology of symbolic exegesis upon himself." " 'What am I but a *word man* '" sets the stage for this generally sensitive book.

vii. Lowell, Wilbur, Dickey, Roethke, Jarrell, Schwartz

It must be somewhat perplexing to have reached that point in one's reputation when dissertations are being completed, but few essays are being published. Only one essay on Roethke appeared in 1972, Jarold Ramsey's "Roethke in the Greenhouse" (*WHR* 26:35–47), a good compilation of the use Roethke made of the father-son and Michigan greenhouse imagery in the poems from the mid period on.

Paul F. Cummins's *Richard Wilbur: A Critical Essay* (Grand Rapids, Mich., Eerdmans, 1971) unfortunately relies more on the author's reaction to Wilbur's personality than on criticism of the poems. A useful work is *Richard Wilbur, a Bibliographical Checklist*, compiled by John P. Field (Kent, Ohio, Kent State Univ. Press, 1971). It contains annotated primary and secondary listings and an itemized catalogue of Wilbur's papers both at Amherst and Buffalo.

Most new essays on Robert Lowell were minor, the criticism itself apparently waiting to see what he produces next in what is obviously a period of change. This is the view of Paul Schwaber writing in "Robert Lowell in Mid-Career (*WHR* 25 [1971]:348–54), although George W. Nitchie's "The Importance of Robert Lowell" (*SoR* 8:

118–32) sees Lowell the poet as secondary to Lowell the moralist and social observer. Nitchie attempts to use both the poems and the plays to prove that it is often their political stance (conveyed through Lowell's use of family and history) that gives them their poetic power. The wisest treatment of Lowell as politically oriented poet, however, occurs in Thomas R. Edwards's book, *Imagination and Power: A Study of Poetry on Public Themes* (New York, Oxford Univ. Press, 1971), pp. 210–26.

More interesting than the single essays are two collections of reprinted criticism. *Critics on Robert Lowell*, edited by Jonathan Price (Coral Gables, Fla., Univ. of Miami Press) is brief, but also relatively cheap. Essays by Tate, Ehrenpreis, Jarrell, W. C. Williams, Richard Poirier, and others give a balanced view of Lowell as poet. *Robert Lowell: A Portrait of the Artist in His Time* (New York, David Lewis, 1970), edited by Michael London and Robert Boyers, contains twenty-seven reprinted essays and the 1961 *Paris Review* interview, plus Jerome Mazzaro's new "Checklist: 1939–1968" of material on Lowell (pp. 293–328).

Mazzaro has also edited *Profile of Robert Lowell* (Columbus, Ohio, Charles E. Merrill, 1971), including less accessible essays by Dudley Fitts, DeSales Standerwick, Charles Altieri, John Reed, A. Alvarez, and Robert Boyers, as well as four interviews with Lowell. To be noted also is Jay Martin's clearly written *Robert Lowell* (UM-PAW 92,1970).

Last year there was a bibliography of James Dickey (see *ALS 1971*, p. 319) and now there is a second: Franklin Ashley's *James Dickey: A Checklist* (Detroit, Gale Research). This listing includes both primary and secondary items, and runs to nearly a hundred pages. Interest in Dickey during 1972 centered mainly on his novel *Deliverance* and the film version of it. The two essays concerned with his poetry were "A Special Kind of Fantasy: James Dickey on the Razor's Edge" by N. Michael Niflis (*SWR* 57:311–17) and Raymond Smith's "The Poetic Faith of James Dickey" (*MPS* 2:259–72). Smith agrees with Dickey's own statement that he is a "born believer," and sees in his work that quality of "acceptance and celebration in the manner of Whitman. Dickey's faith is rooted in nature . . . and his reverence for nature is manifest in a primitive, almost totemic treatment of animals." Smith sees Dickey's use of hunting and animal imagery as his means of achieving his personal myth, his return to "wholeness." Although Niflis terms Dickey's belief system "fantasy," he makes nearly the same points. See also "Craft Interview with James Dickey" (*NYQ* 10:17–35).

M. L. Rosenthal's *Randall Jarrell* (UMPAW 103) is a competent and thorough survey of Jarrell's poetry. Rosenthal sees it as developing thematically from his use of childhood experiences to war to self-search poems, as Jarrell sought to make himself a European poet rather than a Southern one. Rosenthal feels his innate conservatism would have kept him from becoming a radical innovator, but he mourns his death at only fifty-one, and concludes, "he remains a force among us as a poet of defeat and loneliness who nevertheless does not allow himself to become less spirited." In addition to Dure J. Gillikin's "A Checklist of Criticism on Randall Jarrell, 1941–1970" (*BNYPL* 75:176–94), Jerome Mazzaro tried to define several tendencies in Jarrell's poems, only to conclude that as poet he occupied "a notable but not paramount place" among his contemporaries ("Between Two Worlds: The Post-Modernism of Randall Jarrell," *Salmagundi* 17[1971]:92–113).

Perhaps the same fate awaits the reputation of Delmore Schwartz. Even with the publication in 1970 of *Selected Essays of Delmore Schwartz*, edited by Donald A. Dike and David H. Zucker (Univ. of Chicago Press), there has been little critical attention. The essay collection, however, deserves notice. Gentle yet supremely confident, Schwartz writes with the authority of one writer knowing what another writer has done. He wrote urbanely on Gide, Eliot, Faulkner, Hemingway, Dos Passos, Stevens, Pound, Tate, movies, cartoons, and critics.

Lee Valenti has excerpted a few passages from the thousands of pages of notes and essays Schwartz left. "A Poet's Notebooks" contains writing from 1942 to 1959 (*NYQ* 10:111–17).

viii. Plath, Sexton, Levertov, Wakoski, Rich

The essays on the poetry of Sylvia Plath keep coming, though perhaps no one since Hemingway has so divided the critical world. As a rule, Plath's detractors simply write nothing about her; the published comments are generally laudatory (two exceptions are E. D. Blodgett's "Sylvia Plath: Another View," *MPS* 2[1971]:97–106 and Irving Howe, "Sylvia Plath: A Partial Disagreement," *Harper's* Jan.: 88–91).

Robert Phillips's approach in "The Dark Funnel: A Reading of Sylvia Plath" (*MPS* 3:49–74) is to trace "the tragectory of her father's memory" in her poems and *The Bell Jar*. Phillips makes some helpful points about Plath's imagery of Jewishness, queens, and betrayed personae, whether or not his Jungian analyses are completely accurate (see also part I of Alfred Alvarez's *The Savage God: A Study of Suicide*, New York, Random House, and "'Who Is Sylvia?' The Art of Sylvia Plath" by Jan B. Gordon, *MPS* 1[1970]:6–34). There have also been six essays or notes devoted to single poems, two major introductory essays abroad ("La poésie di Sylvia Plath" by Renato Oliva, *SA* 15[1969]:341–81 and "De dichtkunst von Sylvia Plath" by W. Schrick in *DWB* 116:191–210), and Marjorie Perloff's succinct essay "'A Ritual for Being Born Twice': Sylvia Plath's *The Bell Jar*" (*ConL* 13:507–22), important in that it accurately relates the novel to the poetry. Using R. D. Laing as touchstone, Perloff insists that the response to Plath's writing exists because she does depict "the general human condition." We are willing to recognize personal malady, but Plath treats it with detachment and humor, even while showing the malady of the sane world in relation to the insane.

Like Perloff, Pamela A. Smith in "The Unitive Urge in the Poetry of Sylvia Plath" (*NEQ* 45:323–39) uses imagery to prove her interpretation. For Smith, Plath from the early poems of *Colossus* was investing the poem with a unitive purpose: "cleaning up and piecing together fragments, debris, to make something immaculate, superhuman, and whole." Rather naturally, then, Plath's art rested on her prowess with metaphor as a means of this unification. In her early poems, Smith thinks, metaphor was likely to be showy, pretentious. In *Ariel*, however, the metaphors do "put together entirely," if perhaps unpleasantly, the bits and pieces that were Plath's life.

Interviews with Adrienne Rich and Anne Sexton were published this year ("Talking with Adrienne Rich," by Stanley Plumly, Wayne Dodd, and Walter Travis, *OhR* 13:28–48, and John J. Mood's "'A Bird Full of Bones': Anne Sexton—A Visit and a Reading," *ChiR* 23:107–23), both giving evidence to the different perspectives women poets appear to have about some aspects of writing poetry. Emphasis in each is on the poem as a voyage of selfdiscovery, selfknowledge.

Denise Levertov is interviewed by Ian Reid ("'Everyman's Land,'" *SoRA* 5:231–36); she also writes her own description of the

poetic process in "The Poet in the World" (*APR* 1:16–18). Eric Mottram finds, in reviewing Levertov's *To Stay Alive*, that "sincerity is
not enough, that 'lost innocence' and introduction to political awareness . . . need new forms if they are to be re-used" ("The Limits of
Self-Regard," *Parnassus* 1:152–62). Mottram thinks rather more
highly of both Carolyn Kizer's recent work, largely for the technical
prowess of the poems; and also Diane Wakowski's *The Motorcycle
Betrayal Poems*, which he admires because of their metaphoric richness. See also Wakowski's column (*APR* 1: 46–47) and her essays on
Jerome Rothenberg (*Parnassus* 1:142–47) and on Armand Schwerner
(*Parnassus* 1:148–51).

Erica Jong writes on Eleanor Ross Taylor, Eve Merriam, and
Lucille Clifton in "Three Sisters" (*Parnassus* 1:77–88) and finds Clifton the most interesting poet. Jong also speculates that the greatest
artists of the near future will be blacks and women, because, she
claims, these writers appear to be less afraid to "tap the well-springs
of the unconscious."

William Jay Smith has written and compiled *A Woman's Words*,
an eighty-one-page tribute to Louise Bogan (Washington, Library of
Congress, 1971). The pamphlet includes Smith's commemorative
essay, including the laudatory remarks of many other poets, a poem
by Daniel Hoffman, and a lengthy bibliography.

Linda W. Wagner's *Phyllis McGinley* (TUSAS 170[1971]) assesses the poet's prowess chronologically. Wagner offers a chapter on
types of light verse, and evaluates McGinley's work as both light
verse and poetry. The study also includes McGinley's books for children and essays.

ix. Black Poets

The most important recent books on black poetry were *Report from
Part One: The Autobiography of Gwendolyn Brooks* (Detroit, Broadside Press) and Letitia Dace's *LeRoi Jones (Imamu Amiri Baraka):
A Checklist of Works By and About Him* (London, Nether Press,
1971). In an impressionistically casual format, Brooks reminisces
about her life and writers who were important to her, as well as her
newly developed social consciousness. She includes three interviews
and some random observations to close. Recent studies of Brooks's
poems are those by George E. Kent, in two parts ("The Poetry of

Gwendolyn Brooks," *BlackW* 20,xi:30–43; 20,xii:36–48, 68–71) and Houston A. Baker, Jr., "The Achievement of Gwendolyn Brooks" (*CLAJ* 16:23–31).

Most current essays on black poets emphasize the fact that rhythm is being derived more from jazz than from spoken patterns. Annette O. Shands in "The Relevancy of Don L. Lee as a Contemporary Black Poet" (*BlackW* 21,viii:35–48) sees Lee stressing the separation of black culture from white in the very language of his poems. Shands illustrates Lee's expressive use of spelling, abbreviations, vocabulary forms, negative prefixes, and the structural peculiarities of black English. Ronald Walcott writes on Melvin Tolson's 1969 epic *Harlem Gallery* in "Ellison, Gordone and Tolson: Some Notes on the Blues, Style, and Space" (*BlackW* 22,ii:4–29), and Barbara Christian revives interest in Bob Kaufman, one of the "shapers of the Beat movement" and one of the first poets to use jazz rhythms, in "Whatever Happened to Bob Kaufman?" (*BlackW* 21,xi:20–29).

x. Nemerov, Snodgrass, Simpson, E. Olson, Eberhart, Bodenheim, Scott, Francis, Berryman, Cunningham, Kunitz

The Critical Reception of Howard Nemerov: A Selection of Essays and a Bibliography, edited by Bowie Duncan (Metuchen, N.J., Scarecrow, 1971) includes a brief introduction by Reed Whittemore and a major checklist of both primary and secondary materials. The essays reprinted include twenty-two reviews of the various Nemerov books; three longer essays by Julia Randall, Peter Meinke, and Robert Harvey; and a 1960 interview with Nemerov.

The poet's collection of essays, *Reflexions on Poetry and Poetics* (New Brunswick, N.J., Rutgers Univ. Press) is divided between pieces on such single writers as Yeats, Dickey, Aiken, Jarrell, and Burke and pieces which are more general statements of Nemerov's own poetics. Of particular interest are his comments concerning poetry as joke, the uses of metaphor, the "difficult" modern poem, and poetry as a means of contemplation.

Jerome Mazzaro describes the impact of Snodgrass's poems on his readers in "The Public Intimacy of W. D. Snodgrass" (*Salmagundi* 19:96–111). He finds the intimacy of the poet's voice, expressed as it is in skillfully crafted formal poems, highly effective. Ronald Moran's *Louis Simpson* (TUSAS 210) is reasonably comprehensive, but a thesis-ridden book. Moran bases his claim for what he sees as Simpson's major position among American poets on the effectiveness of Simpson's World War II poems. He also insists that Simpson is one of the finest interpreters of America, as country and as culture, writing today. Stressing these two thematic areas, to the exclusion of others, hardly does Simpson's more recent writing justice.

Unfortunately, T. E. Lucas's study of Elder Olson (TUSAS 188) disappoints. Lucas makes very high claims for Olson's poems, but he spends little time discussing them. The bulk of the book describes the Chicago school of criticism and its various excellences. While Lucas's enthusiasm for Olson's prowess as teacher is understandable, the evidence that he presents does little to convince us that Olson is one of our greatest poets.

Bernard Engel's *Richard Eberhart* (TUSAS 194[1971]) is a better blend of poem explication and summation, but Engel's use of the term "Romantic" to describe Eberhart's poems is troublesome. Even if parts of the poet's philosophy suggest a correspondence with the Romantics, such categorization is seldom helpful. Engel's view that Eberhart is a fine poet because "his esthetic origins may be traced to Blake and Wordsworth, even Tennyson," and also because he "was not a participant in the 'modern' poetry movement" also seems too facile to be convincing.

Scott Donaldson's well-written biography, *Poet in America: Winfield Townley Scott* (Austin, Univ. of Texas Press) draws somewhat heavily on Scott's unpublished materials, as well as on his ten collections of poems. The title is apt, for Donaldson's primary theme is the near-futility of a poet's attempting to exist, financially, in America. As Donaldson describes it, Scott's death grew out of his "conflict, as an artist, with a culture in whose system of values the artist (unless he was very, very successful in his lifetime) hardly mattered at all." As possible antidote to this hardly uncommon view, one would do worse than to read *The Trouble with Francis: An Autobiography by Robert Francis* (Amherst, Univ. of Mass. Press, 1971). In addition to Francis's Thoreau-like comments on his financial position, the book includes many aphoristic sentences that carry the thrust of his presentation: that being a poet may not bring a man much recognition, but it does, eventually, bring even that. And Francis's candor is also refreshing: "That I have been published at

all is due largely to luck. Now and then someone with a little influence
has made a move on my behalf."

Richard J. Kelly's *John Berryman: A Checklist* (Metuchen, N.J.,
Scarecrow) is a helpful compilation of all published materials both
by and about the poet. William Meredith's foreword comments on
Berryman's term "crisis poem," and Michael Berryhill's introduction
defends the poet's use of allusions (as predictable, not pretentious),
his incredibly varied idiom, and his choice of personal themes. In
"Berryman's Most Bright Candle" (*Parnassus* 1:180–87), Larry Vo-
nalt finds *Delusions, Etc.* an important book because of its structure.
Opening and closing with poems of prayer, the book contains Berryman's most obviously religious poems as well as questioning ones.

Hayden Carruth, with his usual keen perception, gives readers a
sense of the importance of another of the middle poets in "A Location
of J. V. Cunningham" (*MQR* 11:75–83), and Marjorie Perloff kindles
interest in Stanley Kunitz's new poems ("The Testing of Stanley
Kunitz," *IowaR* 3:93–103). Perloff finds his best poems in *The Testing
Tree*; she likes the loose blank verse and the three-step line, and the
often witty treatment of the self-deprecating narrator; but she misses
in the new personal tone any "passionate sense of history."

xi. O'Hara, Bly, Wright, Strand, Ammons, and Others

Helen Vendler's "The Virtues of the Alterable" (*Parnassus* 1:5–20)
discusses the merits and the dangers of Frank O'Hara's poetic method.
She sees his weaknesses, especially noticeable in the *Collected
Poems*, as being his lack of "a comfortable form" and his "incapacity
for abstraction." She admires O'Hara's having used poems, at his
most successful, as "demonstrations of what mind is by what mind
does." O'Hara saw the poem as process, and his use of the art form in
that way has been widely influential—in fact, "a new species."

Robert Bly, one of the most influential poets today, is taken to
task by Sandra McPherson in "You Can Say That Again. (Or Can
You?)" (*IowaR* 3:70–77). In comparing early collections by Bly and
James Wright, McPherson finds many dictional similarities, and the
same words repeated frequently. She supports her premise by word
counts, and concludes that the poets' early work had in common an
excessive love of the old, enervation of landscape, a somber quality to

all experience, and "some of the sleepiest surrealism around." She does acknowledge that both Wright and Bly have since gone into new directions. It seems no accident, then, that Anthony Libby takes as theme for his essay on Bly's work one of these recurring images. "Robert Bly Alive in Darkness" (*IowaR* 3:78–90) treats Bly's pervasive use of the deep image, the poem as a way in to every man's personal mystery. Despite his often simple imagery, Bly's poems frequently need analysis: as mystical poems, they are often based on paradox. Silence, water, air, politics, death, the feminine principle —Libby uses Bly's recurring images to illustrate his points, and concludes by reading "The Teeth Mother Naked at Last" as an affirmative poem.

Several minor essays on Wright's work appeared this year, those by Madeline DeFrees and John Ditsky published in *MPS* 2:241–59, and the more comprehensive survey by Peter A. Stitt in *MinnR* 2:13–32. Joseph R. McElrath's "Something to Be Said for the Light: A Conversation with James Wright" (*SHR* 6:134–53) is valuable for Wright's judgments about the craft of poetry.

Frederick Garber ("Fat Man at the Margin: The Poetry of Richard Hugo," *IowaR* 3:58–66) sees Hugo as a poetic conservative, "tied deeply into elemental things that never change" and deeply concerned with people. Not a "confessional mode" for all its structural openness, Hugo's voice is his own—intense, constrained, vigorous— but he uses it to give us a sense of what he sees in the world, not necessarily a sense of what he is.

Harold Bloom locates promise in "Dark and Radiant Peripheries: Mark Strand and A. R. Ammons" (*SoR* 8:133–49). He sees their poetry as defining the limits of this younger generation of poets— Ammons as direct heir of Emerson, Strand as "a dark child of Stevens." Because neither poet is afraid of the major and moving themes of great literature, Bloom expects fine poems from them.

John Koethe speaks of the strength of John Ashbery's writing in "Ashbery's Meditations" (*Parnassus* 1:89–93). He finds that the form of the recent prose-like *Three Poems* only reinforces Ashbery's earlier mode. Koethe sees him as a meditative poet, interested primarily not in his method of expression but rather in the question of "whether any expression can be adequate to the need which prompted it." See also the Ashbery interview (*NYQ* 9:11–33).

Crazy Horse 10 is a Theodore Weiss issue, including poems, Phil

Dacey's comment on *The World Before Us: Poems 1950–70*, and a long interview with Weiss. "Joining *The Donner Party*" (*Parnassus* 1:36–46) gives Weiss opportunity to describe the difficulty of writing the long poem. He traces the history of it in America, describing the uses of collage and suite that have characterized it. His most important comments, however, are about the need to attempt the long poem. Rather than being perverse, "the poet who is bitten by the wish to write poems of the first order and who, having read the great works of the past, understands their accomplishment knows, cannot help knowing, that a poem to be major must have magnitude, must accommodate and illuminate as many fundamental themes as possible." Weiss then regrets contemporary poets who feel that they can pour any kind of writing into the mold of the long poem and expect it to jell. His essay is—it seems to me—a plea for sanity, a cry for a return to a normal judicious path in even our "newest" writing: "Skills in themselves of course are hardly sacred. Least of all if the poet's vision changes and he can develop other, deeper, more telling skills closer to and an outcome of that vision. But I am not yet convinced, whatever the failures of intelligence and art (and certainly the inadequacy of intellect alone), that incoherence and the cultivation of chaos are likely to do better; that pyrotechnics, which threatens to burn down the house altogether, is preferable to technique; that madness, even if genuine, however more dramatic and convincing it may appear beside sanity, can illuminate and free us" (p. 46).

Michigan State University

16. Drama

Walter J. Meserve

i. Histories, Encyclopedias, Indexes, Dissertations

Although no single volume dealing with the entire scope of American drama appeared in 1972, a number of general works were published that have some value for the teacher of American drama and theatre. Myron Matlaw's *Modern World Drama: An Encyclopedia* (New York, Dutton), despite omissions that American specialists will soon discover, is a valuable source book for information on plays and play-wrights throughout the world. Vera Mowry Roberts's *The Nature of the Theatre* (New York, Harper and Row, 1971) employs a liberal number of modern American plays to illustrate chapters on dramatic genres. Her objective, however, is a "book about theatre" rather than drama, and her bias shows in her bibliography as well as her section on playwrights. In a more particular view for American drama and theatre specialists, William C. Young's *American Theatrical Arts: A Guide to Manuscripts and Special Collections in the United States and Canada* (Chicago, American Library Assoc., 1971) provides a description of collections in 138 repository institutions. The listings refer to legitimate theatre as well as vaudeville, burlesque, dance, and television and supply information on actors, playwrights, directors, designers, etc. A second very useful volume for researchers is Dean H. Keller's *Index to Plays in Periodicals* (Metuchen, N.J., Scarecrow 1971). Listing his results in two parts—author index, title index—Keller has sifted through 103 different periodicals.

The titles of more than fifty dissertations on topics in American drama and theatre appeared in the *DAI*. Most of them treat some part of American theatre history. Slowly, an assessment of theatre in such varied places as Springfield, Massachusetts; Logan, Utah; Salem, Ohio; Peoria, Illinois; St. Paul, Minnesota; San Francisco, Los Angeles, and Milwaukee is being added to the stacks of theatre history. Other dissertation writers studied the careers of Lawrence Barrett and John Golden, the effect of Kotzebue on the American stage, Augustin Daly's Shakespearean productions, the Federal government's interest in theatre since the Federal Theatre Project and, particularly interesting among the various listed topics, "Landmark Litigation in the American Theatre." Eugene O'Neill was the subject, either wholly or in part, of six dissertations; other Ph.D. recipients treated Henry James, Edward Albee, Tennessee Williams, S. N. Behrman, LeRoi Jones, Philip Barry, Paul Green, and such concepts in American drama as history, tragedy, and despair. With reference to dissertations it should be noted that the British *Journal of American Studies* includes the heading of "Drama" under its "Theses on American Topics in Progress and Completed at British Universities." The April 1972 issue (6:109) lists six dissertations on such topics as commitment, politics and protest in American drama, drama critics, the family in the plays of selected dramatists, and the plays of Edward Albee.

ii. From the Beginning to 1860

The collections of essays clearly reveal certain existing attitudes toward American dramatists writing before World War I. *Major Writers* includes essays on nine writers, one of whom was also a dramatist, but Lewis Leary's "Philip Freneau" (pp. 245–71) does not mention his plays. Among the bibliographic essays in *Fifteen American Authors Before 1900*, edited by Robert A. Rees and Earl N. Harbert (Madison, Univ. of Wis. Press, 1971), those on Cooper, Crane, and Irving neglect the drama completely. Howells is represented by one book, and Longfellow by a single essay. Only C. Hugh Holman's "The Literature of the Old South" (pp. 387–400) gives serious attention to the drama.

For those interested in American drama and theatre of the eighteenth century, *Songs from the Williamsburg Theatre* (Charlottesville, Univ. Press of Va.), introduced and arranged for voice and keyboard by John W. Molnar, will be a revelation. With an historical sketch showing how music became a part of plays and, therefore, necessary to the accomplishments of the theatre company, he prefaces each of the fifty songs with a detailed and well-documented commentary. As the Revolution approached, dramatists joined the conflict. In a well-written essay entitled "Blockheadism and the

Propaganda Plays of the American Revolution" (*EAL* 7,ii:148–62)
John J. Teunissen explains how the "blockhead" metaphor was used
by three dramatists. A few years after the Revolution, Royall Tyler
wrote *The Contrast*. Marius B. Péladeau's edition of *The Prose of
Royall Tyler* (Rutland, Vt., Tuttle) is well prepared although, with
reference to drama, it includes only an essay on *Jane Shore* from
The Polyanthos and Tyler's introduction to his *Sacred Dramas* which
also appears in *America's Lost Plays*. Norman Philbrick has collected
seven plays from the period of the Revolution in *Trumpets Sounding:
Propaganda Plays of the American Revolution* (New York, Benjamin
Blom): *A Dialogue Between a Southern Delegate and His Spouse,
The Fall of British Tyranny, The Blockheads, The Battle of Brooklyn, The Death of General Montgomery, The Patriots*, and *The Motley Assembly*. Although the format of the volume is odd and the
individual introductions more comprehensive than necessary for
one who would read the plays, the editor is helpful in supplying the
historical background and settting for the plays. In another essay,
"The Spy as Hero: An Examination of *André* by William Dunlap"
(*Studies in Theatre and Drama*, pp. 97–119), Professor Philbrick
does not examine the play in terms of hero or structure, but does provide a thorough discussion of historical background and of the details
attendant to its production and reception.

David Ritchey's "Baltimore's Eighteenth Century French Theatre" (*SSCJ* 38:164–67) explains how the Acadians from Nova Scotia
presented French drama in an attempt to contribute a bit of their
own heritage to the culture of their adopted home. Whatever the
drama, however, the actors dominated the scene. Billy J. Harbin
provides new information about the reception of a popular American
actor in "Hodgkinson's Last Years at the Charleston Theatre, 1803–
05" (*TS* 13,ii:20–43). Gresdna Ann Doty adds considerably to our
knowledge of an early actress with her clearly written and carefully
documented account of *The Career of Mrs. Anne Brunton Merry in
the American Theatre* (Baton Rouge, La. State Univ. Press, 1971).
Mainly, Professor Doty assesses Mrs. Merry's twelve-year career
(1796–1808) as an actress and manager of the Chestnut Street Theatre and provides information on seasons, plays, salaries, roles, and
problems at the box office. "A Note on the John Street Theatre" (*TS*
13,ii:100–01) by Barnard Hewitt helps to establish the location of
this theatre.

Management and acting were the subjects of other essays on American theatre and drama during the first half of the nineteenth century. James M. Leonard's "Correspondence and Confrontation Between William Duffy, Manager, and John Hamilton, Actor" (*TS* 13,i:42–51) is slight but provides another view of managerial problems. " 'King Stephen' of the Park and Drury Lane" by Barnard Hewitt, in *The Theatrical Manager in England and America*, edited by Joseph W. Donohue, Jr. (Princeton, N.J., Princeton Univ. Press, 1971), pp. 87–141, follows the career of Stepen Price, who adhered to the great star and box-office procedures of early-nineteenth-century America. The most effective essay in Donohue's volume is Charles H. Shattuck's "The Theatrical Management of Edwin Booth" (pp. 143–88). Carefully researched and written with both charm and wisdom, Shattuck's essay assesses Booth's brief and disastrous career as a theatre manager, concluding that the interlude can only support the fact that Booth's genius was in acting. It should be noted here that Joseph Donohue's introduction provides a well-phrased argument for research in theatre and for the study of plays in performance. Among the actors of mid-nineteenth-century America, few names are easily remembered. The major accomplishments of a minor but very popular actor are presented in Walter J. Meserve's "Barney Williams: A Genuine American Paddy" (*Studies in Theatre and Drama*, pp. 158–76).

Three essays indicative of the steady increase of interest developing among scholars of nineteenth-century drama and theatre treat two significant but poorly understood dramatists. John W. Crowley begins the task of putting "James Nelson Barker in Perspective" (*ETJ* 24:363–69). Paul D. Voelker performs the same scholarly chore for Boker's most successful and best-known play—"George Henry Boker's *Francesca da Rimini*: An Interpretation and Evaluation" (*ETJ* 24: 383–95)—while Alan Woods reviews some thoughts about "Producing Boker's *Francesca da Rimini*" (*ETJ* 24:396–401).

iii. From 1860 Through 1915

At this middle period in the broad history of American drama and theatre it is most convenient to discuss a collection of essays with a view to assessing *The American Theatre: A Sum of Its Parts* (New York, Samuel French, 1971). Initially, the papers were presented for

a symposium, "The American Theatre—A Cultural Process," at the
First American College Theatre Festival, 1969. Among the published
essays, Francis Hodge's "European Influences on American Theatre,
1700–1969" (pp. 3–22) too easily dismisses either originality or distinction in American theatre and drama prior to World War I in order
to dwell upon the New Stagecraft and what followed. Emphasizing
that playwrights of the nineteenth century wrote to reflect an audience that was "critical, romantic, and democratic," Alan Downer's
assessment of pre-O'Neill drama, "Waiting for O'Neill" (pp. 25–39),
is an effective response to Hodge's assumption. For the actors, Richard Moody assembles a great deal of information in "American Actors and Acting Before 1900: The Making of a Tradition" (pp. 41–
80), with an excellent survey and artistic analysis. Alan Hewitt's
concern for the modern period, "Repertory to Residuals, Reflections
on American Acting Since 1900" (pp. 83–123), however, is simply a
mass of episodic reminiscences told with a certain charm and flair.
Helen Krich Chinoy's "The Profession and the Art, Directing in
America, 1860–1920" (pp. 125–51) includes sketchy comments,
mainly on the period after 1900, while Lawrence Carra's "The Influence of the Director—for Good or Bad, Covering the Years 1920–
1969" (pp. 153–69) mainly presents lists and sketches, with little
analysis. A quick view of "The Producer's Many Roles" (pp. 167–79)
is provided by Barnard Hewitt.

Other essays in the volume *The American Theatre* include A. S.
Gillette's "American Scenography—1716–1969" (pp. 181–96); Ned
Bowman's impressive discussion of "American Theatre Architecture:
The Concrete Mirror Held Up to Yankee Nature" (pp. 199–222);
Julian Mates's "American Musical Theatre: Beginnings to 1900" (pp.
225–45); William Green's "Broadway Book Musicals: 1900–1969"
(pp. 247–71); and Randolph Edmonds's "Black Drama in the Ameri-
can Theatre: 1700–1970" (pp. 379–426)—a misleading title in that
Edmonds considers plays with black characters and emphasizes the
contemporary scene. Ralph G. Allen's "Our Native Theatre: Honky-
Tonk, Minstrel Shows, Burlesque" (pp. 273–314) provides enlightenment on a fascinating aspect of American theatre and is also noteworthy for the scripts of "Four Burlesque Bits" that are included.
Elliot Norton's "Puffers, Pundits and Other Play Reviewers: A Short
History of American Dramatic Criticism" (pp. 317–37) sports a fine
title but is weak and terribly disappointing as an essay on dramatic

criticism in America. Two essays in the volume treat the university and the theatre. Both are well written and informative and should be interesting to any teacher of drama and theatre: Bernard Beckerman, "The University Accepts the Theatre, 1800–1925" (pp. 339–55) and James H. Butler, "The University Theatre Begins to Come of Age: 1925–1969" (pp. 357–76). Richard Moody's "American Actors and American Plays on the London Stage in the Nineteenth Century" (*Studies in Theatre and Drama*, pp. 138–57) surveys the major plays and figures with special emphasis upon the activities of the Bateman family.

Particular theatres active in the late nineteenth century and early twentieth century received some attention. Mitzi Friedlander provides a brief story of the Grand Opera House of Louisville in "History of a Theatre" (*FCHQ* 45[1971]:305–14), and Robert Overstreet in "John T. Ford and the Savannah Theatre" (*SSCJ* 38:51–60) explains the theatrical activity in the South of a man whose name generally lives through an event associated with his theatre in Washington. A sketch of "The New Theatre" (*QJS* 58:322–26) is provided by John Perry. Tent theatre developed in the late nineteenth century and emerged with perhaps more than a hundred companies touring during the first decade of the twentieth century. By the 1920s the mold was set, and such rural entertainment boomed with the creation of the Toby and Susie characters and a repertory of plays reminiscent of *The Old Homestead*. In a well-documented and interestingly written book, *Theatre in a Tent: The Development of a Provincial Entertainment* (Bowling Green, Ohio, Bowling Green Univ. Press), that includes many pictures and a fine bibliography, William L. Stout tells the story of this particular kind of American theatre. Barbara Berry's *Let 'Er Buck! The Rodeo* (Indianapolis, Bobbs-Merrill) is mainly for young people as it tells of another rural entertainment that has become a million-dollar business.

No essays appeared on the popular plays written during the Rise of Realism and before World War I, but a number of lesser-known works and literary oddities were discussed. In "Buffalo Bill on Stage" (*Players* 47:80–91) William Coleman describes the events leading up to William F. Cody's 1872 stage debut in *The Scouts of the Prairie* and follows that production to the end of its tour in the spring of 1873. David K. Kirby analyzes "Henry James's *The Other House*: From Novel to Play" (*MarkhamR* 3:49–53), comparing and contrasting the different versions. "Two Unpublished Plays by Stephen Crane" (*RALS* 1[1971]:200–16) were printed and discussed by Lewis H. Fine, who briefly analyzes the manuscript and plot of the first play in " 'The Fire-Tribe and the Pale Face': An Unfinished and Unpublished Play by Stephen Crane" (*Markham R* 3:37–38). The second play remains untitled. A play by Jack London and Herbert Heron, *Gold: A Play in Three Acts* (Oakland, Calif., Holmes Book Co.) is a weak and exceedingly contrived melodrama about a professor who gives up teaching in order to find the "gold of life" and a doctor who loves both gold and the professor's wife. The Klondike provides the background in which right may prevail. Hopefully, this play will turn out to be more authentic than another play, *Daughters of the Rich*, which the Holmes Book Company published in 1971 over London's name, an attribution about which some have grave doubts (see Chapter 12, above).

Three essays on disparate topics in this period deserve mention. In "Towse on Reform in the American Theatre" (*SSCJ* 38:254–60) Tice Miller presents the ideas of a significant critic on ways to improve American theatre. A strong believer in the repertory system, Towse also advocated performances of both classical drama and popular plays. For a revealing commentary on an earlier critic whose work was always interesting to read one should note Thomas K. Wright's "Nym Crinkle: Gadfly Critic and Male Chauvinist" (*ETJ* 24:370–82). Although Percy Mackaye lived past the middle of the century, his best work was created before O'Neill achieved his success. In a well-contrived argument D. Heyward Brock and James M. Welsh analyze Mackaye's theory and practice in the light of Ben Jonson's work—"Percy Mackaye: Community Drama and the Masque Tradition" (*CompD* 6:68–84). They argue well that Mackaye essentially revived an old literary genre and adapted it to his interests in communal drama, where the masque served a social as well as artistic function.

iv. Between the Two World Wars

Quite equal to the distinctive American drama which the dramatists of this period achieved is the innovative experimentation which permeated all aspects of the theatre arts. Norman Bel Geddes was a considerable figure during these years, and George Bogusch presents an authoritative and convincing argument concerning his accomplishments in one part of scenic design—"Norman Bel Geddes and the Art of Modern Theatre Lighting" (*ETJ* 24:415–29). Of a more general nature is Fredrick Hunter's "Norman Bel Geddes: Renaissance Man of the American Theatre," a paper at the Sixth Congress of the International Federation for Theatre Research, 1969, and published in *Innovations in Stage and Theatre Design* edited by Francis Hodge (New York, American Society for Theatre Research and Theatre Library Assn.), pp. 15–28. In the same volume Donald Oenslager presents a sketchy but well-illustrated review of the work of "Robert Edmond Jones: Artist of the Theatre" (pp. 1–14). Among the producing agencies of this period between the two World Wars the Theatre Guild was a giant. Season by season Roy S. Waldau considers the *Vintage Years of the Theatre Guild, 1928–1939* (Cleveland, Ohio, Press of Case Western Reserve Univ.), indicating the problems arising from size, road shows, the Depression, and a conservative directorate. One particular kind of experiment which developed to a high point at this time was the pageant. Gerald Kahan takes "*The Wayfarer*: An American Religious Pageant" (*Players* 47: 170–78), describes it in terms of plot and music, and traces its production history from its first performance at the June–July 1919 Methodist Centenary Missionary Exposition in Columbus, Ohio, to its five-week stand in Madison Square Garden. Another kind of theatrical experimentation is examined by Mardi Valgamae in a slight volume entitled *Accelerated Grimace: Expressionism in the American Drama of the 1920's* (Carbondale, So. Ill. Univ. Press).

a. **Eugene O'Neill.** Dealing with all extant plays written between 1913–1914 and 1941, Travis Bogard traces O'Neill's development as a dramatist in *Contour in Time: The Plays of Eugene O'Neill* (New York, Oxford Univ. Press). Although he considers a lot of ground that has been frequently spaded by others, Bogard's analysis is valuable for his forthright approach to the various influences upon the dramatist as well as for the commentary on lesser-known plays. Two articles by James Milton Highsmith in *Modern Drama* are of considerable value to the O'Neill scholar. In "A Description of the Cornell Collection of Eugene O'Neill's Letters to George Jean Nathan" (*MD* 14:420–25) he lists the letters by date, place, number of pages, etc. "The Cornell Letters: Eugene O'Neill on His Craftsmanship to

George Jean Nathan" (*MD* 15:68–88) provides the necessary analysis of the collection. Ostensibly revealing the tone and content of the
letters, Highsmith argues that they show O'Neill's concern for his
craftsmanship as well as a personal side of the dramatist that is little
known. In another essay, one that would seem little more than an
exercise in comparison, Winifred L. Frazer shows how two playwrights dramatize "by means of a deadly serious joke the curse
under which mankind has ever since labored"—"King Lear and
Hickey: Bridegroom and Iceman" (*MD* 15:267–78). Placing O'Neill
in the currently popular movement, Peter J. Gillett—"O'Neill and the
Racial Myths" (*TCL* 18:111–20)—traces his treatment of black
America and concludes that O'Neill accepted the challenge of creating representative black characters.

b. **Odets, Dos Passos, Didactic Drama.** In "Clifford Odets: A Playwright and His Jewish Background" (*SAQ* 71:225–33) Baird R.
Shuman reviews the Jewish influence in Odets's plays of 1935 and
emphasizes that the dramatist did not again return to a Jewish theme
until *The Flowering Peach* in 1954. One who would have enjoyed
some of Odets's theatrical reputation in the 1930s, John Dos Passos,
is the subject of Melvin Landsberg's book, *Dos Passos' Path to
"U.S.A.": A Political Biography, 1912–1936* (Boulder, Colo. Associated Univ. Press). As the title states, this is an analysis in which
Dos Passos is placed against an historical-political background. His
plays, therefore, are considered only inasmuch as they shed light
upon his creation of *U.S.A.* Landsberg shows, for example, how
Garbage Man helps explain the genesis of *Manhattan Transfer*. He
does comment briefly on the plots of *Airways* and *Fortune Heights*,
but the commentary is slight and sometimes incoherent. Assessment
of Dos Passos's plays as well as his essays and asociations with theatre
people remains incomplete. Another book concerned with the persuasive plays of the 1930s is Sam Smiley's *The Drama of Attack:
Didactic Plays of the American Depression* (Columbia, Univ. of Mo.
Press). Framing his theory in two parts—the genesis and the analysis
of such drama—Smiley presents a particular but convincing argument concerning both the social milieu and the structure of didactic
drama. In order to identify the major structural principles of didactic
drama he considers in some detail over forty plays that were part of
the leftist drama popular on Broadway during the 1930s. Continuing

his argument in an essay on "Thought as Plot in Didactic Drama" (*Studies in Theatre and Drama*, pp. 81–96), Smiley uses American plays to define didactic drama and determine the dual function of thought in this genre. From another point of view Morgan Y. Himelstein considers "Theory and Performance in the Depression Theatre" (*MD* 14:426–35) in an attempt to refute any claim that protest dramatists worked from a significant dramatic theory.

c. **Behrman and Kaufman.** There was also comedy between the two World Wars. One kind was written by S. N. Behrman, whose *Tribulations and Laughter: A Memoir* (London, Hamilton; pub. in Boston, Little, Brown, as *People in a Diary: A Memoir*) is a sentimental but frequently candid and revealing reminiscence (parts of which have been published previously) based on his diary (sixty volumes), which he has kept since 1915. A man of humor, balance, and hope, Behrman reviews his life in the theatre, writing one of his best chapters on the Playwrights' Company. On the other end of the comic spectrum is Kaufman. Howard Teichmann's *George S. Kaufman: An Intimate Portrait* (New York, Atheneum) is mainly laudatory, but the volume is carefully researched. With a well-selected and well-orchestrated bundle of anecdotes, Teichmann moves chronologically through various aspects of Kaufman's life—playwriting, directing, family man, card player, etc. It is worth noting that all of the materials Teichmann gathered in his research will be available at the Wisconsin Center for Theatre Research.

d. **Barry, Wilder, Saroyan.** In "Psychodrama on Broadway: Three Plays of Psychodrama by Philip Barry" (*MarkhamR* 2[1970]:65–74) David C. Gild discusses *In a Garden* as Barry's first attempt to apply the principles of psychodrama, *Here Come the Clowns* as his mature use of the genre, and *Hotel Universe* as his finest work, a play which fulfills almost all of the requirements of clinical psychodrama. Emphasizing their joint concern for theatricalism, intellectual response, and symbolic effect, Douglas Charles Wixson, Jr., discusses "The Dramatic Techniques of Thornton Wilder and Bertold Brecht: A Study in Comparison" (*MD* 15:112–24). Thelma J. Shinn's view of "William Saroyan: Romantic Existentialist" (*MD* 15:185–94) suggests the contradiction in Saroyan's work as he both affirms values in life (*The Cave Dwellers*) and denies them (*Death Along the Wa-*

bash). Ultimately, she shows him to be more romantic than existentialist, but her approach to Saroyan as a perceptive dramatist is effectively presented.

e. Green, Cummings, Anderson, Hellman. Although Vincent S. Kenny's *Paul Green* (TUSAS 186[1971]) presents a great amount of information, there is a bothersome imbalance and inconsistency in the book. His prefacing statement that the symphonic dramas add nothing to Green's stature is contradicted by the amount of space allowed to that part of Green's work. One is bothered by Kenny's conclusion that *Johnny Johnson* is "not an anti-war play, except incidentally" and concerned that he does not consider Green's several essays about theatre and drama. Kenny is most effective in his analysis of Green's folk plays and, with the odd exception of *In Abraham's Bosom*, shows his greatest understanding here. In "Some Notes on Music and Drama" (*Studies in Theatre and Drama*, pp. 73–80) Green has written a delightful and revealing account of his thoughts and experiences in using music in drama. Anecdotal and personal, the essay shows both humor and insight in its final statement. In "Winterset: Four Influences on Mio" (*MD* 14:408–12) Arthur T. Tees contends that the plot and Mio's actions are clearly developed inasmuch as they are based on the influences of Judge Gaunt, Esdras, Mio's father, and Miriamne. Richard Moody's *Lillian Hellman, Playwright* (Indianapolis, Bobbs-Merrill) progresses with wit and ancedote through a play-by-play commentary. Although the progress is sometimes hindered by an unbalanced consideration of particular plays (more space for *My Mother* than for *Toys*, for example), the numerous personal vignettes suggestive of the cooperation which Moody gained from Hellman give the volume both charm and importance as an introduction to the dramatist.

v. After World War II

"Drama and Society, Mid-Century and Before" (pp. 1–14) is the title of Morris Freedman's introductory essay in *American Drama in Social Context* (Carbondale, So. Ill. Univ. Press, 1971), a collection of eight essays, four previously published. Essentially, Freedman refuses to believe that America has a drama, and his opening essay is filled with large gestures of regret and a contempt or misunderstanding of American drama before 1920 which he states, "is not studied except by specialists." Freedman's theme of family tetralogy, which he sees in *Sons, Salesman, Fall,* and *Price* and discusses in "The Jewishness of Arthur Miller; His Family Epic" (pp. 43–58), is a happily conceived argument which he weakens by some pretentious wandering. The essay begins, "Arthur Miller was born in 1915." In "Musical Drama and the American Liberal Impulse" (pp. 59–71) Freedman sees "political intention" and the "liberal impulse" as determining the direction and character of the American musical, which he feels has now reached the ultimate liberal form of nudity. "Toward an American Tragedy" (pp. 113–26) shows Freedman's beliefs that tragedy is political and must involve an historical figure in an epic form—which, for him, only *Indians* illustrates. Generally, Freedman does not reveal either the insight or the writing style that one would equate with a critic of substance.

The only lengthy work on a contemporary dramatist which does not emphasize Miller, Williams, Albee, or the black dramatists is Grover Smith's *Archibald MacLeish* (UMPAW 99). And this work is of little value for the person interested in MacLeish's dramas. Smith is concerned with language, but he has no comment on MacLeish's interest in poetic language and rhythm in drama and allows only four of his final five pages for a summary of his plays.

a. **Arthur Miller.** Three collections of essays suggest the continuing interest that scholars have in Miller's plays. The most complete and satisfying is Gerald Weales's edition of *The Crucible* (New York, Viking, 1971) which includes the text of the play along with the insight and observation that fine criticism should have. John H. Ferres's *Twentieth Century Interpretations of "The Crucible"* (Englewood Cliffs, N.J., Prentice-Hall) provides a strong introduction to the play. Walter J. Meserve's *Merrill Studies in "Death of a Salesman"* (Columbus, Ohio, Charles E. Merrill) has a new introduction to the play by the editor and reprints essays on the play as social problem and tragedy and on the characters, style, and reception of the play. The final section is noteworthy for new translations of important French and German reviews of the play; for new essays on "*Death of a Salesman* in India" by Rajinder Paul, the editor of a monthly drama magazine, *Enact* (Delhi); and *"Death of a Salesman* in England" by Dennis Welland, the author of the first book-length study of Arthur Miller.

Among the articles on Miller's works, B. S. Field, Jr.'s "Hamartia in *Death of a Salesman*" (*TCL* 18:19–24) presents the argument for propriety in catastrophe with the conclusion that Willy was justly punished for the crime he committed. Ronald Hayman, "Arthur Miller: Between Satire and Society" (*Encounter* 37,v:[1971]:75–79), sees Miller as a Sartrean playwright who uses characters to comment on society. The best essay on Miller is Gerald Weales's "All About Talk: Arthur Miller's *The Price*" (*OhR* 13,ii:74–84) in which he effectively argues that the play is about talk, that Miller is "using and questioning the dramatic, social, and therapeutic uses of talk and that an understanding of the play depends upon the degree to which author and audience admit to efficacy in conversation."

b. **Tennessee Williams.** *The Theatre of Tennessee Williams* (4 vols., New York, New Directions, 1971–1972) collects thirteen of his earlier plays, with cast lists, production notes, and his essays pertinent to the plays. Perhaps the best essay published on Williams this year— Donald P. Costello's "Tennessee Williams' Fugitive Kind" (*MD* 15: 26–43)—uses *Orpheus Descending* as a key to understanding his entire work. In terms of major themes, favorite devices, precise language, and images, Costello argues most convincingly that the play presents a clear and concentrated view of the playwright's work. The essay would seem to be an excellent teaching approach to provide a quick and intelligent, if oversimplified, view of Williams's dramas.

Henry Popkin very rapidly traces Williams's reputation in "Tennessee Williams Reexamined" (*Arts in Virginia* 2:2–5), while T. S. Reck discusses the manner and the extent to which Williams drew upon his short fiction in creating his plays—"The Short Stories of Tennessee Williams: Nucleus for His Drama" (*TSL* 16[1971]:141– 54). In "The Distorted Mirror: Tennessee Williams' Self-Portraits" (*MissQ* 25:389–403) Nancy M. Tischler shows herself to be one of the best interpreters of Williams's plays as she explains, primarily through *Battle of Angels,* how he reveals his truth in art and asserts his power as a playwright. Delma E. Pressley approaches Williams from a theological point of view in "The Search for Hope in the Plays of Tennessee Williams" (*MissQ* 25[1971]:31–43), describes the three major theological problems he finds in Williams's plays and suggests *Camino Real* as a turning point in Williams's theological development. After this play Williams began to suggest solutions for his problems.

The Glass Menagerie still draws major attention, but not always deep thought. In "Chloroses—Pâles Roses and Pleurosis—Blue Roses" (*RomN* 13[1971]:250–51) Cora Robey briefly suggests that Williams may have been influenced by Baudelaire's rhyme "chloroses-pâles roses" in "L'Idéal." H. L. Cate and Delma Pressley argue that Williams tried to individualize Amanda as one who possessed a realistic understanding of life—"Beyond Stereotype: Ambiguity in Amanda Wingfield" (*NMW* 3[1971]:91–100). In "Tennessee Williams' Unicorn Broken Again" (*RBPH* 49[1971]:875–85) Gilbert Debusscher attempts to refute a previous interpretation by Gregor Pavlov that the play is simply social melodrama.

c. Edward Albee. Anne Paolucci's brief book-length study of Albee, *From Tension to Tonic: The Plays of Edward Albee* (Carbondale, So. Ill. Univ. Press), is a sensible, clear, rather average interpretation of individual plays. Otherwise, scholarship on Albee's plays is more sparse than in years past. Don D. Moore in "Albee's *The American Dream*" (*Expl* 30:item 44) draws the conclusion that the character of Grandma is the most appealing and wisest for both audiences and critics. John A. Byars applies the "woman as hero test" to "*Taming of the Shrew* and *Who's Afraid of Virginia Woolf?*" (*CimR* 21:41–48) but gives most of his attention to Martha and Albee's play. John Stark attempts to explain *Tiny Alice* in terms of Sontag's critical theories in "Camping Out: *Tiny Alice* and Susan Sontag" (*Players* 47:166–69). Accepting the obscurity in the play and concerned with the reason for creating this obscurity, Stark refers to "Notes on Camp," "Against Interpretation," and the use of religion. His conclusion that *Tiny Alice* is an experiment which exemplifies an alternative to art is not particularly satisfying. In his revised edition of *The Theatre of Protest and Paradox* (New York, N.Y. Univ. Press, 1971) George Wellwarth adds comment to his Albee essay (pp. 321–36) on *Tiny Alice, A Delicate Balance, Box,* and *Quotations* but, as usual in this volume, provides no strong insights or conclusions. In other essays on "Arthur Kopit" (pp. 345–47) and

"Jack Gelber" (pp. 349–52) Wellwarth adds nothing to his original essay; for "Jack Richardson" (pp. 337–44) he provides an extra note on *Xmas in Las Vegas*.

d. **Jean-Claude van Itallie.**   At least a brief mention should be made of a handful of essays on van Itallie which attempt to establish a place for him in the world of scholarship. There is "A Checklist of Jean-Claude van Itallie, 1961–1972" (*Serif* 9,iv:75–77) by Michael J. Brittain and a brief comment by Philip R. Berk entitled "Memories of John [Jean-Claude van Itallie]" (*Serif* 9, iv:9–11), in addition to two essays on different aspects of his work: "Jean-Claude van Itallie: Playwright of the Ensemble: Open Theater" (*Serif* 9,iv:14–17) by Rhea Gaisner, and "Jean-Claude van Itallie: Political Playwright" (*Serif* 9,iv:19–74) by Phyllis J. Wagner.

e. **Black drama.**   There can be no questioning the fact that black drama and theatre are preferred subjects for drama critics, who are then conveniently aided by the number of journals publishing in the area. The scope of the essays now indicates the growth of this movement in theatre, reflecting as it does a political attitude from one point of view and stark propaganda from another, as well as some information about a rapidly developing theatre movement and commentary on a growing number of black dramatists. This growth is shown in a checklist of plays published by Hilda McElroy and Richard A. Willis, "Published Works of Black Playwrights in the United States, 1960–1970" (*BlackW* 21,vi:92–98) as well as James V. Hatch's "A Guide to 200 Years of Drama" (*TDR* 16,iv:5–24) in which black theatre is described as the most vital and exciting theatre in the United States. Some of the particular black theatres are described in one issue of the *Drama Review*: Lisbeth Grant discusses "The New Lafayette Theatre" (*TDR* 16,iv:46–55); Margaret Wilkerson comments on the activities of eight major theatres in "Black Theatre in California" (*TDR* 16,iv:25–38); Jessica Harris describes "The National Black Theatre" (*TDR* 16,iv: 39–45) as a "Temple of Liberation, designed to preserve, maintain and perpetuate the richness of the black life-style." Peter Bailey et al. provide a summary comment in the "Annual Round-Up: Black Theatre in America" (*BlackW* 21,vi: 31–40, 70–74).

The vitality of the subject is also shown by the critical approaches.

Basic for many are the problems of "Teaching Black Drama," which John S. Scott comments upon briefly (*Players* 47:130–31). Difficulties existing between "Educational Theatre and the Black Community" (*BlackW* 21,vi:25–29) are explored by Woodie King, Jr., who does not see relief until there is greater basic understanding. "Black Theater and the African Continuum" (*BlackW* 21,x:42–48) by Paul C. Harrison builds upon an external influence, while a critic from Germany, Eberhard Brüning, sees the political implication in " 'The Black Liberation Movement' und das amerikanische Drama" (*ZAA* 20:46–58).

One of the best articles on black drama this year is Thomas D. Pawley's "The First Black Playwrights" (*BlackW* 21,vi:16–24). With his usual scholarly approach, Pawley discusses early plays, playwrights, and companies. Although Arthur W. Bloom's "The Theatre of Non-Mimetic Propaganda: Critical Criteria" (*XUS* 11,i:29–36) is concerned with all of American drama, he has made good use of black drama in his attempt to show how recent playwrights and performers have recognized the possibility of creating political solutions through theatrical performances. James A. Gilles argues convincingly that although the reality of black life in America destroys man's dreams, there is a tenderness beneath that obvious brutality. His particular example in "Tenderness in Brutality: The Plays of Ed Bullins" (*Players* 48:32–33) is *In the Wine Time*, where he finds an "obligato of tenderness." Another playwright, briefly noted, is "J. E. Franklin, Playwright" (*BlackW* 21,vi:49–50). Providing both play plots and critical commentary, W. Edward Farrison assesses "Lorraine Hansberry's Last Dramas" (*CLAJ* 16:188–97)—*Les Blancs, The Drinking Gourd, What Use Are Flowers?*—and faults Robert Nemiroff, the editor of these newly published plays, for failing to indicate his own additions and changes in the published versions. C. W. E. Bigsby, an English critic, summarizes the decade in "Black Drama in the Seventies" (*KanQ* 3,ii[1971]:10–21).

f. LeRoi Jones. As usual among critics on black drama, LeRoi Jones (Imamu Amiri Baraka) attracted considerable attention. His own essay, "Black Revolutionary Poets Should Be Playwrights" (*BlackW* 21,vi:4–6) may be part of next year's theory, but it can also be considered a subject for analysis by the student of persuasive rhetoric. Along this same line of revolutionary theory, there is Samuel Hay's essay on "Alain Locke and Black Drama" (*BlackW* 21,vi:8–14) in which the author sees revolutionary black drama as "folk drama—fully developed." Continuing on this line of revolution, Walter W. Burford—"LeRoi Jones: From Existentialism to Apostle of Black Nationalism" (*Players* 47:60–64)—sees *The Slave* as Jones's point of turning toward revolutionary art and discusses his four revolutionary plays as illustrative of this change. Grouping "Bullins, Baraka, and Elder: The Dawn of Grandeur in Black Drama" (*CLAJ* 16:32–48), Lance Jeffers acknowledges the artistic responsibilities of these dramatists but sees in their work the explanation, definition, and revelation of a "new black humanity." With reference to particular plays by LeRoi Jones, Albert Bermel sees a new character in "*Dutchman* or the Black Stranger in America" (*ASoc* 9:423–34), while Paul Witherington builds a skeptical but enthusiastic argument around the symbolic and ritualistic use of urination in "Exorcism and Baptism in LeRoi Jones's *The Toilet*" (*MD* 15:159–63).

vi. New Directions

This is the most difficult to determine—new directions. Perhaps there are none, yet a lot of people are attempting to say and do something different. Concerning the trends in scholarship over the past half-dozen years, one can draw a few conclusions: more attention is now being given to the drama and theatre before World War I; concern for those many dramatists who brought America to the attention of the world between the World Wars remains reasonably constant—slight; no new significant dramatist has appeared since Miller and Williams were joined by Albee; and drama critics seem to be searching with some anxiety among the black and avant-garde dramatists.

If there are no obvious new directions, there certainly is a variety of activity among dramatists and within theatre groups. "Women's Theatre Groups" (*TDR* 16,ii:79–89) are, according to Charlotte Rea, developing throughout the United States "as a means of exploring and expressing women's identity, potentialities, and the nature of oppression." Religious theatre and drama continue to be emphasized as a mission. Lael J. Woodbury, "Mormonism and the Commercial Theatre" (*BYUS* 12:234–40), explains how the Mormon Church has progressed in its use of drama to spread the gospel. From another vantage point Oscar Mandel provides "Notes on Ethical Deprivation in Avant-Garde Drama" (*AntigR* 8:43–48), but his notes are pretentious and quite unimpressive. From the comfort of his position on the Broadway stage Neil Simon talks about the drama he knows best in his introduction to a collection of seven of his plays, *The Comedy of Neil Simon* (New York, Random House, 1971). His essay, "Portrait of the Writer as a Schizophrenic" (pp. 3–9), is a light but somewhat revealing analysis of his own evolution as a writer of plays. Gerald M. Berkowitz ("Neil Simon and His Amazing Laugh Machine," *Players* 47:110–13) tries to explain Simon's talent as "a matter of pure technique" but falters badly, explains nothing, and hides behind "*chutzpah*—that is Simon's secret weapon."

For a summary view of activity in the American drama and theatre, read *The American Theatre, 1970–1971* (*Theatre*, vol. 4; New York, Scribner's), underwritten by the International Theatre Institute of the United States. From even a quick reading it could be assumed that the future of American drama is not very promising; but, as Shaw once explained, the drama is always at a low ebb—and contemporary critics illustrate the pattern. "The Season," according to Martin Gottfried was a "sorry state." "Off-Broadway," to use Clive Barnes's one-word description, was "bad!" Arthur Miller, on the other hand, showed hope in an essay on "The Measure of Things Is Men" (pp. 96–97) because "theatre . . . is that last man hand-made thing we have." Although Jean-Claude van Itallie found himself out of key with the times, Rochelle Owens expanded her ego to show a very positive approach—theatre "is the history of me as I grew up to name the world." But perhaps Harold Clurman made the appropriate statement on contemporary drama (he frequently does) when in "New Playwrights: Boys and Girls on the Burning Deck" (pp. 167–77) he applauded the "adventuresomeness" and the "dissent" but, quoting Saul Bellow's *Last Analysis*, concluded: "Now I want insight." Whether that is coming or not, only time will tell, but a tremendous number of plays are being written and produced in America. In a two-part essay, "Premieres in America, 1971" (*Players* 47:120–29, 179–91) Donald Fowle listed 1009 premières of new plays. Somewhere there should be insight.

Indiana University

17. Folklore

John T. Flanagan

The year 1972 saw the appearance of a number of colorful and interesting books about folklore. The folk singer Pete Seeger published
his autobiography, the labor folklorist Archie Green produced his
study of songs of Pennsylvania coal miners, Richard Dorson edited a
collection of essays by various folklorists and anthropologists with a
wide spectrum of interest, and Duncan Emrich compiled an unusual
anthology, *Folklore on the American Land*. These volumes are accorded further discussion below. The bibliography of folklore also
proliferated, ranging from studies of genres and occupations to such
an ambitious survey of an entire region as Vance Randolph's compendium of Ozark folklore.

Sister M. Inez Hilger and Margaret Mondloch collaborated in "A
Source List in Ethnobotany" (*NYFQ* 28:61–78), a collection of materials on plants used for food, shelter, and personal therapy. Many of
the items are definitely folk medicine. Wilcomb Washburn in "History, Anthropology, and the American Indian" (*AmerS* 11:25–36)
lists many folklore articles in a compilation dedicated primarily to
history. In "Bibliography of Mississippi Folklore: 1969 and 1970"
(*MFR* 6:20–33) Abu Saeed Zahurul Haque continues an earlier collection of folklore material dealing with a single state; it is particularly useful because of its inclusion of fugitive newspaper articles. The
annual "Folklore" section which James Penrod and Warren I. Titus
contribute to *American Quarterly* (24:349–53) includes some fifty-
seven articles which appeared in 1971; they are given brief annotations. George W. Boswell in "The Several Folklore Archives at Oxford" (*MFR* 6:9–17) describes the various archives at the University
of Mississippi.

John Horden and James B. Misenheimer, Jr., include some 140
folklore items in their section on mythology, legend, and folklore in
the *Annual Bibliography of English Language and Literature* (Lon-

don, Modern Humanities Research Assn.). There are no annotations, but occasional reviews are cited. Presumably the listings are limited to 1970, but many items dated earlier suggest that the compilation is hardly current.

Harry Joe Jaffe collected "American Negro Folklore: A Check List of Scarce Items" (*SFQ* 36:68–70), items found in rare or privately printed books. Duncan Emrich appended to his amusing treasury of juvenile folklore, *The Hodgepodge Book* (New York, Four Winds Press), a valuable bibliography of some fifty pages (pp. 316–67) of material about beliefs and superstitions, proverbs, and proverbial phrases. The list is arranged alphabetically by authors, and the compiler's evaluations make it highly readable.

The year 1972 saw the publication of the second bibliographical supplement to the *Literary History of the United States* (New York, Macmillan), edited by Richard M. Ludwig. The period covered is 1958–1970 plus some earlier uncollected items and a few 1971 entries. The plan of the original volume is continued here, with such headings as Folk Literature, Negro Folklore, Songs and Ballads, Folktales and Humor, and Indian Lore and Antiquities.

Four issues of *Abstracts of Folklore Studies*, edited by Richard E. Buehler with a corps of assistants, appeared during 1972, and some 1,039 items were listed and annotated. The evaluations are helpful and often surprisingly full, but the coverage is spotty and the index rather hit or miss. Some of the material cited is four years old. The range of journals examined is extraordinary. The cumulative index runs twenty-four pages, but lacks subdivisions. Thus 191 items are listed under "United States" without indication as to what they concern.

Once again the annual folklore bibliography compiled by Merle E. Simmons for the *Southern Folklore Quarterly* deserves special commendation. The 1971 list (36:177–367) is extraordinarily comprehensive and benefits from the careful annotation provided for each item. Simmons retains his eleven-part division of subject matter and his alphabetical list of authors within each division. There is also a twenty-four-page list of contributors. One should note the strong emphasis on Hispanic America and the editorial decision not to segregate the material about the folklore and folk customs of the United States.

Vance Randolph's ambitious *Ozark Folklore: A Bibliography* (Bloomington, Ind. Univ. Press) is probably the most complete list-

ing of printed material for any area or region in the United States.
Among the fifteen divisions, in which the items are arranged alphabetically by authors, are such headings as Songs and Ballads, Folk
Speech, Superstitions, Tall Tales, and Ozark Fiction. Randolph annotates every item, often in an impressionistic and caustic manner
which recalls J. Frank Dobie's book on the Southwest. Thus some
of the novels cited are labeled silly, dreadful, or dreary, "full of cheap
sentiment and bad dialect." Few bibliographies can be called a delight to read; Randolph's is.

i. History and Theory

Few recent books have wider scope and, despite the unevenness of
the essays, greater general utility than *Folklore and Folklife: An
Introduction,* which Richard M. Dorson edited for the University of
Chicago Press. Dorson set out to provide answers to two basic questions: What is folklore? and What do folklorists do? To aid him in his
replies he assembled a team of eighteen experts, many of them his
colleagues in history, anthropology, and literature at Indiana University. The four important sections are oral folklore, social folk custom,
material culture, and folk arts; a closing discussion centers more
narrowly on folk life and field collecting. Dorson's introduction of
some fifty pages is an admirable statement of the fields and skills of
the folklorist, plus a brief exposition of the various schools into which
researchers fall. If the distinctions here are sometimes nebulous or
arbitrary, Dorson is commendably lucid and relatively objective in
his accounts of how the Finnish historical-geographical school, the
ideological group, the functionalists, the psychoanalysts, and the
structuralists arose. He identifies himself as a hemispherist, since he
contends that the history of the New World differs so much from that
of the rest of the world (except possibly Australia) that national traditions notable for their age, stability, and depth cannot be found.
Ethnic and racial mixes as well as geography make the task of the
American folklorist quite special. Because of its breadth and bibliographical suggestions *Folklore and Folklife* will serve both neo-
phytes and professionals. Discussion of some of the essays included
will be reserved for the following pages where it seems more
appropriate.

   A few scattered papers on the general subject of methodology merit citation here. Robert M. Rennick in "The Role of Oral History in Place-Name Research" (*IN* 3:19–26) argues that the collecting techniques of an oral historian and those of a folklorist are substantially the same. The folklorist, of course, values spontaneity more highly, whereas the oral historian sometimes asks the informants to comment on documents. W. F. H. Nicolaisen in "Onomastics—An Independent Discipline?" (*IN* 3:33–47) contends that until recently the folklorist was virtually alone in collecting explanatory place legends; now there is sufficient interest in the field to support onomastics as a separate discipline. Much of his argument rests on the distinction between the lexical and the onomastic meaning of a name—in other words, etymology versus tradition and history. Somewhat the same argument is advanced by Ronald L. Baker in "The Role of Folk Legends in Place-Name Research" (*JAF* 85:367–73). To Baker place-name research is truly interdisciplinary; onomastics can bring the student closer to the common man and can also separate historical "fact" from migratory legend.

On a quite different level Richard S. Tallman in "Folklore in the Schools: Teaching, Collecting, and Publishing" (*NYFQ* 28:163–86) reports his success in guiding high school students in the study of folklore. But despite their zeal in collecting, Tallman believes that folklore should not be taught independently, but rather in conjunction with English, history, or the social sciences.

ii. Ballads

Ballad research in 1972 produced both theories of structure and studies of individual ballads. The famous Child collection provided the usual basis for analysis, but variants collected in the United States and native American ballads also stimulated comment.

In an attempt to establish structural patterns in the ballads Judith W. Turner follows the lead of Vladimir Propp in his morphology of Russian fairy tales, and in "A Morphology of the 'True Love' Ballad" (*JAF* 85:21–31) analyzes such examples as "Sweet William's Ghost," "Lord Thomas and Fair Annet," and "Clerk Saunders." Her thesis that a well-defined morphology for a small group of ballads might serve as a precedent for a scientific analysis of the entire ballad corpus has some validity. But her contention that "the central *event* of a ballad is its theme" is simply a pointless wrenching of language, while her denial of suspense in the singing of a ballad is ridiculous. Certainly "Edward," which is not mentioned here, is as dramatic a narrative as one can find anywhere.

Eleanor R. Long in "Thematic Classification and 'Lady Isabel'" (*JAF* 85:32–41) agrees with George List that a ballad text index is vitally needed, but objects to the "ballad gist" as a basis for cataloguing. "Lady Isabel," she eruditely points out, has analogues in many languages, including such American parallels as "Pearl Bryan" and "Poor Omie Wise," not to mention at least two Grimm household tales. She asserts, moreover, that "Lady Isabel," like other ballads, has really two "gists," the foiling of a multiple murderer and the murder of a pregnant sweetheart. Obviously the reduction of the story to one event is an unsound basis for an index.

Howard Wright Marshall in "'Black Jack David' on Wax: Child 200 and Recorded Hillbilly Music" (*KFQ* 17:133–43) describes what happens to a traditional ballad when it is reduced to a phonograph record. Time compression (two minutes, forty seconds for a 78–rpm disc) requires textual shortening, but often makes the ballad more emotional and more dramatic. Marshall lists twenty-three recordings of Child ballads. Walter D. Haden's "The Scottish 'Tam Lin' in the Light of Other Folk Literature" (*TFSB* 38:42–49) is, on the other hand, a source study. The familiar "Tam Lin" exists in only one North American variant, but includes several universal themes: snake lore, protean changes of form, the Elf Queen versus the Devil. Haden points out the unified, tightly knit plot and the love theme strong enough to overcome both the natural and the supernatural.

Harry B. Caldwell in "Ballad Tragedy and the Moral Matrix: Observations on Tragic Causation" (*NYFQ* 28:209–20) argues that the tragic flaw in the traditional ballads is a social matter first and a personal or individual matter second. Thus "Babylon" reveals the horror of incest, "Glasgerion" the heinous sin committed by the page who is disloyal to his master, and "Earl Brand" the clash of obligations to family and lover. Caldwell adds that the *lex talionis* was important to the ballad people, but often carried with it the seeds of destruction.

In "Ditties of Death in Deseret" (*Lore of Faith*, pp. 153–73) Olive W. Burt discusses little-known murder ballads of the Mormon country, some dealing with figures like Porter Rockwell and Joseph Smith.

The Mormons were singing people and, naturally, sang about the violence of frontier days. Some of these songs were even incorporated into church services, where they helped to bolster sagging spirits and stimulated the will to survive. Mrs. Burt provides one text of a ballad about the most infamous event in Mormon history, "The Mountain Meadows Massacre."

The life of a Western desperado is the theme of a famous ballad discussed by John Q. Anderson in "Another Texas Variant of 'Cole Younger,' Ballad of a Badman" (*WF* 31:103–15). Anderson records the music and words of a version sung by an old-time fiddler in 1962. The ballad, which remains anonymous, illustrates the careful selection of details by the unknown composer. The article summarizes Younger's career in crime and clarifies his relationship with the notorious James brothers.

One of the most interesting studies of a single ballad is Arthur Kyle Davis, Jr.'s " 'Far Fannil Town': A Ballad of Mystery" (*SFQ* 36:1–13), a narrative which seems to have all the earmarks of a Child ballad although it is not part of the collection. Recorded originally in Virginia in 1932, "Far Fannil Town" is set in England and deals with a husband's journey to London in search of his wife; he arrives in time to revive the dying woman with three kisses. Davis points out persuasively that the ballad has the essence of a love tragedy and that its familiar stanza form, its verbal clichés, and its stark drama are characteristic of the better-known Child pieces.

Two articles suggest that ballad-singing families still exist in various parts of the country. Ben Gray Lumpkin's "Folksongs from a Nebraska Family" (*SFQ* 36:14–35) contradicts the theory held by some folklorists that balladry was the exclusive property of the illiterate or uneducated. Members of the Cummings family of Beatrice, Nebraska, all educated and cultured, sang ballads out of pure delight. Their repertory included a few Child pieces like "Robin Hood and Little John" and "The Mermaid" but also "The Nightingale" (a version of "Springfield Mountain") and such nursery favorites as "The Frog's Courtship" and "The Green Grass Grows All 'Round." Patrick B. Mullen's "Folk Songs and Family Traditions" (*Observations and Reflections*, pp. 49–63) gives an account of the author's grandfather, Benjamin Harrison Mullen, who wrote down versions of the ballads he sang for his family. Among his favorites were "Dying Soldier" and

"The Charge of Confederatesburg," two Civil War ballads, variants of which were collected by Vance Randolph in the Ozarks, and an Irish ballad entitled "Barney McCoy."

iii. Folk Songs

Three ambitious collections of folk songs reveal the enormous range of pertinent material and represent also an astonishing diversity of folk-song scholarship. In 1964 Bessie Jones and Bess Lomax Hawes presented a workshop in California in which they strove to teach some of the songs and dances common to the Negro South. The Georgia Sea Island Singers provided much of the material. Subsequently the two teachers edited *Step It Down* (New York, Harper and Rowe) and included in their 233 pages samples of baby games and plays, clapping games (like "Juba"), jumps and skips, singing plays, ring plays, and dances. Bess Lomax Hawes supplied useful headnotes and some interesting personal comments. A bibliography and discography are included.

A more somber but exciting collection of Negro song is *Wake Up Dead Man: Afro-American Worksongs* (Cambridge, Harvard Univ. Press), material collected by Bruce Jackson in Texas prison camps during 1964–1966. The compiler gives biographical data about the singers, discusses at length the tradition of worksongs in the penal camps, and divides the sixty-five songs into basic groups: cotton and cane songs, axe songs, and flat-weeding (hoeing) songs. He excludes spirituals and blues. Worksongs have important functions: they help supply a rhythm for dangerous work, they counteract boredom, and they offer an outlet for tensions and frustrations. Although not fundamentally about the work itself, they help the convicts do their work. *Wake Up Dead Man* is an impressive piece of scholarship. The reader, however, might have trouble imagining how these songs sound when sung; on the printed page, without the setting and the voices, many are endlessly repetitious.

Songs and ballads from a specific occupation and even a specific locale provide the data for Archie Green's *Only a Miner* (Urbana, Univ. of Ill. Press). Green discusses certain carefully selected songs from the coal-mining areas of the United States and deals with those which have been recorded on phonograph records. Particular examples such as "Only a Miner" and "The Death of Mother Jones," as well as two compositions by Merle Travis, "Sixteen Tons" and "Nine Pound Hammer," serve him as case studies. Green considers sources, authorship, music, variants, and recordings. In addition he presents valuable background data derived from interviews, copyright records, and historical accounts. Careful research makes this a model study of a limited area, although there is a plethora of labor and industrial history, much of which reflects a strongly partisan unionist point of view.

Another occupation provided Ann Miller Carpenter with song material. In "The Railroad in American Folk Song, 1865–1920" (*Diamond Bessie*, pp. 103–19) she surveys allusions to railroads in traditional song and distinguishes among ballads of protest, hero ballads, wreck songs, hobo songs, and work songs. Over the years the railroad has symbolized ill-paid employment, the jubilation of isolated communities, the fascination of travel, and even mythical adventure ("The Wabash Cannonball"). It has also produced good music.

Not many investigators turned their attention to hymn singing, but three interesting articles did appear. William Ferris, Jr., in "The Rose Hill Service" (*MFR* 6:37–56) describes a Sunday meeting at a Negro rural church where many hymns were sung by the congregation. Ferris identifies some of the choices, lined out by the preacher in the customary old-fashioned manner, and also presents a profile of the Negro minister giving his emotional and dramatic folk sermon. Francis Edward Abernethy's "Singing All Day and Dinner on the Grounds" (*Observations and Reflections*, pp. 131–40) describes the Sacred Harp singing of a congregation of Primitive Baptists in East Texas. Even without musical accompaniment the volume and enthusiasm of the voices are impressive. A substantial picnic dinner is an essential part of the annual reunion of the singers. In " 'Anxious, Dread Tomorrow' " (*KFQ* 17:11–18) Kay L. Cothran deals with the theme of death in nineteenth-century gospel songs, especially those of the Moody-Sankey collection of 1883. Admittedly trite and poetically trivial, these hymns are nevertheless psychologically powerful. Miss Cothran argues that gospel song "provides equipment for life, death, and afterlife." Moreover, since it appeals chiefly to lower and lower middle-class people who are moving slowly toward urbanization, it has true folk qualities. In an appendix she quotes three excellent examples, notably "Throw Out the Life-Line."

Gospel music is also the subject of William C. Martin's "At the Corner of Glory Avenue and Hallelujah Street" (*Harper's* Jan.:95–

99). Martin describes with gusto a meeting at Houston where the platform was shared by a number of singers, climaxed by the Happy Goodman Family of Madisonville, Kentucky. The audience came from all over southeastern Texas, joined in the singing with fervor, and left the scene with a triumphant catharsis.

A somewhat similar account of a different kind of song is given by Robert Cantwell in "Believing in Bluegrass" (*AtM* March:52–60), an interpretation of Bill Monroe's fifth annual country music festival at Bean Blossom, Indiana. The immense, good-natured crowd came to hear guitars, banjos, fiddles, mandolins, and tenor voices almost continuously for twenty-four hours. Although some fifty bands appeared, Bill Monroe was the dominant figure. Cantwell concludes that bluegrass music is fresh and alive, indeed a kind of traditional life with a growing appeal.

Individual folk singers or composers of folk songs also attracted critical attention. Charles S. Guthrie in " 'Whitey' Stearns: Troubadour of the Cumberland Valley" (*KFR* 18:52–55) summarizes the life of a self-taught Kentucky fiddler who knew an enormous number of fiddle tunes and was a familiar figure in Cumberland County. His repertory included such traditional pieces as "Arkansas Traveler," "Old Joe Clark," "Skip to My Lou," and "Turkey in the Straw." Guthrie makes no comment on the quality of Stearns's fiddling. Craig McGregor contributed a portrait of Bob Dylan to the *New York Times* (7 May, sect. D, p. 15) entitled "Dylan: Reluctant Hero of the Pop Generation." McGregor considers Dylan "the closest thing to a culture hero this generation has." His songs are notable for their strand of Jewishness, their frequent religious themes, and recently their "gay" components. Strictly folk elements are sparse in Dylan's compositions, and his songs have not had time to pass into tradition like Woody Guthrie's. But in many ways he speaks for and to the folk.

One of the most enthusiastic articles to appear is Frederick E. Danker's study of Johnny Cash, "The Repertory and Style of a Country Singer" (*JAF* 85:309–29). In Danker's view Cash is "the most imposing and creative figure in country music and a deeply rooted folk artist." He gives only meager biographical data, but provides a detailed inventory of the singer's repertoire. From the beginning of his career Cash sang traditional ballads ("The Wreck of the Old 97" and "New Mexico," for example); since the mid 1950s he has been a transmitter and creative adapter of folk material. Probably some fifty of Cash's songs might be loosely called ballads; he has also recorded some ninety blues songs. His subjects include railroad songs (the train being both artifact and symbol), sharecropper songs, prison songs, mining songs, cowboy songs, and religious songs (at least sixty in number). Brief comments on Cash's performance style conclude the article. Cash prefers to be accompanied only by a guitar and a string bass. He himself plays the six-string guitar and of late has experimented with the harmonica.

Probably the longest and certainly the most miscellaneous book devoted to American folk song during the year is Pete Seeger's autobiography, *The Incompleat Folksinger* (New York, Simon and Schuster). Edited by Jo Metcalf Schwartz, this compendium offers a little bit of everything, yet is consistently interesting. Seeger tells something of himself, his training, his early singing experiences with the Almanac Singers and Woody Guthrie, his authorship, performances, and travels. He describes the artists he has worked with and the instruments he has played (guitar, banjo, dulcimer, chalil). He also summarizes without conspicuous recrimination his troubles with Congress and the broadcasting media because of his leftist views. The inclusion of material originally published in such journals as *Sing Out* needlessly lengthens the book. Some of these essays retain a historical value, but they are topical and obviously dated. Seeger says in his introduction that his volume has neither plot nor story and that it certainly is not gospel. But even readers who are not his dedicated admirers will find it appealing. An interesting feature article on Seeger was contributed by Jonathan Kwitny to the *Wall Street Journal* which is virtually a review of *The Incompleat Folksinger* (12 June 1973, pp. 1,23).

iv. Folk Tales and Legends

The origin, structure, and diffusion of folk narrative have interested folklorists since the memorable activities of the brothers Grimm. Today, despite the existence of archives and indexes, folktale scholarship has not abated and the varieties of approach have if anything multiplied. Thus such a survey as Linda Degh's "Folk Narrative" in *Folklore and Folklife* (pp. 53–83) has special utility. She not only sketches the achievements of every important folktale scholar but examines the structural elements in tales and defines the important types: märchen, novella, religious tale, animal tale, joke, anecdote, legend, and memorate. Since some of these types do not exist in the United States, most of the examples provided are European, but every reader of the tale can profit from the analysis.

J. Russell Reaver in "From Reality to Fantasy, Opening-Closing Formulas in the Structures of American Tall Tales" (*SFQ* 36:369–82) deals with a narrower field. Reaver uses as his material some 2,378 tall tales collected mostly in the South, 1949–1951. Their most popular theme is the wonderful hunt (Motif X 1110), which describes the killing of a menagerie of animals or birds with one bullet. Many of these tales begin with details about the hunter himself: he goes hunting because of a domestic food shortage, family poverty, a desire for a change of diet, or even absent-mindedness. Reaver comments that the closings show narrative skill in preserving consistency, but leave the audience in various stages of psychological response. The substantial bibliography appended to the article is not always relevant.

Tall tales about the marvelous exploits of nimrods are legion throughout the United States, proof that the spirit if not the person of Baron Münchhausen emigrated across the Atlantic Ocean. Jerry Joines in "Twelve Tall Tales from Wilkes County" (*NCarF* 20:3–10) reports a dozen brief incidents mostly involving talented coon dogs or pointers. One hound will hold a covey of quail in a log and release them one by one for the hunter to shoot; another will point a catfish which has eaten a brood of partridges. The tales are told briefly in colloquial language. In "Edwin Fuller and the Tall Tale" (*NCarF* 20:36–41) Ted Malone revives the fame of a North Carolina writer who published a novel called *Sea-Gift* in 1873. Included in the story is a yarn about a farmer who grew weary of losing pigs to neighborhood thieves. His solution was simple: he neatly bored the pigs' tails and filled them with gunpowder so that when anyone strove to cut off the tails they exploded. Malone adds that Fuller added to his story an early comment about the tall tale. An elephant caught in a spider web is manifestly absurd, but a story with improbabilities close to possibilities is always acceptable. Unnatural natural history is the subject of Gerald Carson's "Fantastic Animals Prowl Tall Timber of Our Mythology" (*Smithsonian* 3,v:20–25). Carson points out that although classical mythology has given us the phoenix and the unicorn, the American imagination has produced the hoop snake, the hodag, the Piasa bird, and the upland trout which nests in trees. Many of these creatures appear in Paul Bunyan's menagerie, to be sure, but others were noted by such writers as Cotton Mather and Audubon. Carson laments that shrinking habitats have endangered or eliminated these species. At least he comments, "No sightings have been reported for years and years."

In *Shingling the Fog and Other Plains Lies* (Chicago, Swallow Press) Roger Welsch has compiled an amusing collection of "windies" chiefly from Nebraska pioneer sources. Periodicals like the *Nebraska Farmer* and books like Mari Sandoz's *Old Jules* afforded many of his examples, but he supplements this material with personal interviews with old settlers. The book is divided by subject matter rather than by types, with the weather, topography, and adverse economic conditions suggesting most of the tall tales. Welsch lists all oral informants and assigns motif numbers to his entries.

Another type of tale prevalent throughout the United States is the story of the vanishing hitchhiker. Douglas J. McMillan in an article entitled "The Vanishing Hitchhiker in Eastern North Carolina" (*NCarF* 20:123–28) presents five versions of the ubiquitous narrative garnered from the folklore archives at East Carolina University. All concern a girl, often in a long dress, who requests a ride on a dark and gloomy night, gets into a car, converses with the driver, sometimes even leaves a purse or card behind, and then when the car stops vanishes. Philip Brandt George in "The Ghost of Cline Avenue: 'La Llorona' in the Calumet Region" (*IF* 5:56–91) reports that the hitchhiker story is known to residents of a suburban area of Gary, Indiana, but that the Mexicans who dominate the population group often seem to confuse it with the legend of La Llorona, the woman who killed her children and then sought for their bodies. A more elaborate discussion of the hitchhiking theme is provided by Katharine Luomala in "Disintegration and Regeneration: The Hawaiian Phantom Hitchhiker Legend" (*Fabula* 13:20–59). Here the central figure is usually identified as Pele, the volcano goddess of Hawaiian mythology, who is variously represented as a girl or old woman. Miss Luomala cites some fifty-one versions of the story going back as far as 1933, compares them, and emphasizes salient details in the incidents. It is rather amusing to discover that Pele has not disappeared into the mysterious past; indeed she has been alleged to be visible in certain Honolulu luxury hotels.

A somewhat similar theme, the disappearing corpse, is the subject of a psychological study by L. Veszy-Wagner, "The Corpse in the Car: A Minor Myth Creation" (*AI* 29:53–69). Basically the story involves a fatally injured person who asks for help, is assisted into an automobile, and dies shortly afterward; the hero-driver of course survives. The article also discusses a dream in which the driver is tortured by the presence of the passenger and looks upon the car as a prison.

Wanda Ensor in "Tales of the Supernatural Collected in Mitchell and Yancey Counties, North Carolina" (*TFSB* 38:61–71) presents narratives from Relief, North Carolina, collected from an older group of rural natives. She gives biographical data but neither comment nor analysis. In an interesting theoretical article entitled "Women's Tall Tales: A Problem of the Social Structure of Fantasy" (*StAR* 2:21–27) Kay L. Cothran contends that women, despite assumptions to the contrary, both tell and enjoy tall tales. In southeastern Georgia, where she did field work, men "talk trash" (tell yarns) as a leisure-time activity, but female tale-telling is certainly not unknown. Miss Cothran's argument would be more persuasive if she had provided examples.

Two Indian stories received special attention from students of the legend. C. E. Schorer in "Indian Tales of C. C. Trowbridge: The Bad Man" (*SFQ* 36:160–75) prints another tale from the collection made by Trowbridge in the 1820s near Detroit. He identifies "The Bad Man" as an Orpheus-type narrative, a theme not unknown to aboriginal storytellers. In a long introduction Schorer compares this tale with other Orpheus stories and points out differences; here the girl (wife) is dead before the narrative begins and she is successfully rescued and restored to life by sweating (an interesting incorporation of a familiar Indian custom into a myth). Ruth M. Boyer in "A Mescalero Apache Tale: The Bat and the Flood" (*WF* 36:189–97) suggests that a simple story might well have social and economic implications. In 1958 an Apache woman on a New Mexico reservation told the story of a bat sitting in a tree who was derided by a group of bats on the ground. When a flood inundated the area the bat in the tree flew away but the bats on the ground were engulfed. Apaches apparently do not have the aversion for bats which white people commonly feel and even use bat wings medicinally. But the story was sometimes employed didactically to teach children that mockery is cruel and usually self-defeating.

In 1971 Harold Courlander published *The Fourth World of the Hopis* (New York, Crown Publishers), a collection of myths, legends, and personal recollections which the editor obtained on visits to the Hopi mesas, 1968–1970. A few had been published previously. The twenty legends deal with the four worlds of Hopi mythology, Hopi migrations, the kachinas, the Navajo attack on Oraibi, and the arrival of the Tewas. The language is somewhat streamlined and, although Courlander provides notes and interpretations, he identifies his sources only by their residences. A glossary and pronunciational guide are most helpful.

v. Folk Speech

W. Edson Richmond's essay on "Folk Speech" in *Folklore and Folklife* (pp. 145–57) provides a helpful survey of linguistic study in the United States. Richmond defines the differences between cultivated and common speech on the one hand and folk speech on the other; he also points out the existence of at least seven dialect areas, principally in New England and the South. Folk speech reveals differences in vocabulary, grammar, idiom, and phonetics. Richmond selects vivid examples to confirm his distinctions and also contends that folk speech is the fountain of all language.

Indeed students of folk speech cast their nets widely to be certain they are aware of all possible ramifications. Thus George W. Boswell in "Tongue Twisters and a Few Other Examples of Linguistic Folklore" (*KFR* 18:49–51) assembles some mnemonic devices and verbal tricks ("better baby buggy bumpers"). Alfred F. Rosa and Paul A. Eschholz in "Bunkerisms: Archie's Suppository Remarks in *All in the Family*" (*JPC* 6:271–78) scrutinize a popular television show and select examples of Archie Bunker's malapropisms, spoonerisms, and laughable analogies. Archie's blunders are of course contrived, but at the same time plausible for a character supposedly prejudiced and ignorant. One remembers "welfare incipients," "like the immaculate connection," and "on the sperm of the moment." Robert K. Dodge surveys the famous compilations of Nathaniel Ames, Benjamin Franklin, and Robert B. Thomas in "Didactic Humor in the Almanacs of Early America" (*JPC* 5:592–605) and discusses the proverbs and aphorisms to which the almanac gave wide currency. Dodge reiterates the point that although Franklin originated few proverbs, he rewrote and improved many; he made good use of such technical devices as ellipsis, inversion, and repetition.

In "Language Loyalty and Folklore Studies: The Mexican- American" (*WF* 31:77–86) Rosan Jordan de Caro uses the speech habits of Mexican-Americans in Texas to show how cultural and linguistic loyalties influence the preservation of ethnic folkways. Mexican-Americans in cities like Fort Worth are bilingual and bicultural; their dual language heritage produces conflicts of identity and even social problems.

In *The Old Ball Game: Baseball in Folklore and Fiction* (New York, Herder and Herder [1971]) Tristram P. Coffin gives the history of baseball but devotes much of his attention to its folklore—nicknames of clubs and players, customs, legends, and particularly the language of the diamond. Superstitions are many, but only a few are peculiar to baseball, whereas terms like "charley horse," "southpaw," and "bush league" have passed from this one sport into general circulation. One remark commonly attributed to Leo Durocher has become an American tradition: "Nice guys finish last."

The collecting and interpretation of graffiti continue to attract attention. In 1971 Robert Reisner published *Graffiti: Two Thousand Years of Wall Writing* (New York, Cowles Book Co.) in which he surveyed graffiti in Europe, ethnic graffiti, latrinalia, and graffiti in literature and art. His section called "Collector's Choice" is a long compilation of examples garnered from night clubs, taverns, universities, subways, and doors. Not all are pornographic and many are politically topical. In general, graffiti are literate and witty: for example, "Life is a hereditary disease" and "Nuns—kick the habit."

In "Graffiti and Slogans: Flushing the Id" (*JPC* 6:351–56) Paul D. McGlynn contends that graffiti have a common psychic origin, a need for expression; they also have a singular ring of authority ("God's will is still in probate") and quickly reach wide currency ("Jesus saves but Moses invests"). McGlynn believes that slogans are merely respectable graffiti, sometimes mass-produced by Madison Avenue. The article "Social Analysis of Graffiti" (*JAF* 85:356–66) under the multiple authorship of Terrance L. Stocker, Linda W. Dutcher, Stephen M. Hargrove, and Edwin A. Cook argues that wall writing can be used "as an unobtrusive measure to reveal patterns of customs and attitudes of a society." The four collectors examined graffiti from three universities, Southern Illinois, Missouri, and Western Kentucky, in order to evaluate the liberality of the campus populations. Their data confirmed their feeling that the Carbondale institution was most liberal, the Missouri school tended toward liberalism, and the Kentucky college was ultraconservative. Tables of homosexual, heterosexual, and racist graffiti and an appendix with specific examples complete the study. The interesting point is made that at the Missouri and Kentucky schools so few women's graffiti were collected that any meaningful analysis was impossible.

vi. Cures, Beliefs, and Superstitions

Don Yoder's chapter entitled "Folk Medicine" in *Folklore and Folklife* (pp. 191–215) is a useful survey of popular beliefs about cures and therapeutic practices. Yoder distinguished two basic varieties: natural folk medicine, involving the general use of herbs, plants, minerals, and animal substances, some of which have been preserved by scientific medicine; and magico-religious or occult folk medicine which relies on charms and holy words or actions for its efficacy. Much of Yoder's material is European. But he calls attention to the work of Vance Randolph in *Ozark Superstitions* and to the excellent compilation by Wayland D. Hand in vols. 6 and 7 of the *Frank C. Brown Collection of North Carolina Folklore*. Yoder remarks also that the twentieth century has shown if anything an increase in irrational medical attitudes, as confirmed by the popularity of astrology, food fads, faith healers, and even chain letters.

Recent articles seem to substantiate his point of view since, although folk medicine was undoubtedly widely prevalent among recently arrived immigrants and on the frontier, it is by no means wanting in modern urban society.

Wayland D. Hand in "The Common Cold in Utah Folk Medicine" (*Lore of Faith*, pp. 243–50) ransacked various folk archives to compile a list of cures for the common cold once familiar to the early Mormon settlers. They do not differ greatly from practices elsewhere; among the remedies utilized was a dirty sock, a bag of asafetida, or a bunch of garlic or onions hung around the neck. Various ointments, plasters, and potions were employed, as well as the widely known vinegar and honey. Hand reports the old adage: "Feed a cold and starve a fever." Tom Waller and Gene Killion in "Georgia Folk Medicine" (*SFQ* 36:71–92) list a number of cures garnered from WPA

collections in Georgia from 1935 to 1941. Only a few informants, all
Negro, were identified. The cures pertain to almost every minor ail-
ment from arthritis to boils and from dysentery to malaria. Some of
the nostrums, such as the blood of a black cat or hen for shingles,
somehow do not suggest great efficacy. About twenty-one cures for
warts are included. Lydia Fish in "The Old Wife in the Dormitory—
Sexual Folklore and Magical Practices from the State University
College" (NYFQ 28:30–36) discusses menstrual beliefs and methods
to prevent conception or to produce abortion familiar to female
students at Buffalo. She believes that despite the supposed sophisti-
cation of college today, many girls remember and use traditional
customs. Among the common terms for the monthly period are falling
off the roof, flying the flag, being on the rag, the curse, the Red Baron,
and having grandmother to visit. Some girls will not bathe, shower, or
wash their hair during this time. Contraceptive practices involve pills,
prayers, and home-made prophylactics (even Saran Wrap), while
such douches as vinegar, lemon juice and water, and especially in
the South Coca-Cola are well known. One reported stimulant to
abortion was violent exertion, even blows in the stomach.

According to Helen Z. Papanikolas in "Greek Folklore of Carbon
County" (Lore of Faith, pp. 61–77), the Greek miners who came to
Utah imported and preserved many customs and beliefs. Thus wom-
en who had just given birth were considered unclean and could not
leave the house for forty days. Protective amulets were worn and the
Evil Eye was feared, but persons with special powers could cure it.
Commonly used folk medicine included leeches, plasters, cupping,
and various potions, while chicken droppings were supposed to cure
sties or a sore throat and a silver coin or knife pressed against a bump
would reduce swelling. Marilyn Powe reported "Black 'Isms' " from
Mississippi (MFR 6:76–82) and divided her compilation of Negro
sayings and beliefs into five categories: dreams, predictions, death
signs, bad luck, and miscellaneous cures and charms. According to
the author, both blacks and whites cherish these superstitions and
many are still taken seriously. Patricia S. McLean turned her attention
to voodooism in North Carolina, and in "Conjure Doctors in Eastern
North Carolina" (NCarF 20:21–29) she describes practitioners who
were famous for their knowledge of simples and potions. In a region
with few doctors, sick people visited conjurers and sometimes even
benefited. One interesting custom is reported here: shrouding mirrors

after a death for fear that the departed spirit might try to communicate with the living by appearing as a reflection in the glass.

In "The Cycle of Life Among the Folk" (*Lore of Faith*, pp. 223–41) Austin E. Fife and Alta S. Fife report beliefs collected in Moab, Utah, in 1953. They refer to divination, taboos, and predictions and range from foretelling the occupation of a girl's future husband to the cause of a sty (urinating in the middle of a road). To the Moabites long, tapering fingers suggested a future pianist or doctor, while thick fat hands were lazy hands. Tickling a person could cause stuttering, while amputated parts of the body could still produce pain in the stubs left behind and thus should be burned or buried.

Individual plants even stimulated articles. Thus hemp is the subject of Lawrence S. Thompson's "*Cannabis sativa* and Traditions Associated with It" (*KFR* 18:1–4). Thompson reports that hemp was a staple crop in Kentucky with various uses: as feed for hens, as a poultice against bleeding, as a cure for a cold, and as an aphrodisiac.

Animals too in popular belief had multiple functions. Thus the American bison was not merely a food source for both Indians and whites. According to Larry Barsness in "Superbeast and the Supernatural" (*AW* 9,iv:62–63) prairie travelers thought that the buffalo had curative powers. A gill of buffalo gall mixed with water would aid digestion or cure an ulcerated stomach, buffalo meat had a desirable laxative effect, and buffalo soap would relieve rheumatism and moderate tuberculosis. Some early Westerners even argued that buffalo by their numbers and strength had changed the topography of the West by wallowing, debarking trees, and polishing prairie boulders.

Folk beliefs of a very different kind were collected by John J. Poggie and Carl Gersung in "Risk and Ritual" (*JAF* 85:66–72). The two authors by means of a questionnaire circulated among the residents of an unnamed New England coastal town endeavored to identify superstitions held by lobster fishermen and workers in a textile factory. The factory workers functioning in an environment without physical danger admitted few superstitions, but the fishermen, exposed to the perils of weather and sea, listed a substantial number, although they sometimes disclaimed belief in them. The authors point out that fishing is perhaps the most dangerous of American occupations; ritual which enjoins certain behavior is commonly followed even when the workers profess scepticism.

Robert L. Dluge, Jr., in "My Interview with a Powwower" (*PF* 21,iv:39–42) describes a faith healer of eastern Pennsylvania who treats patients for erysipelas, skin cancer, and dermatitis. To him an inflammation is nothing but "fire and corruption," and his cures frequently consist of speaking Biblical texts. Dluge attributes the continued existence of such powwows to the scarcity of doctors and a kind of revival of belief in occultism.

vii. Literary Use of Folklore

The discussion of folklore themes in literary work continues to be an important area of folklore scholarship. While general studies, because of their nature and scope, have not been common, analyses of individual works and authors become more frequent.

Jerry W. Ward in "Folklore and the Study of Black Literature" (*MFR* 6:83–90) devotes only a few pages to a vast subject but deals thoughtfully with the need to understand Negro folklore in order to evaluate black literature. Darwin Turner, a Negro critic, has already emphasized the significance of the "dozens" and the role of the trickster in some black writing. Other critics have pointed out that Negro authors like Charles Chesnutt, Richard Wright, Chester Himes, and Langston Hughes have employed speech patterns, customs, and folkways for the purpose of authenticating their work; while the folk sermon and the blues have even been utilized as structural devices in fiction. Ward contends that folklore concerns what he calls the "core-of-being" of a group and that it is much more important to be aware of this fact than to immerse oneself in the study of comparative texts.

A more debatable point of view underlies Carol Anne French's "Western Literature and the Myth-Makers" (*Montana* 22:76–81). She complained about the inaccurate picture of Western life afforded by both Hollywood motion pictures and western novelists. Basically she argues that Western life was not always rural nor was it always associated with ranches. She also condemns the emphasis on violence and gunplay, and she scorns the tendency to depict women as absurd, cowering creatures. One of the few western writers to merit her praise is A. B. Guthrie, Jr., whose literary artistry she finds comparable to the artistry of Remington and Russell on canvas. William W. Savage wrote a rejoinder to Miss West's article, which he termed superficial and based on inadequate knowledge of the field. In "Western Literature as Myths: A Rejoinder" (*Montana* 22:78–81) he observes that since Hamlin Garland, Willa Cather, Frank Waters, and Walter Van Tilburg Clark were ignored, the author obviously overstated her case.

Readers are becoming increasingly aware that American playwrights, poets, and novelists have used folklore frequently and successfully in their work. Thus Rictor Norton points out in "Folklore and Myth in 'Who's Afraid of Virginia Woolf'?" (*Renascence* 23 [1971]:159–67) that Edward Albee in his most famous play utilized nursery rhymes, ritual, and myth. Indeed the original title was "The Exorcism," suggesting a ritual of purgation and purification. Norton asserts ingeniously that in the play Honey is pig number one, Martha is pig number two, George is the third little pig who builds his house of brick and survives, while Nick is the big bad wolf who huffs and puffs but is eventually defeated.

Two articles deal with Longfellow. Joseph S. Pronechen in "The Making of *Hiawatha*" (*NYFQ* 28:151–60) reviews the composition of *Hiawatha* in a superficial and inaccurate essay. Much more important is Donald A. Sears's "Folk Poetry in Longfellow's Boyhood" (*NEQ* 45:96–105), convincing proof that a strong tradition of folk poetry in the Portland of Longfellow's boyhood very likely influenced the young poet. In particular a farmer-poet named Thomas Shaw peddled his own broadside ballads about local drownings, schooner wrecks, and crimes. Although of small artistic merit, these pieces did combine melodrama, sentimentality, and moralism in a way familiar to every ballad singer. Probably no clear indebtedness can be established, but Longfellow as a successful storyteller in verse undoubtedly was influenced by such once-popular works.

Cynthia J. Andes in "The Bohemian Folk Practise in 'Neighbor Rosicky'" (*WAL* 7:63–64) suggests that the picnic in Willa Cather's most famous short story may reflect her knowledge of an old Bohemian folk tradition of burning leftovers from breadmaking on Good Friday in order to insure plentiful yields from fruit trees. Certainly Miss Cather was well acquainted with the traditions of her Czech neighbors. Two essays about John Steinbeck deal with his use of talismans. Todd M. Lieber in "Talismanic Patterns in the Novels of John Steinbeck" (*AL* 44:262–75) attempts to prove the structural value of such devices in his fiction. Kyra Jones in "Myth in *The Winter*

of Our Discontent" (*Diamond Bessie*, pp. 93–102) observes that the
author frequently wrote about people living in a kind of enclave
apart from the world, a mythological state or earthly paradise. Here
myth vanquishes reality, but in *The Winter of Our Discontent* the
reverse is true. Yet Steinbeck employs a cave where rituals take place,
a round stone which symbolizes a *yoni* and can change colors, and
multilayered Biblical parallels. The novel, however, contains no
savior; the closest approach to a god figure is a sterile, materialistic
banker. In "The Gourd and Regional Writing" (*MFR* 6:5–8) Ovid S.
Vickers deals with allusions to gourds in some Southern novels and
takes most of her evidence from Carolyn Miller's *Lamb in His Bosom*
and Vinnie Williams's *Walk Egypt*. Gourds can function as recepta-
cles, storage pots, and dippers; traditions about these all-purpose
plants are incorporated into the stories.

Folk language is the subject matter of critical essays dealing with
William Faulkner and Jesse Stuart. Gerald W. Walton's "A Word List
of Southern Farm Terms from Faulkner's *The Hamlet*" (*MFR* 6:60–
75) is a thoughtful compilation of nouns and verbs in common rural
usage which appear in one of Faulkner's best-known novels. Walton
lists his examples and defines them more from personal familiarity
than from a lexicon. Faulkner's use of terms like baling wire, bottom
land, heifers, middle buster, singletree, traces, yearling (male cow),
coal oil (kerosene), and hands (farm workers) confirms his knowledge of farm diction and helps to provide the desired local color.
James E. Spears in "William Faulkner, Folklorist; A Note" (*TFSB*
38:95–96) calls attention to the amount of folklore in *Sartoris*. In an
article entitled "Place Names in the Writings of Jesse Stuart" (*WF*
31:169–77) Eugene L. Huddleston observes that the Kentucky writer
acquired from a lifetime of residence in Greenup County an astonishing fund of proper names, many of which he utilized in his fiction.
Terms like hollow, branch, grove, lick, gap, and ridge appear frequently, with singular appropriateness, while other topographical
names are marked by their assertion of the kinds or numbers of trees.
Huddleston observes that Stuart is more than a provincial and less
than a symbolist; his regional importance rests in part on his ability
to achieve the spirit of place in his work, the result of his extensive
uoo of local nomenclature.

Nathaniel Hawthorne is one nineteenth-century writer who constantly seems to attract attention from critics interested in the literary

use of folklore and legend. At least three recent articles deserve comment here. Robert Moore's "Hawthorne's Folk-Motifs and *The House of the Seven Gables*" (*NYFQ* 28:221–33) does not do justice to its subject, but it does emphasize how a variety of familiar folklore motifs underscore the notion of witchcraft in one of Hawthorne's major novels. After pointing out that Hawthorne derived his ideas of folklore from personal experience and from reading, Moore comments briefly on some of the short stories and then discusses the curse, the bewitched well, the ominous portrait, and the blighted garden in the novel. None of this is exactly new. Karl P. Wentersdorf examines elements of witchcraft in *The Scarlet Letter* in *Folklore* and Daniel R. Barnes, Hawthorne's use of the "bosom serpent" legend in *JAF*. Both articles are discussed in Chapter 2, above.

In a valuable article entitled "The Structure and Dynamics of Folklore in the Novel Form: The Case of John O. Killens" (*KFQ* 17:92–118), William H. Wiggins, Jr., shows how one Negro writer of fiction has employed folklore for structural purposes. Killens, the author of four novels, three of which deal with the Negro's achievement of manhood, wrote in *'Sippi* a story virtually based on a folktale. Like other black writers Killens previously employed folktales for humorous or ornamental purposes, but in his third novel he created a protagonist who rejected in sequence Southern racial customs (especially titles for all white persons), the superiority of white men, the superiority of white women, and cowardice in the face of racial violence, precisely as the hero of the original folktale had done. In addition Wiggins points out that Killens borrowed certain techniques from African and Anglo-American folklore. Thus *'Sippi* reveals conscious repetition, parataxis, and parallel phrasing.

viii. Material Culture

Warren E. Roberts, Henry Glassie, and Don Yoder all contributed essays on various aspects of folk life or material culture to *Folklore and Folklife* (pp. 233–350), their subjects ranging from architecture and crafts to costumes and cookery. Each author discusses the theory and the tangible results, and each provides a brief bibliography. This multiplicity of interest is also apparent elsewhere.

Thus Austin E. Fife and Alta S. Fife in "Unsung Craftsmen" (*Lore of Faith*, pp. 216–74) deal with the artisans of early Utah and describe the dugouts and stone houses built functionally without reference to blueprints. Even the quilts, rugs, lariats, bridles, and gates of frontier days had aesthetic qualities as well as utility. The Fifes treat early farm dwellings more specifically in another article: "Stone Houses of Utah" (*UHQ* 40:6–23) confirms the skill of early Utah masons who built so economically and symmetrically that many of their houses still stand. Pennsylvania also produced stone houses, several of which Robert A. Barakat describes in "The Herr and Zeller Houses" (*PF* 21,iv:2–22). These early-eighteenth-century dwellings proved remarkably sturdy. One important element in house construction is the subject of Beulah M. D'Olive Price's "Riving Shingles in Alcorn County" (*MFR* 6:108–14). In a country where wood is plentiful, shinglemaking is traditional. The article describes and illustrates such tools as the froe, the maul, and the draw knife.

Michael Owen Jones continues to get mileage from his nine-hundred-page dissertation at Indiana University on Appalachian chairmaking, and there is considerable repetition in such articles as " 'If You Make a Simple Thing, You Gotta Sell It at a Simple Price': Folk Art Production as a Business" (*KFR* 18:5–12,31–40) and " 'There's Gotta Be New Designs Once in Awhile': Culture Change and the 'Folk' Arts" (*SFQ* 36:43–60). But Jones analyzes questions of merchandizing and taste. His account of the costs in time and money of chairmaking and the small profits earned by the folk craftsman is revealing.

Folk art surfaces in many places. David J. Winslow in "New York Duck Decoys" (*KFQ* 17:119–32) discusses the skill of guides and hunters in fashioning commercial decoys in northern New York state. Wooden ducks occasionally were given such unusual features as long necks, broad bills, and hunchbacks. Mac E. Barrick in "Central Pennsylvania Fishing Spears" (*PF* 21,iii:32–35) describes the spears or gigs which were used for generations in fishing for carp or suckers. Earl F. Robacker and Ada F. Robacker in "Quilting Traditions of the Dutch Country" (*PF* 21sup:31–38) recount the history of quiltmaking and pay special attention to designs and colors. The names of quilts—Oak Leaf, Pine Tree, Missouri Rose, Feather Crown, Indiana Puzzle—are intriguing. Wasyl O. Luciw and George Wynnysky in "The Ukrainian Pysanka and Other Decorated Easter Eggs in Pennsylvania" (*PF* 21,iii:2–7) summarize the history of coloring Easter eggs (*pysanky*) in the Ukraine. Immigrants to the Pennsylvania coalfields brought the tradition with them, and their descendants still preserve the practice, using such methods as scratching, painting, or dropping wax on the shells. The popular designs are geometrical or involve the outlines of plants and animals. For centuries the egg symbolized the sun and the perpetuation of life, and the exchange of eggs at Easter was a common greeting.

Two articles in *Pennsylvania Folklife* deal with fraktur work. Monroe H. Fabian's "The Eastern Bible Artist Identified" (22,ii:2–14) gives biographical data about Johannes Spangenberg, the hitherto unknown creator of musician and gentleman figures on the borders of birth and baptism certificates. Carroll Hopf's "Calligraphic Drawing and Pennsylvania German Fraktur" (22,i:2–9) traces the history of calligraphic "flourishing" as it developed in eastern Pennsylvania a century ago. According to Hopf, fraktur artists hoped to preserve vital statistics, emphasize a religious truth, or present colorful and interesting designs. Particularly impressive were the "flourished" lions.

Food habits represent another kind of folk tradition. In "Moon Cake in Chinatown, New York City: Continuity and Change" (*NYFQ* 28:83–117) Janet Langlois discusses the ancient Oriental custom of eating moon cake on the fifteenth day of the eighth month. The special cake, a feature of Cantonese cookery, is often baked with a whole egg yolk inside to symbolize the autumn moon. Today the cake and the custom of eating it survive in New York's Chinatown, but as a business enterprise rather than a ritual. The Nebraska pioneer food habits interested Roger L. Welsch. In " 'Sorry Chuck'—Pioneer Foodways" (*NH* 53:99–113) he points out that no immigrant train lacked flour, bacon, molasses, and loaf sugar, nor a cast-iron Dutch oven. Later settlers utilized wild fruits and berries and learned to make pemmican, although they borrowed very few dietary habits from the Indians. Game was dried, corn pickled, jellies and jams reduced to butter. Many unfortunate pioneers had to learn to make apple pie without apples and to roast anything brown for coffee.

Kay L. Cothran examines the food habits of Southern piney woods inhabitants in "Talking with Your Mouth Full: A Communications Approach to Food Rules" (*TFSB* 38:33–38). She suggests various criteria. Some foods, corn and pork, are always appropriate. Some are only occasionally suitable, often as remedies (burned chicken feathers to avoid heart pounding, whiskey with honey or pine tar to

reduce coughs). But a woman following childbirth should avoid fish
and honey, and foods that must never be eaten include raccoon,
opossum, alligator, snake, sea gull, and even bear. Miss Cothran
contends that food taboos reveal interesting sociological data.

Ellen J. Gehret and Alan G. Keyser trace the history of a plant in
"Flax Processing in Pennsylvania from Seed to Fiber" (*PF* 22,i:10–
34). Flax, once common in the Quaker state, was driven out by cotton
and virtually disappeared from the fields by 1870. The authors describe methods of harvesting, retting, hackling, and bleaching.

The entire December issue of the *New York Folklore Quarterly*
(28:242–313) is given over to student collections made around Sche-
nectady. The material deals with Polish cooking, New York State
lumbering, and Slavic Easter eggs. Further south the students of a
northeastern Georgia high school also collect and their data have
appeared periodically in a magazine entitled *Foxfire*. Thus the summer issue (6:77–172) is devoted to weaving and describes the procedure from the pasturing and shearing of sheep, through the card-
ing and spinning of the wool, to the making of shuttles and warps for
the actual production of cloth. Diagrams and photographs of the
weavers are included as well as fragments of interviews: one worker
claimed "I'd rather weave as eat" but another admitted that "Sometimes I just get plumb frazzled." Eliot Wigginton, the teacher who
originally inspired the project, edited the *Foxfire Book* (Garden
City, N.Y., Doubleday) which has attracted wide attention. A fascinating miscellany of recipes, cures, weather signs, hunting tales,
nostrums, snake lore, and ghost stories from the hill country, it also
includes instructions on how to make shingles, chairs, soap, quilts,
and moonshine whiskey. The reader derives from the *Foxfire Book*
an excellent picture of the isolated, self-sufficient, largely illiterate
mountain folk who still take pleasure in what they can make and do.
Donald Johnston wrote an interesting commentary on the book and
the folk in "*Foxfire*: They Learned, and They Loved It," *New York
Times* (9 April, sect. E, p. 13).

The most impressive American work on material culture to appear
during 1972 is the *Treasury of American Design*, edited by Clarence
P. Hornung (New York, Abrams). Magnificently printed in Japan,
this two-volume study touches almost every aspect of folk craft and
provides lavish color illustrations. Pictures of figureheads, decanters,
weathervanes, tea canisters, crocks, chests, mirrors, toys, butter

moulds, and tavern signs help the reader to visualize the compact and informative descriptions. The bulk and expense of the work probably place it beyond the reach of the ordinary reader, but it is an invaluable reference tool.

ix. Minor Varieties of Folklore

Minor varieties of folklore such as riddles, jokes, nicknames, and chain letters continue to stimulate discussion and apparently have a wide currency. Roger D. Abrahams and Alan Dundes contributed an essay on riddles to *Folklore and Folklife* (pp. 129–43) in which they trace the scholarship on the subject and describe riddles which are explanations, jokes, or parodies. The many foreign items in their bibliography might suggest that the riddle is not a common genre in the United States today. In a further essay, "The Literary Study of the Riddle" (*TSLL* 14:177–97), Abrahams remarks that, although riddle study has attracted literary critics, it has also produced serious errors in interpretation. Abrahams terms the riddle "a special form of surface metaphor." He cites material collected from the island of St. Vincent, where riddles are often chiefly a contest in wit.

James E. Spears in "Proverbs Common to Tennessee: A Note and a Glossary" (*TFSB* 38:72–76) lists some 132 proverbs familiar in Tennessee. They relate to animals, plants, minerals, cosmic elements, and behavior. He identifies informants but provides no annotations. In "Syriac Proverbs from California" Joyce Bynum Lethin presents some thirty proverbs or *masale* collected from Assyrian communities in California (*WF* 31:87–101). Provided for each proverb are the Syrian original, a literal translation, and an interpretation or fuller statement. The proverbs generally deal with the need for caution, patience, and discretion.

Jan Harold Brunvand's article "The Study of Contemporary Folklore: Jokes" (*Fabula* 13:1–19) complains that jokes have been neglected by serious students although they demand the same kind of scrutiny given other folklore forms. Brunvand believes that jokes can reveal attitudes towards nationalism, politics, religion, history, and technology. He develops his argument by citing six pairs of jokes, American and Romanian, and pointing out their similarities and differences. Andrea Greenberg considers racial slurs in "Form and Function of the Ethnic Joke" (*KFQ* 17:144–61), with Jewish and Negro

stories providing her chief data. She feels that ethnic jokes provide
an outlet for frustration, hostility, and psychic tension and contends
that stories with some narrative content reveal more about the narrator than do riddles. Jewish jokes often pivot on the conflict between
loyalty to Jewish tradition and assimilation into the American way
of life. Black jokes told by whites often stress the supposed Negro
traits of laziness, superstition, sexuality, and violence; but if told by
blacks they are either a defense mechanism or a positive, self-
conscious weapon against current racism.

Bruce Jackson in "Circus and Street" (*JAF* 85:123–39) considers
the Negro "toast," which he defines as "a folk literature of the lower
class black male," and points out the strong elements of violence and
sexuality in this racial form. Important characters in the toasts are
Badman (Stackolee for example) and Trickster. Jackson draws a
parallel between the activities of the circus and the behavior described in the toasts and gives texts of the familiar "Titanic" and
"Signifying Monkey."

In an essay entitled "Folk Children's Pejorative Nicknames and
Epithets" (*KFR* 18:70–74) James E. Spears provides a list of terms
collected from juveniles and emphasizes that they are stimulated by
physical stature and coloring, facial features, and special mannerisms.
Most of them are familiar and are neither specifically regional nor
rural.

A quite different subject interested Mac E. Barrick in "The Typescript Broadside" (*KFQ* 17:27–38), which he subtitled "An Un-
wonted View of Erotica." Typed broadsides or flying sheets which
circulated among schools and manufacturing firms in Pennsylvania
in the 1950s were read avidly because of their erotic or obscene material. Barrick prints examples but observes that the surviving texts
are generally unique and do not permit comparisons.

x. Miscellaneous

A few items which do not conveniently fit into the preceding categories will be grouped here. Kathleen M. Kavanagh provides a capsule biography of a famous jumping hero in "The Limited Fame of
Sam Patch" (*NYFQ* 28:118–34) and notes that Patch combined the
Yankee Brother Jonathan character with that of the Western brag-
gart. But the article is largely a rehash of familiar material.

Juliana Roth in "Travel Journals as a Folklife Research Tool; Impressions of the Pennsylvania Germans" (*PF* 21,iv:28–38) discusses the vast amount of material about rural life available in accounts of such travelers as Peter Kalm, Thomas Ashe, and John Bradbury. Quite naturally these men recorded their impressions of barns, houses, fences, and taverns, with scattered details concerning food, dress, and language.

Myrna King collected playground jingles from white and black girls in a poverty-stricken area of Tennessee and in "Skip-Rope Rhymes in Bell Buckle, Tennessee" (*TFSB* 38:11–19) presents her findings. She gathered sixty-seven rhymes, for which she provides brief annotations.

Two essays from Texas treat folklore in unusual fields. C. L. Sonnichsen in "The Folklore of Texas Feuds" (*Observations and Reflections*, pp. 35–47) outlines some famous frontier feuds and comments that such vendettas are not only an expression of traditional customs and beliefs but actually folklore in action. He adds that among belligerent factions revenge is a compulsion and violence begets violence. On the other hand, tradition also decreed that feudists must never talk or fraternize with the enemy. Today feuds seem obsolete but Sonnichsen suggests that they could occur again if civil justice should break down. A milder form of folklore attracted Sarah Greene. Her "From Amnesia to Illegitimacy: The Soap Opera as Contemporary Folklore" (pp. 79–90) deals with the extraordinary appeal that soap operas have to the television audience and contends that, although they have known authors and do not enter tradition, they are concocted out of American folk beliefs and customs. Certainly the characters represent modern folk types and heroes. Interviews with viewers in Upshur County, Texas, sustain her evaluations.

In "Asiatic Parallels in North American Star Lore" (*JAF* 85:236–47) William B. Gibbon observes that aboriginal folklore contains many references to the constellations that are similar to Old World star beliefs. Thus the concept of the Milky Way as a path of birds or as the track of departed spirits, widely spread among the American Indians, also appears in eastern Europe. Again, the Pleiades, interpreted either as a group of women or of dancing youths, and the exploits of Orion, the classic figure of the hunter shooting at game, are motifs common on both sides of the Atlantic. Gibbons refrains from asserting a direct line of transmittal but strongly suggests that the star names themselves indicate an early relationship between linguistically similar peoples long out of geographical contact. An extensive bibliography supports his essay.

One of the most attractive volumes to appear during the year is Duncan Emrich's *Folklore on the American Land* (Boston, Little, Brown). Despite its 707 pages and a substantial list of references, this is less a work of scholarship than a fascinating selection of American verbal and material traditions. Diverse folk themes interest Emrich, for many years chief of the folklore section of the Library of Congress. His anthology touches on folk speech, folk proverbs, American names, cattle brands, street cries, and autograph album rhymes. Substantial sections of the book present legends and tales, songs and ballads. The final pages offer examples of weatherlore, folk medicine, and beliefs about birth and death. Carefully chosen pictures document some of the activities and places commemorated in the text. This jaunty book is a delight for the casual reader and certainly not without value for the professional folklorist.

University of Illinois

18. Themes, Topics, and Criticism

George Monteiro
and Neil K. Fitzgerald

i. Textual Editing

The textual editing of nineteenth-century American books, despite the sharp reduction in recent years of public funds available to the Center for Editions of American Authors, continues to occupy the time of a rather large number of scholars and technicians. Edmund Wilson's well-known attack on the entire project (see *ALS 1968*, pp. 68–70) seems in the long run to have had little or no effect on the intentions and actions of those involved. Closely edited volumes of Howells, Crane, Hawthorne, and Melville appear regularly, more or less on schedule. If Wilson's objection to the wholesale editing of a given author's complete works has been shunted aside, as we think it has, there have arisen new questions concerning the ways in which such editing has been carried out. Rather than questioning whether or not all or any of a given author's books should be subjected to the rigorous editing required by the CEAA, interested parties have taken to questioning the validity and the universal applicability of those very principles.

The most cogent attack on the current practices of editing is Donald Pizer's "On the Editing of Modern American Texts" (*BNYPL* 75[1971]:147–53). Objecting to "the absolutism of copy-text procedures," he observes that what editors finally produce is an eclectic text which by its very nature is one that has never before existed. Rather than getting at exactly what a writer has written and has presumably seen into print, we are invariably given the result of an editor's (or editors') decision as to what the author might have intended his text to be. Pizer's essay provoked replies, all but one published in succeeding issues of the same journal in the same year. Norman Grabo vigorously defends the applicability of the Greg-

Bowers copy-text theory to nineteenth- and twentieth-century writers
("Pizer vs Copy-Text," 75:171–73). Insisting that "there is no single
theory of copy-text," Hershel Parker defends, with an editor's intensity, his preference for "an unpublished version of copy-text" on which
to base the final published version ("In Defense of 'Copy-Text Editing,'" 75:337–44). In "How Not to Edit American Authors: Some
Shortcomings of the CEAA Editions" (75:419–23) John Freehafer
concentrates on what he finds to be the three major deficiencies of the
CEAA editions: "a failure to learn from the best editorial practice of
the past" (from nearly three and a half centuries of Shakespearean
editing, for example), "a failure to present literary works as such"
(CEAA editions are "almost totally concerned with bibliographical
questions," not the broadly literary matters which attract readers in
the first place), and "a failure to use Greg's theory of copy-text with
sufficient boldness and imagination to reconstruct ideal authorial
texts of many of the works being edited." Pizer himself reentered the
lists with "'On Editing of Modern American Texts': A Final Comment" (75:504–05), reaffirming his contention that as a uniform, general principle imposed upon every text desiring CEAA support and
endorsement, adherence to Greg's theory of copy-text "represents primarily the bias of a contemporary school of textual editing rather than
a response either to the distinctive nature of modern American texts
or to the needs of the general professional audience for whom the
texts are being edited." In what could have been entitled "A Final
Final Comment," Parker returned in 1972 to reply to Freehafer that
the "Historical Notes" to the various volumes of the Newberry-
Northwestern Melville edition fully satisfy his call for critical prefaces
which are "both valuable and highly verifiable" ("Historical Introductions vs Personal Interpretations," BNYPL 76:19).

Something further will undoubtedly follow.

ii. Bibliography

Of lasting importance to students of American literature, with long-
term implications for the nature of literary scholarship, is the rapidly
expanding concern with the intimate relationship between all facets
of bookmaking and publication and the making of literature. The
difficulty has been that all such information has not always been
readily accessible to the critic or the editor who most needs it. As we

are almost daily reminded, for most authors and publishers this information is either currently unavailable or, when it does exist, not in immediately usable form.

Long an advocate for putting all bibliographical information in such order that it can be measured and improved upon, G. Thomas Tanselle offers us a most useful essay on "The State of Reference Bibliography in American Literature" (*RALS* 1[1971]:3–16). After surveying the principal tools now available, such as annual bibliographies and review indexes, he moves to a consideration of the strengths and weaknesses of various selective lists (unannotated and annotated) for topics, genres, periods, and individuals, calling, in the meantime, for more bibliographical essays on individual writers. Because of the sheer bulk of proliferating materials, however, he cautions that there is immediate need for refining bibliographical guides to existing bibliographies.

Tanselle's own *Guide to the Study of United States Imprints* (Cambridge, Mass., Harvard Univ. Press, 1971) is a model of the kind of reference work we sorely need. In a lucid, no-nonsense introduction he offers the rationale behind the organization of this checklist intended as an aid to those interested in the development of printing and publishing in the United States. The two volumes are organized into sections on regional lists, genre lists, author lists, copyright records, catalogues (auction, dealers', exhibition, library), book-trade directories, studies of individual printers and publishers, general studies ("any material in discursive form which takes up American printing and publishing with an emphasis on a locality, a period, or a group of men rather than on a single figure"), lists of secondary material, and an appendix describing a basic collection of two hundred and fifty titles on printing and publishing in the United States.

When *Proof: The Yearbook of American Bibliographical and Textual Studies* was announced in 1971, its editor, Joseph Katz, promised that it would be "devoted to the study of books and manuscripts and their contributions to the American cultural experience." Judging from the two volumes which have so far appeared, for 1971 and 1972, this self-proclaimed charge has been followed closely. Besides pieces devoted to individual writers and single books, *Proof* has published William S. Kable's "The Serif Series: Bibliographies and Checklists" (1[1971]:368–76), Tanselle's "Some Remarks on Bibliographical Non-Proliferation" (1[1971]:169–79), in which he warns against the danger of accumulating raw data for its own sake, Calhoun Winton's "The Colonial South Carolina Book Trade" (2:71–87), and Joseph Katz and James B. Meriwether's "A Redefinition of 'Issue'" (2:61–70), a welcome attempt to bring light to a murky subject. A continuing feature of *Proof* is its carefully organized "Register of Current Publications."

Some sense of the wide variety of serious bibliographical study currently under way can be gained by looking briefly at a few notable examples. Conrad A. Balliet's "White on Black: A Check List of Poetry by White Americans About the Black Experience, 1708–1970" (*BNYPL* 75[1971]:424–64) lists and annotates poems by, at our quick count, some one hundred and fifty poets, from Amos B. Alcott to Louis Zukofsky. In *"The Reviewer*: A Bibliographical Guide to a Little Magazine" (*RALS* 1[1971]:58–103) Maurice Duke provides a history of this Richmond, Virginia, semimonthly of the 1920s, along with a full listing of each issue's contents and contributors. Henry Christian makes it possible to begin to study a neglected writer of the 1930s and 1940s with his *Louis Adamic: A Checklist* (Kent, Ohio, Kent State Univ. Press, 1971). George Robert Minkoff's *A Bibliography of The Black Sun Press* (Great Neck, N.Y., Minkoff, 1970) is a handsome descriptive bibliography of the books published by Caresse and Harry Crosby's press. Jeffery Dane Kluewer's "An Annotated Check List of Writings on Linguistics and Literature in the Sixties" (*BNYPL* 76:36–91) offers not only an alphabetically ordered list of articles, books, and reviews but also indexes which break that list down into bibliographies and collections, theories of language, linguistics and literary criticism, linguistic schools, prosody, psycholinguistics, quantitative studies, style and stylistics, syntax and grammar, and, finally, non-prosodic analyses of literary periods and of authors and their works. One final example results from the peaceful application of the computer: C. Edward Wall's *Cumulative Author Index for Poole's Index to Periodical Literature, 1802–1906* (Ann Arbor, Mich., Pierian Press, 1971). The value of this standard guide, originally organized only by subject, has now been greatly enhanced.

iii. Henry Adams and Edmund Wilson

The last time that Henry Adams received anything more than passing mention in these pages his case was taken up under the subheading of

"American Studies" (*ALS 1968*, pp. 300–02). If we are to attend to the scholarship on Adams since then, however, we would do well to consider giving him full status as a literary figure, perhaps as one of our major writers.

That Adams's "primary contributions to our literature were aesthetic" is the main thrust of Louis Auchincloss's excellent introduction to Adams (UMPAW 93[1971]). His complementary theme is that Adams, lusting for the recognition of scientists for his curious, often outmoded or disproved theories, "always misconceived his principal talent." These ideas do not, of course, originate with Auchincloss, but the insistence and force with which he pursues them is symptomatic of the direction in which Adams studies are already headed.

Focusing on Adams's acknowledged aesthetic masterpieces, John J. Conder's *A Formula of His Own: Henry Adams's Literary Experiment* (Chicago Univ. Press, 1970) takes Adams at his own word that *Mont-Saint-Michel and Chartres* and *The Education* are to be seen, as he insisted to William James, "chiefly as a literary experiment, hitherto, as far as I know, never tried or never successful." The task Conder sets for himself is to link the basic issue of Adams's career, the "connection between the forms of literary endeavor he followed and his changing attitudes toward determinism," to the highly experimental form of his two masterworks. What he seeks is a way of accounting for the artistic coherence which Adams achieves despite the complexities inherent in his materials.

That *Mont-Saint-Michel and Chartres* is less a textbook, a guidebook, or a work of history than a work of art is Robert Mane's point in *Henry Adams on the Road to Chartres* (Cambridge, Mass., Harvard Univ. Press, 1971). Insisting that Adams's "true life" was that of the artist, Mane painstakingly reconstructs the way Adams went about preparing himself for the task of writing his book. About half of Mane's text deals with the chief personal influences upon Adams's artistic education, including John La Farge, Clarence King, and Henry Hobson Richardson. Structurally, however, this book is oddly out of balance. To show that Chartres is a work of art and not history, Mane spends a great deal of time impugning Adams as historian and even as an observing tourist. Adams, it turns out, depended heavily upon certain printed sources, kept no valuable notes on his visits to the French cathedrals, and distorted or ignored much of the scholarship on the literature of the Middle Ages, particularly the work on the fabliaux, which show women of the time as much abused and as, in turn, abusers. "Never has any advocate better succeeded in suppressing the hostile evidence," writes Mane. "For these chapters on mediaeval literature—it is now obvious—are a plea, a clever, biased, impassioned plea, not a tableau." As for Adams's concept of the "historical" Virgin, decides Mane, she is nothing more than a poetic configuration drawn almost entirely from his experience with his wife Marian and his friend Elizabeth Cameron.

Two other recent books deserve brief mention. Melvin Lyon's *Symbol and Idea in Henry Adams* (Lincoln, Univ. of Nebr. Press, 1970) focuses on the pervasive and consistent role myth and symbol play in all Adams's writings. Ernst Scheyer's *The Circle of Henry Adams: Art and Artists* (Detroit, Wayne State Univ. Press, 1970), done in the elaborate style of German scholarship, investigates in exhaustive detail Adams's extensive intimacy with the world of European and American art. As an art historian, Scheyer brings new light to that long underemphasized side of Adams's aesthetic experience.

When we turn to the periodicals we discover once again that it is the Adams who thought of his work and himself in literary terms that receives the most attention. In a neat tour de force Charles Vandersee in "Henry Adams and the *Atlantic*: Pattern for a Career" (*PLL* 7 [1971]:351–73) explains why a young man, hoping for a literary career and with a prestigious new magazine at his doorstep, chose not to contribute to it. Although there is ample evidence to indicate that Adams at various stages in his career flirted with the idea of sending the *Atlantic* some sample of his work, he could never overcome his conviction that the magazine's editors lacked the courage to confront frankly the more important contemporary, chiefly political, issues. In a second search into the complexities of Adams's character, "The Hamlet in Henry Adams" (*ShS* 24[1971]:87–104), Vandersee builds on Adams's own allusions to Hamlet. In *The Education*, he argues, Adams actually intended to portray himself as Hamlet, "that unlikeliest of characters in nineteenth-century America." With Hamlet, Adams shared the theme of "consciousness and its role in alienation."

As for the meaning and the quality of Adams's own novels, the debate is still on. Two of the more valuable essays of recent years are Henry Wasser's "Science and Religion in Henry Adams' *Esther*" (*MarkhamR* 2,iii[1970]:[4–6]), which follows the trend of seeing Esther as a composite of competing beliefs within Adams himself, and that of Neil Schmitz, "The Difficult Art of American Political Fiction: Henry Adams' *Democracy* as Tragical Satire" (*WHR* 25 [1971]:147–62). Schmitz reads the book in terms of the American political novel and its tradition. Since Adams was aware of the nature of that tradition, Schmitz argues, he was able to avoid descending to the kind of caricature which characterizes it. In judging Senator Silas P. Ratcliffe, proposes Schmitz, Mrs. Madeleine Lee is attempting a fair analysis of American democracy—not a stereotyped jeremiad on the advent of Jacksonian politics. Taken in this way, Schmitz reveals an Adams—and all Adamses were Jackson-haters—who comes to turn upon himself. Here is the wounded idealist contending with the cynical realist. Adams came to see no viable alternatives to Ratcliffean democracy and left the subject. "Yet if the novel constitutes his farewell address to American politics," concludes Schmitz, "it also represents an opening for a new form of political fiction, one through which the novelist could go disburdened by illusions."

The best single recent piece on *The Education* is probably Henry B. Rule's "Henry Adams' Satire on Human Intelligence: Its Method and Purpose" (*CentR* 15[1971]:430–44). Rule sees the value and significance of Adams's satire on the human mind in his creation of a literary Adams, the man transforming what he really is, or at least aspects of what he really is, through artistic imagination to produce a more clear-cut moral. That ultimate moral, Rule supposes, is that increased powers of thought are needed to control increased technology.

There now exist two fine surveys of Adams scholarship: Charles Vandersee's "Henry Adams (1838–1918)" (*ALR* 2[1969]:89–120), and Earl N. Harbert's chapter in *Fifteen American Authors Before 1900*, edited by Robert A. Rees and Earl N. Harbert (Madison, Univ. of Wis. Press, 1971).

The publication of *Upstate: Records and Recollections of Northern New York* (New York, Farrar, Straus and Giroux), Edmund Wilson's wistful, sometimes rueful, more or less ordered reflections, provided the *TLS* with the occasion for an assessment and a summing-up of Wilson's career ("Edmund Wilson and the End of the American Dream," 19 May: 561–64). The reviewer praises Wilson's "exhaustively prepared" books, such as *The Shock of Recognition* and *Patriotic Gore*, calls attention to his "crucially important attack" in *The Fruits of the MLA*, and marvels at Wilson's prescience in *Axel's Castle* (1931), particularly in his comments on T. S. Eliot. Taking his lead

from Alfred Kazin, the reviewer proposes that Wilson at his best (and
he is often at his best) is to be compared with "the literary artists
driven by historical imaginations—men like Carlyle," for Wilson is
nothing less than "one of the great men of letters in our century."

"The American as a man of letters" is what Leonard Kriegel calls
him in *Edmund Wilson* (Carbondale, So. Ill. Univ. Press, 1971). The
author of this valuable book, a measured assessment of the Wilson
canon, does not hesitate to point out shortcomings where he finds
them. In *Patriotic Gore*, for example, he scores Wilson for his inaccurate, unreal view of Southern slavery, as well as for his heavy
reliance on undigested lumps of quotation to make dubious points.
Kriegel sees *To the Finland Station* as quite possibly Wilson's masterpiece. It constitutes the high point of his involvement with the social
and political contradictions of his times. After that monumental
work, however, so runs the argument, Wilson slips more and more
into the past and into his own personal, often idiosyncratic and
quirky, concerns. When he writes about contemporary writers in the
1940s and the 1950s, Wilson is never on the main path, as he had
always been in the 1920s and the 1930s, and when he writes about
contemporary society, he produces, much too late and in absolutely
the wrong key, books like *The Cold War and the Income Tax*.
Over Kriegel's book hovers the literary ghost of Henry Adams, another writer driven by an acute historical imagination. Like the aging
Adams, Wilson at the last, as *Upstate* amply documents, retreats to
an earlier age. But, as Kriegel decides, "there is, finally, something
altogether too passive, too complacent, in the sight of one of our
great men, perhaps our greatest literary figure, simply deciding that
'this country, whether or not I continue to live in it, is no longer any
place for me.'"

In "Edmund Wilson on *The New Republic*" (*New Republic*
1 July: 25–28) Malcolm Cowley writes judiciously of the man who
"dreamed of having all literature as his imperium" and who lived long
enough and wrote well enough to become "a mixture of Samuel Johnson, William Hazlitt, and Burton the traveller." The conclusion
reached by Mark Taylor in "Edmund Wilson and Literature" (*Commonweal* 96:386–87) is that Wilson will be remembered for his studies of literature. *Axel's Castle*, though narrower in chronological
scope, belongs with Erich Auerbach's *Mimesis*. Yet, because he seldom wrote about "the giants of literature," Wilson is denied "full

membership in the tiny community of great modern philologists—along with Auerbach, E. R. Curtius, Leo Spitzer, a few more Europeans, and perhaps a single American, Kenneth Burke."

Anyone in pursuit of Wilson, either as literary critic, historian, dramatist, or even poet, will find Richard David Ramsey's *Edmund Wilson: A Bibliography* (New York, David Lewis, 1971) invaluable. It includes sections on books, essays, book reviews, plays and dialogues, stories, poems, translations (of Wilson's works and by Wilson), miscellanea (editorial comments, periodicals edited, drawings), manuscript locations, correspondence (by Wilson, to Wilson, and about him), and theses and dissertations. Oddly—it now occurs to us—there exists nothing comparable for Henry Adams.

iv. Criticism, Reviewing, Scholarship, and Polemics

At this early stage of the game, we need undergo little of what Harold Bloom has since termed "anxiety" (*The Anxiety of Influence*, 1973) in tracing those social and intellectual currents responsible for the rise of certain recognizable types of polemic criticism. For instance, most of us assume, usually tacitly, that the rightful demands of minority groups seeking a separate ethnic voice, the emphasis upon "relevance," and the outspoken and iconoclastic militancy of the 1960s show themselves clearly and understandably in the outpouring of articles bluntly arguing an end to the bondage of white letters. The role of the critic, of course, can change with the spirit of an era, and there is nothing unusual in the idea of criticism being used as a vehicle for social or political change.

But there is something odd about the ready acceptance of such use as scholarship. For—be he new critic, source-hunter, or influence-tracer—the scholar (if Richard Altick and all those wonderful, pride-inducing epigraphs that embellish his *The Art of Literary Research* can still be trusted) begins his task with the sharpened spade of inquiry and presumably not with an axe to grind. In the paragraphs to follow, a few examples should suggest that the unspoken trend of polemic-as-scholarship may have its analogue in a seemingly unrelated trend—the attention scholars increasingly give to modern reviewers. In their scholarly criticisms of fellow critics, many writers are reluctant to ignore spokesmen of views simply popular. If popular reviewer, then, is to be considered critic, and critic is somehow scholar, scholarly writing may stand in danger of accidentally redefining itself as nothing more than the glorified editorial.

A spate of articles in those journals which lend themselves to yearly review by *ALS* field contributors attempt even yet to distinguish between the critic and the reviewer. There seems nothing unnatural or prodigal about so doing; for the distinction is always an important one. The function of the reviewer traditionally makes him some kind of arbiter of the current taste, while the critic is generally thought of as something of an illuminator or explicator of enduring aesthetic merit. But then where do you place, say, a Conrad Aiken? Definitions must be settled, and that is decidedly a part of the scholarly task. This business of differentiating closely related and mutually ancillary literary functions is admittedly a sticky one, but toughminded or even modestly useful distinctions seem not to be the most arduous task or telling trait of these articles.

What is unnatural about this trend is that its practitioners seem increasingly unwilling to profit by their individual successes. They most often arrive at a useful definition only to go on without it or, at least, to issue a disclaimer. Witness, for example, René Wellek's unremarkable "American Criticism of the Last Ten Years" (*YCGL* 20 [1971]:5–14). A sketchy but useful lecture on main categories and trends (originally delivered at Yale on April 3, 1971), it leaves out virtually all "books of critical importance about periods, genres and individual authors" for the sake of space, and then includes discussion of Susan Sontag. Whether or not this fulfills Wellek's goal to focus on academic criticism in terms of theory is something each reader apparently has to decide for himself. But, like other criticism-oriented articles, Wellek's distinguishes reviewing activity from criticism proper but goes on to include the former as worthy of scholarly attention.

It is not too difficult to understand why Wellek and others feel the need to allow so much latitude in choosing just whom to consider in the limited space under the rubric "criticism." During the same year in which he overviewed the previous decade of American criticism, he also worked over his "Kenneth Burke and Literary Criticism" (*SR* 79:171–88). Nobody who has tackled Burke, however fleetingly, would have the temerity to assert he was anything but critic or scholar, but few of us have had the gumption to specify just what kind.

But after accepting him as part of the brotherhood of critics, both Wellek and Howard Nemerov ("Everything, Preferably All at Once: Coming to Terms with Kenneth Burke," *SR* 79[1971]:189–201) leave their readers with some haunting evidence that Burke's theories aid and abet an illicit crossing of the border between scholarly criticism and personal release from repression. For Burke, as some of us claim to understand him, argues that the critic creates himself in his criticism of a literary work as well as a piece of explication. If this is true, at least of Burke, it comes very close to reading oneself into a book and out again.

If the slippery terms of Burke's critical theory tend to put his analysts off balance, so do reviewers who seem to be something more than reviewers. Sliding over the no-man's-land between criticism and reviewing from the other side, an article by Arthur Waterman ("Conrad Aiken as Critic: The Consistent View," *MissQ* 24[1971]:91–110) is a specimen of another type. Again part of the larger trend to define the function of the critic, Waterman says that delay (until 1958) in assembling Aiken's scattered criticism and reluctance to accept him as a poet of major stature has obscured the body of his 238 critical pieces as unusually consistent in approach, durable, and occasionally prophetic. (Aiken was among the first to give recognition to Faulkner.)

Waterman finds in the corpus of Aiken's work a theory always founded on criticism as both a release from repression for the writer and a search for illusion by the reader. This psychological base turns Aiken himself conservative towards the latter, however, seeing the average reader's psyche as the norm. Still his preoccupation with psychology frequently made Aiken recognize both his own bias and the need to tolerate the peculiar structure of a writer's individual consciousness. In order to make a world-view from the chaos of the period and literary circles in which he lived, Aiken consistently linked writers he reviewed to accepted ones of past tradition, in this sense defining himself as critic and not mere reviewer.

Aiken is not a critic in the sense of Eliot's reflective placing of subjects in a philosophical tradition. Rather, he compares the writer under review to a previously accepted writer—Katherine Mansfield with Chekhov, for example. He is a reviewer, clicking off short-term appraisals and immediate judgments of going literary people. But because his judgments were consistent and stood up so well, he is somewhere on the middle ground, and near enough to "critic" for Waterman to consider him such.

The trouble with all of this is not that the likes of Aiken do not deserve to be viewed in proper perspective in the history of literary criticism, but that others seemingly with the same outward qualifications as an Aiken are moving up towards canonization as literary critic, a term which still bears (and should) the connotation of illuminator and explicator. Already lurking in notes in our journals is the suggestion that H. L. Mencken so qualifies. Admittedly most of these devote themselves to analysis of Mencken's effective prose (Thomas C. Bonner, "Mencken as Whangdoodle: One Aspect of H. L. Mencken's Prose Style," *MarkhamR* 3[1971]:14–17) and focus upon his biased "reviewing." But an anonymous note (*BNYPL* 75 [1971]:63–65) suggests his "critical" acumen, calling him "A Scout for the Scholars: H. L. Mencken." Nobody doubts that Mencken was critical in the popular sense of "hypercritical" or that he was "scholarly" as the word is generally used in society, for he did write three tomes of the incredibly detailed *The American Language*. But if he qualifies as a critic of the past among recent articles, then, indeed, there can be no complaint with the polemic critics of the present.

In these pages two years ago (*ALS 1970*, pp. 376–81,400–01) G. R. Thompson wrote that "militance, one soon becomes convinced after reading recent black criticism, is indeed a necessary stage in the acceptance of blackness by both whites and blacks." This may, or it may not, be true; but militance has no place in scholarship. One becomes even sooner convinced that Thompson was "convinced" not so much by his reading of black letters as by the force exerted by prevailing societal attitudes. We all hate to admit it, but one of the most prevalent trends in our scholarship is to tread lightly on or around the work of and on minority writers, for fear, undoubtedly, that we will aggravate social tension if we mention anything as other than mostly a success. All of Thompson's reluctance about black militance in criticism in his twenty-six-page discussion was ultimately chalked up to the alien and unclear idea of blackness that whites perforce must have. He hedged his bets on the last two pages with a single paragraph to the effect that "This is not to say that black New Criticism does not have serious faults." He then cited the faults from a black critic.

The end result of such questionable liberalism is that scholarly journals lend their pages to a deal of sheer polemics masquerading, with and without footnotes, as scholarship. Following on the very heels of Thompson's tolerance is the likes of an article the next year by Lewis H. Fenderson, "The New Breed of Black Writers and Their Jaundiced View of Tradition" (*CLAJ* 15[1971]:18–24). There is nothing unusual about his tack in the piece (it mirrors many of the same traits of articles discussed the year previous by Thompson), but in Fenderson the paradigm is unusually and patently clear. Literature is simply the springboard to politics; blacks must liberate themselves from the shackles of white literary forms, like grammar.

As evidence of this, Fenderson talks at length of Sidney Smith's slur on early American letters, as if to say that because the ground that spawned a Mrs. Susanna Rowson eventually turned out a Faulkner, any variety of literature will eventually and automatically flower. Tripping through the history of modern black literature, Fenderson sounds like he is doing a parody of American literary history. Except that he is deadly serious. Quotations chosen to illustrate his points have, in many instances, literally nothing to do with them. At one turn a particularly empty passage from an obscure piece is labeled as the strident-voiced beacon of "neo-hoodooism." All of this is well and good for one man's commonplace book, but it is neither criticism nor scholarship; it is simply another outlet for polemic protest.

This is not to say that other minority "scholars" do not as well read their political stance of the present in and out of their literature of the past (cf., for example, Edward Simmen, "'We Must Make This Beginning': The Chicano Leader Image in the Short Story," *SWR* 57:126–33). And it is absolutely impossible to construe all of this to mean that all such critics are polemicists. Not all are, but some decidedly tend towards the use of the literary scholarship forum as rallying podium. Literary criticism may well be becoming more and more personal and less and less illuminating.

Wallace Kaufman, in "Revolution, Environment, and Poetry" (*SAQ* 71:137–48), finds Wordsworth the apostle of ecology. And no wonder for his Whiggish discovery, for he read his definition into the poet in order to read it out again: "Man's dissociation of his own self-aware personality from the workings of the natural environment has been the mainsail of Western culture." It comes as little surprise to find that the author, besides teaching at Chapel Hill, runs a "conservation-oriented real estate development."

There is no telling when the trend towards confusing polemic editorializing from literature with scholarly criticism began, but it is relatively clear already where it will end. It will end with the popular reviewer in the chair of the working scholar, and it will end with release from personal or political repression overtaking what Howard Mumford Jones defined as our business as he understood it (SR 39[1931]:76)—"to find out in a humble spirit of inquiry what literary masterpieces really say."

It will all probably sound a good deal like an article by Lester G. Crocker, "Professor Babbitt Revisited" (SIR 10[1971]:260–82). Crocker's piece is a picking and piqueing, point-by-point blue-penciling of Irving Babbitt's *Rousseau and Romanticism* which severely belies Crocker's avowed purpose—to show that it can be useful to look back on a book then significant and now neglected. Most of the piece emerges as a pointed blast at Babbitt's slips and methodological errors. Babbit is taken over the coals for misusing terms and for failing to be perceptive. After all of this, he is briefly praised, in a paragraph, for his "erudition and intellectual power." In a final sweeping stroke both Babbitt and Rousseau are labeled "Puritans." Perhaps the study is, after all, only the product of someone once forced in graduate school days to read *Rousseau and Romanticism,* one who has had a grudge ever since. It doesn't matter, for it is in the drift of things. We need only be reviewers now.

Brown University

The authors' work was supported by a grant from the General Faculty Research Reserve Fund of Brown University. George Monteiro is primarily responsible for sections i–iii, Neil K. Fitzgerald for section iv.

Afterword: The CEAA Program

In the summer of 1973 Matthew J. Bruccoli, Director of the Center for Editions of American Authors, was able to announce the publication of the one-hundredth volume bearing the CEAA seal. These hundred volumes represent the near completion of the CEAA editions of some authors, notably Stephen Crane, Hawthorne, and Melville, for whom editions of ten to fifteen volumes had been projected. The editions of more prolific authors, such as Irving and Howells, while highly productive (the seal having been awarded to twelve Irving volumes and to fourteen Howells volumes) are further from completion of their respective projections of twenty-seven and thirty-two volumes. A few of the editions, particularly those of Thoreau, Emerson (works), and Twain (works), lag far behind initial expectations. But however uneven the progress of the thirteen editions either funded through or otherwise associated with CEAA, the fact of the publication of the one-hundredth CEAA volume represents a significant achievement in American literary scholarship.

Over two hundred scholars have contributed to the bibliographic, textual, historical, and critical scholarship involved in these volumes. For the first time the federal government has acknowledged, through substantial grants from the National Endowment for the Humanities in support of the textual work, that the preservation and restoration of the nation's literary heritage is a goal worthy of sustained public support. Not all reviewers have grasped the fact that these volumes are essentially scholarly tools—volumes that present not only the textual editors' best efforts to restore the texts as the authors wished them to appear, but also, and more important, tables and lists recording the evidence upon which the editors' decisions are based. Because reasonable editors may differ in their interpretation of the textual evidence, critics may dispute the use of the term "definitive edition" in reference to the CEAA texts. But the thorough bibliographic research, the explicit reporting of all textual variants, and the meticulous proofreading required to earn the CEAA seal assure that the textual apparatus that accompanies the texts *is* definitive and need never be compiled again. Future scholars, be their bent psychoanalytic, mythic, sociological, structural, or biographical, will have secure information about the genesis and mutations of their authors' texts.

The existence of these hundred volumes has changed the tools and techniques of American literary scholarship. Scholars are using these carefully prepared volumes as the standard texts for reference in their articles, and as the editions become more complete we can expect this practice to become standard. The appearance of these authoritative texts in paperback, issued without textual apparatus by commercial publishers, will enable teachers both to have confidence that their students are reading what the author wrote and to apply the most recent scholarship directly to the texts they are teaching. The CEAA has promoted an awareness of the degree of corruption in most literary texts widely in use, has provoked spirited discussion that has raised immeasurably the standards of textual scholarship in this country, and through its support of centers for textual study, is helping to train the young scholars who will continue the decontamination of our literary texts.

In 1973 the CEAA began the inspection and sealing of facsimile editions and of textual apparatus published independent of the literary work to which it refers. The first two facsimile editions published with the CEAA seal were the holograph manuscripts of *The Red Badge of Courage* and *The Great Gatsby*. The publication of CEAA approved textual apparatus without text is of advantage in dealing with twentieth-century literature still under copyright. When copyright runs out on these works, as it is about to do on early Hemingway, Fitzgerald, and Faulkner for instance, edited texts that restore the author's original intention can be issued quickly and inexpensively. *The Great Gatsby* is the first of these twentieth-century texts to be so treated.

The CEAA has also been encouraging scholars to undertake the textual editing of single volumes, independent of any series or extended edition. There are authors whose reputations rest on a small body of writing or a single work; Joseph Kirkland and E. W. Howe are instances. By encouraging individual textual scholars, or doctoral candidates working under the supervision of textual scholars, to undertake such "one-shot" independent projects, the CEAA hopes to foster the extension of the careful textual editing accorded major authors to lesser figures and to do so in a way that will avoid the need for massive subvention to meet publishing costs.

While the subject is not of inherent scholarly interest, the cost of publishing (as opposed to editing) the CEAA volumes is emerging as a vital issue and one that could well determine which authors and titles will, in fact, become available in textually reliable editions. Several of the editions have backlogs of volumes in standing type or in full preparation for the printer. But some university presses find themselves unable to publish these completed volumes because of steadily inflating production costs, reduced university budgets, and the sharp cutback in federal funds to libraries, their chief market. Such titles as *The Sketch Book of Geoffrey Crayon, Gent.* and *A Hazard of New Fortunes* are kept out of the hands of scholars for this reason. The National Endowment for the Humanities has used its full powers of encouragement to urge the CEAA to complete all of the presently funded editions by September 1976. The completion of this vast cultural project in the bicentennial year would be a suitable and impressive symbol of the concern of the federal government for the cultural life of the nation. Several of the editions are likely to be able to complete their textual work by this deadline. But unless funds, federal or other, are found to meet the publishing costs of these volumes, a good deal of the literary heritage that the NEH has done so much to preserve and restore will continue to gather dust in printers' shops and filing cabinets while students and scholars continue to employ corrupt texts of our classic American authors.

Don L. Cook

Indiana University

Index

Broughton, Panthea Reid, 128
Brown, Alice, 192–93
Brown, Calvin, 122
Brown, Charles Brockden, 180–81, 283
Brown, Harry M., 195
Brown, Slater, 324
Brown, William Wells, 191
Browne, Charles Farrar, 195
Browne, Ray B., 74
Browning, Preston M., Jr., 29
Browning, Robert, 317
Bruccoli, Matthew J., 131–32, 134, 200, 415
Brumm, Ursula, 120, 155, 156
Brüning, Eberhard, 369
Bruns, Roger A., 281
Brunvand, Jan Harold, 397
Bryan, C. D. B., 145
Bryant, Jerry H., 307
Bryant, William Cullen, 188, 231, 233
Brydone, Patrick, 175
Bryer, Jackson R., 131
Buber, Martin, 142
Bucco, Martin, 249
Bucke, Richard M., 56
Buckingham, Willis J., 66
Budd, Louis J., 82, 199
Buehler, Richard E., 373
Buell, Lawrence J., 11, 52–53
Bufano, Randolph J., 8
Bulgheroni, Marisa, 287
Bullins, Ed, 369–70
Bungert, Hans, 198
Bunn, Alfred, 289
Bunting, Charles T., 289
Burford, Walter W., 370
Burg, B. Richard, 162
Burgess, Anthony, 340
Burgoyne, General John, 179
Burke, Edmund, 171
Burke, Kenneth, 343–44, 349, 409–11
Burke, T. A., 194
Burke, Thomas, 176
Burlinghame, Roger, 134
Burns, Graham, 86
Burns, Robert, 61
Burns, Stuart, 279
Burroughs, William, 265, 294, 311
Burt, Olive W., 376–77
Burtner, H. W., 337
Burton, Sir Richard F., 408
Bush, George E., 311
Bush, Robert, 80

Bush, Sargent, Jr., 161, 179
Butler, Joseph T., 187
Butler, James H., 359
Butor, Michel, 120
Butterfield, R. W., 106
Buttitta, Anthony, 135
Byars, John A., 367
Byers, John R., Jr., 248
Byles, Mather, 182
Byrd, Scott, 287
Byrd, William, 155, 165

Cabell, James Branch, 248–49, 331
Cable, George Washington, 192
Cady, Edwin H., 198
Cage, John, 334
Cahill, Daniel J., 308
Caldwell, Harry B., 376
Calhoun, Douglas, 341
Calhoun, Robert M., 178
Calisher, Hortense, 264
Callahan, John F., 138
Cameron, Elizabeth, 406
Cameron, Kenneth W., 16, 47–48, 55–57, 71, 231
Campbell, Harry M., 38
Campbell, Jeff H., 124
Campbell, Killis, 230
Camus, Albert, 92, 101, 151, 285, 307
Canaday, Nicholas, Jr., 32–33
Canny, James R., 209
Cantwell, Robert, 380
Capellán, Ángel, 151
Capote, Truman, 136, 169, 243, 268, 271, 288, 290–91
Carey, George, 231
Carey, Glenn O., 121, 129
Cargill, Oscar, 94–95
Carlson, Eric W., 212–13
Carlyle, Thomas, 408
Carothers, Robert L., 47
Carpeaux, Otto, 151
Carpenter, Ann Miller, 379
Carr, John, 267
Carra, Lawrence, 358
Carroll, Charles, 172
Carroll, Lewis, 282
Carruth, Hayden, 351
Carruthers, Clifford M., 134, 247
Carruthers, William A., 186
Carson, Gerald, 382–83
Carter, Elliott, 325

Zall, P. M., 170
Zardoya, Concha, 65
Zenger, John Peter, 167
Ziff, Larzer, 161
Zimmer, Anne Young, 176
Zimmer, Dieter E., 256

Zimmer, Jeanne M., 8
Zola, Emile, 204
Zucker, David H., 346
Zuckerman, Michael, 195
Zukofsky, Louis, 334, 339–40, 404